INSIDE
VISUAL C++™

SECOND EDITION
VERSION 1.5

DAVID J.
KRUGLINSKI

PUBLISHED BY
Microsoft Press
A Division of Microsoft Corporation
One Microsoft Way
Redmond, Washington 98052-6399

Library of Congress Cataloging-in-Publication Data
Kruglinski, David J.
    Inside visual C++ / David J. Kruglinski. -- 2nd ed.
       p.   cm.
    Includes index.
    ISBN 1-55615-661-8 : $39.95 ($53.95 Can.)
    1. C++ (Computer program language)   2. Microsoft Visual C++.
  I. Title.
  QA76.73.C153K78   1994
  005.265--dc20   94-19212
                             CIP

Printed and bound in the United States of America.

1 2 3 4 5 6 7 8 9 MLML 9 8 7 6 5 4

Distributed to the book trade in Canada by Macmillan of Canada, a division of Canada Publishing Corporation.

A CIP catalogue record for this book is available from the British Library.

Microsoft Press books are available through booksellers and distributors worldwide. For further information about international editions, contact your local Microsoft Corporation office. Or contact Microsoft Press International directly at fax (206) 936-7329.

Acquisitions Editor: Dean Holmes
Project Editor: Jack Litewka
Technical Editor: Jim Fuchs

CONTENTS SUMMARY

TABLE OF CONTENTS

CHAPTER TWENTY-FOUR

DATABASE MANAGEMENT WITH MICROSOFT ODBC 501

CHAPTER TWENTY-SIX

DYNAMIC LINK LIBRARIES (DLLs) 635

ACKNOWLEDGMENTS

A lot of people contributed to the first edition of this book, and many of those same souls worked hard on this edition too. Special thanks go to Chuck Sphar, who provided advance copies of the MFC documents, and to Dean McCrory of the AFX development group, who endured and patiently answered dozens of technical questions, many of which were really stupid. More stupid questions were cheerfully answered by Russell Williams and Eric Wells of the Excel group. Not to be ignored are those folks out in cyberspace, especially John Arnold, who pointed out far too many glitches and mistakes in the first edition.

On the Microsoft Press side, there's technical editor Jim Fuchs, who put in the usual long hours and checked every line of my source code, and project editor Jack Litewka, who applied his large magnifying glass to each of my screen dumps. Special thanks go to Dean McCrory (the same Dean mentioned above), Kraig Brockschmidt, and Charlie Kindel, who reviewed the manuscripts for Chapters 24 and 25.

INTRODUCTION

It isn't often that a truly new software product category comes along. The "application framework" is such a category, and Visual C++ contains what is arguably the most powerful Windows-based application framework to date. The product has substantial credibility because it comes from Microsoft, the author of Windows itself. Even though the Microsoft Visual C++ application framework is quite different from anything else you might have used, it builds on elements you might be familiar with already, including the C++ language, the Windows Software Development Kit (SDK) for the C language, the original Microsoft Foundation Class Library version 1.0 that was delivered with Microsoft C/C++ version 7.0, and the Microsoft Foundation Class Library version 2.0 that was part of Visual C++ version 1.0.

Microsoft Foundation Class (MFC) Library version 2.5—which I'll often refer to as "the MFC library," for short—is an important part of Visual C++ version 1.5 and the core of the application framework. The MFC library consists of a library of C++ classes and global functions with source code included. Other Visual C++ components—including AppWizard, ClassWizard, App Studio, Visual Workbench, the compiler, and the linker—are the tools you'll use to construct your applications.

This book explains the MFC library classes, and it shows you how to use the classes and the tools to build Windows-based applications. If you already own Visual C++, *Inside Visual C++* provides useful techniques, points of view, examples, and theory that are not included in the product documentation. If you're contemplating buying Visual C++, this book gives you an overall picture of the product's capabilities.

Who Can Use This Book

When I started working with version 1.0 of the MFC library, after a not-so-successful attempt to learn Windows SDK programming, I realized that C++ and Windows were a natural fit and that it was actually easier to learn Windows-based programming the C++ way. Why not try to teach it that way? Why not assume that the reader has a programming background and then bypass all the "ugly stuff" that beginning SDK programmers have to learn?

My editors agreed, but they also said, "Don't forget the experienced Windows programmers, the ones who have been buying all the Petzold books." "OK," I said, and set my sights on an approach that would serve those with and without prior Windows experience.

Next there was the question of C++ knowledge. Surely, with so many C++ books out there, everyone would know the language by now. "Everyone has bought at least one C++ book" would be a truer statement, however. Perhaps you began to read a book, did a few of the examples, and then lost interest and dropped back to C. The Visual C++ application framework is a good excuse to become really proficient at C++, and this book will help.

As a writer, it was easier to assume that my readers didn't know Windows than it was to assume that they didn't know C++. Given the prototype for an ellipse function, for example, it's pretty easy for any programmer to write code that draws an ellipse on the screen, with either an ordinary C function or a C++ member function. But if the programmer doesn't understand C++ classes and objects, he or she is in trouble. For this reason, I've included a C++ crash course in Appendix A. If you're new to C++, read through Appendix A, but keep those other C++ books handy. You might finally be motivated to read them!

Notice that I've been talking about programmers. Yes, you do have to be one, or at least a student of programming. Compilers, tools, and operating systems have become so complex in recent years that it's impossible to go from zero to expert Windows programmer within one book. A background in C is the absolute minimum because even Appendix A assumes that you can read C code.

Oh, I almost forgot. You should know how to run Windows-based applications. If you don't know what a program for Windows is supposed to do, how can you design and write one? If you're looking for an application to start with, try Microsoft Word for Windows. It's a good example of a modern Windows-based program. Besides that, it's a darn good word processor, and you can write help files with it. I used it to write this book.

How to Use This Book

When you're starting off with Visual C++, you can use this book as a tutorial by going through it sequentially. Later you can use it as a reference by looking up topics in the table of contents or the index. Because of the tight interrelationships among many application framework elements, it wasn't possible to cleanly isolate each concept in its own chapter, so the book really isn't an encyclopedia. When you use this book, you'll definitely want the *Class Library Reference* by your side.

The Organization of this Book

As the table of contents shows, there are four main parts to this book:

Part I: Windows, Visual C++, and Application Framework Fundamentals

In this part, I try to strike a balance between abstract theory and practical application. After a quick review of modern Windows and of the Visual C++ components, you'll be introduced, in a gentle way, to the application framework and the document–view architecture. You'll see a simple "Hello, world!" program, built with the MFC library classes, that requires only 30 lines of code.

Part II: The MFC Library View Class

The MFC library documentation presents all the application framework elements in quick succession, with the assumption that you already know Windows SDK programming. Here you're confined to one major application framework component—the "view," which is really a window. It's here that you'll learn what SDK programmers know already, but in the context of C++ and the MFC library classes. There's something for Windows gurus too, because the MFC library view environment supports extras such as dialog data exchange, graphical buttons, and Visual Basic controls. You'll use the Visual C++ tools a lot, and that in itself eliminates much of the coding drudgery in the life of SDK programmers.

Part III: The Document–View Architecture

Now the real core of application framework programming is introduced— the document–view architecture. You'll learn what a document is (think of it as something much more general than a word processing document), and you'll see how to connect it to the view that you learned about in Part II. You'll be amazed, once you have written a document class, at how the MFC library simplifies file I/O and printing.

Along the way, you'll learn about command message processing, toolbars and status bars, splitter frames, and context-sensitive help. You'll also be introduced to the Windows Multiple Document Interface (MDI) that's featured so prominently in MFC library applications.

Pay special attention to the section "Speeding Up the Build Process" on page 43 because the speed-up hints will help you save time as you work through the book's examples.

Part IV: Advanced Topics

This part is a catchall for many useful Windows programming techniques directly supported by the MFC library. You'll start with several bare-bones Windows-based applications that bypass the document–view architecture, and then you'll see a useful class for device-independent bitmaps. In Chapter 24, you'll see examples that use the Microsoft Open Database Connectivity (ODBC) programming interface. Chapter 25 introduces OLE, and Chapter 26 explains MFC library–style dynamic link libraries (DLLs).

Going Further with Windows: The Purpose of the "For SDK Programmers" Sidebars

This book can't offer the kind of detail—the tricks and hidden features—found in the newer, specialized books about Windows. Most of these books are written from the point of view of a C-language SDK programmer. In order to use these books, you'll have to understand the underlying SDK application programming interface (API) and its relationship to the MFC library.

This book's "For SDK Programmers" sidebars, scattered throughout the text, help you make the connection to the Windows SDK. These specially formatted boxes help experienced Windows C programmers relate new MFC library concepts to SDK principles they already know. If you're unfamiliar with SDK programming, you should skip these notes the first time through, but you should read them on your second pass through the book because they'll help you understand the mainstream literature about Windows after you get up to speed with the MFC library.

If You've Worked with Other Application Frameworks

You're probably already aware of other application framework products. (The best known is *MacApp*, for the Apple Macintosh.) The MFC library is similar to and different from these other products; therefore, please don't make any assumptions about terminology or the function of any similarly named class.

Hardware Requirements

If you haven't discovered this already, your Windows development machine needs more horsepower than a standard target machine. Because your time is valuable, go for a fast 80486 or Pentium computer with 8 megabytes (MB) or more of random access memory (RAM). Extra RAM can be used for a disk cache and a RAM disk that will work together to speed compiles and links. Chapter 3 shows you how to configure your extra RAM.

As far as disk space is concerned, plan on 50 MB for the Visual C++ programs alone. Each project can require as much as 4 MB (including precompiled headers, map files, and a browser database), and you'll have lots of projects. A 200-MB hard disk drive is the minimum; a 500-MB hard disk drive is more realistic. By the way, you'll also need a CD-ROM drive. Visual C++ is shipped only on CD-ROM, and you'll probably want to access sample code and documentation directly from the CD-ROM.

Also consider a large-screen monitor with a super VGA board. With the large monitor, you can simultaneously display Visual Workbench, the Help window, and a Windows-based program that's being debugged.

Using the CD-ROM Companion Disc

The companion disc that's bound into the inside back cover of this book contains the source code files and make files for all the sample programs. The executable program files are not included, so you won't have to build the samples that you're interested in. To install the companion disc's files, insert the disc in your CD-ROM drive, and run the Setup program. Follow the on-screen instructions.

With a conventional C-language Windows SDK program, the source code files tell the whole story. With the MFC library application framework, things are not so simple. Much of the C++ code is generated by AppWizard, and the resources originate in App Studio. The examples in the early chapters include step-by-step instructions for using the tools to generate and customize the source code files. You'd be well advised to walk through those instructions for the first few examples. There's very little code to type. For the middle chapters, use the code from the companion disc, but read through the steps anyway in order to appreciate the role of App Studio and the Wizards. For the final chapters, not all the source code is listed. You'll need to examine the companion disc's files for those later examples.

Technical Notes and Sample Programs

You can access a Visual C++ help file that contains 46 useful technical notes. These notes cover advanced MFC library features not discussed in the documentation. This book contains references to technical notes that are identified by numbers. To read a technical note in the help file, you have two options: You can run WINHELP and then select \MSVC\HELP\MFC-NOTES.HLP, or you can double-click the MFC Tech Notes icon in the Microsoft Visual C++ Program Manager group.

The \MSVC\MFC\SAMPLES subdirectory contains 30 useful MFC library sample programs. These programs, documented in the \MSVC-\HELP\MFCSAMP help file (accessible from the MFC Samples Help icon in the Visual C++ Program Manager group), illustrate more advanced MFC library features. This book contains occasional references to these sample programs.

Visual C++ Version 1.5

This book is a revision of an edition that was written for Visual C++ version 1.0. The changes made are numerous and occur throughout the book. Also, text and screen changes reflect general improvements in AppWizard and ClassWizard. Chapters 24 and 25 have been completely rewritten because of the addition of the Open Database Connectivity (ODBC) classes and the major revision of the OLE classes to accommodate OLE version 2.0.

Both ODBC and OLE 2 are such complex subjects that books have been written on each. This book will discuss these subjects in a way that relates to the focus of this book—namely, Visual C++. Chapter 24 is an introduction to C++ database programming rather than a thorough explanation of client-server computing. Chapter 25 concentrates on basic OLE 2 theory and OLE Automation; other OLE 2 features such as in-place editing, linking, and drag-and-drop are not covered.

P A R T I

WINDOWS, VISUAL C++, AND APPLICATION FRAMEWORK FUNDAMENTALS

C H A P T E R   O N E

MICROSOFT WINDOWS AND VISUAL C++

Enough has already been written about the acceptance of Microsoft Windows and the benefits of the graphical user interface (GUI). This chapter summarizes the Windows programming model and shows you how the Visual C++ components work together to help you write applications for Windows. Along the way, you'll learn some new things about Windows. We'll be looking toward the future rather than dwelling on the past.

The Windows Programming Model

No matter which development tools you use, programming for Windows is different from old-style batch or transaction-oriented programming. To get started, you need to know some Windows fundamentals. As a frame of reference, we'll use the well-known MS-DOS programming model. Even if you don't currently program for plain MS-DOS, you're probably familiar with it.

Message Processing

When you write an MS-DOS application in C, the only absolute requirement is a function named *main*. The operating system calls *main* when the user runs the program, and from that point on, you can use any programming structure you want. If your program needs to get user keystrokes or otherwise use operating system services, it calls an appropriate function such as *getchar* or perhaps uses a character-based windowing library.

When the Windows operating system launches a program, it calls the program's *WinMain* function. Somewhere your application must have *WinMain*, which performs some specific tasks. The most important task is creating the application's "main window," which must have its own code to process messages that Windows sends it. An essential difference between a program written for Windows and a program written for MS-DOS is that an MS-DOS program calls the operating system to get user input, but a Windows program processes user input via messages from the operating system.

> NOTE: Many development environments for Windows, including Microsoft Visual C++ with the Microsoft Foundation Class (MFC) Library version 2.5, simplify programming by hiding the *WinMain* function and structuring the message-handling process. When you use the MFC library, you need not write a *WinMain* function, but understanding the link between the operating system and your programs is helpful.

Many messages in Windows are strictly defined and apply to all applications. For example, a WM_CREATE message is sent as a window is being created, a WM_LBUTTONDOWN message is sent when the user presses the left mouse button, a WM_CHAR message is sent when the user types a character, and a WM_CLOSE message is sent when the user closes a window. Other messages ("command" messages) are sent to an application window in response to user menu choices. These messages depend on the application's menu layout. The programmer can define still other messages, known as "user messages."

Don't worry about how your code processes these messages yet. That's the job of the application framework. Be aware, though, that the Windows message processing requirement imposes a lot of structure on your program. Don't try to force your Windows programs to look like your old MS-DOS programs. Study the examples in this book, and then be prepared to start fresh.

The Windows Graphics Device Interface (GDI)

Many MS-DOS programs wrote directly to the video memory and the printer port. The disadvantage of this technique was the need to supply driver software for every display card and every printer model. Windows introduced a layer of abstraction called the Graphics Device Interface (GDI). Windows provides the display and printer drivers, so your program doesn't need to know the type of display card and printer attached to the system. Instead of addressing the hardware, your program calls GDI functions that reference a data structure called a device context. Windows maps the device context structure to a physical device and issues the appropriate input/output instructions. The GDI is almost as fast as direct video access, and it allows different applications written for Windows to share the display.

Resource-Based Programming

To do data-driven programming in MS-DOS, you have to code the data as initialization constants, or you have to provide separate data files for your program to read. When you program for Windows, you store data in a resource file using a number of formats. Windows merges a resource file into a linked program through a process called "binding." Resource files can include bitmaps, icons, menu definitions, dialog box layouts, and strings. They can even include custom resource formats that you define.

You use a text editor to edit a program, but you generally use "what you see is what you get" (wysiwyg) tools to edit resources. If you're laying out a dialog box, for example, you select elements from an array of icons called a control palette, and you position and size the buttons, list boxes, and so forth with the mouse. With the Visual C++ App Studio resource editor program, you can effectively edit most resource formats. (Note: In Microsoft Visual Basic and in Microsoft Access, the control palette is called a toolbox.)

Memory Management

In the old days, the MS-DOS conventional memory limit of 640 kilobytes (KB) restricted the size of your programs. You could use various overlay management techniques and extended/expanded memory managers to allow larger programs, but all had shortcomings. An 80386SX-based (or better) computer usually has 4 megabytes (MB) or more of memory, and its CPU has built-in memory management hardware. Windows, together with the Visual C++ compiler, offers additional memory management features. The net result is that memory usually isn't a problem anymore.

Chapter 9 describes current memory management techniques for Windows. If you've heard horror stories about locking memory handles, thunks, and burgermasters, don't worry. That's all in the past. Today you simply allocate the memory you need, and Windows takes care of the details. Parts of your program, including resources, can be automatically swapped to and from disk and then shuffled in physical memory, but chances are your computer has so much memory that your entire program will fit into physical memory.

Dynamic Link Libraries (DLLs)

In the MS-DOS environment, all a program's object modules were statically linked during the build process. Windows allows dynamic linking, which means that specially constructed libraries can be loaded and linked at runtime. Multiple applications can share dynamic link libraries (DLLs), which saves memory and disk space. Dynamic linking increases program modularity because you can compile and test DLLs separately.

Designers originally created DLLs for use with the C language, and C++ has added some complications. After considerable effort, the Microsoft Foundation Class Library developers succeeded in combining all the application framework classes into a single DLL. Thus, you can statically or dynamically link the application framework classes into your application. In addition, you can create your own DLLs that build on the Microsoft Foundation Class Library. Chapter 26 includes information about creating DLLs.

Windows NT

Windows NT is a new 32-bit operating system that has an advanced file system with security features, multithreading, true preemptive multitasking, enhanced network access, and portability to selected RISC computers. Windows NT can run both existing Windows-based 16-bit applications (including Visual C++ version 1.5) and new high-performance Windows-based 32-bit applications.

How do you develop Windows 32-bit applications? Early beta testers had to use the Win32 SDK, which includes a new C-language application programming interface (API). Because of the need for 32-bit parameters, most Win32 function prototypes are different from their 16-bit equivalents. In addition, many functions are new, particularly in the area of disk I/O. Windows 32-bit applications access files through the Win32 API rather than through the MS-DOS API.

Existing C-language 16-bit applications for Windows will need extensive conversion to become true 32-bit applications. A Microsoft Foundation Class (MFC) Library application, on the other hand, will require only recompilation because the MFC library was designed with the Win32 API in mind. There is a separate 32-bit Visual C++ version for Windows NT. You can use the 32-bit version to produce applications targeted for Windows NT and other 32-bit versions of Windows. See Appendix D for information about Visual C++ for Windows NT.

The Visual C++ Components

Microsoft Visual C++ is two complete Windows application development systems in one product. If you so choose, you can develop C-language Windows programs using the API first introduced in the Windows SDK. Windows SDK programming techniques are well known and have been documented in many books, including Charles Petzold's *Programming Windows 3.1* (Microsoft Press, 1992). You can use many tools newly introduced in Visual C++, including App Studio, to make Windows SDK–style programming easier.

This book is not about Windows SDK–style programming, however. It's about C++ programming within the MFC library application framework that's part of Visual C++. You'll be using the C++ classes that are documented in the *Class Library Reference,* and you'll also be using application framework–specific Visual C++ tools such as AppWizard and ClassWizard.

> NOTE: Use of the Microsoft Foundation Class (MFC) Library programming interface doesn't cut you off from the Windows SDK functions. In fact, you'll almost always need some direct Windows SDK calls in your MFC library programs.

Two Visual C++ Versions: Standard Edition and Professional Edition

Visual C++ is available in two versions: the Standard Edition and the Professional Edition. The Standard Edition is actually an entry-level variation of Visual C++ version 1.0. This book does not address the Standard Edition.

A quick run-through of the Visual C++ components will help you get your bearings before you zero in on the application framework. Figure 1-1 on the following page shows an overview of the Visual C++ application build process.

Visual Workbench and the Build Process

The Visual Workbench is a Windows-hosted interactive development environment that's a direct descendant of Microsoft QuickC for Windows. If you're accustomed to running a compiler from the command line, please try Visual Workbench. Trust me. It's really good. I avoided the old character-mode Programmer's Workbench, but I use Visual Workbench now for all my projects. All examples in this book are built with Visual Workbench.

If you've used QuickC for Windows, Programmer's Workbench, or the Borland IDE, you already understand how Visual Workbench operates. But if you're new to integrated development environments, you'll need to know what a project is. A project is a collection of interrelated source files that are compiled, linked, and bound to make up a working Windows program. Project source files are generally stored in a separate subdirectory. A project depends on many files outside the project subdirectory too, such as include files and library files.

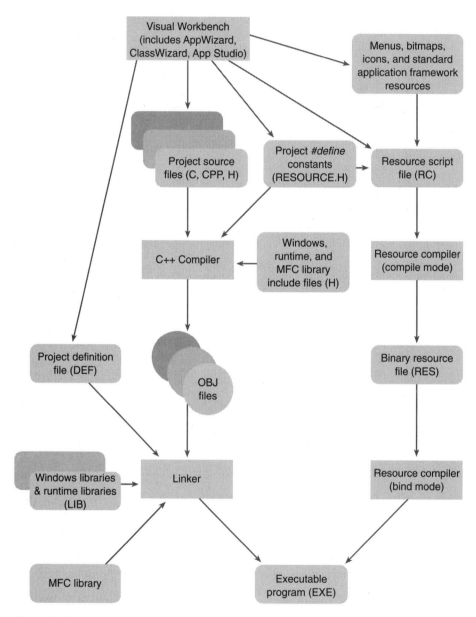

Figure 1-1.
The Visual C++ application build process.

Experienced programmers are familiar with make files. A make file expresses all the interrelationships among source files. (A source code file needs specific include files, an executable file requires certain object modules and libraries, and so forth.) A make program reads the make file and then invokes the compiler, assembler, linker, and resource compiler to produce the final output, which is generally an executable file. The make program uses built-in "inference rules" that tell it, for example, to invoke the compiler to generate an OBJ file from a specified CPP file.

In a command-line environment, you need to code the make file by hand. Visual Workbench automatically generates the make file, known as a "project file." In most cases, you want your project to include all the source files in the project subdirectory, but you can exclude files in the project subdirectory and use files from other subdirectories. After you create a project, you can edit source code files in individual child windows. Visual Workbench "remembers" which source code files you were working with and maintains a list of most recently used projects. As part of the project, you can save compiler and linker switch settings as specified through a series of dialog boxes. To generate the executable program, you simply choose the Build command from the Visual Workbench Project menu.

Visual Workbench contains a useful text editor that follows Windows interface standards and uses color to highlight C++ syntax. Unfortunately, you can't fully customize this editor or install your own editor. If you do decide to use your own editor, you'll forfeit the smooth integration that the integrated development environment provides. For example, Visual Workbench highlights lines containing errors in your source code files when you build a project and allows you to set debugging breakpoints.

The App Studio Resource Editor

The original Windows SDK included separate tools for editing dialog boxes, bitmaps, and fonts. With Visual C++, you use App Studio to edit most resources. Chapter 3 shows some App Studio windows. (See pages 39 and 40.) App Studio includes both a wysiwyg menu editor and a powerful dialog box editor that is far superior to the old Windows SDK DIALOG program. You can use App Studio as your resource editor for Windows SDK–style programming, but when you use App Studio for MFC library programming, you can interactively insert Microsoft Visual Basic controls in your dialog boxes for later connection to your C++ code.

App Studio's native file format is the ASCII Windows resource (RC) file format, and each project usually has one RC file with *#include* statements to bring in resources from other subdirectories. Editing the RC file outside App Studio is not recommended. App Studio can also process EXE and DLL files, so you can use the clipboard to "steal" resources, such as bitmaps and icons, from other Windows applications.

App Studio compares favorably to the best applications written for Windows, so it's significant that App Studio was written using the Visual C++ tools and the MFC library. App Studio can even edit its own resources! Try it. (You'll need to copy App Studio to another file and load the copy.)

The C/C++ Compiler

The Visual C++ compiler can process both C source code and C++ source code. It determines the language by looking at the source code filename extension. A C extension indicates C source code, and CPP or CXX indicates C++ source code. The compiler is compliant with ANSI version 2.1 and has additional Microsoft extensions. Template and exception syntax are not supported in Visual C++ version 1.5. The Visual Workbench's Use Microsoft Foundation Classes option (in the Project Options dialog box) determines whether the compiler uses the Microsoft Foundation Class Library include files.

The Linker

To generate an EXE file, the Visual C++ linker processes the OBJ files that the compiler produces. If you specify the Visual Workbench option Use Microsoft Foundation Classes, the linker uses the MFC library file for the appropriate memory model.

The Resource Compiler

The Visual C++ resource compiler operates in either compile mode or bind mode. In compile mode, an ASCII resource (RC) file from App Studio is compiled into a binary RES file. In bind mode, the RES file is merged with an executable (EXE) file. If you update a RES file, you can rebind it to its EXE file without relinking.

The Debugger

If your program works the first time, you don't need the debugger. The rest of us might need one from time to time. The Visual C++ debugger is the first-ever Windows-hosted C++ debugging environment. The debugger works closely with Visual Workbench to ensure that breakpoints are saved on disk. Toolbar buttons toggle breakpoints and control single-step execution. Figure 1-2 illustrates the Visual C++ debugger in action. Note that the Locals

Figure 1-2.
The Visual C++ debugger window.

window can expand an object pointer to show all data members of the derived class and base classes. To debug a program, you must build the program with the compiler and linker options set to generate debugging information.

In addition to the Windows-hosted Visual C++ debugger, you get the character-mode CodeView debugger. CodeView for Windows debugs p-code, and it has several other useful features.

AppWizard

AppWizard is a code generator that creates a working skeleton of a Windows application with features, class names, and source code filenames that you specify through dialog boxes. You'll use AppWizard extensively as you work through the examples in this book. Don't confuse AppWizard with conventional code generators such as Caseworks CASE:W and Blue Sky WindowsMAKER. AppWizard code is minimalist code; the functionality is inside the application framework base classes. Its purpose is to get you started quickly with a new application.

ClassWizard

ClassWizard is a program (implemented as a DLL) that operates both inside the Visual Workbench and inside App Studio. ClassWizard takes the drudgery out of maintaining Visual C++ class code. Need a new class or a new function to handle a Windows message? ClassWizard writes the prototypes, function bodies, and code to connect the messages to the application framework. ClassWizard can update class code that you write, so you avoid maintenance problems common to ordinary code generators.

The Source Browser

If you write an application from scratch, you probably have a good mental picture of your source code files, classes, and member functions. If you take over someone else's application, you'll need some assistance. The Visual C++ Source Browser (the "browser," for short) lets you examine (and edit) an application from the class or function viewpoint instead of from the file viewpoint. It's a little like the "inspector" tools available with other object-oriented libraries such as Smalltalk. The browser has the following viewing modes:

- Definitions and References—You select any function, variable, type, macro, or class and then see where it's defined and used in your project.

- Call Graph/Caller Graph—For a selected function, you get a graphical representation of the functions it calls or the functions that call it.

- Derived Class Graph/Base Class Graph—These are graphics class hierarchy diagrams. For a selected class, you see the derived classes or the base classes. You can control the hierarchy expansion with the mouse.

A typical browser window is shown on page 34 in Chapter 3.

NOTE: If you rearrange the lines in any source code file, you must rebuild the browser database.

Online Help

The entire contents of the Windows SDK reference manuals and the MFC library reference manuals are included in the Visual C++ online Help. Help is also available for App Studio, AppWizard, and ClassWizard. Don't underestimate the value of Help. Many programmers at Microsoft use it exclusively. If you want help on a function, simply click on (or move the cursor to) the function in the Visual Workbench editor and press F1; you'll see a Help window, as shown in Figure 1-3.

Visual C++ Help resolves conflicts between Windows SDK function names and identical Microsoft Foundation Class (MFC) Library names. If you select a function name that corresponds to member functions in several classes, you can choose the class from a list box. If you ask for help on a class, you'll see a member function and data member list in functional order.

Windows Diagnostic Tools

Visual C++ contains the same set of diagnostic tools that were included with the Windows SDK when it was a separate product: SPY for observing Windows messages, HEAPWALK for examining memory, HC31 for compiling help files, STRESS for artificially limiting available memory, and a profiler program that alerts you to bottlenecks in code.

Figure 1-3.
The Visual C++ Help window.

Also included are the DBWIN utility, which displays diagnostic output, and the NMAKE program, which processes hand-coded make files. NMAKE is used to build nonstandard versions of the Microsoft Foundation Class Library.

The Microsoft Foundation Class Library Version 2.5

The Microsoft Foundation Class Library version 2.5 (aka the MFC library) is really the subject of this book. It defines the application framework that you'll be getting to know intimately. Chapter 2 gets you started with actual code and some important concepts.

CHAPTER TWO

THE MICROSOFT FOUNDATION CLASS LIBRARY APPLICATION FRAMEWORK

This chapter introduces the Microsoft Foundation Class Library version 2.5 (aka the MFC library) application framework by explaining its benefits. Early on, you'll see a stripped-down but fully operational MFC library program for Windows that should help you understand what application framework programming is all about. Theory is kept to a minimum here, but the message mapping and document–view sections contain important information that will help you with the examples that follow in later chapters.

Why Use the Application Framework?

If you're going to develop applications for Windows, you've got to choose a development environment. Assuming you've already rejected the interactive options such as Microsoft Visual Basic, you must choose among the following options:

- The tried-and-true Windows SDK (Software Development Kit)
- The new MFC library application framework
- Other Windows-based application frameworks such as Borland's Object Windows Library (OWL)

If you're starting from scratch, any option involves a big learning curve. If you're already a Windows SDK programmer, you'll still have a learning curve with the MFC library. So what benefits can justify this effort?

The Microsoft Press editors told me not to make this section sound like a marketing brochure, but I couldn't help it. I'm really enthusiastic about the product. It's the application development environment I've been waiting on for 10 years.

Here are the MFC library benefits as I see them.

MFC library version 2.5 is the C++ Microsoft Windows API.   Your acceptance of this premise depends on your acceptance of the C++ language. If C++ takes over from C—and many people expect it to—then it's natural for Windows to have a C++ programming interface. It's highly unlikely that the Windows–C++ interface standard will come from any company other than Microsoft, the producer of Windows itself.

I believe C++ will take over because it's the only universally accepted object-oriented language, and object-oriented programming is necessary for large software projects that require reusable, modular components. As more users demand more sophisticated software, we can't keep writing bigger C programs!

Application framework applications use a standard structure.   Any programmer starting on a large project develops some kind of structure for the code. The problem is that each programmer's structure is different, and for a new team member to learn the structure and conform to it is difficult. The MFC library application framework includes its own application structure—one that's been proven in many software environments and in many projects. If you write a program for Windows that uses the MFC library, you can safely retire to a Caribbean island, knowing that your minions can easily maintain and enhance your code back home.

Don't think that the MFC library's structure makes your programs inflexible. With the MFC library, your program can do anything that a Windows SDK program can do, and that means you can take maximum advantage of Windows.

Application framework applications are small and fast.   Function for function, MFC library programs are almost as small as Windows SDK programs. An MFC library "Hello, world!" program is only 80 KB with the MFC library functions statically linked. The same program is 23 KB with the MFC library dynamic link library (DLL). As for speed, in some circumstances an MFC library application is actually faster than its Windows SDK equivalent.

MFC library application framework is feature-rich. The MFC library version 1.0 classes, supplied with Microsoft C/C++ version 7.0, were essentially a C++ programming interface for Windows. Some significant features were added, however:

- General-purpose classes (non-Windows-specific), including
  - ❑ Collection classes for lists, arrays, and maps
  - ❑ A useful and efficient string class
  - ❑ Time, time span, and date classes
  - ❑ File access classes for operating system independence
  - ❑ Support for systematic object storage and retrieval to and from disk
- A "common root object" class hierarchy
- Streamlined Multiple Document Interface (MDI) application support
- Support for OLE (Object Linking and Embedding) version 1.0

The MFC library version 2.0 classes picked up where the version 1.0 classes left off by supporting many user interface features that are found in current Windows-based applications. Application framework architecture aside, here's a summary of the important new features:

- Full support for File Open, Save, and Save As menu items with the most recently used file list
- Print preview and printer support
- Scrolling windows and splitter windows
- Toolbars and status bars
- Access to Microsoft Visual Basic controls
- Context-sensitive help
- Automatic processing of data entered in a dialog box
- An improved interface to OLE version 1.0
- DLL support

The version 2.5 classes contribute the following:

- ODBC (Open Database Connectivity) support that allows your application to access and update data stored in many popular databases such as Microsoft Access, FoxPro, and SQL Server.

- An interface to OLE version 2.01, with support for in-place editing, linking, drag-and-drop, and OLE Automation.

You'll see examples that exploit all these features, but to appreciate what the MFC library offers, consider print preview and printer support. The Windows SDK offers no support for print preview. Charles Petzold devotes 60 pages to printer support in *Programming Windows 3.1;* other books about Windows ignore the subject completely. The MFC library contains several thousand lines of "invisible" code that makes print preview and printing "automatic." The Print Preview and Printer support features alone might justify the use of the MFC library.

The Visual C++ tools reduce coding drudgery.   App Studio, AppWizard, and ClassWizard significantly reduce the time needed to write code that is specific to your application. For example, App Studio creates a header file that contains assigned values for *#define* constants. AppWizard generates skeleton code for your entire application, and ClassWizard generates prototypes and function bodies for message handlers.

The Learning Curve

All the benefits listed above sound great, don't they? You're probably thinking that "you don't get something for nothing." Yes, that's true. To use the application framework effectively you have to learn it thoroughly, and that takes time. If you have to learn C++, Windows, and the MFC library (without OLE 2) all at the same time, it will be at least six months before you're really productive. Interestingly, that's close to the learning time for the Windows SDK alone.

How can that be if the MFC library offers so much more? For one thing, you can avoid many programming details that Windows SDK programmers are forced to learn. From my own experience, I can say that an object-oriented application framework makes programming for Windows easier to learn—that is, once you understand object-oriented programming.

The MFC library won't bring real Windows programming down to the masses. Windows programmers have usually commanded higher salaries than other programmers, and that situation will continue. The MFC library learning curve, together with the application framework's power, should ensure that MFC library programmers will be in strong demand.

What's an Application Framework?

One definition of an application framework is "an integrated collection of object-oriented software components that offers all that's needed for a generic application." That isn't a very useful definition, is it? If you really want to know what an application framework is, you'll have to read the rest of this book. The application framework example that you'll familiarize yourself with later in this chapter is a good starting point.

The Application Framework vs. the MFC library

One reason that C++ is a popular language is that it can be "extended" with class libraries. Some class libraries are delivered with C++ compilers, others are sold by third-party software firms, and still others are developed in-house. A class library is a set of related C++ classes that can be used in an application. A matrix class library, for example, might perform common mathematical operations involving matrices, and a communications class library might support the transfer of data over a serial link. Sometimes you construct objects of the supplied classes; sometimes you derive your own classes—it all depends on the design of the particular class library.

An application framework is a superset of a class library. An ordinary library is an isolated set of classes designed to be incorporated into any program, but an application framework defines the structure of the program itself. This sounds like a fine distinction, and it is. Most Windows development class libraries, including Microsoft Foundation Class library version 1.0, Borland OWL, and Microsoft Foundation Class Library version 2.5, are considered application frameworks. Microsoft Foundation Class (MFC) Library version 2.5, however, provides significantly more features than the others.

An Application Framework Example

Enough generalizations. It's time to look at some code—not pseudocode but real code that actually compiles and runs with the MFC library. Guess what? It's the good old "Hello, world!" application with a few additions. (If you've used version 1.0 of the MFC library, this code will be familiar except for the frame window base class.) It's about the minimum amount of code for a working MFC library application for Windows. Contrast it with the equivalent Windows SDK application! You don't have to understand every line now. Don't bother to type it in and test it. Wait for the next chapter, where you'll start using the "real" application framework.

NOTE: By convention, MFC library class names begin with the letter C.

Following is the source code for the header and implementation files for our MYAPP application. The two classes, *CMyApp* and *CMyFrame,* are each derived from the MFC library base classes. First the MYAPP.H header file for the MYAPP application:

```
// application class
class CMyApp : public CWinApp
{
public:
    virtual BOOL InitInstance();
};

// frame window class
class CMyFrame : public CFrameWnd
{
public:
    CMyFrame();
protected:
    // 'afx_msg' indicates that the next two functions are part
    // of the MFC library message dispatch system.
    afx_msg void OnLButtonDown(UINT nFlags, CPoint point);
    afx_msg void OnPaint();
    DECLARE_MESSAGE_MAP()
};
```

And now the MYAPP.CPP implementation file for the MYAPP application:

```
#include <afxwin.h> // MFC library header file declares base classes
#include "myapp.h"

CMyApp NEAR theApp; // the one and only CMyApp object

BOOL CMyApp::InitInstance()
{
    m_pMainWnd = new CMyFrame();
    m_pMainWnd->ShowWindow(m_nCmdShow);

    m_pMainWnd->UpdateWindow();
    return TRUE;
}
```

```
BEGIN_MESSAGE_MAP(CMyFrame, CFrameWnd)
    ON_WM_LBUTTONDOWN()
    ON_WM_PAINT()
END_MESSAGE_MAP()

CMyFrame::CMyFrame()
{
    Create("AfxFrameOrView", "MYAPP Application");
}

void CMyFrame::OnLButtonDown(UINT nFlags, CPoint point)
{
    TRACE("Entering CMyFrame::OnLButtonDown - %lx, %d, %d\n",
          (long) nFlags, point.x, point.y);
}

void CMyFrame::OnPaint()
{
    CPaintDC dc(this);
    dc.TextOut(0, 0, "Hello, world!");
}
```

Here are some of the program elements:

The *WinMain* function.   Remember that Windows requires your application to have a *WinMain* function. You don't see *WinMain* here because it's hidden inside the application framework.

The *CMyApp* class.   An object of class *CMyApp* represents an application. The program defines a single global *CMyApp* object, *theApp*. The *CWinApp* base class determines most of *theApp*'s behavior.

Application startup.   When the user starts the application, Windows calls the application framework's built-in *WinMain* function, and *WinMain* looks for your globally constructed application object of a class derived from *CWinApp*. Don't forget that, in C++, global objects are constructed <u>before</u> the main program is executed.

The *CMyApp::InitInstance* member function.   When *WinMain* finds the application object, it calls the *InitInstance* member function, which makes the calls needed to construct and display the application's main frame window. You must override *InitInstance* in your derived application class because the *CWinApp* base class doesn't have the slightest idea about what kind of main frame window you want.

The *CWinApp::Run* member function.   The *Run* function is hidden in the base class, but it dispatches the application's messages, thus keeping the application running. *WinMain* calls *Run* after it calls *InitInstance*.

The *CMyFrame* class.   An object of class *CMyFrame* represents the application's main frame window. When the constructor calls the *Create* member function of the base class *CFrameWnd*, Windows creates the actual window structure and the application framework links it to the C++ object. The *ShowWindow* and *UpdateWindow* functions, also member functions of the base class, must be called in order to display the window.

The *CMyFrame::OnLButtonDown* function.   This is a sneak preview of the MFC library's message-handling capability. We've elected to "map" the left mouse button down event to a *CMyFrame* member function. You'll learn the details of the MFC library's message mapping in Chapter 4. For the time being, accept that this function gets called when the user presses the left mouse button. The function invokes the MFC library *TRACE* macro to display a message in the debugging window.

The *CMyFrame::OnPaint* function.   The application framework calls this important mapped member function of class *CMyFrame* every time it's necessary to repaint the window: at the start of the program, when the user resizes the window, and when all or part of the window is newly exposed. The *CPaintDC* statement relates to the Graphics Device Interface (GDI) and is explained in later chapters. The *TextOut* function displays "Hello, world!"

Application shutdown.   The user shuts down the application by closing the frame window. This action initiates a sequence of events, which ends with the destruction of the *CMyFrame* object, the exit from *Run*, the exit from *WinMain*, and the destruction of the *CMyApp* object.

Look at the example again. This time try to get the big picture. Most of the application's functionality is in the MFC library base classes *CWinApp* and *CFrameWnd*. In writing MYAPP, we've followed a few simple structure rules, and we've written key functions in our derived classes. C++ lets us "borrow" a lot of code without copying it. Think of it as a partnership between us and the application framework. The application framework provided the structure, and we provided the code that made the application unique.

Now you're beginning to see why the application framework is more than a class library. Not only does the application framework define the application structure but it also encompasses more than C++ base classes.

You've already seen the hidden *WinMain* function at work. Other elements support message processing, diagnostics, DLLs, and so forth.

MFC Library Message Mapping

Refer to the *OnLButtonDown* member function in the previous example. You might think that *OnLButtonDown* would be an ideal candidate for a virtual function. A window base class would define virtual functions for mouse event messages and other standard messages, and derived window classes could override the functions as necessary. Some Windows class libraries do work this way.

The MFC library application framework doesn't use virtual functions for messages used in Windows. Instead, it uses macros to "map" specified messages to derived class member functions. Why the rejection of virtual functions? Consider this situation: You have a hierarchy of five window classes in Windows, and the base class defines virtual functions for 140 messages. C++ requires a virtual function dispatch structure called a "vtbl" that has a 4-byte entry for each class–virtual function combination, regardless of whether the functions are actually overridden in the base classes. Thus, for each distinct type of window or control, the application needs a 2.8-KB table to support virtual message handlers.

What about message handlers for menu command messages and messages from button clicks? You couldn't define these as virtual functions in a window base class because each application might have a different set of menu commands and buttons. The MFC library message map system avoids large vtbls, and it accommodates application-specific command messages. It also allows selected nonwindow classes, such as document classes and the application class, to handle command messages. Unlike the "dynamic dispatch table" system that Borland supplied as part of the early versions of OWL, message maps require no extensions to the C++ language.

An MFC library message handler requires a function prototype, a function body, and an entry in the message map. ClassWizard helps you add message handlers to your classes. You select a Windows message ID from a list box, and the Wizard generates the code with the correct function parameters and return values.

Documents and Views

The previous example used an application object and a frame window object. Most of your MFC library applications will be more complex. Typically, they'll contain application and frame classes plus two other classes that represent the "document" and the "view." This "document–view architecture" is not new. It originated in the early 1980s in the academic world and was then adopted by Apple Computer in 1985 for the MacApp application framework product.

In simple terms, the document–view architecture separates data from the user's view of the data. One obvious benefit is multiple views of the same data. Consider a document that consists of a month's worth of stock quotes stored on disk. Suppose there are a table view and a chart view of the data. The user updates values through the table view window, and the chart view window changes because both windows display the same information (but in different views).

In the MFC library, documents and views are represented by C++ classes and objects. Figure 2-1 shows three objects of class *CStockDoc* corresponding to three companies: AT&T, IBM, and GM. All three documents have a table view attached, and one document also has a chart view. As you can see, there are four view objects—three of class *CStockListView* and one of class *CStockChartView*.

The document base-class code interacts with the File Open and File Save menu items; the derived document class does the actual reading and writing of the document object's data. (The application framework does

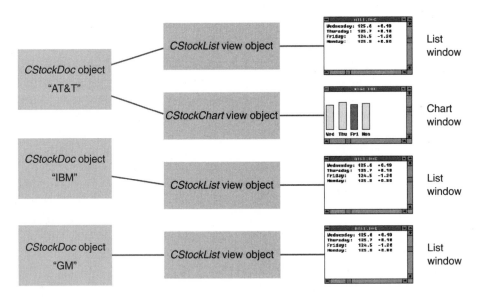

Figure 2-1.
The document–view relationship.

most of the work of displaying the File Open and File Save dialog boxes and opening, closing, reading, and writing files.) The view base class represents a window that is contained inside a frame window; the derived view class interacts with its associated document class and does the application's display and printer I/O. The derived view class and its base classes handle messages in Windows. The MFC library orchestrates all interactions among documents, views, and frame windows, and the application object, mostly through virtual functions.

Don't think that a document object must be associated with a disk file that is read entirely into memory. If a "document" were really a database, for example, you could override selected document class member functions, and the File Open menu item would bring up a list of databases instead of a list of files.

PART II

THE MFC LIBRARY
VIEW CLASS

C H A P T E R   T H R E E

GETTING STARTED WITH APPWIZARD— "HELLO, WORLD!"

Chapter 2 sketched the Microsoft Foundation Class (MFC) Library version 2.5 document–view architecture. This hands-on chapter shows you how to build a functioning MFC library application, but it insulates you from the complexities of the class hierarchy and object interrelationships. You'll work with only one document–view program element, the "view class" that is closely associated with a window. For the time being, you can ignore elements such as the application class, the frame window, and the document. Of course, your application won't be able to save its data on disk, and it won't support multiple views, but Part III of this book provides plenty of opportunity to exploit those features.

> TIP: It's easy to copy a whole project, either with the Windows File Manager or from the DOS prompt (XCOPY /S). There's a trap that's easy to fall into, though. If your original project has open child windows associated with source files, the child windows in the new project will be associated with files in the <u>original</u> project. If you're not careful, you'll be changing the original project inadvertently when you meant to change the copy. (I've fallen into this trap too many times.) To avoid this problem, close all the project's child windows, either before or after the copy.

Because resources are so important in Windows-based applications, you'll use the App Studio resource editor to visually explore the resources of your new program. You'll also get some hints for setting up your Windows environment for maximum build speed and optimal debugging output.

REQUIREMENTS: To compile and run the examples presented in this and the following chapters, you must have successfully installed Microsoft Windows (version 3.1 or later) and all the Visual C++ components. Be sure that the Visual Workbench binary, include, and library directories are set correctly. (You can change the directories by choosing Directories from the Options menu.) If you have any problems with the following steps, please refer to your Visual C++ documentation and README files for troubleshooting instructions.

What's a View?

From the user's standpoint, a "view" is an ordinary window that he or she can size, move, and close in the same way as any other Windows-based application window. From the programmer's perspective, a view is a C++ object of a class derived from the MFC library *CView* class. Like any C++ object, the view object's behavior is determined by the member functions (and data members) of the class—both the application-specific functions in the derived class and the standard functions inherited from the base classes.

With Visual C++, you can produce interesting applications for Windows by simply adding code to the derived view class that the AppWizard code generator produces. When your program runs, the MFC library application framework constructs an object of the derived view class, and it displays a window that is tightly linked to the C++ view object. As is customary in C++ programming, the MFC library view class is divided into two source modules—the header file (H) and the implementation file (CPP).

Single Document Interface (SDI) vs.
Multiple Document Interface (MDI)

The MFC library supports two distinct application types, SDI and MDI. An SDI application has, from the user's point of view, only one window. If the application depends on disk-file "documents," only one document can be loaded at a time. Windows Notepad is an example of an SDI application. An MDI application has multiple "child windows," each of which corresponds to individual documents. The Visual Workbench is a good example of an MDI application.

When you run AppWizard, MDI is the default application type. For the early examples in this book, we'll be generating SDI applications because fewer classes and features are involved. Be sure you uncheck the AppWizard

Multiple Document Interface option for these examples. Starting with Chapter 17, we'll be generating MDI applications. The MFC library application framework architecture ensures that most SDI examples can be upgraded easily to MDI applications.

The "Do-Nothing" Application

The AppWizard program generates the code for a functioning MFC library application. This working application simply brings up an empty window with a menu attached. Later you'll add code that draws inside the window. Follow these steps to build the application:

1. Run AppWizard to generate SDI application source code. Choose AppWizard from the Visual Workbench Project menu. When AppWizard starts, you'll see the MFC AppWizard dialog box, as shown here:

Type the program name as shown, but do not press Enter or click the OK button. You can enter a different name if you want, but AppWizard uses the program name when it creates files and classes. If you enter a different name, your files and classes will have a name that is different from that of the files and classes shown in this AppWizard dialog box example.

Next click the Options button, and specify the options in the Options dialog box, as shown at the top of the following page:

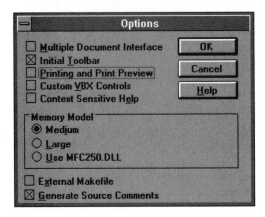

Click the OK buttons in the Options and MFC AppWizard dialog boxes.

AppWizard generates files based on the parameters you type in the MFC AppWizard dialog box. Immediately before AppWizard generates your code, it displays the New Application Information dialog box shown here:

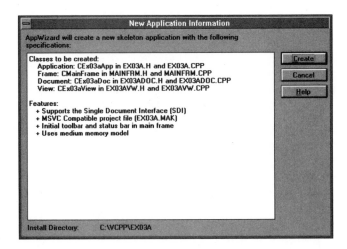

Click the Create button, and AppWizard begins to create your application's subdirectory, files, and classes. When AppWizard is finished, look in the application's subdirectory. The following files are of interest (for now):

File	Description
EX03A.DEF	Windows module definition file
EX03A.MAK	Project file that allows Visual Workbench to build your application
EX03A.RC	Resource script file
EX03AVW.CPP	View class implementation file that contains *CEx03aView* class member functions
EX03AVW.H	View class header file that contains the *CEx03aView* class declaration
README.TXT	Text file that explains the purpose of all generated files
RESOURCE.H	*#define* constant definitions

Open the EX03AVW.CPP and EX03AVW.H files and look at the source code. Together these files define the *CEx03aView* class, which is central to the application. An object of class *CEx03aView* corresponds to the application's view window, where all the "action" takes place.

2. **Compile and link the generated code.** AppWizard, in addition to generating code, creates a custom project file for your application. This file, EX03A.MAK, specifies all the file dependencies together with the compile and link option flags. Because the new project becomes Visual Workbench's current project, you can now build the application by choosing Build EX03A.EXE from the Project menu.

> NOTE: The Compile, Build, and Execute items on the Project menu display the current project's name.

If the build is successful, an executable program called EX03A.EXE is created in the application's subdirectory.

The EX03A.DEF file provides useful information to the linker. Most important is the name of the application, contained in the DEF file's first noncomment line:

```
NAME        EX03A
```

> TIP: If you have two or more programs with the same DEF file NAME parameter, Windows won't let you run them simultaneously. (You'll probably see two copies of the application you run first.) Be careful.

3. **Test the resulting application.** Choose Execute EX03A.EXE from the Project menu. Experiment with the program. It really doesn't do much, does it? (What do you expect for no coding, anyway?) Actually, as you might be able to tell from the size of the EXE file, the program has a lot of features—you simply haven't activated them yet. Close the program window when you've finished experimenting.

4. **Browse the application.** You can use the Visual C++ browser only after you have successfully compiled an application. Choose Open EX03A.BSC from the Browse menu, and the browser window appears. Set the following parameters:

Type:	Base Class Graph
Subset:	Classes (default)
Symbol:	CEx03aView

> NOTE: The Symbol text box is case-sensitive, so be sure to enter the information exactly as shown.

Now click the Display Result button and expand the class hierarchy by clicking on the icons. The browser window with *CEx03aView* and base classes should eventually look similar to this:

The *CEx03aView* View Class

AppWizard generated the *CEx03aView* view class, and this class is specific to the EX03A application. (AppWizard generates classes using the project name you entered in the MFC AppWizard dialog box.) *CEx03aView* is at the bottom of a long inheritance chain of MFC library classes, as illustrated previously in the browser window. The class picks up member functions and data members all along the chain. You can learn about these classes in the *Class Library Reference* document, but you must be sure to look at the descriptions for every base class because the descriptions of inherited member functions aren't repeated for derived classes.

The most important *CEx03aView* base classes are *CWnd* and *CView*. *CWnd* provides *CEx03aView*'s "windowness," and *CView* provides the hooks to the rest of the application framework, particularly to the document and to the frame window that you'll see in Part III of this book.

Drawing Inside the View Window— The Windows Graphics Device Interface

Now you're ready to write code to draw inside the view window. You'll be making a few changes directly to the EX03A source code.

The *OnDraw* Member Function

Specifically, you'll be fleshing out the *OnDraw* member function in EX03AVW.CPP. *OnDraw* is a virtual member function of the *CView* class that the application framework calls every time the view window needs to be repainted. A window needs repainting if the user resizes the window or reveals a previously hidden part of the window, or if the application changes the window's data. If the user resizes the window or reveals a hidden area, the application framework calls *OnDraw*, but if a function in your program changes the data, it must inform Windows of the change by calling the view's inherited *Invalidate* (or *InvalidateRect*) member function. This call to *Invalidate* triggers a later call to *OnDraw*.

Even though you can draw inside a window at any time, it's strongly recommended that you let window changes accumulate and then process them all together in the *OnDraw* function. That way your program can respond to program-generated events and to Windows-generated events such as size changes.

The Windows Device Context

Remember from Chapter 1 that Windows doesn't allow direct access to the display hardware but communicates through an abstraction called a "device context" that is associated with the window. In the MFC library, the device context is a C++ object of class *CDC* passed (by pointer) as a parameter to *OnDraw*. After you have the device context pointer, you can call the many *CDC* member functions that do the work of drawing.

Adding Draw Code to the EX03A Program

Now let's write the code to draw some text and a circle inside the view window. Be sure that the project EX03A.MAK is open in Visual Workbench. You can use the browser to locate the code for the function (double-click on *CEx03a View::On Draw*), or you can open the source code file EX03AVW.CPP and locate the function yourself.

1. **Edit the *OnDraw* function in EX03AVW.CPP.** Find the AppWizard-generated *OnDraw* function in EX03AVW.CPP:

```
void CEx03aView::OnDraw(CDC* pDC)
{
    CEx03aDoc* pDoc = GetDocument();
    ASSERT_VALID(pDoc);

    // TODO: add draw code here
}
```

The following screened code (which you type in) replaces the previous code:

```
void CEx03aView::OnDraw(CDC* pDC)
{
    pDC->TextOut(0, 0, "Hello, world!"); // prints in default font
                                         //  & size, top left corner
    pDC->SelectStockObject(GRAY_BRUSH);  // selects a brush for the
                                         //  circle interior
    pDC->Ellipse(CRect(0, 20, 100, 120)); // draws a gray circle 100
                                          //  units in diameter
}
```

You can safely remove the call to *GetDocument* because we're not dealing with documents yet. The functions *TextOut*, *SelectStockObject*, and *Ellipse* are all member functions of the application framework's device context class *CDC*. The *Ellipse* function draws a circle if the bounding rectangle's length is equal to its width.

The MFC library provides a handy utility class, *CRect*, for Windows rectangles. A temporary *CRect* object serves as the bounding rectangle argument for the ellipse drawing function. You'll see more use of the *CRect* class later in this book.

2. **Recompile and test EX03A.** Choose Build from the Project menu, and, if there are no compile errors, test the application again. Now you have a program that visibly does something!

For Windows SDK Programmers

Rest assured that the standard Windows *WinMain* and *WndProc* functions are hidden away inside the application framework. You'll see those functions later in this book, when the MFC library frame and application classes are examined. In the meantime, you're probably wondering what happened to the WM_PAINT message, aren't you? You would expect to do your window drawing in response to this Windows message, and you would expect to get your device context handle from a *PAINTSTRUCT* structure that the Windows *BeginPaint* function returns.

It so happens that the application framework has done all the dirty work for you and served up a device context (in object pointer form) in the virtual function *OnDraw*. As explained in Chapter 2, true virtual functions in window classes are an MFC library rarity. MFC library message map functions that the application framework dispatches handle most Windows messages. Microsoft Foundation Class Library version 1.0 programmers always defined an *OnPaint* message map function for their derived window classes. In version 2.5, however, *OnPaint* is defined in the *CView* class, and it calls *OnDraw*. Why? Because *OnDraw* needs to support the printer as well. Both *OnPaint* and *OnPrint* call *OnDraw*, thus enabling the same drawing code to accommodate both the printer and the display.

A Preview of App Studio—Resources Introduced

Now that you have a complete application program, it's a good time for a quick look at the App Studio resource editor. Although the application's resource script, EX03A.RC, is an ASCII file, modifying it with a text editor is not a good idea. That's App Studio's job.

The Contents of EX03A.RC

The resource file determines much of the EX03A application's "look and feel." The file EX03A.RC contains (or points to) the Windows resources listed on the following page:

Resource	Description
Accelerators	Definitions for keys that simulate menu and toolbar selections
Toolbar bitmap	The row of buttons immediately below the menu
Dialog	Layout and contents of dialog boxes—the About dialog box for EX03A
Icon	The AFX logo you see in the application's About dialog box
Menu	The application's main menu and associated pop-up menus
String table	Strings that are not part of the C++ source code

In addition to the resources listed above, EX03A.RC contains the statement

```
#include  "afxres.h"
```

which brings in some special MFC library resources common to all applications. These special resources include strings, graphical buttons, and elements needed for printing and OLE.

EX03A.RC also contains the statement

```
#include  "resource.h"
```

This statement brings in the application's *#define* constants, which are *IDR_MAINFRAME* (identifying the menu, icon, string list, and accelerator table) and *IDD_ABOUTBOX* (identifying the About dialog box). This same RESOURCE.H file is included indirectly by the application's source code files. If you use App Studio to add more constants (symbols), the definitions ultimately show up in RESOURCE.H. If you use a text editor to add your own constants to RESOURCE.H, App Studio does not disturb them.

NOTE: The file EX03A.RC2, located in the project's RES subdirectory, contains resources that App Studio doesn't edit. The version resource falls into this category.

Running App Studio

Although you can run App Studio from the Windows File Manager or Program Manager, running it from within Visual Workbench is easiest.

1. Start the App Studio program. In Visual Workbench, choose App Studio from the Tools menu. You will see the following App Studio window:

TIP: You can also activate App Studio by choosing the project's RC file in the Open File dialog box. For this to work, you must first choose Editor from Visual Workbench's Options menu and check the Open .RC Files Using App Studio check box in the Editor dialog box.

For Windows SDK Programmers

App Studio replaces the Windows SDK Dialog Editor and SDK Paint. In addition to handling dialog boxes, icons, cursors, and bitmaps, App Studio edits string tables and accelerator tables, and it has a wysiwyg menu editor. You no longer need to edit resource script files—indeed, you shouldn't because you might trip up App Studio with a syntax error.

With the SDK Dialog Editor, you must manually assign an integer and corresponding #*define* constant name to each control. App Studio assigns #*define* constants to windows, buttons, menu items, and so forth. (You can change the constants if you want.) App Studio generates and maintains a single include file, named RESOURCE.H, that contains all the definitions with sequential integer values.

2. Examine the application's resources. Now take some time to explore the individual resources. Notice that resource selection is a two-step process: First you click on the resource type on the left, and then you double-click on a specific resource on the right. When you select a resource, another window opens with tools appropriate for the selected resource. (The control palette might also open.)

3. **Modify the About dialog box.** Make some changes to the About dialog box, shown here in App Studio:

You can change the size of the window by dragging the right and bottom borders, move the OK button, change the text, and so forth. Simply click on an element to select it. When you're done, save the file and exit App Studio.

4. **Rebuild the application with the modified resource file.** In Visual Workbench, choose Build from the Project menu. Notice that no actual C++ recompilation or linking is necessary. Visual Workbench saves the edited resource file on disk, and then the Resource Compiler (RC.EXE) processes EX03A.RC to produce a compiled version, EX03A.RES. Then RC.EXE runs again to bind the compiled resources to the EX03A.EXE file, replacing the resources that were there before.

5. **Test the new version of the application.** Run the EX03A program again, and then choose About from the application's Help menu to confirm that your dialog box was changed as expected.

The Windows Debug Kernel and DBWIN

As a developer, you should run the Windows Debug kernel at all times. (The sidebar on the facing page gives instructions for installing the kernel.) The Debug kernel provides important error messages that you would miss with the regular version of Windows.

Installing the Windows Debug Kernel

You must specifically tell the Visual C++ Setup program to install the Windows Debug kernel files. To do so, run the Visual C++ Setup program. A dialog box similar to this one appears:

(If you've previously installed Visual C++, you can uncheck all check boxes except the Tools check box.) Click the Tools button. A dialog box similar to this one appears:

Check the Debug Kernel check box. (If you've previously installed Visual C++, you can uncheck the other check boxes.) Click the OK button in the second dialog box, and then click the Continue button in the first dialog box.

To activate the Debug kernel after it is installed, run the N2D batch file (located in the \MSVC\BIN subdirectory). This batch file copies files from the \MSVC\DEBUG subdirectory to your WINDOWS subdirectory. The message "Enhanced Mode Debug Windows 3.1" at the bottom of Windows' background screen indicates that the Debug kernel is properly installed. (This message should appear the next time you start Windows.)

If your computer is equipped with dual monitors, the error messages appear on the auxiliary monitor. If you don't have dual monitors, you should definitely run the Windows DBWIN program, located in the \MSVC\BIN subdirectory, to see the error messages in a window. DBWIN is useful not only for displaying messages from the Windows Debug kernel but also for displaying output from the application framework diagnostic macros *TRACE*, *ASSERT*, and *VERIFY*. The *TRACE* macro is explained in Chapter 15, on page 278. Consider inserting the line

```
load=dbwin
```

in your WIN.INI file to load DBWIN when Windows starts. You can also add a DBWIN program item in your STARTUP group.

Do You Need to Use the Debugger?

Using the debugger with programs for Windows is more complicated than using the debugger with MS-DOS programs. You can't use the debugger to trace through an entire program because Windows-based programs don't execute sequentially. You must put breakpoints at the start of the message-handling functions that you need to debug.

TIP: To avoid stepping through the code in the MFC library, use the Step Over button, shown here,

to step to the next statement in the function you are debugging.

You might find that you can do most of your debugging without the Visual C++ debugger. If you find that you're using the debugger infrequently, you can save considerable compile, link, and load time by eliminating debugging information from your program. The last "speedup" hint (#6 on page 47) shows you how.

Enabling the Diagnostic Macros

The application framework *TRACE* macros are particularly useful for monitoring program status. These macros, together with the *ASSERT* and *VERIFY* macros, require the Debug build option (but do not require debugging information). In addition, the *TRACE* macros require that tracing be enabled. You can enable tracing by inserting the statement

```
afxtrace = TRUE;
```

in your program. Alternatively, you can insert the statement

```
TraceEnabled = 1
```

in the [Diagnostics] section of the AFX.INI file in your WINDOWS subdirectory. You can control this trace option, together with other trace options, with the TRACER utility that is included with Visual C++. If you're using the Visual Workbench debugger, TRACE output appears in the Debug Output window. Otherwise, you need an auxiliary monitor or the DBWIN program.

Speeding Up the Build Process

As you saw with the application you created earlier in this chapter, Visual C++ can be slow when building an application. This section's information will help you speed up the process of compiling and linking applications. The speedup hints are presented here instead of in an appendix because you can begin saving time right away as you build the sample applications.

The procedures described here are optional, but their combined effect is to cut build time by more than half. Most procedures depend on your computer having sufficient installed memory.

1. Be sure that SMARTDRV is installed. SMARTDRV is the disk caching utility that is normally installed during MS-DOS or Windows setup. The line SMARTDRV in your AUTOEXEC.BAT file starts the utility when your computer boots. The default cache size is usually sufficient. (The default cache size is based on the amount of memory in your computer.)

SMARTDRV generally improves the performance of all Windows-based programs. SMARTDRV comes with both MS-DOS and Windows; you should use whichever version is newer. Be sure to use SMARTDRV's double-buffering option if your hard disk requires double buffering. (See your MS-DOS or Windows manual for more information.)

2. Set up a RAM drive. If your computer has 16 MB or more of memory available, set up a RAM drive. The following line in your CONFIG.SYS file sets up a 6-MB RAM drive:

```
devicehigh=c:\windows\ramdrive.sys 6144 512 1024 /e
```

> NOTE: The RAMDRIVE.SYS device driver comes with both MS-DOS and Windows. You should use whichever version is newer. Also note that this example assumes you're using MS-DOS or a third-party memory manager to create upper memory blocks. If you're not using memory management software to create upper memory blocks, change *devicehigh* to *device* in the line above. (For more information about MS-DOS's memory management capabilities, see *The Microsoft Guide to Managing Memory with MS-DOS 6,* by Dan Gookin, Microsoft Press, 1993.)

If C is your only hard disk drive, the RAM drive will be drive D. Exit all applications and reboot the computer to be sure that the RAM drive is installed.

3. Set the TMP and TEMP environment variables to D:\. If you have successfully installed a RAM drive, these environment variables instruct the compiler and linker (and possibly other programs) to store temporary files in the RAM drive. Set these environment variables in your AUTOEXEC.BAT file:

```
set tmp=D:\
set temp=D:\
```

(Note: Change the drive letter if your RAM drive is not drive D.)

4. Modify your MFC library project files to use the RAM drive for precompiled headers. This procedure must be performed for each generated MFC library project file, but the results are worth the effort. First, though, you need to know about precompiled headers and the way the MFC library uses them.

> NOTE: Visual C++ has two precompiled header "systems": automatic and manual. Automatic precompiled headers, activated with the /Yx compiler switch, are new, but manual precompiled headers, first introduced with C/C++ version 7.0, are still available. The make files in this book, as generated by AppWizard, use the manual precompiled headers.

Precompiled headers represent compiler "snapshots" taken at a particular source code line. In all MFC library programs, the snapshot is taken immediately after the statement

```
#include "stdafx.h"
```

The file STDAFX.H contains *#include* statements for the MFC library header files. The file's contents depend on the options that you select when you run AppWizard, but the file <u>always</u> contains the following statements:

```
#include <afxwin.h>
#include <afxext.h>
```

If you're using OLE, STDAFX.H contains the statement

```
#include <afxole.h>
```

Occasionally you'll need the "private" header file that is accessed by the statement

```
#include <afxpriv.h>
```

The source file STDAFX.CPP contains only the statement

```
#include "stdafx.h"
```

and is used to generate the precompiled header file in the project directory. The MFC library headers included by STDAFX.H never change, but they do take a long time to compile. The compiler switch /Yc, used only with STDAFX.CPP, causes <u>creation</u> of the precompiled header (PCH) file. The switch /Yu, used with all the other source code files, causes <u>use</u> of an existing PCH file. The switch /Fp specifies the PCH filename that would otherwise default to STDAFX.PCH in the project subdirectory.

AppWizard sets the /Yc and /Yu switches for you. To change these switches, choose Project from Visual Workbench's Options menu, and click the Compiler button; then click on the Precompiled Headers category, and check or uncheck the Automatic Use Of Precompiled Headers check box as necessary.

> NOTE: You need to choose Rebuild All from the Project menu to create the precompiled header in the RAM drive.

You must manually set the /Fp switch to force the PCH file to reside in the RAM drive. To do so, choose Project from Visual Workbench's Options menu, and click the Compiler button; then click on the Custom Options category, and add the expression

```
/Fp"D:\STDAFX.PCH"
```

in the Other Options text box, as shown here:

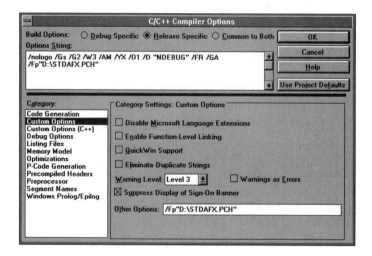

NOTE: Most of the projects on the book's companion disc use the /Fp switch to store the PCH file in the \VCPP subdirectory. This reduces the disk space required when all the projects are compiled, but it doesn't require a RAM drive. You can convert these projects to use a RAM drive by replacing the expression

```
/Fp"..\STDAFX.PCH"
```

in the Other Options text box in the Custom Options category of the C/C++ Compiler Options dialog box with the expression

```
/Fp"D:\STDAFX.PCH"
```

If you're working on several projects simultaneously, those projects can share the same STDAFX.PCH file because that file isn't application-dependent. Not only will you save time, but you'll save disk space because you'll eliminate duplicate copies of the very large PCH file.

> NOTE: You can share the precompiled header file among projects only if the contents of STDAFX.H are the same. A project that uses OLE, for example, can't use the PCH file from a project that doesn't use OLE. See the Visual C++ documentation for more information.

> NOTE: Obviously, the PCH file won't stay in the RAM drive when the computer is rebooted or turned off. You can set up batch files to save and restore this file from disk, or you can force Visual Workbench to regenerate the PCH file by choosing Rebuild All from the Project menu.

5. **Store the library files in the RAM drive.** You'll reduce link time by about 25 percent if you keep the library files in the RAM drive. Use a batch file to copy the appropriate LIB files to the RAM drive when your computer boots. (If you're using the medium-model debug library, you'll want to copy MLIBCEW.LIB and MAFXCWD.LIB to the RAM drive.) Finally, tell Visual C++ to look for the library files in the RAM drive. To do so, choose Directories from the Options menu. In the Directories dialog box that appears, set the Library Files Path text box to point to the RAM drive. (Unless you have a very large RAM drive, you'll probably want to leave the MFC library files on your hard disk. Be sure the Library Files Path text box in the Directories dialog box still points to the MFC library subdirectory on your hard disk.)

6. **If you're not using the debugger, eliminate the debugging information.** You might want to get the benefits of the *TRACE, VERIFY,* and *ASSERT* macros without using the debugger. AppWizard generates project files with the compiler and linker switches for debugging information. You can save build time by turning off these switches as follows:

❑ Choose Project from the Options menu. The Project Options dialog box appears. Click the Compiler button. The C/C++ Compiler Options dialog box appears. Click on the Debug Options category, and then click the None radio button. Your screen now looks like the one shown at the top of the following page:

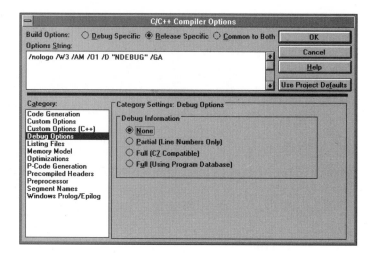

❑ Click OK to close the C/C++ Compiler Options dialog box.

❑ Click the Linker button in the Project Options dialog box. The Linker Options dialog box appears. Click on the Output category, and then uncheck the Generate Debugging Information check box. Your screen now looks like this:

❑ Close the Linker Options and Project Options dialog boxes.

NOTE: The Debug radio button in the Build Mode section of the Project Options dialog box enables a set of compiler and linker options that relate to debugging.

These options include the generation of debugging information for Visual Workbench and CodeView for Windows debuggers, the definition of the _DEBUG preprocessor constant (which activates certain diagnostic features in the MFC library), and the selection of the debug version of the MFC library (MAFXCWD.LIB for medium-memory-model applications).

It's possible to separately enable and disable each of these debugging options through the Compiler Options and Linker Options dialog boxes. If, for example, you want the MFC library diagnostic features, such as the *TRACE* macro, but you don't want to use the debugger, you must individually adjust the compiler and linker options.

7. If you aren't using the browser, don't build the browser database.
The project's browser database (BSC file) must be rebuilt every time you change any source code. If you don't need the browser, you can save build time by turning off browser information. To do so, choose Project from the Options menu. The Project Options dialog box appears. Click the Compiler button. The C/C++ Compiler Options dialog box appears. Click on the Listing Files category, and then uncheck the Browser Information check box. Your screen now looks like this:

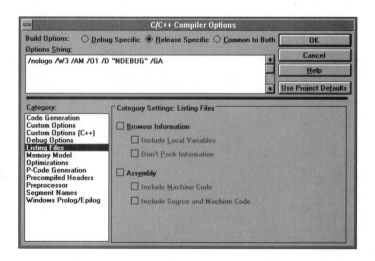

Close the C/C++ Compiler Options and Project Options dialog boxes.

Creating a New MAK File

Sooner or later you'll need to create your own MAK file for an existing project. Perhaps the MAK file from AppWizard was lost, or perhaps you prefer not to use AppWizard. Simply do the following:

1. Choose Close All from Visual Workbench's Window menu. When you start a new project, Visual Workbench leaves your old windows open, which is probably not what you want.

2. Choose New from Visual Workbench's Project menu. A subdirectory must exist for the project. If you're starting from scratch, use File Manager to create a new subdirectory. Select the subdirectory using the New Project dialog box, and then type the makefile name. You'll see a list of any CPP and C files that already exist in the selected subdirectory.

3. Add the necessary source files. Click the Add All button (or double-click on individual files). Doing so adds the files to the project. Also add the DEF file (you might have to write one) and the RC file.

4. Set up manual precompiled headers. Assuming your project has STDAFX.CPP and STDAFX.H files, fill in the Precompiled Headers category of the C/C++ Compiler Options dialog box, as shown here:

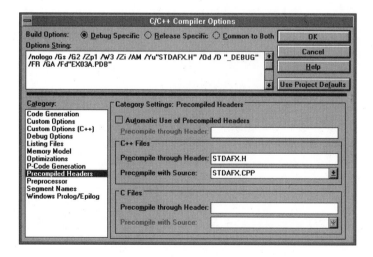

C H A P T E R F O U R

BASIC EVENT HANDLING— USING CLASSWIZARD

In Chapter 3, you saw how the Microsoft Foundation Class (MFC) Library application framework called the view class's virtual *OnDraw* function. Take a look at the *Class Library Reference* now. If you look at the documentation for the *CView* class and its base class, *CWnd*, you'll see several hundred member functions. Functions with names beginning with *On*—such as *OnKeyDown* and *OnLButtonUp*—are member functions that the application framework calls in response to various Windows "events" such as keystrokes and mouse clicks.

Most of these application framework–called functions aren't virtual functions such as *OnDraw* and thus require more effort to program. This chapter explains how to use the Visual C++ ClassWizard to set up the "message map" structure necessary for connecting the application framework to your functions' code. You'll see the practical application of message map functions.

The first two examples use an ordinary *CView* class. More often than not, you'll want a "scrolling" view. The last example uses *CScrollView* in place of the *CView* base class. Now the MFC library application framework inserts scroll bars and "hooks them up" to the view.

Getting User Input—Message Map Functions

Your EX03A application from Chapter 3 did not accept user input (other than the standard Microsoft Windows resizing and window close commands). The window contained menus and a toolbar, but these were not "connected" to the view code. The menus and the toolbar must wait until Part III of this book because they depend on the frame class, but plenty of other Windows input sources will keep you busy until then. Before you can process any Windows event, even a mouse click, however, you must learn how to use the MFC library message map system.

The Message Map

When the user clicks the left mouse button in a view window, Windows sends a message—specifically WM_LBUTTONDOWN—to that window. If your program needs to take action in response to WM_LBUTTONDOWN, your view class must have a member function that looks like this:

```
void CMyView::OnLButtonDown(UINT nFlags, CPoint point)
{
    // event processing code here
}
```

Your class header file must also have the corresponding prototype:

```
afx_msg void OnLButtonDown(UINT nFlags, CPoint point);
```

The *afx_msg* notation is a "no-op" that alerts you that this is a prototype for a message map function. Finally, your code file needs a message map macro that connects your *OnLButtonDown* function to the application framework:

```
BEGIN_MESSAGE_MAP(CMyView, CView)
    ON_WM_LBUTTONDOWN() // entry specifically for OnLButtonDown
    // other message map entries
END_MESSAGE_MAP()
```

and your class header file needs the statement

```
DECLARE_MESSAGE_MAP()
```

How do you know which function goes with which Windows message? Appendix B (and the MFC library online Help file) includes a table that lists all standard Windows messages and corresponding member function prototypes. You can manually code the message-handling functions—indeed, that was the only option for Microsoft Foundation Class Library version 1.0 programmers. Fortunately, Visual C++ provides a tool, ClassWizard, that automates the coding of message map functions.

Saving the View's State—Class Data Members

If your program accepts user input, you'll want the user to have some visual feedback. The view's *OnDraw* function draws an image based on the view's current "state," and user actions can alter that state. In a full-blown MFC library application, the document object holds the state of the application, but you're not to that point yet. For now, you'll use a view class "data member," *m_ellipseRect*, an object of class *CRect*, to hold the current bounding rectangle of an ellipse. Then you'll make the member function toggle that rectangle (the view's state) between small and large. (The toggle is activated by pressing the mouse's left button.) The initial value of *m_ellipseRect* is set in the *CMyView* constructor, and it is changed in the *OnLButtonDown* member function.

NOTE: By convention, MFC library nonstatic class data member names begin with *m_*.

TIP: Why not use a global variable for the view's state? Because if you did, you'd be in trouble if your application had multiple views. Besides, encapsulating data in objects is a big part of what object-oriented programming is all about.

Initializing a View Class Data Member

As Appendix A points out, the most efficient place to initialize a class data member is in the constructor, like this:

```
CMyView::CMyView() : m_ellipseRect(0, 0, 200, 200) { }
```

Invalidating the Rectangle

The *OnLButtonDown* function could toggle the value of *m_ellipseRect* all day, but the *OnDraw* function won't get called unless the user resizes the view window. The *OnLButtonDown* function must call the *InvalidateRect* function (a member function that the *CMyView* class inherits from *CWnd*). *InvalidateRect* triggers a call to *OnDraw*, and *OnDraw* can access the "invalid rectangle" parameter that was passed to *InvalidateRect*.

For Windows SDK Programmers

The MFC library makes it easy to attach your own "state variables" to a window through C++ class data members. In Windows SDK programming, the *WNDCLASS* members *cbClsExtra* and *cbWndExtra* are available for this purpose, but the code for using this mechanism is so complex that few developers bother with it.

The smaller the invalid rectangle, the faster Windows draws the window, even if your *OnDraw* function issues drawing instructions for all elements in the window. If your *OnDraw* function is smart enough to draw only the items that are inside the invalid rectangle, the display update will be even faster.

The Window's Client Area

A window has a rectangular "client area" that excludes the border, caption bar, and menu. The *CWnd* member function *GetClientRect* supplies you with the client area dimensions. Normally, you're not allowed to draw outside the client area, and most mouse messages are received only when the mouse cursor is in the client area.

The EX04A Example Program

In the EX04A example, a circle changes size when the user clicks the left mouse button while the mouse cursor is inside the view window. You'll see the use of a view class data member to hold the view's state, and you'll use the *InvalidateRect* function.

In the Chapter 3 example, drawing in the window depended on only one function, *OnDraw*. The EX04A example requires three customized functions (including the constructor) and one data member. The complete *CEx04aView* header and source code files are listed in Figure 4-1. (The steps for creating the program are shown after the program listings.) All changes to the original AppWizard output are screened in gray.

EX04AVW.H

```
class CEx04aView : public CView
{
private:
    CRect m_ellipseRect;
protected: // create from serialization only
    CEx04aView();
    DECLARE_DYNCREATE(CEx04aView)

// Attributes
public:
    CEx04aDoc* GetDocument();
```

Figure 4-1. *(continued)*
The CEx04aView *header and source code files.*

Figure 4-1. *continued*

```
// Operations
public:

// Implementation
public:
    virtual ~CEx04aView();
    virtual void OnDraw(CDC* pDC); // overridden to draw this view
#ifdef _DEBUG
    virtual void AssertValid() const;
    virtual void Dump(CDumpContext& dc) const;
#endif

// Generated message map functions
protected:
    //{{AFX_MSG(CEx04aView)
    afx_msg void OnLButtonDown(UINT nFlags, CPoint point);
    //}}AFX_MSG
    DECLARE_MESSAGE_MAP()
};

#ifndef _DEBUG  // debug version in ex04avw.cpp
inline CEx04aDoc* CEx04aView::GetDocument()
    { return (CEx04aDoc*) m_pDocument; }
#endif
```

EX04AVW.CPP

```
#include "stdafx.h"
#include "ex04a.h"

#include "ex04adoc.h"
#include "ex04avw.h"

#ifdef _DEBUG
#undef THIS_FILE
static char BASED_CODE THIS_FILE[] = __FILE__;
#endif

/////////////////////////////////////////////////////////////////////
// CEx04aView

IMPLEMENT_DYNCREATE(CEx04aView, CView)

BEGIN_MESSAGE_MAP(CEx04aView, CView)
    //{{AFX_MSG_MAP(CEx04aView)
    ON_WM_LBUTTONDOWN()
```

(continued)

Figure 4-1. *continued*

```
        //}}AFX_MSG_MAP
END_MESSAGE_MAP()


/////////////////////////////////////////////////////////////////////
// CEx04aView construction/destruction

CEx04aView::CEx04aView() : m_ellipseRect(0, 0, 200, 200)
{
}


CEx04aView::~CEx04aView()
{
}


/////////////////////////////////////////////////////////////////////
// CEx04aView drawing

void CEx04aView::OnDraw(CDC* pDC)

{
    pDC->SelectStockObject(GRAY_BRUSH);
    pDC->Ellipse(m_ellipseRect);
}


/////////////////////////////////////////////////////////////////////
// CEx04aView diagnostics

#ifdef _DEBUG
void CEx04aView::AssertValid() const
{
    CView::AssertValid();
}


void CEx04aView::Dump(CDumpContext& dc) const
{
    CView::Dump(dc);
}


CEx04aDoc* CEx04aView::GetDocument() // non-debug version is inline
{
    ASSERT(m_pDocument->IsKindOf(RUNTIME_CLASS(CEx04aDoc)));
    return (CEx04aDoc*) m_pDocument;
}


#endif //_DEBUG
```

(continued)

Figure 4-1. *continued*

```
/////////////////////////////////////////////////////////////////////////
// CEx04aView message handlers

void CEx04aView::OnLButtonDown(UINT nFlags, CPoint point)
{
    if (m_ellipseRect == CRect(0, 0, 200, 200)) {
      m_ellipseRect = CRect(0, 0, 100, 100); // little circle
    }
    else {
      m_ellipseRect = CRect(0, 0, 200, 200); // big circle
    }
    InvalidateRect(CRect(0, 0, 200, 200));
}
```

Using ClassWizard with EX04A

Look at the following EX04AVW.H source code:

```
//{{AFX_MSG(CEx04aView)
afx_msg void OnLButtonDown(UINT nFlags, CPoint point);
//}}AFX_MSG
```

Now look at the following EX04AVW.CPP source code:

```
//{{AFX_MSG_MAP(CEx04aView)
ON_WM_LBUTTONDOWN()
//}}AFX_MSG_MAP
```

AppWizard generated the funny-looking comment lines for the benefit of Class Wizard. ClassWizard adds message handler prototypes between the *AFX_MSG* "brackets," and it also adds message map entries between the *AFX_MSG_MAP* brackets. In addition, ClassWizard generates a skeleton *OnLButtonDown* member function in EX04AVW.CPP, complete with the correct parameter declarations and return type.

Notice how the AppWizard-ClassWizard combination is different from a conventional code generator. You run a conventional code generator only once and then edit the resulting code. You run AppWizard to generate the application only once, but you can run ClassWizard as many times as necessary, and you can edit the code at any time. You're safe as long as you don't alter what's inside the *AFX_MSG* and *AFX_MSG_MAP* brackets.

Using AppWizard and ClassWizard Together

The following steps illustrate how you use AppWizard and ClassWizard together to create this application:

1. **Run AppWizard to create EX04A.** Choose AppWizard from the Visual Workbench Project menu. Use AppWizard to generate a program named EX04A in the \VCPP\EX04A subdirectory. The options and the default class names are shown here:

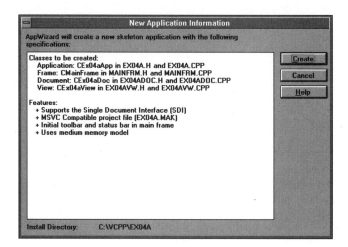

Click on the Options and the Classes buttons in the MFC AppWizard dialog box to set these options.

2. **Use ClassWizard to add a *CEx04aView* class message handler.** Be sure you have opened the EX04A project, and choose ClassWizard from the Browse menu of the Visual Workbench. The ClassWizard dialog box appears. Now click on *CEx04aView* at the top of the Object IDs list box, and then double-click on WM_LBUTTONDOWN in ClassWizard's Messages list box. The *OnLButtonDown* function name should appear in the Member Functions list box, and a hand symbol should appear next to the message name in the Messages list box. Here's the ClassWizard dialog box:

3. **Edit the *OnLButtonDown* code in EX04AVW.CPP.** Click on the Edit
   Code button. ClassWizard opens an edit window for EX04AVW.CPP in
   the Visual Workbench and positions the cursor on the newly generated
   OnLButtonDown member function. The following screened code (which
   you type in) replaces the previous code:

```
void CEx04aView::OnLButtonDown(UINT nFlags, CPoint point)
{
    if (m_ellipseRect == CRect(0, 0, 200, 200)) {
      m_ellipseRect = CRect(0, 0, 100, 100); // little circle
    }
    else {
      m_ellipseRect = CRect(0, 0, 200, 200); // big circle
    }
    InvalidateRect(CRect(0, 0, 200, 200));
}
```

4. **Edit the constructor and the *OnDraw* function in EX04AVW.CPP.** The
   following screened code (which you type in) replaces the previous code:

```
CEx04aView::CEx04aView() : m_ellipseRect(0, 0, 200, 200)
{
}
void CEx04aView::OnDraw(CDC* pDC)
{
    pDC->SelectStockObject(GRAY_BRUSH);
    pDC->Ellipse(m_ellipseRect);
}
```

5. **Add the *m_ellipseRect* data member in EX04AVW.H.** Insert the following code at the start of the *CEx04aView* class declaration:

```
private:
    CRect m_ellipseRect;
```

6. **Build and run the EX04A program.** In the Visual Workbench, choose Build from the Project menu and then choose Execute. The resulting program responds to left-button mouse clicks by shrinking and expanding a circle in the view window. (Don't press the mouse's left button quickly in succession; Windows interprets this as a double-click rather than two single clicks.)

For Windows SDK Programmers

A standard Windows SDK application registers a "window class" and, in the process, assigns a *WndProc* function to all windows of that class. The *WndProc* function is called each time Windows sends a message, and it usually has a *switch* statement for processing the incoming messages.

The MFC library takes care of window class registration by assigning a window class (not to be confused with a C++ class) to each type of window. All view windows, for example, share the same window class. The MFC library contains only one "hidden" *WndProc* function for all view windows. This function works with the message map system to call the appropriate class member function in response to a Windows message.

EX04B—Dragging a Circle with the Mouse

Let's do something a little more sophisticated with the mouse. The object of the next example is to draw a circle in the window and then allow the user to drag the circle with the mouse. As you study the program, you'll learn a few more things about Windows.

Mouse message handlers are necessary for the following three mouse messages:

■ The WM_LBUTTONDOWN message begins the tracking process if the left mouse button is pressed when the mouse cursor is positioned over the circle.

■ The WM_MOUSEMOVE message, received periodically while the mouse moves, causes the circle to follow the mouse cursor position. This message is processed only when the left mouse button is held down and the tracking process was successfully started. (See WM_LBUTTONDOWN at the bottom of the facing page.)

■ The WM_LBUTTONUP message, received when the left mouse button is released, ends the tracking process if it was successfully started.

Now follow these steps to produce the working EX04B example.

1. **Run AppWizard to create EX04B.** Close the EX04A project, and use AppWizard to generate a program named EX04B in the \VCPP\EX04B subdirectory. The options and the default class names are shown here:

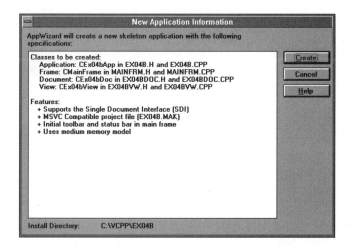

2. **Edit the *CEx04bView* class header in the file EX04BVW.H.** In the file EX04BVW.H, add the following lines in the class *CEx04bView* declaration:

```
private:
    CRect   m_ellipseRect;
    CPoint  m_mousePos;
    BOOL    m_bCaptured;
```

3. **Use ClassWizard to add three message handlers.** Add message-handling functions for the three mouse messages previously described. A list of Windows messages and their associated member functions is shown in the table at the top of the following page:

Message	Member Function Name
WM_LBUTTONDOWN	*OnLButtonDown*
WM_LBUTTONUP	*OnLButtonUp*
WM_MOUSEMOVE	*OnMouseMove*

4. Edit the *CEx04bView* mouse message-handling functions in the file EX04BVW.CPP. ClassWizard generated the skeletons for the functions previously listed. Find them in the file EX04BVW.CPP, and then type in the screened code (replacing the existing code) as follows:

```
void CEx04bView::OnLButtonDown(UINT nFlags, CPoint point)
{
    CRect rect;
    CRgn  circle;

    TRACE("entering CEx04bView::OnLButtonDown - point = %d, %d\n",
            point.x, point.y);
    circle.CreateEllipticRgnIndirect(m_ellipseRect);
    if (circle.PtInRegion(point)) {
        // capturing mouse ensures subsequent LButtonUp message
        SetCapture();
        m_bCaptured = TRUE;
        m_mousePos = point;
        // "cross" mouse cursor is active while mouse is captured
        ::SetCursor(::LoadCursor(NULL, IDC_CROSS));
    }
}


void CEx04bView::OnLButtonUp(UINT nFlags, CPoint point)
{
    if (m_bCaptured) {
        ReleaseCapture();
        m_bCaptured = FALSE;
    }
}


void CEx04bView::OnMouseMove(UINT nFlags, CPoint point)
{
    CSize offset;
    CRect tempRect, newRect, invalidRect, clientRect;

    if (m_bCaptured) {
        GetClientRect(clientRect);
        // don't move the circle outside the client window
        if (clientRect.PtInRect(point)) {
```

```
        offset = point - m_mousePos;
        newRect = m_ellipseRect + (CPoint(0, 0) + offset);
        tempRect.UnionRect(m_ellipseRect, newRect);
        invalidRect.IntersectRect(tempRect, clientRect);
        InvalidateRect(invalidRect, TRUE);
        m_mousePos = point;
        m_ellipseRect = newRect;
    }
  }
}
```

5. Edit the constructor and the *OnDraw* function in the file EX04B-VW.CPP. AppWizard generated these skeleton functions. Find them and type in the following code:

```
CEx04bView::CEx04bView() : m_ellipseRect(0, 0, 100, 100) // constructor
{
    m_bCaptured = FALSE;
}

void CEx04bView::OnDraw(CDC* pDC)
{
    pDC->SelectStockObject(GRAY_BRUSH);
    pDC->Ellipse(m_ellipseRect);
}
```

6. Build and run the EX04B program. In Visual Workbench, choose Build from the Project menu and then choose Execute. The resulting program allows a circle to be dragged with the mouse.

The EX04B Program Elements

Following is a discussion of the major elements in the EX04B program.

The *m_ellipseRect* Data Member

This object of class *CRect* holds the current (as of the last mouse move) bounding rectangle of the moving circle. The *OnDraw* member function uses it.

The *m_mousePos* Data Member

The *OnMouseMove* member function must compare the current mouse position with the previous mouse position to know how far to move the circle. This object of class *CPoint* stores the previous mouse position.

The *m_bCaptured* Data Member

This Boolean variable is set to TRUE when mouse tracking is in progress.

The *SetCapture* and *ReleaseCapture* Member Functions

SetCapture is the *CWnd* member function that "captures" the mouse such that mouse movement messages are sent to this window even if the mouse cursor is outside the window. An unfortunate side effect of this function is that the circle can be moved outside the window and "lost," but I'll show you how to fix that problem in the first paragraph on the facing page. A desirable and necessary effect is that <u>all</u> subsequent mouse messages are sent to the window, including the WM_LBUTTONUP message, which would otherwise be lost. *ReleaseCapture* turns off mouse capture.

The *SetCursor* and *LoadCursor* Windows Functions

The MFC library does not "wrap" some Windows functions. By convention, we use the C++ scope resolution operator (::) when directly calling Windows functions. In this case, there is no potential of conflict with a *CView* member function, but you can deliberately choose to call a Windows function in place of a class member function with the same name. In that case, the :: operator ensures that you call the globally scoped Windows function.

With the first parameter NULL, the *LoadCursor* function creates a "cursor resource" from the specified predefined mouse cursor that Windows uses. The *SetCursor* function activates the specified cursor resource. This cursor remains active as long as the mouse is captured.

CRect, *CPoint*, and *CSize* Arithmetic

If you look in the *Class Library Reference,* you will see that the *CRect*, *CPoint*, and *CSize* classes have a number of overloaded operators. (Overloaded operators are explained in Appendix A.) You can, among other things, do the following:

- Add a *CSize* object to a *CPoint* object
- Subtract a *CSize* object from a *CPoint* object
- Subtract one *CPoint* object from another, yielding a *CSize* object
- Add a *CPoint* object to a *CRect* object
- Subtract a *CPoint* object from a *CRect* object

From this list, you can begin to see that a *CSize* object is the "difference between two *CPoint* objects" and that you can "bias" a *CRect* object by a *CPoint* object. The C++ compiler enforces the rules above; it will not, for example, let you add a *CSize* object to a *CRect* object.

The *OnMouseMove* member function uses *CRect*, *CPoint*, and *CSize* objects to move the circle's bounding rectangle based on the last mouse move.

Is a Point Inside the Client Area?

A captured mouse can move the circle outside the client area, but that's not what we want. The *OnMouseMove* message handler uses the *CRect::PtInRect* function to see whether the mouse position is truly inside the client area. If the mouse cursor is outside the client area, the circle isn't moved.

Is a Point Inside a Circle?

The Windows GDI provides an element called a "region" that can be used for clipping and for hit testing. Regions consist of combinations of polygons (including rectangles) and ellipses. The *OnLButtonDown* function creates a temporary *CRgn* object corresponding to the circle, and then it calls the *PtInRgn* function to find out whether the mouse cursor was inside the circle when the mouse button was pressed.

The Minimum Invalid Rectangle

The previous example, EX04A, invalidated the entire view client area each time the circle size was changed. The EX04B example invalidates only the area known to have changed. This rectangular area is computed by first performing a union operation on the rectangle for the circle's new position and on the rectangle for the circle's old position and then by performing an intersection operation with the window's client area. Figure 4-2 illustrates the process.

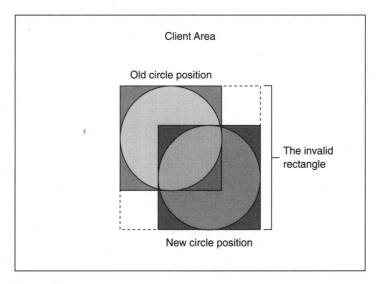

Figure 4-2.
Calculating the minimum invalid rectangle.

The *CRect LPRECT* Operator

If you read the *Class Library Reference* carefully, you will notice that the *CWnd InvalidateRect* member function takes an *LPRECT* parameter, not a *CRect* parameter. It so happens that *LPRECT* is a pointer to a Windows *RECT* structure and that *CRect* is derived from *RECT*. (Yes, C++ lets you derive a class from a structure.) This derivation ensures that a *CRect** parameter is passed to the function, not a *CRect* argument.

A *CRect* argument is allowed because the *CRect* class defines an overloaded operator *LPRECT()* that takes the address of a *CRect* object. Thus, the compiler converts *CRect* arguments to *LPRECT* arguments when necessary. You call functions as though they had *CRect* reference parameters. The view member function code

```
CRect clientRect;
GetClientRect(clientRect);
```

retrieves the client rectangle coordinates and stores them in *clientRect*.

Device Coordinates—Necessary for This Example

In the Windows default device coordinates mode, units map to display pixels with the origin at the top left. Vertical (*y*-axis) values increase from top to bottom. Because they call underlying Windows functions, many *CRect* operators work properly only with coordinates that have non-negative values. Also, the mouse message function *point* parameter is always in device coordinates. Chapter 5 illustrates the use of other Windows mapping modes and the appropriate conversion strategies.

A Scrolling View Window

As the lack of scroll bars in EX04A and EX04B indicates, the MFC library *CView* class, the base class of *CEx04bView*, doesn't directly support scrolling. The MFC library has another class, *CScrollView*, that does support scrolling. *CScrollView* is derived from *CView*. We'll create a new program that uses *CScrollView* in place of *CView*. The new program, EX04C, does not accept mouse input because the necessary coordinate transformation functions aren't covered until Chapter 5. The program does process keyboard messages, and it introduces an important Windows message, WM_CREATE.

A Window Is Larger than What You See

If you use the mouse to shrink the size of an ordinary window, the contents of the window remain anchored at the top left of the window, and items at the bottom and/or on the right of the window disappear. When you expand the window, the items reappear. You can correctly conclude that a window is larger than the "viewport" that you see on the screen. The viewport doesn't have to be anchored at the top left of the window area. Through the use of the *CWnd* functions *ScrollWindow* and *SetViewportOrg*, the *CScrollView* class allows you to move the viewport anywhere in the window, and that includes areas above and to the left of the origin.

Scroll Bars

Microsoft Windows makes it easy to display scroll bars at the edges of a window, but Windows by itself doesn't make any attempt to connect those scroll bars to their window. That's where the *CScrollView* class fits in. *CScrollView* member functions process the WM_HSCROLL and WM_VSCROLL messages sent by the scroll bars to the view. Those functions move the viewport within the window and do all the necessary housekeeping.

Scrolling Alternatives

The *CScrollView* class supports a particular kind of scrolling—one in which there is one big window and a small viewport. Each item is assigned a unique position in this big window. What if you have 10,000 address lines to display? Instead of having a window 10,000 lines long, you probably want a smaller window with scrolling logic that selects only as many lines as the screen can display. In that case, you should write your own scrolling view class derived from *CView*.

> NOTE: As you'll see in Chapter 24, a *CScrollView*-derived view can easily and efficiently accommodate as many as 2000 lines.

The EX04C Scrolling Example

The goal of EX04C is to make a window twice as wide and twice as high as the screen. The program draws a large circle at the exact center of this window such that the upper left quadrant of the circle is visible when the window is maximized. The user can scroll the window with the mouse and the direction keys.

1. **Run AppWizard to create EX04C.** Use AppWizard to generate a program named EX04C in the \VCPP\EX04C subdirectory. In the Classes dialog box, select *CEx04cView* and set the base class to *CScrollView*, as shown at the top of the following page.

The options and the default class names are shown here:

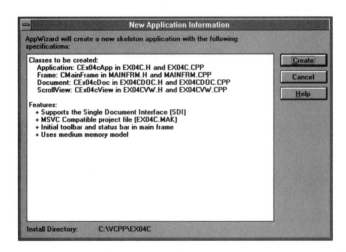

2. Modify the AppWizard-generated *OnInitialUpdate* function in EX04CVW.CPP as follows:

```
void CEx04CView::OnInitialUpdate()
{
    CScrollView::OnInitialUpdate();

    CSize totalSize = CSize(::GetSystemMetrics(SM_CXSCREEN) * 2,
                            ::GetSystemMetrics(SM_CYSCREEN) * 2);
    CSize pageSize = CSize(totalSize.cx / 2,
                           totalSize.cy / 2);
```

```
CSize lineSize = CSize(totalSize.cx / 100,
                       totalSize.cy / 100);
SetScrollSizes(MM_TEXT, totalSize,
               pageSize, lineSize);
}
```

3. **Use ClassWizard to add message handlers for the WM_KEYDOWN message.** ClassWizard generates the member function *OnKeyDown* along with the necessary message map entries and prototypes.

4. **Edit the *CEx04cView* message handler function.** ClassWizard generated the skeleton for the *OnKeyDown* function. Find it in file EX04C-VW.CPP, and then type in the following code:

```
void CEx04cView::OnKeyDown(UINT nChar, UINT nRepCnt, UINT nFlags)
{
    switch (nChar) {
    case VK_HOME:
      OnVScroll(SB_TOP, 0, NULL);
      OnHScroll(SB_LEFT, 0, NULL);
      break;
    case VK_END:
      OnVScroll(SB_BOTTOM, 0, NULL);
      OnHScroll(SB_RIGHT, 0, NULL);
      break;
    case VK_UP:
      OnVScroll(SB_LINEUP, 0, NULL);
      break;
    case VK_DOWN:
      OnVScroll(SB_LINEDOWN, 0, NULL);
      break;
    case VK_PRIOR:
      OnVScroll(SB_PAGEUP, 0, NULL);
      break;
    case VK_NEXT:
      OnVScroll(SB_PAGEDOWN, 0, NULL);
      break;
    case VK_LEFT:
      OnHScroll(SB_LINELEFT, 0, NULL);
      break;
    case VK_RIGHT:
      OnHScroll(SB_LINERIGHT, 0, NULL);
      break;
    default:
      break;
    }
}
```

5. **Edit the *CEx04cView OnDraw* function.** Change the AppWizard-generated *OnDraw* function in EX04CVW.CPP by typing in the following code:

```
void CEx04CView::OnDraw(CDC* pDC)
{
    int x = ::GetSystemMetrics(SM_CXSCREEN);
    int y = ::GetSystemMetrics(SM_CYSCREEN);

    pDC->SelectStockObject(GRAY_BRUSH); // selects a brush for
                                        //   the circle interior
    // draw a circle centered in the scrolling window
    pDC->Ellipse(CRect(x - 300, y - 300, x + 300, y + 300));
}
```

6. **Build and run the EX04C program.** In the Visual Workbench, choose Build from the Project menu and then choose Execute. The program shows a large circle in a scrolling window as shown here:

You might need to scroll to see the circle.

The EX04C Program Elements

Following is a discussion of the major elements in the EX04C program.

The Windows *GetSystemMetrics* Function

The Windows *GetSystemMetrics* function returns the widths and heights of various Windows display elements, including the screen itself. *OnDraw* uses the screen size to determine the circle's center.

The Virtual *OnInitialUpdate* Function

OnInitialUpdate is called by the framework soon after the window is created. This is a good place to initialize the window. Be sure to call the base class function. (*OnInitialUpdate* is explained in greater detail in Chapter 15.)

The *SetScrollSizes* Function

SetScrollSizes is a *CScrollView* member function that <u>must</u> be called during the initialization of a scrolling window. This function specifies the map mode, total window size, and page and line sizes for scrolling. The *MM_TEXT* mapping mode corresponds to device coordinates where one unit equals one pixel.

Handling Keystrokes

Most of the time, you'll get keyboard input through Windows edit controls, keyboard accelerators, or the *CEditView* class, all of which will be described later. Sometimes, though, you need to process raw keystrokes. The Windows WM_KEYDOWN message gives you the exact, untranslated code for a pressed key. The message map function *OnKeyDown* handles this message with a *switch* statement that the *nChar* parameter controls.

Keystrokes that represent normal ASCII characters also generate a WM_CHAR message that delivers the translated ASCII character. We cannot use WM_CHAR here because the direction keys don't generate ASCII characters.

Connecting Scroll Keys to *CScrollView*

In a *CScrollView* window, the scroll bars send a WM_HSCROLL message and a WM_VSCROLL message in response to the user's mouse actions. The handlers for these messages call the *CScrollView::OnHScroll* and *CScrollView::OnVScroll* virtual member functions. If you want only mouse scrolling, you don't need to write any code because the base class does the work. If you want keyboard-actuated scrolling, however, you can use the *OnKeyDown* function to simulate scroll messages. All that's necessary is a direct call to the *OnVScroll* function. The Up direction key, for example, with code *VK_UP*, calls *OnVScroll* with the parameters that specify "scroll up one line." The size of a line was set in the *SetScrollSizes* function called in *OnInitialUpdate*.

Coordinate Transformations—Not Yet

EX04C is an introductory *CScrollView* example. Coordinate transformations are going on in the base class, so don't try any transformations yourself. See EX05A in the next chapter for a complete scrolling example with alternate mapping modes.

Other Windows Messages

The MFC library directly supports about 130 Windows message-handling functions. In addition, you can define your own messages. You will see plenty of message-handling examples in later chapters, including handlers for menu items, child window controls, and so forth. In the meantime, five special Windows messages deserve special attention.

The WM_CREATE Message

This is the first message that Windows sends to a view. It is sent when the window's *Create* function is called by the framework, so the window creation is not finished and the window is not visible. Therefore, your *OnCreate* handler cannot call Windows functions that depend on the window being completely alive. You can call such functions in an overridden *OnInitialUpdate* function, but you must be aware that, in an SDI application, *OnInitialUpdate* can be called more than once in a view's lifetime.

The WM_CLOSE Message

Windows sends the WM_CLOSE message when the user closes a window from the system menu and when a parent window is closed. If you implement the *OnClose* message map function in your derived view class, you can control the closing process. If, for example, you need to prompt the user to save changes to a file, you do it in *OnClose*. Only when you have determined that it is safe to close the window do you call the base class *OnClose* function, which continues the close process. The view object and the corresponding window are both still active.

> TIP: When you're using the full application framework, you probably won't use the WM_CLOSE message handler. As Chapter 24 illustrates, you'll override the *CDocument::SaveModified* virtual function instead, as part of the application framework's highly structured program exit procedure.

The WM_QUERYENDSESSION Message

Windows sends the WM_QUERYENDSESSION message to all running applications when the user exits Windows. The *OnQueryEndSession* message map function handles it. If you write a handler for WM_CLOSE, write one for WM_QUERYENDSESSION too.

The WM_DESTROY Message

Windows sends this message after the WM_CLOSE message, and the *OnDestroy* message map function handles it. When your program receives this message, it should assume that the view window is no longer visible on the screen but that it is still active and its child windows are still active. Use this message handler to do cleanup that depends on the existence of the underlying window. Be sure to call the base class *OnDestroy* function. You cannot "abort" the window destruction process in your view's *OnDestroy* function. *OnClose* is the place to do that.

The WM_NCDESTROY Message

This is the last message that Windows sends when the window is being destroyed. All child windows have already been destroyed. You can do final processing in *OnNcDestroy* that doesn't depend on a window being active. Be sure to call the base class *OnNcDestroy* function.

> **TIP:** Do not try to destroy a dynamically allocated window object in *OnNcDestroy*. That job is reserved for a special *CWnd* virtual function, *PostNcDestroy*, that the base class *OnNcDestroy* calls. Technical Note # 17 in the MFCNOTES.HLP Help file gives hints on when it's appropriate to destroy a window object.

CHAPTER FIVE

THE GRAPHICS DEVICE INTERFACE (GDI)

You've already seen some elements of the GDI. Any time your program draws directly on the display or printer, it must use the GDI functions. The GDI has functions for drawing points, lines, rectangles, polygons, ellipses, bitmaps, and text. This chapter gives you the information you need to use the GDI effectively in the Visual C++ environment. It emphasizes the use of text because graphics programming for Microsoft Windows is often intuitive. We'll cover in detail the "mapping modes" that determine the size of displayed objects.

The Device Context Classes

In Chapters 3 and 4, the *OnDraw* member function of the view class was passed a pointer to a device context object. *OnDraw* selected a brush and then drew a circle. The Windows device context is the key GDI element that represents a physical device. Each C++ device context has an associated Windows device context, identified by a handle of type *HDC*.

Microsoft Foundation Class (MFC) Library version 2.5 has a number of device context classes. The base class *CDC* has all the member functions (some virtual) you'll need for drawing. Except for the oddball *CMetaFileDC* class, derived classes are distinct only in their constructors and destructors. If you (or the application framework) construct an object of a derived device context class, you can pass a *CDC* pointer to a function such as *OnDraw*. For the display, the usual derived classes are *CClientDC* and *CWindowDC*. For other devices, such as a printer or a memory buffer, you construct an object of the base class *CDC*.

The "virtualness" of the *CDC* class is an important feature of the application framework. In Chapter 18, you'll see how easy it is to write code that works with both the printer and the display. A statement in *OnDraw* such as

```
pDC->TextOut(0, 0, "Hello");
```

sends text to the display, the printer, or the Print Preview window depending on the class of the object referenced by the *CView::OnDraw* function's *pDC* parameter.

For display and printer device context objects, the application framework attaches the handle to the object. For other device contexts, such as the memory device context that you'll see in Chapter 10, you must call a member function after construction in order to attach the handle.

The Display Context Classes *CClientDC* and *CWindowDC*

Remember that a window's client area excludes the border, the caption bar, and the menu bar. If you create a *CClientDC* object, you have a device context that is mapped only to this client area—you can't draw outside it. The point *(0, 0)* usually refers to the upper left corner of the client area. As you'll see later, an MFC library *CView* object corresponds to a "child window" that is contained in a separate frame window, often along with a toolbar, a status bar, and scroll bars. The client area of the view, then, does <u>not</u> include these other windows. If the window contains a toolbar, for example, point *(0, 0)* refers to the point immediately <u>under</u> the left edge of the toolbar.

If you construct an object of class *CWindowDC*, point *(0, 0)* is at the upper left corner of the nonclient area of the window. With this "whole window" device context, you can draw in the window's border, in the caption area, and so forth. Don't forget that the view window doesn't have a nonclient area, so *CWindowDC* is more applicable to frame windows than to view windows.

Constructing and Destroying *CDC* Objects

After you construct a CDC object, it is important to destroy it promptly when you're done with it. Windows limits the number of available device contexts, and if you fail to destroy a device context object, the Debug kernel gives you a nasty *FatalExit* message in the debug window. Most frequently, you'll construct a device context object inside a message handler function such as *OnLButtonDown*. The easiest way to ensure that the device context object is destroyed (and the underlying Windows device context is released) is to construct the object on the stack like this:

```
void CMyView::OnLButtonDown(UINT nFlags, CPoint point)
{
    CRect rect;

    CClientDC dc(this);  // constructs dc on the stack
    dc.GetClipBox(rect); // retrieves the clipping rectangle
} // dc automatically destroyed
```

Notice that the *CClientDC* constructor takes a window pointer as a parameter. The destructor for the *CClientDC* object is called upon return from the function. You can also get a device context pointer by using the *CWnd::-GetDC* member function. You must be careful here to call the *ReleaseDC* function to release the device context.

```
void CMyView::OnLButtonDown(UINT nFlags, CPoint point)
{
    CRect rect;

    CDC* pDC = GetDC();      // a pointer to an internal dc
    pDC->GetClipBox(rect); // retrieves the clipping rectangle
    ReleaseDC(pDC);         // don't forget this
}
```

WARNING: You must not destroy the *CDC* object passed by the pointer to *OnDraw*. The application framework handles the destruction for you.

The State of the Device Context

You know already that a device context is required for drawing. When you use a *CDC* object to draw an ellipse, for example, what you see on the screen (or the printer's hard copy) depends on the current "state" of the device context. This state includes

■ Attached GDI drawing objects such as pens, brushes, and fonts.

■ The mapping mode that determines the scale of items when they are drawn.

■ Various details such as text alignment parameters and polygon filling mode. You have already seen, for example, that choosing a gray brush prior to drawing an ellipse results in the ellipse having a gray interior.

When you create a device context object, it has certain default characteristics, such as a black pen for shape boundaries. All other state characteristics are assigned through *CDC* class member functions. GDI objects are "selected into the device context" by means of the overloaded *SelectObject* functions. A device context can, for example, have one pen, one brush, or one font selected at any given time.

The *CPaintDC* Class

You'll need this class only if you override your view's *OnPaint* function. The default *OnPaint* calls *OnDraw* with a properly set up device context, but sometimes you'll need display-specific drawing code. The *CPaintDC* class is special because its constructor and destructor do housekeeping unique to *OnPaint*. Once you have a *CDC* pointer, however, you can use it as you would any other device context pointer.

Here's a sample *OnPaint* function that creates a *CPaintDC* object:

```
void CMyView::OnPaint()
{
    CPaintDC dc(this);
    OnPrepareDC(&dc); // explained later
    dc.TextOut(0, 0, "for the display, not the printer");
    OnDraw(&dc);      // stuff that's common to the display and printer
}
```

For Windows SDK Programmers

The *CPaintDC* constructor calls *BeginPaint* for you, and the destructor calls *EndPaint*. If you construct your device context on the stack, the *EndPaint* call is completely automatic.

GDI Objects

A Windows GDI object type is represented by an MFC library class. *CGdiObject* is the abstract base class for the GDI object classes. A "Windows GDI object" is represented by a C++ object of a class derived from *CGdiObject*. Here's a list of the GDI derived classes:

- *CBitmap*—A bitmap is an array of bits in which one or more bits correspond to each display pixel. You can use bitmaps to represent images, including icons and cursors, and you can use them to create brushes.

- *CBrush*—A brush defines a bitmapped pattern of pixels that is used to fill areas with color.

■ *CFont*—A font is a complete collection of characters of a particular typeface and a particular size. Fonts are generally stored on disk as resources, and some are device-specific.

■ *CPalette*—A palette is a color mapping interface that allows an application to take full advantage of the color capability of an output device without interfering with other applications.

■ *CPen*—A pen is a tool for drawing lines and shape borders. You can specify a pen's color and thickness and whether it draws solid, dotted, or dashed lines.

■ *CRgn*—A region is an area that is a combination of polygons and ellipses. You can use regions for filling, clipping, and mouse hit-testing.

Constructing and Destroying GDI Objects

You never construct an object of class *CGdiObject*, but rather you construct objects of the derived classes. Constructors for some GDI derived classes, such as *CPen* and *CBrush*, allow you to specify enough information to create the object in one step. Others, such as *CFont* and *CRgn*, require a second creation step. For these classes, you first construct the C++ object with the default constructor, and then you call a create function such as *CreateFont* or *CreatePolygonRgn*.

The *CGdiObject* class has a virtual destructor. The derived class destructors delete the Windows GDI objects that are attached to the C++ objects. If you construct an object of a class derived from *CGdiObject*, you must delete it prior to exiting the program. If you don't, Windows doesn't release the memory, and you'll get another nasty message in the debug window. To delete a GDI object, you must first separate it from the device context. You'll see an example in the next section.

Tracking GDI Objects

OK, so you know that you have to delete your GDI objects and that they must first be disconnected from their device context. How do you disconnect them? Members of the *CDC SelectObject* family of functions do the work of selecting a GDI object into the device context and, in the process, return a pointer to the previously selected object (which gets deselected in the process). Trouble is, you can't deselect the old object without selecting a new object. One easy way to track the objects is to "save" the original GDI object when you select your own GDI object and "restore" the original object when you're finished. Then you'll be ready to delete your own GDI object. Here's an example:

```
void CMyView::OnDraw(CDC* pDC)
{
    CPen newPen(PS_DASHDOTDOT, 2, (COLORREF) 0);  // black pen,
                                                  //  2 pixels wide
    CPen* pOldPen = pDC->SelectObject(&newPen);

    pDC->MoveTo(10, 10);
    pDC->Lineto(110, 10);
    pDC->SelectObject(pOldPen);                    // newPen is deselected
} // newPen automatically destroyed on exit
```

When a device context object is destroyed, all its GDI objects are deselected. Thus, if you know that a device context will be destroyed before its selected GDI objects are destroyed, then you don't have to deselect the objects. If, for example, you declare a pen as a view class data member (and you initialize it when you initialize the view), you don't have to deselect the pen inside *OnDraw* because the device context, controlled by the view base class's *OnPaint* handler, will be destroyed first.

Stock GDI Objects

Windows contains a number of "stock GDI objects" that you can use. Because these objects are inside Windows, you don't have to worry about deleting them. (Windows ignores requests to delete stock objects.) The MFC library function *SelectStockObject* gives you a *CGdiObject* pointer that you can select into a device context. These stock objects are handy when you want to deselect your own nonstock GDI object prior to its destruction. You can use a stock object as an alternative to the "old" object you used in the previous example.

```
void CMyView::OnDraw(CDC* pDC)
{
    CPen newPen(PS_DASHDOTDOT, 2, (COLORREF) 0);  // black pen,
                                                  //  2 pixels wide

    pDC->SelectObject(&newPen);
    pDC->MoveTo(10, 10);
    pDC->Lineto(110, 10);
    pDC->SelectStockObject(BLACK_PEN);             // newPen is deselected
} // newPen destroyed on exit
```

The *Class Library Reference* lists the stock objects available for pens, brushes, fonts, and palettes.

The Lifetime of a GDI Selection

For the <u>display</u> device context, you get a <u>fresh</u> device context at the beginning of each message-handling function. No GDI selections (or mapping modes or other device context settings) persist after your function exits. You must, therefore, set up your device context from scratch each time. The *CView* class virtual member function *OnPrepareDC* is useful for setting the mapping mode, but you must take care of your own GDI objects.

For other device contexts, such as those for printers and memory buffers, your assignments can last longer. For these long-life device contexts, things get a little more complicated. The complexity results from the temporary nature of GDI C++ object pointers returned by the *SelectObject* function. (The temporary C++ object will be destroyed by the application framework during the idle loop processing of the application, sometime after the handler function returns the call. See Technical Note #3 in the MFCNOTES.HLP Help file.) You can't simply store the pointer in a class data member; rather you must convert it to a Windows handle (the only permanent GDI identifier) with the *GetSafeHdc* member function. Here's an example:

```
// m_pPrintFont is a CFont pointer initialized in the CMyView constructor
// m_hOldFont is a CMyView data member of type HFONT, initialized to 0

void CMyView::SwitchToCourier(CDC* pDC)
{
    m_pPrintFont->CreateFont(30, 10, 0, 0, 400, FALSE, FALSE,
                             0, ANSI_CHARSET, OUT_DEFAULT_PRECIS,
                             CLIP_DEFAULT_PRECIS, DEFAULT_QUALITY,
                             DEFAULT_PITCH œ FF_MODERN,
                             "Courier New"); // TrueType
    CFont* pOldFont = pDC->SelectObject(m_pPrintFont);
    // m_hObject is the CGdiObject public data member that contains
    //  the handle
    m_hOldFont = (HFONT) pOldFont->GetSafeHandle();
}


void CMyView:SwitchToOriginalFont(CDC* pDC)
{
    // FromHandle is a static member function that returns an
    //  object pointer
    if (m_hOldFont) {
      pDC->SelectObject(CFont::FromHandle(m_hOldFont));
    }
}


// m_pPrintFont is deleted in the CMyView destructor
```

> NOTE: Be careful when deleting an object whose pointer is re-
> turned by *SelectObject*. If you've allocated the object yourself, you
> can delete it. If the pointer is temporary, as it will be for the object
> initially selected into the device context, you cannot delete the
> C++ object.

A Permanent Device Context for the Display—
Registering Window Classes

You've learned that you get a fresh display device context each time a Windows message handler function is called. An exception to this rule, however,
is that at window creation time you can specify a permanent device context
that lasts for the life of the window. The permanent device context retains its
settings, including GDI object selections and mapping mode, but not its
color palette.

You request a permanent Windows device context with a call to the
AfxRegisterWndClass function, with the *nClassStyle* parameter *CS_OWNDC* or
CS_CLASSDC. Even though the Windows device context is permanent, you
must still ensure that it is released at the end of each message handler that
uses it.

The *AfxRegisterWndClass* function is useful for assigning other special
characteristics to a window. For example, you can use this function to inhibit
mouse double-click messages or to prevent the user from closing the window
from the system menu. To call *AfxRegisterWndClass*, override the *CWnd* virtual
PreCreateWindow member function for the window you want to customize.
Here's an example in a derived view class:

```
BOOL CMyView::PreCreateWindow(CREATESTRUCT& cs)
{
    cs.lpszClass = AfxRegisterWndClass(CS_HREDRAW œ CS_VREDRAW œ
                                       CS_OWNDC, NULL);
    return TRUE;
}
```

Of course, you'll need a prototype for the *PreCreateWindow* member
function in your view class declaration.

Windows Color Mapping

The Windows GDI provides a "hardware-independent" color interface. Your
program supplies an "absolute" color code, and the GDI maps that code to a
suitable color or color combination on your computer's video display. Most

Windows programmers try to optimize their applications' color display for a few common video board categories.

Standard Video Graphics Array (VGA) Display Boards

A standard VGA display board uses 18-bit color registers, and thus it has a palette of 262,144 colors. Because of video memory constraints, however, the standard VGA board accommodates 4-bit color codes, which means it can display only 16 colors at a time. Because Windows needs fixed colors for captions, borders, scroll bars, and so forth, your programs can use only 16 "standard" pure colors. You cannot conveniently access the other colors that the board can display.

Each Windows color is represented by a combination of 8-bit "red," "green," and "blue" values. The 16 standard VGA "pure" (nondithered) colors are shown in the following table:

Red	Green	Blue	Color
0	0	0	Black
0	0	255	Bright blue
0	255	0	Bright green
0	255	255	Cyan
255	0	0	Bright red
255	0	255	Magenta
255	255	0	Bright yellow
255	255	255	White
0	0	128	Dark blue
0	128	0	Dark green
0	128	128	Blue-green
128	0	0	Brown
128	0	128	Dark purple
128	128	0	Olive
128	128	128	Dark gray
192	192	192	Light gray

Color-oriented GDI functions accept 32-bit *COLORREF* parameters that contain 8-bit color codes each for red, green, and blue. The Windows *RGB* macro converts 8-bit red, green, and blue values to a *COLORREF* parameter. The following statement, when executed on a system with a standard VGA board, constructs a brush with a dithered color (one that consists of a pattern of pure-color pixels):

```
CBrush brush(RGB(128, 128, 192));
```

The following statement (in your view's *OnDraw* function) sets the text background to bright red:

```
pDC->SetBkColor(RGB(255, 0, 0));
```

The *CDC* functions *SetBkColor* and *SetTextColor* don't always display dithered colors as the brush-oriented drawing functions do. If the dithered color pattern is too complex, the closest matching pure color is displayed.

256-Color Display Boards

Many display boards can accommodate 8-bit color codes, which means they can display 256 colors simultaneously. If you have one of these "super VGA" boards, you need to install a special Windows display driver, supplied by Microsoft or your board's manufacturer, to activate the 256-color mode. Because 8-bit color images require twice as much memory as 4-bit color images, Windows display updates can be noticeably slower in 256-color mode.

If Windows is configured for a 256-color display board, your programs are limited to 20 standard colors unless you activate the Windows "color palette" system as supported by the MFC library *CPalette* class and the Windows API. Windows color palette programming is covered briefly in Chapter 23. In this chapter, we'll assume that the Windows default color mapping is in effect.

With a 256-color display driver installed, you get the 16 VGA colors listed in the table on the previous page, plus 4 more, for a total of 20. The following table lists the 4 additional colors:

Red	Green	Blue	Color
192	220	192	Pale green
166	202	240	Light blue
255	251	240	Off-white
160	160	164	Medium gray

The *RGB* macro works much the same as it does with the standard VGA. If you specify one of the 20 standard colors for a brush, you get a pure color; otherwise, you get a dithered color. If you use the *PALETTERGB* macro instead, you don't get dithered colors; you get the closest matching standard pure color.

24-Bit Color Display Boards

Other display boards, mostly in the high-end category (which are becoming more widely used), use 24-bit color codes. This 24-bit capability enables the display of 16.7 million pure colors. If you're using a 24-bit color board, you have full access to all the colors. The *RGB* macro allows you to specify the exact colors you want.

Mapping Modes

Up to now, our drawing units have been display pixels, also known as device coordinates. The statement

```
pDC->Rectangle(CRect(0, 0, 200, 200));
```

draws a square 200 pixels by 200 pixels, with its top left corner at the top left of the window's client area (with positive *y* values increasing as you move down the window). This square would look smaller on a high-resolution display of 1024 by 768 pixels than it would on a standard VGA display that is 640 by 480 pixels, and it would look tiny if printed on a laser printer with 600-dpi resolution.

What if you want the square to be 2 inches by 2 inches, regardless of the display device? Windows provides a number of mapping modes, or coordinate systems, that can be associated with the device context. If you assign the *MM_LOENGLISH* mapping mode, for example, a logical unit is $1/100$ inch instead of 1 pixel. In the *MM_LOENGLISH* mapping mode, the *y*-axis runs in the opposite direction to that in the *MM_TEXT* mode: *y* values decrease as you move down. Thus, a 2-inch-by-2-inch square is drawn in logical coordinates this way:

```
pDC->Rectangle(CRect(0, 0, 200, -200));
```

Looks easy, doesn't it? Well, it isn't, because you can't work only in logical coordinates. Your program is always switching between device coordinates and logical coordinates, and you need to know when to convert between them. This chapter gives you a few rules that could make your programming life easier. First you need to know what mapping modes Windows gives you.

The *MM_TEXT* Mapping Mode

At first glance, *MM_TEXT* appears to be no mapping mode at all, but rather another name for device coordinates. Almost. In *MM_TEXT*, coordinates map to pixels, values of *x* increase as you move right, and values of *y* increase as you move down, but you're allowed to change the origin through calls to the *CDC* functions *SetViewportOrg* and *SetWindowOrg*. Here's some code that sets the origin to (*100, 100*) and draws a 200-pixel-by-200-pixel square. (An illustration of the output is shown in Figure 5-1.) Now the logical point (*0, 0*) maps to the device point (*100, 100*).

```
void CMyView::OnDraw(CDC* pDC)
{
    pDC->SetMapMode(MM_TEXT);
    pDC->SetViewportOrg(CPoint(100, 100));
    pDC->Rectangle(CRect(0, 0, 200, 200));
}
```

The "Fixed Scale" Mapping Modes

One important group of Windows mapping modes provides fixed scaling. With these mapping modes, you can change the viewport origin, but you cannot change the scale factor. You have already seen that, in the *MM_LOENGLISH* mapping mode, *x* values increase as you move right, and *y* values decrease as you move down. All fixed mapping modes follow this convention, and you can't change it. The only difference among the fixed mapping modes is the actual scale factor, listed in the table on the facing page.

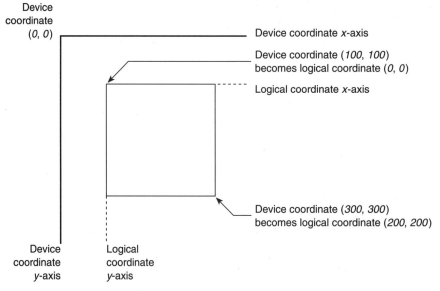

Figure 5-1.
A square drawn after the origin has been moved to (100, 100).

Mapping Mode	Logical Unit
MM_LOENGLISH	0.01 inch
MM_HIENGLISH	0.001 inch
MM_LOMETRIC	0.1 mm
MM_HIMETRIC	0.01 mm
MM_TWIPS	$\frac{1}{1440}$ inch

The last mapping mode, *MM_TWIPS*, is most often used with printers. One "twip" unit is $\frac{1}{20}$ point. (A point is a type measurement unit that is approximately $\frac{1}{72}$ inch.) If the mapping mode is *MM_TWIPS*, and you want, for example, 12-point type, set the character height to 12 × 20, or 240 twips.

The "Variable Scale" Mapping Modes

Windows provides two mapping modes, *MM_ISOTROPIC* and *MM_ANISO-TROPIC*, that allow you to change the scale factor as well as the origin. With these mapping modes, your drawing can change size as the user changes the size of the window. Also, if you invert the scale of one axis, you can "flip" an image about the other axis, and you can define your own arbitrary fixed scale factors.

With the *MM_ISOTROPIC* mode, a 1:1 aspect ratio is always preserved. In other words, a circle is always a circle as the scale factor changes. With the *MM_ANISOTROPIC* mode, the *x* and *y* scale factors can change independently. Circles can be squished into ellipses.

Here's an *OnDraw* function that draws an ellipse that fits exactly in its window:

```
void CMyView::OnDraw(CDC* pDC)
{
    CRect clientRect;

    GetClientRect(clientRect);
    pDC->SetMapMode(MM_ANISOTROPIC);
    pDC->SetWindowExt(1000, 1000);
    pDC->SetViewportExt(clientRect.right, -clientRect.bottom);
    pDC-SetViewportOrg(clientRect.right / 2, clientRect.bottom / 2);

    pDC->Ellipse(CRect(-500, -500, 500, 500));
}
```

What's going on here? The functions *SetWindowExt* and *SetViewportExt* work together to set the scale, based on the window's current client rectangle returned by the *GetClientRect* function. The resulting window size is exactly 1000 by 1000 logical units. The *SetViewportOrg* function sets the origin to the center of the window. Thus, a centered ellipse with a radius of 500 logical units fills the window exactly as illustrated in Figure 5-2.

Here are the formulas for converting logical units to device units:

x scale factor = x viewport extent / x window extent
y scale factor = y viewport extent / y window extent
device x = logical $x \times x$ scale factor + x origin offset
device y = logical $y \times y$ scale factor + y origin offset

Suppose the window is 448 pixels wide (*clientRect.right*). The right edge of the ellipse's client rectangle is 500 logical units from the origin. The x scale factor is 448 / 1000, and the x origin offset is 448 / 2 device units. If you use the formulas above, the right edge of the ellipse's client rectangle comes out to 448 device units, the right edge of the window. The x scale factor is expressed as a ratio (viewport extent / window extent) because Windows device coordinates are integers, not floating-point values. The extent values are meaningless by themselves.

If you substitute *MM_ISOTROPIC* for *MM_ANISOTROPIC* in the example above, the "ellipse" is always a circle, as shown in Figure 5-3. It expands to fit the smallest dimension of the window rectangle.

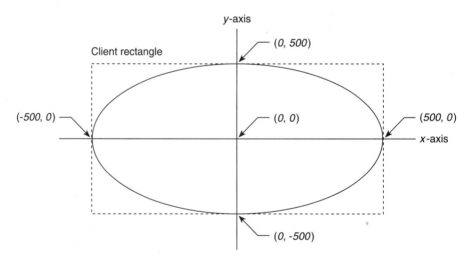

Figure 5-2.
A centered ellipse drawn in the MM_ANISOTROPIC *mapping mode.*

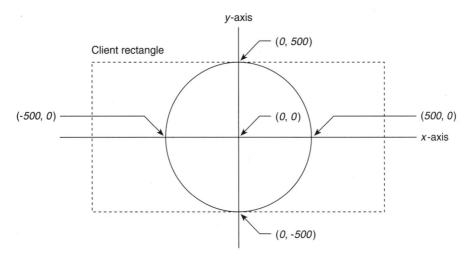

Figure 5-3.
A centered ellipse drawn in the MM_ISOTROPIC *mapping mode.*

Coordinate Conversion

Once you set the mapping mode (plus the origin and scale) of a device context, you can use logical coordinate parameters for most (but not all) *CDC* member functions. If you get the mouse cursor coordinates from a WM_MOUSEMOVE message, for example, you're dealing with device coordinates. Many other MFC library functions, particularly the member functions of class *CRect*, work correctly only with device coordinates.

Furthermore, you're likely to need a third set of coordinates that we'll call "physical coordinates." Why another set? Suppose you're using the *MM_LOENGLISH* mapping mode in which a logical unit is 0.01 inch, but an inch on the screen represents a foot (12 inches) in the real world. Now suppose the user works in inches and decimal fractions. A user measurement of 26.75 inches translates into 223 logical units, which must be ultimately translated to device coordinates. You'll want to store the physical coordinates as either floating-point numbers or scaled long integers to avoid rounding-off errors.

For the physical-to-logical translation, you're on your own, but the Windows GDI takes care of the logical-to-device translation for you. The *CDC* functions *LPtoDP* and *DPtoLP* translate between the two systems, assuming the device context mapping mode and associated parameters have already been set. Your job is to decide when to use each system. Here are a few rules of thumb:

■ Assume *CDC* member functions take logical coordinate parameters.

■ Assume *CWnd* member functions take device coordinate parameters.

■ Do all hit-test operations in device coordinates. Define regions in device coordinates. Functions such as the *CRect::PtInRect* function work only with non-negative coordinates. Windows, not the MFC library, imposes this last restriction.

■ Store long-term values in logical or physical coordinates. If you store a point in device coordinates and the user scrolls a window, that point is no longer valid.

Suppose you need to know whether the mouse cursor is inside a rectangle when the user presses the left mouse button. Here's the code:

```
// m_rect is CRect data member of CMyView in MM_LOENGLISH
//  logical coordinates

void CMyView::OnLButtonDown(UINT nFlags, CPoint point)
{
    CRect rect = m_rect; // rect is a temporary copy of m_rect;

    CClientDC dc(this);
    dc.SetMapMode(MM_LOENGLISH);
    dc.LPtoDP(rect);      // rect is now in device coordinates
    if (rect.PtInRect(point)) {
      TRACE("mouse cursor is inside the rectangle\n");
    }
}
```

Notice the use of the *TRACE* macro (discussed in Chapter 3).

NOTE: As you get further into application framework programming, you'll see that it's better to set the mapping mode in the virtual *CView* function *OnPrepareDC* instead of in the *OnDraw* function.

Fonts

Old-fashioned character-mode applications could display only the boring system font on the screen. Windows provides multiple, device-independent fonts in variable sizes. The effective use of these Windows fonts can significantly energize an application with minimum programming effort. The new Windows version 3.1 TrueType fonts are even more effective and easier to program than the previous device-dependent fonts. You'll see several example programs that use fonts later in this chapter.

Fonts Are GDI Objects

Fonts are an integral part of the Windows GDI. This means that fonts behave in the same way as other GDI objects. They can be scaled and clipped, and they can be selected into a device context as a pen or a brush can be selected. All GDI rules about deselection and deletion apply to fonts.

Choosing a Font

Choosing a Windows font used to be like going to a fruit stand and asking for "a piece of reddish-yellow fruit, with a stone inside, that weighs about 4 ounces." You might have gotten a peach or a plum or even a nectarine, and you could be sure that it wouldn't have weighed exactly 4 ounces. Once you took possession of the fruit, you could weigh it and check the fruit type. Now, with TrueType, you can specify the fruit type, but you still can't specify the exact weight.

Today you can choose between two font types—TrueType device-independent fonts and device-dependent fonts such as the Windows display System font and the LaserJet LinePrinter font—or you can specify a font category and size and let Windows select the font for you. If you let Windows select the font, it will choose a TrueType font if possible. The MFC library provides a font selection dialog box tied to the currently selected printer, so there's little need for printer font guesswork. You let the user select the exact font and size for the printer, and then you approximate the display the best you can.

Printing with Fonts

For text-intensive applications, you'll probably want to specify printer font sizes in points. (1 point = $\frac{1}{72}$ inch.) Why? Most, if not all, built-in printer fonts are defined in terms of points. The LaserJet LinePrinter font, for example, comes in one size, 8.5 point. You can specify TrueType fonts in any point size. If you work in points, you need a mapping mode that easily accommodates points. That's what *MM_TWIPS* is for. An 8.5-point font is 8.5 × 20, or 170, twips, and that's the character height you'll want to specify.

Displaying Fonts

If you're not worried about the display matching the printed output, you have a lot of flexibility. You can choose any of the scalable Windows TrueType fonts, or you can choose the fixed-size system fonts (stock objects). With the TrueType fonts, it doesn't much matter what mapping mode you use; simply choose a font height and go for it. No need to worry about points.

Matching printer fonts to make printed output match the screen presents some problems, but TrueType makes it easier than it was before. Even if you're printing with TrueType fonts, however, you'll never quite get the display to match the printer output. Why? Characters are ultimately displayed in pixels, and the width of a string of characters is equal to the sum of the pixel widths of its characters, possibly adjusted for kerning. The pixel width of the characters depends on the font, the mapping mode, and the resolution of the output device. Only if both the printer and the display were set to *MM_TEXT* mode (1 pixel or dot = 1 logical unit) would you get an exact correspondence. If you're using the *CDC GetTextExtent* function to calculate line breaks, the screen breakpoint will occasionally be different from the printer breakpoint.

> **NOTE:** In the MFC library Print Preview mode, which we'll examine closely in Chapter 18, the line breaks occur exactly as they do on the printer, but the print quality suffers in the process.

If you're matching a printer-specific font on the screen, TrueType again makes the job easier. Windows substitutes the closest matching TrueType font. For the 8.5-point LinePrinter font, Windows comes pretty close with its Courier New font.

Points in a Window—Logical Twips

If you use twips units (1/20 point, 1/1440 inch) for printing, the obvious thing to do is set the window device context mapping mode to *MM_TWIPS*. Doing so is undesirable, however, because 10-point type that looks fine on paper is too small to read when transferred inch for inch to a VGA screen. If, instead, you use what Charles Petzold (in *Programming Windows 3.1*) calls the "logical twips" mapping mode, things work better.

The following statements set the mapping mode to logical twips.

```
pDC->SetMapMode(MM_ANISOTROPIC);
pDC->SetWindowExt(1440, 1440);
pDC->SetViewportExt(pDC->GetDeviceCaps(LOGPIXELSX),
                    -pDC->GetDeviceCaps(LOGPIXELSY));
```

Don't worry too much about the theory behind this mapping mode. Simply remember that, if you use logical twips on the display, 12-point type (with a character height of 240 twips) will look the same as it does in Visual Workbench and other Windows-based programs. The minus sign on the second *SetViewportExt* parameter ensures that *y* values decrease as you move down, as in the *MM_TWIPS* mode.

Computing Character Height

Five font height measurement parameters are available through the *CDC* function *GetTextMetrics*, but only three are significant. The *tmHeight* parameter represents the full height of the font, including descenders (for the characters g, j, p, q, and y) and any diacritics that appear over capital letters. The *tmExternalLeading* parameter is the distance between the top of the diacritic and the bottom of the descender from the line above. The sum of *tmHeight* and *tmExternalLeading* is the total character height. The value of *tmExternalLeading* is often 0.

You would think that *tmHeight* would represent the font size in points. Wrong! Another *GetTextMetrics* parameter, *tmInternalLeading*, comes into play. The point size corresponds to the difference between *tmHeight* and *tmInternalLeading*. With the *MM_TWIPS* mapping mode in effect, a selected 12-point font might have a *tmHeight* value of 295 logical units and a *tmInternalLeading* value of 55. The font's net height of 240 corresponds to the point size of 12. Figure 5-4 shows the important font measurements.

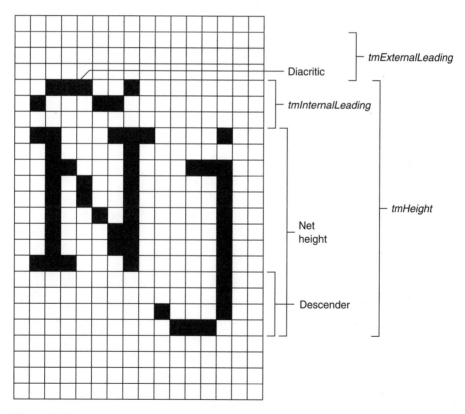

Figure 5-4.
Font height measurements.

The EX05A Program

This example sets up a view window with the logical twips mapping mode. A text string is displayed in 10 point sizes with the Arial TrueType font. Here are the steps for building the application:

1. **Run AppWizard to generate a project called EX05A.** Choose App-Wizard from Visual Workbench's Project menu. The options and the default class names are shown here:

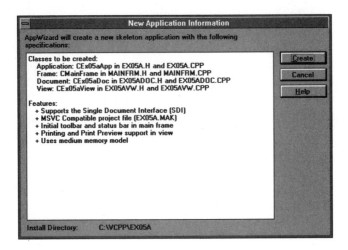

Notice that this time we're accepting the default Printing And Print Preview option.

2. **Add function prototypes in file EX05AVW.H.** *ShowFont* is a new private member function in the *CEx05aView* class. *OnPrepareDC* is an override of a *CView* base class function. The class declaration needs prototypes for both.

```
private:
    void ShowFont(CDC* pDC, int& nPos, int nPoints);
protected:
    void OnPrepareDC(CDC* pDC, CPrintInfo* pInfo = NULL);
```

3. **Add the *OnPrepareDC* and *ShowFont* functions in file EX05AVW.CPP.** These are new functions. You've already added the prototypes in the class header.

```
void CEx05aView::OnPrepareDC(CDC* pDC, CPrintInfo* pInfo /* = NULL */)
{
```

```
    pDC->SetMapMode(MM_ANISOTROPIC);
    pDC->SetWindowExt(1440, 1440);
    pDC->SetViewportExt(pDC->GetDeviceCaps(LOGPIXELSX),
                        -pDC->GetDeviceCaps(LOGPIXELSY));
}

void CEx05aView::ShowFont(CDC* pDC, int& nPos, int nPoints)
{
    TEXTMETRIC  tm;
    CFont       testFont;
    char        text[100];
    CSize       tExtent;

    testFont.CreateFont(-nPoints * 20, 0, 0, 0, 400, FALSE, FALSE, 0,
                        ANSI_CHARSET, OUT_DEFAULT_PRECIS,
                        CLIP_DEFAULT_PRECIS, DEFAULT_QUALITY,
                        DEFAULT_PITCH œ FF_SWISS, "Arial");
    CFont* pOldFont = (CFont*) pDC->SelectObject(&testFont);
    pDC->GetTextMetrics(&tm);
    TRACE("points = %d, tmHeight = %d, tmInternalLeading = %d,"
          " tmExternalLeading = %d\n", nPoints, tm.tmHeight,
          tm.tmInternalLeading, tm.tmExternalLeading);
    wsprintf(text, "This is %d-point Arial", nPoints);
    tExtent = pDC->GetTextExtent(text, strlen(text));
    TRACE("String width = %d, string height = %d\n", tExtent.cx,
          tExtent.cy);
    pDC->TextOut(0, nPos, text);
    pDC->SelectObject(pOldFont);
    nPos -= tm.tmHeight + tm.tmExternalLeading;
}
```

4. **Edit the *OnDraw* function in EX05AVW.CPP.** AppWizard always
   generates a skeleton *OnDraw* function for your view class. Find the
   function and edit the code as follows:

```
void CEx05aView::OnDraw(CDC* pDC)
{
    int nPosition = 0;

    for (int i = 6; i <= 24; i += 2) {
        ShowFont(pDC, nPosition, i);
    }
}
```

5. **Build and run the EX05A program.** In Visual Workbench, choose
   Build from the Project menu, and then choose Execute. The resulting
   output looks like the screen on the following page on a standard VGA
   card:

Notice that the output string sizes don't quite correspond to the point sizes. This discrepancy results from the font engine's conversion of logical units to pixels. The program's trace output, partially shown below, shows the display of font metrics (the numbers depending on your display driver and your video driver):

```
points = 6, tmHeight = 134, tmInternalLeading = 14, tmExternalLeading = 5
string width = 1032, string height = 134
points = 8, tmHeight = 182, tmInternalLeading = 24, tmExternalLeading = 5
string width = 1325, string height = 182
points = 10, tmHeight = 226, tmInternalLeading = 24, tmExternalLeading = 5
string width = 1829, string height = 226
points = 12, tmHeight = 274, tmInternalLeading = 34, tmExternalLeading = 10
string width = 2208, string height = 274
```

Try Print Preview. Notice, as shown below, that the printer font metrics are different from the display font metrics, particularly the value of *tmInternalLeading*:

```
points = 6, tmHeight = 150, tmInternalLeading = 30, tmExternalLeading = 0
string width = 1065, string height = 150
points = 8, tmHeight = 210, tmInternalLeading = 45, tmExternalLeading = 0
string width = 1380, string height = 210
points = 10, tmHeight = 240, tmInternalLeading = 45, tmExternalLeading = 0
string width = 1770, string height = 240
points = 12, tmHeight = 270, tmInternalLeading = 30, tmExternalLeading = 15
string width = 2130, string height = 270
```

No attempt was made here to set a print scale factor different from the display scale factor. In Chapter 18, you'll learn how to control the print scale factor separately.

The EX05A Program Elements

Mapping Mode Set in the *OnPrepareDC* Function

The application framework calls *OnPrepareDC* prior to calling *OnDraw*, so the *OnPrepareDC* function is the logical place to prepare the device context. If you had other message handlers that needed the correct mapping mode, those functions would have contained calls to *OnPrepareDC*.

The *ShowFont* Private Member Function

ShowFont contains code that is executed 10 times in a loop. With C, you would have made this a global function, but with C++ it's better to make it a private class member function, sometimes known as a "helper function."

This function creates the font, selects it into the device context, prints a string to the window, and then deselects and deletes the font. If you choose to include debug information in the program, *ShowFont* also displays useful font metrics information, including the actual width of the string.

The Call to *CFont::CreateFont*

This call includes lots of parameters, but the important ones are the first two—the font height and width. A width value of 0 means that the aspect ratio of the selected font will be set to a value specified by the font designer. If you put a nonzero value here, as you'll see in the next example, you can change the font's aspect ratio.

> TIP: If you want your font to be a specific point size, the *CreateFont* font height parameter (the first parameter) must be <u>negative</u>. If you're using the *MM_TWIPS* mapping mode, for example, a height parameter of −240 ensures a 12-point font with $tmHeight - tmInternalLeading = 240$. A +240 height parameter gives you a smaller font with $tmHeight = 240$.

The last *CreateFont* parameter specifies the font name, in this case the Arial TrueType font. If you had used *NULL* for this parameter, the *FF_SWISS* specification (which indicates a proportional font without serifs) would have caused Windows to choose the "best matching" font, which, depending on the specified size, might have been the System font or the Arial TrueType font. The font name takes precedence. If you had specified *FF_ROMAN* (which indicates a proportional font with serifs) with Arial, you would have gotten Arial.

The EX05B Program

This program is similar to EX05A except that it shows multiple fonts. The mapping mode is *MM_ANISOTROPIC*, but this time the scale depends on the window size. The characters change size along with the window. This program effectively shows off some TrueType fonts and contrasts them with the old-style fonts. Here are the steps for building the application:

1. **Run AppWizard to generate a project called EX05B.** Choose App-Wizard from Visual Workbench's project menu. The options and the default class names are shown here:

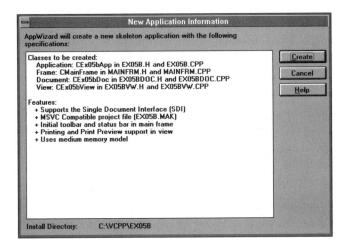

```
New Application Information

AppWizard will create a new skeleton application with the following
specifications:

Classes to be created:
    Application: CEx05bApp in EX05B.H and EX05B.CPP
    Frame: CMainFrame in MAINFRM.H and MAINFRM.CPP
    Document: CEx05bDoc in EX05BDOC.H and EX05BDOC.CPP
    View: CEx05bView in EX05BVW.H and EX05BVW.CPP

Features:
    + Supports the Single Document Interface (SDI)
    + MSVC Compatible project file (EX05B.MAK)
    + Initial toolbar and status bar in main frame
    + Printing and Print Preview support in view
    + Uses medium memory model

Install Directory:    C:\VCPP\EX05B
```

Notice that again we're accepting the default Printing And Print Preview option.

2. **Add function prototypes in file EX05BVW.H.** *TraceMetrics* is a new private member function in the *CEx05bView* class. *OnPrepareDC* is an override of a *CView* base class function. The class declaration needs prototypes for both.

```
private:
    void TraceMetrics(CDC* pDC);
protected:
    void OnPrepareDC(CDC* pDC, CPrintInfo* pInfo = NULL);
```

3. **Add the *OnPrepareDC* and *TraceMetrics* functions in EX05BVW.CPP.**

```
void CEx05bView::OnPrepareDC(CDC* pDC, CPrintInfo* pInfo /* = NULL */)
{ // called by the application framework prior to OnDraw
    CRect clientRect;

    GetClientRect(&clientRect);
    pDC->SetMapMode(MM_ANISOTROPIC);
    pDC->SetWindowExt(400, 400);
    pDC->SetViewportExt(clientRect.right, clientRect.bottom);
    // +y = down
    pDC->SetViewportOrg(0, 0);
}


void CEx05bView::TraceMetrics(CDC* pDC)
{
    TEXTMETRIC tm;
    char szFaceName[100];

    pDC->GetTextMetrics(&tm);
    pDC->GetTextFace(99, szFaceName);
    TRACE("font = %s, tmHeight = %d, tmInternalLeading = %d,"
        " tmExternalLeading = %d\n", szFaceName, tm.tmHeight,
            tm.tmInternalLeading, tm.tmExternalLeading);
}
```

4. **Edit the *OnDraw* function in EX05BVW.CPP.** AppWizard always
   generates a skeleton *OnDraw* function for your view class. Find the
   function and edit the code as follows:

```
void CEx05bView::OnDraw(CDC* pDC)
{
    CFont testFont1, testFont2, testFont3, testFont4;

    testFont1.CreateFont(50, 0, 0, 0, 400, FALSE, FALSE, 0,
                        ANSI_CHARSET, OUT_DEFAULT_PRECIS,
                        CLIP_DEFAULT_PRECIS, DEFAULT_QUALITY,
                        DEFAULT_PITCH œ FF_SWISS, "Arial");
    CFont* pOldFont = pDC->SelectObject(&testFont1);
    TraceMetrics(pDC);
    pDC->TextOut(0, 0, "This is Arial, default width");

    testFont2.CreateFont(50, 0, 0, 0, 400, FALSE, FALSE, 0,
                        ANSI_CHARSET, OUT_DEFAULT_PRECIS,
                        CLIP_DEFAULT_PRECIS, DEFAULT_QUALITY,
                        DEFAULT_PITCH œ FF_MODERN, "Courier");
```

(continued)

```
    pDC->SelectObject(&testFont2);
    TraceMetrics(pDC);
    pDC->TextOut(0, 100, "This is Courier, default width");

    testFont3.CreateFont(50, 10, 0, 0, 400, FALSE, FALSE, 0,
                         ANSI_CHARSET, OUT_DEFAULT_PRECIS,
                         CLIP_DEFAULT_PRECIS, DEFAULT_QUALITY,
                         DEFAULT_PITCH œ FF_ROMAN, NULL);
    pDC->SelectObject(&testFont3);
    TraceMetrics(pDC);
    pDC->TextOut(0, 200, "This is generic Roman, variable width");

    testFont4.CreateFont(50, 0, 0, 0, 400, FALSE, FALSE, 0,
                         ANSI_CHARSET, OUT_DEFAULT_PRECIS,
                         CLIP_DEFAULT_PRECIS, DEFAULT_QUALITY,
                         DEFAULT_PITCH œ FF_MODERN, "LinePrinter");
    pDC->SelectObject(&testFont4);
    TraceMetrics(pDC);
    pDC->TextOut(0, 300, "This is LinePrinter, default width");

    pDC->SelectObject(pOldFont);
}
```

The *OnDraw* function displays character strings in four fonts as follows:

- testFont1—The TrueType font Arial with default width selection.

- testFont2—The old-style font Courier with default width selection. Notice how jagged the font is in larger sizes.

- testFont3—The generic Roman font for which Windows supplies the TrueType font Times New Roman with programmed width selection. The width is tied to the horizontal window scale, so the font stretches to fit the window.

- testFont4—The LinePrinter font is specified, but because this is not a Windows font for the display, the font engine falls back on the *FF_MODERN* specification and chooses the TrueType Courier New font.

5. **Build and run the EX05B program.** In Visual Workbench, choose Build from the Project menu, and then choose Execute. The program output is shown in the screen at the top of the facing page:

Resize the window to make it smaller, and watch the font sizes change. Compare this screen with the previous one:

If you continue to downsize the window, notice how the Courier font stops shrinking after a certain size, and notice how the Roman font width changes.

Now choose Print Preview from the File menu. The output, as shown in Figure 5-5 on the following page, is very different from the window display output because the Courier and LinePrinter fonts are not TrueType fonts. The Windows Courier font maps to one of the printer's built-in fixed-size Courier fonts, and the printer's LinePrinter font is available only in 8.5 point. The other fonts appear small because the *MM_TEXT* mapping mode causes printer dots to be mapped directly to display pixels—which is clearly undesirable. In Chapter 18, you'll learn more about scaling your printer output.

Figure 5-5.
The EX05B Print Preview output.

The EX05C Example—*CScrollView* Revisited

You saw the *CScrollView* class in Chapter 4 (in EX04C), but you couldn't do much with it because you hadn't learned about mapping modes. Even with the *MM_TEXT* mode, you could not have done mouse hit-testing because the *CScrollView* class changes the origin behind your back. Now we'll revisit the scrolling view in another example that's an amalgam of programs EX04B and EX04C. The new program allows the user to move a circle with a mouse, but it does so in a scrolling window with the *MM_LOENGLISH* mapping mode. Keyboard scrolling is left out, but you can add it by borrowing the *OnKeyDown* member function from EX04C.

Instead of a stock brush, we'll use a pattern brush for the circle—a real GDI object. There's one complication with pattern brushes: They have to be "unrealized" as the window scrolls; otherwise, strips of the pattern don't line up, and the effect is ugly.

As with EX04C, this example involves a view class derived from *CScrollView*. Here are the steps to create the application:

1. Run AppWizard to generate a project called EX05C. Choose App-Wizard from Visual Workbench's Project menu. Be sure to set the view base class to *CScrollView*. The options and the default class names are shown in the screen at the top of the facing page:

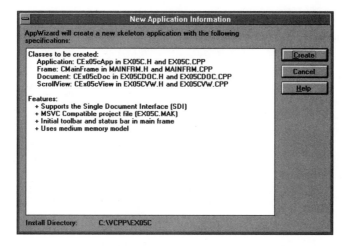

2. **Edit the *CEx05cView* class header in file EX05CVW.H.** Add the following lines in the class *CEx05cView* declaration:

```
private:
    CRect   m_ellipseRect;
    CPoint  m_mousePos;
    BOOL    m_bCaptured;
```

3. **Use ClassWizard to add four message handlers.** Add the message handlers as follows:

Message	Member Function Name
WM_LBUTTONDOWN	*OnLButtonDown*
WM_LBUTTONUP	*OnLButtonUp*
WM_MOUSEMOVE	*OnMouseMove*

4. **Edit the *CEx05cView* message handler functions.** ClassWizard generated the skeletons for the functions listed above. Find them in EX05CVW.CPP and code them as follows:

```
void CEx05cView::OnLButtonDown(UINT nFlags, CPoint point)
{
    CRect ellipseRect;
    CRgn  circle;

    ellipseRect = m_ellipseRect;
    CClientDC dc(this);
```

(continued)

```
   OnPrepareDC(&dc);
   dc.LPtoDP(ellipseRect);
   circle.CreateEllipticRgnIndirect(ellipseRect);
   if (circle.PtInRegion(point)) {
      // capturing mouse ensures subsequent LButtonUp message
      SetCapture();
      m_bCaptured = TRUE;
      dc.DPtoLP(&point);
      m_mousePos = point;
      // new mouse cursor is active while mouse is captured
      ::SetCursor(::LoadCursor(NULL, IDC_CROSS));
   }
}
```

```
void CEx05cView::OnLButtonUp(UINT nFlags, CPoint point)
{
   if (m_bCaptured) {
      ReleaseCapture();
      m_bCaptured = FALSE;
   }
}
```

```
void CEx05cView::OnMouseMove(UINT nFlags, CPoint point)
{
   CSize  offset;
   CPoint mousePos;
   CRect  ellipseRect, newRect, invalidRect, clientRect, tempRect;

   CClientDC dc(this);
   OnPrepareDC(&dc);
   GetClientRect(clientRect);
   if (m_bCaptured) {
      ellipseRect = m_ellipseRect;
      mousePos = m_mousePos;
      dc.LPtoDP(ellipseRect);
      dc.LPtoDP(&mousePos);
      offset = point - mousePos;
      newRect = ellipseRect + (CPoint(0, 0) + offset);
      tempRect.UnionRect(ellipseRect, newRect);
      invalidRect.IntersectRect(tempRect, clientRect);
      InvalidateRect(invalidRect, TRUE);
      dc.DPtoLP(&point);
      dc.DPtoLP(newRect);
      m_mousePos = point;
      m_ellipseRect = newRect;
   }
}
```

5. **Edit the** *CEx05cView* **constructor,** *OnDraw* **function, and** *OnInitial-Update* **function.** AppWizard generated these skeleton functions. Find them in EX05CVW.CPP and code them as follows:

```
CEx05cView::CEx05cView() : m_ellipseRect(0, 0, 100, -100)
{
    m_bCaptured = FALSE;
}

void CEx05cView::OnDraw(CDC* pDC)
{
    CBrush hatchBrush(HS_DIAGCROSS, RGB(255, 0, 0));
    CPoint tempPoint(0, 0); // logical 0,0

    hatchBrush.UnrealizeObject();
    pDC->LPtoDP(&tempPoint);            // In device coordinates,
    pDC->SetBrushOrg(tempPoint);       //   align the brush with
                                       //   the window origin.
    pDC->SelectObject(&hatchBrush);
    pDC->Ellipse(m_ellipseRect);
    pDC->SelectStockObject(BLACK_BRUSH); // deselect hatchBrush
}

void CEx05cView::OnInitialUpdate
{
    CScrollView::OnInitialUpdate();
    CSize totalSize = CSize(800 * 2. 800 * 2);   // 8 inch by 8 inch
    CSize pageSize = CSize(totalSize.cx / 2, totalSize.cy / 2);
    CSize lineSize = CSize(totalSize.cx / 100, totalSize.cy / 100);
    SetScrollSizes(MM_LOENGLISH, totalSize, pageSize, lineSize);
}
```

6. **Build and run the EX05C program.** In the Visual Workbench, choose Build from the Project menu, and then choose Execute. The program allows a circle to be dragged with the mouse, and it allows the window to be scrolled.

The EX05C Program Elements

Following is a discussion of the major elements in the EX05C program.

The *CScrollView::OnPrepareDC* Member Function

The *CView* class has a virtual *OnPrepareDC* function that does nothing. The *CScrollView* class implements the function for the purpose of setting up the view's mapping mode, scale factor, and origin, based on the parameters that you passed to *SetScrollSizes* in *OnCreate*. The application framework calls

OnPrepareDC for you prior to calling *OnDraw*, so you don't need to worry about it. You must call *OnPrepareDC* yourself in any other message handler function that uses the view's device context, such as *OnLButtonDown* and *OnMouseMove*.

The *OnMouseMove* Coordinate Transformation Code

As you can see, this function contains quite a few translation statements. The logic can be summarized by the following steps:

1. Convert the previous ellipse rectangle and mouse point (stored in data members) from logical to device coordinates.

2. Update the mouse point and the ellipse rectangle.

3. Generate an invalid rectangle.

4. Convert the ellipse rectangle and mouse point to logical coordinates.

The *OnDraw* Function

The *UnrealizeObject* and *SetBrushOrg* calls are necessary to ensure that all of the circle's interior pattern lines up when the view is scrolled. The brush is aligned with a reference point *tempPoint*, which is at top left of the logical window, converted to device coordinates. This is a notable exception to the rule that CDC member functions require logical coordinates.

The *CScrollView SetScaleToFitSize* Mode

The *CScrollView* class has a stretch-to-fit mode that displays the entire scrollable area in the view window. The Windows *MM_ANISOTROPIC* mapping mode comes into play, with one restriction: Positive *y* values always increase in the down direction, as in *MM_TEXT* mode.

To use the stretch-to-fit mode, make the following call in your view's function in place of the call to *SetScrollSizes*:

```
SetScaleToFitSize(totalSize);
```

The example in Chapter 23 makes this call in *OnInitialUpdate*, and it also makes it in response to a Shrink To Fit menu item. Thus, the display can toggle between scrolling mode and shrink-to-fit mode.

THE MODAL DIALOG

Almost every program for Windows uses a dialog window to interact with the user. The dialog might be a simple OK message box, or it might be a complex data entry form. Calling this powerful element a dialog "box" is an injustice. As you'll see, the dialog is truly a window that receives messages, that can be moved and closed, and that can even accept drawing instructions in its client area.

The two kinds of dialogs are "modal" and "modeless." This chapter explores the most common type, the modal dialog. You'll be working with a single dialog example that includes most typical dialog "controls" plus a few not-so-typical ones. Chapter 7 introduces the modeless dialog and the special-purpose COMMDLG modal dialogs for opening files, selecting fonts, and so forth.

Modal vs. Modeless Dialogs

The *CDialog* base class supports both modal and modeless dialogs. With a modal dialog, such as the Open File dialog, the user cannot work elsewhere in the application until the dialog is closed. With a modeless dialog, the user can work in another window in the application while the dialog remains on the screen. The Visual Workbench Find dialog is a good example of a modeless dialog; you can edit your program during a global search (once the search is started).

Your choice of a modal or a modeless dialog depends on the application. Modal dialogs are much easier to program, which might influence your decision.

FYI: The Microsoft Foundation Class Library version 1.0 supported two dialog classes: *CDialog* for modeless dialogs and *CModalDialog* for modal dialogs. The Microsoft Foundation Class (MFC) Library versions 2.0 and 2.5 *CDialog* class accommodate both modal and modeless dialogs, but *CModalDialog* still existed as a macro for compatibility. Do not use the *CModalDialog* class in new Microsoft Foundation Class Library version 2.5 programs.

System Modal Dialogs

All modal dialogs restrict the user from working elsewhere in the application that opens the dialog. With an ordinary modal dialog, however, the user can switch to another program. One type of modal dialog, the system modal dialog, absolutely restricts the user to the dialog; the user must close the dialog before continuing with any other Windows task.

NOTE: System modal dialogs are not allowed in 32-bit Windows.

Resources and Controls

So now you know a dialog is a window. What makes the dialog different from the *CView* windows you've seen already? For one thing, a dialog window is almost always tied to a Windows resource that identifies the dialog's elements and specifies their layout. Because you can use App Studio to create and edit a dialog resource, you can quickly and efficiently produce dialogs in a visual manner.

A dialog consists of a number of elements called controls. Dialog controls include edit controls (aka text boxes), buttons, list boxes, combo boxes, and static text (aka labels). Windows manages these controls through special grouping and tabbing logic, and that relieves you of a major programming burden. The dialog controls can be referenced either by a *CWnd* pointer (because they themselves are really windows) or by an index number (with an associated #*define* constant) assigned in the resource. Controls can send messages to their dialog in response to user actions such as typing text or clicking a button.

The MFC library and ClassWizard work together to enhance the dialog logic that Windows provides. With ClassWizard, you can associate dialog class data members with dialog controls, and you can specify editing parameters such as maximum text length and numeric high and low limits. ClassWizard generates calls to the MFC library data exchange and data validation functions that move information back and forth between the screen and the data members.

Programming a Modal Dialog

Modal dialogs are the most frequently used dialogs. A user action (a menu choice, for example) brings up a dialog on the screen, the user enters data in the dialog, and then the user closes the dialog. Here's a summary of the steps to add a modal dialog to an existing project:

1. Use App Studio to create a dialog resource that contains various controls. App Studio updates the project's resource script (RC) file to include your new dialog resource, and the RESOURCE.H file is updated to include corresponding *#define* constants.

2. Use ClassWizard to create a dialog class that is derived from *CDialog* and attached to the resource created in step 1. ClassWizard adds the associated code and header file to the Visual Workbench project.

3. Use ClassWizard to add data members, exchange functions, and validation functions to the dialog class.

4. Use ClassWizard to add message handlers for the dialog's buttons and special controls.

5. Write the code for special control initialization (in *OnInitDialog*) and for the message handlers. Be sure the *CDialog* virtual member function *OnOK* is called when the user closes the dialog (unless the user cancels the dialog). (Note: *OnOK* is called by default.)

6. Write the code in your view class to activate the dialog. This code consists of a call to your dialog class's constructor followed by a call to the *DoModal* dialog class member function. *DoModal* returns only when the user exits the dialog window.

Now we'll proceed with a real example, one step at a time.

The Dialog That Ate Cincinnati—
The EX06A Example

Let's not mess around with wimpy little dialogs. We'll build a monster dialog that contains almost every kind of control. The job will be easy because App Studio is there to help us. The finished product is shown in Figure 6-1.

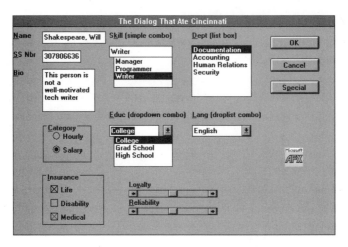

Figure 6-1.
The finished dialog in action.

As you can see, the dialog supports a human resources application. These kinds of business programs are fairly boring, so the challenge is to produce something that could not have been done with 80-column punched cards. The program is brightened a little by the use of scroll bar controls for "loyalty" and "reliability." Here is a classic example of direct action and visual representation of data! Visual Basic controls could add more interest, but they aren't covered until Chapter 8.

Here are the steps for building the dialog resource:

1. Run AppWizard to generate a project called EX06A. Choose App-Wizard from Visual Workbench's Project menu. The options and the default class names are shown here:

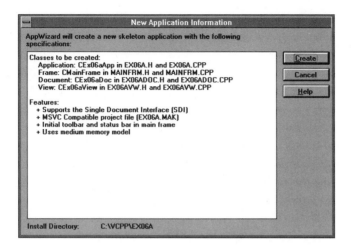

As usual, AppWizard sets the new project to be the Visual Workbench current project.

2. **From the Visual Workbench, open the file EX06A.RC.** Choose App Studio from Visual Workbench's Tools menu. This starts App Studio with the EX06A resource file that AppWizard generated.

3. **Create a new dialog with ID *IDD_DIALOG1*.** Click the New button in the EX06A.RC (MFC Resource Script) window. The New Resource dialog appears. Click on Dialog, and then click on OK. App Studio creates a new dialog resource, as shown here:

App Studio assigns the resource ID *IDD_DIALOG1* to the new dialog. Notice that App Studio inserts OK and Cancel buttons for the new dialog.

4. **Size the dialog and assign a caption.** When you double-click on the new dialog, or if you choose Show Properties from App Studio's Window menu, the Dialog Properties dialog appears. Type the caption for the new dialog as shown in the following screen. The state of the pushpin button determines whether the Dialog Properties dialog stays on top of other windows. (When the pushpin is "pushed," the dialog stays on top of other windows.) Click the Snap To Grid button to reveal the grid and to help align controls.

5. **Set the dialog style.** Choose Styles from the drop-down list box at the top right of the Dialog Properties dialog, and then set the style properties as shown here:

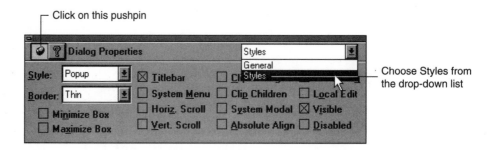

6. Add the dialog's controls. Use the control palette to add each control. Drag controls from the control palette to the new dialog with the mouse, and then position and size the controls, as shown in Figure 6-1 on page 110. (You don't have to be precise when positioning the controls.) Here are the control palette's controls:

Pointer — Picture
Static text — Edit box
Group box — Pushbutton
Check box — Radio button
Combo box — List box
Horizontal scroll bar — Vertical scroll bar
User-defined — Grid (VBX control)

NOTE: App Studio displays the position and size of each control in the status bar. The position units are special "dialog units," or DLUs, not device units. A horizontal DLU is the average width of the dialog font divided by 4. A vertical DLU is the average height of the font divided by 8. The dialog font is normally 8-point MS Sans Serif.

Here's a brief description of the dialog's controls:

❑ **The static text control for the Name field.** A static text control simply paints characters on the screen. No user interaction occurs at runtime. You can type the text after you position the bounding rectangle, and you can resize the rectangle as needed. This is the only static text control you'll see listed in text, but you should also create the other static text controls as shown in Figure 6-1. Follow the same procedure for the other static text controls in the dialog. All static text controls have the same ID, but that doesn't matter because the program doesn't need to access any of them.

❑ **The Name edit control.** An edit control is the primary means of entering text in a dialog. Change this control's ID from *IDC_EDIT1* to *IDC_NAME*. Accept the defaults for the rest of the properties. Notice that the default sets Auto HScroll, which means that the text scrolls horizontally when the box is filled.

113

- ❑ **The SSN (social security number) edit control.** As far as App Studio is concerned, this control is exactly the same as the Name edit control. Simply change its ID to *IDC_SSN*. Later you will use ClassWizard to make this a numeric field.

- ❑ **The Biography edit control.** This is a multiline edit control. Change its ID to *IDC_BIO*, and then set its properties as shown here:

- ❑ **The Category group box.** This control serves only to group two radio buttons visually. Type in the caption *Category*. The default ID is sufficient.

- ❑ **The Hourly and Salary radio buttons.** Position these radio buttons inside the Category group box. Set the Hourly button's ID to *IDC_CAT*, and set the other properties, as shown here:

Be sure that both buttons have the Auto property set (the default) and that only the Hourly button has the Group property set. When these properties are set correctly, Windows ensures that only one of the two buttons can be selected at a time. The Category group box has no effect on the buttons' operation.

❑ **The Insurance group box.** This control holds three check boxes. Type in the caption *Insurance.*

❑ **The Life, Disability, and Medical check boxes.** Place these controls inside the Insurance group box. Accept the default properties, but change the IDs to *IDC_LIFE, IDC_DIS,* and *IDC_MED.* Unlike radio buttons, check boxes are independent; the user can set any combination.

> **NOTE:** You must also set the Group property for the control that <u>follows</u> the radio button group, in this case the Life check box.

❑ **The Skill combo box.** This is the first of three types of combo boxes. Change the ID to *IDC_SKILL*; otherwise, accept all the defaults. Add three skills (terminating each line with Ctrl-Enter) in the Enter List Choices box, as shown here:

This is a combo box of type Simple. The user can type anything in the top edit control, use the mouse to select an item

---

Aligning Controls

To align two or more controls, select the controls by clicking on the first control and Shift-clicking on the other controls you want aligned. Next choose one of the alignment commands (Left, Right, Top, or Bottom) from the Align Controls pop-up menu on the Layout menu.

from the attached list box, or use the Up or Down direction key to select an item from the attached list box.

❑ **The Education combo box.** Change the ID to *IDC_EDUC*, and then set the Type option to Dropdown. Add three education levels in the Enter List Choices box, as shown in Figure 6-1 on page 110. With this combo box, the user can type anything in the edit box, click on the arrow and then select an item from the drop-down list box, or use the Up or Down direction key to select an item from the attached list box.

> NOTE: To set the size for the drop-down portion of a combo box, click on the box's arrow and pull down from the bottom center of the rectangle.

❑ **The Department list box.** Change the ID to *IDC_DEPT*; otherwise, accept all the defaults. In this list box, the user can select only a single item by using the mouse, by using the Up or Down direction key, or by typing the first character of a selection.

❑ **The Language combo box.** Change the ID to *IDC_LANG*, and then set the Type option to Drop List. Add three languages (English, French, and Spanish) to the Enter List Choices box. With this combo box, the user can select only from the attached list box. To select, the user can click on the arrow and then select an entry from the drop-down list, or the user can type the first letter of the selection and then refine the selection with the Up or Down direction key.

Selecting a Group of Controls

To quickly select a group of controls, position the mouse cursor above and to the left of the group. Hold down the left mouse button and drag to a point below and to the right of the group, as shown here:

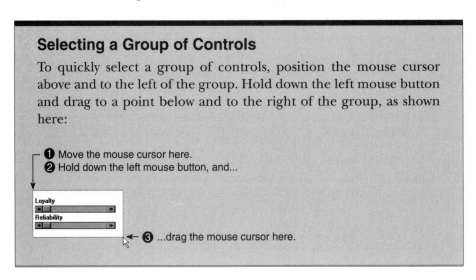

❶ Move the mouse cursor here.
❷ Hold down the left mouse button, and...

Loyalty

Reliability

❸ ...drag the mouse cursor here.

❑ **The Loyalty and Reliability scroll bars.** Do not confuse scroll bar controls with a window's built-in scroll bars as seen in scrolling views. A scroll bar control behaves in the same manner as do other controls and can be resized at design time. Position and size the horizontal scroll bar controls as shown in Figure 6-1 on page 110, and then assign the IDs *IDC_LOYAL* and *IDC_RELY*.

❑ **The OK, Cancel, and Special pushbuttons.** Type the button captions *OK*, *Cancel*, and *Special*, and then assign the *IDC_- SPECIAL* ID to the Special button. Later you'll learn about special meanings that are associated with the default *IDOK* and *IDCANCEL* IDs.

❑ **Any icon. (The AFX icon is shown as an example.)** You can display any icon in a dialog, as long as the resource script defines the icon. We'll use the program's AFX icon, identified as *IDR_- MAINFRAME*. Set the Type option to Icon, and set the icon to *IDR_MAINFRAME*. Leave the ID as *IDC_STATIC*.

7. **Check the dialog's tabbing order.** Choose Set Tab Order from the App Studio Layout menu. Use the mouse to set the tabbing order, as shown here:

Click on each control in the order shown and then press Enter.

> TIP: If you mess up the tab sequence part way through, you can recover with a Ctrl-left mouse click on the <u>last correctly sequenced</u> control. Subsequent mouse clicks will start with the next sequence number.

> NOTE: Static text controls (such as Name and Skill) have ampersands (&) embedded in the text for their captions. The ampersands appear as underscores under the following character at runtime. (See Figure 6-1 on page 110.) This enables the user to jump to selected controls by holding down the Alt key and pressing the key corresponding to the underlined character. (The related control must immediately follow the static text in the tabbing order.) Thus, Alt-N jumps to the Name edit control, and Alt-K jumps to the Skill combo box. Needless to say, designated jump characters should be unique within the dialog. The Skill control uses *K* because the SS Nbr control uses *S*.

8. **Save the resource file on disk.** Choose Save from the File menu or click the Save button on the toolbar to save EX06A.RC. Keep App Studio running, and keep the newly built dialog on the screen.

ClassWizard and the Dialog Class

You have now built a dialog resource, but you can't use it without a corresponding dialog class. (The section titled "Understanding the EX06A Application" later in this chapter explains the relationship between the dialog window and the underlying classes.) The ClassWizard DLL works in conjunction with App Studio to create that class as follows:

1. **Choose ClassWizard from the App Studio Resource menu.** Be sure that you still have the newly built dialog, *IDD_DIALOG1*, selected in App Studio and that \VCPP\EX06A\EX06A is the current Visual Workbench project.

2. **Add the *CEx06aDialog* class.** Fill in the Add Class dialog, as shown at the top of the facing page:

Be sure to enter the information exactly as shown; some of this information is case-sensitive.

Because your newly built dialog was selected in App Studio, Class-Wizard knew enough to choose *CDialog* as the base class for *CEx06a-Dialog* and to make *IDD_DIALOG1* the corresponding resource. Click the Create Class button.

3. **Add the *CEx06aDialog* variables.** After ClassWizard creates the *CEx06aDialog* class, the MFC Class Wizard dialog appears. Click the Member Variables tab, and the Member Variables page appears, as shown here:

You need to associate data members with each of the dialog's controls. To associate a data member with one of the dialog's controls, click on a control ID and then click the Add Variable button. The Add Member Variable dialog appears, as shown on the following page:

Type in the member variable name and choose the variable type according to the following table. Be sure to type the member variable name exactly as shown; the case of each letter is important. Click OK to return to the MFC Class Wizard dialog. Repeat this process for each of the listed controls.

Control ID	Data Member	Type
IDC_BIO	m_bio	CString
IDC_CAT	m_nCat	int
IDC_DEPT	m_dept	CString
IDC_DIS	m_bInsDis	BOOL
IDC_EDUC	m_educ	CString
IDC_LANG	m_lang	CString
IDC_LIFE	m_bInsLife	BOOL
IDC_MED	m_bInsMed	BOOL
IDC_NAME	m_name	CString
IDC_SKILL	m_skill	CString
IDC_SSN	m_lSsn	long

As you select controls in the MFC Class Wizard dialog, various edit boxes appear at the bottom of the dialog. If you select a *CString* variable, you can set its maximum number of characters; if you select a numeric variable, you can set its high and low limits. Set the minimum value for *IDC_SSN* to *0* and the maximum value to *999999999*.

Most relationships between control types and variable types are obvious. The way in which radio buttons correspond to variables is not so intuitive, however. The *CDialog* class associates an integer variable with each radio button group, with the first button corresponding to value 0, the second to 1, and so forth.

4. Add the message-handling function for the Special button.
CEx06aDialog doesn't need many message-handling functions because the *CDialog* base class, with the help of Windows, does most of the dialog management. When you specify the *IDOK* ID for the OK button (Class-Wizard's default), for example, the virtual *CDialog* function *OnOK* gets called when the user clicks the button. For other buttons, however, you need message handlers. Click the Message Maps tab.

The MFC Class Wizard dialog should contain an entry for *IDC_SPE-CIAL* in the Object IDs list box. Click on this entry, and double-click on the BN_CLICKED message that appears in the Messages list box. Class-Wizard invents a member function name, *OnSpecial*, and opens the Add Member Function dialog, as shown here:

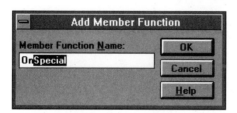

You could type your own function name here, but this time accept the default and click OK. Next click the Edit Code button in the ClassWizard dialog. This opens the file EX06ADLG.CPP in Visual Workbench and moves to the *OnSpecial* function. Insert a *TRACE* statement in the *OnSpecial* function by typing in the screened code, which replaces the existing code.

```
void CEx06aDialog::OnSpecial()
{
    TRACE("CEx06aDialog::OnSpecial\n");
}
```

5. Use ClassWizard to add an *OnInitDialog* message-handling function. As you'll see in a moment, ClassWizard generates code that initializes a dialog's controls. This DDX (Dialog Data Exchange) code won't initialize the list box choices, however, so you must override the *CDialog::OnInitDialog* function. Although *OnInitDialog* is a virtual member function, ClassWizard can generate the prototype if you map the

WM_INITDIALOG message in the derived dialog class. To do so, choose ClassWizard from Visual Workbench's Browse menu. Click on *CEx06a-Dialog* in the Object IDs list box, and then double-click on the WM_-INITDIALOG message in the Messages list box. Click the Edit Code button in the ClassWizard dialog to edit the *OnInitDialog* function. Type in the screened code, which replaces the existing code:

```
BOOL CEx06aDialog::OnInitDialog()
{
    CListBox* pLB = (CListBox*) GetDlgItem(IDC_DEPT);
    pLB->InsertString(-1, "Documentation");
    pLB->InsertString(-1, "Accounting");
    pLB->InsertString(-1, "Human Relations");
    pLB->InsertString(-1, "Security");

    return CDialog::OnInitDialog(); // call after initialization
    // initialize any VB controls after base class OnInitDialog call
}
```

You could use the same initialization technique for the combo boxes if you wanted, in place of the initialization in the resource.

Connecting the Dialog to the View

Now we've got the resource and the code for a dialog, but it's not connected to the view. In most applications, you would probably use a menu choice to activate a dialog, but we haven't studied menus yet. Here we'll use the familiar mouse click message WM_LBUTTONDOWN to start the dialog. The steps are as follows:

1. **In ClassWizard, select the *CEx06aView* class.** At this point, be sure that \VCPP\EX06A\EX06A is the current Visual Workbench project.

2. **Use ClassWizard to add the *OnLButtonDown* member function.** You've done this in the examples in earlier chapters. Simply select the *CEx06aView* class name, click on the *CEx06aView* object ID, and then double-click on WM_LBUTTONDOWN.

3. **Add code to the virtual *OnDraw* function in file EX06AVW.CPP.** To prompt the user to press the left mouse button, code the *CEx06aView* *OnDraw* function. (The skeleton was generated by AppWizard.) The following screened code (which you type in) replaces the existing code:

```
void CEx06aView::OnDraw(CDC* pDC)
{
    pDC->TextOut(0, 0, "Press the left mouse button here.");
}
```

4. Write the code for *OnLButtonDown* in file EX06AVW.CPP. Most of the code consists of *TRACE* statements to print the dialog data members after the user exits the dialog. The *CEx06aDialog* constructor call and the *DoModal* call are the critical statements, however:

```
void CEx06aView::OnLButtonDown(UINT nFlags, CPoint point)
{
    CEx06aDialog dlg;

    dlg.m_name     = "Shakespeare, Will";
    dlg.m_lSsn     = 307806636;
    dlg.m_nCat     = 1;   // 0 = hourly, 1 = salary
    dlg.m_bio      = "This person is not a well-motivated tech writer";
    dlg.m_bInsLife = TRUE;
    dlg.m_bInsDis  = FALSE;
    dlg.m_bInsMed  = TRUE;
    dlg.m_dept     = "Documentation";
    dlg.m_skill    = "Writer";
    dlg.m_lang     = "English";
    dlg.m_educ     = "College";
//  dlg.m_nLoyal   = dlg.m_nRely = 50;
    int ret = dlg.DoModal();
    TRACE("DoModal return = %d\n", ret);
    TRACE("name = %s, ssn = %ld, nCat = %d\n",
        (const char* ) dlg.m_name, dlg.m_lSsn, dlg.m_nCat);
    TRACE("dept = %s, skill = %s, lang = %s, educ = %s\n",
        (const char* ) dlg.m_dept, (const char* ) dlg.m_skill,
        (const char* ) dlg.m_lang, (const char* ) dlg.m_educ);
    TRACE("life = %d, dis = %d, med = %d, bio = %s\n",
        dlg.m_bInsLife, dlg.m_bInsDis, dlg.m_bInsMed,
        (const char* ) dlg.m_bio);
//  TRACE(" loyalty = %d, reliability = %d\n",
//      dlg.m_nLoyal, dlg.m_nRely);
}
```

NOTE: The statements that are "commented out" will be used later in this chapter.

5. To EX06AVW.CPP, add the dialog class include statement. The *OnLButtonDown* function above depends on the declaration of class *CEx06aDialog.* You must insert the include statement

```
#include "ex06adlg.h"
```

at the top of the *CEx06aView* class source code file (EX06AVW.CPP), after the statement

```
#include "ex06avw.h"
```

6. Build and test the application. If you have done everything right, you should be able to build and run the EX06A application through Visual Workbench. Try entering data in each control, and then click the OK button and observe the *TRACE* results. Notice that the scroll bar controls don't do much yet, but we'll attend to them later. Notice what happens when you press Enter while entering text data in a control: The dialog closes immediately.

Understanding the EX06A Application

When your program calls *DoModal*, control is returned to your program only when the user closes the dialog. If you understand that, you understand modal dialogs. When you get to modeless dialogs, you'll begin to appreciate the programming simplicity of modal dialogs. A lot happens "out of sight" as a result of that *DoModal* call, however. Here's a "what calls what" summary:

```
CDialog::DoModal
    CEx06aDialog::OnInitDialog
        ...additional initialization...
        CDialog::OnInitDialog
            CWnd::UpdateData(FALSE)
                CEx06aDialog::DoDataExchange
    user enters data...
    user clicks the OK button
    CEx06aDialog::OnOK
        ...additional validation...
        CDialog::OnOK
            CWnd::UpdateData(TRUE)
                CEx06aDialog::DoDataExchange
            CDialog::EndDialog(IDOK)
```

OnInitDialog and *DoDataExchange* are virtual functions overridden in the *CEx06a Dialog* class. Windows calls *OnInitDialog* as part of the dialog initialization process, and that results in a call to *DoDataExchange*, a function that was generated by ClassWizard. Here is a listing of that function:

```
void CEx06aDialog::DoDataExchange(CDataExchange* pDX)
{
    CDialog::DoDataExchange(pDX)
    //{{AFX_DATA_MAP(CEx06aDialog)
    DDX_Text(pDX, IDC_BIO, m_bio);
    DDX_Radio(pDX, IDC_CAT, m_nCat);
```

```
        DDX_LBString(pDX, IDC_DEPT, m_dept);
        DDX_Check(pDX, IDC_DIS, m_bInsDis);
        DDX_CBString(pDX, IDC_EDUC, m_educ);
        DDX_CBString(pDX, IDC_LANG, m_lang);
        DDX_Check(pDX, IDC_LIFE, m_bInsLife);
        DDX_Check(pDX, IDC_MED, m_bInsMed);
        DDX_Text(pDX, IDC_NAME, m_name);
        DDX_CBString(pDX, IDC_SKILL, m_skill);
        DDX_Text(pDX, IDC_SSN, m_lSsn);
        DDV_MinMaxLong(pDX, m_lSsn, 0, 999999999);
        //}}AFX_DATA_MAP
    }
```

DoDataExchange and the *DDX_* (exchange) and *DDV_* (validation) functions are "bi-directional." If *UpdateData* is called with a *FALSE* parameter, the functions transfer data from the data members to the dialog controls. If the parameter is *TRUE*, the functions transfer data from the dialog controls to the data members. *DDX_Text* is overloaded to accommodate a variety of data types.

The *EndDialog* function is critical to the dialog exit procedure. *DoModal* returns the parameter passed to *EndDialog*. *IDOK* accepts the dialog's data, and *IDCANCEL* cancels the dialog.

> **TIP:** You can write your own "custom" DDX functions and wire them into App Studio. This feature is useful if you're using a unique data type throughout your application. See Technical Note #26 in the MFCNOTES.HLP file.

Enhancing the Dialog Program

The EX06A program required little coding for a lot of functionality. Now we'll make a new version of this program that uses some hand-coding to add extra features. We'll eliminate EX06A's rude habit of dumping the user in response to the Enter key, and we'll hook up the scroll bar controls.

Taking Control of the *OnOK* Exit

In the original EX06A program, the *CDialog::OnOK* virtual function handled the OK button, which triggered data exchange and the exit from the dialog. The Enter key happens to have the same effect, and that might or might not be what you want. If the user presses Enter in the Name edit control, for example, he or she is immediately bounced out of the dialog.

What's going on here? When the user presses Enter, Windows looks to see which pushbutton has the "input focus" as indicated by a dotted rectangle. If no button has the focus, Windows looks for the "default push-button" that the program or the resource specifies. (The default pushbutton has a thicker border.) If the dialog has no default button, the *OnOK* function is called, even if the dialog does not contain an OK button.

You can disable the Enter key simply by writing a do-nothing *CEx06aDialog::OnOK* function and adding the exit code to a new function that responds to the OK button. Here are the steps:

1. **Use App Studio to change the OK button ID.** Open the resource file EX06A.RC, select dialog *IDD_DIALOG1*, and then select the OK button. Change its ID from *IDOK* to *IDC_OK*, and uncheck its Default Button property.

For Windows SDK Programmers

Dialog controls send WM_COMMAND "notification messages" to their parent dialogs. For a single button click, for example, *wParam* is the button ID, and *lParam* contains both the button handle and the BN_CLICKED notification code. Most *WndProc* programs process these notification messages with a nested switch statement. Microsoft Foundation Class Library version 2.0 "flattened out" the message processing logic by "promoting" control notification messages to the same level as other Windows messages.

ClassWizard generates notification message map entries similar to this:

```
ON_BN_CLICKED(IDC_DELETE, OnDeleteButtonClicked)
ON_BN_DOUBLECLICKED(IDC_DELETE, OnDeleteButtonDblClicked)
```

Button events are special because they generate "command messages" if your dialog class doesn't have notification handlers like the ones above. As Chapter 13 explains, the application framework routes these command messages, and they are ultimately processed by ON_COMMAND message-handling entries mapped like this:

```
ON_COMMAND(IDC_DELETE, OnDelete)
```

In this case, the *OnDelete* function is unable to distinguish between a single click and a double click, but that's no problem because few Windows-based programs utilize double clicks for buttons.

---

2. **Use ClassWizard to create a member function called *OnClickedOk*.**
   This *CEx06aDialog* class member function is keyed to the BN_CLICKED
   message from control *IDC_OK*.

3. **Write the body of the *OnClickedOk* function.** This function calls the
   base class *OnOK* function, as did the original *CEx06aDialog::OnOK*
   function. Here is the code:

```
void CEx06aDialog::OnClickedOk()
{
    TRACE("CEx06aDialog::OnClickedOk\n");
    CDialog::OnOK();
}
```

4. **Create a dummy *OnOK* function.** Add the following prototype to
   EX06ADLG.H:

```
protected
    virtual void OnOK();
```

   Now add the following code in EX06ADLG.CPP:

```
void CEx06aDialog::OnOK()
{
    // dummy OnOK function
    TRACE("CEx06aDialog::OnOK\n");
}
```

   Pressing Enter while entering text data in one of the dialog's controls
   now calls this function.

5. **Build and test the application.** Try the Enter key now. Nothing should
   happen, but the OK button should work as before.

OnCancel Processing

Just as the Enter key triggers a call to *OnOK*, the Escape key triggers a call to
OnCancel, which results in an exit from the dialog with a *DoModal* return
code of *IDCANCEL*. EX06A does no special processing for *IDCANCEL*;
therefore, the Esc key (and the system menu Close command) closes the dialog. You can circumvent this process by substituting a dummy *OnCancel* function, following the same procedure you used for the OK button.

Hooking Up the Scroll Bar Controls

The App Studio dialog editor allows you to put scroll bar controls in your
dialog, but ClassWizard doesn't provide any direct support for these con-

trols. You will now add the code that makes the Loyalty and Reliability scroll bars work.

Scroll bar controls have position and range values that can be read and written. If you set the range to (0, 100), for example, and you call the *CScrollBar* member function *SetScrollPos* with parameter 50, the scroll box is positioned at the center of the bar. The scroll bars send the WM_HSCROLL and WM_VSCROLL messages to the dialog when the user drags the scroll box or clicks on the arrows. The dialog's message handlers must decode these messages and position the scroll box accordingly.

One tricky thing about scroll bar controls is that all horizontal bars send the same message, WM_HSCROLL, and all vertical bars send the WM_VSCROLL message. Because this monster dialog contains two horizontal scroll bars, the one and only WM_HSCROLL message handler must figure out which scroll bar sent the scroll message.

Also, scroll bars have no data exchange functions. You must code your own data exchange in the *OnInitDialog* and *OnOK* (or rather *OnClickedOK*) functions.

Here are the steps for adding the scroll bar logic to EX06A:

1. **Add the class data members *m_nLoyal* and *m_nRely*.** Add the following code to the class declaration in EX06ADLG.H, placing the statements <u>outside</u> the *AFX_DATA* brackets:

```
public:
    int m_nLoyal;
    int m_nRely;
```

These data members are made public so that they are consistent with the ClassWizard-generated public data members. Also add *enum* statements for the minimum and maximum scroll range:

```
enum { nMin = 0 };
enum { nMax = 100 };
```

2. **Change the *OnInitDialog* function to add data exchange logic.** The *OnInitDialog* function must set the positions of the scroll boxes according to percentage values stored in the *CEx06aDialog* data members. A value of 100 means "Set the scroll box to the extreme right"; a value of 0 means "Set the scroll box to the extreme left."

Add the following code to the *CEx06aDialog* member function *OnInitDialog* in the file EX06ADLG.CPP:

```
CScrollBar* pSB = (CScrollBar*) GetDlgItem(IDC_LOYAL);
pSB->SetScrollRange(nMin, nMax);
pSB->SetScrollPos(m_nLoyal);

pSB = (CScrollBar*) GetDlgItem(IDC_RELY);
pSB->SetScrollRange(nMin, nMax);
pSB->SetScrollPos(m_nRely);
```

3. **Change the *OnClickedOK* function to add data exchange logic.**
   Here is the new *OnClickedOK* function (in EX06ADLG.CPP) that "reads" the scroll box positions and sets the values of *m_nLoyal* and *m_nRely*:

```
void CEx06aDialog::OnClickedOK()
{
    CScrollBar* pSB;

    TRACE("CEx06aDialog::OnClickedOK\n");
    pSB = (CScrollBar*) GetDlgItem(IDC_LOYAL);
    m_nLoyal = pSB->GetScrollPos();

    pSB = (CScrollBar*) GetDlgItem(IDC_RELY);
    m_nRely = pSB->GetScrollPos();

    CDialog::OnOK(); // does data exchange
}
```

4. **Use ClassWizard to add a scroll bar message handler to *CEx06a-Dialog*.** Choose the WM_HSCROLL message, and then add the member function *OnHScroll*. Enter the following code:

```
void CEx06aDialog::OnHScroll(UINT nSBCode, UINT nPos,
                            CScrollBar* pScrollBar)
{
    int nTemp1, nTemp2;

    nTemp1 = pScrollBar->GetScrollPos();
    switch(nSBCode) {
    case SB_THUMBPOSITION:
        pScrollBar->SetScrollPos(nPos);
        break;
    case SB_LINEUP: // left arrow button
        nTemp2 = (nMax - nMin) / 10;
        if ((nTemp1 - nTemp2) > nMin) {
            nTemp1 -= nTemp2;
        }
```

(continued)

```
      else {
        nTemp1 = nMin;
      }
      pScrollBar->SetScrollPos(nTemp1);
      break;
  case SB_LINEDOWN: // right arrow button
      nTemp2 = (nMax - nMin) / 10;
      if ((nTemp1 + nTemp2) < nMax) {
        nTemp1 += nTemp2;
      }
      else {
        nTemp1 = nMax;
      }
      pScrollBar->SetScrollPos(nTemp1);
  }
}
```

5. **In EX06AVW.CPP, add initialization code to *OnLButtonDown*.** To test the data exchange logic, you'll want to set the values of *m_nLoyal* and *m_nRely*. In *OnLButtonDown*, remove the comment characters in front of the lines that relate to *m_nLoyal* and *m_nRely*.

6. **Build and test the application.** Build and run EX06A again. Do the scroll bars work this time? The scroll boxes should "stick" after you drag them with the mouse, and they should move when you click the scroll bars' arrows. (Notice that we haven't added logic for when the user clicks on the scroll bar itself.)

Identifying Controls:
CWnd Pointers and Control IDs

When you lay out a dialog resource in App Studio, you identify controls by IDs such as *IDC_SSN*. In your program code, however, you often need access to a control's underlying window object. The MFC library provides the *CWnd::GetDlgItem* function for converting an ID to a *CWnd* pointer. You've seen this already in the *OnInitDialog* and *OnClickedOK* member functions of class *CEx06aDialog*. The application framework "manufactured" this returned *CWnd* pointer because there never was a constructor call for the control objects. This pointer is temporary and should not be stored for later use.

> TIP: If you need to convert a *CWnd* pointer to a control ID, use the MFC library *GetDlgCtrlID* member function of class *CWnd*.

Setting the Color for the Dialog Background and for Controls

It's very easy to select a new color for <u>all</u> the dialogs in your application. Just edit the call to *SetDialogBkColor* in your derived application class *InitInstance* function. The following line causes all dialogs to have a green background and white static text:

SetDialogBkColor(RGB(0, 255, 0), RGB(255, 255, 255));

If you want to change the background color of individual dialogs or specific controls in a dialog, you have to work a little harder. There is no *SetDlgItemColor* function. Instead, each control sends a WM_CTLCOLOR message to the parent dialog immediately before the control is displayed. A WM_CTLCOLOR message is also sent on behalf of the dialog itself. If you map this message in your derived dialog class, you can set the foreground and background text colors, and you can select a brush for the control or dialog nontext area.

Here's a sample *OnCtlColor* function that sets all edit control backgrounds to yellow and the dialog background to red. The *m_hYellowBrush* and *m_hRedBrush* variables are data members of type *HBRUSH*, initialized in the dialog's *OnInitDialog* function. The *nCtlColor* parameter indicates the type of control, and the *pWnd* parameter identifies the specific control. If you wanted to set the color for an individual edit control, you would convert *pWnd* to a child window ID and test it.

```
HBRUSH CMyDialog::OnCtlColor(CDC* pDC, CWnd* pWnd, UINT nCtlColor)
{
    if (nCtlColor == CTLCOLOR_EDIT) {
        pDC->SetBkColor(RGB(255, 255, 0));  // yellow
        return m_hYellowBrush;
    }
    if (nCtlColor == CTLCOLOR_DLG) {
        pDC->SetBkColor(RGB(255, 0, 0));    // red
        return m_hRedBrush;
    }
    return CDialog::OnCtlColor(pDC, pWnd, nCtlColor);
}
```

Painting Inside the Dialog Window

You can paint directly in the client area of the dialog window, but you'll avoid overwriting dialog elements if you paint only inside a control window. If you want to display only text, use App Studio to create a blank static control with a unique ID, and then call the *CWnd::SetDlgItemText* function in a dialog member function such as *OnInitDialog* to place text in the control.

Displaying graphics is more complicated. You must use ClassWizard to add an *OnPaint* member function to the dialog; this function converts the static control's ID to a *CWnd* pointer and gets its device context. The trick is to draw inside the control window while preventing Windows from overwriting your work later. The *Invalidate/UpdateWindow* sequence achieves this. Here is an *OnPaint* function that paints a small black square in a static control:

```
void CMyDialog::OnPaint()
{
    CPaintDC dc(this);                          // keeps Windows happy
    CWnd* pWnd = GetDlgItem(IDC_STATIC1);       // IDC_STATIC1 specified
                                                //  in App Studio

    CDC* pControlDC = pWnd->GetDC();

    pWnd->Invalidate();
    pWnd->UpdateWindow();
    pControlDC->SelectStockObject(BLACK_BRUSH);
    pControlDC->Rectangle(0, 0, 10, 10);        // black square bullet
    pWnd->ReleaseDC(pControlDC);
}
```

As with all windows, the dialog's *OnPaint* function is called only if some part of the dialog is invalidated. You can force the *OnPaint* call from another dialog member function with the following statement:

```
Invalidate();
```

Using Other Control Features

You've seen how to "extend" one control class, *CScrollBar*, with code in the *OnInitDialog* member function and the dialog's exit function. You can extend the other controls in similar fashion. Look in the *Class Library Reference* at the control classes, particularly *CListBox* and *CComboBox*. Each has a number of features that ClassWizard does not directly support. List boxes and some combo boxes, for example, can support multiple selections. If you want to use these features, don't use ClassWizard to add data members, but define your own data members and add your own exchange code in *OnInitDialog* and *OnClickedOK*.

C H A P T E R   S E V E N

THE MODELESS DIALOG AND THE COMMDLG DIALOG CLASSES

In Chapter 6, you saw the ordinary modal dialog and most of the controls for Microsoft Windows. Now you'll move on to the modeless dialog and the Windows COMMDLG classes. Modeless dialogs, as you'll remember, allow the user to work elsewhere in the application while the dialog is active. The COMMDLG classes are the C++ programming interface to the group of Windows utility dialogs that include File Open, Printer Setup, Color Selection, and so forth, which are supported by the dynamic link library COMMDLG.DLL.

In this chapter's first example, you'll build a simple modeless dialog that is controlled from a view. In the second example, you'll derive a class from the COMMDLG *CFileDialog* class, which allows file deletion.

Modeless Dialogs

In Microsoft Foundation Class (MFC) Library versions 2.0 and 2.5, modal and modeless dialogs share the same base class, *CDialog*, and they both use a dialog resource that you can build with App Studio. If you're using a modeless dialog with a view, then you'll need some specialized programming techniques.

Creating Modeless Dialogs

You've already learned that you display a modal dialog window by calling the *DoModal* function and that the window ceases to exist as soon as *DoModal* returns. You can construct a modal dialog object on the stack knowing that the

Windows dialog has been destroyed by the time the C++ dialog object goes out of scope. Modeless dialogs are more complicated. You start by constructing a dialog object, but then to create the dialog window you call the *CDialog::Create* member function instead of *DoModal*. Control returns immediately with the dialog still on the screen. Now you must worry about exactly when to construct the dialog object, when to create the dialog window, when to destroy the dialog, and when to process user-entered data.

User-Defined Messages

Suppose you want the modeless dialog window destroyed when the user clicks the dialog's OK button. This presents a problem. How does the view know that the user has clicked the OK button? The dialog could call a view class member function directly but that would "marry" the dialog to a particular view class. A better solution is for the dialog to send the view a user-defined message as the result of a call to the OK button message-handling function. When the view gets the message, it can destroy the dialog window (but not the object). This sets the stage for the creation of a new dialog.

You have two options for sending Windows messages. You can use the *CWind::SendMessage* function or the *PostMessage* function. The former causes an immediate call to the message-handling function, and the latter posts a message in the Windows message queue. With the *PostMessage* option, there's a slight delay, so it's reasonable to expect that the dialog is completely gone by the time the view gets the message.

Dialog Ownership

Now suppose you've accepted the dialog default pop-up style, which means the dialog isn't confined to the view's client area. As far as Windows is concerned, the dialog's "owner" is the application's main frame window (introduced in Chapter 12), not the view. You need to know the dialog's view to send the view a message. Therefore, your dialog class must track its own view through a data member that the constructor sets.

A Modeless Dialog Example—EX07A

We could convert the Chapter 6 monster dialog to a modeless dialog, but starting from scratch with a simpler dialog is easier. Example EX07A uses a dialog with one edit control, an OK button, and a Cancel button. As in the Chapter 6 example, pressing the left mouse button while the mouse cursor is inside the view window brings up the dialog, but now we have the option of destroying it in response to another event—pressing the <u>right</u> mouse button when the mouse cursor is inside the view window. We'll allow only one dialog at a time, so we must be sure that a second left button press doesn't bring up a duplicate dialog.

To summarize the upcoming steps, the EX07A view class has a single associated dialog object that is constructed on the heap when the view is constructed. The dialog window is created and destroyed in response to user actions, but the dialog object is not destroyed until the application terminates.

Here are the steps to create the EX07A example:

1. **Run AppWizard to produce \VCPP\EX07A\EX07A.** Choose AppWizard from Visual Workbench's Project menu. The options and the default class names are shown here:

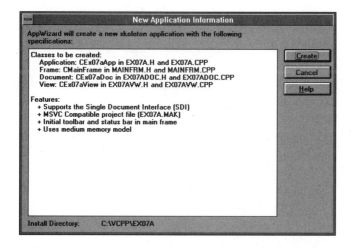

2. **Use App Studio to create a new dialog.** Choose App Studio from Visual Workbench's Tools menu. When App Studio starts up, click the New button and then choose Dialog. App Studio assigns the ID *IDD_-DIALOG1* to the new dialog. Change the dialog caption to *Modeless Dialog.* Accept the default OK and Cancel buttons with IDs *IDOK* and *IDCANCEL,* and then add a static text control and an edit control with the default ID *IDC_EDIT1.* Change the static text control's caption to *Edit 1.* The completed dialog is shown at the top of the following page:

3. Use ClassWizard to create the *CEx07aDialog* class. Choose Class-Wizard from the App Studio Resource menu. Fill in the Add Class dialog as shown here, and then click the Create Class button.

Add the message-handling functions shown below. To add a message-handling function, click on an object ID, click on a message, and click the Add Function button. The Add Member Function dialog box appears. Type the function name and click the OK button.

Object ID	Message	Member Function Name
IDCANCEL	BN_CLICKED	*OnCancel*
IDOK	BN_CLICKED	*OnOK*

4. Add a variable to the *CEx07aDialog*. While in ClassWizard, click the Member Variables tab, and then click the Add Variable button to add the *CString* variable *m_edit1* to the *IDC_EDIT1* control.

5. Edit EX07ADLG.H to add a view pointer and function prototypes.
Type in the following screened code in the *CEx07aDialog* class declaration:

```
public:
    CView* m_pView;
```

Also, add the function prototypes as follows:

```
public:
    CEx07aDialog(CView* pView);
    BOOL Create();
```

> **NOTE:** Using the *CView* class rather than the *CEx07a-View* class allows the dialog class to be used with any view class.

6. Add the modeless constructor in file EX07ADLG.CPP. You could modify the existing *CEx07aDialog* constructor, but if you add a separate one, the dialog class can serve for both modal and modeless dialogs.

```
CEx07aDialog::CEx07aDialog(CView* pView)   // modeless constructor
    : CDialog()
{
    m_pView = pView;
}
```

You should also add the following line to the AppWizard-generated modal constructor:

```
m_pView = NULL;
```

The C++ compiler is clever enough to distinguish between the modeless constructor *CEx07aDialog(CView*)* and the modal constructor *CEx07aDialog(CWnd*)*. If the compiler sees an argument of class *CView* or a derived *CView* class, it generates a call to the modeless constructor. If it sees an argument of class *CWnd* or another derived *CWnd* class, it generates a call to the modal constructor.

7. Add the *Create* function in EX07ADLG.CPP. This derived dialog class *Create* function calls the base class function with the dialog resource ID as a parameter.

```
BOOL CEx07aDialog::Create()
{
    return CDialog::Create(CEx07aDialog::IDD);
}
```

8. Edit the *OnOK* and *OnCancel* functions in EX07ADLG.CPP. These virtual functions generated by ClassWizard are called in response to dialog button clicks.

```
void CEx07aDialog::OnOK()           // not really a message handler
{   // Do not call base class OnOk
    UpdateData(TRUE);
    if (m_pView != NULL) {
      m_pView->PostMessage(WM_GOODBYE, IDOK);
    }
}

void CEx07aDialog::OnCancel()     // not really a message handler
{   // Do not call base class OnCancel
    if (m_pView != NULL) {
      m_pView->PostMessage(WM_GOODBYE, IDCANCEL);
    }
}
```

If the dialog is being used as a modeless dialog, it sends the user-defined message WM_GOODBYE to the view. We'll worry about handling the message later.

> NOTE: For a modeless dialog, be sure you do <u>not</u> call the *CDialog::OnOK* or *CDialog::OnCancel* function. This means you <u>must</u> override these virtual functions in your derived class; otherwise, using the Esc key, the Enter key, or a button click would result in a call to the base class functions, which call the Windows *EndDialog* function. *EndDialog* is appropriate only for modal dialogs. In a modeless dialog, you must call *DestroyWindow* instead, and, if necessary, you must call *UpdateData* to transfer data from the dialog controls to the class data members.

9. Edit RESOURCE.H to define the *WM_GOODBYE* message ID. Add the following line of code:

```
#define WM_GOODBYE     WM_USER + 5
```

The Windows constant WM_USER is the first message ID available for user-defined messages. The application framework uses a few of these messages, so we'll skip over the first five messages.

> NOTE: App Studio does not understand constants based on other constants. When App Studio reads

RESOURCE.H, it ignores *WM_GOODBYE,* and thus you won't see it in the list of symbols. App Studio does rewrite the *WM_GOODBYE* definition back to RESOURCE.H on exit, however, so it's not lost.

10. **Modify the *CEx07aView* constructor and destructor in EX07A-VW.CPP.** The *CEx07aView* class has a data member *m_pDlg* that points to the view's *CEx07aDialog* object. The view constructor constructs the dialog object on the heap, and the view destructor deletes it.

```
CEx07aView::CEx07aView()
{
    m_pDlg = new CEx07aDialog(this);
}

CEx07aView::~CEx07aView()
{
    delete m_pDlg; // destroys window if not already destroyed
}
```

11. **Add code to the virtual *OnDraw* function in file EX07AVW.CPP.** The *CEx07aView OnDraw* function (the skeleton was generated by AppWizard) should be coded as follows in order to prompt the user to press the mouse button:

```
void CEx07aView::OnDraw(CDC* pDC)
{
    pDC->TextOut(0, 0, "Press the left mouse button here.");
}
```

12. **Use ClassWizard to add *CEx07aView* mouse message handlers.** Add handlers for the WM_LBUTTONDOWN and WM_RBUTTON-DOWN messages. Now edit the code in file EX07AVW.CPP as follows:

```
void CEx07aView::OnLButtonDown(UINT nFlags, CPoint point)
{
    // creates the dialog if not created already
    if (m_pDlg->GetSafeHwnd() == 0) {
      m_pDlg->Create(); // displays the dialog window
    }
}

void CEx07aView::OnRButtonDown(UINT nFlags, CPoint point)
{
    m_pDlg->DestroyWindow();
    // no problem if window was already destroyed
}
```

For almost all window types except main frame windows, the *Destroy-Window* function does not destroy the C++ object. We want this behavior because we'll take care of the dialog object's destruction in the view destructor.

13. Add the dialog header include statement to file EX07AVW.CPP.
While you're in EX07AVW.CPP, add the following dialog header include statement after the view header include statement.

```
#include "ex07avw.h"
#include "ex07adlg.h"
```

14. Add your own message code for the WM_GOODBYE message.
Because ClassWizard does not support user-defined messages, you must write the code yourself. This task makes you appreciate the work Class-Wizard does for the other messages.

❑ In EX07AVW.CPP, add the following line after the *BEGIN_MES-SAGE_MAP* statement but outside the *AFX_MSG_MAP* brackets:

```
ON_MESSAGE(WM_GOODBYE, OnGoodbye)
```

❑ In EX07AVW.CPP, add the message handler function itself:

```
LONG CEx07aView::OnGoodbye(UINT wParam, LONG lParam)
{
    // message received in response to modeless dialog OK
    // and Cancel buttons
    TRACE("CEx07aView::OnGoodbye %x, %lx\n", wParam, lParam);
    TRACE("Dialog edit1 contents = %s\n", (const char*) m_pDlg->m_edit1);
    m_pDlg->DestroyWindow();
    return 0L;
}
```

❑ In EX07AVW.H, add the function prototype:

```
LONG OnGoodbye(UINT wParam, LONG lParam);
```

With the Windows SDK, the *wParam* and *lParam* parameters are the usual means of passing message data. In a mouse button down message, for example, the mouse *x*- and *y*-coordinates are packed into the *lParam* value. With the MFC library, message data is passed in more meaningful parameters. The mouse position is passed as a *CPoint* object. User-defined messages must use *wParam* and *lParam*; so you can use these two variables however you want. In this example, we've put the button ID in *wParam*.

15. Edit the EX07AVW.H header file. You need a data member to hold the dialog pointer:

```
private:
    CEx07aDialog* m_pDlg;
```

If you add the forward declaration

```
class CEx07aDialog;
```

at the beginning of EX07AVW.H, you won't have to include EX07A-DLG.H in every module that includes EX07AVW.H.

16. Build and test the application. Build and run EX07A. Try pressing the mouse's left mouse button and then its right button. (Be sure the mouse cursor is outside the dialog window when you press the right mouse button.) Also enter some data and click the dialog's OK button. Does the view's *TRACE* statement correctly list the edit control's contents?

> NOTE: If you use the EX07A view and dialog classes in an MDI application, each MDI child window can have one modeless dialog. When the user closes an MDI child, the child's modeless dialog is destroyed because the view's destructor calls the dialog destructor, which, in turn, destroys the dialog window.

The *CFormView* Class— A Modeless Dialog Alternative

If you need an application based on a single modeless dialog, the *CFormView* class will save you a lot of work. You'll have to wait until Chapter 15, however, because the *CFormView* class is most useful when coupled with the *CDocument* class, and we haven't progressed that far in our exploration of the application framework.

COMMDLG Dialogs

Windows provides a group of standard user interface dialogs, and these are supported by the MFC library classes. You are probably familiar with all or most of these dialogs because so many Windows-based applications, including Visual C++, already use them. A list of the COMMDLG classes is in the table at the top of the following page:

Class	Purpose
CFileDialog	Allows the user to open a new file or an existing file
CFontDialog	Allows the user to select a font from a list of available fonts
CColorDialog	Allows the user to select or create a color
CPrintDialog	Allows the user to set up the printer and print a document
CFindReplaceDialog	Allows the user to substitute one string for another

The resources for these dialogs are buried inside the COMMDLG.DLL dynamic link library in the \WINDOWS\SYSTEM directory. You can access these resources through App Studio, but you shouldn't try to update them directly. You can use the clipboard to copy the dialogs to your own resource script if you want to.

Using the *CFileDialog* Class Directly

Using the *CFileDialog* class to open a file is easy. Here is some code that opens a file that the user has selected through the dialog:

```
CFileDialog dlg(TRUE, "bmp", "*.bmp");
if (dlg.DoModal() == IDOK){
  CFile file;
  VERIFY(file.Open(dlg.GetPathName(), CFile::modeRead)));
}
```

The first constructor parameter (*TRUE*) specifies that this object is a "File Open" dialog instead of a "File Save" dialog, and "bmp" is the default file extension. The *CFileDialog::GetPathName* function returns a *CString* object that contains the full pathname of the selected file.

Adding Dialog Controls at Run Time

You can use the App Studio resource editor to create dialog controls at build time. If you need to add a dialog control at run time, here are the programming steps:

1. Add an embedded control window data member to your dialog class. The MFC library control window classes include *CButton*, *CEdit*, *CListBox*, and *CComboBox*. An embedded control window is constructed and destroyed along with the dialog.

2. Use the App Studio symbol editor to add an ID constant for the control.

3. Override the *CDialog* function *OnInitDialog* to call the embedded control window's *Create* member function. This call displays the new control in the dialog.

4. In your derived dialog class, manually add the necessary message handlers for your new control.

Deriving from the COMMDLG Classes

Most of the time you can use the COMMDLG classes directly. If you derive your own COMMDLG classes, however, you can add functionality without duplicating code. You have to be careful, though, because quite a lot happens inside the Windows code before class member functions such as *OnOK* are called. Sometimes you must innovate to get the features you want.

A *CFileDialog* Example—EX07B

In this example, you will derive a class *CEx07bDialog* that adds a working Delete button to the standard file dialog. It also changes the dialog's caption and changes the OK button's caption to Open. The example illustrates how you can create dialog controls "on the fly" without a corresponding resource entry. The new file dialog is activated as in the previous examples—by pressing the left mouse button when the mouse cursor is in the view window. Because you should be gaining skill with Visual C++, the following steps won't be as detailed as those for the earlier examples. Figure 7-1 shows what the dialog looks like.

Figure 7-1.
The File Delete dialog in action.

Follow these steps to build the EX07B application:

1. Run AppWizard to produce \VCPP\EX07B\EX07B. Choose App-Wizard from Visual Workbench's Project menu. The options and the default class names are shown at the top of the following page:

143

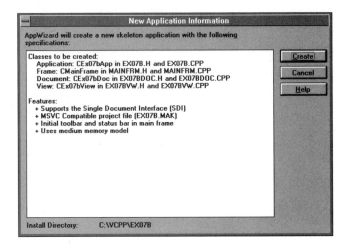

2. Use ClassWizard to create the *CEX07bDialog* class. ClassWizard
won't let you specify *CFileDialog* as a base class, so you'll have to choose
CDialog. Fill in the Add Class dialog, as shown here:

Be sure to leave the Dialog ID edit control empty in the Add Class
dialog. When you click the Create Class button, ClassWizard displays
this dialog:

This is OK. Click the Yes button to continue.

ClassWizard produces the files EX07BDLG.H and EX07BDLG.CPP and adds them to the project.

3. Edit the file EX07BDLG.H. Change the line

```
class CEx07bDialog : public CDialog
```

to

```
class CEx07BDialog : public CFileDialog
```

to change the *CEx07BDialog* base class.

In the *CEx07BDialog* class declaration, replace the following lines

```
// Dialog Data
    //{{AFX_DATA(CEx07bDialog)
    enum { IDD = _UNKNOWN_RESOURCE_ID_ };
        // NOTE: the ClassWizard will add data members here
    //}}AFX_DATA
```

with the following data member declarations:

```
public:
    CButton m_deleteButton;
    BOOL    m_bDeleteFlag;
```

And, finally, add the following function prototypes:

```
virtual BOOL OnInitDialog();
afx_msg void OnDeleteButton();
```

4. Use App Studio to add a define constant for the Delete button. Choose Symbols from the Edit menu, and then click the New button in the Symbol Browser dialog. In the New Symbols dialog, add the constant *IDC_DELETE*. (You can accept the default value.)

5. Replace *CDialog* with *CFileDialog* in EX07BDLG.CPP. Choose Replace from the Visual Workbench Edit menu and replace this name globally.

6. Replace the *CEx07bDialog* constructor in EX07BDLG.CPP. The constructor for the *CFileDialog* class takes a long string of optional parameters. We set the first parameter, *bOpenFileDialog*, to *TRUE* (for the File Open dialog) because we want to select an existing file. The third parameter, *lpszFileName*, is the initial filename. If you set it to "*.*", you will see a list of all files in the current directory. The body of the constructor sets the dialog caption by accessing an internal structure called *m_ofn*.

```
CEx07bDialog::CEx07bDialog(CWnd* pParent /*=NULL*/)
    : CFileDialog(TRUE, NULL, "*.*")
{
    m_ofn.lpstrTitle = "File Delete"; // dialog caption
}
```

7. **Add the *OnInitDialog* function in file EX07BDLG.CPP.** This member function calls the *CButton Create* member function to create the new Delete button window and insert it in the dialog. The function sets the position, size, and font of the new button based on the existing Cancel button. The *SetDlgItemText* function changes the title of the existing OK button.

```
BOOL CEx07bDialog::OnInitDialog()
{
    m_bDeleteFlag = FALSE;
    CRect rect; // button location in dialog window
    CWnd* pWndCancel = GetDlgItem(IDCANCEL);   // look at the Cancel button
    pWndCancel->GetWindowRect(&rect);          // get its size and position
    int nDiff = (rect.bottom - rect.top) * 2;  // move down from it
    rect.top += nDiff;                         // delete button's top...
    rect.bottom += nDiff;                      //  ...and bottom
    ScreenToClient(rect);                      // convert back to dialog
    CFont* pFont = pWndCancel->GetFont();      // get Cancel button's font

    m_deleteButton.Create("Delete",
                    WS_CHILD | WS_VISIBLE | BS_PUSHBUTTON,
                    rect, this, IDC_DELETE);
    GetDlgItem(IDC_DELETE)->SetFont(pFont, TRUE);   // set up font
    SetDlgItemText(IDOK, "Open");                   // change OK button's
                                                    // caption

    return CFileDialog::OnInitDialog();
}
```

8. **Add the Delete button message handler in file EX07BDLG.CPP.** The Windows COMMDLG code does important processing before calling the dialog class's *OnOK* function. Therefore, the dialog must simulate clicking the OK button by sending itself an IDOK button-click message. Calling *EndDialog* or the base class *OnOK* doesn't work. The data member *m_bDeleteFlag* tells the view that the Delete button was clicked rather than the Open button.

```
void CEx07bDialog::OnDeleteButton()
{
    m_bDeleteFlag = TRUE;
    SendMessage(WM_COMMAND, IDOK, BN_CLICKED);
}
```

ClassWizard supports only control handlers that are defined in the dialog resource. This means you'll have to manually insert the following entry in the EX07BDLG.CPP message map:

```
BEGIN_MESSAGE_MAP(CEx07bDialog, CFileDialog)
    //{{AFX_MSG_MAP(CEx07bDialog)
        // NOTE: the ClassWizard will add message map macros here
    ON_BN_CLICKED(IDC_DELETE, OnDeleteButton)
    //}}AFX_MSG_MAP
END_MESSAGE_MAP()
```

You've already put the function prototype in the header file.

9. **Add code to the virtual *OnDraw* function in file EX07BVW.CPP.** The *CEx07bView OnDraw* function (the skeleton was generated by App-Wizard) should be coded as follows to prompt the user to press the mouse button:

```
void CEx07bView::OnDraw(CDC* pDC)
{
    pDC->TextOut(0, 0, "Press the left mouse button here.");
}
```

10. **Add the *OnLButtonDown* message handler to the *CEx07bView* class.** Use ClassWizard to create the message handler for WM_L-BUTTONDOWN, and then edit the code as follows:

```
void CEx07bView::OnLButtonDown(UINT nFlags, CPoint point)
{
    CEx07bDialog dlg;

    if (dlg.DoModal() != IDCANCEL) {
        CString filename = dlg.GetPathName(); // CFileDialog function
        if (dlg.m_bDeleteFlag) {
            char text[200];
            wsprintf (text, "Are you sure you want to delete %s?",
                    (LPCSTR) filename);
            if (AfxMessageBox(text, MB_YESNO) == IDYES) {
                CFile::Remove(filename);
            }
        }
        else {
            TRACE("Open file %s\n", (const char*) filename);
        }
    }
}
```

Using the global *AfxMessageBox* function is a convenient way to pop up a simple dialog that displays some text and that queries the user for a *Yes/No* answer. The *Class Library Reference* describes all the message box variations and options.

Of course, you'll need the statement

```
#include "ex07bdlg.h"
```

after the line

```
#include "ex07bvw.h"
```

11. **Build and test the application.** Build and run EX07B. Pressing the left mouse button should bring up the Delete dialog, and you should be able to use it to navigate through the disk directory and to delete files.

C H A P T E R   E I G H T .

VISUAL BASIC CONTROLS

Microsoft Visual Basic, introduced in 1991, has proven to be a very popular and successful application development system for Microsoft Windows. Part of its success is attributable to its open-ended nature. You can extend the Basic language by adding Visual Basic "controls"—special dynamic link libraries (DLLs), written in C, that are available from Microsoft and from third-party software developers. You can now use these same Visual Basic controls with Visual C++, and App Studio fully supports them. The Professional Edition of Microsoft Visual Basic 3.0 includes a Control Development Kit (CDK) that allows you to write your own custom controls.

Unfortunately, it was not possible for Microsoft to port Visual Basic controls to 32-bit Windows. Visual Basic controls are in the process of being replaced with "OLE controls," which will work in both the 16-bit and the 32-bit environments. The 16-bit VBX controls described in this chapter will probably remain the standard for 16-bit applications for Windows. The new OLE controls will be integrated into future 32-bit versions of App Studio and the Microsoft Foundation Classes. You will be able to write custom OLE controls in C++, and you can call on Control Wizards for help.

In this chapter, you'll learn why Visual Basic controls are different from standard Windows controls and custom Windows controls, and you'll learn how to integrate these controls into a Microsoft Foundation Class (MFC) Library version 2.5 program. An example, built with the Visual Basic GRID control included with Visual C++, illustrates the use of control properties, methods, and events. The end result is a crude but workable spreadsheet program.

NOTE: See Technical Note #27 in the MFCNOTES.HLP file for detailed documentation on each standard VBX event, each standard VBX property, and specific properties and events for the Visual Basic GRID control.

Standard Controls for Windows and Ordinary Custom Controls

You've already seen the standard Windows controls as represented by the classes *CEdit, CButton, CScrollBar,* and so forth. These controls are built into Windows, and the MFC library fully supports them. You can also use ordinary custom controls (written in C and usually implemented as DLLs) with the MFC library. With App Studio you can size and position ordinary custom controls in a dialog, but at design time you can't see what the controls look like.

Consider any control a "smart window" that's usually (but not always) embedded in a dialog. Many controls accept input, but all controls provide some sort of visual output. Controls can support extensive interaction with the user without the involvement of your application. The Windows *CEdit* control, for example, processes cursor movements and backspace keystrokes, and it supports wordwrap—all by itself. The more work a control does, the less programming you have to do.

C++ Classes and Visual Basic Controls

C++ is a totally flexible object-oriented programming language, but a C++ program's features must be specified at compile time. Visual Basic limits your flexibility, but it allows interactive program development. Visual Basic controls are the closest thing Visual Basic has to classes. These controls are stand-alone modules that interact, both at design time and at run time, with the Visual Basic environment. With Visual C++, you can use both compiled C++ classes and Visual Basic controls. Comparing the behavior of these two diverse programming elements is useful.

Methods vs. Member Functions

If you write your own C++ class, it can have a member function called *DanceAroundTheTable* if you want it to. Of course, the other classes in your application must know, at compile time, specifically what *DanceAroundThe-Table* does and what its parameters are. Classes for Windows controls use

150

hard-coded notification messages and member functions. Some member functions, such as the *CEdit::GetLineCount* function, apply to only one control class, but others, such as *CWnd::GetDlgItemText*, apply to all controls.

Visual Basic controls have "methods" that are similar to class member functions. These methods are limited to a predefined set that includes *AddItem, RemoveItem, Move,* and *Refresh* (among others). Not all Visual Basic controls respond to all the methods. The *Move* method, though, works with all controls.

Properties vs. Data Members

At first the limited set of Visual Basic control methods seems restrictive. Fortunately, Visual Basic controls have "properties" in addition to methods. You could say that Visual Basic properties correspond to C++ data members. Each Visual Basic control can define its own set of properties, which can include strings, long integers, or floating-point numbers. You could create a Visual Basic control with a string property called "DanceAroundTheTable" that could be set to "waltz" or "foxtrot." Most Visual Basic controls recognize a standard set of properties, such as BackColor and FontName. The control will list its collection of properties when interrogated.

Properties are limited to three data types, but using a property instead of a fixed data type offers a significant advantage in Visual Basic—namely, that the run-time system requires no advance knowledge of a control's properties when it executes the application program. Other programs besides the Visual Basic run-time system can take advantage of this run-time property access. App Studio, for example, can present a list of a control's properties, and it allows you to set initial values.

Some Visual Basic controls support array properties. A graph control, for example, might have an array of numeric points that can be individually set and retrieved.

Visual Basic Control Events vs. Windows Control Notifications

Standard controls send notification messages to a dialog in response to events. A pushbutton sends a BN_CLICKED message, for example. ClassWizard helps you define a dialog class member function to handle the message. Visual Basic controls work in exactly the same way. Most Visual Basic controls send standard messages (called events) such as VBN_CLICK and VBN_KEYDOWN. Some Visual Basic controls send unique messages such as VBN_ROWCOLCHANGE. When you run ClassWizard from inside App Studio (with a dialog selected), Class Wizard knows which Visual Basic control you're using, and it presents a list of the events for the selected control.

Visual Basic Event Registration

Your program must call the global MFC library function *AfxRegisterVBEvent* for each Visual Basic control event that needs handling. When ClassWizard creates a dialog that uses an event-oriented Visual Basic control, it generates the *AfxRegisterVBEvent* call for you in your program's main module (MYAPP.CPP). If your control uses the GRID control's ROWCOLCHANGE event, the generated code looks like this:

```
//{{AFX_VBX_REGISTER_MAP()
    UINT NEAR VBN_ROWCOLCHANGE = AfxRegisterVBEvent("ROWCOLCHANGE");
//}}AFX_VBX_REGISTER_MAP
```

A corresponding *extern* statement is in the main header file (MYAPP.H) and is included by the programs that use the Visual Basic control:

```
//{{AFX_VBX_REGISTER()
    extern UINT NEAR VBN_ROWCOLCHANGE;
//}}AFX_VBX_REGISTER
```

For every dialog class that uses the Visual Basic control, ClassWizard generates a message map entry such as this:

```
ON_VBXEVENT(VBN_ROWCOLCHANGE, IDC_GRID1, OnRowcolchangeGrid1)
```

The *CVBControl* Class

You've seen that the MFC library provides classes for the standard Windows controls. As you've probably guessed, it also provides a class for Visual Basic controls. This class, *CVBControl*, is derived from *CWnd* and thus has the characteristics of a window, as do *CEdit*, *CButton*, and so forth. The *CVBControl* class serves all Visual Basic controls.

In a dialog class member function, you can get a temporary pointer to a *CVBControl* object with a statement such as this:

```
CVBControl* pVBC = GetDlgItem(IDC_GRID1); // IDC_GRID1 defined
                                          //  in RESOURCE.H
```

A better option, though, is to let ClassWizard define a Visual Basic control pointer variable that is initialized in the dialog's *DoDataExchange* member function. The application framework cleans up the *CVBControl* objects when the dialog closes, so don't try to delete a *CVBControl* object unless you have constructed it yourself.

As the *Class Library Reference* shows, the *CVBControl* class contains all the member functions you'll need to access Visual Basic controls. The *Move,*

Refresh, GetItem, and *RemoveItem* functions activate a control's methods, and there are functions for setting and getting the different kinds of properties based on data type. You use the *CVBControl::Create* member function when you need a Visual Basic control outside a dialog.

The EX08A Example

One Visual Basic control included with Visual C++ is the GRID control, which was originally distributed with the Visual Basic CDK. The EX08A program uses the GRID control to create a simple spreadsheet. Remember that this is only an example, so don't erase Microsoft Excel from your hard disk. Figure 8-1 shows the EX08A program containing data.

	A	B	C	D	E	F	G
1	2.00	3.00	4.00	5.00	6.00	7.00	8.00
2	3.00	4.00	5.00	6.00	7.00	8.00	9.00
3	4.00	5.00	6.00	7.00	8.00	9.00	10.00
4	5.00	6.00	7.00	8.00	9.00	10.00	11.00
5	6.00	7.00	8.00	9.00	10.00	11.00	12.00
6	7.00	8.00	9.00	10.00	11.00	12.00	13.00
7	8.00	9.00	10.00	11.00	12.00	13.00	14.00
8	9.00	10.00	11.00	12.00	13.00	14.00	15.00
9	10.00	11.00	12.00	13.00	14.00	15.00	16.00
10	11.00	12.00	13.00	14.00	15.00	16.00	17.00
11	65.00	75.00	85.00	95.00	105.00	115.00	125.00

Grid Test

[OK] [Cancel] [Add Row] [Delete Row] [2.00] [Update Value]

Figure 8-1.
The EX08A window.

The EX08A spreadsheet consists of 12 rows and 8 columns. The top row and the left column are used for labels, and the bottom row is used for column sums that the program updates. When the user selects a cell with the mouse, the cell's value is copied to the dialog's edit control. The user can then edit the value, which is copied back into the grid when the user presses Enter.

The Visual Basic GRID Control

The Visual Basic GRID control consists of a rectangular array of addressable cells. The host program sets the initial number of rows and columns, and it stores data in and retrieves data from the individual cells. At run time, the user can use the mouse (but not the direction keys) to select an individual cell or a range of cells. The GRID control is more an "output control" than

153

an "input control" because the user cannot type directly into the cells. As you'll see in the example, however, you can make it reasonably easy for the user to enter and edit cell data.

> **NOTE:** The Visual C++ VBCHART example application, located in the \MSVC\MFC\SAMPLES\VBCHART subdirectory, demonstrates the GRID control's ability to be customized. Because of some clever tricks, such as moving an edit window, the program's grid behaves the same as a real spreadsheet. Be sure to build and run VBCHART to see what is possible with some creative programming.

The GRID control supports most standard Visual Basic control properties, events, and methods, and it has a number of unique properties and events. The ones you'll use in EX08A are listed here:

Name	Description
Property	
CellSelected (numeric)	True (−1) if a cell is selected; False (0) otherwise
Col (numeric)	Current column
ColAlignment (numeric, indexed)	Non-fixed cells/row labels (0 = left aligned, 1 = right aligned, 2 = centered)
*Cols (numeric)	Total number of columns
ColWidth (numeric, indexed)	Column width in "logical twips"
FixedAlignment (numeric, indexed)	Fixed cells/row labels (0 = left aligned, 1 = right aligned, 2 = centered)
Row (numeric)	Current row
RowHeight (numeric, indexed)	Row height in "logical twips"
*Rows (numeric)	Total number of rows
Text (string)	The text in the selected cell, defined by Col and Row
Event	
SelChange	Notifies the program when the user uses the mouse to select a new cell
Method	
AddItem	Inserts a row
RemoveItem	Deletes a row

*These properties can be set in App Studio; others can be set and read only at run time.

Building the EX08A Example Program

Before you begin to build the EX08A program, be sure that the files GRID.VBX and VB.LIC are present in the \WINDOWS\SYSTEM subdirectory. Now follow these steps to build the program:

1. **Run AppWizard to produce \VCPP\EX08A\EX08A.** Choose App-Wizard from Visual Workbench's Project menu. The options and the default class names are shown here:

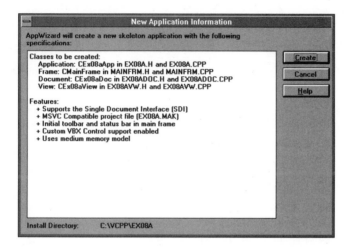

Be sure to check the Custom VBX Controls option.

> TIP: If you forget to check the Custom VBX Controls option, or if you want to add VBX capability to an existing application, simply insert the line

```
EnableVBX();
```

at the start of the *InitInstance* member function in your derived application class.

2. **Add a WM_LBUTTONDOWN message handler to *CEx08aView* in EX08AVW.CPP.** Use ClassWizard to add the *OnLButtonDown* function, and then edit the function. The following screened code (which you type in) replaces the existing code:

```
void CEx08aView::OnLButtonDown(UINT nFlags, CPoint point)
{
    int         i, j;
    CEx08aDialog dlg;             // constructs the dialog
```

(continued)

```
for (i = 1; i < 8; i++) {   // fills the data array with test data
  for (j = 1; j < 11; j++) {
    dlg.m_dArray[i][j] = i + j;
  }
}

dlg.DoModal();              // starts the dialog

for (j = 1; j < 11; j++) { // prints the modified array
  for (i = 1; i < 8; i++) {
    TRACE("%8.2f ", dlg.m_dArray[i][j]);
  }
  TRACE("\n");
}
}
```

This function brings up the modal dialog when the user presses the left mouse button while the mouse cursor is in the view window. It also initializes and prints the data array.

3. Edit the *OnDraw* function in EX08AVW.CPP. The following screened code replaces the existing code:

```
void CEx08aView::OnDraw(CDC*pDC)
{
  pDC->TextOut(0,0,"Press the left mouse button here.");
}
```

While you're in EX08AVW.CPP, add the following include statement near the top of the file:

```
#include "ex08adlg.h"
```

4. Install the GRID control in App Studio. Start App Studio by choosing App Studio from Visual Workbench's Tools menu. Choose Install Controls from the App Studio File menu, and specify \WINDOWS\SYSTEM\GRID.VBX. A Grid button will appear in the control palette when you edit the dialog.

5. Use App Studio to create the dialog *IDD_DIALOG1*. Use the dialog pictured in Figure 8-1 on page 153 as a model. Click on Dialog in the Type list, and then click the New button. The New Resource dialog appears. Click on Dialog in the Resource Type list, and then click the OK button. A new window appears, showing the *IDD_DIALOG1* dialog, and the control palette also appears, containing the Grid button, as shown at the top of the facing page:

Draw a large GRID control on the *IDD_DIALOG1* dialog. Double-click on the *IDD_DIALOG1* dialog to open the Properties window. Set the GRID control's Rows property to *12* and the Cols property to *8*. Notice that there are many GRID properties you can't set at design time, including the column width, row height, and initial cell text. The GRID control ID defaults to *IDC_GRID1*.

Add buttons to the dialog, and then assign button and edit control IDs as follows:

Control	ID	Caption
OK button	*IDOK* (the default)	OK (the default)
Cancel button	*IDCANCEL* (the default)	Cancel (the default)
Add Row button	*IDC_ADDROW*	Add Row
Delete Row button	*IDC_DELETEROW*	Delete Row
Edit window	*IDC_VALUE*	
Update Value button	*IDC_UPDATEVALUE* (default button)	Update Value

6. **Use ClassWizard to create the *CEx08aDialog* class.** Choose Class-Wizard from the App Studio Resource menu. Fill in the Add Class dialog, as shown at the top of the following page:

Click the Create Class button. The MFC ClassWizard dialog appears, as shown here:

Add message-handling functions as shown in the following table. To add a message-handling function, click on an object ID, click on a message, and then click the Add Function button. The Add Member Function dialog appears. Type the function name, and click the OK button.

Object ID	Message	Function Name
CEx08aDialog	WM_INITDIALOG	OnInitDialog
IDC_ADDROW	BN_CLICKED	OnAddrow
IDC_DELETEROW	BN_CLICKED	OnDeleterow
IDC_GRID1	VBN_SELCHANGE	OnSelchangeGrid1
IDC_UPDATEVALUE	BN_CLICKED	OnUpdatevalue
IDCANCEL	BN_CLICKED	OnCancel
IDOK	BN_CLICKED	OnOK

Now click the Edit Variables button and add the following two dialog data members:

Control ID	Member Variable Name	Property	Variable Type
IDC_VALUE	*m_cellValue*	Value	CString
IDC_GRID1	*m_pVBGrid*	Control	CVBControl*

Save changes and exit App Studio when you're done.

7. **Add an array data member in EX08ADLG.H.** The *m_dArray* data member is a two-dimensional array of doubles that correspond to the values in the Grid control. Put the array inside the *CEx08aDialog* declaration but outside the *AFX_DATA* brackets.

```
// Dialog Data
    double m_dArray[8][12];
    //{{AFX_DATA(CEx08aDialog)
    enum { IDD = IDD_DIALOG1 };
    CVBControl*  m_pVBGrid;
    CString      m_cellValue;
    //}}AFX_DATA
```

8. **Add a member function prototype in EX08ADLG.H.** Add the function prototype as shown:

```
// Implementation
private:
    void ComputeSums();
```

9. **Code the *OnInitDialog* function in EX08ADLG.CPP.** Visual Basic controls use a measurement system called "logical twips." If you want to convert between pixels and logical twips, you can't rely on the *CDC* functions *DPtoLP* and *LPtoDP*; rather, you must do the conversions yourself using values returned by the *CDC::GetDeviceCaps* function.

The first part of the *OnInitDialog* function sets the column widths to $1/8$ of the control's client-area width, and it sets the row height to $1/12$ of the total control height. The client-area width in logical twips is computed according to the following formula:

client logical twips = client pixels × 1440 / logical pixels per inch

The *CWnd::GetClientRect* function retrieves a rectangle whose width is the width of the client rectangle in device coordinates (pixels).

Now look at the first *for* loop. This code cycles through all 8 columns and sets the column width and column heading, using the *CVBControl::-SetNumProperty* and the *CVBControl::SetStrProperty* member functions.

ColWidth is an indexed property, so you must use the index parameter to set the element's value. Text is not indexed but depends on both the Col and Row properties having been set to point to a particular cell.

The second *for* loop sets the row heights and row labels. It also sets the indexed FixedAlignment and ColAlignment properties of all the fixed cells (top row, left column) to centered alignment and the ColAlignment property of the other cells to right alignment.

The nested *for* loops near the end of the function set a grid cell's text to the value in the corresponding *m_dArray* data member. The double values must be converted to strings before they can be used to set the cells' Text property. The following screened code replaces the existing code:

```
BOOL CEx08aDialog::OnInitDialog()
{
    CRect rect;
    char    temp[20];
    int     i, j;
    long    lColWidth, lRowHeight;

    VERIFY(CDialog::OnInitDialog());
    VERIFY(m_pVBGrid->GetNumProperty("Cols") == 8L); // set in App Studio
    VERIFY(m_pVBGrid->GetNumProperty("Rows") == 12L);
    CClientDC dc(this);
    m_pVBGrid->GetClientRect(rect); // device coordinates
    lColWidth  = m_pVBGrid->GetNumProperty("ColWidth", 0);
    lRowHeight = m_pVBGrid->GetNumProperty("RowHeight", 0);
    lColWidth  = (1440L * (long) rect.right) /
                 (8L * (long) dc.GetDeviceCaps(LOGPIXELSX)) - 20L;
    lRowHeight = (1440L * (long) rect.bottom) /
                 (12L * (long) dc.GetDeviceCaps(LOGPIXELSY)) - 20L;

    m_pVBGrid->SetNumProperty("Row", 0);
    for (i = 0; i < 8; i++) {

      m_pVBGrid->SetNumProperty("ColWidth", lColWidth, i);
      if (i) { // column headings
        m_pVBGrid->SetNumProperty("Col", i);
        m_pVBGrid->SetStrProperty("Text", CString('A' + i - 1));
      }
    }

    m_pVBGrid->SetNumProperty("Col", 0);
    for (j = 0; j < 12; j++) {
      m_pVBGrid->SetNumProperty("RowHeight", lRowHeight, j);
```

```
    m_pVBGrid->SetNumProperty("FixedAlignment", 2, j); // centered
    m_pVBGrid->SetNumProperty("ColAlignment", 1, j);   // right
    if (j) {  // row headings
      m_pVBGrid->SetNumProperty("Row", j);
      sprintf(temp, "%d", j);
      m_pVBGrid->SetStrProperty("Text", temp);
    }
  }
  // sets the spreadsheet values from m_dArray
  for (i = 1; i < 8; i++) {
    m_pVBGrid->SetNumProperty("Col", i);
    for (j = 1; j < 11; j++) {
      m_pVBGrid->SetNumProperty("Row", j);
      sprintf(temp, "%8.2f", m_dArray[i][j]);
      m_pVBGrid->SetStrProperty("Text", temp);
    }
  }
  ComputeSums();
  // be sure there's a selected cell
  m_pVBGrid->SetNumProperty("Col", 1L);
  m_pVBGrid->SetNumProperty("Row", 1L);
  m_cellValue = m_pVBGrid->GetStrProperty("Text");
  UpdateData(FALSE); // calls DoDataExchange to update edit control
  return TRUE;
}
```

10. **Code the *OnOK* function in EX08ADLG.CPP.** This function retrieves the grid cell values and stores them in the *m_dArray* data member. The following screened code replaces the existing code:

```
void CEx08aDialog::OnOK()
{
    int i, j;

    for (i = 1; i < 8; i++) {
      m_pVBGrid->SetNumProperty("Col", i);
      for (j = 1; j < 11; j++) {
        m_pVBGrid->SetNumProperty("Row", j);
        m_dArray[i][j] = atof(m_pVBGrid->GetStrProperty("Text"));
      }
    }
    CDialog::OnOK();
}
```

11. **Code the *OnAddrow* and *OnDeleterow* functions in EX08ADLG.CPP.** To add or delete a row, a cell must be currently selected. Notice the use of the *AddItem* and *RemoveItem* method functions. The screened code on the following page replaces the existing code:

161

```
void CEx08aDialog::OnAddrow()
{
    if (m_pVBGrid->GetNumProperty("CellSelected") == 0) {
      AfxMessageBox("No cell selected");
      return;
    }
    LONG i = m_pVBGrid->GetNumProperty("Row");
    m_pVBGrid->AddItem("new row", i);
    ComputeSums();
}


void CEx08aDialog::OnDeleterow()
{
    if (m_pVBGrid->GetNumProperty("CellSelected") == 0) {
      AfxMessageBox("No cell selected");
      return;
    }
    LONG i = m_pVBGrid->GetNumProperty("Row");
    m_pVBGrid->RemoveItem(i);
    ComputeSums();
}
```

12. **Code the *OnUpdatevalue* function in EX08ADLG.CPP.** This function
    is activated by the Update Value button, which is the dialog's default
    button. Its main duty is to transfer the edit control value to the selected
    grid cell. It also computes the sum of each column and stores the results
    in row 11. The program takes advantage of the fact that pressing Enter
    sends the same message as clicking the default button. When the user
    enters a value in the one-and-only edit control, he or she can press Enter
    to make *OnUpdatevalue* process the value. The following screened code
    replaces the existing code:

```
void CEx08aDialog::OnUpdatevalue()
{
    char    temp[30];
    double value;
    LONG    lRow, lCol;

    if (m_pVBGrid->GetNumProperty("CellSelected") == 0) {
      AfxMessageBox("No cell selected");
      return;
    }
    UpdateData(TRUE);
    value = atof(m_cellValue);
    sprintf(temp, "%8.2f", value);
```

```
    // saves current cell selection
    lCol = m_pVBGrid->GetNumProperty("Col");
    lRow = m_pVBGrid->GetNumProperty("Row");

    m_pVBGrid->SetStrProperty("Text", temp); // copies new value
                                             //  to selected cell
    ComputeSums();

    // restores current cell selection
    m_pVBGrid->SetNumProperty("Col", lCol);
    m_pVBGrid->SetNumProperty("Row", lRow);
}
```

13. **Code the *OnSelchangeGrid1* function in EX08ADLG.CPP.** This
    function handles the GRID control's SelChange event. It copies the
    selected cell's value to the edit control so that the user can update it.
    The *m_pVBGrid* pointer must be tested for a NULL value because the
    first SelChange event occurs before the pointer is initialized. The fol-
    lowing screened code replaces the existing code:

```
void CEx08aDialog::OnSelchangeGrid1(UINT, int, CWnd*, LPVOID)
{
    if (m_pVBGrid) {
        m_cellValue = m_pVBGrid->GetStrProperty("Text");
        UpdateData(FALSE); // calls DoDataExchange to update edit control
        GotoDlgCtrl(GetDlgItem(IDC_VALUE)); // position to edit control
    }
}
```

14. **Code the private *ComputeSums* function in EX08ADLG.CPP.** Type
    in the following screened code:

```
void CEx08aDialog::ComputeSums()
{
    int    i, j, nRows;
    double sum;
    char   temp[30];

    // add up each column and put the sum in bottom row
    // row count could have been changed by add row/delete row
    nRows = (int) m_pVBGrid->GetNumProperty("Rows");
    for (i = 1; i < 8; i++) {
        m_pVBGrid->SetNumProperty("Col", i);
        sum = 0.0;
        for (j = 1; j < nRows - 1; j++) {
            m_pVBGrid->SetNumProperty("Row", j);
            sum += atof(m_pVBGrid->GetStrProperty("Text"));
        }
```

(continued)

163

```
    sprintf(temp, "%8.2f", sum);
    m_pVBGrid->SetNumProperty("Row", nRows - 1);
    m_pVBGrid->SetStrProperty("Text", temp);
  }
}
```

15. Build and run the EX08A program. In Visual Workbench, choose Build from the Project menu, and then choose Execute. The resulting output looks like that shown in Figure 8-1 on page 153. Try updating values, and then try deleting and adding rows. Check that the sums in the bottom row are correct.

> NOTE: If you don't see all the numbers in the grid, you need to make the grid larger in App Studio.

Using Other Visual Basic Controls

The GRID control is not the best example of a Visual Basic control, but it is a good learning tool. Many sophisticated Visual Basic controls are available from third-party software firms. Until the Visual C++ installed base grows, the documentation for these controls will be oriented only to Visual Basic. You will have to "translate" the Visual Basic calling sequences to C++, but this shouldn't be too difficult if you have studied the EX08A example. A few Visual Basic methods, such as *Drag* and *SetFocus*, aren't directly supported by the MFC library.

Chapter 11 uses another Visual Basic control, CNTR.VBX. This control is available on the companion disc included with this book.

Visual Basic Picture Properties

Some Visual Basic controls, GRID included, support picture properties. Technical Note #27 in the MFCNOTES.HLP file explains how the MFC library supports these Visual Basic picture properties.

Advantages and Disadvantages of Writing and Using Visual Basic Controls

If a developer writes a Visual Basic control, that control can be sold to both Visual Basic and Visual C++ programmers. That in itself should be reason enough to write a Visual Basic control instead of an ordinary custom control. Also, App Studio directly supports Visual Basic controls. Once a Visual Basic control is installed in App Studio, a corresponding button appears in the control palette, the control is visible in a dialog, and the design-time properties can be set.

On the negative side, Visual Basic controls are less efficient than ordinary DLLs because of the need to communicate via properties instead of directly by function calls. You can improve efficiency if you use property index numbers instead of property name strings. The *CVBControl* member function *GetPropIndex* returns a property's index value, which you can use subsequently for getting and setting properties.

Also, Visual Basic controls aren't very compatible with the MFC library document–view architecture. A GRID control, for example, stores all its spreadsheet data inside itself. This makes it difficult to support multiple views of spreadsheet data.

For the time being, if you write your own Visual Basic controls, you'll have to use C, and that means you won't get the benefit of the MFC library classes. Of course, you must write ordinary custom control DLLs in C too.

C H A P T E R   N I N E

WINDOWS MEMORY MANAGEMENT— JUST SAY "NEW"

If you've read about memory management in other books on the Microsoft Windows operating system, you'll wonder whether I'm talking about the same operating system here. Yes, indeed I am, but I'm talking about "post real mode" Windows—versions 3.1 and later. The old Intel 8088 microprocessor chips, as found in the original IBM PC, are no longer supported. As the 8088 chip fades from view, so does real mode with its 1-MB memory limitation and lack of hardware memory management. In its place is 16-bit protected mode with a much larger address space and two levels of hardware memory management.

Many of the ugly things the older books about Windows discuss—memory handles, locking, burgermasters, thunks, and so forth—are no longer relevant. Some nasties remain, particularly segments, but even segments are due to disappear when we move to 32-bit Windows.

You were able to get started with Visual C++ programming without knowing anything about Windows memory management. If you've followed the examples up to this point, you've used the C++ *new* operator when you wanted heap memory, and your applications have worked fine. As you write larger and more sophisticated Windows programs, you'll still use *new*, but you'll need to know what Windows does behind the scenes to make some basic decisions. Should you use the medium memory model or the large memory model? What's the difference between far and near declarations? Must your program periodically reorganize its heap memory?

This chapter starts with an advance look at 32-bit programming for Windows and suggests a strategy for migration to this up-and-coming environment. Not left out, however, is the here-and-now 16-bit protected mode environment. You'll learn about segments, the near heap, the far heap, and near vs. far function calls. You'll also learn how to make your large-model application run in "multiple instance" mode.

A Memory Model Review

If you've been writing C programs for Intel microprocessors, you're no doubt familiar with the four standard "memory models." The following table shows the relationships between memory models and address lengths:

	16-Bit Data Addresses	32-Bit Data Addresses
16-Bit Code Addresses	Small	Compact
32-Bit Code Addresses	Medium	Large

You'll learn more about the composition of these address fields later.

We're very close to the age of 32-bit Windows, with its flat 32-bit address space. Indeed, Microsoft Foundation Class Library version 2.5 was designed with 32-bit Windows in mind, and it has already been tested with the Windows NT operating system. Most MFC library applications you write now should be portable to Windows NT with a simple recompilation and relink—that is, unless you make your code too dependent on the current 16-bit memory architecture.

How do you eliminate 16-bit dependencies? For a start, you can use the large memory model for all your applications. This might sound like heresy because other books have warned you specifically to avoid the large model for Windows-based programs. There were some good reasons not to use the large model in the old real mode, but the real mode wicked witch is dead. The 16-bit large memory model generally uses 32-bit addresses for both programs and data, and this closely matches what you'll find in the 32-bit versions of Windows.

Yes, your large-model compiled program will be a bit larger than the medium-model equivalent, and execution will be a little slower, but you will save development time because you won't have to worry about the distinction between 16-bit "near" and 32-bit "far" pointers. If you apply the development time savings to profiling and otherwise optimizing your application, you'll come out ahead, plus you'll have a program that is easily portable to the 32-bit environment.

16-Bit Windows

Now it's back to reality. Users will have Windows version 3.1 for a while, and you'll have to produce 16-bit applications to run on that operating system. So you're stuck learning about segments, near heap memory management, and the various 16-bit memory models.

The Intel Segment Architecture

The Intel 80286, 80386, and 80486 families of microprocessor chips support the 16-bit protected mode. The segment is the basic memory allocation unit, and it can have a maximum size of 64 KB. All memory addresses are composed of a 16-bit segment address (also known as a "selector") and a 16-bit offset within the segment. The microprocessors listed above all support a hardware memory management scheme that uses a descriptor table in memory. Each entry in the table maps a 13-bit descriptor table index, contained in the selector, to a physical memory address range. Windows can shuffle segments in physical memory if it updates the base address in the descriptor table accordingly. If necessary, you can specify that particular segments be fixed in physical memory.

The size of segments can change too. If your program is using a 20-KB segment, for example, and it needs that segment "expanded" to 40 KB, the operating system allocates a new 40-KB segment, copies the contents from the original 20-KB segment, and then frees the original 20-KB segment for subsequent use by other programs. Because the selector does not change (only the base address in the descriptor table changes), your program can continue to use the data in the bottom 20 KB of the new segment as though the data had never moved. Figure 9-1 on the following page is a simplified illustration of the descriptor table in action.

Segments store code or data. Code segments are considered "read-only" because their contents don't change during program execution. Data segments are usually "read/write" because a running program changes memory variables. The Windows memory manager takes an active role in writing and reading segments to and from disk during program execution. If memory is full, the Windows memory manager can discard a code segment that hasn't been used in a while. Windows reloads a discarded code segment when a program needs it. (Discarding an infrequently used code segment is not usually necessary in 386 enhanced mode because of Windows' virtual memory manager.)

Figure 9-1.
Protected mode addressing for the 80386 microprocessor.

The DGROUP Segment and Multi-Instance Programs

All Windows and MS-DOS programs use one special segment: the "default data segment," known as the DGROUP segment. This segment contains the stack together with some (or all) of the application's static data plus data in the local heap (explained later). When a program is running, the data segment (DS) and stack segment (SS) registers are loaded with the DGROUP segment address, in such a manner that subsequent memory reference instructions access data in the DGROUP segment.

> NOTE: You specify the maximum stack size in the program's Memory Image category of the Linker Options dialog. AppWizard uses a default value of 10,240.

Under certain conditions, a Windows program can run in multi-instance mode. This means you can start several instances of a program, but only one copy of the program's code will be loaded into memory. Windows Notepad is a good example of a multi-instance program. Each instance of the program has its own DGROUP segment, assigned at startup. For a program to run in multi-instance mode, all its data (with some exceptions) must fit into one segment. This restriction is necessary because the DS register, loaded once for each instance, can address only one segment at a time.

Windows can move a DGROUP segment to another location in physical memory because it is accessed through the descriptor table the same way as any other segment.

Memory Models—One Code Segment or Many?

In the "small" and "compact" memory models, all the application's code must fit into one code segment. Simple Windows SDK programs can be compiled for the small or compact models because most of their functionality is contained in the Windows kernel and DLLs. MFC library programs are generally too large for the small model because many MFC library functions must be statically linked. With the medium and large models, the code is split into several code segments. Therefore, you'll see most Windows programs use these large-code models.

With the medium and large models, the default compiler behavior is to make one code segment for each C or C++ source module. This is fine for applications that typically have three or four source modules. If you used the same strategy for libraries, however, you might have too many code segments. (This would be very rare—the descriptor table can contain up to 8192 8-byte entries.) The compiler directive *#pragma code_seg* enables you to combine the code from multiple source modules into a single code segment. The *__based* keyword or the compiler directive *#pragma alloc_text* allows you to split a C source module's code into several segments.

If you need a Windows application to run on a computer with limited memory, you can "swap-tune" the program by matching functions with code segments according to the program's execution pattern. The Module Definition File (DEF) defines the attributes of the segments. You can, for example, select which segments are initially loaded into memory when the application starts. (See the *Command-Line Utilities User's Guide* for more information.)

> NOTE: Generally, you cannot mix modules compiled for different memory models. If you compile a module for the medium model, for example, you cannot link it with another module compiled for the small or large model.

Near Function Calls

By default, in the medium and large memory models, function calls use 32-bit addresses (selector plus offset). This rule applies even to calls within a single segment. If you know that a particular function won't be called from outside its segment, you can declare it near and thus make the compiler generate a shorter, faster, 16-bit calling sequence. Near declarations are handy for private class member functions. If you follow the convention of placing all of a class's member functions in one source file, you know that a private function can't be called from outside that module (unless the class or function is declared a *friend*). Following is an example:

```
class CMyView : public CView
{
// constructor, macros, etc. not shown
private:
    void NEAR NearTest();
    void FarTest();
public:
    virtual void OnDraw(CDC* pDC);
};

void CMyView::OnDraw(CDC* pDC)
{
    NearTest();
    FarTest();
}

void NEAR CMyView::NearTest()
{
    int i = 0; // force compiler to generate some code
}

void CMyView::FarTest()
{
    int i = 0; // force compiler to generate some code
}
```

It's interesting to look at the generated code for the calls to *NearTest* and *FarTest*. Here is what you get with the medium model:

```
    NearTest();
2737:0271 56               PUSH     SI
2737:0272 E8E700           CALL     CEx12View::NearTest (035C)
    FarTest();
2737:0275 56               PUSH     SI
2737:0276 9A7E033727       CALL     CEx12View::FarTest (2737:037E)
```

You saved 2 bytes by using a near function—big deal.
Here is the equivalent large-model code:

```
    NearTest();
252F:02B7 FF7608           PUSH     WORD PTR [BP+08]
252F:02BA FF7606           PUSH     WORD PTR [This]
252F:02BD E81601           CALL     CEx12View::NearTest (03D6)
    FarTest();
252F:02C0 FF7608           PUSH     WORD PTR [BP+08]
252F:02C3 FF7606           PUSH     WORD PTR [This]
252F:02C6 9AF4032F25       CALL     CEx12View::FarTest (252F:03F4)
```

As you can see, the large model has even more code, and you still save 2 bytes by using a near function.

Memory Models—One Data Segment or Many?

You might think that the small and medium models imply one data segment and that the large and compact models imply several data segments. The rules, however, are more complex than that. A medium-model application, for example, might use several data segments, and a large-model application might use only one data segment. What's going on?

Here is a summary of the data access rules by memory model:

■ *Small and medium models*

❏ The default pointer size is 16 bits.

❏ The stack, all static variables, and the local heap are in the DGROUP segment.

❏ The C++ *new* operator allocates memory from the Windows local heap.

■ *Large and compact models*

❏ The default pointer size is 32 bits.

❏ The stack is in the DGROUP segment.

❏ Static variables, excluding non-near C++ objects, are in the DGROUP segment when possible.

❏ DGROUP static variables are accessed via 16-bit addresses where possible.

❏ Large static items are located in their own data segments.

❏ C++ non-near static objects are located in a data segment associated with their code module.

❏ The C++ *new* operator allocates memory from the Windows global heap.

But what do these rules mean to the average programmer? First of all, the medium memory model doesn't give you much data space. You're limited to 64 KB total, and all of that isn't usable. (Some of this memory is used by the stack, uninitialized global and static near data, and compiler-generated near data.) If you want, you can do "mixed-model" programming, which involves declaring far (32-bit) pointers to data in other data segments and using the Windows global memory allocation functions instead of *new*. Perhaps the large model isn't such a bad idea after all!

If you're using the large model, you can make your program run multi-instance if you ensure that it has only one data segment. The project's map file (MAP) specifies how many data segments are in your program. To ensure one data segment, don't declare large amounts of static data (either large individual objects or numerous small ones), and be sure that all global C++ objects (particularly your *CWinApp* object) are declared near.

> **NOTE:** With the large model, you can force a module's static data to reside in a particular data segment by using the *#pragma data_seg* statement. Be careful when referencing extern static data that is not in the DGROUP segment. You must declare the variables far, or you must check the Assume 'Extern' And Uninitialized Data 'Far' check box in the Memory Model category of the Compiler Options dialog (/Gx- switch).

Now that you're beginning to understand the difference between near (16-bit offset only) and far (segment address plus offset) addressing, it's time to look at some more compiler-generated code. Assume that *i* is a static integer variable. With the medium model (and, most of the time, with the large model), static variables are stored in the DGROUP segment, and you get the following machine instruction:

```
i = 0;
247F:02CB C7067E140000   MOV       WORD PTR [?I@@3HE (147E)],0000
```

Now, with the large model and the variable *i* in a different data segment, you get two instructions instead of one:

```
i = 0;
252F:02CB 8E060C10       MOV       ES,[100C]
252F:02CF 26C70636140000 MOV       WORD PTR ES:[?I@@3HE (1436)],0000
```

The extra MOV instruction loads the extended data segment (ES) register with the segment selector value that is stored in a temporary variable (100C) in the DGROUP segment. Notice the addition of 5 bytes of code. These bytes do add up in a large application. In 32-bit Windows, however, the code will be simpler and shorter.

The Local Heap

If you use the small or medium memory model, the C++ *new* operator is mapped to the compiler's *_nmalloc* (that is, near *malloc*) function, which in turn is mapped directly to the Windows *LocalAlloc* function. What does this mean? It means that you're using the "local heap" that is entirely contained in your application's DGROUP segment. The initial size of the heap is specified in the module definition file.

When you get memory from the local heap, the underlying DGROUP segment can move and change size, but the allocated memory blocks have fixed offsets within the segment. This means that local heap memory can become fragmented. In the old days, Windows programmers would call *LocalAlloc* themselves and then carefully lock and unlock the returned "memory handles" to allow Windows to shuffle the individual blocks within the heap. There's still some benefit to doing this, but the technique excludes use of the *new* operator. Most fragmentation problems disappear when you switch to the large model and the Windows global heap.

The Global Heap

With the large and compact memory models, the C++ *new* operator is mapped to the compiler's _*fmalloc* function. In Microsoft C version 6.0, _*fmalloc* called the Windows *GlobalAlloc* function directly, and *GlobalAlloc* allocated a brand-new movable segment on the "global heap" each time it was called. Because the number of descriptor table entries is limited (4096 segment selectors with 80286 computers and 8192 selectors with 80386- and 80486-based computers), you couldn't afford to use _*fmalloc* every time you needed a little bit of memory.

With Microsoft C/C++ version 7.0 and with Visual C++, the _*fmalloc* function works differently (as does the *new* operator). The _*fmalloc* function now does "subsegment allocation," which means that it can satisfy many memory requests by allocating a single large segment. The Windows *GlobalAlloc* function is called only when necessary to get a new segment. The amount of memory actually allocated is rounded up to the nearest 4-KB boundary. If a segment needs to grow, it is reallocated with the Windows *GlobalReAlloc* function, also to the nearest 4-KB boundary.

> **NOTE:** The 4-KB minimum allocation and reallocation sizes are subject to change. You can set internal Windows variables, and future versions of Windows might change the default values.

Global heap segments are completely movable and resizable through their descriptor table selectors, but the memory offsets within the segments are fixed. This means that you can still have fragmentation within a segment.

There's another problem too. Suppose your program allocates five memory blocks in three segments and then frees blocks 2, 3, and 5, as shown in Figure 9-2 on the following page.

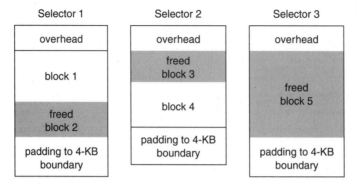

Figure 9-2.
Memory allocation with freed blocks.

All freed memory is available to your program, but the third segment is not returned to Windows, even though your program is not using it. You can avoid this condition if your program frequently calls the *_heapmin* function. Figure 9-3 shows the effects of *_heapmin* on the three segments above.

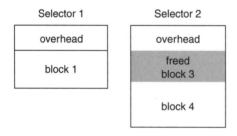

Figure 9-3.
The third segment (Selector 3, shown in Figure 9-2) has been returned to Windows.

Now the second segment has been reallocated, and the third segment has been returned to Windows with the *GlobalFree* function. The padding bytes have been removed too.

Location of the Program's vtbl

The "vtbl" is the data structure that dispatches calls to C++ virtual functions. In all MFC library applications, whatever the memory model, the vtbl is stored in a code segment. You never have to worry about the vtbl using up valuable space in your DGROUP segment.

Direct Use of Windows Memory Allocation Functions

In many Windows applications, you can get away with not directly using any Windows memory allocation functions. (Just say "new.") In a few cases, however, you need them. If you're using the Windows clipboard or dynamic data exchange (DDE), you need sharable memory. You can call *GlobalAlloc* directly with the flag parameter set to *GMEM_DDESHARE*, but then you're stuck using one of those obsolete Windows memory handles. Try using *GlobalAllocPtr* instead. This macro, defined in WINDOWSX.H, allocates memory, locks the handle, and returns a pointer to the locked memory block. The companion *GlobalFreePtr* macro unlocks and frees the memory identified by a pointer. See Chapter 23 for a global memory usage example.

Suppose you've been asked to write a Windows-based program to control the neighborhood nuclear plant. You absolutely can't afford to have the program crash as a result of memory fragmentation. In this case, you might be forced to write your own memory manager, based on *GlobalAllocPtr* and *GlobalFreePtr*. This memory manager might allocate memory in fixed-size chunks, or it might periodically perform garbage collection to compact the heap. The *_fheapwalk* function is helpful if you want to know what memory your program has allocated on the global heap.

The 80386/80486 Virtual Memory Manager

Now that you think you have memory management all figured out, I'm going to throw a whole new memory management system at you. This 386 enhanced mode virtual memory allocation system works separately and <u>on top of</u> the segment scheme you've seen already. Once physical memory fills up, memory pages, each 4 KB in size, are swapped to and from disk. The net result is a linear memory address space that can be as large as 64 megabytes (MB). Usually, the address space is much smaller. It's limited by the size of the Windows swap file (386SPART.PAR, SPART.PAR, or WIN386.SWP), which depends on the amount of physical memory and the space available on the hard disk. Figure 9-4 on the following page illustrates 386 enhanced mode memory management.

This virtual memory manager pretty much defeats the Windows segment management capability. Because Windows thinks it has, say, 20 MB of RAM, it won't have to discard or even move its segments until the 20 MB are used up. The virtual memory manager is in control, swapping (but not discarding) 4-KB blocks. This puts a different spin on swap-tuning. The new goal is to combine related code and data in 4-KB chunks. This, incidentally, is the same strategy that you'll need for 32-bit Windows.

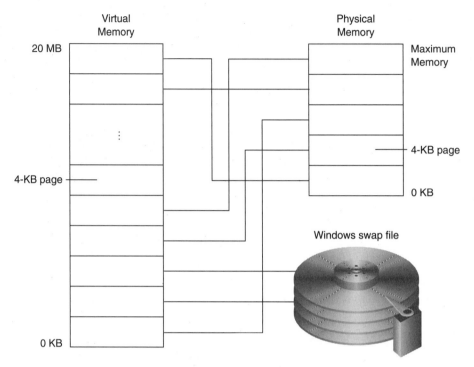

Figure 9-4.
386 enhanced mode memory management.

Detecting Memory Leaks

Memory fragmentation can affect program performance, but memory "leaks" frequently cause programs to crash. A memory leak occurs when your program fails to free an allocated memory block. If you consistently use the *new* operator for allocating heap memory, you can benefit from the application framework's diagnostic memory manager. When you use the Debug build option, *new* is overloaded to write signature bytes for the blocks it allocates. Thus, you can request a "snapshot" of the heap at any time. This dump identifies all C++ objects and non-object blocks.

If you need even more information about allocated memory, add the following line in each applicable source module:

#define new DEBUG_NEW

This tracks the source module name and source line number where the *new* operator was used.

Chapter 15 explains the memory dump process, which requires a knowledge of the *CObject* and *CDumpContext* classes. You'll see that the application framework automatically dumps all allocated memory blocks that have not been freed when the program terminates. Remember that you must allocate memory with *new* to take advantage of this application framework diagnostic feature; if you use *GlobalAlloc*, you can rely on the Windows Debug kernel to tell you about unfreed allocation units.

What to Do When You Run Out of Memory

Before you can plan your strategy for this unhappy situation, you must first learn how to detect the out-of-memory condition. I've encountered three separate out-of-memory conditions, but there are probably more. Here are the three conditions:

■ *Full local heap*—This is usually detected by the exception-processing code built into the MFC library. (A message box appears when memory runs out.) Don't even bother with recovery strategies; just recompile your program for the large model.

■ *Full global heap*—You don't get an exception with this condition; Windows just bogs down, usually after about 12 megabytes of memory have been used up. This usually indicates a logic problem, and you have to fix your program.

■ *The exhausting of Windows resources, usually in the USER.EXE component of Windows*—This condition is more common, and it's also detected by an exception. Perhaps the end user opens up 20 form view windows, each with a dozen controls. One solution is to write your own exception-processing code, which frees all known allocated memory and gracefully shuts down the program. This is difficult because Windows might not be able to perform the operations you need. A more effective strategy is to have your program limit the number of windows that the user can open. The 32-bit versions of Windows have more resource memory available, so this problem should disappear eventually.

BITMAPS

Without graphics images, Windows-based applications would be pretty dull. Some applications depend on images for their usefulness, but any application can be spruced up with the addition of decorative clip art from a variety of sources. Windows bitmaps are arrays of bits mapped to display pixels. That might sound simple, but you have to learn a lot about bitmaps before you can use them to create professional Windows-based applications.

This chapter starts with the simplest bitmap program—one that loads and displays a bitmap from a resource. The second example shows you how to use bitmaps for smooth movement of items on the screen. You'll have to wait until Chapter 23, however, to see the real power of bitmaps. There you'll save bitmaps on disk and print them out, and you'll also transfer them to other applications by means of the clipboard.

GDI Bitmaps and Device-Independent Bitmaps (DIBs)

The two kinds of Windows bitmaps are GDI bitmaps and DIBs. GDI bitmap objects are represented by the Microsoft Foundation Class (MFC) Library version 2.5 *CBitmap* class. The bitmap object has an associated Windows data structure, maintained inside the Windows GDI module, that is device-dependent. Your program can get a copy of the bitmap data, but the bit arrangement depends on the display hardware. GDI bitmaps can be freely transferred among programs on a single computer, but because of the device dependency, transferring them by disk or modem doesn't make sense.

The DIB is an alternative bitmap format that solves the interchangeability problem. Any computer running Windows can process DIBs, which are usually stored in BMP disk files. The wallpaper that forms your background is read from a BMP file when you start Windows. The primary storage format for Windows Paintbrush is the BMP file, and App Studio uses BMP files for toolbar buttons and other images. When a BMP file is read from disk, it's often translated into a GDI bitmap, but programs can work directly from the DIB format if necessary.

Using GDI Bitmaps

A GDI bitmap is simply another GDI object, such as a pen or a font. You must somehow create a bitmap, and then you must select it into a device context. When you're done with the object, you must deselect it and delete it. You know the drill.

There's a catch, though, because the "bitmap" of the display or printer device is effectively the display surface or the printed page itself. Therefore, you can't select a bitmap into a display device context or a printer device context. You have to create a special memory device context for your bitmaps, using the *Create::CompatibleDC* function. You must then use the *CDC* member function *StretchBlt* or *BitBlt* to copy the bits from the memory device context to the "real" device context. These "bit-blitting" functions are generally called in your view class's *OnDraw* function. Of course, you mustn't forget to clean up the memory display context when you're done.

Color Bitmaps and Monochrome Bitmaps

Now might be a good time to reread the "Windows Color Mapping" section in Chapter 5. As you'll see here, Windows deals with color bitmaps a little differently from the way it deals with brush colors.

Most color bitmaps are 16-color. A standard VGA board has 4 contiguous "color planes," with 1 corresponding bit from each plane combining to represent a pixel. The 4-bit color values are set when the bitmap is created. With a standard VGA board, bitmap colors are limited to the standard 16 colors. Windows does not use dithered colors in bitmaps.

With monochrome bitmaps, you have more flexibility. A monochrome bitmap has only one plane. Each pixel is represented by a single bit that is either on or off. The *CDC SetTextColor* function sets the "on" display color, and *SetBkColor* sets the "off" color. You can specify both of these pure colors with the Windows *RGB* macro.

Loading a GDI Bitmap from a Resource

The easiest way to use a bitmap is to load it from a resource. If you open a resource script with App Studio, you'll find a list of bitmap resources. If you select any bitmap and examine its properties, you'll see a filename. Here's an example entry in an RC file, when viewed by a text editor:

```
IDB_LEAVES              BITMAP  DISCARDABLE    "RES\\LEAVES.BMP"
```

IDB_LEAVES is the resource ID, and the file is LEAVES.BMP in the project's RES subdirectory. (LEAVES is one of the Windows 3.0 wallpaper bitmaps, normally located in the WINDOWS directory.) The resource compiler reads the DIB from disk and stores it in the RES file. The resource-binding process copies the DIB into the program's EXE file. The LEAVES bitmap must be in device-independent format because the EXE can be run with any display board that Windows supports.

The *CDC LoadBitmap* function converts a resource-based DIB to a GDI bitmap. Below is the simplest possible self-contained *OnDraw* function that displays the LEAVES bitmap.

```
CMyView::OnDraw(CDC* pDC)
{
    CDC* pDisplayMemDC = new CDC;
    CBitmap* pBitmap = new CBitmap;
    pBitmap->LoadBitmap(IDB_LEAVES);
    pDisplayMemDC->CreateCompatibleDC(pDC);
    pDisplayMemDC->SelectObject(pBitmap);
    pDC->BitBlt(100, 100, 200, 150, pDisplayMemDC, 0, 0, SRCCOPY);
    delete pDisplayMemDC; // deselects bitmap
    delete pBitmap;
}
```

The *BitBlt* function copies the LEAVES pixels from the memory display context to the display (or printer) device context. The LEAVES bitmap is 200 pixels by 150 pixels, and, on the display, it occupies a rectangle 200 logical units by 150 logical units, offset 100 units down and to the right of the upper left corner of the window's client area.

> N O T E : The code shown above works fine for the display. As you'll see in Chapter 18, the application framework calls the *OnDraw* function for printing, in which case *pDC* points to a printer device context. The bitmap here, unfortunately, is configured specifically for the display and thus cannot be selected into the printer-compatible memory device context. If you want to print a bitmap,

you can create a display-compatible memory device context in the view's *OnInitialUpdate* function and then call *BitBlt* in *OnDraw* to copy the bits to the printer device context. The EX10A program in this chapter demonstrates this technique. Even this technique isn't perfect, however, because bitmap colors aren't converted to gray shades on the printer. Chapter 23 introduces the *CDib* class, which allows you to make a DIB from a bitmap and then print the DIB directly.

The Effect of the Display Mapping Mode

If the display mapping mode in the LEAVES example is *MM_TEXT*, each bitmap pixel maps to a display pixel, and the bitmap looks nice. If the mapping mode is *MM_LOENGLISH*, the bitmap size is 2.0 inches by 1.5 inches, or 192 pixels by 144 pixels on a VGA screen, and the GDI must do some bit-crunching to make the bitmap fit. Consequently, the bitmap won't look as good with the *MM_LOENGLISH* mapping mode.

Stretching the Bits

What if we want LEAVES to occupy a rectangle exactly 200 pixels by 150 pixels, even though the mapping mode is <u>not</u> *MM_TEXT*? The *StretchBlt* function is the answer. If we replace the *BitBlt* call with the following three statements, LEAVES is displayed cleanly, whatever the mapping mode.

```
CRect rect(0, 0, 320, 240);
pDC->DPtoLP(&rect);
pDC->StretchBlt(0, 0, rect.Width(), rect.Height(),
        pDisplayMemDC, 0, 0, 200, 150, SRCCOPY);
```

With either *BitBlt* or *StretchBlt*, the display update is slow if the GDI has to actually stretch or compress bits. If the GDI determines, as in the case above, that no conversion is necessary, the update is fast.

The EX10A Program

The EX10A example displays a resource-based bitmap in a scrolling view with mapping mode set to *MM_LOENGLISH*. The program uses the *StretchBlt* logic described above, except that the memory device context and the bitmap are created in the view's *OnCreate* member function and last for the life of the program. Also, the program reads the bitmap size through a call to the *CGdiObject* member function *GetObject*, so it's not using hard-coded values as in the examples above.

Here are the steps for building the example:

1. **Run AppWizard to produce \VCPP\EX10A\EX10A.** Choose App-Wizard from Visual Workbench's Project menu. The options and the default class names are shown below. Be sure to specify the view's base class as *CScrollView* and to specify *CScrollView* on the view's base class.

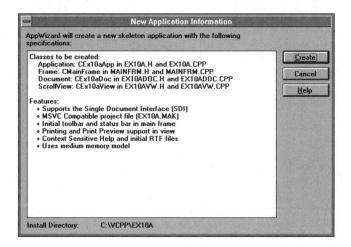

Be sure to select the Context Sensitive Help option in the Options dialog and accept the Printing And Print Preview default.

2. **Add the following data members to class *CEx10aView*.** Edit the file EX10AVW.H. The memory device context lasts for the life of the view. The integers in the code are the source (bitmap) dimensions and the destination (display) dimensions.

```
private:
    CDC*    m_pDisplayMemDC;
    HBITMAP m_hOldDisplayBitmap;
    int     m_nSWidth, m_nSHeight, m_nDWidth, m_nDHeight;
```

3. **Edit the following member functions in class *CEx10aView*.** Edit the file EX10AVW.CPP. The *OnInitialUpdate* function sets up the memory display context and the bitmap; the *OnDraw* function has only to call *BitBlt*. When *OnInitialUpdate* sets the bitmap destination dimensions, it multiplies the pixel values by 4 to make a giant-size bitmap. *OnInitial-Update* must save the old bitmap handle in the data member *m_hOld-DisplayBitmap* so that the destructor can restore it later. You've already seen this technique used for fonts.

185

```
void CEx10aView::OnInitialUpdate()
{
    CScrollView::OnInitialUpdate();
    CSize totalSize(800, 1050); // 8" x 10"
    CSize lineSize = CSize(totalSize.cx / 100, totalSize.cy / 100);
    SetScrollSizes(MM_LOENGLISH, totalSize, totalSize, lineSize);

    BITMAP bm; // Windows BITMAP data structure (see Win 3.1 help)
    if (m_pDisplayMemDC == NULL) {
      CClientDC dc(this);
      OnPrepareDC(&dc); // necessary
      CBitmap* pBitmap = new CBitmap;
      pBitmap->LoadBitmap(IDB_APPEXIT);
      m_pDisplayMemDC->CreateCompatibleDC(&dc);
      CBitmap* pOldBitmap = (CBitmap*)
                            (m_pDisplayMemDC->SelectObject(pBitmap));
      m_hOldDisplayBitmap = (HBITMAP) pOldBitmap->GetSafeHandle();

      pBitmap->GetObject(sizeof(bm), &bm);
      m_nSWidth = bm.bmWidth;
      m_nSHeight = bm.bmHeight;
      CRect rect(0, 0, m_nSWidth, m_nSHeight); // size of the bitmap
      dc.DPtoLP(&rect);
      m_nDWidth = rect.Width() * 4;
      m_nDHeight = rect.Height() * 4; // display bitmap dimensions
    }
}


void CEx10aView::OnDraw(CDC* pDC)
{
    pDC->StretchBlt(100, -100, m_nDWidth, m_nDHeight,
                    m_pDisplayMemDC, 0, 0, m_nSWidth,
                    m_nSHeight, SRCCOPY);
}


CEx10aView::CEx10aView()
{
    m_pDisplayMemDC = new CDC;
}


CEx10aView::~CEx10aView()
{
    // clean up the memory display context and the bitmap
    delete m_pDisplayMemDC->SelectObject(CBitmap::FromHandle
                                (m_hOldDisplayBitmap));
    delete m_pDisplayMemDC;
}
```

4. **In App Studio, import the *IDB_APPEXIT* bitmap.** Choose App Studio from Visual Workbench's Tools menu, and then choose Import from App Studio's Resource menu. Select the file \VCPP\EX10A\HLP\APP-EXIT.BMP. AppWizard generated this file when you asked for context-sensitive help. Now App Studio will copy it into the project's RES subdirectory. Assign the ID *IDB_APPEXIT* and save the changes.

5. **Build and test the EX10A application.** Your screen should look like this:

The bitmap "bits" are now exactly 4 pixels by 4 pixels.

6. **Try the Print Preview function.** The bitmap prints to scale because the application framework applies the *MM_LOENGLISH* mapping mode to the printer device context just as it does to the display device context.

Using Bitmaps to Improve the Screen Display

You've seen an example program that displayed a bitmap that originated outside the program. Now you'll see an example program that generates its own bitmap to support smooth motion on the screen. The principle is simple: You draw on a memory device context with a bitmap selected, and then you "zap" the bitmap onto the screen.

187

The EX10B Program

In the EX05C example in Chapter 5, the user dragged a circle with the mouse. As the circle moved, the display flickered because the circle was erased and redrawn on every mouse move message. EX10B uses a GDI bitmap to correct the problem. The EX05C custom code for mouse message processing carries over almost intact; most of the new code is in the *OnPaint* and *OnCreate* functions.

In summary, the EX10B *OnCreate* function creates a memory device context and a bitmap that are compatible with the display. The *OnPaint* function prepares the memory device context for drawing, passes *OnDraw* a handle to the memory device context, and copies the resulting bitmap from the memory device context to the display.

Here are the steps to build EX10B from scratch:

1. **Run AppWizard to produce \VCPP\EX10B\EX10B.** Choose App-Wizard from Visual Workbench's Project menu. The options and the default class names are shown below. Be sure to specify *CScrollView* on the view's base class.

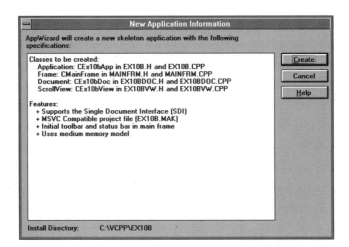

2. **Use ClassWizard to add *CEx10bView* message handlers.** Add message handlers for the following messages:

   ❑ WM_LBUTTONDOWN

   ❑ WM_LBUTTONUP

   ❑ WM_MOUSEMOVE

   ❑ WM_PAINT

3. **Edit the EX10BVW.H header file.** Add the private data members shown here to the *CEx10bView* class:

```
private:
    CRect    m_ellipseRect;
    CPoint   m_mousePos;
    BOOL     m_bCaptured;
    CDC*     m_pMemDC;
    CBitmap* m_pBitmap;
```

4. **Code the *CEx10bView* constructor and destructor in EX10BVW.CPP.** You need a memory device context object and a bitmap GDI object. These are constructed in the view's constructor and destroyed in the view's destructor.

```
CEx10bView::CEx10bView() : m_ellipseRect(0, 0, 100, -100) // constructor
{
        m_bCaptured = FALSE;
        m_pMemDC    = new CDC;
        m_pBitmap   = new CBitmap;
}

CEx10bView::~CEx10bView()           // destructor
{
    delete m_pBitmap;               // already deselected
    delete m_pMemDC;
}
```

5. **Add code for the *OnInitialUpdate* function in EX10BVW.CPP.** The C++ memory device context and bitmap objects are already constructed. This function creates the corresponding Windows objects. Both the device context and the bitmap are compatible with the display context *dc*, but you must explicitly set the memory display context's mapping mode to match the display context. You could create the bitmap in the *OnPaint* function, but the program runs faster if you create it once here.

```
void CEx10bView::OnInitialUpdate()
{
    CScrollView::OnInitialUpdate();

    // sets the scrolling parameters as in EX05C
    CSize totalSize = CSize(800 * 2, 800 * 2);
    CSize pageSize  = CSize(totalSize.cx / 2, totalSize.cy / 2);
    CSize lineSize  = CSize(totalSize.cx / 100, totalSize.cy / 100);
    SetScrollSizes(MM_LOENGLISH, totalSize, pageSize, lineSize);

    // creates the memory device context and the bitmap
```

(continued)

189

```
if (m_pMemDC->GetSafeHdc() == NULL) {
  CClientDC dc(this);
  OnPrepareDC(&dc);
  CRect rectMax(0, 0, totalSize.cx, -totalSize.cy);
  dc.LPtoDP(rectMax);
  m_pMemDC->CreateCompatibleDC(&dc);
  // makes the bitmap the same size as the display window
  m_pBitmap->CreateCompatibleBitmap(&dc, rectMax.right,
                                         rectMax.bottom);
  m_pMemDC->SetMapMode(MM_LOENGLISH);
}
CScrollView::OnInitialUpdate();
}
```

6. Add code for the *OnPaint* function in EX10BVW.CPP. Normally, it isn't necessary to override *OnPaint* to reduce screen flicker through the use of a memory display context. The *CView* version of *OnPaint* contains the following code:

```
CPaintDC dc(this);
OnPrepareDC(&dc);
OnDraw(&dc);
```

In this example, you will be overriding *OnPaint* to reduce screen flicker through the use of a memory display context. *OnDraw* is passed this memory display context for the display, and it is passed the printer device context for printing. Thus *OnDraw* can perform tasks common to the display and the printer. You don't need to use the bitmap with the printer because the printer has no speed constraint.

The overridden *OnPaint* must perform three steps to prepare the memory device context for drawing. Here are the three steps, in order:

❏ Select the bitmap into the memory device context.

❏ Transfer the invalid rectangle (as calculated by *OnMouseMove*) from the display context to the memory device context. There is no *SetClipRect* function, but the *CDC IntersectClipRect* function, when called after the *CDC SelectClipRgn* function (with a *NULL* parameter), has the same effect. If you don't set the clipping rectangle to the minimum size, the program runs slower.

❏ Initialize the bitmap to the current window background color. The *CDC PatBlt* function fills the specified rectangle with a pattern. In this case, the pattern is the brush pattern for the current window background. That brush must first be constructed and selected into the memory device context.

After the memory device context is prepared, *OnPaint* can then call *OnDraw* with a memory device context parameter. Afterward, the *CDC BitBlt* function copies the updated rectangle from the memory device context to the display device context.

```
void CEx10bView::OnPaint()
{
    CRect updateRect;

    CPaintDC dc(this);
    OnPrepareDC(&dc);
    dc.GetClipBox(&updateRect);
    CBitmap* pOldBitmap = (CBitmap*) (m_pMemDC->SelectObject(m_pBitmap));

    m_pMemDC->SelectClipRgn(NULL);
    m_pMemDC->IntersectClipRect(&updateRect);
    CBrush backgroundBrush((COLORREF) ::GetSysColor(COLOR_WINDOW));
    CBrush* pOldBrush = m_pMemDC->SelectObject(&backgroundBrush);
    m_pMemDC->PatBlt(updateRect.left, updateRect.top,
                     updateRect.Width(), updateRect.Height(), PATCOPY);
    OnDraw(m_pMemDC);
    dc.BitBlt(updateRect.left, updateRect.top,
              updateRect.Width(), updateRect.Height(), m_pMemDC,
              updateRect.left, updateRect.top, SRCCOPY);
    m_pMemDC->SelectObject(pOldBitmap);
    m_pMemDC->SelectObject(pOldBrush);
}
```

7. **Code the *OnDraw* function in EX10BVW.CPP.** This *CEx10bView* member function is similar to the EX05C *OnDraw* function except that it draws a stationary black square in addition to the moving circle. In EX10B, *OnDraw* is passed a pointer to a memory device context by the *OnPaint* function. For printing, *OnDraw* is passed a pointer to the printer device context.

```
void CEx10bView::OnDraw(CDC* pDC)
{
    pDC->SelectStockObject(BLACK_BRUSH);
    pDC->Rectangle(100, -100, 200, -200);
    pDC->SelectStockObject(GRAY_BRUSH);
    pDC->Ellipse(m_ellipseRect);
}
```

8. **Copy mouse message-handling code from EX05CVW.CPP.** Copy the functions shown on the following page from EX05CVW.CPP to EX10BVW.CPP. Be sure to change the class names of these functions from *CEx05cView* to *CEx10bView*.

❑ *OnLButtonDown*

❑ *OnLButtonUp*

❑ *OnMouseMove*

9. **Change one line in the *OnMouseMove* function in EX10BVW.CPP.** Change the line

```
InvalidateRect(invalidRect, TRUE);
```

to

```
InvalidateRect(invalidRect, FALSE);
```

If the second *CWnd::InvalidateRect* parameter is *TRUE*, Windows erases the background before repainting the invalid rectangle. That's what you needed in EX05C, but the background erasure is what causes the flicker. Because the entire invalid rectangle is being copied from the bitmap, you no longer need to erase the background. The *FALSE* parameter prevents this erasure.

10. **Build and run the application.** Here is the EX10B program output:

Is the circle's movement smoother now?

Other Uses for GDI Bitmaps

GDI bitmaps are often used in animation. At the start of a program, you might create a series of bitmaps that correspond to states of an animated object. Logic in the *OnPaint* function would then select the appropriate bitmap into the memory display context, and then *OnPaint* would use the *BitBlt* function to copy from the memory device context to a specific rectangular region in the display context. If the moving object is not itself rectangular, you must use some of the more esoteric *BitBlt* "raster operation codes" (ROPs) to merge the moving object with the rest of the display image. You might even need a separate "mask" bitmap. The *BitBlt SRCCOPY* ROP parameter in EX10B causes the source bitmap to be copied directly to the destination bitmap. See the *Class Library Reference* for information about other raster operation codes.

BITMAP BUTTONS, THE TIMER, AND ON-IDLE PROCESSING

This chapter presents a few useful Microsoft Foundation Class (MFC) Library programming techniques that don't depend on the document–view architecture. First you'll build a dialog that contains graphical bitmap buttons, and then you'll exercise the Windows timer. Last you'll see two places to attach "on-idle" code. (On-idle code can be used to perform background tasks while no messages are being processed.) The on-idle example introduces the application framework's main frame class, thus making this chapter a lead-in to Part III of this book.

Bitmap Buttons

The MFC library's *CBitmapButton* class allows you to easily create buttons that are labeled with graphics instead of text. You <u>don't</u> have to call *BitBlt* or *StretchBlt*. This chapter's first example shows you how to add bitmap buttons to a dialog.

The EX11A Program

In this example, you'll build a dialog with three bitmap buttons. These buttons use Copy, Cut, and Paste bitmaps "stolen" from the help system. So that you'll know that the buttons are working, the program displays appropriate text in a static text control and sets a dialog data member when you click the buttons.

Follow these steps closely to construct the example:

1. **Run AppWizard to produce \VCPP\EX11A\EX11A.** Choose AppWizard from Visual Workbench's Project menu. The options and the default class names are shown at the top of the next page:

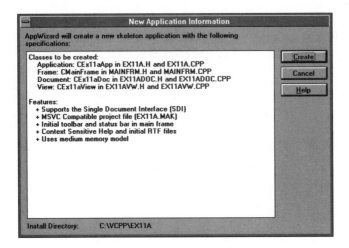

Be sure to specify the Context Sensitive Help option to create the bitmap files that the example needs.

2. **Start App Studio, and then import the button bitmaps.** Choose Import from App Studio's Resource menu to import and name the following bitmap files. You'll be importing each resource <u>twice</u>, once for the button's up (U) state and again for the button's down (D) state.

File	First Resource ID	Second Resource ID
HLP\EDITCOPY.BMP	"COPYU"	"COPYD"
HLP\EDITCUT.BMP	"CUTU"	"CUTD"
HLP\EDITPAST.BMP	"PASTEU"	"PASTED"

Be sure to use quotation marks in the ID field of the Bitmap Properties dialog to ensure that the resources are identified by strings instead of constants. The IDs will thus not appear in the RESOURCE.H file.

3. **Invert the colors for the "down" bitmaps.** Select the COPYD bitmap, and choose Invert Colors from the App Studio Image menu. Repeat for the CUTD and PASTED bitmaps. At run time, when a bitmap button changes from the up state to the down state, the U (noninverted) bitmap is replaced with the D (inverted) bitmap, which changes the button's colors. The screen at the top of the facing page shows the COPYD bitmap in App Studio:

4. Use App Studio to produce the dialog IDD_BITMAP. Create the
dialog shown here:

Notice the highlighted static text control in the dialog.

The three bitmap buttons are defined at the top of the following
page:

Button ID	Caption*
IDC_EDIT_COPY	COPY
IDC_EDIT_CUT	CUT
IDC_EDIT_PASTE	PASTE

*Note: Be sure to use uppercase for the captions.

Check the Owner Draw check box in the Push Button Properties dialog for each bitmap button.

The button captions correspond to the bitmap resource names. When the application framework draws the button COPY, it looks for bitmap resources named COPYD and COPYU.

Change the static text control's ID to *IDC_MESSAGE*.

5. **Use ClassWizard to generate the *CEx11aDialog* class.** If you run Class Wizard from inside App Studio, you won't have to specify the dialog ID. Fill in the Add Class dialog as shown here:

After the class is generated, define the following message handlers:

Object ID	Message	Member Function Name
CEx11aDialog	WM_INITDIALOG	*OnInitDialog*
IDC_EDIT_COPY	BN_CLICKED	*OnEditCopy*
IDC_EDIT_CUT	BN_CLICKED	*OnEditCut*
IDC_EDIT_PASTE	BN_CLICKED	*OnEditPaste*

Don't bother to define any dialog class data members with ClassWizard.

6. **Add data members to the *CEx11aDialog* class.** In the EX11ADLG.H file, add the following *friend* statement and private data members in the *CEx11aDialog* class declaration:

```
friend class CEx11aView;
private:
    CBitmapButton m_editCopy;
    CBitmapButton m_editCut;
    CBitmapButton m_editPaste;
    int m_nButton; // 1=copy, 2=cut, 3=paste, 0=none
```

7. **Edit the EX11ADLG.CPP file.** The *CBitmapButton AutoLoad* function initializes a button by loading the bitmap and sizing the button to fit the bitmap. Call it in the dialog's *OnInitDialog* function.

```
BOOL CEx11aDialog::OnInitDialog()

{
    VERIFY(m_editPaste.AutoLoad(IDC_EDIT_PASTE, this));
    VERIFY(m_editCut.AutoLoad(IDC_EDIT_CUT, this));
    VERIFY(m_editCopy.AutoLoad(IDC_EDIT_COPY, this));
    m_nButton = 0;
    return CDialog::OnInitDialog();
}
```

The following button message handlers set the text in the dialog's static control, and they set the value of *m_nButton*, which is available to the view class:

```
void CEx11aDialog::OnEditCopy()
{
    SetDlgItemText(IDC_MESSAGE, "Copy");
    m_nButton = 1;
}
```

```
void CEx11aDialog::OnEditCut()
{
    SetDlgItemText(IDC_MESSAGE, "Cut");
    m_nButton = 2;
}
```

```
void CEx11aDialog::OnEditPaste()
{
    SetDlgItemText(IDC_MESSAGE, "Paste");
    m_nButton = 3;
}
```

Typically, you use these functions to set dialog data members that would be returned to the view.

8. **Edit the *CEx11aView* class in EX11AVW.CPP to accommodate the dialog.** With ClassWizard, add a message handler for the WM_L-BUTTONDOWN message for the view, and then edit the code, as shown at the top of the following page:

```
void CEx11aView::OnLButtonDown(UINT nFlags, CPoint point)
{
    CEx11aDialog dlg;

    if (dlg.DoModal() == IDOK) {
        TRACE("Result = %d\n", dlg.m_nButton);
    }
}
```

Pressing the left mouse button while the mouse cursor is inside the view window activates the dialog.

Add the following *#include* statement to EX11AVW.CPP:

```
#include "ex11adlg.h"
```

While you are in EX11AVW.CPP, edit the *OnDraw* function to display a message:

```
void CEx11bView::OnDraw(CDC* pDC)
{
    pDC->TextOut(0, 0, "Press the left mouse button here.");
}
```

9. **Build and test the program.** When you press the left mouse button while the mouse cursor is inside the view window, you should see the EX11A dialog shown here:

A message appears when you click on a bitmap button. The bitmap buttons are smaller than the rectangles you specified in App Studio. (See the dialog shown in step 4.) They shrank because the application framework maps the bitmap bits to pixels in the dialog.

Going Further with Bitmap Buttons

Bitmap buttons can assume "focused" and "disabled" states in addition to the "up" and "down" states you've already seen. If the button has a bitmap resource name that ends in *F*, that bitmap appears when the button has the input focus. If the resource name ends in *X*, that bitmap appears when the button is disabled (through a call to the *CWnd::EnableWindow* function, for example). See the *Class Library Reference* for additional details on the *CBitmapButton* class.

Using a Timer and Yielding Control

You can program a Windows timer to send your program messages at regular intervals independent of microprocessor speed. You can use timers to control animation speed, to trigger alarms, to implement pseudo-multitasking, or, as illustrated by the example beginning on page 203, to provide a visual status indication during a long compute process.

Timers

Timers are easy to use. You simply call the *CWnd* function *SetTimer* with an interval parameter, and then you provide, with the help of ClassWizard, a message handler function for the WM_TIMER message. If you set the timer interval to, say, 200 milliseconds, WM_TIMER messages will be generated at that interval until you call the *CWnd* function *KillTimer* or until the timer's window is destroyed.

A simple timer-based animation program is trivial. The view's *OnCreate* function starts the timer, and the timer message handler updates position variables and invalidates a rectangle. The *OnDraw* function paints the image according to the position variables. The EX11B sample program later in this chapter is a little more interesting because you'll be using the timer to interrupt a long compute process. While you experiment with the timer, you'll learn more about Windows message processing, and you'll gain some insights for building your own multitasking applications.

Simultaneous Timers

Windows version 3.1 allows a total of 32 simultaneous timers. In a real application, you must be prepared for the possibility that all timers are in use, as indicated by a *0* return code from *SetTimer*.

Yielding Control

The 16-bit Windows model is definitely not a preemptive multitasking operating system. If your program enters a long compute loop, it takes complete control of the computer unless it is nice enough to yield control. So why yield control? Maybe the user needs to click a Cancel button to terminate the process, or maybe the user would like the ability to switch to another application. In case you haven't guessed, the timer won't work unless your program yields control.

How do you yield control? To understand the answer, you must delve a little deeper into the Windows message-handling process. You've already seen the tail end of the process—your message-handling member functions are called in response to messages such as BN_CLICKED (actually a WM_COMMAND message). Windows provides access to these messages, directly from the message queue, at an early stage in their development. If you put the following code almost anywhere in a Windows program, you can see the raw messages as they come in.

```
MSG Message; // Windows message structure
while (1) {  // infinite loop
    if (::PeekMessage(&Message, NULL, 0, 0, PM_REMOVE)) {
        TRACE("message = %x, wParam = %x, lParam = %lx\n",
                Message.message, Message.wParam, Message.lParam);
        ::TranslateMessage(&Message);
        ::DispatchMessage(&Message);
    }
}
```

If you look for WM_COMMAND or WM_CHAR messages after the *PeekMessage* call, you'll never see any because they don't come into existence until after the call to *TranslateMessage*. This translation function converts WM_KEYDOWN messages to WM_CHAR messages, and, if the user clicks a dialog button, the resulting WM_LBUTTONDOWN message is converted to the appropriate WM_COMMAND message. You'll never see a WM_PAINT message either because these messages bypass the message queue.

The application framework, while in control, gets the raw messages from the queue and calls *TranslateMessage* and *DispatchMessage*. If your program takes control, it must do the dispatch work to keep the messages flowing. All you need to do, every once in a while, is make the calls to *PeekMessage*, *TranslateMessage*, and *DispatchMessage*.

The EX11B Program

Suppose your application has a process that takes several minutes. If you let your program take control of the computer during that interval, even if it displays an hourglass cursor, the user is likely to get frustrated and reboot the machine. It's customary to provide a visual "percent complete" indicator to relieve the user's anxiety. In EX11B, we'll use a scroll bar control as an indicator, and we'll use a timer to update the thumbtrack every 100 milliseconds. (Of course, a real application would never use a scroll bar for this purpose, but it serves as a useful example.) We'll tie the compute process to this EX11B modal dialog:

Here are the steps for building the EX11B application:

1. Run AppWizard to produce \VCPP\EX11B\EX11B. Choose AppWizard from Visual Workbench's Project menu. The options and the default class names are shown here:

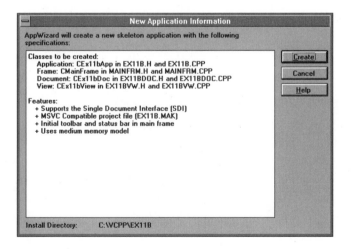

2. **Add a WM_LBUTTONDOWN message handler to *CEx11bView* in EX11BVW.CPP.** First edit the virtual *OnDraw* function to display a message:

```
void CEx11bView::OnDraw(CDC* pDC)
{
    pDC->TextOut(0, 0, "Press the left mouse button here.");
}
```

Then use ClassWizard to add the *OnLButtonDown* function, and add the following code:

```
void CEx11bView::OnLButtonDown(UINT nFlags, CPoint point)
{
    CEx11bDialog dlg;
    dlg.DoModal();
}
```

This code brings up the modal dialog whenever the user presses the left mouse button while the mouse cursor is in the view window.

While you're in EX11BVW.CPP, add the following *#include* statement:

```
#include "ex11bdlg.h"
```

3. **Use App Studio to create the dialog *IDD_DIALOG1*.** Use the dialog shown in step 1 as a model. Keep the default control ID for the Cancel button, but use *IDC_START* for the Start button. Change the scroll bar ID from *IDC_STATIC* to *IDC_SCROLLBAR1*. Save the resource script when you're finished.

4. **Use ClassWizard to create the *CEx11bDialog* class.** Choose Class-Wizard from the App Studio Resource menu. Fill in the Add Class dialog as shown here:

After the class is generated, add message-handling functions for *IDC_START*, *IDCANCEL*, and WM_TIMER. (Add BN_CLICKED message handlers for *IDC_START* and *IDCANCEL*. Accept the default names *OnStart* and *OnCancel*.)

5. Add the following data members in EX11BDLG.H:

```
private:
    long m_lCount;
    static const long lMaxCount;
```

The *m_lCount* data member of class *CEx11bDialog* is incremented during the compute process. It serves as a percent complete measurement when divided by the static variable *m_lMaxCount.*

6. Add a static variable to EX11BDLG.CPP. The static data member *lMaxCount* was declared in the class header, but it must be defined in the EX11BDLG.CPP file.

```
const long NEAR CEx11bDialog::lMaxCount = 500L;
```

7. Add initialization code to the *CEx11bDialog* constructor in EX11BDLG.CPP. Add the following line to the constructor to ensure that the Cancel button works if the compute process was not started:

```
m_lCount = 0L;
```

8. Code the *OnStart* function in EX11BDLG.CPP. This code is executed when the user clicks the Start button.

```
void CEx11bDialog::OnStart()
{
    MSG Message;
    int nTemp;
    int nTimer;

    nTimer = SetTimer(1, 100, NULL); // 1/10 second
    ASSERT(nTimer != 0);
    GetDlgItem(IDC_START)->EnableWindow(FALSE);
    for (m_lCount = 0L; m_lCount < lMaxCount; m_lCount++) {
        for (nTemp = 0; nTemp < 30000; nTemp++) {} // simulate computation
        if (::PeekMessage(&Message, NULL, 0, 0, PM_REMOVE)) {
            ::TranslateMessage(&Message);
            ::DispatchMessage(&Message);
        }
    }
    KillTimer(nTimer);
    CDialog::OnOK();
}
```

The main *for* loop is controlled by the value of *m_lCount.* Each time through the loop, *PeekMessage* allows other messages, including WM_-TIMER, to be processed. The *EnableWindow(FALSE)* call disables the Start button during the computation. If we didn't take this precaution, the *OnStart* function could be reentered.

9. **Code the *OnTimer* function in EX11BDLG.CPP.** When the timer fires, the scroll bar's scroll box is set according to the value of *m_lCount*.

```
void CEx11bDialog::OnTimer(UINT nIDEvent)
{
    CScrollBar* pBar = (CScrollBar*) GetDlgItem(IDC_SCROLLBAR1);
    pBar->SetScrollRange(0, (int) lMaxCount);
    pBar->SetScrollPos((int) m_lCount);
}
```

10. **Update the *OnCancel* function in EX11BDLG.CPP.** When the user clicks the Cancel button during computation, we don't destroy the dialog, but we set *m_lCount* to its maximum value, which causes *OnStart* to exit the dialog. If the computation hasn't started, it's OK to exit directly.

```
void CEx11bDialog::OnCancel()
{
    TRACE("entering CEx11bDialog::OnCancel\n");
    if (m_lCount == 0L) {      // prior to Start button
      CDialog::OnCancel();
    }
    else { // computation in progress
      m_lCount = lMaxCount;  // force exit from OnStart
    }
}
```

11. **Build and run the application.** Press the left mouse button while the mouse cursor is inside the view window to bring up the dialog. Try the Start button, and then try Cancel. The scroll bar's scroll box should move during the computation.

On-Idle Processing

When it doesn't have anything else to do, the application framework calls an on-idle function that is, by default, a dummy function. If you have a long computation that can be conveniently broken into chunks or if you must regularly update an element on the screen, you should consider hooking into this on-idle function. Remember that any on-idle function should complete its work and return to Windows as soon as possible; otherwise, the performance of other applications will suffer.

CWinApp::OnIdle is the application framework's standard on-idle function. You can override this function in your derived application class if you need to do special processing. *OnIdle* doesn't get called, however, when the menu system or a modal dialog is active. If you need to do on-idle processing for modal dialogs and menus, you'll have to add a message handler function for the WM_ENTERIDLE message, but you must add it to the <u>frame</u> class rather than to the view class. That's because pop-up dialogs are always "owned" by the application's main frame window, not by the view window.

The EX11C Program

This example uses CNTR, a cute little Visual Basic control that acts like an automobile odometer. CNTR.VBX is not included with Visual C++, but a copy of it is on the companion disc. After you install the companion disc, you'll find a copy of the file CNTR.VBX in your \VCPP\EX11C subdirectory. Copy this file to your \WINDOWS\SYSTEM subdirectory. The CNTR control appears twice in the EX11C example—once in the view window and once in a dialog. Here is EX11C in action:

When the program starts, the view's counter runs. When the dialog comes up (in response to a mouse click), the dialog's counter starts and the view's counter stops.

Here are the steps for building the EX11C application:

1. Run AppWizard to produce \VCPP\EX11C\EX11C. Choose AppWizard from Visual Workbench's Project menu. The options and the default class names are shown at the top of the following page:

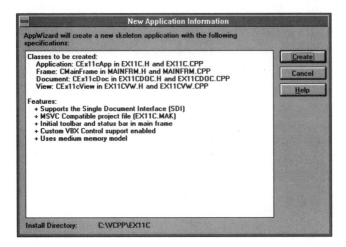

Be sure to select the Custom VBX Controls option.

2. **Add a data member and function prototype to *CEx11cApp*.** The derived application class is declared in the file EX11C.H. For the view's CNTR control, we need an object of class *CVBControl*. The application class is the best place for the control because the application class's *OnIdle* function must be able to access the control. It's easy for the view object to find the application object when it's time to create the CNTR control window. Because the control object is embedded, we don't have to worry about its destruction.

```
public:
    CVBControl m_cntr;
```

We're going to override the *CWinApp::OnIdle* function; so we'll need a function prototype in the application's class.

```
    virtual BOOL OnIdle(LONG lCount);
```

3. **Add the *CEx11cApp OnIdle* function in *EX11C.CPP*.** The application framework calls this overridden *OnIdle* function whenever the application's modal dialog and menu are not active. Each time it's called, the function increments the value of the CNTR control, which is a child of the view window.

```
BOOL CEx11cApp::OnIdle(LONG lCount)
{
    CWinApp::OnIdle(lCount);
    float val = m_cntr.GetFloatProperty("value");
    val += (float) .001;
    m_cntr.SetFloatProperty("value", val);
    return TRUE;
}
```

4. Use ClassWizard to add message handlers in *CEx11cView*.
In EX11CVW.H, add message handlers for WM_CREATE and WM_LBUTTONDOWN.

5. Code the *CEx11cView OnCreate* message-handling function.
In EX11CVW.CPP, find the ClassWizard-generated skeleton and add code as shown:

```
int CEx11cView::OnCreate(LPCREATESTRUCT lpCreateStruct)
{
    if (CView::OnCreate(lpCreateStruct) == -1)
        return -1;

    CVBControl* pCntr = &((CEx11cApp*) AfxGetApp())->m_cntr;
    pCntr->Create("CNTR.VBX;Counter;", WS_VISIBLE | WS_CHILD | WS_BORDER,
                CRect(50, 175, 180, 208), this, 1);
    pCntr->SetNumProperty("DigitsLeft", 3);
    pCntr->SetNumProperty("DigitsRight", 2);
    pCntr->SetFloatProperty("Value", 123.45);

    return 0;
}
```

This function actually creates the CNTR control window for the *CVBControl* object that's embedded in the application object.

6. Code the *CEx11cView OnLButtonDown* message-handling function. First, in EX11CVW.CPP, edit the virtual *OnDraw* function to display a message:

```
void CEx11cView::OnDraw(CDC* pDC)
{
    pDC->TextOut(0, 0, "Press the left mouse button here.");
}
```

Then find the ClassWizard-generated skeleton and add code as shown:

```
void CEx11cView::OnLButtonDown(UINT nFlags, CPoint point)
{
    CEx11cDialog dlg;

    dlg.DoModal();
}
```

This function activates the dialog that will contain the other CNTR control.

While you're in EX11CVW.CPP, add the following *#include* statement:

```
#include "ex11cdlg.h"
```

7. **Use App Studio to create a dialog.** Use the dialog shown on page 207 as a model. Accept the default ID *IDD_DIALOG1*. Be sure you first install the Visual Basic control CNTR.VBX. (Choose Install Controls from the App Studio File menu to do so.) Position the CNTR control, and then double-click on it to bring up its Counter Properties dialog. Set its DigitsRight property to *2*. Save the changes when you're finished.

8. **Use ClassWizard to create the *CEx11cDialog* class.** Choose ClassWizard from the App Studio Resource menu.

    Fill in the Add Class dialog, as shown here:

    You don't need any message handlers, but you must add data members for the dialog's CNTR control. Click the Edit Variables button, and then add the following variables for the *IDC_COUNTER1* control:

Variable	Property	Type	Description
m_fCntrValue	Value	*float*	Control's floating-point value
m_pVBCntr	Control	*CVBControl**	CNTR control pointer

9. **Use ClassWizard to add a WM_ENTERIDLE message handler to *CMainFrame* in MAINFRM.CPP.** The frame class *OnEnterIdle* function is called when <u>any</u> menu or modal dialog is active. In this example, it updates the dialog's CNTR control. Both the *CEx11cDialog* dialog and the system menu can trigger a call to *OnEnterIdle*. Because there are two dialogs in this program (*IDD_ABOUTBOX* and *IDD_DIALOG1*), the program must be sure that this *OnEnterIdle* call is associated with the dialog that contains the counter. Only the *IDD_DIALOG1* dialog has a control with ID *IDC_COUNTER1*.

```
void CMainFrame::OnEnterIdle(UINT nWhy, CWnd* pWho)
{
    CVBControl* pVBc = (CVBControl*) pWho->GetDlgItem(IDC_COUNTER1);
    if (pVBc != NULL) {
      float val = pVBc->GetFloatProperty("value");
      val += (float) .001;
      pVBc->SetFloatProperty("Value", val);
    }
}
```

While you're in MAINFRM.CPP, add the following *#include* statement:

```
#include "ex11cdlg.h"
```

10. **Build and test the application.** As pictured in the screen on page 207, the lower view CNTR should come up and run when the program starts. When you click inside the view window, the dialog's CNTR dialog should appear and the counter should run. Dismiss the dialog, and then close the main window.

> FYI: Try starting a second instance of the application. This is really interesting. The dialog's counter blocks the view's counter in its own instance, but Windows permits counters to run simultaneously in the other instances.

PART III

THE DOCUMENT–VIEW ARCHITECTURE

C H A P T E R   T W E L V E

MENUS AND KEYBOARD ACCELERATORS

In all the examples to this point, mouse clicks have triggered most program activity. Even though menu selections might have been more appropriate, we've used mouse clicks because mouse click messages are handled simply and directly within the Microsoft Foundation Class (MFC) Library version 2.5 view window. If you want program activity to be triggered when the user chooses a command from a menu, you must first become familiar with the other application framework elements.

This chapter concentrates on menus and the "command routing architecture." Along the way, it introduces frames and documents, explaining the relationships between these new application framework elements and the already-familiar view element. You'll use App Studio to lay out a menu visually, and you'll use ClassWizard to link document and view member functions to menu items. You'll learn how to use special update command user interface member functions to check and disable menu items, and you'll see how to use keyboard accelerators as menu shortcut keys.

At the end of the chapter is an example that shows you how to create dynamic menus whose content is determined at run time. Here you'll bypass App Studio and instead use the low-level menu elements together with the extended command message handlers. In case you're tired of the circles used in earlier examples, this chapter introduces the *CEditView* class, which has the functionality of a simple text editor.

The Main Frame Window and Document Classes

Up to now, you've been using a view window as if it were the application's only window. In an SDI application, the view window sits inside another window—the application's main frame window. It's the main frame window that has the title bar and the menu bar. Various child windows, including the view window, the toolbar window, and the status bar window, occupy the main frame window's client area. (See Figure 12-1.) The application framework controls the interaction between the frame and the view by routing messages from the frame to the view.

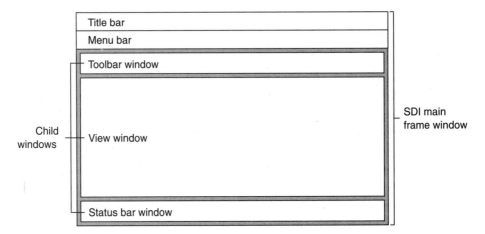

Figure 12-1.
The child windows within an SDI main frame window.

Look again at the files generated by AppWizard. The MAINFRM.H and MAINFRM.CPP files contain the code for the application's main frame window class, derived from the class *CFrameWnd*. Other files, with names such as EX12ADOC.CPP and EX12ADOC.H, contain code for the application's document class, which is derived from *CDocument*. Starting with this chapter, you'll be modifying those frame and document files a lot.

Windows Menus

A Windows menu is the familiar application element that consists of a top-level horizontal list of items with associated pop-up menus that appear when the user selects a top-level item. Most of the time, you define a default menu resource for a frame window that loads when the window is created. You can also define a menu resource independently of a frame window. In that case, your program must call the functions necessary to load and activate the menu.

A menu resource completely defines the initial appearance of a menu. Menu items can be grayed or have check marks, and bars can separate groups of menu items. Multiple levels of pop-up menus are possible. If a first-level menu item is associated with a subsidiary popup, the menu item carries a right-pointing arrowhead symbol, as shown in Figure 12-2, next to the Load Workspace menu item.

App Studio includes an easy-to-use menu resource editing tool. With this tool, you edit menus in a wysiwyg environment. Each menu item has a properties dialog that defines all the characteristics of that item. The resulting resource definition is stored in the application's resource script (RC) file. Each menu item is associated with an ID, such as *ID_FILE_OPEN*, that is defined in the RESOURCE.H file.

Figure 12-2.
Multilevel pop-up menus (from Microsoft Visual C++).

Version 2.5 of the Microsoft Foundation Class Library extends the functionality of the standard menus for Windows. Each menu item can have a prompt string that appears in the frame's status bar when the item is highlighted. These prompts are really Windows string resource elements linked to the menu item by a common ID. From the point of view of App Studio, they appear to be part of the menu item definition.

Keyboard Accelerators

You have probably noticed that one letter is underlined in most menu items. In Visual Workbench (and most other applications), pressing Alt-F followed by S activates the File Save menu item. This is the standard Windows method of using the keyboard to choose from menus. If you looked at the application's menu resource script (or the App Studio properties dialog), you would see ampersands (&) in front of the characters that are underlined in the application's menu items.

Windows offers an alternative way of linking keystrokes to a menu item. The keyboard accelerator resource consists of a table of key combinations with associated command IDs. The Edit Copy menu item, for example (with command ID *ID_EDIT_COPY*), might be linked to the Ctrl-C key combination through a keyboard accelerator entry. A keyboard accelerator entry does not have to be associated with a menu item. If there were no Edit Copy menu item, the Ctrl-C key combination would nevertheless activate the *ID_EDIT_COPY* command.

NOTE: If a keyboard accelerator is associated with a menu item, the accelerator key is disabled when the menu item is disabled.

Command Processing

As Chapter 2 pointed out, the application framework provides a sophisticated routing system for command messages. These messages originate from menu selections, keyboard accelerators, and toolbar and dialog button clicks. Also, command messages can be sent by calls to the *CWnd::SendMessage* function. Each message is identified by a *#define* constant that is often assigned by App Studio. The application framework has its own set of internal command message IDs, such as ID_FILE_PRINT and ID_FILE_OPEN. Your project's RESOURCE.H file contains IDs that are unique to your application.

Most command messages originate in the application's frame window, and, without the application framework in the picture, that's where you would put the message handlers. With command routing, however, you can handle the message almost anywhere. When the application framework sees a frame window command message, it starts looking for message handlers in one of the sequences listed below:

SDI Application	MDI Application
View	View
Document	Document
SDI main frame	MDI child frame
Application	MDI main frame
	Application

Most applications have a particular command handler in only one class, but suppose your one-view application has an identical handler in both the view and the document classes. Because the view is higher in the command route, only the view's command handler function will be called.

What does it take to install a command handler function? The requirements are similar to those of the window message handlers you've already seen. You need the function itself, a corresponding message map entry, and the function prototype. Suppose you have a menu item called Zoom (with *IDM_ZOOM* as the associated ID) that you want your view class to handle. First you add the following code to your view implementation file:

```
BEGIN_MESSAGE_MAP(CMyView, CView)
    ON_COMMAND(IDM_ZOOM, OnZoom)
END_MESSAGE_MAP()

void CMyView::OnZoom()
{
    // command message processing code
}
```

Now add the following function prototype to the *CMyView* class header file:

```
afx_msg void OnZoom();
```

Of course, ClassWizard automates the process of inserting command message handlers the same way that it facilitates the insertion of window message handlers. You'll learn how in the next example.

Command Message Handling in Derived Classes

The command routing system is one dimension of command message handling. The class hierarchy is a second dimension. If you look at the source code for the MFC library classes, you'll see lots of ON_COMMAND message map entries. When you derive a class from one of these base classes—*CView*, for example—the derived class inherits all the *CView* message map functions, including the command message functions. To override one of the base class message map functions, you must add both a function and a message map entry to your derived class.

Update Command User Interface (UI) Messages

You often need to change the appearance of a menu item to match the internal state of your application. If you have a Clear All item in your application's Edit menu, for example, you might want to disable that item if there's nothing to clear. You've undoubtedly seen such grayed menu items in Windows-based applications. You've probably seen check marks next to menu items too.

With SDK programming for Windows, it's difficult to keep menu items synchronized with the application's state. Every piece of code that changes the internal state must contain statements to update the menu. The MFC library takes a different approach by sending a special update command UI message whenever a pop-up menu is first displayed. That message is generally routed to the same object that was the target of the menu item. The message handler function's argument is a *CCmdUI* object, which contains a pointer to the corresponding menu item. The handler function can then use this pointer to modify the menu item's appearance. Update command UI messages apply only to items in pop-up menus, not to top-level menu items that are permanently displayed. You couldn't use an update command UI message to disable the File menu item, for example.

The update command UI coding requirements are similar to those for commands. You need the function itself, a special message map entry, and, of course, the prototype. The associated ID, *IDM_ZOOM* in this case, is the same constant used for the command. Here is an example of the necessary additions to the view class code file:

```
BEGIN_MESSAGE_MAP(CMyView, CView)
    ON_UPDATE_COMMAND_UI(IDM_ZOOM, OnUpdateZoom)
END_MESSAGE_MAP()

void CMyView::OnUpdateZoom(CCmdUI* pCmdUI)
{
    pCmdUI->SetCheck(m_bZoomed); // m_bZoomed is a class data member
}
```

Here is the function prototype that you must add to the class header:

```
afx_msg void OnUpdateZoom(CCmdUI* pCmdUI);
```

Needless to say, ClassWizard automates the process of inserting update command UI messages.

Commands That Originate in Dialogs

Suppose you have a pop-up dialog with buttons, and you want a particular button to send a command message. Command IDs must be in the range 0x8000–0xDFFF, the same ID range that App Studio uses for your menu items. If you assign a dialog button an ID in this range, the button will generate a routable command. The application framework first routes this command to the main frame window because the frame window owns all pop-up dialogs. Then the command routing proceeds normally; if your view has a handler for the button's command, that's where it will be handled. It's not so easy to use update command UI handlers for dialog buttons. See the code in the example program \MSVC\MFC\SRC\BARCORE.CPP for some hints.

To ensure that the ID is in the range 0x8000–0xDFFF, you must use the App Studio symbol editor to enter the ID prior to assigning it to a button.

The Application Framework's Built-In Menu Items

You don't have to start each frame menu from scratch because the MFC library defines some useful menu items for you, along with all the command handler functions, as shown in Figure 12-3.

Figure 12-3.
The standard SDI frame menus. (Font is not a built-in menu.)

The menu items and command message handlers you get depend on the options you choose in AppWizard. If you don't select printing, for example, you don't get the Print and Print Preview menu items. Because printing is optional, the message map entries are not defined in the *CView* class but are generated in your derived view class. That's why entries such as

```
ON_COMMAND(ID_FILE_PRINT, CView::OnFilePrint)
ON_COMMAND(ID_FILE_PRINT_PREVIEW, CView::OnFilePrintPreview)
```

are defined in your *CMyView* class instead of in the *CView* class.

Enabling/Disabling of Menu Items

The application framework can disable a menu item if it does not find a command message handler in the current command route. This feature saves you the trouble of having to write *ON_UPDATE_COMMAND_UI* message handlers. You can disable the feature if you set the *CFrameWnd* data member *m_bAutoMenuEnable* to *FALSE* (the default).

Suppose you have two views for one document, but only the first view class has a message handler for the *IDM_ZOOM* command. The frame menu's Zoom item will be enabled only when the first view is active. For another example, consider the application framework–supplied Edit Cut, Copy, and Paste menu items. These will be disabled if you have not provided message handlers in your derived view or document classes.

The *CEditView* Class

This chapter focuses on command messages, but the *CEditView* class plays a prominent role. This class, itself derived from *CView*, serves as the base class for an application's custom view class. An object of a class derived from *CEditView* is like a *CView* object because it can process command messages. It's also like a *CEdit* object because it permits text editing and formatting. A *CEditView* object is really an ordinary view object with the functionality of an edit control window. The class member functions make the two related windows act as one object—an ideal tool when you need text input.

As is an edit control, the *CEditView* object's text is contained deep within the *CEdit* part of the object. To access that text (and otherwise interact with the window), you must use specific *CEditView* functions together with functions inherited from *CWnd* and (indirectly) from *CEdit*. The *CEditView* class does not employ C++ multiple inheritance but rather provides the *GetEditCtrl* member function for access to the *CEdit* member functions.

Don't try to build a full-featured word processor with *CEditView*. The class has many limitations that are imposed by the underlying Windows edit control. You cannot mix fonts within the window, for example, and you are limited to a text buffer size of about 64 KB. *CEditView* does implement the clipboard Cut, Copy, and Paste commands, however. These are connected to the standard application framework Edit menu items.

> **NOTE:** If you need to intercept control notification messages from the *CEditView* internal edit control, manually set up message map entries such as the following:

```
ON_EN_CHANGE(AFX_IDW_PANE_FIRST, OnEditChange)
```

> The constant *AFX_IDW_PANE_FIRST* identifies the view's edit control.

The EX12A Example

This example illustrates the routing of menu and keyboard accelerator commands to both documents and views. The application's view class is derived from *CEditView*. View-directed menu commands, originating from a Font menu, alter the view's font, and a document-directed Clear All menu item erases the document's contents. The Font menu contains items for System and Fixed fonts with the capability of displaying a check mark next to the selected font. The Clear All item, located on the Edit menu, is grayed when the document is empty. Figure 12-4 shows the EX12A program in use.

Figure 12-4.
The EX12A program in use.

If we exploited the document–view architecture fully, we would keep the edit view's text inside the document, but that's a little too advanced for this chapter. Instead, we'll define a "phony" document *CString* data member called *m_text* that won't be reflected in the view. The initial value of *m_text* is

223

"Hello," and choosing Clear All from the Edit menu sets it to empty. At least you'll start to get the idea about the separation of the document and the view.

The EX12A example exercises the App Studio wysiwyg menu editor and keyboard accelerator editor together with the ClassWizard. You'll need to do very little C++ coding. Simply follow these steps:

1. Run AppWizard to generate \VCPP\EX12A\EX12A. Choose App-Wizard from Visual Workbench's Project menu. In the Classes dialog, set the view's base class to *CEditView*, as shown below:

The options and the default class names are shown here:

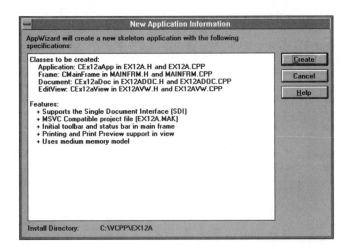

2. Use App Studio to edit the application's main menu. Choose App Studio from Visual Workbench's Tools menu. Edit the *IDR_MAINFRAME* menu resource to add a Clear All item to the Edit menu so that it looks like this:

> NOTE: The App Studio menu resource editor is intuitive, but you might need some help the first time you insert an item in the middle of a menu. Each menu has a blank item at the bottom. Use the mouse to drag the blank item to the insertion position to define a new item. A new blank item will appear at the bottom when you've finished.

Now add a Font menu, and then define the underlying System and Fixed items as shown here:

Use the following command IDs for your new menu items:

Menu	Item	Command ID
Edit	Clear All	*ID_EDIT_CLEARALL*
Font	&System\tF2	*ID_FONT_SYSTEM*
Font	&Fixed\tF3	*ID_FONT_FIXED*

The MFC library has defined the first choice, *ID_EDIT_CLEARALL*. (Note: \t is a tab character—but type \t, don't press the Tab key.)

When you add the menu items, type appropriate prompt strings in the Menu Item Properties dialog. These prompts will appear in the status window when the menu item is highlighted.

3. **Use App Studio to add keyboard accelerators.** Open the *IDR_MAIN-FRAME* accelerator table, and then add the following items:

Accelerator ID	Key
ID_FONT_SYSTEM	*VK_F2*
ID_FONT_FIXED	*VK_F3*

Be sure to turn off the Ctrl, Alt, and Shift modifiers. The App Studio Accelerator Properties dialog is shown below:

Save the resource file on disk when you are finished.

4. **Use ClassWizard to add the view class command and update command UI message handlers.** Select the *CEx12aView* class, and then add the following member functions:

Object ID	Message	Member Function Name
ID_FONT_FIXED	COMMAND	*OnFontFixed*
ID_FONT_FIXED	UPDATE_COMMAND_UI	*OnUpdateFontFixed*
ID_FONT_SYSTEM	COMMAND	*OnFontSystem*
ID_FONT_SYSTEM	UPDATE_COMMAND_UI	*OnUpdateFontSystem*

5. **Use ClassWizard to add the document class command and update command UI message handlers.** Select the *CEx12aDoc* class, and then add the following member functions:

Object ID	Message	Member Function Name
ID_EDIT_CLEARALL	COMMAND	*OnEditClearall*
ID_EDIT_CLEARALL	UPDATE_COMMAND_UI	*OnUpdateEditClearall*

6. **Add a data member in file EX12ADOC.H.** Add the following code in the *CEx12aDoc* class definition.

```
private:
    CString m_text; // representation of edit text
```

7. **Add a data member and a function prototype in file EX12AVW.H.** Add the following code in the *CEx12aView* class definition:

```
private:
    int m_nFont; // ID of currently selected stock font
```

Add the following function prototype:

```
    virtual BOOL PreCreateWindow(CREATESTRUCT& cs);
```

8. **Edit the document class member functions in EX12ADOC.CPP.** Remember that we're faking the document view interaction in this example. The constructor sets the initial value of *m_text* for only one reason—so that the Edit Clear All menu item is initially enabled.

```
CEx12aDoc::CEx12aDoc() : m_text("Hello")
{
}
```

The Edit Clear All message handler sets *m_text* to empty. You get only one chance to clear the document—once it's cleared, it stays cleared, and the menu item becomes gray (disabled).

A pop-up message box indicates that the function was called.

```
void CEx12aDoc::OnEditClearall()
{
    AfxMessageBox("Document cleared");
    m_text = "";
}
```

If *m_text* is empty, the Edit Clear All menu item is disabled.

```
void CEx12aDoc::OnUpdateEditClearAll(CCmdUI* pCmdUI)
{
    pCmdUI->Enable(!m_text.IsEmpty());
}
```

9. **Edit the view class member functions in EX12AVW.CPP.** The constructor initializes the font data member so that the font menu check marks match the initial font.

```
CEx12aView::CEx12aView()
{
    m_nFont = SYSTEM_FONT;
}
```

The following two functions are called in direct response to the ID_-FONT_SYSTEM and ID_FONT_FIXED menu command messages. They set the *m_nFont* data member to support the update command UI functions.

```
void CEx12aView::OnFontSystem()
{
    CFont font;

    font.CreateStockObject(SYSTEM_FONT);
    SetFont(&font);
    m_nFont = SYSTEM_FONT;
}
```

```
void CEx12aView::OnFontFixed()
{
    CFont font;

    font.CreateStockObject(SYSTEM_FIXED_FONT);
    SetFont(&font);
    m_nFont = SYSTEM_FIXED_FONT;
}
```

The following two functions are called when the user chooses an item from the Font menu. The System and Fixed items are checkmarked according to the contents of the *m_nFont* data member.

```
void CEx12aView::OnUpdateFontSystem(CCmdUI* pCmdUI)
{
    pCmdUI->SetCheck(m_nFont == SYSTEM_FONT);
}


void CEx12aView::OnUpdateFontFixed(CCmdUI* pCmdUI)
{
    pCmdUI->SetCheck(m_nFont == SYSTEM_FIXED_FONT);
}
```

If we didn't override the *CWnd* virtual *PreCreateWindow* function, the edit view would have a horizontal scroll bar and would not support wordwrap. This *CEx12aView* function, called by the application framework, sets the style parameter appropriately.

```
BOOL CEx12aView::PreCreateWindow(CREATESTRUCT& cs)
{
    cs.style = AFX_WS_DEFAULT_VIEW | WS_VSCROLL |
               ES_AUTOVSCROLL | ES_MULTILINE | ES_NOHIDESEL;
    return CEditView::PreCreateWindow(cs);
}
```

10. **Build and test the EX12A application.** When the application starts, the Clear All item on the Edit menu should be enabled, and the System menu item on the Font menu should be checkmarked. Type some text, and then change the font. Try pressing the F2 and F3 keys. Next, choose Clear All from the Edit menu. The text won't be cleared, but you should get the pop-up message box, and the Clear All item should be disabled. Note that the *CEditView* class supports printing and Print Preview as well as clipboard operations.

The *CMenu* Class

Up to this point, the application framework and App Studio have shielded you from the menu class, *CMenu*. A *CMenu* object can represent each Windows menu, including the top-level menu items and associated popups. Most of the time, the menu's resource is directly attached to a frame window when the window's *Create* function is called, and a *CMenu* object is never explicitly constructed. The *CWnd* member function *GetMenu* returns a temporary *CMenu* pointer. Once you have this pointer, you can freely access and update the menu object.

Suppose you want to switch menus sometime after the application starts. *IDR_MAINFRAME* always identifies the initial menu in the resource script. If you want a second menu, you use App Studio to create a menu resource with your own ID. Then, in your program, you construct a *CMenu* object, use the *CMenu::LoadMenu* function to load the menu from the resource, and call the *CWnd::SetMenu* function to attach the new menu to the frame window.

You can use a resource to define a menu, and then your program can modify the menu items at run time. If necessary, however, you can build the whole menu at run time, without benefit of a resource. In either case, you can use *CMenu* member functions such as *ModifyMenu*, *InsertMenu*, and *DeleteMenu*. Each of these functions operates on an individual menu item identified by ID or by a relative position index.

A menu object is actually composed of a nested structure of submenus. You can use the *GetSubMenu* member function to get a *CMenu* pointer to a pop-up menu contained in the main *CMenu* object. Inserting a new pop-up menu is more difficult because you must use a Windows menu handle (HMENU) instead of a *CMenu* pointer. The *CMenu::GetMenuString* function returns the menu item string based on a zero-based index or a command ID. If you use the command ID option, the menu is searched, together with any submenus.

It's possible to use graphics inside menus, and there is a special "free-floating" type of pop-up menu. See the *Class Library Reference* for details on these seldom-used menu features.

Extended Command Processing

In addition to the *ON_COMMAND* message map macro you've seen already, the MFC library provides an extended variation, *ON_COMMAND_EX*. The extended command message map macro provides two features that are not supplied by the regular command message—a command ID function parameter, and the ability to reject a command at run time, sending it to the next object in the command route. If the extended command handler returns *TRUE*, the command goes no further; if it returns *FALSE*, the application framework looks for another command handler.

The command ID parameter is useful, as you'll see in EX12B, when you want one function to handle several related command messages. The rejection feature is used in the Help system (introduced in Chapter 20). If a view can't handle a Help request, for example, the request can be passed to the document or the application. You might invent some of your own uses for this feature.

ClassWizard can't help you with extended command handlers, so you'll have to do the coding yourself, outside the *AFX_MSG_MAP* brackets. Assume *IDM_ZOOM_1* and *IDM_ZOOM_2* are related command IDs defined in RESOURCE.H. Here's the class code you'll need to process both messages with one function, *OnZoom*:

```
BEGIN_MESSAGE_MAP(CMyView, CView)
    ON_COMMAND_EX(IDM_ZOOM_1, OnZoom)
    ON_COMMAND_EX(IDM_ZOOM_2, OnZoom)
END_MESSAGE_MAP()

BOOL CMyView::OnZoom(UINT nID)
{
    if (nID == IDM_ZOOM_1) {
        // code specific to first zoom command
    }
    else {
        // code specific to second zoom command
    }
    // code common to both commands
    return TRUE; // command goes no further
}
```

Here's the function prototype:

```
afx_msg BOOL OnZoom(UINT nID);
```

The EX12B Example

This example uses the *CEditView* class, but with a twist. A new top-level menu item lets the user change the size of the edit window's font. We could hard-code the size choices in the menu resource, but instead we dynamically create the Size popup with eight font sizes, and then we use extended command macros to route the eight distinct command messages to one member function. Figure 12-5 on the following page shows the EX12B program in use.

> NOTE: If you're serious about font and size selection, you'll probably use the COMMDLG class *CFontDialog*. EX12B illustrates the use of menu commands, which is not an ideal font-selection technique.

Because menus are always associated with an application's frame window, we must build the font popup in the *CMainFrame* class. We depend on the application framework's command routing to send the resulting command messages to the *CEx12bView* class. We won't attempt to use the extended command's rejection mechanism, though.

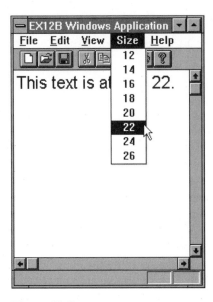

Figure 12-5.
The EX12B program in use.

Follow these steps to build the EX12B example:

1. Run AppWizard to generate \VCPP\EX12B\EX12B. Choose App-
Wizard from Visual Workbench's Project menu. The options and the
default class names are shown here:

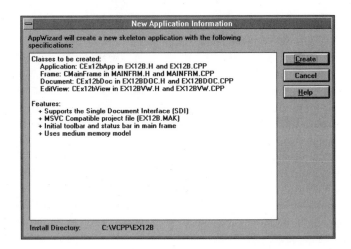

Note that the view's base class is *CEditView.*

2. Use App Studio to edit the application's main menu. Choose App Studio from Visual Workbench's Tools menu. Edit the *IDR_MAIN-FRAME* menu resource to create a menu that looks like this:

You need the dummy Base menu item in the Size menu to force Size to be a pop-up menu rather than an ordinary top-level menu item. This menu item will be replaced at run time. Use *IDM_SIZE_BASE* for the dummy menu item ID.

> NOTE: This application requires eight sequential command IDs, starting with *IDM_SIZE_BASE*. If you add menu items, they might overlap the range of size commands. Be sure that App Studio doesn't assign command IDs inside the range *IDM_SIZE_BASE* through *IDM_SIZE_BASE + 7.*

3. Add code to the *OnCreate* function in MAINFRM.CPP. When the application's frame window is created, the *CMainFrame::OnCreate* function alters the associated menu, specified in the *IDR_MAINFRAME* resource. The function first locates the Size pop-up submenu, and then it deletes the Base menu item that was defined in the resource. Finally it adds eight font size entries and creates the initial font. Because the *CEditView* class uses the *MM_TEXT* mapping mode, the font sizes are arbitrary and are not related to points.

```
int CMainFrame::OnCreate(LPCREATESTRUCT lpCreateStruct)
{
    char temp[10];
    int i, j;
```

(continued)

```
if (CFrameWnd::OnCreate(lpCreateStruct) == -1)
    return -1;

if (!m_wndToolBar.Create(this) ||
    !m_wndToolBar.LoadBitmap(IDR_MAINFRAME) ||
    !m_wndToolBar.SetButtons(buttons,
      sizeof(buttons)/sizeof(UINT)))
{
    TRACE("Failed to create toolbar\n");
    return -1;      // fail to create
}

if (!m_wndStatusBar.Create(this) ||
    !m_wndStatusBar.SetIndicators(indicators,
      sizeof(indicators)/sizeof(UINT)))
{
    TRACE("Failed to create status bar\n");
    return -1;      // fail to create
}
```

```
CMenu* pMenu = GetMenu();
CMenu* pSubMenu = pMenu->GetSubMenu(3); // Size pop-up menu
// clear out the existing popup  (assume single item)
pSubMenu->DeleteMenu(0, MF_BYPOSITION);
for (i = 0; i < 8; i++) {
  j = 12 + i * 2; // size 12, 14, 16, 18, 20, 22, 24, 26
  pSubMenu->AppendMenu(MF_ENABLED | MF_STRING,
                       (UINT) IDM_SIZE_BASE + i,
                       itoa(j, temp, 10));
}
```

```
    return 0;
}
```

4. **Use ClassWizard to add a *CEx12bView* class message handler.** Add a message handler for WM_CREATE.

5. **Edit the EX12BVW.H header.** You must add the *CEx12bView* function prototype for *OnCommandSize* because ClassWizard doesn't do it for you.

```
afx_msg BOOL OnCommandSize(UINT nID);
```

You also need a font data member in class *CEx12bView*.

```
private:
    CFont* m_pFont;
```

6. Add the extended command message map entries in EX12BVW.CPP.
Add the following entries after the *BEGIN_MESSAGE_MAP* statement
but outside the *AFX_MSG_MAP* brackets:

```
ON_COMMAND_EX(IDM_SIZE_BASE, OnCommandSize)
ON_COMMAND_EX(IDM_SIZE_BASE + 1, OnCommandSize)
ON_COMMAND_EX(IDM_SIZE_BASE + 2, OnCommandSize)
ON_COMMAND_EX(IDM_SIZE_BASE + 3, OnCommandSize)
ON_COMMAND_EX(IDM_SIZE_BASE + 4, OnCommandSize)
ON_COMMAND_EX(IDM_SIZE_BASE + 5, OnCommandSize)
ON_COMMAND_EX(IDM_SIZE_BASE + 6, OnCommandSize)
ON_COMMAND_EX(IDM_SIZE_BASE + 7, OnCommandSize)
```

7. Edit the *OnCreate* member function in EX12BVW.CPP. The *OnCreate*
function creates the edit view's initial TrueType font:

```
int CEx12bView::OnCreate(LPCREATESTRUCT lpCreateStruct)
{
    if (CEditView::OnCreate(lpCreateStruct) != 0) {
        return -1;
    }

    ASSERT(m_pFont->CreateFont(-12, 0, 0, 0, 400, FALSE, FALSE, 0,
                               ANSI_CHARSET, OUT_DEFAULT_PRECIS,
                               CLIP_DEFAULT_PRECIS, DEFAULT_QUALITY,
                               DEFAULT_PITCH | FF_SWISS, "Arial"));
    SetFont(m_pFont);
    return 0;
}
```

8. Add the *OnCommandSize* member function to EX12BVW.CPP. This
single function is called for all size command messages. The *nID* parameter corresponds to the command ID and thus ranges between *IDM_-*
SIZE_BASE and *IDM_SIZE_BASE + 7*. Simple arithmetic converts *nID* to
a reasonable font size, and then a Windows font object is created. This
font must be available when the view's *OnDraw* function paints the text,
so the C++ font object can't be defined on the stack. The class data member *m_pFont* holds a pointer to the heap-based *CFont* object.

The temporary *CFont* object font exists only for housekeeping purposes. As pointed out in Chapter 5, font GDI objects must be deleted
eventually, and they can't be deleted as long as they're selected. If the
SYSTEM_FONT stock object is selected, the prior font is released.

```
BOOL CEx12bView::OnCommandSize(UINT nID)
{
    int    nFontSize;
    CFont font;

    font.CreateStockObject(SYSTEM_FONT);
    SetFont(&font); // deselects any prior special font
    m_pFont->DeleteObject(); // deletes the deselected font

    nFontSize = 12 + (nID - (UINT) IDM_SIZE_BASE) * 2;
    VERIFY(m_pFont->CreateFont(-nFontSize, 0, 0, 0, 400, FALSE, FALSE, 0,
                        ANSI_CHARSET, OUT_DEFAULT_PRECIS,
                        CLIP_DEFAULT_PRECIS, DEFAULT_QUALITY,
                        DEFAULT_PITCH | FF_SWISS, "Arial"));
    SetFont(m_pFont);
    return TRUE;
}
```

9. **Edit other view constructor and destructor in EX12BVW.CPP.** The *CEx12bView* constructor allocates memory for the font object.

```
CEx12bView::CEx12bView()
{
    m_pFont = new CFont;
}
```

Because the *CEditView* class deselects the font, you don't have to. You do have to destroy the font object, however. The destructor takes care of deleting the attached GDI font.

```
CEx12bView::~CEx12bView()
{
    delete m_pFont;
}
```

10. **Build and test the EX12B application.** Test the compiled application by typing in the window and then selecting a font size from the menu. Does the text change size? Are there any unpleasant "undeleted font" messages in the Debug window?

TOOLBARS AND STATUS BARS

All the Visual C++ examples up to this point have included toolbars and status bars. AppWizard generated the code that initialized these application framework elements as long as you accepted the AppWizard default option Initial Toolbar. The default toolbar provides graphics equivalents for many of the standard application framework menu selections, and the default status bar displays menu prompts together with the keyboard state indicators CAP, NUM, and SCRL.

This chapter shows you how to customize the toolbar and status bar for your application. You'll be able to add your own toolbar graphical buttons and control their appearance. You'll also learn how to disable the status bar's normal display of menu prompts and keyboard indicators. This allows your application to take over the status bar for its own use.

Control Bars and the Application Framework

The toolbar is an object of class *CToolBar*, and the status bar is an object of class *CStatusBar*. Both these classes are derived from class *CControlBar*, which is itself derived from *CWnd*. The *CControlBar* class supports control bar windows that are positioned inside frame windows. These control bar windows resize and reposition themselves as the parent frame moves and changes size. The application framework takes care of the construction, window creation, and destruction of the control bar objects. AppWizard generates control bar code for its derived frame class located in the files MAINFRM.CPP and MAINFRM.H.

In a typical SDI application, a *CToolBar* object occupies the top portion of the *CMainFrame* client area, and a *CStatusBar* object occupies the bottom portion. The view occupies the remaining (middle) part of the frame.

Assuming that AppWizard has generated the control bar code for your application, the user can enable and disable the toolbar and the status bar individually by choosing commands in the application's View menu. When a control bar is disabled, it disappears, and the view size is recalculated. Apart from the common behavior just described, toolbar and status bar objects operate independently of each other and have rather different characteristics.

The Toolbar

A toolbar object is a window consisting of a number of horizontally arranged graphical buttons that might be clustered in groups. The programming interface determines the grouping. The graphical images for the buttons are stored in a single bitmap that is attached to the application's resource file. When the buttons are clicked, they send command messages, as do menus and keyboard accelerators. Update command UI message handlers are used to update the buttons' states, which, in turn, are used by the application framework to modify the buttons' graphical images.

The Toolbar Bitmap

Each button in a toolbar appears to have its own bitmap, but actually there is a single bitmap for the entire toolbar. The toolbar bitmap has a tile, 15 pixels high and 16 pixels wide, for each button. The application framework supplies the button borders, and it modifies those borders, together with the button's bitmap tile color, to reflect the current button state. Figure 13-1 shows the relationship between the toolbar bitmap and a typical toolbar. (The last image in each toolbar is for a context-sensitive Help button, which has not been discussed yet.)

The toolbar bitmap is stored in the file TOOLBAR.BMP in the application's RES subdirectory. It's identified in the RC file as *IDR_MAIN-FRAME*. You can use App Studio to edit the toolbar bitmap.

Figure 13-1.
A toolbar bitmap and an actual toolbar.

THIRTEEN: Toolbars and Status Bars

Button States

Each button can assume the following states:

State	Meaning
0	Normal, unpressed state (up)
TBBS_PRESSED	Currently selected (pressed) with the mouse
TBBS_CHECKED	In the checked (down) state
TBBS_DISABLED	Unavailable for use
TBBS_INDETERMINATE	Enabled, but neither up nor down
*TBBS_CHECKED	TBBS_DISABLED*	In the checked state, but unavailable for use

A button can behave in either of two ways. It can be a pushbutton, which is down only when currently selected by the mouse, or it can be a check box button, which can be toggled up and down with mouse clicks. All buttons in the standard application framework toolbar are pushbuttons.

The Toolbar and Command Messages

When the user clicks a toolbar button with the mouse, a command message is generated. This message is routed like the menu command messages you saw in Chapter 12. Most of the time, a toolbar button matches a menu choice. In the standard application framework toolbar, for example, the Disk button is equivalent to the File Save menu choice because both generate the ID_FILE_SAVE message. The object receiving the command message doesn't need to know whether the message was produced by a click in the toolbar or by a choice from the menu.

A toolbar button doesn't have to mirror a menu item. If you don't provide the equivalent menu item, however, you are advised to define a keyboard accelerator for the button so that the user can activate the command with the keyboard or with a Windows keyboard macro product. If your application has toolbar buttons without corresponding menu items, ClassWizard can't define command and update command UI message handlers. You'll have to add the functions, message map entries, and prototypes yourself.

The static *buttons* array, defined in the application's main frame class, associates commands with buttons. On the following page is the code, found in MAINFRM.CPP, that AppWizard normally generates:

```
static UINT BASED_CODE buttons[] =
{
    // same order as in the bitmap 'toolbar.bmp'
    ID_FILE_NEW,
    ID_FILE_OPEN,
    ID_FILE_SAVE,
        ID_SEPARATOR,

    ID_EDIT_CUT,
    ID_EDIT_COPY,
    ID_EDIT_PASTE,
        ID_SEPARATOR,
    ID_FILE_PRINT,
    ID_APP_ABOUT,
    ID_CONTEXT_HELP,
};
```

The *ID_SEPARATOR* constants serve to group the buttons by inserting corresponding spaces in the toolbar. If the number of toolbar bitmap panes exceeds the number of *buttons* array elements (excluding separators), the extra buttons are not displayed.

Toolbar Update Command UI Messages

You remember from Chapter 12 that update command UI message handlers were used to disable or check menu items. These same message handlers apply to toolbar buttons. If your update command UI message handler calls the *CCmdUI::Enable* member function with a *FALSE* parameter, the corresponding button is set to the disabled (grayed) state and no longer responds to mouse clicks.

With menu items, the *CCmdUI::SetCheck* member function displays a check mark next to the menu item. For the toolbar, the *SetCheck* function implements check box buttons. If the update command UI message handler calls *SetCheck* with a parameter value of 1, the button is toggled to the down (checked) state; if the parameter is 0, the button is toggled up (unchecked).

NOTE: If the *SetCheck* parameter value is 2, the button is set to the "indeterminate" state. This state looks like the disabled state, but the button is still active and its color is a bit brighter. Microsoft Word for Windows uses the up, down, and indeterminate states for its boldface toolbar button. If the user has selected some text that contains only boldface characters, the boldface button is down. If no selected characters are boldface, the button is up; but if the selected characters are mixed, the button is indeterminate.

The update command UI message handlers for menu items are called only when the items' drop-down menu is painted. The toolbar is displayed all the time, so when are its update command UI message handlers called? They're called during the application's idle processing, so the buttons can be updated continuously. If the same handler covers a menu item and a toolbar button, it is called both during idle processing and when the drop-down menu is displayed.

NOTE: Even though a toolbar button is disabled, keyboard accelerators can still send the associated command messages. Your command handlers, therefore, must be able to ignore these accelerator keys and other spurious commands. In other words, you can't count on the command UI message handler totally disabling the command.

Locating the Main Frame Window

The toolbar and status bar objects you'll be working with are attached to the application's main frame window, not to the view window. How does your view find its main frame window? In an SDI application, you can use the *CWnd::GetParentFrame* function. Unfortunately, this function won't work in an MDI application because the view's parent frame is the MDI child frame, not the MDI frame window.

If you want your view class to work in both SDI and MDI applications, you must find the main frame window through the application object. The *AfxGetApp* global function returns a pointer to the application object, and you can use that pointer to get the *CWinApp* data member *m_pMainWnd*. In an MDI application, AppWizard generates code that sets *m_pMainWnd*, but in an SDI application, the framework sets *m_pMainWnd* during the view creation process. Once *m_pMainWnd* is set, you can use it in a view class to get the frame's toolbar with a statement such as this:

```
CToolBar* pToolBar = (CToolBar*)
    AfxGetApp()->m_pMainWnd->GetDescendantWindow(AFX_IDW_TOOLBAR);
```

You can use the same logic to locate menu objects, status bar objects, and dialog objects.

NOTE: In an SDI application, the value of *m_pMainWnd* is not set when the view's *OnCreate* message handler is called. If you need to access the main frame window in your *OnCreate* function, you must use the *GetParentFrame* function.

The EX13A Toolbar Example

In this example, you will replace the standard application framework Edit Cut, Copy, and Paste toolbar buttons with three special-purpose buttons that control drawing in the view window. You will also construct a Draw menu with three corresponding menu items as follows:

Menu Item	Function
Circle	Draws a circle in the view window
Square	Draws a square in the view window
Pattern	Toggles a diagonal line fill pattern for new squares and circles

The menu and toolbar choices force the user to alternate between drawing circles and squares. After the user draws a circle, the Circle menu item and toolbar button are disabled; after the user draws a square, the Square menu item and toolbar button are disabled.

In the application's Draw menu, the Pattern menu item gets a check mark when pattern fill is active. In the toolbar, the corresponding button is a check box button that is down when pattern fill is active and up when it is not active.

Figure 13-2 shows the application in action. The user has drawn a circle with pattern fill. Note the states of the three drawing buttons.

Figure 13-2.
The EX13A program in action.

The EX13A example introduces the App Studio bitmap editor. You'll need to do very little C++ coding. Simply follow these steps:

1. **Run AppWizard to generate \VCPP\EX13A\EX13A.** Choose App-Wizard from Visual Workbench's Project menu. The options and the default class names are shown here:

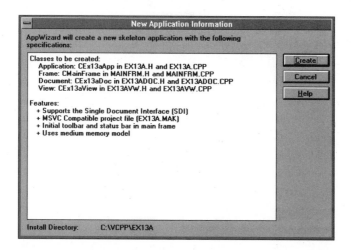

2. **Use App Studio to edit the application's main menu.** Choose App Studio from Visual Workbench's Tools menu. Edit the *IDR_MAINFRAME* menu resource to make a menu that looks like this (which means you'll need to remove the Edit menu):

Use the following command IDs for your new menu items:

Menu	Menu Item	Command ID
Draw	Circle	*ID_DRAW_CIRCLE*
Draw	Square	*ID_DRAW_SQUARE*
Draw	Pattern	*ID_DRAW_PATTERN*

When you're in the Menu Item Properties dialog, add some appropriate prompt strings.

3. **Use App Studio to edit the application's toolbar.** Edit the *IDR_-MAINFRAME* bitmap resource to create a bitmap that looks like this:

You'll be erasing the Edit Cut, Copy, and Paste tiles (fourth, fifth, and sixth from the left) and replacing them with new patterns. Here's a close-up of the three new tiles:

The trick here is to turn on App Studio's tile grid. Choose Grid Settings from the Image menu, and then check the Tile Grid check box and accept the 16-pixel width and 15-pixel height default values. The resulting grid lines separate the individual button images. Remember that you're working with a general-purpose bitmap editor with the tile grid added as a special feature for toolbar buttons.

Use the rectangle and ellipse tools from the bitmap editor's palette. Experiment with different line widths. You can change the magnification by selecting the magnifying glass icon in the Graphics Palette. (To open the Graphics Palette, press F2 or choose Show Graphics Palette from the Window menu.) Save the resource file when you're done.

4. **Edit the MAINFRM.CPP file.** Replace the original *buttons* array with the following:

```
static UINT BASED_CODE buttons[] =
{
    // same order as in the bitmap 'toolbar.bmp'
    ID_FILE_NEW,
    ID_FILE_OPEN,
    ID_FILE_SAVE,
        ID_SEPARATOR,
    ID_DRAW_SQUARE,
    ID_DRAW_CIRCLE,
        ID_SEPARATOR,
    ID_DRAW_PATTERN,
        ID_SEPARATOR,
    ID_FILE_PRINT,
    ID_APP_ABOUT,
};
```

5. **Use ClassWizard to add *CEx13aView* view class message handlers.** Add message handlers for the following command and update command UI messages, and accept the default function names:

Object ID	Message	Member Function Name
ID_DRAW_CIRCLE	COMMAND	*OnDrawCircle*
ID_DRAW_CIRCLE	UPDATE_COMMAND_UI	*OnUpdateDrawCircle*
ID_DRAW_PATTERN	COMMAND	*OnDrawPattern*
ID_DRAW_PATTERN	UPDATE_COMMAND_UI	*OnUpdateDrawPattern*
ID_DRAW_SQUARE	COMMAND	*OnDrawSquare*
ID_DRAW_SQUARE	UPDATE_COMMAND_UI	*OnUpdateDrawSquare*

6. **Edit the EX13AVW.H file.** Add the following data members to the *CEx13aView* class header.

```
private:
    CRect m_rect;
    BOOL  m_bCircle;
    BOOL  m_bPattern;
```

7. Edit the EX13AVW.CPP file. The *CEx13aView* constructor simply initializes the class data members.

```
CEx13aView::CEx13aView() : m_rect(0, 0, 100, 100)
{
    m_bCircle = TRUE;
    m_bPattern = FALSE;
}
```

The *OnDraw* function draws an ellipse or a rectangle, depending on the value of the *m_bCircle* flag. The brush is plain white or a diagonal pattern, depending on the value of *m_bPattern*.

```
void CEx13aView::OnDraw(CDC* pDC)
{
    CBrush brush(HS_BDIAGONAL, 0L); // brush with diagonal pattern

    if (m_bPattern) {
        pDC->SelectObject(&brush);
    }
    else {
        pDC->SelectStockObject(WHITE_BRUSH);
    }
    if (m_bCircle) {
        pDC->Ellipse(m_rect);
    }
    else {
        pDC->Rectangle(m_rect);
    }
    pDC->SelectStockObject(WHITE_BRUSH); // deselects brush if selected
}
```

The *OnDrawCircle* function handles the ON_DRAW_CIRCLE command message, and the *OnDrawSquare* function handles the ON_DRAW_-SQUARE command message. These two functions move the drawing rectangle down and to the right, and then they invalidate the rectangle, causing the *OnDraw* function to redraw it. The effect of this invalidation strategy is a diagonal cascading of alternating squares and circles.

```
void CEx13aView::OnDrawCircle()
{
    m_bCircle = TRUE;
    m_rect += CPoint(25, 25);
    InvalidateRect(m_rect);
}

void CEx13aView::OnDrawSquare()
{
```

246

```
    m_bCircle = FALSE;
    m_rect += CPoint(25, 25);
    InvalidateRect(m_rect);
}
```

The following two update command UI functions alternately enable
and disable the Circle and Square buttons and corresponding menu
items. Only one item can be enabled at a time.

```
void CEx13aView::OnUpdateDrawCircle(CCmdUI* pCmdUI)
{
    pCmdUI->Enable(!m_bCircle);
}


void CEx13aView::OnUpdateDrawSquare(CCmdUI* pCmdUI)
{
    pCmdUI->Enable(m_bCircle);
}
```

The *OnDrawPattern* function toggles the state of the *m_bPattern* flag.
It also accesses the toolbar object to dump a list of the button characteristics.

```
void CEx13aView::OnDrawPattern()
{
    UINT id, style;
    int nCount, i, image;

    m_bPattern = m_bPattern ^ 1;
    // the following code lists the attributes of all toolbar buttons
    // GetParentFrame works in SDI applications only
    CToolBar* pTool = (CToolBar*)
        GetParentFrame()->GetDescendantWindow(AFX_IDW_TOOLBAR);
    TRACE("Toolbar entries:\n");
    nCount = pTool->GetCount();
    for (i = 0; i < nCount; i++) {
        pTool->GetButtonInfo(i, id, style, image);
        TRACE(" index = %d, command ID = %x, button style = %x\n",
        i, id, style);
    }
}
```

The *OnUpdateDrawPattern* function updates the Pattern button and
menu item according to the state of the *m_bPattern* flag. The toolbar
button appears to move in and out, and the menu item check mark
appears and disappears.

```
void CEx13aView::OnUpdateDrawPattern(CCmdUI* pCmdUI)
{
    pCmdUI->SetCheck(m_bPattern);
}
```

8. Build and test the EX13A application. Notice the behavior of the toolbar buttons. Try the corresponding menu items, and notice that they too are enabled, disabled, and checked as the application's state changes.

The Status Bar

The status bar window neither accepts user input nor generates command messages. Its job is simply to display text in panes under program control. The status bar supports two types of text panes—a message line pane and a status indicator pane. To use the status bar for application-specific data, you must first disable the standard status bar that displays the menu prompt and keyboard status.

The Status Bar Definition

The static *indicators* array that AppWizard generates in the MAINFRM.CPP file defines the application's status bar. The constant *ID_SEPARATOR* identifies a message line pane; the other constants are string resource IDs that identify indicator panes. Here is the *indicators* array for the standard framework status bar:

```
static UINT BASED_CODE indicators[] =
{
    ID_SEPARATOR,            // status line indicator
    ID_INDICATOR_CAPS,
    ID_INDICATOR_NUM,
    ID_INDICATOR_SCRL,
};
```

The *CStatusBar::SetIndicators* member function, called in the application's derived frame class, configures the status bar according to the contents of the *indicators* array.

The Message Line

A message line pane displays a string that the program supplies dynamically. To set the value of the message line, you must first get access to the status bar object, and then you must call the *CStatusBar::SetPaneText* member function with a zero-based index parameter. Pane 0 is the leftmost pane, 1 is the next pane to the right, and so forth.

The following code fragment is part of a view class member function. Because the view window is not always a sibling of the status bar window, it's necessary to access the parent frame window through the application object. The *CWnd::GetDescendantWindow* function retrieves a pointer to the status bar that is identified by the constant *ID_MY_STATUS_BAR.*

```
CStatusBar* pStatus = (CStatusBar*)
    AfxGetApp()->m_pMainWnd->GetDescendantWindow(ID_MY_STATUS_BAR);
pStatus->SetPaneText(0, "message line for first pane");
```

Normally, the length of a message line pane is exactly one-fourth the width of the display. If, however, the message line is the first (index 0) pane, it is a stretchy pane without a beveled border. Its minimum length is one-fourth the display width, and it expands if room is available in the status bar.

The Status Indicator

A status indicator pane is linked to a single resource-supplied string that is displayed or hidden by logic in an associated update command UI message handler function. Indicators are identified by a string resource ID, and that same ID is used to route update command UI messages. The Caps Lock indicator is handled in the frame class by the following message map entry and handler function. The *Enable* function turns on the indicator if the Caps Lock mode is set.

```
ON_UPDATE_COMMAND_UI(ID_INDICATOR_CAPS, OnUpdateKeyCapsLock)

void CMainFrame::OnUpdateKeyCapsLock(CCmdUI* pCmdUI)
{
    pCmdUI->Enable(::GetKeyState(VK_CAPITAL) & 1);
}
```

The status bar update command UI functions are called during idle processing so that the status bar is updated continuously.

The length of a status indicator pane is the exact length of the corresponding resource string.

Taking Control of the Status Bar

In the standard application framework implementation, the status bar has the child window ID *AFX_IDW_STATUS_BAR.* The application framework looks for this ID when it wants to display a menu prompt. The update command UI handlers for the keyboard state indicators, embedded in the frame window base class, are linked to three string IDs: *ID_INDICATOR_CAPS*, *ID_INDICATOR_NUM*, and *ID_INDICATOR_SCRL*. To take control of the status bar, you must use a different child window ID, and you must use different indicator ID constants.

The status bar window ID is assigned in the *CStatusBar::Create* function called by the derived frame class *OnCreate* member function. That function is contained in the MAINFRM.CPP file that AppWizard generates. The window ID is the third *Create* parameter, and it defaults to *AFX_IDW_STATUS_BAR*.

To assign your own ID, you must replace this call:

```
m_wndStatusBar.Create(this);
```

with this call:

```
m_wndStatusBar.Create(this, WS_CHILD | WS_VISIBLE | CBRS_BOTTOM,
                      ID_MY_STATUS_BAR);
```

You must also, of course, define the *ID_MY_STATUS_BAR* constant in the RESOURCE.H file (using App Studio).

We forgot one thing. The standard application framework's View menu allows the user to turn the status bar on and off. That logic is pegged to the *AFX_IDW_STATUS_BAR* window ID, so you'll have to change the menu logic too. In your derived frame class, you must write message map entries and handlers for the *ID_VIEW_STATUS_BAR* command and update command UI messages. *ID_VIEW_STATUS_BAR* is the ID of the Status Bar menu item. The derived class handlers override the standard handlers in the *CFrameWnd* base class. See the EX13B example for code details.

The EX13B Status Bar Example

The EX13B example replaces the standard application framework status bar with a new status bar with the following text panes:

Pane Index	String ID	Type	Description
0	*ID_SEPARATOR* (0)	Message line	*x* cursor coordinate
1	*ID_SEPARATOR* (0)	Message line	*y* cursor coordinate
2	*ID_INDICATOR_SHIFT*	Status indicator	Keyboard Shift key status
3	*ID_INDICATOR_CTRL*	Status indicator	Keyboard Ctrl key status
4	*ID_INDICATOR_ALT*	Status indicator	Keyboard Alt key status

The resulting status bar is shown in Figure 13-3.

Figure 13-3.
The status bar of the EX13B example.

The leftmost pane stretches past its normal ¼-screen length as the displayed frame window expands to fill more than ¾-screen width.

Follow these steps to produce the EX13B example:

1. Run AppWizard to generate \VCPP\EX13B\EX13B. Choose App-
Wizard from Visual Workbench's Project menu. The options and the default class names are shown here:

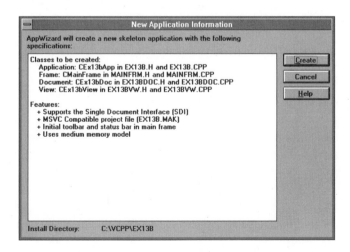

2. Use App Studio to edit the application's string table resource.
Select any string table segment, and then add the following three strings:

String ID	String Caption
ID_INDICATOR_SHIFT	SHIFT
ID_INDICATOR_CTRL	CTRL
ID_INDICATOR_ALT	ALT

This process adds the three IDs to the symbol table stored in the project's RESOURCE.H file.

3. Use App Studio to edit the application's symbols. Click the symbol toolbar button or choose Symbols from the Edit menu. Add the new status bar identifier, *ID_MY_STATUS_BAR*, and accept the default value.

4. Use ClassWizard to add View menu command handlers in class *CMainFrame*. Add the following command message handlers:

Object ID	Message	Member Function Name
ID_VIEW_STATUS_BAR	COMMAND	*OnViewStatusBar*
ID_VIEW_STATUS_BAR	UPDATE_COMMAND_UI	*OnUpdateViewStatusBar*

5. Add the following function prototypes to MAINFRM.H. You must add these *CMainFrame* message handler prototypes manually because Class-Wizard doesn't recognize the associated command message IDs.

```
afx_msg void OnUpdateKeyShift(CCmdUI* pCmdUI);
afx_msg void OnUpdateKeyCtrl(CCmdUI* pCmdUI);
afx_msg void OnUpdateKeyAlt(CCmdUI* pCmdUI);
```

Add the message handler statements inside the *AFX_MSG* brackets so that ClassWizard will let you access and edit the code later.

6. Edit the MAINFRM.CPP file. Replace the original *indicators* array with the following:

```
static UINT BASED_CODE indicators[] =
{
    ID_SEPARATOR,   // first message line pane
    ID_SEPARATOR,   // second message line pane
    ID_INDICATOR_SHIFT,
    ID_INDICATOR_CTRL,
    ID_INDICATOR_ALT,
};
```

Next, edit the *OnCreate* member function as shown here:

```
int CMainFrame::OnCreate(LPCREATESTRUCT lpCreateStruct)
{
    if (CFrameWnd::OnCreate(lpCreateStruct) == -1)
        return -1;

    if (!m_wndToolBar.Create(this) ||
        !m_wndToolBar.LoadBitmap(IDR_MAINFRAME) ||
        !m_wndToolBar.SetButtons(buttons,
          sizeof(buttons)/sizeof(UINT)))
    {
        TRACE("Failed to create toolbar\n");
        return -1;      // fail to create
    }

    if (!m_wndStatusBar.Create(this,
        WS_CHILD | WS_VISIBLE | CBRS_BOTTOM, ID_MY_STATUS_BAR) ||
        !m_wndStatusBar.SetIndicators(indicators,
        sizeof(indicators)/sizeof(UINT)))
    {
        TRACE("Failed to create status bar\n");
        return -1;      // fail to create
    }

    return 0;
}
```

The modified call to *Create* uses our own status bar ID, *ID_MY_-
STATUS_BAR*, instead of *AFX_IDW_STATUS_BAR* (the application
framework's status bar object).

Now add the following message map entries for class *CMainFrame*.
ClassWizard can't add these for you because it doesn't recognize the
string table IDs and the constant *ID_VIEW_STATUS_BAR* as object IDs.

```
ON_UPDATE_COMMAND_UI(ID_INDICATOR_SHIFT, OnUpdateKeyShift)
ON_UPDATE_COMMAND_UI(ID_INDICATOR_CTRL, OnUpdateKeyCtrl)
ON_UPDATE_COMMAND_UI(ID_INDICATOR_ALT, OnUpdateKeyAlt)
```

Next, add the following *CMainFrame* member functions that update
the three status indicators:

```
void CMainFrame::OnUpdateKeyShift(CCmdUI* pCmdUI)
{
    pCmdUI->Enable(::GetKeyState(VK_SHIFT) < 0);
}

void CMainFrame::OnUpdateKeyCtrl(CCmdUI* pCmdUI)
{
```

(continued)

```
    pCmdUI->Enable(::GetKeyState(VK_CONTROL) < 0);
}


void CMainFrame::OnUpdateKeyAlt(CCmdUI* pCmdUI)
{
    pCmdUI->Enable(::GetKeyState(VK_MENU) < 0);
}
```

Finally, edit the following View menu functions that ClassWizard originally generated in MAINFRM.CPP:

```
void CMainFrame::OnViewStatusBar()
{
    CWnd* pBar;

    if (pBar = GetDescendantWindow(ID_MY_STATUS_BAR)) {
        // toggle visible state
        pBar->ShowWindow((pBar->GetStyle() & WS_VISIBLE) == 0);
        RecalcLayout();
    }
}
```

```
void CMainFrame::OnUpdateViewStatusBar(CCmdUI* pCmdUI)
{
    CWnd* pBar;

    if (pBar = GetDescendantWindow(ID_MY_STATUS_BAR)) {
        pCmdUI->SetCheck((pBar->GetStyle() & WS_VISIBLE) != 0);
    }
}
```

These functions ensure that the View menu Status Bar command is properly linked to the new status bar.

7. **Use ClassWizard to add a *CEx13bView* class message handler for WM_MOUSEMOVE.** The mouse move message handler updates the status bar with the current mouse cursor position.

8. **Edit the *OnDraw* function in EX13BVW.CPP.** The *OnDraw* function displays a message in the view window.

```
void CEx13bView::OnDraw(CDC* pDC)
{
    pDC->TextOut(0, 0, "Watch the status bar while you move the mouse.");
}
```

9. **Edit the *OnMouseMove* function in EX13BVW.CPP.** This function gets a pointer to the status bar object and then calls the *SetPaneText* function to update the first and second message line panes.

```
void CEx13bView::OnMouseMove(UINT nFlags, CPoint point)
{
    char text[100];

    CStatusBar* pStatus = (CStatusBar*)
        AfxGetApp()->m_pMainWnd->GetDescendantWindow(ID_MY_STATUS_BAR);
    if (pStatus) {
        wsprintf(text, "x = %d", point.x);
        pStatus->SetPaneText(0, text); // first pane
        wsprintf(text, "y = %d", point.y);
        pStatus->SetPaneText(1, text); // second pane
    }
}
```

10. **Build and test the EX13B application.** Move the mouse, and observe that the left two status bar panes accurately reflect the mouse cursor's position. Also, press Shift and Ctrl. Do the status bar indicators operate correctly? Does Alt toggle the ALT status indicator? Remember that, in Windows, Alt doesn't work like Ctrl and Shift. You don't have to hold Alt down to Alt-Shift another key. Can you toggle the status bar on and off from the View menu?

> NOTE: If you want the first (*0*th) status bar pane to have a beveled border like the other panes, include the following line in the *CMainFrame::OnCreate* function, after the call to the status bar *Create* function:
>
> ```
> m_wndStatusBar.SetPaneInfo(0, 0, SBPS_STRETCH, 0);
> ```

n("del_info"):
l_lock(info cnt, &info_pkt, CURR_DB) ==
wait until locks are available */
nect and delete abstract */

CHAPTER FOURTEEN

A REUSABLE BASE CLASS

A promise of C++ is its ability to produce "software Lego blocks" that can be taken "off the shelf" and fitted easily into an application. The Microsoft Foundation Class (MFC) Library version 2.5 classes are a good example of reusable software. This chapter shows you how to build your own reusable base class that builds on what the MFC library already provides.

In the process of building the reusable class, you'll learn a few more things about Windows and the MFC library. In particular, you'll see how the application framework allows access to the Windows "initialization" (INI) file, you'll learn more about the mechanics of the *CFrameWnd* class, and you'll get more exposure to static class variables and the *CString* class.

Why Reusable Base Classes Are Difficult to Write

In a normal application, you write software components that solve particular problems. It's usually a simple matter of meeting the project specification. With reusable base classes, however, you must anticipate future programming needs, both your own and those of others. You have to write a class that's general and complete yet efficient and easy to use.

This chapter's example showed me the difficulty in building reusable software. I started out with the intention of writing a frame class that would "remember" its window size and position. When I got into the job, I discovered that existing Windows-based programs such as Notepad remember whether they have been iconized or whether they have been maximized to full screen. Then there was the oddball case of a window that was both iconized and maximized. After that, I had to worry about the toolbar and the status bar, plus the class had to work in a dynamic link library (DLL). In short, it was surprisingly difficult to write a frame class that would do everything that a programmer might expect.

257

In a production programming environment, reusable base classes might fall out of the normal software development cycle. A class written for one project might be extracted and further generalized for another project. There's always the temptation, though, to cut and paste existing classes without asking, "What can I factor out into a base class?" If you're in the software business for the long term, it's really beneficial to start building your library of truly reusable components.

The *CPersistentFrame* Class

In this chapter, you'll be making a class called *CPersistentFrame* that is derived from the *CFrameWnd* class. This *CPersistentFrame* class supports a persistent SDI (Single Document Interface) frame window that remembers the following characteristics:

- Window size
- Window position
- Maximized status
- Iconized status
- Toolbar enablement
- Status bar enablement

When you terminate an application that's built with the *CPersistentFrame* class, the above information is saved on disk in the application's private INI file. When the application starts again, it reads the INI file and restores the frame to its state at the previous exit.

You can use the persistent view class in any SDI application, including the examples in this book. All you have to do is substitute *CPersistentFrame* for *CFrameWnd* in your application's derived frame class files.

The *CFrameWnd* Class and the *ActivateFrame* Member Function

Why choose *CFrameWnd* as the base class for a persistent window? Why not have a persistent view instead? In an MFC library SDI application, the main frame window is always the parent of the view window. This frame window is created first, and then the control bars and the view are created as child windows. The application framework ensures that the child windows shrink and expand appropriately as the user changes the size of the frame window. It wouldn't make sense to change the view size after the frame was created.

The key to controlling the frame's size is the *CFrameWnd::ActivateFrame* member function. The application framework calls this virtual function during the SDI main frame creation process (and in response to the File New and File Open menu items). Its job is to call the *CWnd::ShowWindow* function with the parameter *nCmdShow*. *ShowWindow* makes the frame window visible, along with its menu, view window, and control bars. The *nCmdShow* parameter determines whether the window is maximized or iconized or both.

If you override *ActivateFrame* in your derived frame class, you can change the value of *nCmdShow* before passing it to the *CFrameWnd::Activate-Frame* function. Also, you can call the *CWnd::SetWindowPlacement* function that sets the size and position of the frame window, and you can set the visible status of the control bars. Because all changes are made before the frame window becomes visible, there is no annoying flash on the screen.

You must be careful not to reset the frame window's position and size after every File New or File Open command. A first-time flag data member ensures that your *CPersistentFrame::ActivateFrame* function operates only when the application starts.

The Windows INI File

If you've used Windows-based applications before, you've probably seen INI files. The WIN.INI and SYSTEM.INI files, located in the WINDOWS directory, hold important profile information. Older Windows-based applications stored their private profile data in WIN.INI, but current applications store their own INI files in the WINDOWS directory. An application generally reads its INI file on startup and writes it back on exit.

The MFC library application framework uses an INI file to store a list of most recently used files. The INI file is usually named after the application. The Windows Clock program's INI file is called CLOCK.INI, for example. In an MFC library program, the INI file is managed by member functions in the *CWinApp* application class. These functions are available for your use. Before you study the functions, however, you should know something about the structure of the INI file.

A Windows INI file is divided into sections, each identified by a heading name in square brackets. Each section consists of a series of entry names with associated string or numeric values. Both heading names and entry names are case-independent. At the top of the following page is a listing of a hypothetical INI file:

```
[Text formatting]
Font=Helvetica Narrow
Points=12
Tabs=5
[Numeric formatting]
MaxDigits=16.2
Radix=10
```

Heading names are "Text formatting" and "Numeric formatting," and entry names are "Font," "Points," "Tabs," "MaxDigits," and "Radix."

By default, the application framework reads and writes the INI file for you. The MFC library provides four *CWinApp* member functions for accessing INI file entries:

- *GetProfileInt*
- *WriteProfileInt*
- *GetProfileString*
- *WriteProfileString*

These functions treat INI file entries as either *CString* objects or unsigned integers. If you need floating-point values as entries, you must use the string functions and do the conversion yourself. All the functions take a heading name and an entry name as parameters. Now the INI file is starting to look like a mini hierarchical database.

To use the INI file entry access functions, you need a pointer to the application object. The global function *AfxGetApp* does the job. With the previous sample INI file, you can change the Font and Points entries with the following code:

```
AfxGetApp()->WriteProfileString("Text formatting", "Font",
                                "Times Roman");
AfxGetApp()->WriteProfileInt("Text formatting", "Points", 10);
```

For Windows SDK Programmers

Windows provides three functions for INI file entries: *WritePrivate-ProfileString*, *GetPrivateProfileString*, and *GetPrivateProfileInt*. Each of these requires the INI filename as a parameter. For strings, the parameters are long pointers to conventional zero-terminated character arrays. The MFC library INI file entry access functions wrap these Windows functions and thus eliminate the need to assemble the INI filename.

Using the *CString* Class

The MFC library *CString* class is a significant de facto extension to the C++ language. As the *Class Library Reference* points out, the *CString* class has many useful operators and member functions, but perhaps its most important feature is its dynamic memory allocation. You never have to worry about the size of a *CString* object. The following statements represent typical uses of *CString* objects:

```
CString firstName("Elvis");
CString lastName("Presley");
CString truth = firstName + " " + lastName; // concatenation
truth += " is alive";
ASSERT(truth == "Elvis Presley is alive");
ASSERT(truth.Left(5) == firstName);
ASSERT(truth[2] == 'v'); // subscript operator
```

In a perfect world, C++ programs would always use all *CString* objects and never use ordinary zero-terminated character arrays. Unfortunately, many runtime library functions still use character arrays, so programs must always mix and match their string representations. Fortunately, the *CString* class provides a *const char* ()* operator that converts a *CString* object to a character pointer. Many of the MFC library functions have *const char* parameters. Take the global *AfxMessageBox* function, for example. Here is one of its prototypes:

```
int AFXAPI AfxMessageBox(LPCSTR lpszText, UINT nType = MB_OK,
                         UINT nIDHelp = 0);
```

(Note: LPCSTR is not a pointer to a *CString* object but rather is a replacement for *const char FAR*.*)

You can call *AfxMessageBox* this way:

```
char szMessageText[] = "Unknown error";
AfxMessageBox(szMessageText);
```

Or you can call it this way:

```
CString messageText("Unknown error");
AfxMessageBox(messageText);
```

Now, suppose you want to use the *wsprintf* function to generate a formatted string. You can easily use a character array such as this:

```
int nError = 23;
char szMessageText[50];
wsprintf(szMessageText, "Error number %d", nError);
AfxMessageBox(szMessageText);
```

It would be inappropriate to use a *CString* object here because it would be awkward to convert the output from *wsprintf* to a *CString* object. What if you really want a *CString*? How do you use *wsprintf* to format to a *CString* object? You can't use a *CString* object as the first parameter because the compiler expects a *char**, not the *const char** that the *CString* class provides.

To use a *CString* object as a function <u>output</u> parameter, you must use the *CString GetBuffer* and *ReleaseBuffer* functions. The *GetBuffer* function locks down a *CString* object and fixes its size. The *ReleaseBuffer* function makes the *CString* object dynamic again. Here is some code that allows *wsprintf* to send its output to a *CString* object.

```
CString fontFamily("Helvetica");
CString fontModifier("Narrow");
CString font;
wsprintf(font.GetBuffer(20), "%s %s", (LPCSTR) fontFamily,
        (LPCSTR) fontModifier);
font.ReleaseBuffer();
ASSERT(font.MakeUpper() == "HELVETICA NARROW");
```

The *GetBuffer* parameter value of *20* was chosen because the font string is not expected to exceed 20 characters (not counting the null terminator). The *ReleaseBuffer* call is not absolutely necessary here because we're not calling any *CString* member functions that would change the length of the *font* object.

Differences Between *sprintf* and *wsprintf*

Both *sprintf* and *wsprintf* work with Windows, and both require *CString* input parameters to be cast to character pointers. Some differences exist between the two functions, however. The *wsprintf* function does not support floating-point formatting and thus does not require linking of the floating-point library functions. The *sprintf* function, on the other hand, is less fussy about the casting of character pointer input parameters; you can, for example, write

```
char text[50];
CString string("test");
sprintf(text, "%s\n", (const char*) string);
```

But with *wsprintf* you need a stricter cast with a medium model:

```
wsprintf(text, "%s\n", (LPCSTR) string);
```

The *const char** operator takes care of converting a *CString* to a constant character pointer (except for special functions such as *sprintf*), but what about conversion in the other direction? It so happens that the *CString* class has a constructor that converts a constant character pointer to a *CString* object, and it has a set of overloaded operators for these pointers. That's why statements such as this work:

```
truth += " is alive";
```

The special constructor works with functions that take a *CString* reference parameter, such as *CDC::TextOut*. In the following statement, a *CString* object is created on the calling program's stack and then its address is passed to *TextOut*.

```
pDC->TextOut(0, 0, "Hello world");
```

The Position of a Maximized Window

As a Windows user, you know that you can maximize a window from the system menu or by clicking a button at the top right corner of the window. You can return a maximized window to its original size in a similar fashion. It's obvious that a maximized window remembers its original size and position.

The *CWnd* function *GetWindowRect* retrieves the screen coordinates of a window. If a window is maximized, *GetWindowRect* returns the coordinates of the screen rather than the window's unmaximized coordinates. If a persistent frame class is to work for maximized windows, it has to know the window's unmaximized coordinates. The *CWnd::GetWindowPlacement* function retrieves the window's unmaximized coordinates together with some flags that indicate whether the window is currently iconized or maximized or both.

Static Data Members

If your application uses constants that are associated with a particular class, it makes sense to declare these constants as static data members. This strategy avoids name conflicts, and it makes your programs more modular. Appendix A shows you how to declare and define static data members, but it avoids the issue of memory models. The static data members in the MFC library are all declared NEAR. In the small and medium models, this designation has no effect, but in the large and compact models, the statics are placed in the DGROUP segment for efficiency and to facilitate multi-instance applications.

You should follow this convention in your own classes unless you know that you have a full DGROUP.

> NOTE: Chapter 26 will discuss the implications of using static data members in a DLL. For now, avoid using initialized *CString* static data members in any class that you might place in an extension DLL.

The Default Window Rectangle

You're used to defining rectangles with device or logical coordinates. A *CRect* object constructed with the statement

```
CRect rect(CW_USEDEFAULT, CW_USEDEFAULT, 0, 0);
```

has a special meaning. When Windows creates a new window with this special rectangle, it positions the window in a cascade pattern with the top left corner below and to the right of the window most recently created. The right and bottom edges of the window are always within the display's boundaries.

The *CFrameWnd* static *rectDefault* data member contains the special rectangle in the previous example. The *CPersistentFrame* class declares its own *rectDefault* default window rectangle with a fixed size and position as a static data member, thus hiding the base class member.

The EX14A Example

The EX14A program illustrates the use of a persistent frame window class, *CPersistentFrame*. Figure 14-1 shows the contents of the files PERSIST.H and PERSIST.CPP, which are included in the EX14A project. In the example, you'll insert the new frame class into an AppWizard-generated SDI application. EX14A is a "do-nothing" application, but you can easily insert the persistent frame class into any of your own SDI "do-something" applications.

PERSIST.H

```
class CPersistentFrame : public CFrameWnd
{ // remembers where it was on the desktop
    DECLARE_DYNAMIC(CPersistentFrame)
private:
    static const CRect NEAR rectDefault;
```

Figure 14-1. *(continued)*
The CPersistentView *class listing.*

Figure 14-1. *continued*

```
    CString m_profileHeading, m_profileRect, m_profileIcon;
    CString m_profileMax, m_profileTool, m_profileStatus;
    BOOL    m_bFirstTime;
protected: // create from serialization only
    CPersistentFrame();
    ~CPersistentFrame();
    virtual void ActivateFrame(int nCmdShow = -1);
    //{{AFX_MSG(CPersistentFrame)
    afx_msg void OnDestroy();
    //}}AFX_MSG
    DECLARE_MESSAGE_MAP()
};
```

PERSIST.CPP

```
#include "stdafx.h"
#include "persist.h"

#ifdef _DEBUG
#undef THIS_FILE
static char BASED_CODE THIS_FILE[] = __FILE__;
#endif
/////////////////////////////////////////////////////////////////////
// CPersistentFrame

const CRect NEAR CPersistentFrame::rectDefault(10, 10, 500, 400);
// static

IMPLEMENT_DYNAMIC(CPersistentFrame, CFrameWnd)

BEGIN_MESSAGE_MAP(CPersistentFrame, CFrameWnd)
    //{{AFX_MSG_MAP(CPersistentFrame)
    ON_WM_DESTROY()
    //}}AFX_MSG_MAP
END_MESSAGE_MAP()


/////////////////////////////////////////////////////////////////////
CPersistentFrame::CPersistentFrame() :
    m_profileHeading("Window size"), m_profileRect("Rect"),
    m_profileIcon("icon"), m_profileMax("max"),
    m_profileTool("tool"), m_profileStatus("status")
{
    m_bFirstTime = TRUE;

}
```

(continued)

Figure 14-1. *continued*

```
///////////////////////////////////////////////////////////////
CPersistentFrame::~CPersistentFrame()
{
}


///////////////////////////////////////////////////////////////
void CPersistentFrame::OnDestroy()
{
    CString text, temp;
    CWnd*  pBar;
    BOOL   bIconic, bMaximized;

    WINDOWPLACEMENT wndpl;
    wndpl.length = sizeof(WINDOWPLACEMENT);
    // gets current window position and iconized/maximized status
    BOOL bRet = GetWindowPlacement(&wndpl);
    if (wndpl.showCmd == SW_SHOWNORMAL) {
      bIconic = FALSE;
      bMaximized = FALSE;
    }
    else if (wndpl.showCmd == SW_SHOWMAXIMIZED) {
      bIconic = FALSE;
      bMaximized = TRUE;
    }
    else if (wndpl.showCmd == SW_SHOWMINIMIZED) {
      bIconic = TRUE;
      if (wndpl.flags) {
        bMaximized = TRUE;
      }
      else {
        bMaximized = FALSE;
      }
    }
    wsprintf(text.GetBuffer(20), "%04d %04d %04d %04d",
        wndpl.rcNormalPosition.left, wndpl.rcNormalPosition.top,
        wndpl.rcNormalPosition.right, wndpl.rcNormalPosition.bottom);

    text.ReleaseBuffer();
    AfxGetApp()->WriteProfileString(m_profileHeading,
                                    m_profileRect, text);
    AfxGetApp()->WriteProfileInt(m_profileHeading,
                                 m_profileIcon, bIconic);
    AfxGetApp()->WriteProfileInt(m_profileHeading,
                                 m_profileMax, bMaximized);
```

(continued)

Figure 14-1. *continued*

```
    if (pBar = GetDescendantWindow(AFX_IDW_TOOLBAR)) {
        AfxGetApp()->WriteProfileInt(m_profileHeading, m_profileTool,
            (pBar->GetStyle() & WS_VISIBLE) != 0L);
    }
    if (pBar = GetDescendantWindow(AFX_IDW_STATUS_BAR)) {
        AfxGetApp()->WriteProfileInt(m_profileHeading,
            m_profileStatus, (pBar->GetStyle() & WS_VISIBLE) != 0L);
    }
    CFrameWnd::OnDestroy();
}

//////////////////////////////////////////////////////////////////////
void CPersistentFrame::ActivateFrame(int nCmdShow)
{
    CWnd*           pBar;
    CString         text;
    BOOL            bIconic, bMaximized, bTool, bStatus;
    UINT            flags;
    WINDOWPLACEMENT wndpl;
    CRect           rect;

    if (m_bFirstTime) {
      m_bFirstTime = FALSE;
      text = AfxGetApp()->GetProfileString(m_profileHeading,
                                           m_profileRect);
      if (!text.IsEmpty()) {
        // can't use sscanf in a DLL
        rect.left = atoi((const char*) text);
        rect.top = atoi((const char*) text + 5);
        rect.right = atoi((const char*) text + 10);
        rect.bottom = atoi((const char*) text + 15);
      }
      else {
        rect = rectDefault;
      }

      bIconic = AfxGetApp()->GetProfileInt(m_profileHeading,
                                           m_profileIcon, 0);
      bMaximized = AfxGetApp()->GetProfileInt(m_profileHeading,
                                              m_profileMax, 0);

      if (bIconic) {
        nCmdShow = SW_SHOWMINNOACTIVE;
        if (bMaximized) {
```

(continued)

267

Figure 14-1. *continued*

```
        flags = WPF_RESTORETOMAXIMIZED;
    }
}
else {
  if (bMaximized) {
    nCmdShow = SW_SHOWMAXIMIZED;
    flags = WPF_RESTORETOMAXIMIZED;
  }
  else {
    nCmdShow = SW_NORMAL;
    flags = 0;
  }
}
wndpl.length = sizeof(WINDOWPLACEMENT);
wndpl.showCmd = nCmdShow;
wndpl.flags = flags;
wndpl.ptMinPosition = CPoint(0, 0);
wndpl.ptMaxPosition = CPoint(-::GetSystemMetrics(SM_CXBORDER),
                             -::GetSystemMetrics(SM_CYBORDER));
wndpl.rcNormalPosition = rect;

bTool = AfxGetApp()->GetProfileInt(m_profileHeading,
                                   m_profileTool, 1);
if (pBar = GetDescendantWindow(AFX_IDW_TOOLBAR)) {
    pBar->ShowWindow(bTool);
}
bStatus = AfxGetApp()->GetProfileInt(m_profileHeading,
                                     m_profileStatus, 1);
if (pBar = GetDescendantWindow(AFX_IDW_STATUS_BAR)) {
    pBar->ShowWindow(bStatus);
}
// sets window's position and iconized/maximized status
BOOL bRet = SetWindowPlacement(&wndpl);
}
CFrameWnd::ActivateFrame(nCmdShow);
}
```

Here are the steps for building the EX14A example program:

1. Run AppWizard to generate \VCPP\EX14A\EX14A. Choose App-Wizard from Visual Workbench's Project menu. The options and the default class names are shown in the screen at the top of the facing page:

2. Modify MAINFRM.H. You must change the base class of *CMainFrame*. To do this, simply change the line

```
class CMainFrame : public CFrameWnd
```

to

```
class CMainFrame : public CPersistentFrame
```

3. Modify MAINFRM.CPP. Globally replace all occurrences of *CFrameWnd* with *CPersistentFrame*. Also, add the line

```
#include "persist.h"
```

immediately <u>before</u> the line

```
#include "mainfrm.h"
```

4. Modify EX14A.CPP. Add the line

```
#include "persist.h"
```

immediately <u>before</u> the line

```
#include "mainfrm.h"
```

> NOTE: As an alternative to modifying EX14A.CPP, you can insert
>
> ```
> #include "persist.h"
> ```
>
> at the top of the MAINFRM.H file. If you do this, you won't need to add the *#include* statements in MAIN-FRM.CPP and EX14A.CPP.

269

5. **Add the file PERSIST.CPP to the project.** Use Visual Workbench's Project Edit dialog to add the file PERSIST.CPP.

6. **Use ClassWizard to import the new *CPersistentFrame* class.** Choose ClassWizard from Visual Workbench's Browse menu, and then add the class *CPersistentFrame* with the base class *CFrameWnd*. Fill in the Import Class dialog as shown here:

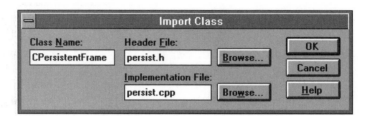

Be sure that the class header file is PERSIST.H and that the implementation file is PERSIST.CPP.

7. **Build and test the EX14A application.** Size and move the application's frame window, and then close the application. When you restart the application, does its window open at the same location where it was closed? Experiment with maximizing and iconizing, and then change the status of the control bars. Does the persistent frame remember its settings? Examine the file EX14A.INI in the WINDOWS directory. Does it look similar to this?

```
[Window size]
rect=0480 0005 0598 0378
icon=0
max=0
tool=1
status=1
```

Persistent Frames in MDI Applications

You won't get to MDI applications until Chapter 17, but if you're using this book as a reference, you might want to apply the persistent frame technique to MDI applications.

The *CPersistentFrame* class, as presented in this chapter, won't work in an MDI application because the MDI main frame window's *ShowWindow* function is called, not by a virtual *ActivateFrame* function, but by the application class's *InitInstance* member function. If you need to control the characteristics of an MDI main frame window, add the necessary code to *InitInstance*.

The *ActivateFrame* function is called, however, for *CMDIChildWnd* objects. This means your MDI application could remember the sizes and positions of its child windows. You could store the information in the INI file, but you would have to accommodate multiple windows. You would have to modify the *CPersistentFrame* class for this purpose.

C H A P T E R   F I F T E E N

SEPARATING THE DOCUMENT FROM ITS VIEW

Now you're finally going to see the interaction between documents and views. Chapter 12 gave you a preview of this interaction when it showed the routing of command messages to both view objects and document objects. In this chapter, you'll see how the document maintains the application's data and how the view presents the data to the user. You'll also learn how the document and view objects talk to each other while the application executes.

The two examples in this chapter both use the *CFormView* class as the base class for their views. The first example is as simple as possible, with the document holding only one simple object of class *CStudent*, which represents a single student record. The view shows the student's name and grade and allows editing. With the *CStudent* class, you'll get some practice writing classes to represent real-world entities. You'll also get to use the Microsoft Foundation Class (MFC) Library version 2.5 diagnostic dump functions.

The second example goes further by introducing collection classes, the *CObList* class in particular. Now the document holds a collection of student records, and the view allows the sequencing, insertion, and deletion of individual records. The frame class gets involved too because it contains the toolbar that generates command messages for the view.

Document–View Interaction Functions

You already know that the document object holds the data and that the view object displays the data and allows editing. An SDI application has a document class derived from *CDocument*, and it has one or more view classes, each ultimately derived from *CView*. A complex handshaking process takes place among the document, the view, and the rest of the application framework. To understand this process, you need to know about four important member functions in the document and view classes. Two are virtual functions that you often override in your derived classes; two are nonvirtual base class functions that you call in your derived classes. Let's look at these functions one at a time.

The *CView::GetDocument* Function

A view object has only one associated document object. The *GetDocument* function allows an application to navigate from a view to its document. Suppose a view object gets a message that the user has entered new data into an edit control. The view must tell the document object to update its internal data accordingly. The *GetDocument* function provides the document pointer that can be used to access document class member functions or public data members.

The *CDocument::GetNextView* function navigates from the document to the view, but because a document can have more than one view, it's necessary to call this member function once for each view, inside a loop. The *GetDocument* function is used more frequently than *GetNextView*.

When AppWizard generates a derived *CView* class, it creates a special "type-safe" version of the *GetDocument* function that returns not a *CDocument* pointer but a pointer to your derived class. This function is an inline function and looks something like this:

```
CMyDoc* GetDocument()
{
    return (CMyDoc*) m_pDocument;
}
```

When the compiler sees a call to *GetDocument* in your view class code, it uses the derived class version instead of the *CDocument* version, so you do not have to cast the returned pointer to your derived document class. Because the *CView::GetDocument* function is <u>not</u> a virtual function, a statement such as

```
pView->GetDocument(); // pView is declared CView*
```

calls the base class *GetDocument* function and thus returns a pointer to a *CDocument* object.

The *CDocument::UpdateAllViews* Function

If the document data changes for any reason, all views must be notified so that they can update their representations of that data. If *UpdateAllViews* is called from a member function of a derived document class, its first parameter, *pSender*, is *NULL*. If *UpdateAllViews* is called from a member function of a derived view class, set the *pSender* parameter to the current view like this:

```
GetDocument()->UpdateAllViews(this);
```

The non-null parameter prevents the application framework from notifying the current view. The assumption is that the current view has already updated itself.

The function has optional "hint" parameters that can be used to give the view specific and application-dependent information about which parts of the view to update. This is an advanced use of the function.

How exactly does a view get notified when *UpdateAllViews* gets called? Take a look at the next function, *OnUpdate*.

The *CView::OnUpdate* Function

This is a virtual function that the application framework calls in response to your application's call to the *CDocument::UpdateAllViews* function. You can, of course, call it directly within your derived *CView* class. Typically, your derived view class's *OnUpdate* function accesses the document, gets the document's data, and then updates the view's data members or controls to reflect the changes. Alternatively, *OnUpdate* can invalidate a portion of the view, causing the view's *OnDraw* function to use document data to draw in the window. The *OnUpdate* function might look something like this:

```
void CMyView::OnUpdate(CView* pSender, LPARAM lHint, CObject* pHint)
{
    CMyDocument* pMyDoc = GetDocument();
    CString lastName = pMyDoc->GetLastName();
    m_pNameStatic->SetWindowText(lastName); // m_pNameStatic is
                                            //  a CMyView data member
}
```

The hint information is passed through directly from the call to *UpdateAllViews*. The default *OnUpdate* implementation invalidates the entire window rectangle. In your overridden version, you can choose to define a smaller invalid rectangle as specified by the hint information.

If the *CDocument* function *UpdateAllViews* is called with the *pSender* parameter pointing to a specific view object, *OnUpdate* is called for all the document's views <u>except</u> the specified view.

The *CView::OnInitialUpdate* Function

This virtual *CView* function is called when the application starts, when the user chooses New from the File menu, and when the user chooses Open from the File menu. The *CView* base class version of *OnInitialUpdate* does nothing but call *OnUpdate*. If you override *OnInitialUpdate* in your derived view class, be sure it calls the base class's *OnInitialUpdate* function or the derived class's *OnUpdate* function.

275

You can use your derived class's *OnInitialUpdate* function to initialize your view object. When the application starts, the application framework calls *OnInitialUpdate* immediately after *OnCreate* (if you've mapped *OnCreate* in your view class). *OnCreate* is called only once, but *OnInitialUpdate* can be called many times.

The Simplest Document–View Application

Suppose that you don't need multiple views of your document but you plan to take advantage of the application framework's file support. In this case, you can forget about the *UpdateAllViews* and *OnUpdate* functions. Simply follow these steps when you develop the application:

1. In your derived document class header file (generated by AppWizard), declare your document's data members. These data members are the primary data storage for your application. You can make these data members public, or you can declare the derived view class a <u>friend</u> of the document class.

2. In your derived view class, override the *OnInitialUpdate* virtual member function. The application framework calls this function when the document data has been initialized or read from disk. (Chapter 16 discusses disk file I/O.) *OnInitialUpdate* should update the view to reflect the current document data.

3. In your derived view class, let your window message and command message handlers update the document data members directly, using *GetDocument* to access the document object.

Here is the sequence of events for this simplified document–view environment:

Application starts	*CMyDocument* object constructed
	CMyView object constructed
	View window created
	CMyView::OnCreate called (if mapped)
	CMyView::OnInitialUpdate called
	View object initialized
	View window invalidated
User edits data	*CMyView* functions update *CMyDocument* data members
User exits application	*CMyView* object destroyed
	CMyDocument object destroyed

The *CFormView* Class

The *CFormView* class is a useful view class that has many of the characteristics of a modeless dialog window. Like a class derived from *CDialog*, a derived *CFormView* class is associated with a dialog resource that defines the frame characteristics and enumerates the controls. The *CFormView* class supports the same dialog data exchange and validation (DDX and DDV) functions that you saw in the *CDialog* examples in Chapter 7.

> WARNING: If you use App Studio to make a dialog for a form view, you <u>must</u> specify the following items in the Dialog Properties dialog:
>
> Style = Child
> Border = None
> Visible = unchecked

A *CFormView* object receives notification messages directly from its controls, and it receives command messages from the application framework. This application framework command-processing ability clearly separates *CFormView* from *CDialog*, and it makes controlling the view from the frame's main menu or toolbar easy.

The *CFormView* class is derived from *CView* (actually, from *CScrollView*) and not from *CDialog*. You can't, therefore, assume that *CDialog* member functions are supported. *CFormView* does <u>not</u> have virtual *OnInitDialog*, *OnOK*, and *OnCancel* functions. *CFormView* does not call *UpdateData* and the DDX functions. You have to call these functions yourself at the appropriate times, usually in response to control notification messages or command messages.

Even though the *CFormView* class is not derived from the *CDialog* class, it is built around the Windows dialog. For this reason, you can use many of the *CDialog* class member functions such as *GotoDlgCtrl* and *NextDlgCtrl*. All you have to do is cast your *CFormView* pointer to a *CDialog* pointer. The following statement, extracted from a member function of a class derived from *CFormView*, sets the focus to a specified control. *GetDlgItem* is a *CWnd* function and is thus inherited by the derived *CFormView* class.

```
((CDialog*) this)->GotoDlgCtrl(GetDlgItem(IDC_NAME));
```

AppWizard, through its Classes dialog, gives you the option of using *CFormView* as the base class for your view. When you select *CFormView*, AppWizard generates an empty dialog with the correct style properties set. The next step is to use ClassWizard to add control notification message handlers, command message handlers, and update command UI handlers. (The example steps beginning on page 284 show you what to do.) You can also define data members and validation criteria.

NOTE: If you want ClassWizard to add menu command message handlers to a *CFormView* derived class, you must run ClassWizard from inside App Studio after selecting the appropriate menu.

The *CObject* Class

If you study the MFC library hierarchy, you'll notice that the *CObject* class is at the top. All other classes, except *CString* and trivial classes such as *CRect* and *CPoint*, are derived from the *CObject* "root" class. When a class is derived from *CObject*, it inherits a number of important characteristics. The many benefits of *CObject* derivation will become clear as you read the chapters that follow.

In this chapter, you'll see how *CObject* derivation allows objects to participate in the diagnostic dumping scheme and to be elements in the collection classes.

Diagnostic Dumping

The MFC library gives you some useful tools for diagnostic dumping. You enable these tools when you use the Debug project build option. When you use the Release build option, diagnostic dumping is disabled, and the diagnostic code is not linked to your program.

The *TRACE* Macro

You've seen the *TRACE* macro used throughout the preceding examples in this book. *TRACE* statements are active whenever the constant *_DEBUG* is defined (when you use the Debug project build option and when the *afxTraceEnabled* variable is set to *TRUE*). *TRACE* statements work like C language *printf* statements, but they're completely disabled in the release version of the program. The output from *TRACE* statements goes to the AUX output device, the debugger's output window, or, more commonly, to the Debug Window (DBWIN.EXE). Here's a typical *TRACE* statement:

```
int nCount = 9;
CString desc("total");
TRACE("Count = %d, Description = %s\n", nCount, (const char*) desc);
```

NOTE: You must use the *(const char*)* cast for *CString* objects in a *TRACE* statement. Be careful to match all *TRACE* format strings to variables because the compiler's type checking is turned off in this situation. If the formats are mismatched, the *TRACE* statement will give you incorrect results and thus hinder your debugging efforts.

NOTE: The *TRACE* macro takes a variable number of parameters and is thus easy to use. If you look at the Microsoft Foundation Class (MFC) source code, you won't see *TRACE* macros but rather *TRACE0*, *TRACE1*, *TRACE2*, and *TRACE3* macros. These macros take 0, 1, 2, and 3 parameters respectively, and they have the advantage of storing their strings in a code segment rather than in the program's DGROUP segment. If your program is pushing the limits of the DGROUP segment in Debug mode, use the *TRACEn* macros instead of *TRACE*.

The *afxDump* Object

An alternative to the *TRACE* statement is more compatible with the C++ language. The MFC library *afxDump* object accepts program variables with a syntax similar to that of *cout*, the C++ output stream. You don't need complex formatting strings; instead, overloaded operators control the output format. (Overloaded operators are explained in Appendix A.) The *afxDump* output goes to the same destination as *TRACE* output, but the *afxDump* object is defined only in the Debug version of the MFC library. Here is a typical stream-oriented diagnostic statement that produces the same output as the *TRACE* statement above:

```
int nCount = 9;
CString desc("total");
#ifdef _DEBUG
   afxDump << "Count = " << nCount << ", Description = " << desc << "\n";
#endif
```

Although both *afxDump* and *cout* use the same insertion operator (<<), they don't share any code. The *cout* object is part of the Visual C++ iostream library, and *afxDump* is part of the MFC library. Don't assume that any of the *cout* formatting capability is available through *afxDump*.

Classes that aren't derived from *CObject*, such as *CString, CTime*, and *CRect*, contain their own overloaded insertion operators for *CDumpContext* objects. The *CDumpContext* class, of which *afxDump* is an instance, includes the overloaded insertion operators for the native C++ data types (*int, double, char**, and so on). The *CDumpContext* class also contains insertion operators for *CObject* references and pointers, and that's where things get interesting.

The Dump Context and the *CObject* Class

If the *CDumpContext* insertion operator accepts *CObject* pointers and references, it must also accept pointers and references to derived classes. Consider a trivial class, *CEvent*, that is derived from *CObject*:

```
class CEvent : public CObject
{
public:
    int m_nTime;
};
```

What happens when the following statement executes?

```
#ifdef _DEBUG
    afxDump << event; // event is an object of class CEvent
#endif
```

The virtual *CObject::Dump* function gets called. If you haven't overridden *Dump* for *CEvent*, you don't get much except for the address of the object. If you have overridden *Dump*, however, you can get the internal state of your object. Here's a *CEvent::Dump* function:

```
#ifdef _DEBUG
void CEvent::Dump(CDumpContext& dc) const
{
    CObject::Dump(dc); // always call the base class function
    dc << "\ntime = " << m_nTime << "\n";
}
#endif
```

The base class (*CObject*) *Dump* function prints a line such as this:

```
a CObject at $4498
```

If you have called the *DECLARE_DYNAMIC* macro in your *CEvent* class definition and the *IMPLEMENT_DYNAMIC* macro in your *CEvent* declaration, you will see the name of the class in your dump, like this:

```
a CEvent at $4498
```

even if your dump statement looks like this:

```
#ifdef _DEBUG
    afxDump << (CObject*) pEvent;
#endif
```

The two macros work together to include the MFC library runtime class code in your derived *CObject* class. With this code in place, your program can determine an object's class name at runtime (for the dump, for example), and it can obtain class hierarchy information.

> **NOTE:** The macro pairs (*DECLARE_SERIAL, IMPLEMENT_-SERIAL*) and (*DECLARE_DYNCREATE, IMPLEMENT_DYNCRE-ATE*) provide the same runtime class features as those provided by the (*DECLARE_DYNAMIC, IMPLEMENT_DYNAMIC*) pair.

Automatic Dump of Undeleted Objects

With the Debug build mode set, the application framework dumps all objects that are undeleted when your program exits. This dump is a useful diagnostic aid, but if you want it to be really useful, you must be sure to delete <u>all</u> your objects, even the ones that would normally disappear after the exit. This object cleanup is good programming discipline.

Window Subclassing for Enhanced Data Entry Control

What if you want an edit control (in a dialog or form view) that accepts only numeric characters? The MFC library provides a convenient way to change the behavior of any standard control, including the edit control. Actually, there are several ways. You can derive your own classes from *CEdit*, *CListbox*, and so forth (with their own message handler functions), and then create control objects at runtime. Or you can register a special window class, as an SDK programmer would do, and integrate it into the project's resource file with the Visual Workbench editor. Neither of these methods, however, allow you to use App Studio to position controls in the dialog resource.

The easy way to modify a control's behavior is to use the MFC library's "window subclassing" feature. You use App Studio to position a normal control in a dialog resource, and then you write a new C++ class that contains message handlers for the events that you want to handle yourself. Here are the steps for subclassing an edit control:

1. With App Studio, position an edit control in your dialog resource. Assume it has the child window ID *IDC_EDIT1*.

2. Write a new class, for example *CNumericEdit*, derived from *CEdit*. Map the WM_CHAR message, and write a handler like this:

```
void CNumericEdit::OnChar(UINT nChar, UINT nRepCnt,
                          UINT nFlags)
{
    if (nChar >= '0' && nChar <= '9') {
      CEdit::OnChar(nChar, nRepCnt, nFlags);
    }
}
```

(continued)

continued

3. In your derived dialog or form view class header, declare a data member of class *CNumericEdit* in this way:

```
private:
    CNumericEdit m_numericEdit;
```

4. If you're working with a dialog class, add the following line to your *OnInitDialog* override function:

```
m_numericEdit.SubclassDlgItem(IDC_EDIT1, this);
```

5. If you're working with a form view class, add the following code to your *OnInitialUpdate* override function:

```
if (m_numericEdit.m_hWnd == NULL) {
    m_numericEdit.SubclassDlgItem(IDC_EDIT1, this);
}
```

The *CWnd SubclassDlgItem* member function ensures that all messages are routed through the application framework's message dispatch system before being sent to the control's built-in window procedure. This technique is called "dynamic subclassing" and is explained in more detail in Technical Note #1 in the MFCNOTES.HLP file.

The EX15A Example

The first of this chapter's two examples shows a very simple document–view interaction. The *CEx15aDoc* document class, derived from *CDocument*, allows for a single embedded *CStudent* object. The *CStudent* class represents a student record that is composed of a *CString* name and a long integer grade. The *CEx15aView* view class is derived from *CFormView*. It is a visual representation of a student record that has edit controls for the name and grade. The default Enter pushbutton updates the document with data from the edit controls. Figure 15-1 shows the EX15A window.

Figure 15-2 shows the code for the *CStudent* class. Most of the class's features serve EX15A, but a few items carry forward to EX15B and the programs discussed in Chapter 16. For now, take note of the two data members, the default constructor, the operators, and the *Dump* function declaration. The *DECLARE_DYNAMIC* and *IMPLEMENT_DYNAMIC* macros ensure that the class name is available for the diagnostic dump.

Figure 15-1.
The EX15A program in action.

STUDENT.H

```
class CStudent : public CObject
{
    DECLARE_DYNAMIC(CStudent)
public:
    CString m_name;
    LONG m_lGrade;

    CStudent() {
        m_lGrade = 0L;
    }

    CStudent(const char* szName, long lGrade) : m_name(szName) {
        m_lGrade = lGrade;
    }

    CStudent(const CStudent& s) : m_name(s.m_name) { // copy constructor
        m_lGrade = s.m_lGrade;
    }

    const CStudent& operator =(const CStudent& s) {
        m_name = s.m_name;
        m_lGrade = s.m_lGrade;
        return *this
    }
```

Figure 15-2.
CStudent class listing.

(continued)

Figure 15-2. *continued*

```
    BOOL operator ==(const CStudent& s) const
    {
        if ((m_name == s.m_name) && (m_lGrade == s.m_lGrade)) {
          return TRUE;
        }
        else {
          return FALSE;
        }
    }

    BOOL operator !=(const CStudent& s) const
    {
        // Let's make use of the operator we just defined!
        return !(*this == s);
    }
#ifdef _DEBUG
    void Dump(CDumpContext& dc) const;
#endif
};
```

STUDENT.CPP

```
    #include "stdafx.h"
    #include "student.h"

    IMPLEMENT_DYNAMIC(CStudent, CObject)

    #ifdef _DEBUG
    void CStudent::Dump(CDumpContext& dc) const
    {
        CObject::Dump(dc);
        dc << "\nm_name = " << m_name << "\nm_lGrade = " << m_lGrade;
    }
    #endif
```

In Figure 15-2, the grade data member is declared to be of type *LONG* instead of type *int* to enable the same *CStudent* class to be used for disk input and output in the following chapters.

Follow these steps to build the EX15A example:

1. Run AppWizard to generate \VCPP\EX15A\EX15A. Choose AppWizard from Visual Workbench's Project menu. In the Classes dialog, change the view's base class to *CFormView*, as shown in the screen at the top of the following page:

The options and the default class names are shown here:

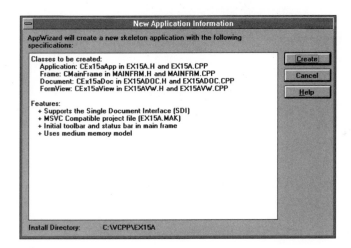

2. Use App Studio to replace the Edit menu choices. Delete the current Edit menu items, and replace them with a Clear All choice, as shown here:

Use the default constant *ID_EDIT_CLEARALL*, which is assigned by the application framework.

3. Use App Studio to modify the *IDD_EX15A_FORM* dialog. Open the AppWizard-generated dialog *IDD_EX15A_FORM,* and add controls as shown here:

Be sure the Style properties are set <u>exactly</u> as shown in the Dialog Properties dialog (Style = Child, Border = None, Visible is unchecked).

Use the following IDs for the controls:

Control	ID
Name edit control	*IDC_NAME*
Grade edit control	*IDC_GRADE*
Enter pushbutton	*IDC_ENTER*

4. Use ClassWizard to add message handlers for *CEx15aView*.

> NOTE: You must run ClassWizard from App Studio (with the menu *IDR_MAINFRAME* selected) to see the menu's Object ID.

Select the *CEx15aView* class, and then add handlers for the following messages. Accept the default function names.

Object ID	Message	Member Function Name
IDC_ENTER	BN_CLICKED	*OnEnter*
ID_EDIT_CLEARALL	COMMAND	*OnEditClearall*
ID_EDIT_CLEARALL	UPDATE_COMMAND_UI	*OnUpdateEditClearall*

5. Use ClassWizard to add variables for *CEx15aView*. Click the Member Variables tab in the MFC Class Wizard dialog, and then add the following variables:

Control	Member Variable Name	Property Type	Variable Type
IDC_GRADE	m_lGrade	Value	long
IDC_NAME	m_name	Value	CString

For *m_lGrade*, enter a minimum value of *0* and a maximum value of *100*. Notice that ClassWizard generates the code necessary to validate data entered by the user.

6. Add member function prototypes to EX15AVW.H. ClassWizard has written a very complete header file for class *CEx15aView*, but you must add two function prototypes:

```
protected:
    virtual void OnInitialUpdate();
private:
    void UpdateEntry();
```

7. Edit EX15AVW.CPP. Because the view class uses the *CStudent* class, you must include the *CStudent* class declaration. You must enter the following two functions from scratch because AppWizard did not generate skeleton code for them. The application framework calls the *OnInitialUpdate* function when the application starts. The *UpdateEntry* function is a private "helper" member function that transfers data from the document to the *CEx15aView* data members and then to the dialog edit controls. It also sets the focus to the Name edit control.

```
void CEx15aView::OnInitialUpdate()
{   // called on startup
    UpdateEntry();
}
```

```
void CEx15aView::UpdateEntry()
{   // called from OnInitialUpdate and OnEditClearall
    CEx15aDoc* pDoc = GetDocument();
    m_lGrade = pDoc->m_student.m_lGrade;
    m_name = pDoc->m_student.m_name;
    UpdateData(FALSE); // calls DDX
    ((CDialog*) this)->
      GotoDlgCtrl(GetDlgItem(IDC_NAME)); // note parentheses usage
}
```

Add the statement

```
#include "student.doc"
```

<u>before</u> the statement that reads

```
#include "ex15adoc.h"
```

The *OnEnter* function replaces the *OnOK* function you'd expect to see in a dialog class. The function transfers data from the edit controls to the view's data members and then to the document.

```
void CEx15aView::OnEnter()
{
    CEx15aDoc* pDoc = GetDocument();
    UpdateData(TRUE);
    pDoc->m_student.m_lGrade = m_lGrade;
    pDoc->m_student.m_name = m_name;
}
```

In a complex multiview application, the Edit Clear All command would be routed directly to the document. In this simple example, it's routed to the view. The update command UI handler disables the menu item if the document's student object is already blank.

```
void CEx15aView::OnEditClearall()
{
    GetDocument()->m_student = CStudent(); // "blank" student
                                           //  object
    UpdateEntry();
}
void CEx15aView::OnUpdateEditClearall(CCmdUI* pCmdUI)
{
    pCmdUI->Enable(((CEx15aDoc*) GetDocument())->m_student !=
      CStudent()); // blank?
}
```

8. **Edit the EX15ADOC.H file.** The *CEx15aDoc* class provides for an embedded *CStudent* object. The *CStudent* default constructor is called when the document object is constructed, and the *CStudent* destructor is called when the document object is destroyed.

```
public:
    CStudent m_student;
```

9. **Edit the EX15ADOC.CPP file.** Because the document class incorporates the *CStudent* class, you must include its declaration. <u>Before</u> the statement

```
#include "ex15adoc.h"
```

add the statement

```
#include "student.h"
```

Let's use the *CEx15aDoc* constructor to set some initial values for the student object.

```
CEx15aDoc::CEx15aDoc()
{
    TRACE("Document object constructed\n");
    m_student.m_name = "default value";
    m_student.m_lGrade = 0L;
}
```

We can't tell whether the EX15A program worked properly unless we dump the document when the program exits. We'll use the destructor to call the document's *Dump* function, which calls the *CStudent::Dump* function.

```
CEx15aDoc::~CEx15aDoc()
{
#ifdef _DEBUG
    Dump(afxDump);
#endif
}

void CEx15aDoc::Dump(CDumpContext& dc) const
{
    CDocument::Dump(dc);
    dc << "\n" << m_student << "\n";
}
```

10. **Edit the EX15A.CPP file.** <u>Before</u> the statement

```
#include "ex15adoc.h"
```

add the statement

```
#include "student.h"
```

11. **Edit the EX15A project to add STUDENT.CPP.** You must tell Visual Workbench that you are adding the *CStudent* code to the project. When you add the STUDENT.CPP source code file, Visual Workbench will analyze the other project files and establish the STUDENT.H dependencies.

12. **Build and test the EX15A application.** Type a name and a grade, and then click the Enter button. Now exit the application. Does the debug window show messages similar to those shown at the top of the following page?

```
a CEx15aDoc at $4472
m_strTitle = Ex15a
m_strPathName =
m_bModified = 0
m_pDocTemplate = $438E
a CStudent at $4498
m_name = default value
m_lGrade = 0
```

NOTE: You must compile the application with the Debug project build option to see these messages.

A More Advanced Document–View Interaction

If you're laying the groundwork for a multiview application, the document–view interaction must be more complex than the simple interaction in example EX15A. The fundamental problem is this: The user edits in view #1, so view #2 (and any other views) must be updated to reflect the changes. Now you need the *UpdateAllViews* and *OnUpdate* functions because the document is going to act as the clearinghouse for all view updates. The development steps are as follows:

1. In your derived document class header file (generated by App-Wizard), declare your document's data members. If you want, you can make these data members private, and you can define member functions to access them or declare the view class as a <u>friend</u> of the document class.

2. In your derived view class, override the *OnUpdate* virtual member function. The application framework calls this function whenever the document data has changed for any reason. *OnUpdate* should update the view to reflect the current document data.

3. Evaluate all your command messages. Determine whether each is document-specific or view-specific. (A good example of a document-specific command is the Clear All command on the Edit menu.) Now map the commands to the appropriate classes.

4. In your derived view class, allow the appropriate command message handlers to update the document data. Be sure that these message handlers call the *CDocument::UpdateAllViews* function before they exit. Use the *CView::GetDocument* member function to access the view's document.

5. In your derived document class, allow the appropriate command message handlers to update the document data. Be sure that these message handlers call the *CDocument UpdateAllViews* function before they exit.

The sequence of events for the complex document–view interaction is shown here:

Application starts	*CMyDocument* object constructed
	CMyView object constructed
	Other view objects constructed
	View windows created
	CMyView::OnCreate called (if mapped)
	CView::OnInitialUpdate called
	Calls *CMyView::OnUpdate*
	Initializes the view
User executes	*CMyView* functions update *CMyDocument* data members
view command	Calls *CDocument::UpdateAllViews*
	Other views' *OnUpdate* function called
User executes	*CMyDocument* functions update data members
document	Calls *CDocument::UpdateAllViews*
command	*CMyView::OnUpdate* called
	Other views' *OnUpdate* called
User exits	View objects destroyed
application	*CMyDocument* object destroyed

The *CDocument::DeleteContents* Function

At some point, you'll need a function to delete the contents of your document. You could write your own private member function, but it happens that the application framework declares a virtual *DeleteContents* function for the *CDocument* class. The application framework calls your overridden *Delete-Contents* function when the document is closed and, as you'll see in the next chapter, at other times as well.

The *CObList* Collection Class

Once you get to know the collection classes, you'll wonder how you ever got along without them. The *CObList* class is a useful representative of the collection class family. If you're familiar with this class, it's easy to learn the other list classes, the array classes, and the map classes.

You might think that collections are something new, but the C programming language has always supported one kind of collection—the array. C arrays must be fixed in size, and they do not support insertion of elements. Many C programmers have written function libraries for other collections, including linked lists, dynamic arrays, and indexed dictionaries. For implementing collections, the C++ class is an obvious and better alternative than a C function library. A list object, for example, neatly encapsulates the list's internal data structures.

The *CObList* class supports ordered lists of pointers to objects of classes derived from *CObject*. Why is the *CObject* class involved at all? Suppose there weren't a *CObject* root class, and you needed a general-purpose list class for storing pointers to objects. How would you declare the return values and parameters of your list class member functions? You could use *void* pointers, but that would require a lot of casting. The *CObject* class solves the problem. If you derive all your collectable object classes from *CObject*, you can store their pointers in a list of *CObject* pointers. You can even mix and match pointers to objects of different derived classes.

Instead of a collection of *CObject* pointers, why not define a collection for a specific derived class such as *CMyObject*? A collection of *CMyObject* pointers would be type-safe because it would accept pointers only to those objects and require no casting whatsoever. Indeed, you could derive your own *CMyObList* class from *CObList*, or you could use the Microsoft Foundation Class Library collection template tool (TEMPLDEF) documented in Technical Note #4 in the MFCNOTES.HLP file. Both alternatives are probably more trouble than they're worth. Besides, the template tool is more useful for generating collection classes for native types such as floats and doubles.

The *CObList* class and the other collection classes provide special benefits when you do diagnostic dumping and serialization. You'll see the dump context in this chapter, but you must wait until Chapter 16 to see serialization.

Using the *CObList* Class for a First-In, First-Out (FIFO) List

One of the easiest ways to use a *CObList* object is to add new elements to the tail, or bottom, of the list, and to remove elements from the head, or top, of the list. The first element added to the list will always be the first element removed from the head of the list. Suppose you're working with element objects of class *CEvent*, which is your own custom class derived from *CObject*. An MS-DOS program that puts five elements into a list and then retrieves them in the same sequence is shown at the top of the facing page:

```
#include <afx.h>
#include <afxcoll.h>
class CEvent : public CObject
{
private:
    int m_nTime;
public:
    CEvent(int nTime) { m_nTime = nTime; } // constructor
                                           //  stores integer time value
    void PrintTime() { TRACE("time = %d\n", m_nTime); }
};

int main()
{
    CEvent* pEvent;
    CObList eventList; // event list constructed on the stack
    int     i;

    // inserts event objects in sequence {0, 1, 2, 3, 4}
    for (i = 0; i < 5; i++) {
      pEvent = new CEvent(i);
      eventList.AddTail(pEvent); // no cast necessary for pEvent
    }

    // retrieves and removes event objects in sequence {0, 1, 2, 3, 4}
    while (!eventList.IsEmpty()) {
      pEvent = (CEvent*) eventList.RemoveHead(); // cast required for
                                                 //  return value
      pEvent->PrintTime();
      delete pEvent;
    }

    return 0;
}
```

Here's what's going on in the program. First a *CObList* object, *eventList*, is constructed. Then the *CObList::AddTail* member function inserts pointers to newly constructed *CEvent* objects. No casting is necessary for *pEvent* because *AddTail* takes a *CObject* pointer parameter, and *pEvent* is a pointer to a derived class.

Next the *CEvent* object pointers are removed from the list of the objects deleted. A cast is necessary for the returned value of *RemoveHead* because *RemoveHead* returns a *CObject* pointer that is <u>higher</u> in the class hierarchy than *CEvent*.

When you remove an object pointer from a collection, the object is not automatically deleted. The *delete* statement is necessary for deleting the *CEvent* objects.

CObList Iteration—The *POSITION* Variable

Suppose you want to iterate through the elements in a list. The *CObList* class provides a *GetNext* member function that returns a pointer to the "next" list element, but using it is a little tricky. *GetNext* takes a parameter of type *POSITION*, which is simply a long integer. The *POSITION* variable is an internal representation of the retrieved element's position in the list. Because the *POSITION* parameter is declared as a reference (&), the function can change its value.

GetNext does the following:

1. Returns a pointer to the "current" object in the list, identified by the incoming value of the *POSITION* parameter.

2. Increments the value of the *POSITION* parameter to the next list element.

Here's what a *GetNext* loop looks like, assuming that you're using the list generated in the previous example:

```
POSITION pos = eventList.GetHeadPosition();
while (pos != NULL) {
  pEvent = (CEvent*) GetNext(pos);
  pEvent->PrintTime();
}
```

Now, suppose you have an interactive Windows program that uses toolbar buttons to sequence forward and backward through the list, one element at a time. You can't use *GetNext* to retrieve the entry because *GetNext* always <u>increments</u> the *POSITION* variable, and you don't know in advance whether the user is going to want the next element or the previous element. Here's a sample view class command message handler function that gets the next list entry. In the *CMyView* class, *m_eventList* is an embedded *CObList* object, and the *m_position* data member is a *POSITION* variable that holds the current list position.

```
CMyView::OnCommandNext()
{
    POSITION pos;
    CEvent*  pEvent;
```

```
     if ((pos = m_position) != NULL) {
       m_eventList.GetNext(pos);
       if (pos != NULL) { // pos is NULL at end of list
         pEvent = (CEvent*) m_eventList.GetAt(pos);
         pEvent->PrintTime();
         m_position = pos;
       }
       else {
         AfxMessageBox("End of list reached");
       }
     }
}
```

Now *GetNext* is called first to increment the list position, and the *CObList GetAt* member function is called to retrieve the entry. The *m_position* variable is updated only when we're sure we're not at the tail of the list.

The Dump Context and Collection Classes

The *Dump* function for *CObList* and the other collection classes has a useful property. If you call *Dump* for a collection object, you can get a display of each object in the collection. If the element objects employ the *DECLARE_DYNAMIC* and *IMPLEMENT_DYNAMIC* macros, the dump will show the class name for each object.

The default behavior of the collection *Dump* functions is to display only class names and addresses of element objects. If you want the collection *Dump* functions to call the *Dump* function for each element object, you must, somewhere at the start of your program, make the following call:

```
#ifdef _DEBUG
     afxDump.SetDepth(1);
#endif
```

Now the statement

```
#ifdef _DEBUG
     afxDump << eventList;
#endif
```

produces output such as this:

```
a CObList with 4 elements

    a CEvent at $4CD6
time = 0
    a CEvent at $5632
time = 1
    a CEvent at $568E
time = 2
    a CEvent at $56EA
time = 3
```

The EX15B Example

This second *SDI* example improves on EX15A in the following ways:

- Instead of a single embedded *CStudent* object, the document now contains a list of *CStudent* objects.

- Toolbar buttons allow the user to sequence through the list.

- The application is structured to allow the addition of extra views. The Edit Clear All command is now routed to the document object, so the document's *UpdateAllViews* function and view's *OnUpdate* function are brought into play.

- The student-specific view code is isolated so that the *CEx15bView* class can later be transformed into a base class that contains only general-purpose code. Derived classes can override selected functions to accommodate lists of application-specific objects.

The EX15B window, shown in Figure 15-3, looks a little different from the EX15A window (shown in Figure 15-1 on page 283). The toolbar buttons are enabled only when appropriate. The Next (arrow-down graphic) button, for example, is disabled when we're positioned at the bottom of the list.

Figure 15-3.
The EX15B program in action.

The toolbar buttons function as follows:

Button	Function
⭱	Retrieves the first student record
⭳	Retrieves the last student record
⭡	Retrieves the previous student record
⭣	Retrieves the next student record
☒	Deletes the current student record
☐	Inserts a new student record

The Clear button in the view window clears the contents of the Name and Grade edit controls. The Clear All command on the Edit menu deletes all the student records in the list and clears the view's edit controls.

This example deviates from the step-by-step format in the previous examples. Because there's now more code, we'll simply list selected code and the resource requirements. In the listing figures, shaded code indicates that the user entered additional code or entered other changes to the output from AppWizard and ClassWizard. The frequent use of *TRACE* statements lets you follow the program's execution in the debugging window.

Here's a list of the files and classes in the EX15B example:

Header File	Source Code File	Classes	Description
EX15B.H	EX15B.CPP	*CEx15bApp*	Application class (from AppWizard)
		CAboutDlg	About dialog
MAINFRM.H	MAINFRM.CPP	*CMainFrame*	SDI main frame
STUDOC.H	STUDOC.CPP	*CStudentDoc*	Student document
STUVIEW.H	STUVIEW.CPP	*CStudentView*	Student form view (derived from *CFormView*)
STUDENT.H	STUDENT.CPP	*CStudent*	Student record (from EX15A)
STDAFX.H	STDAFX.CPP		Includes the standard precompiled headers

CEx15bApp

EX15B.CPP is standard AppWizard output except for the following line:

```
#include "student.h"
```

included immediately <u>before</u> the statement

```
#include "studoc.h"
```

CMainFrame

The code for the *CMainFrame* class in *MAINFRM.CPP* is the standard output from AppWizard except for the toolbar button array:

```
static UINT BASED_CODE buttons[] =
{
    // same order as in the bitmap "toolbar.bmp"
    ID_FILE_NEW,
    ID_FILE_OPEN,
    ID_FILE_SAVE,
        ID_SEPARATOR,
    ID_POS_HOME,
    ID_POS_END,
    ID_POS_PREV,
    ID_POS_NEXT,
    ID_POS_DEL,
    ID_POS_INS,
        ID_SEPARATOR,
    ID_FILE_PRINT,
    ID_APP_ABOUT,
};
```

CStudentDoc

AppWizard originally generated the *CStudentDoc* class. Figure 15-4 shows the code used in the EX15B example.

STUDOC.H

```
// studoc.h : interface of the CStudentDoc class

class CStudentDoc : public CDocument
{
```

Figure 15-4.   *(continued)*
The CStudentDoc *class listing.*

Figure 15-4. *continued*

```
      DECLARE_DYNCREATE(CStudentDoc)
private:
    CObList m_studentList;
protected: // create from serialization only
    CStudentDoc();

// Attributes
public:
    CObList* GetList() {
        return &m_studentList;
    }

// Operations
public:

// Implementation
public:
    virtual ~CStudentDoc();
    virtual void Serialize(CArchive& ar); // overridden for document
                                          //  i/o
#ifdef _DEBUG
    virtual void AssertValid() const;
    virtual void Dump(CDumpContext& dc) const;
#endif
protected:
    virtual BOOL OnNewDocument();
    virtual void DeleteContents();
// Generated message map functions
protected:
    //{{AFX_MSG(CStudentDoc)
    afx_msg void OnEditClearAll();
    afx_msg void OnUpdateEditClearAll(CCmdUI* pCmdUI);
    //}}AFX_MSG
    DECLARE_MESSAGE_MAP()
};


/////////////////////////////////////////////////////////////////////
```

STUDOC.CPP

```
// studoc.cpp : implementation of the CStudentDoc class

#include "stdafx.h"
#include "resource.h"

#include "student.h"
#include "studoc.h"
```

(continued)

Figure 15-4. *continued*

```
#ifdef _DEBUG
#undef THIS_FILE
static char BASED_CODE THIS_FILE[] = __FILE__;
#endif


/////////////////////////////////////////////////////////////////////
// CStudentDoc

//IMPLEMENT_SERIAL(CStudentDoc, CDocument, 0)
IMPLEMENT_DYNCREATE(CStudentDoc, CDocument)

BEGIN_MESSAGE_MAP(CStudentDoc, CDocument)
    //{{AFX_MSG_MAP(CStudentDoc)
    ON_COMMAND(ID_EDIT_CLEAR_ALL, OnEditClearAll)
    ON_UPDATE_COMMAND_UI(ID_EDIT_CLEAR_ALL, OnUpdateEditClearAll)
    //}}AFX_MSG_MAP
END_MESSAGE_MAP()


/////////////////////////////////////////////////////////////////////
// CStudentDoc construction/destruction

CStudentDoc::CStudentDoc()
{
#ifdef _DEBUG
    afxDump.SetDepth(1); // ensure dump of list elements
#endif
}


CStudentDoc::~CStudentDoc()
{
}


/////////////////////////////////////////////////////////////////////
BOOL CStudentDoc::OnNewDocument()
{
    TRACE("Entering CStudentDoc::OnNewDocument\n");
    if (!CDocument::OnNewDocument())
      return FALSE;
    return TRUE;
}


/////////////////////////////////////////////////////////////////////
// CStudentDoc serialization

void CStudentDoc::Serialize(CArchive& ar)
{
```

(continued)

Figure 15-4. *continued*

```
    if (ar.IsStoring()) {
      // any other document variables to archive
    }
    else {
      // any other document variables from archive
    }
}

/////////////////////////////////////////////////////////////////
void CStudentDoc::DeleteContents()
{
#ifdef _DEBUG
    Dump(afxDump);
#endif
    while (m_studentList.GetHeadPosition()) {
      delete m_studentList.RemoveHead();
    }
}

/////////////////////////////////////////////////////////////////
// CStudentDoc diagnostics

#ifdef _DEBUG
void CStudentDoc::AssertValid() const
{
    CDocument::AssertValid();
}

void CStudentDoc::Dump(CDumpContext& dc) const
{
    CDocument::Dump(dc);
    dc << "\n" << m_studentList << "\n";
}

#endif //_DEBUG

/////////////////////////////////////////////////////////////////
// CStudentDoc commands


void CStudentDoc::OnEditClearAll()
{
    DeleteContents();
    UpdateAllViews(NULL);
}
```

(continued)

Figure 15-4. *continued*

```
////////////////////////////////////////////////////////////////////////
void CStudentDoc::OnUpdateEditClearAll(CCmdUI* pCmdUI)
{
        pCmdUI->Enable(!m_studentList.IsEmpty());
}
```

ClassWizard and *CStudentDoc*

The Edit Clear All command is handled in the document class. The following message handlers were added through ClassWizard:

Object ID	Message	Member Function Name
ID_EDIT_CLEAR_ALL	COMMAND	*OnEditClearAll*
ID_EDIT_CLEAR_ALL	ON_UPDATE_COMMAND_UI	*OnUpdateEditClearAll*

Data Members

The document class provides for an embedded *CObList* object, *m_studentList*, that holds pointers to *CStudent* objects. The list object is constructed when the *CStudentDoc* object is constructed, and it is destroyed at program exit.

Constructor and Destructor

The document constructor sets the depth of the dump context so that a dump of the list causes a dump of the individual list elements.

GetList

The inline *GetList* function helps isolate the view from the document. The document class must be specific to the type of object in the list, in this case objects of the class *CStudent*. A view base class, however, can use a member function to get a pointer to the list without knowing the name of the list object.

DeleteContents

The *DeleteContents* function is a virtual override function that is called by other document functions and by the application framework. Its job is to remove all student object pointers from the document's list and to delete those student objects. An important point to remember here is that *SDI* document objects are reused after they are closed. *DeleteContents* also dumps the student list.

Dump

AppWizard generates the *Dump* function skeleton between the lines *#ifdef _DEBUG* and *#endif.* Because the *afxDump* depth was set to *1* in the document constructor, all the *CStudent* objects contained in the list are dumped.

CStudentView

Figure 15-5 shows the code for the *CStudentView* class. This code will be carried over into the next two chapters.

STUVIEW.H

```
// stuview.h : interface of the CStudentView class

class CStudentView : public CFormView
{
    DECLARE_DYNCREATE(CStudentView)
protected: // create from serialization only
    CStudentView();
// Form data
public:
    //{{AFX_DATA(CStudentView)
    enum { IDD = IDD_STUDENT };
    CString m_name;
    long    m_lGrade;
    //}}AFX_DATA

// Attributes
public:
    CStudentDoc* GetDocument()
    {
        ASSERT(m_pDocument->IsKindOf(RUNTIME_CLASS(CStudentDoc)));
        return (CStudentDoc*) m_pDocument;
    }

// Operations
public:

// Implementation
protected:
    POSITION m_position; // current position in document list
    CObList* m_pList;    // copied from document
public:
    virtual ~CStudentView();
```

Figure 15-5.   *(continued)*

The CStudentView *class listing.*

Figure 15-5. *continued*

```
    virtual void DoDataExchange(CDataExchange* pDX);    // DDX/DDV
                                                        //  support
    virtual void OnDraw(CDC* pDC);  // overridden to draw this view
#ifdef _DEBUG
    virtual void AssertValid() const;
    virtual void Dump(CDumpContext& dc) const;
#endif

    // Printing support
protected:
    virtual void OnInitialUpdate();
    virtual void OnUpdate(CView* pSender, LPARAM lHint, CObject*
                          pHint);

// Generated message map functions
protected:
    //{{AFX_MSG(CStudentView)
    afx_msg void OnCommandHome();
    afx_msg void OnUpdateCommandHome(CCmdUI* pCmdUI);
    afx_msg void OnCommandEnd();
    afx_msg void OnUpdateCommandEnd(CCmdUI* pCmdUI);
    afx_msg void OnCommandPrev();
    afx_msg void OnUpdateCommandPrev(CCmdUI* pCmdUI);
    afx_msg void OnCommandNext();
    afx_msg void OnUpdateCommandNext(CCmdUI* pCmdUI);
    afx_msg void OnCommandDel();
    afx_msg void OnUpdateCommandDel(CCmdUI* pCmdUI);
    afx_msg void OnCommandIns();
    afx_msg void OnClear();
    //}}AFX_MSG
protected:
    virtual void GetEntry(POSITION position);
    virtual void InsertEntry(POSITION position);
    virtual void ClearEntry();

    DECLARE_MESSAGE_MAP()
};


/////////////////////////////////////////////////////////////////
```

STUVIEW.CPP

```
// stuview.cpp : implementation of the CStudentView class

#include "stdafx.h"
#include "resource.h"
```

(continued)

Figure 15-5. *continued*

```
#include "student.h"
#include "studoc.h"
#include "stuview.h"

#ifdef _DEBUG
#undef THIS_FILE
static char BASED_CODE THIS_FILE[] = __FILE__;
#endif

/////////////////////////////////////////////////////////////////
// CStudentView

IMPLEMENT_DYNCREATE(CStudentView, CFormView)

BEGIN_MESSAGE_MAP(CStudentView, CFormView)
    //{{AFX_MSG_MAP(CStudentView)
    ON_COMMAND(ID_POS_HOME, OnCommandHome)
    ON_UPDATE_COMMAND_UI(ID_POS_HOME, OnUpdateCommandHome)
    ON_COMMAND(ID_POS_END, OnCommandEnd)
    ON_UPDATE_COMMAND_UI(ID_POS_END, OnUpdateCommandEnd)
    ON_COMMAND(ID_POS_PREV, OnCommandPrev)
    ON_UPDATE_COMMAND_UI(ID_POS_PREV, OnUpdateCommandPrev)
    ON_COMMAND(ID_POS_NEXT, OnCommandNext)
    ON_UPDATE_COMMAND_UI(ID_POS_NEXT, OnUpdateCommandNext)
    ON_COMMAND(ID_POS_DEL, OnCommandDel)
    ON_UPDATE_COMMAND_UI(ID_POS_DEL, OnUpdateCommandDel)
    ON_COMMAND(ID_POS_INS, OnCommandIns)
    ON_BN_CLICKED(IDC_CLEAR, OnClear)
    //}}AFX_MSG_MAP
    // Standard printing commands
END_MESSAGE_MAP()

/////////////////////////////////////////////////////////////////
// CStudentView construction/destruction

CStudentView::CStudentView()
    : CFormView(CStudentView::IDD)
{
    TRACE("Entering CStudentView constructor\n");
    //{{AFX_DATA_INIT(CStudentView)
    m_lGrade = 0;
    //}}AFX_DATA_INIT
    m_position = NULL;
}
```

(continued)

Figure 15-5. *continued*

```
CStudentView::~CStudentView()
{
}


/////////////////////////////////////////////////////////////////////
void CStudentView::OnInitialUpdate()
{
    // called on startup, on File New, and on File Open
    TRACE("Entering CStudentView::OnInitialUpdate\n");
    OnUpdate(this, NULL, NULL);
}


/////////////////////////////////////////////////////////////////////
void CStudentView::OnUpdate(CView* pSender, LPARAM lHint, CObject*
                           pHint)
{
    // called by OnInitialUpdate and by UpdateAllViews
    TRACE("Entering CStudentView::OnUpdate\n");
    m_pList = GetDocument()->GetList();
    m_position = m_pList->GetHeadPosition();
    GetEntry(m_position); // initial data for view
}


/////////////////////////////////////////////////////////////////////
void CStudentView::OnDraw(CDC* pDC)
{
    CStudentDoc* pDoc = GetDocument();

    // TODO: add draw code here
}


/////////////////////////////////////////////////////////////////////
// CStudentView diagnostics

#ifdef _DEBUG
void CStudentView::AssertValid() const
{
    CFormView::AssertValid();
}

void CStudentView::Dump(CDumpContext& dc) const
{
    CFormView::Dump(dc);
}

#endif //_DEBUG
```

(continued)

Figure 15-5. *continued*

```
//////////////////////////////////////////////////////////////
// CStudentView commands

void CStudentView::DoDataExchange(CDataExchange* pDX)
{
    TRACE("Entering CStudentView::DoDataExchange\n");
    CFormView::DoDataExchange(pDX);
    //{{AFX_DATA_MAP(CStudentView)
    DDX_Text(pDX, IDC_NAME, m_name);
    DDV_MaxChars(pDX, m_name, 20);
    DDX_Text(pDX, IDC_GRADE, m_lGrade);
    DDV_MinMaxLong(pDX, m_lGrade, 0, 100);
    //}}AFX_DATA_MAP
}


//////////////////////////////////////////////////////////////
void CStudentView::OnCommandHome()
{
    // need to deal with the list empty condition
    TRACE("Entering CStudentView::OnCommandHome\n");
    if (!m_pList->IsEmpty()) {
      m_position = m_pList->GetHeadPosition();
      GetEntry(m_position);
    }
}


//////////////////////////////////////////////////////////////
void CStudentView::OnCommandNext()
{
    POSITION pos;

    TRACE("Entering CStudentView::OnCommandNext\n");
    if ((pos = m_position) != NULL) {
      m_pList->GetNext(pos);
      if (pos) {
        GetEntry(pos);
        m_position = pos;
      }
    }
}


//////////////////////////////////////////////////////////////
void CStudentView::OnCommandEnd()
```

(continued)

Figure 15-5. *continued*

```
{
    TRACE("Entering CStudentView::OnCommandEnd\n");
    if (!m_pList->IsEmpty()) {
      m_position = m_pList->GetTailPosition();
      GetEntry(m_position);
    }
}


/////////////////////////////////////////////////////////////////////
void CStudentView::OnCommandPrev()
{
    POSITION pos;

    TRACE("Entering CStudentView::OnCommandPrev\n");
    if ((pos = m_position) != NULL) {
      m_pList->GetPrev(pos);
      if (pos) {
        GetEntry(pos);
        m_position = pos;
      }
    }
}


/////////////////////////////////////////////////////////////////////
void CStudentView::OnCommandDel()
{
    // deletes current entry and positions to next one or head
    POSITION pos;

    TRACE("Entering CStudentView::OnCommandDel\n");
    if ((pos = m_position) != NULL) {
      m_pList->GetNext(pos);
      if (pos == NULL) {
        pos = m_pList->GetHeadPosition();
        TRACE("GetHeadPos = %ld\n", pos);
        if (pos == m_position) {
          pos = NULL;
        }
      }
      GetEntry(pos);
      CObject* ps = m_pList->GetAt(m_position);
      m_pList->RemoveAt(m_position);
      delete ps;
      m_position = pos;
```

(continued)

Figure 15-5. *continued*

```
            GetDocument()->SetModifiedFlag();
            GetDocument()->UpdateAllViews(this);
        }
    }


    /////////////////////////////////////////////////////////////////
    void CStudentView::OnCommandIns()
    {
        TRACE("Entering CStudentView::OnCommandIns\n");
        InsertEntry(m_position);
        GetDocument()->SetModifiedFlag();
        GetDocument()->UpdateAllViews(this);
    }


    /////////////////////////////////////////////////////////////////
    void CStudentView::OnUpdateCommandHome(CCmdUI* pCmdUI)
    {
        // called during IDLE processing
        POSITION pos;

        // enables button if list not empty and not at home already
        pos = m_pList->GetHeadPosition();
        pCmdUI->Enable((m_position != NULL) && (pos != m_position));
    }


    /////////////////////////////////////////////////////////////////
    void CStudentView::OnUpdateCommandEnd(CCmdUI* pCmdUI)
    {
        // called during IDLE processing
        POSITION pos;
        // enables button if list not empty and not at end already
        pos = m_pList->GetTailPosition();
        pCmdUI->Enable((m_position != NULL) && (pos != m_position));
    }


    /////////////////////////////////////////////////////////////////
    void CStudentView::OnUpdateCommandPrev(CCmdUI* pCmdUI)
    {
        // called during IDLE processing
        POSITION pos;

        // enables button if list not empty and previous item(s) exist
        if ((pos = m_position) != NULL) {
          m_pList->GetPrev(pos);
        }
```

(continued)

Figure 15-5. *continued*

```
        pCmdUI->Enable((m_position != NULL) && (pos != NULL));
    }


    //////////////////////////////////////////////////////////////////
    void CStudentView::OnUpdateCommandNext(CCmdUI* pCmdUI)
    {
        // called during IDLE processing
        POSITION pos;

        // enables button if list not empty and following item(s) exist
        if ((pos = m_position) != NULL) {
          m_pList->GetNext(pos);
        }
        pCmdUI->Enable((m_position != NULL) && (pos != NULL));
    }


    //////////////////////////////////////////////////////////////////
    void CStudentView::OnUpdateCommandDel(CCmdUI* pCmdUI)
    {
        // called during IDLE processing
        pCmdUI->Enable(m_position != NULL);
    }


    //////////////////////////////////////////////////////////////////
    void CStudentView::OnClear()
    {
        TRACE("Entering CStudentView::OnClear\n");
        ClearEntry();
    }


    //////////////////////////////////////////////////////////////////
    // protected virtual functions

    void CStudentView::GetEntry(POSITION position)
    {
        if (position) {
          CStudent* pStudent = (CStudent*) m_pList->GetAt(position);
          m_name = pStudent->m_name;
          m_lGrade = pStudent->m_lGrade;
        }
        else {
          ClearEntry();
        }
        UpdateData(FALSE);
    }
```

(continued)

Figure 15-5. *continued*

```
/////////////////////////////////////////////////////////////////
void CStudentView::InsertEntry(POSITION position)
{
    if (UpdateData(TRUE)) {
      // UpdateData returns FALSE if it detects a user error
      CStudent* pStudent = new CStudent;
      pStudent->m_name = m_name;
      pStudent->m_lGrade = m_lGrade;
      m_position = m_pList->InsertAfter(m_position, pStudent);
    }
}


/////////////////////////////////////////////////////////////////
void CStudentView::ClearEntry()
{
    m_name = "";
    m_lGrade = 0;
    UpdateData(FALSE);
    ((CDialog*) this)->GotoDlgCtrl(GetDlgItem(IDC_NAME));
}
```

ClassWizard and *CStudentView*

ClassWizard was used to map the *CStudentView* Clear pushbutton notification message as follows:

Object ID	Message	Member Function Name
IDC_CLEAR	**BN_CLICKED**	*OnClear*

Because *CStudentView* is derived from *CFormView*, ClassWizard supports the definition of dialog data members. The variables shown here were added with the Edit Variables button:

Control ID	Member Variable Name	Property Type	Variable Type
IDC_GRADE	*m_lGrade*	*Value*	*long*
IDC_NAME	*m_name*	*Value*	*CString*

Set the minimum value of the *m_lGrade* data member to *0* and its maximum value to *100*.

Because the toolbar buttons aren't duplicated by menu items, Class-Wizard won't help you with the message handlers. You must add the command and update command UI function prototypes manually.

Data Members

The *m_position* data member is a kind of cursor for the document's collection. It points to the *CStudent* object that is currently displayed. The *m_pList* variable provides a quick way to get at the student list in the document.

OnInitialUpdate

The virtual *OnInitialUpdate* function is called when you start the application. It sets the view's *m_pList* data member for subsequent access to the document's list object.

OnUpdate

The virtual *OnUpdate* function is called both by *OnInitialUpdate* and by the *CDocument::UpdateAllViews* function. It resets the list position to the head of the list, and it displays the head entry. In this example, the *UpdateAllViews* function is called only in response to the Edit Clear All command. In a multiview application, you might need a different strategy for setting the *CStudentView m_position* variable in response to document updates from another view.

Toolbar Button Command Message Handlers

These functions are called in response to toolbar button clicks:

> *OnCommandHome*
> *OnCommandEnd*
> *OnCommandPrev*
> *OnCommandNext*
> *OnCommandDel*
> *OnCommandIns*

Each function has built-in error checking.

Toolbar Button Update Command UI Message Handlers

These functions are called during idle processing to update the state of the toolbar buttons:

> *OnUpdateCommandHome*
> *OnUpdateCommandEnd*
> *OnUpdateCommandPrev*

OnUpdateCommandNext
OnUpdateCommandDel

For example, this button,

which retrieves the first student record, is disabled when the list is empty and when the *m_position* variable is already set to the head of the list. Because a delay sometimes occurs in calling the update command UI functions, the command message handlers must check for error conditions.

Protected Virtual Functions

These three functions are protected virtual functions that deal specifically with *CStudent* objects:

GetEntry
InsertEntry
ClearEntry

Move these to a derived class if you want to isolate the general-purpose list-handling features in a base class.

Resource Requirements

The file EX15B.RC defines the application's resources as follows.

Symbols

Because the toolbar buttons aren't duplicated by menu items, you must add the command symbols manually. If you click the App Studio ID= toolbar button, you'll see the following symbols (among others):

Symbol	Value
ID_POS_DEL	0x8005
ID_POS_END	0x8002
ID_POS_HOME	0x8001
ID_POS_INS	0x8006
ID_POS_NEXT	0x8004
ID_POS_PREV	0x8003

Edit Menu

On the Edit menu, the clipboard menu items are replaced by the Clear All menu item. See step 2 on page 285 for an illustration of the Edit menu.

The *IDD_STUDENT* Dialog

The *IDD_STUDENT* dialog, shown here, is similar to the EX15A dialog shown in Figure 15-1 except that the Enter pushbutton has been replaced by the Clear pushbutton:

The following IDs identify the controls:

Control	ID
Name edit control	*IDC_NAME*
Grade edit control	*IDC_GRADE*
Clear pushbutton	*IDC_CLEAR*

The controls' styles are the same as for the *EX15A* program.

Toolbar

Here's the *IDR_MAINFRAME* bitmap resource:

314

The bitmap was created by erasing the Edit Cut, Copy, and Paste tiles (fourth, fifth, and sixth from the left) and replacing them with six new patterns. The Flip Vertical command (on the Image menu) was used to duplicate some of the tiles.

Testing the EX15B Application

Fill in the student name and grade fields, and then click this button

to insert the entry into the list. Repeat this action several more times, using the Clear push button to erase the data from the previous entry. When you exit the application, the debug output should look similar to this:

```
a CStudentDoc at $48EE
m_strTitle = Ex15b
m_strPathName =
m_bModified = 0
m_pDocTemplate = $46AE
a CObList with 4 elements

    a CStudent at $4DC2
m_name = Fisher, Lon
m_lGrade = 67
    a CStudent at $50FA
m_name = Meyers, Brian
m_lGrade = 80
    a CStudent at $5152
m_name = Seghers, John
m_lGrade = 92
    a CStudent at $51AA
m_name = Anderson, Bob
m_lGrade = 87
```

315

Two Exercises for the Reader

You might have noticed the absence of a modify toolbar button. Without such a button, you can't modify an existing student record. Can you add the necessary toolbar button and message handlers? The most difficult task might be designing a graphic for the button's tile.

Recall that the *CStudentView* class is just about ready to be a general-purpose base class. Try separating the *CStudent*-specific virtual functions into a derived class. After that, make another derived class that uses a new element class other than *CStudent*.

CHAPTER SIXTEEN

READING AND WRITING DOCUMENTS—SDI

As you've probably noticed, every AppWizard-generated program has a File menu that contains the familiar New, Open, Save, and Save As commands. In this chapter, you'll learn how to make your application respond to read and write documents.

Here we'll stick with the Single Document Interface (SDI) application because it's familiar territory. Chapter 17 introduces the Multiple Document Interface (MDI) application, which is more flexible in its handling of documents and files. In both chapters, you'll get a heavy but necessary dose of application framework theory; you'll learn a lot about the various helper classes that have been concealed up to this point. The going will be rough, but, believe me, you really have to know the details to get the most out of the application framework.

This chapter's example, EX16A, is an SDI application based on EX15B in the previous chapter. It uses the student list document with a *CFormView*-derived view class minus some of the frills such as the Edit Clear All command. Now the student list can be written to and read from disk through a process called serialization. Chapter 17 shows you how to use the same view and document classes to make an MDI application, and it shows how to retrofit an SDI application with the drag-and-drop file capability that is normally reserved for MDI applications.

Serialization—What Is It?

The term "serialization" might be new to you, but it's already seen some use in the world of object-oriented programming. The idea is that objects can be persistent, which means they can be saved on disk when a program exits and restored when the program is restarted. The process of saving and restoring objects is called serialization. In the Microsoft Foundation Class (MFC) Library, designated classes have a member function named *Serialize*. When the application framework calls *Serialize* for a particular object—for example, an object of class *CStudent*—the data for the student is either saved on disk or read from disk.

In the MFC library, serialization is not a substitute for a database management system. All the objects associated with a document are <u>sequentially</u> read from or written to a single disk file. It's not possible to access individual objects at random disk file addresses. If you need database capability in your application, consider using the Microsoft Open Database Connectivity (ODBC) software. Chapter 24 shows you how to use ODBC with the MFC library application framework.

Disk Files and Archives

How do you know whether *Serialize* should read or write data? How is *Serialize* connected to a disk file? With the MFC library, disk files are represented by objects of class *CFile*. A *CFile* object encapsulates the file handle that you get through the *CRuntime* function *_open*. This is <u>not</u> the buffered *FILE* pointer that you'd get with a call to *fopen*; rather, it's a handle to a binary file. This file handle is used by the application framework for *_read*, *_write*, and *_lseek* calls.

If your application does no direct disk I/O but instead relies on the serialization process, you can avoid direct use of *CFile* objects. Between the *Serialize* function and the *CFile* object is an archive object (of class *CArchive*), as shown in Figure 16-1.

The *CArchive* object buffers data for the *CFile* object, and it maintains an internal flag that indicates whether the archive is storing (writing to disk) or loading (reading from disk). Only one active archive is associated with a file at any one time. The application framework takes care of constructing the *CFile* and *CArchive* objects, opening the disk file for the *CFile* object, and associating the archive object with the file. All you have to do, in your *Serialize* function, is load data from or store data in the archive object. The application framework calls the document's *Serialize* function during the File Open and File Save processes.

Making a Class Serializable

A serializable class must be derived directly or indirectly from *CObject*. In addition, the class declaration must contain the *DECLARE_SERIAL* macro call,

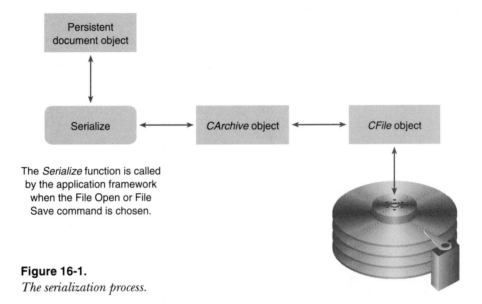

Figure 16-1.
The serialization process.

and the class implementation file must contain the *IMPLEMENT_SERIAL* macro call. (See the *Class Library Reference* for a description of these macros.) The *CStudent* class, which you'll be using in this chapter's examples, already uses these macros.

Writing a *Serialize* Function

In Chapter 15, you saw a *CStudent* class, derived from *CObject*, with these data members:

```
public:
    CString m_name;
    LONG    m_lGrade;
```

Now your job is to write a *Serialize* member function for *CStudent*. Because *Serialize* is a virtual member function of class *CObject*, you must be sure that the return value and parameter types match the *CObject* declaration. Here's the *Serialize* function for the *CStudent* class:

```
void CStudent::Serialize(CArchive& ar)
{
    if (ar.IsStoring())
        ar << m_name << m_lGrade;
    else
        ar >> m_name >> m_lGrade;
}
```

Serialization functions generally call the *Serialize* function of their base class. If *CStudent* were derived from *CPerson*, for example, the first line of the *Serialize* function would be

```
CPerson::Serialize(ar);
```

The *Serialize* functions for *CObject* and *CDocument* don't do anything useful, so there's no need to call them.

Notice that *ar* is a *CArchive* reference parameter that identifies the application's archive object. The *CArchive::IsStoring* member function tells us whether the archive is currently being used for storing or loading. The *CArchive* class has overloaded insertion operators (<<) and extraction operators (>>) for many of the C++ built-in types. MFC library classes that are not derived from *CObject*, such as *CString* and *CRect*, have their own overloaded insertion and extraction operators for *CArchive*.

Loading from an Archive—Embedded Objects vs. Pointers

Now, suppose your *CStudent* object has other objects embedded in it, and these objects are not instances of standard classes such as *CString*, *CTime*, and *CRect*. Let's add a new data member to the *CStudent* class:

```
public:
    CTranscript m_transcript;
```

Assume that *CTranscript* is a custom class, derived from *CObject*, with its own *Serialize* member function. The *CStudent::Serialize* function now becomes

```
void CStudent::Serialize(CArchive& ar)
{
    if (ar.IsStoring())
        ar << m_name << m_lGrade;
    else
        ar >> m_name >> m_lGrade;
    m_transcript.Serialize(ar);
}
```

Before the *CStudent::Serialize* function can be called to load a student record from the archive, a *CStudent* object must be constructed somewhere. The embedded *CTranscript* object *m_transcript* is constructed along with the *CStudent* object before the call to the *CTranscript::Serialize* function. When the *CTranscript::Serialize* function does get called, it can load the archived transcript data into the embedded *m_transcript* object.

Suppose that, instead of an embedded object, your *CStudent* object contained a *CTranscript* <u>pointer</u> data member such as this:

```
public:
    CTranscript* m_pTranscript;
```

Making Persistent Object Data Portable

A design goal for Microsoft Foundation Class Library version 2.5 was to make persistent object data portable between 16-bit Windows systems and 32-bit Windows systems (for example, Microsoft Windows NT). For this reason, *CArchive* does not have overloaded insertion operators and extraction operators for word-width-dependent types such as *int*. *CArchive* does support the following types, however:

Type	Description
BYTE	8 bits unsigned
WORD	16 bits unsigned
LONG	32 bits signed
DWORD	32 bits unsigned
float	32 bits
double	64 bits, IEEE standard

If you need to use word-width-dependent types, cast them to one of the supported types, as shown here:

```
void CStudent::Serialize(CArchive& ar)
{
    WORD w;

    if (ar.IsStoring()) {
      ar << (WORD) m_nMyInt;
    }
    else {
      ar >> w;
      m_nMyInt = (int) w;
    }
}
```

You could write your *Serialize* function as shown below, but as you can see, you must construct a new *CTranscript* object yourself:

```
void CStudent::Serialize(CArchive& ar)
{
    if (ar.IsStoring())
        ar << m_name << m_lGrade;
```

(continued)

```
    else {
        m_pTranscript = new CTranscript;
        ar >> m_name >> m_lGrade;
    }
    m_pTranscript->Serialize(ar);
}
```

Because the *CArchive* insertion and extraction operators are overloaded for *CObject* pointers, you could write *Serialize* this way instead:

```
void CStudent::Serialize(CArchive& ar)
{
    if (ar.IsStoring())
        ar << m_name << m_lGrade << m_pTranscript;
    else
        ar >> m_name >> m_lGrade >> m_pTranscript;
}
```

In the second case, use of the *DECLARE_SERIAL* and *IMPLEMENT_SERIAL* macros in the *CTranscript* class ensures that a *CTranscript* object will be constructed even though the archive extraction operator is overloaded for the *CObject* base class. Once the *CTranscript* object is constructed, the overridden *Serialize* function for *CTranscript* can be called to do the work of reading the student data from the disk file. Finally, the the *CTranscript* pointer is stored in the *m_pTranscript* data member. To avoid a memory leak, you must be sure that *m_pTranscript* does not already contain a pointer to a *CTranscript* object. If the *CStudent* object was just constructed and thus was not previously loaded from the archive, the transcript pointer will be null.

The insertion and extraction operators do <u>not</u> work with embedded objects of classes derived from *CObject*.

```
ar >> m_name >> m_lGrade >> &m_transcript; // don't try this
```

Serializing Collections

Because all collection classes are derived from the *CObject* class and the collection class declarations contain the *DECLARE_SERIAL* macro call, you can conveniently serialize collections with a call to the collection class's *Serialize* member function. If you call *Serialize* for a *CObList* collection of *CStudent* objects, for example, the *Serialize* function for each *CStudent* object will be called in turn. You should, however, know the following specific things about loading collections from an archive:

■ If a collection contains pointers to objects of mixed classes (all derived from *CObject*), the individual class names in essence are stored in the archive so that the objects can be properly constructed with the appropriate class constructor.

■ If a container object, such as a document, contains an <u>embedded</u> collection, loaded data is appended to the existing collection. You might need to empty the collection before loading from the archive. This is usually done in a *DeleteContents* function, which is called by the application framework.

■ If a container object contains a pointer to a collection, a new collection object is constructed when the extraction operator loads data from the archive. A pointer to the new collection is stored in the container object's pointer data member. You might need to destroy the old collection object (after emptying it) before loading from the archive.

■ When a collection of *CObject* pointers is loaded from an archive, the following processing steps take place for each object in the collection:

❑ The object's class is identified.

❑ Heap storage is allocated for the object.

❑ The object's data is loaded into the newly allocated storage.

❑ A pointer to the new object is stored in the collection.

The EX16A example, beginning on page 331, shows serialization of an embedded *CObList* collection.

The *Serialize* Function and the Application Framework

OK, so you know how to write serialize functions, and you know that these function calls can be nested. But do you know when the first *Serialize* function gets called to start the serialization process? With the application framework, everything is keyed to the document (the object of a class derived from *CDocument*). When you choose Save or Open from the File menu, the application framework creates a *CArchive* object (and underlying *CFile* object) and then calls your document class's *Serialize* function, passing a reference to the *CArchive* object. Your derived document class *Serialize* function then serializes each of its nontemporary data members.

NOTE: If you take a close look at any AppWizard-generated document class, you will notice that the class includes the *DECLARE_DYNCREATE* and *IMPLEMENT_DYNCREATE* macros instead of the *DECLARE_SERIAL* and *IMPLEMENT_SERIAL* macros. The *SERIAL* macros are not needed because document objects are never used in conjunction with the *CArchive* extraction operator or included in collections; the application framework calls the document's *Serialize* member function directly. You should include the *DECLARE_SERIAL* and *IMPLEMENT_SERIAL* macros in all other serializable classes.

The SDI Application

You've seen many SDI applications that have one document class and one view class. We'll stick to a single view class in this chapter, but we'll explore the interrelationships among the application object, the main frame window, the document, the view, the document template object, and the associated string and menu resources.

The Windows Application Object

For each of your applications, AppWizard has been quietly generating a class derived from *CWinApp*. It has also been generating a statement such as this:

```
CMyApp theApp;
```

What you're seeing here is the mechanism that starts an MFC library application. The class *CMyApp* is derived from the class *CWinApp*, and *theApp* is a globally declared instance of the class. This global object is called the Windows application object. Here's a summary of the startup steps in a Microsoft Windows MFC library application:

1. Windows loads your program into memory.

2. The global object *theApp* is constructed. (All globally declared objects are constructed immediately when the program is loaded.)

3. Windows calls the global function *WinMain*, which is part of the MFC library. (*WinMain* is equivalent to the non-Windows *main* function—each is a main program entry point.)

4. *WinMain* searches for the one and only instance of a class derived from *CWinApp*.

5. *WinMain* calls the *InitInstance* member function for *theApp*, which is overridden in your derived application class.

6. Your overridden *InitInstance* function starts the process of loading a document and displaying the main frame and view windows.

7. *WinMain* calls the *Run* member function for *theApp*, which starts the processes of dispatching window messages and command messages.

You can override another important *CWinApp* member function. The *ExitInstance* function is called when the application terminates, after all its windows are closed.

NOTE: Under certain conditions, Windows allows multiple instances of programs to run. Code is shared, but read/write data is not shared. The *InitInstance* function is called each time a program instance starts up. Another *CWinApp* function, *InitApplication,* is called when the <u>first</u> instance starts up. You can override *Init-Application* in your derived application class, but there's seldom a reason to do so.

The Document Template Class

If you look at the *InitInstance* function that AppWizard generates for your derived application class, you'll see that the following statement is featured prominently:

```
AddDocTemplate(new CSingleDocTemplate(IDR_MAINFRAME,
              RUNTIME_CLASS(CMyDoc),
              RUNTIME_CLASS(CMainFrame),    // main SDI frame window
              RUNTIME_CLASS(CMyView)));
```

Unless you start doing fancy things with splitter windows and multiple views, this is the only time you'll actually see a document template object. In this case it's an object of the class *CSingleDocTemplate*, which is derived from *CDocTemplate*. The *CSingleDocTemplate* class applies only to SDI applications because SDI applications are limited to one document object. *AddDoc-Template* is a member function of class *CWinApp*.

The *AddDocTemplate* call, together with the document template constructor call, establishes the relationships among <u>classes</u>—the application class, the document class, the view window class, and the main frame window class. The application object exists, of course, before template construction, but the document, view, and frame objects are <u>not</u> constructed at this time. The application framework later dynamically constructs these objects when they are needed.

This dynamic construction is a sophisticated use of the C++ language. Through the use of the *DECLARE_DYNCREATE* and *IMPLEMENT_DYN-CREATE* macros in the class declaration and implementation, the MFC library is able to construct objects of specified classes dynamically. If this dynamic construction capability weren't present, more relationships among your application's classes would have to be hard-coded. Your derived application class, for example, would need code for constructing document, view, and frame objects of your specific derived classes. This would compromise the object-oriented nature of your program.

With the template system, all that's required in your application class is use of the *RUNTIME_CLASS* macro, which converts a class name to a special pointer that the MFC library runtime mechanism can process. Notice that the target class's declaration must be included for this macro to work.

Figure 16-2 illustrates the relationships among the various classes, and Figure 16-3 illustrates the object relationships. The application can have more than one template (and associated class groups), but when the SDI program is running there can be only one document object and only one main frame window object.

Figure 16-2.
Class relationships.

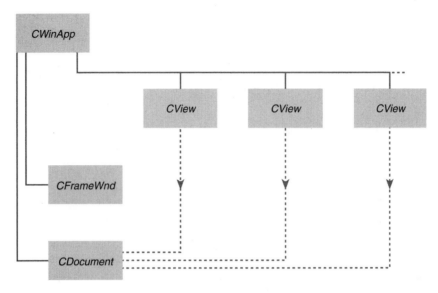

Figure 16-3.
Object relationships.

The Document Template Resource

The first *AddDocTemplate* parameter is *IDR_MAINFRAME*, the identifier for a string table resource. Here is the corresponding string that AppWizard might generate in the application's RC file:

```
IDR_MAINFRAME
    "MYAPP Windows Application\n"      // application window caption
    "MYAPP\n"                          // root for default document name
    "MYAPP Document\n"                 // document type name
    "MYAPP Files (*.xyz)\n"            // document type description & filter
    ".xyz"                             // extension for documents of this type
```

(Note: The resource compiler won't accept the string concatenations as shown above. If you examine the EX16A.RC file, you'll see the substrings combined in one large string.)

IDR_MAINFRAME specifies one string that is separated into substrings by \n. The substrings show up in various places when the application executes. The string *xyz* is the default document file extension specified to AppWizard.

The *IDR_MAINFRAME* ID, in addition to specifying the application's strings, identifies the application's icon, toolbar bitmap, and menus. AppWizard generates these resources, and App Studio maintains them.

So now you've seen how the *AddDocTemplate* call ties all the application elements together. Be aware, though, that no windows have been created yet, and therefore nothing appears on the screen.

Multiple Views of an SDI Document

Providing multiple views of an SDI document is a little more complicated. You could simply provide a menu item that allows the user to choose a view, or you could allow multiple views in a splitter window. Chapter 19 shows you how to use a splitter window.

Creating an Empty Document—The *CWinApp::OnFileNew* Function

After your application class's *InitInstance* function calls *AddDocTemplate*, it calls *OnFileNew*, another important *CWinApp* member function. *OnFileNew*, through a call to another *CWinApp* function, *OpenDocumentFile*, sorts through the web of interconnected class names and does the following:

1. Constructs the document object but does not attempt to read data from disk.

2. Constructs the main frame object (of class *CMainFrame*); also creates the main frame window but does not show it. The main frame window includes the *IDR_MAINFRAME* menu, the toolbar, and the status bar.

3. Constructs the view object; also creates the view window but doesn't show it.

4. Establishes connections among the document, main frame, and view <u>objects</u>. Do not confuse these object connections with the <u>class</u> connections established by the call to *AddDocTemplate*.

5. Calls the virtual *OnNewDocument* member function for the document object, which calls the virtual *DeleteContents* function.

6. Calls the virtual *OnInitialUpdate* member function for the view object.

7. Calls the virtual *ActivateFrame* for the frame object to show the main frame window together with the menus, view window, and control bars.

NOTE: Some of the functions listed above are not called directly by *OpenDocument* but are called indirectly through the application framework.

In an SDI application, the document, main frame, and view objects are created only once, and they last for the life of the program. The *CWinApp::-OnFileNew* function is called by *InitInstance*. It's also called in response to the File New menu item. In this case, *OnFileNew* must behave a little differently. It can't construct the document, frame, and view objects because they're already constructed. Instead, it reuses the existing document object and performs steps 5, 6, and 7 on the facing page. Notice that *OnFileNew* always calls *DeleteContents* to empty the document.

The Document Class's *OnNewDocument* Function

You've seen the view class *OnInitialUpdate* member function in Chapter 15, but the document class *OnNewDocument* member function is new. If an SDI application didn't reuse the same document object, you wouldn't need *OnNewDocument* because you could perform all document initialization in your document class constructor. Now you must override *OnNewDocument* to initialize your document object each time the user chooses File New or File Open. AppWizard helps you by providing a skeleton function in the derived document class it generates.

Connecting File Open to Your Serialization Code—*OnFileOpen*

When AppWizard generates an application, it maps the File Open menu item to the *CWinApp OnFileOpen* member function, which, through a call to the *CWinApp* function *OpenDocumentFile*, does the following:

1. Calls the virtual *OnOpenDocument* member function for the already existing document object. This function prompts the user to select a file and then opens the file, constructs a *CArchive* object set for loading, and calls *DeleteContents*.

2. Calls the document's *Serialize* function, which loads data from the archive.

3. Calls the view's *OnInitialUpdate* function.

NOTE: Some of the functions listed above are not called directly by *OpenDocument* but are called indirectly through the application framework.

The Most Recently Used (MRU) file list is a handy alternative to the File Open menu item. The application framework tracks the four most recently used files and displays their names on the File menu. These filenames are stored in the application's INI file between program executions.

The Document Class's *DeleteContents* Function

When you load an existing SDI document object from a disk file, you must somehow erase the existing contents of the document object. The best way to do this is to override the *CDocument::DeleteContents* virtual function in your derived document class. The overridden function, as you've seen in Chapter 15, does whatever is necessary to clean up your document class's data members. In response to both the File New and the File Open menu items, the *CDocument OnFileNew* and *OnFileOpen* functions both call the *DeleteContents* function, which means *DeleteContents* is called immediately after the document object is first constructed. It's called again when you close a document.

If you want your document classes to work in SDI applications, plan on emptying the document's contents in the *DeleteContents* member function rather than in the destructor. Use the destructor only to clean up items that last for the life of the object.

Connecting File Save and File Save As to Your Serialization Code

When AppWizard generates an application, it maps the File Save menu item to the *OnFileSave* member function of the *CDocument* class. *OnFileSave* calls the *CDocument* function *OnSaveDocument*, which in turn calls your document's *Serialize* function with an archive object set for storing. The File Save As menu item is handled in a similar manner; it is mapped to the *CDocument* function *OnFileSaveAs*, which calls *OnSaveDocument*. Here the application framework does all the file management necessary to save a document on disk.

> NOTE: Yes, it is true that the File New and File Open menu choices are mapped to <u>application</u> class member functions, but File Save and File Save As are mapped to <u>document</u> class member functions. File New is mapped to *OnFileNew*. The SDI version of *InitInstance* also calls *OnFileNew*. No document object exists when the application framework calls *InitInstance,* so *OnFileNew* can't possibly be a member function of *CDocument*. When a document is saved, however, a document object certainly exists.

The Document's *IsModified* Flag

Many document-oriented applications for Windows track the user's modification of a document. If the user tries to close a document or exit the program, a message box asks whether the user wants to save the document. The MFC library application framework directly supports this behavior with the *CDocument* data member *m_bModified*. This Boolean variable is *TRUE* if the document has been modified; otherwise, it is *FALSE*.

The protected *m_bModified* flag is accessed through the *CDocument* member functions *SetModifiedFlag* and *IsModified*. A document object's flag is set to *FALSE* when the document is created or read from disk and when it is saved on disk. You, the programmer, must use the *SetModifiedFlag* function to set the flag to *TRUE* when the document data changes.

In Visual Workbench, the toolbar disk button, which corresponds to the File Save menu item, is disabled whenever the currently selected document has not been modified. In the EX16A example, you'll see how a one-line update command UI function can use *IsModified* to control the state of the disk button and the corresponding menu item.

NOTE: In one respect, Microsoft Foundation Class Library version 2.5 SDI applications behave a little differently from other Windows SDI applications such as Notepad and Paintbrush. Here's a typical sequence of events:

1. The user creates a document and saves it on disk under the name, say, TEST.DAT.

2. The user modifies the document.

3. The user chooses File Open and then specifies TEST.DAT.

When the user chooses File Open, both Notepad and Paintbrush ask whether the user wants to save the changes made to the document (in step 2, above). If the user says no, the program rereads TEST.DAT from disk. A Microsoft Foundation Class Library version 2.5 application, on the other hand, assumes the changes are permanent and does not reread the file.

EX16A—An SDI Example with Serialization

This example is similar to example EX15B. The student dialog and bitmaps are the same, and the view class is the same. Serialization has been added, together with an update command UI function for File Save. The header and implementation files for the view and document classes will be reused in example EX17A in the next chapter.

All the new code (code that is different from EX15B) is listed, with additions and changes to the AppWizard-generated code and ClassWizard code shaded.

A list of the files and classes in the EX16A example is shown in the table on the following page:

Header File	Source Code File	Class	Description
EX16A.H	EX16A.CPP	*CEx16aApp*	Application class (from AppWizard)
		CAboutDlg	About dialog
MAINFRM.H	MAINFRM.CPP	*CMainFrame*	SDI main frame
STUDOC.H	STUDOC.CPP	*CStudentDoc*	Student document
STUVIEW.H	STUVIEW.CPP	*CStudentView*	Student form view (from EX15B)
STUDENT.H	STUDENT.CPP	*CStudent*	Student record
STDAFX.H	STDAFX.CPP		Precompiled headers

CStudent

The EX16A STUDENT.H file is based on the file in the EX15A project (shown in Figure 15-2 on page 283) and contains a prototype added for the *Serialize* function, as shown in Figure 16-4. The *CStudent* implementation file, STUDENT.CPP, now has the *Serialize* member function added, as shown in Figure 16-4.

STUDENT.H

```
// student.h
class CStudent : public CObject
{
    DECLARE_SERIAL(CStudent)
public:
    CString m_name;
    LONG    m_lGrade;

    CStudent() {
        m_lGrade = 0;
    }

    CStudent(const char* szName, int lGrade) : m_name(szName) {
        m_lGrade = lGrade;
    }

    CStudent(const CStudent& s) : m_name(s.m_name) {
        m_lGrade = s.m_lGrade;
    }
```

Figure 16-4.　　　　　　　　　　　　　　　　　　　　　　　*(continued)*
The STUDENT.H and STUDENT.CPP listings.

Figure 16-4. *continued*

```
    const CStudent& operator =(const CStudent& s)
    {
        m_name   = s.m_name;
        m_lGrade = s.m_lGrade;
        return *this;
    }

    BOOL operator ==(const CStudent& s) const
    {
        if ((m_name == s.m_name) && (m_lGrade == s.m_lGrade)) {
          return TRUE;
        }
        else {
          return FALSE;
        }
    }

    BOOL operator !=(const CStudent& s) const
    {
        // Let's make use of the operator we just defined!
        return !(*this == s);
    }

    virtual void Serialize(CArchive& ar);
#ifdef _DEBUG
    void Dump(CDumpContext& dc) const;
#endif
};
```

STUDENT.CPP

```
#include "stdafx.h"
#include "student.h"

IMPLEMENT_SERIAL(CStudent, CObject, 0)

void CStudent::Serialize(CArchive& ar)
{
    TRACE("Entering CStudent::Serialize\n");
    if (ar.IsStoring()) {
        ar << m_name << m_lGrade;
    }
    else {
        ar >> m_name >> m_lGrade;
    }
}
```

(continued)

Figure 16-4. *continued*

```
#ifdef _DEBUG
    void CStudent::Dump(CDumpContext& dc) const {
        CObject::Dump(dc);
        dc << "\nm_name = " << m_name << "\nm_lGrade = " << m_lGrade;
    }
#endif
```

CEx16aApp

Look carefully at the AppWizard-generated application class, shown in Figure 16-5, because it illustrates much of what we talked about earlier in this chapter. Your input to AppWizard determines how the application class opens documents. If you specify a file extension in the Classes dialog for the document class, you get the following code:

```
// simple command line parsing
if (m_lpCmdLine[0] == '\0')
{
    // create a new (empty) document
    OnFileNew();
}
else
{
    // open an existing document
    OpenDocumentFile(m_lpCmdLine);
}
```

In this case, the application accepts a document name on the command line. You can start the program from File Manager, and you can specify a file when setting up a Program Manager icon.

If you leave the file extension blank (the default case), you get this code:

```
// create a new (empty) document
OnFileNew();

if (m_lpCmdLine[0] != '\0')
{
    // TODO: add command line processing here
}
```

Now the application won't accept a filename command-line argument.

EX16A.H

```
#ifndef __AFXWIN_H__
    #error include 'stdafx.h' before including this file for PCH
#endif

#include "resource.h"        // main symbols

/////////////////////////////////////////////////////////////////////////////
// CEx16aApp:
// See ex16a.cpp for the implementation of this class
//

class CEx16aApp : public CWinApp
{
public:
    CEx16aApp();

// Overrides
    virtual BOOL InitInstance();

// Implementation

    //{{AFX_MSG(CEx16aApp)
    afx_msg void OnAppAbout();
        // NOTE - The ClassWizard will add and remove member functions here.
        //    DO NOT EDIT what you see in these blocks of generated code !
    //}}AFX_MSG
    DECLARE_MESSAGE_MAP()
};
```

EX16A.CPP

```
#include "stdafx.h"
#include "ex16a.h"

#include "mainfrm.h"
#include "studoc.h"
#include "stuview.h"

#ifdef _DEBUG
#undef THIS_FILE
static char BASED_CODE THIS_FILE[] = __FILE__;
#endif
```

Figure 16-5.   (*continued*)

The CEx16aApp *class listing.*

Figure 16-5. *continued*

```
///////////////////////////////////////////////////////////////////////////
// CEx16aApp

BEGIN_MESSAGE_MAP(CEx16aApp, CWinApp)
    //{{AFX_MSG_MAP(CEx16aApp)
    ON_COMMAND(ID_APP_ABOUT, OnAppAbout)
        // NOTE - the ClassWizard will add and remove mapping macros here.
        //    DO NOT EDIT what you see in these blocks of generated code !
    //}}AFX_MSG_MAP
    // Standard file based document commands
    ON_COMMAND(ID_FILE_NEW, CWinApp::OnFileNew)
    ON_COMMAND(ID_FILE_OPEN, CWinApp::OnFileOpen)
END_MESSAGE_MAP()


///////////////////////////////////////////////////////////////////////////
// CEx16aApp construction

CEx16aApp::CEx16aApp()
{
    // TODO: add construction code here,
    // Place all significant initialization in InitInstance
}


///////////////////////////////////////////////////////////////////////////
// The one and only CEx16aApp object

CEx16aApp NEAR theApp;

///////////////////////////////////////////////////////////////////////////
// CEx16aApp initialization

BOOL CEx16aApp::InitInstance()
{
    // Standard initialization
    // If you are not using these features and wish to reduce the size
    //  of your final executable, you should remove from the following
    //  the specific initialization routines you do not need.

    SetDialogBkColor();            // set dialog background color to gray
    LoadStdProfileSettings();  // Load standard INI file options
                               //  (including MRU)

    // Register the application's document templates.  Document templates
    //  serve as the connection between documents, frame windows, and views.
```

(continued)

Figure 16-5. *continued*

```
    AddDocTemplate(new CSingleDocTemplate(IDR_MAINFRAME,
            RUNTIME_CLASS(CStudentDoc),
            RUNTIME_CLASS(CMainFrame),      // main SDI frame window
            RUNTIME_CLASS(CStudentView)));

    // simple command line parsing
    if (m_lpCmdLine[0] == '\0')
    {
        // create a new (empty) document
        OnFileNew();
    }
    else
    {
        // open an existing document
        OpenDocumentFile(m_lpCmdLine);
    }

    return TRUE;
}
/////////////////////////////////////////////////////////////////////
// CAboutDlg dialog used for App About

class CAboutDlg : public CDialog
{
public:
    CAboutDlg() : CDialog(CAboutDlg::IDD)
        {
            //{{AFX_DATA_INIT(CAboutDlg)
            //}}AFX_DATA_INIT
        }

// Dialog Data
    //{{AFX_DATA(CAboutDlg)
        enum { IDD = IDD_ABOUTBOX };
    //}}AFX_DATA

// Implementation
protected:
    virtual void DoDataExchange(CDataExchange* pDX);    // DDX/DDV support
    //{{AFX_MSG(CAboutDlg)
        // No message handlers
    //}}AFX_MSG
    DECLARE_MESSAGE_MAP()
};
```

(continued)

337

Figure 16-5. *continued*

```
void CAboutDlg::DoDataExchange(CDataExchange* pDX)
{
    CDialog::DoDataExchange(pDX);
    //{{AFX_DATA_MAP(CAboutDlg)
    //}}AFX_DATA_MAP
}

BEGIN_MESSAGE_MAP(CAboutDlg, CDialog)
    //{{AFX_MSG_MAP(CAboutDlg)
        // No message handlers
    //}}AFX_MSG_MAP
END_MESSAGE_MAP()

// App command to run the dialog
void CEx16aApp::OnAppAbout()
{
    CAboutDlg aboutDlg;
    aboutDlg.DoModal();
}
```

CFrameWnd

The main frame window class code, shown in Figure 16-6, is almost unchanged from the code that AppWizard generated. The toolbar button constants are added, and the overridden *ActivateFrame* function exists solely for trace purposes.

MAINFRM.H

```
class CMainFrame : public CFrameWnd
{
protected: // create from serialization only
    CMainFrame();
    DECLARE_DYNCREATE(CMainFrame)

// Attributes
public:

// Operations
public:

// Implementation
public:
```

Figure 16-6. *(continued)*

The CMainFrame *class listing.*

Figure 16-6. *continued*

```
        virtual ~CMainFrame();
        virtual void ActivateFrame(int nCmdhow = -1);

protected:      // control bar embedded members
    CStatusBar      m_wndStatusBar;
    CToolBar        m_wndToolBar;

// Generated message map functions
protected:
    //{{AFX_MSG(CMainFrame)
    afx_msg int OnCreate(LPCREATESTRUCT lpCreateStruct);
        // NOTE - the ClassWizard will add and remove member functions here.
        //     DO NOT EDIT what you see in these blocks of generated code !
    //}}AFX_MSG
    DECLARE_MESSAGE_MAP()
};
```

MAINFRM.CPP

```
#include "stdafx.h"
#include "ex16a.h"

#include "mainfrm.h"

#ifdef _DEBUG
#undef THIS_FILE
static char BASED_CODE THIS_FILE[] = __FILE__;
#endif

/////////////////////////////////////////////////////////////////////////
// CMainFrame

IMPLEMENT_DYNCREATE(CMainFrame, CFrameWnd)

BEGIN_MESSAGE_MAP(CMainFrame, CFrameWnd)
    //{{AFX_MSG_MAP(CMainFrame)
        // NOTE - the ClassWizard will add and remove mapping macros here.
        //     DO NOT EDIT what you see in these blocks of generated code !
    ON_WM_CREATE()
    //}}AFX_MSG_MAP
END_MESSAGE_MAP()

/////////////////////////////////////////////////////////////////////////
// arrays of IDs are used to initialize control bars.
```

(continued)

Figure 16-6. *continued*

```
// toolbar buttons - IDs are command buttons
static UINT BASED_CODE buttons[] =
{
    // same order as in the bitmap 'toolbar.bmp'
    ID_FILE_NEW,
    ID_FILE_OPEN,
    ID_FILE_SAVE,
        ID_SEPARATOR,
    ID_POS_HOME,
    ID_POS_END,
    ID_POS_PREV,
    ID_POS_NEXT,
    ID_POS_DEL,
    ID_POS_INS,
        ID_SEPARATOR,
    ID_FILE_PRINT,
    ID_APP_ABOUT,
};

static UINT BASED_CODE indicators[] =
{
    ID_SEPARATOR,               // status line indicator
    ID_INDICATOR_CAPS,
    ID_INDICATOR_NUM,
    ID_INDICATOR_SCRL,
};


/////////////////////////////////////////////////////////////////////////////
// CMainFrame construction/destruction

CMainFrame::CMainFrame()
{
    // TODO: add member initialization code here
}

CMainFrame::~CMainFrame()
{
}

void CMainFrame::ActivateFrame(int nCmdShow)
{
    // overridden here only for tracing
    TRACE("Entering CMainFrame::ActivateFrame\n");
    CFrameWnd::ActivateFrame(nCmdShow);
}
```

(continued)

Figure 16-6. *continued*

```
int CMainFrame::OnCreate(LPCREATESTRUCT lpCreateStruct)
{
    if (CFrameWnd::OnCreate(lpCreateStruct) == -1)
        return -1;

    if (!m_wndToolBar.Create(this) ||
        !m_wndToolBar.LoadBitmap(IDR_MAINFRAME) ||
        !m_wndToolBar.SetButtons(buttons,
          sizeof(buttons)/sizeof(UINT)))
    {
        TRACE("Failed to create toolbar\n");
        return -1;         // fail to create
    }

    if (!m_wndStatusBar.Create(this) ||
        !m_wndStatusBar.SetIndicators(indicators,
          sizeof(indicators)/sizeof(UINT)))
    {
        TRACE("Failed to create status bar\n");
        return -1;         // fail to create
    }

    return 0;
}
```

CStudentDoc

The *CStudentDoc* class is the same as the *CStudentDoc* class from the previous chapter (shown in Figure 15-4 on page 298) except for three functions: *Serialize, OnOpenDocument,* and *OnUpdateFileSave.*

Serialize

One line has been added to the AppWizard-generated function to serialize the document's student list.

```
/////////////////////////////////////////////////////////////////////////
// CStudentDoc serialization

void CStudentDoc::Serialize(CArchive& ar)
{
    if (ar.IsStoring())
    {
        // TODO: add storing code here for other data members
    }
```

(continued)

```
    else
    {
        // TODO: add loading code here for other data members
    }
    m_studentList.Serialize(ar);
}
```

OnOpenDocument

This virtual function is overridden only for the purpose of displaying a *TRACE* message.

```
BOOL CStudentDoc::OnOpenDocument(const char* pszPathName)
{
    TRACE("Entering CStudentDoc::OnOpenDocument\n");
    if (!CDocument::OnOpenDocument(pszPathName))
        return FALSE;
    return TRUE;
}
```

OnUpdateFileSave

This is a message map function that grays the File Save toolbar button when the document is in the unmodified state. The view controls this state by calling the document's *SetModifiedFlag* function.

```
void CStudentDoc::OnUpdateFileSave(CCmdUI* pCmdUI)
{
    // disable disk toolbar button if file is not modified
    pCmdUI->Enable(IsModified());
}
```

CStudentView

The code for the *CStudentView* class comes from the previous chapter. Figure 15-5 on page 303 shows the code.

AppWizard and EX16A

If you were using AppWizard to start the EX16A project, you would specify document type name *Student* and file extension *16a* in the Classes dialog as shown in Figure 16-7.

Figure 16-7.
The EX16A AppWizard Classes dialog.

This ensures that the document template resource string contains the correct default extension.

Testing the EX16A Application

Build the program, and then test it by typing some data and saving it on disk with the filename *TEST.16A*. (You don't need to type the *.16A*.) Now the window should look similar to Figure 16-8.

Figure 16-8.
The EX16A window.

Exit the program, and then restart it and open the file you saved. Did the names come back? Take a look at the Debug Messages window and observe the sequence of function calls. Is the following sequence produced when you start the application?

```
Entering CStudentDoc constructor
Entering CMainFrame constructor
Entering CStudentView constructor
Entering CStudentDoc::OnNewDocument
Entering CStudentDoc::DeleteContents
Entering CStudentView::OnInitialUpdate
Entering CStudentView::OnUpdate
Entering CMainFrame::ActivateFrame
```

File Manager Document Association

Start the Windows File Manager, and then open the directory \VCPP\EX16A. Widen the file search to include Other Files, and then select the file TEST.16A. Choose Associate from the File menu. Fill in the dialog as shown in Figure 16-9.

Figure 16-9.
File Manager window with File Manager Associate dialog.

Now narrow the File Manager's search to Documents. Only files with the 16A suffix will be shown, denoted by this document symbol:

Double-click TEST.16A. Does the EX16A program start up? If you look in WIN.INI, you'll see the line

```
16A=c:\vcpp\ex16a\ex16a.exe ^.16A
```

File Manager also inserts a new (redundant) entry in the Windows Registration Database; you'll learn more about that in the next chapter.

READING AND WRITING DOCUMENTS—MDI

This chapter introduces the Microsoft Foundation Class (MFC) Library version 2.5 Multiple Document Interface (MDI) application and explains how it reads and writes its document files. The MDI application is really the preferred MFC library program style. AppWizard endows only MDI applications with capabilities such as File Manager drag and drop, and most of the sample programs that come with Microsoft Visual C++ are MDI applications.

Here you'll learn the similarities and differences between Single Document Interface (SDI) and MDI applications, and you'll see how the MDI application handles files dragged and dropped from Windows File Manager. You'll also learn how, with little effort, you can retrofit SDI applications with this drag-and-drop capability. Be sure you thoroughly understand the SDI application, as described in Chapter 16, before you attack the MDI application.

The MDI Application

Before you look at the class library code for MDI applications, you should be familiar with the operation of Windows MDI programs. Take a close look at the Visual C++ Visual Workbench now. It's an MDI application whose "multiple documents" are program source code files. Visual Workbench is not the most typical MDI application, though, because it collects its documents into projects. It's better to examine Microsoft Word for Windows or, better yet, to examine a real class library MDI application—the kind that AppWizard generates.

A Typical MDI Application, MFC Library Style

This chapter's first example, EX17A, is an MDI version of EX16A. Look back at Figure 16-8 on page 343 to see an illustration of the SDI version after the user has selected a file. Now look at the MDI equivalent, shown in Figure 17-1.

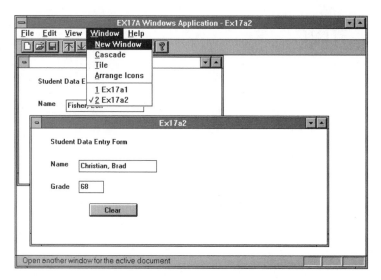

Figure 17-1.
The EX17A application with two files open and the Window menu shown.

The user has two separate document files open, each in a separate MDI child window, but only one child window is active—the lower window, which lies on top of the other child window. The application has only one menu and one toolbar, and all commands are routed to the active child window. The main window's title bar reflects the name of the active child window's document file.

The child window's minimize box allows the user to reduce the child window to an icon in the main window. The application's Window menu (shown in Figure 17-1) lets the user control the presentation through the following items:

Menu Item	Action
New Window	Opens an additional child window for the selected document
Cascade	Arranges the existing windows in an overlapped pattern
Tile	Arranges the existing windows in a nonoverlapped, tiled pattern
Arrange Icons	Arranges iconized windows in the frame window
(document names)	Selects the corresponding child window and brings it to the top

If the user saves and closes both child windows (and opens the File menu), the application looks like Figure 17-2 on the next page.

The menu is different: Most toolbar buttons are disabled, and the window caption does not show a filename. About the only thing the user can do is start a new document or open an existing document from disk.

Figure 17-3 on the next page shows the application when it first starts up and a new document is created. The single child window has been maximized.

For Windows SDK Programmers

Starting with version 3.0, Windows has directly supported MDI applications. The Microsoft Foundation Class (MFC) Library version 2.5 builds on this Windows support to make an MDI environment that parallels the SDI environment. In an SDK MDI application, a main application frame window contains the menu and a single "client window." The client window manages various child windows that correspond to documents. The MDI client window has its own preregistered window class (not to be confused with a C++ class) with a procedure that handles special messages such as WM_MDICASCADE and WM_MDITILE. An MDI child window procedure is similar to the window procedure for an SDI main window.

In the MFC library, the *CMDIFrameWnd* class encapsulates the functions of both the main frame window and the MDI client window. This class has message handlers for all the Windows MDI messages and thus can manage its child windows, which are represented by objects of class *CMDIChildWnd*.

Figure 17-2.
EX17A with no child windows.

Figure 17-3.
EX17A with initial child window.

The single, empty child window has the default document name Ex17a1. This name is based on the Doc Type Name you selected in the AppWizard Classes dialog, Ex17a. The first new file is Ex17a1, the second is Ex17a2, and so forth. The user normally chooses a different name when saving the document.

MFC library MDI applications, like many commercial MDI applications, start up with a new, empty document. (Visual Workbench is an exception.) If you want your application to start up with a blank frame, you can remove the *OnFileNew* call in the application class file as shown in example EX17A.

The MDI Application Object

You're probably wondering how an MDI application works and what code makes it different from an SDI application. Actually, the startup sequences are pretty much the same. An application object, of a class derived from class *CWinApp*, has an overridden *InitInstance* member function. This *InitInstance* function is somewhat different from the SDI *InitInstance*, starting with the call to *AddDocTemplate*.

The MDI Document Template Class

The MDI template construction call in *InitInstance* looks like this:

```
AddDocTemplate(new CMultiDocTemplate(IDR_MYDOCTYPE,
        RUNTIME_CLASS(CMyDoc),
        RUNTIME_CLASS(CMDIChildWnd),    // standard MDI child frame
        RUNTIME_CLASS(CMyView)));
```

Like the *CSingleDocTemplate* class you saw in Chapter 16, the *CMultiDocTemplate* class allows an application to use multiple document types, but, unlike the *CSingleDocTemplate* class, it allows the simultaneous existence of more than one document object. This is the essence of the MDI application.

The single *AddDocTemplate* call shown above permits the MDI application to support multiple child windows, each connected to a document object and a view object. It's possible to have several child windows (and corresponding view objects) connected to the same document object. In this chapter, we'll start with only one view class and one document class. You'll see multiple view classes and multiple document classes in Chapter 19.

The MDI Frame Window and Child Window

The SDI examples had only one frame window class and only one frame window object. For SDI applications, AppWizard generated a class called *CMainFrame*, which was derived from the class *CFrameWnd*. An MDI application has two frame window base classes and many frame objects, as shown in the table on the following page. The MDI frame–view window relationship is shown in Figure 17-4 on the following page.

Base Class	AppWizard-Generated Class	Number of Objects	Menu and Control Bars	Contains a View	Object Constructed
CMDIFrameWnd	*CMainFrame*	1 only	Yes	No	In application class's *InitInstance* function
CMDIChildWnd	No derivation	1 per child window	No	Yes	By application framework when a new child window is opened

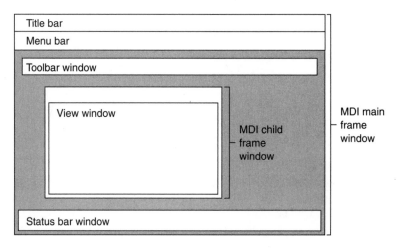

Figure 17-4.
The MDI frame–view window relationship.

In an SDI application, the *CMainFrame* object framed the application <u>and</u> contained the view object. In an MDI application, the two roles are separated. Now the *CMainFrame* object is constructed in *InitInstance*, and the *CMDIChildWnd* object contains the view. AppWizard generates code as shown here:

```
CMainFrame* pMainFrame = new CMainFrame;
if (!pMainFrame->LoadFrame(IDR_MAINFRAME))
    return FALSE;
pMainFrame->ShowWindow(m_nCmdShow);
pMainFrame->UpdateWindow();
m_pMainWnd = pMainFrame;
```

The application framework can create the *CMDIChildWnd* objects dynamically because the *CMDIChildWnd* class is passed to the *CMultiDoc-Template* constructor.

(Note: The MDI *InitInstance* function sets the *CWinApp* data member *m_pMainWnd* to point to the application's main frame window. This means you can access *m_pMainWnd* through the global *AfxGetApp* function any time you need to get your application's main frame window.)

The Main Frame and Document Template Resources

An MDI application has two separate string and menu resources, identified by the constants *IDR_MAINFRAME* and *IDR_MYDOCTYPE*. The first resource set goes with the empty main frame window; the second set goes with the occupied main frame window. Here are the two string resources with substrings broken out:

```
IDR_MAINFRAME
    "MYAPP Windows Application"       // application window caption

IDR_MYDOCTYPE
    "\nn                             // application window caption
    "MYAPP\n"                        // root for default document name
    "MYAPP Document\n"               // document type name
    "MYAPP Files (*.17a)\n"          // document type description and filter
    ".17a\n"                         // extension for documents of this type
    "MYAPPFileType\n"                // registration database document ID
    "MYAPP File Type"                // registration database document
                                     //  description
```

(Note: The resource compiler won't accept the string concatenations as shown above. If you examine the EX17A.RC file, you'll see the substrings combined in one large string.)

The application window caption comes from the *IDR_MAINFRAME* string. When a document is open, the document filename is appended. The last two substrings in the *IDR_MYDOCTYPE* string are there to support drag and drop.

Creating an Empty Document—The *CWinApp::OnFileNew* Function

The MDI *InitInstance* function calls *OnFileNew*, as did the SDI *InitInstance* function. This time, however, the main frame window has already been created. *OnFileNew*, through a call to the *CWinApp* function *OpenDocumentFile*, now does the following:

1. Constructs a document object but does not attempt to read data from disk.

2. Constructs a child frame window object (of class *CMDIChildWnd*). Also creates the child frame window but does not show it. In the main frame window, the *IDR_MAINFRAME* menu is replaced by the *IDR_MYDOCTYPE* menu. *IDR_MYDOCTYPE* also identifies an icon resource that is used when the child window is minimized within the frame.

3. Constructs a view object. Also creates the view window but does not show it.

4. Establishes connections among the document, the main frame, and view <u>objects</u>. Do not confuse these object connections with the <u>class</u> associations established by the call to *AddDocTemplate*.

5. Calls the virtual *OnNewDocument* member function for the document object.

6. Calls the virtual *OnInitialUpdate* member function for the view object.

7. Calls the virtual *ActivateFrame* for the child frame object to show the frame window and view window.

The *OnFileNew* function is also called in response to the File New menu command. In an MDI application, *OnFileNew* performs the exact same steps as it does when called from *InitInstance*.

NOTE: Some functions listed above are not called directly by *OpenDocumentFile* but are called indirectly through the application framework.

Creating an Additional View for an Existing Document

If you choose New Window from the Window menu, the application framework opens a new child window that's linked to the currently selected document. The associated *CMDIFrameWnd* function, *OnWindowNew*, does the following:

1. Constructs a child frame object (of class *CMDIChildWnd*). Also creates the child frame window but does not show it.

2. Constructs a view object. Also creates the view window but does not show it.

3. Establishes connections between the new view object and the existing document and main frame objects.

4. Calls the virtual *OnInitialUpdate* member function for the view object.

5. Calls the virtual *ActivateFrame* for the child frame object to show the frame window and the view window.

Loading and Storing Documents

In MDI applications, documents are loaded and stored the same way as in SDI applications, but with two important differences: A new document object is constructed each time a document file is loaded from disk, and the document object is destroyed when the child window is closed. Don't worry about clearing a document's contents before loading—but you should override the *CDocument::DeleteContents* function anyway to make the class portable to the SDI environment.

Multiple Document Templates

An MDI application can support multiple document templates through multiple calls to the *AddDocTemplate* function. Each template can specify a different combination of document, view, and MDI child frame classes. When the user chooses New from the File menu, the application framework displays a list box that allows the user to choose a template by name as specified in the string resource. Multiple *AddDocTemplate* calls are not fully supported in SDI applications because the document, view, and frame objects are constructed once for the life of the application.

Drag and Drop—Programs and Documents

In the IBM PC world, users are accustomed to starting up a program and then selecting a disk file (sometimes called a document) that contains data the program understands. All MS-DOS programs worked this way, and Windows improved things by allowing the user to double-click on a program icon instead of typing a program name. Meanwhile the Apple Macintosh users were double-clicking on a document icon, and the Macintosh operating system figured out which program to run.

Windows version 3.1 also allows users to double-click on a document icon to run programs. But how does Windows know which program to run when a user double-clicks a document icon? In Chapter 16, you used File Manager to manually associate a file type with a program. This association process placed a line in the [Extensions] section of WIN.INI that linked a three-character file extension with the program name. When File Manager started the program, it put the selected filename in the command line, and the program opened the file on startup.

Now we'll take this process to a new level. No longer will we (or the user) need to manually associate a document type with a program. After the user executes the program the first time as part of the installation process, he or she will be able to drag a file from File Manager and drop it into a running application's main window. The user can still double-click on a document icon in File Manager, but the program launch process is significantly different.

Program Registration

Windows maintains a database of program information in a file called REG.DAT. This registration database supports both OLE and File Manager drag and drop. As far as drag and drop is concerned, each database entry contains program parameters, including the program identifier, the file type description, and the command line. A Windows utility program, REGEDIT, allows editing of the registration database. Figure 17-5 shows a typical REGEDIT window for an MFC library MDI program.

You and your user don't have to mess with REGEDIT because Windows provides a function to register a program, and the application framework wraps this function with a *CWinApp* member function. The following line in your derived application class *InitInstance* function does the job:

```
RegisterShellFileTypes();
```

The first time your MDI program is run (from Visual Workbench or from Program Manager), the registration database is updated to include the program's identifier and command line parameters, and the WIN.INI file is updated to associate the file extension with the program identifier. You might notice a slight delay while the files are updated.

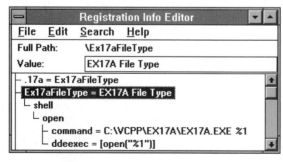

Figure 17-5.
The REGEDIT window.

NOTE: REGEDIT was run with the /v switch.

Enabling Drag and Drop

If you want your already-running program to open files dragged from File Manager, you must call the *CWnd* function *DragAcceptFiles* for the application's main frame window. The application object's public data member *m_pMainWnd* points to the *CMDIFrameWnd* object. The following line in *Init-Instance* enables drag and drop:

```
m_pMainWnd->DragAcceptFiles();
```

Enabling Embedded Launch

In the SDI example EX16A, File Manager started an associated program by including the document filename in the program's command line. File Manager can also start a program through an embedded launch procedure, and that's what AppWizard sets up for MDI applications. An embedded launch is a two-step process. First, the program is executed with the *-e* parameter as specified in the registration database. After it's running, the program gets a message via Windows' Dynamic Data Exchange (DDE) that tells it to load a file.

The following call to a *CWinApp* member function is included in *InitInstance*:

```
EnableShellOpen();
```

This function does the setup necessary for the program to accept DDE messages.

Program Startup Parameters

When an MFC library MDI program is run from Program Manager, there is usually no command line parameter. When it's run from File Manager (an embedded launch), the registration database ensures that the program is run with the *-e* parameter. Here's the code in the derived application class *InitInstance* function that processes the command line:

```
if (m_lpCmdLine[0] == '\0')
{
    // Create a new (empty) document.
    OnFileNew();
}
```

(continued)

```
else if ((m_lpCmdLine[0] == '-' || m_lpCmdLine[0] == '/') &&
         (m_lpCmdLine[1] == 'e' || m_lpCmdLine[1] == 'E'))
{
    // program launched embedded - wait for DDE or OLE open
}
else
{
    // open an existing document
    OpenDocumentFile(m_lpCmdLine);
}
```

If there's no command line argument, the program creates a new, empty child window. If the command line contains something that looks like a filename, the program creates a new child window and loads that file. In an embedded launch, the program waits for a DDE message.

Responding to DDE Messages

The base classes take care of the DDE messages that result from drag and drop and File Manager embedded launch (with the *-e* command line parameter). In drag and drop, the application framework calls the *CWinApp* function *OpenDocumentFile* with the filename as a parameter. In an embedded launch, the application framework calls two *CWinApp* functions: *OnDDE-Command* and *OpenDocumentFile*. You normally don't need to override these functions in your derived application class. Let the application framework do the work.

The EX17A Example

This example is the MDI version of EX16A from the previous chapter. It uses exactly the same document and view class code and the same resources (except for the program name). The application code and main frame class code are different, however. All the new code is listed here, including the code that AppWizard generates.

Here's a list of the files and classes in the EX17A example:

Header File	Source Code File	Class	Description
EX17A.H	EX17A.CPP	*CEx17aApp*	Application class (from AppWizard)
		CAboutDlg	About dialog
MAINFRM.H	MAINFRM.CPP	*CMainFrame*	MDI main frame

(continued)

Header File	Source Code File	Class	Description
STUDOC.H	STUDOC.CPP	*CStudentDoc*	Student document (from EX16A)
STUVIEW.H	STUVIEW.CPP	*CStudentView*	Student form view (from EX15B)
STUDENT.H	STUDENT.CPP	*CStudent*	Student record (from EX16A)
STDAFX.H	STDAFX.CPP		Precompiled headers

CEx17aApp

Two functions, *OpenDocumentFile* and *OnDDECommand*, are overridden only for the purpose of inserting *TRACE* statements. Also, the *OnFileNew* call in *InitInstance* has been commented out to prevent the creation of an empty document window on startup. Figure 17-6 shows the source code.

EX17A.H

```
#ifndef __AFXWIN_H__
    #error include 'stdafx.h' before including this file for PCH
#endif

#include "resource.h"        // main symbols

/////////////////////////////////////////////////////////////////////
// CEx17aApp:
// See ex17a.cpp for the implementation of this class
//

class CEx17aApp : public CWinApp
{
public:
    CEx17aApp();

// Overrides
    virtual BOOL InitInstance();
    // open named file
    virtual CDocument* OpenDocumentFile(LPCSTR lpszFileName);
    virtual BOOL OnDDECommand(char* pszCommand);
```

Figure 17-6. *(continued)*

The CEx17aApp source listing.

Figure 17-6. *continued*

```
// Implementation

    //{{AFX_MSG(CEx17aApp)
    afx_msg void OnAppAbout();
        // NOTE - the ClassWizard will add and remove member functions
        // here.
        //    DO NOT EDIT what you see in these blocks of generated code !
    //}}AFX_MSG
    DECLARE_MESSAGE_MAP()
};
```

EX17A.CPP

```
#include "stdafx.h"
#include "ex17a.h"

#include "mainfrm.h"
#include "student.h"
#include "studoc.h"
#include "stuview.h"

#ifdef _DEBUG
#undef THIS_FILE
static char BASED_CODE THIS_FILE[] = __FILE__;
#endif

/////////////////////////////////////////////////////////////////////////
// CEx17aApp

BEGIN_MESSAGE_MAP(CEx17aApp, CWinApp)
    //{{AFX_MSG_MAP(CEx17aApp)
    ON_COMMAND(ID_APP_ABOUT, OnAppAbout)
        // NOTE - the ClassWizard will add and remove mapping macros here.
        //    DO NOT EDIT what you see in these blocks of generated code !
    //}}AFX_MSG_MAP
    // Standard file based document commands
    ON_COMMAND(ID_FILE_NEW, CWinApp::OnFileNew)
    ON_COMMAND(ID_FILE_OPEN, CWinApp::OnFileOpen)
END_MESSAGE_MAP()

/////////////////////////////////////////////////////////////////////////
// CEx17aApp construction

CEx17aApp::CEx17aApp()
{
```

(continued)

Figure 17-6. *continued*

```
    // TODO: add construction code here
    // Place all significant initialization in InitInstance
}

/////////////////////////////////////////////////////////////////
// The one and only CEx17aApp object

CEx17aApp NEAR theApp;

/////////////////////////////////////////////////////////////////
// CEx17aApp initialization

BOOL CEx17aApp::InitInstance()
{
    // Standard initialization
    // If you are not using these features and wish to reduce the size
    //   of your final executable, you should remove from the following
    //   the specific initialization routines you do not need.

    SetDialogBkColor();          // set dialog background color to gray
    LoadStdProfileSettings();    // Load standard INI file options
                                 //   (including MRU)

    // Register the application's document templates.  Document templates
    //   serve as the connection between documents,
    //   frame windows, and views.

    AddDocTemplate(new CMultiDocTemplate(IDR_EX17ATYPE,
            RUNTIME_CLASS(CStudentDoc),
            RUNTIME_CLASS(CMDIChildWnd),      // standard MDI
                                              //   child frame
            RUNTIME_CLASS(CStudentView)));

    // create main MDI Frame window
    CMainFrame* pMainFrame = new CMainFrame;
    if (!pMainFrame->LoadFrame(IDR_MAINFRAME))
        return FALSE;
    pMainFrame->ShowWindow(m_nCmdShow);
    pMainFrame->UpdateWindow();
    m_pMainWnd = pMainFrame;

    // enable file manager drag/drop and DDE Execute open
    m_pMainWnd->DragAcceptFiles();
    EnableShellOpen();
    RegisterShellFileTypes();
```

(continued)

Figure 17-6. *continued*

```
        // simple command line parsing
        if (m_lpCmdLine[0] == '\0')
        {
            // create a new (empty) document
//          OnFileNew();
        }
        else if ((m_lpCmdLine[0] == '-' || m_lpCmdLine[0] == '/') &&
            (m_lpCmdLine[1] == 'e' || m_lpCmdLine[1] == 'E'))
        {
            // program launched embedded - wait for DDE or OLE open
        }
        else
        {
            // open an existing document
            OpenDocumentFile(m_lpCmdLine);
        }

        return TRUE;
}


/////////////////////////////////////////////////////////////////////////
CDocument* CEx17aApp::OpenDocumentFile(LPCSTR lpszFileName)
{
    TRACE("Entering CEx17aApp::OpenDocumentFile - %s\n", lpszFileName);
    return CWinApp::OpenDocumentFile(lpszFileName);
}


/////////////////////////////////////////////////////////////////////////
BOOL CEx17aApp::OnDDECommand(char* pszCommand)
{
    TRACE("Entering CEx17aApp::OnDDECommand - %s\n", pszCommand);
    return CWinApp::OnDDECommand(pszCommand);
}


/////////////////////////////////////////////////////////////////////
// CAboutDlg dialog used for App About

class CAboutDlg : public CDialog
{
public:
    CAboutDlg();

// Dialog Data
    //{{AFX_DATA(CAboutDlg)
    enum { IDD = IDD_ABOUTBOX };
    //}}AFX_DATA
```

(continued)

Figure 17-6. *continued*

```
// Implementation
protected:
    virtual void DoDataExchange(CDataExchange* pDX); // DDX/DDV support
    //{{AFX_MSG(CAboutDlg)
        // No message handlers
    //}}AFX_MSG
    DECLARE_MESSAGE_MAP()
};

CAboutDlg::CAboutDlg() : CDialog(CAboutDlg::IDD)
{
    //{{AFX_DATA_INIT(CAboutDlg)
    //}}AFX_DATA_INIT
}

void CAboutDlg::DoDataExchange(CDataExchange* pDX)
{
    CDialog::DoDataExchange(pDX);
    //{{AFX_DATA_MAP(CAboutDlg)
    //}}AFX_DATA_MAP
}

BEGIN_MESSAGE_MAP(CAboutDlg, CDialog)
    //{{AFX_MSG_MAP(CAboutDlg)
        // No message handlers
    //}}AFX_MSG_MAP
END_MESSAGE_MAP()

// App command to run the dialog
void CEx17aApp::OnAppAbout()
{
    CAboutDlg aboutDlg;
    aboutDlg.DoModal();
}

/////////////////////////////////////////////////////////////////
// CEx17aApp commands
```

CMainFrame

This main frame class, listed in Figure 17-7 beginning on the following page, is almost identical to the SDI version, except that it is derived from *CMDIFrameWnd* instead of from *CFrameWnd*. The same toolbar definitions are included.

MAINFRM.H

```
class CMainFrame : public CMDIFrameWnd
{
    DECLARE_DYNAMIC(CMainFrame)
public:
    CMainFrame();

// Attributes
public:

// Operations
public:

// Implementation
public:
    virtual ~CMainFrame();

protected:    // control bar embedded members
    CStatusBar    m_wndStatusBar;
    CToolBar      m_wndToolBar;

// Generated message map functions
protected:
    //{{AFX_MSG(CMainFrame)
    afx_msg int OnCreate(LPCREATESTRUCT lpCreateStruct);
        // NOTE - the ClassWizard will add and remove member functions here.
        //    DO NOT EDIT what you see in these blocks of generated code !
    //}}AFX_MSG
    DECLARE_MESSAGE_MAP()
};
```

MAINFRM.CPP (the class implementation file)

```
#include "stdafx.h"
#include "ex17a.h"

#include "mainfrm.h"

#ifdef _DEBUG
#undef THIS_FILE
static char BASED_CODE THIS_FILE[] = __FILE__;
#endif
```

Figure 17-7.   *(continued)*

The CMainFrame *class listing.*

Figure 17-7. *continued*

```
/////////////////////////////////////////////////////////////////
// CMainFrame

IMPLEMENT_DYNAMIC(CMainFrame, CMDIFrameWnd)

BEGIN_MESSAGE_MAP(CMainFrame, CMDIFrameWnd)
    //{{AFX_MSG_MAP(CMainFrame)
        // NOTE - the ClassWizard will add and remove mapping macros here.
        //    DO NOT EDIT what you see in these blocks of generated code !
    ON_WM_CREATE()
    //}}AFX_MSG_MAP
END_MESSAGE_MAP()


/////////////////////////////////////////////////////////////////
// arrays of IDs used to initialize control bars

// toolbar buttons - IDs are command buttons
static UINT BASED_CODE buttons[] =
{
    // same order as in the bitmap 'toolbar.bmp'
    ID_FILE_NEW,
    ID_FILE_OPEN,
    ID_FILE_SAVE,
        ID_SEPARATOR,
    ID_POS_HOME,
    ID_POS_END,
    ID_POS_PREV,
    ID_POS_NEXT,
    ID_POS_DEL,
    ID_POS_INS,
        ID_SEPARATOR,
    ID_FILE_PRINT,
    ID_APP_ABOUT,
};

static UINT BASED_CODE indicators[] =
{
    ID_SEPARATOR,              // status line indicator
    ID_INDICATOR_CAPS,
    ID_INDICATOR_NUM,
    ID_INDICATOR_SCRL,
};
```

(continued)

Figure 17-7. *continued*

```
////////////////////////////////////////////////////////////////////////
// CMainFrame construction/destruction

CMainFrame::CMainFrame()
{
    // TODO: add member initialization code here
}

CMainFrame::~CMainFrame()
{
}

int CMainFrame::OnCreate(LPCREATESTRUCT lpCreateStruct)
{
    if (CMDIFrameWnd::OnCreate(lpCreateStruct) == -1)
        return -1;

    if (!m_wndToolBar.Create(this) ||
        !m_wndToolBar.LoadBitmap(IDR_MAINFRAME) ||
        !m_wndToolBar.SetButtons(buttons,
          sizeof(buttons)/sizeof(UINT)))
    {
        TRACE("Failed to create toolbar\n");
        return -1;        // fail to create
    }

    if (!m_wndStatusBar.Create(this) ||
        !m_wndStatusBar.SetIndicators(indicators,
          sizeof(indicators)/sizeof(UINT)))
    {
        TRACE("Failed to create status bar\n");
        return -1;        // fail to create
    }

    return 0;
}


/////////////////////////////////////////////////////////////////////
// CMainFrame diagnostics

#ifdef _DEBUG
void CMainFrame::AssertValid() const
{
    CMDIFrameWnd::AssertValid();
}
```

(continued)

Figure 17-7. *continued*

```
void CMainFrame::Dump(CDumpContext& dc) const
{
    CMDIFrameWnd::Dump(dc);
}


#endif //_DEBUG


/////////////////////////////////////////////////////////////////////
// CMainFrame message handlers
```

Testing the EX17A Application

Do the build, run the program from Visual Workbench, and then make several documents. Try saving the documents on disk, closing them, and reloading them. Now exit the program and start File Manager. The files you created should show up with File Manager document icons. Double-click on a document icon and see whether the EX17A program starts up. Now, with both File Manager and EX17A on the screen, drag a document from File Manager to EX17A. Was the file opened?

> NOTE: If File Manager is already running when you first start EX17A, it won't recognize the changes made to the registration database. You must exit File Manager and restart or drag a file into the EX17A main frame window for File Manager to recognize the changes made to the registration database.

The EX17B Example

In this example, you'll retrofit the embedded launch and drag-and-drop capabilities into an SDI application. You need to modify only the application class and the main frame class. The resulting program does nothing, but you can apply the same changes to any SDI program, including EX16A. We'll go back to the old step-by-step method because so little code is new.

1. Run AppWizard to generate \VCPP\EX17B\EX17B. Choose AppWizard from Visual Workbench's Project menu. The options and default class names are shown in the screen at the top of the following page:

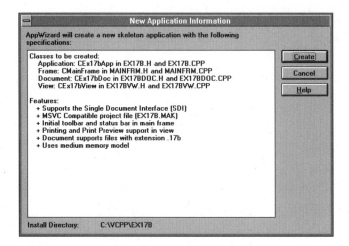

Be sure you turn off the Multiple Document Interface check box. For the document class, specify a file extension of *17b*.

2. Edit the derived application class *InitInstance* function in EX17B.CPP. After updating the registration database and enabling an embedded launch, this function calls *OnFileNew* when it detects an embedded launch. This call constructs, creates, and shows all the necessary windows. The application framework *CWinApp* functions *OnDDECommand* and *OpenDocumentFile* can then handle the DDE messages.

```
BOOL CEx17bApp::InitInstance()
{
    // Standard initialization
    // If you are not using these features and wish to reduce the size
    //  of your final executable, you should remove from the following
    //  the specific initialization routines you do not need.

    SetDialogBkColor();        // set dialog background color to BTNFACE
    LoadStdProfileSettings();  // load standard INI file options
                               //  (including MRU)

    // Register the application's document templates.  Document templates
    //  serve as the connection between documents,
    //  frame windows and views.

    AddDocTemplate(new CSingleDocTemplate(IDR_MAINFRAME,
            RUNTIME_CLASS(CEx17bDoc),
            RUNTIME_CLASS(CMainFrame),      // main SDI frame window
            RUNTIME_CLASS(CEx17bView)));
```

```
    EnableShellOpen();
    RegisterShellFileTypes();

// create a new (empty) document
    if (m_lpCmdLine[0] == '\0')
    {
        // create a new (empty) document
        TRACE("create a new empty document\n");
        OnFileNew();
    }
    else if ((m_lpCmdLine[0] == '-' || m_lpCmdLine[0] == '/') &&
             (m_lpCmdLine[1] == 'e' || m_lpCmdLine[1] == 'E'))
    {
        TRACE("program launched embedded\n");
        OnFileNew();
        // Program launched embedded - Wait for DDE or OLE to open.
    }
    else
    {
        TRACE("open an existing document - %s\n", m_lpCmdLine);
        // open an existing document
        OpenDocumentFile(m_lpCmdLine);
    }

    return TRUE;
}
```

3. Use App Studio to edit the IDR_MAINFRAME string resource.

Choose String Table, and then select the IDR_MAINFRAME string.
Add the following text to the end of the AppWizard-generated string:

```
\nEX17BFileType\nEx17B File Type
```

The resulting string should look like this:

```
EX17B Windows Application\nEx17b\nEX17B Document\nEX17B Files
(*.17b)\n.17b\nEX17BFileType\nEx17B File Type
```

4. Edit the main frame window *OnCreate* function in MAINFRM.CPP.

Add the following line at the end of the *CMainFrame OnCreate* function,
immediately before the return statement:

```
DragAcceptFiles();
```

When the frame window is created, the drag-and-drop capability is
activated.

5. **Build and test the resulting application.** It's not interesting to test a do-nothing application, but you can create zero-length files and load them later. Run the program first from Visual Workbench to update the registration database. Save a file, exit the program, and then run File Manager. The newly saved file should show up in File Manager as a document icon, and you should be able to execute EX17B by double-clicking on the document icon. Drag and drop should work too.

PRINTING AND PRINT PREVIEW

If you're depending on the Windows SDK alone, printing is one of the tougher programming jobs you'll have. If you don't believe me, just skim through the 60-page chapter ("Using the Printer") in Charles Petzold's *Programming Windows*. Other books about Microsoft Windows ignore the subject completely. The Microsoft Foundation Class (MFC) Library version 2.5 application framework goes a long way toward making printing easy. As a bonus, it adds a print preview capability that behaves like the print preview functions in commercial Windows-based programs such as Microsoft Word for Windows and Microsoft Excel.

In this chapter, you'll learn how to use the MFC library Print and Print Preview functions. In the process, you'll get a feeling for what's involved in Windows printing and how it's different from MS-DOS printing. First you'll do some wysiwyg printing, in which the printer output matches the screen display (except for the scale factor). This option requires careful use of Windows' mapping modes. Later you'll print a paginated data processing style report that doesn't reflect the screen display at all. In that example, you will learn how to structure your document so that the program can print any specified range of pages on demand.

Windows Printing

In the old days, programmers had to worry about configuring their applications for dozens of printers. Now Windows makes life easy because it provides all the printer drivers you'll ever need. It also supplies a consistent user interface for printing.

Standard Printer Dialogs

When the user chooses Print from the File menu of an application for Windows, the standard Print dialog appears, as shown in Figure 18-1.

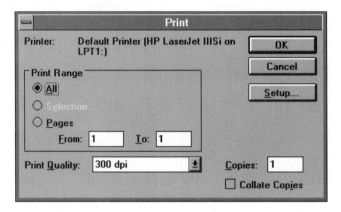

Figure 18-1.
The standard Print dialog.

If the user clicks the Setup button, the standard Print Setup dialog appears, as shown in Figure 18-2.

Figure 18-2.
The standard Print Setup dialog.

During the printing process, the application displays a standard printer status dialog, as shown in Figure 18-3.

Interactive Print Page Selection

If you've worked in the data processing field, you're used to batch-mode printing. A program reads a record and then formats and prints selected information as a line in a report. Every time, say, 50 lines have been printed,

Figure 18-3.
The standard printer status dialog.

the program ejects the paper and prints a new page heading. The programmer assumes that the whole report will be printed at one time and makes no allowance for interactively printing selected pages.

As Figure 18-1 shows, page numbers are important in Windows-based printing. A program must respond to a user's page selection by calculating which information to print and then printing the selected pages. If you're aware of this page selection requirement, you can design your application's data structures accordingly.

Remember the student list from Chapter 16? What if there were 1000 students and the user wanted page 5 of a student report? If you assumed that each student record required one print line and that a page held 50 lines, page 5 would include records 201 through 250. With the *CObList* class, you're stuck iterating through the first 200 list elements before you can start printing. Maybe the list isn't the ideal data structure. How about an array instead? With the *CObArray* class, you can directly access the 201st student record.

Not every application has elements that map to a fixed number of print lines. Suppose the student record contained a multiline text biography field? Because you don't know how many biography lines each record has, you'd have to search through the whole file to determine the page breaks. If your program remembered those page breaks as it calculated them, its efficiency would increase.

Display Pages vs. Printed Pages

In many cases, you'll want a printed page to correspond to a display page. As you learned in Chapter 5, you cannot guarantee that objects will be printed exactly as they are displayed. With TrueType fonts, however, and some extra margin room, you can get pretty close. If you're working with full-size paper and you want the corresponding display to be readable, you'll certainly want a display window that's larger than the screen. Thus, the *CScrollView* class is ideal for your printable views.

Sometimes, however, you might not care about display pages. Perhaps your view holds its data in a list box, or maybe you don't need to display the data at all. In these cases, your program can contain stand-alone print logic that simply extracts data from the document and sends it to the printer. Of course, the program must properly respond to a user's page range request. If you query the printer to find out the paper size and portrait/landscape configuration, you can adjust the pagination accordingly.

Print Preview

The Microsoft Foundation Class Library version 2.5 Print Preview feature shows you on screen the <u>exact</u> page breaks and line breaks you'll get when you print your document on the selected printer. The fonts might look a little funny, especially in the smaller sizes, but it's not a problem. Look now at the print preview windows that appear on pages 381 and 383.

Print Preview is an MFC library feature, not a Windows feature. Don't underestimate how much effort went into programming Print Preview. The Print Preview program examines each character individually, determining its position based on the printer's device context. After selecting an approximating font, the program displays the character in the print preview window at the proper location.

Programming for the Printer

The application framework does most of the work for printing and print preview. To use the printer effectively, you must understand the sequence of function calls and know which functions to override.

The Printer Device Context and the *CView::OnDraw* Function

When your program prints on the printer, it uses a device context object of class *CDC*. Don't worry about where the object comes from; the application framework constructs it and passes it as a parameter to your view's *OnDraw* function. If your application uses the printer to duplicate the display, the *OnDraw* function can do double duty. If you're displaying, *OnPaint* calls *On-Draw*, and the device context is the display context. If you're printing,

OnDraw is called by another *CView* function, *OnPrint*, with a printer device context. The *OnPrint* function is called once to print an entire page.

In print preview mode, the *CDC* object is linked to another device context object of class *CPreviewDC*, but that linkage is transparent. Your *OnPrint* and *OnDraw* functions work the same regardless of whether you're printing or previewing.

The *CView::OnPrint* Function

You know that *OnPrint* calls *OnDraw*, and that *OnDraw* can use both a display device context and a printer device context. The mapping mode should be set before *OnPrint* is called. You can override *OnPrint* to print items that you don't need on the display, such as a title page, headers, and footers. The *OnPrint* parameters are

- A pointer to the device context

- A pointer to a print information structure (*CPrintInfo*) that includes page dimensions, the current page number, and the maximum page number

In your overridden *OnPrint* function, you can elect not to call *OnDraw* at all to support print logic that is totally independent of the display logic. The application framework calls the *OnPrint* function once for each page to be printed, with the current page number in the *CPrintInfo* structure. You're about to find out how the application framework determines the page number.

Preparing the Device Context—The *CView::OnPrepareDC* Function

If you need a display mapping mode other than *MM_TEXT* (and you usually do), that mode is generally set in the view's *OnPrepareDC* function. You override this function yourself if your view class is derived directly from *CView*, but it's already overridden if your view is derived from *CScrollView*. The *OnPrepareDC* function is called in *OnPaint* immediately before the call to *OnDraw*. If you're printing, the same *OnPrepareDC* function is called, this time immediately before the application framework calls *OnPrint*. Thus, the mapping mode is set before both the painting of the view and the printing of a page.

The second parameter of the *OnPrepareDC* function is a pointer to a *CPrintInfo* structure. This pointer is valid only if *OnPrepareDC* is being called prior to printing. You can test for this condition by calling the CDC member function *IsPrinting*. The *IsPrinting* function is particularly handy if you're using *OnPrepareDC* to set different map modes for the display and the printer.

If you do not know in advance how many pages your print job requires, your overridden *OnPrepareDC* function can detect the end of the document and reset the *m_bContinuePrinting* flag in the *CPrintInfo* structure. When this flag is *FALSE*, the *OnPrint* function won't be called, and control will pass to the end of the print loop.

> TIP: If your view class is derived from the *CScrollView* class and your *OnPrepareDC* function sets the *m_bContinuePrinting* flag, the base class *OnPrepareDC* function must be called <u>before</u> the flag is set.

The Start and End of a Print Job

When a print job starts, the application framework calls two *CView* functions, *OnPreparePrinting* and *OnBeginPrinting*. The first function, *OnPreparePrinting*, is called before the display of the Print dialog. You must override this function to enable printing and print preview. (AppWizard generates the *OnPreparePrinting*, *OnBeginPrinting*, and *OnEndPrinting* functions for you if you select the Printing And Print Preview option.) If you know the minimum and maximum page numbers, call *SetMinPages* and *SetMaxPages* in *OnPreparePrinting*. The numbers you pass to these functions will appear in the Print dialog for the user to override.

The second function, *OnBeginPrinting*, is called after the Print dialog exits. Override this function to create Graphics Device Interface (GDI) objects, such as fonts, that you need for the entire print job. A program runs faster if you create a font once instead of creating it repetitively for each page.

The *CView* function *OnEndPrinting* is called at the end of the print job, after the last page has been printed. Override this function to get rid of GDI objects created in *OnBeginPrinting*.

The following table summarizes the important overridable *CView* print loop functions:

OnPreparePrinting	Sets minimum and maximum page numbers
OnBeginPrinting	Creates GDI objects
OnPrepareDC (for each page)	Sets mapping mode and optionally detects end of print job
OnPrint (for each page)	Does print-specific output and then calls *OnDraw*
OnEndPrinting	Deletes GDI objects

Example EX18A—A Wysiwyg Print Program

This example displays and prints a single page of text stored in a document. The printed image is supposed to match the displayed image. In the first iteration, the program uses the *MM_TWIPS* mapping mode for both the printer and the display. Because the application uses a 10-point font, the text is too small to read on the display. The second iteration changes the display's mapping mode to logical twips, making the display text legible.

Here are the steps for building the example:

1. Run AppWizard to produce \VCPP\EX18A\EX18A. Choose App-Wizard from Visual Workbench's Project menu. The options and the default class names are shown here:

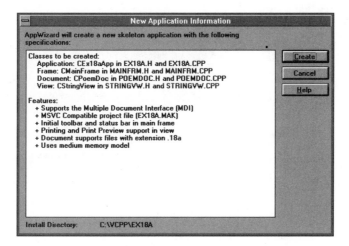

Be sure to select *CScrollView* as the view's base class. Also, be sure to accept the Printing And Print Preview default option. Name the document and view classes exactly as specified. You will be using them again in later chapters. Remember that we're accepting the MDI option this time.

2. Edit the POEMDOC.H header file. The document data is stored in a string array. You need not set a maximum dimension in the declaration because the array is dynamic. Add the following lines to the *CPoemDoc* class declaration:

```
public:
    CStringArray m_stringArray;
```

Also add a prototype for the virtual *DeleteContents* function:

```
virtual void DeleteContents();
```

3. Edit three *CPoemDoc* member functions in file POEMDOC.CPP.
We'll initialize the poem document in the overridden *OnNewDocument* function. *DeleteContents* is called in *CDocument::OnNewDocument,* so we're sure the poem won't be deleted. (The poem, by the way, is an excerpt from the 20th poem in Lawrence Ferlinghetti's book *A Coney Island of the Mind.*) Type 10 lines of your choice. It could be another poem or maybe your favorite Windows function description.

```
BOOL CPoemDoc::OnNewDocument()
{
    if (!CDocument::OnNewDocument())
        return FALSE;

    m_stringArray.SetSize(10);
    m_stringArray[0] = "The pennycandystore beyond the El";
    m_stringArray[1] = "is where I first";
    m_stringArray[2] = "                    fell in love";
    m_stringArray[3] = "                        with unreality";
    m_stringArray[4] = "Jellybeans glowed in the semi-gloom";
    m_stringArray[5] = "of that september afternoon";
    m_stringArray[6] = "A cat upon the counter moved among";
    m_stringArray[7] = "                    the licorice sticks";
    m_stringArray[8] = "                    and tootsie rolls";
    m_stringArray[9] = "            and Oh Boy Gum";

    return TRUE;
}
```

(Note: The *CStringArray* class supports dynamic arrays, but here we're using the *m_stringArray* object as though it were a static array of 10 elements. You'll see arrays used more dynamically in examples EX21A and EX26B.)

The application framework calls the document's virtual *DeleteContents* function when it closes the document; this action deletes the strings in the array. A *CStringArray* contains actual objects, and a *CObArray* contains pointers to objects. This distinction is important when it is time to delete the array elements. Here the *RemoveAll* function actually deletes the string objects.

```
void CPoemDoc::DeleteContents()
{
    // called before OnNewDocument and when document is closed
    m_stringArray.RemoveAll();
}
```

Serialization isn't important in this example, but the following function illustrates how easy it is to serialize strings. The application framework calls the *DeleteContents* function before loading from the archive, so you don't have to worry about emptying the array.

```
void CPoemDoc::Serialize(CArchive& ar)
{
    m_stringArray.Serialize(ar);
}
```

4. **Edit the *OnInitialUpdate* function in STRINGVW.CPP.** You must override the function for all classes derived from *CScrollView*. This function's job is to set the logical window size and the mapping mode.

```
void CStringView::OnInitialUpdate()
{
    CScrollView::OnInitialUpdate();
    CSize totalSize = CSize(11520, 15120);      // 8" x 10.5"
    CSize pageSize = CSize(totalSize.cx / 2,
                           totalSize.cy / 2);   // page scroll
    CSize lineSize = CSize(totalSize.cx / 100,
                           totalSize.cy / 100); // line scroll
    SetScrollSizes(MM_TWIPS, totalSize, pageSize,
                   lineSize);                   // CScrollView function
}
```

5. **Edit the *OnDraw* function in STRINGVW.CPP.** The *OnDraw* function of class *CStringView* draws on both the display and the printer. In addition to displaying the poem text lines in 10-point roman font, it draws a border around the printable area together with a crude ruler along the top and left margins. The function assumes an HP LaserJet printer that has a printable area of 8 inches by 10.5 inches offset from the upper left corner of the paper. Also assumed is the *MM_TWIPS* mapping mode, in which 1 inch = 1440 units.

> NOTE: A more general function could call the Windows *Get-DeviceCaps* function to retrieve the actual dimensions of the printable area, and then it could adjust the printed output accordingly.

```
void CStringView::OnDraw(CDC* pDC)
{
    int       i, j, nHeight;
    char      temp[10];
    CFont     font;
    TEXTMETRIC tm;

    CPoemDoc* pDoc = GetDocument();
    // draw a border 8 x 10.5
    pDC->Rectangle(CRect(0, 0, 11505, -15105));
    // draw horizontal and vertical rulers
    for (i = 0; i <= 8; i++) {
        wsprintf(temp, "%02d", i);
        pDC->TextOut(i * 1440, 0, temp);
    }
    for (i = 0; i <= 10; i++) {
        wsprintf(temp, "%02d", i);
        pDC->TextOut(0, -i * 1440, temp);
    }
    // print the poem 0.5 inch down and over
    // use 10-point roman font
    font.CreateFont(-200, 0, 0, 0, 400, FALSE, FALSE, 0, ANSI_CHARSET,
                    OUT_DEFAULT_PRECIS, CLIP_DEFAULT_PRECIS,
                    DEFAULT_QUALITY, DEFAULT_PITCH | FF_ROMAN,
                    "Times New Roman");
    CFont* pOldFont = (CFont*) pDC->SelectObject(&font);
    pDC->GetTextMetrics(&tm);
    nHeight = tm.tmHeight + tm.tmExternalLeading;
    TRACE("font height = %d, internal leading = %d\n",
          nHeight, tm.tmInternalLeading);
    j = pDoc->m_stringArray.GetSize();
    TRACE("array size = %d\n", j);
    for (i = 0; i < j; i++) {
        pDC->TextOut(720, -i * nHeight - 720, pDoc->m_stringArray[i]);
    }
    pDC->SelectObject(pOldFont);
}
```

6. Edit the *OnPreparePrinting* function in STRINGVW.CPP. This function sets the maximum number of pages in the print job. This example has only one page. It's absolutely necessary to call the base class *DoPreparePrinting* function in your overridden *OnPreparePrinting* function.

```
BOOL CStringView::OnPreparePrinting(CPrintInfo* pInfo)
{
    pInfo->SetMaxPage(1);
    return DoPreparePrinting(pInfo);
}
```

7. Build and test the application. When you start the EX18A application, your MDI child window should look like this:

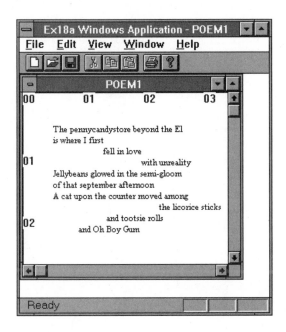

The window text is too small, isn't it? Go ahead and choose Print Preview from the File menu, and then use the magnifying glass to zoom in on the text in the upper left corner. The window should look like this:

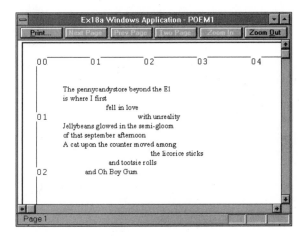

Remember "logical twips" from Chapter 5? Now we're going to use logical twips to enlarge type on the display while keeping the printed text the same size. This requires some extra work because the *CScrollView* class wasn't designed for nonstandard mapping modes. The techniques you'll see here will be helpful if you write an OLE in-place-editing application.

8. **Edit the STRINGVW.H header file.** Now we're going to override the *CStringView OnPrepareDC* function, and we're going to add the helper function *SetScrollInfo*:

```
protected:
    virtual void OnPrepareDC(CDC* pDC, CPrintInfo* pInfo = NULL);
    void SetScrollInfo();
```

9. **Add the functions *OnPrepareDC* and *SetScrollInfo* in STRING-VW.CPP.** The *OnPrepareDC* function sets the mapping mode to *MM_TWIPS* if the program is printing; otherwise, it sets the mode to logical twips.

```
void CStringView::OnPrepareDC(CDC* pDC, CPrintInfo* pInfo /* = NULL */)
{
    if (pDC->IsPrinting()) {
        pDC->SetMapMode(MM_TWIPS);
    }
    else {
        CScrollView::OnPrepareDC(pDC, pInfo);
        pDC->SetMapMode(MM_ANISOTROPIC);
        pDC->SetWindowExt(1440, 1440);
        pDC->SetViewportExt(pDC->GetDeviceCaps(LOGPIXELSX),
                            -pDC->GetDeviceCaps(LOGPIXELSY));
    }
}


void CStringView::SetScrollInfo()
{
    CClientDC dc(NULL);
    OnPrepareDC(&dc);
    CSize totalSize = CSize(11520, 15120);       // 8" x 10.5"
    dc.LPtoDP(&totalSize);
    CSize pageSize = CSize(totalSize.cx / 2,
                           totalSize.cy / 2);    // page scroll
    CSize lineSize = CSize(totalSize.cx / 100,
                           totalSize.cy / 100);  // line scroll
    SetScrollSizes(MM_TEXT, totalSize, pageSize, lineSize);
}
```

10. Use ClassWizard to map the view's *WM_SIZE* message.

11. Modify the *CStringView* functions, as shown.

```
CStringView::CStringView()
{
    SetScrollSizes(MM_TEXT, CSize(0, 0));
}

void CStringView::OnInitialUpdate()
{
    SetScrollInfo();
    CScrollView::OnInitialUpdate();
}

void CStringView::OnSize(UINT nType, int cx, int cy)
{
    SetScrollInfo();
    CScrollView::OnSize(nType, cx, cy);
}
```

12. Build and test the application. This time the text should be larger. Here's what the child window should look like now (though the appearance depends on the resolution of your video board):

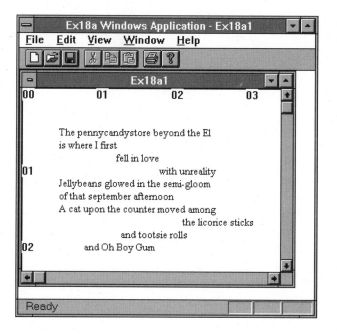

Example EX18B—A Multipage Print Program

In this example, the document contains an array of 50 *CRect* objects that define circles. The circles are randomly positioned in a 6-by-6-inch area and have random diameters of as much as 0.5 inch. The circles, when drawn on the display, look like two-dimensional simulations of soap bubbles. Instead of drawing the circles on the printer, the application prints the corresponding *CRect* coordinates in numeric form, 12 to a page with headers and footers.

1. **Run AppWizard to produce \VCPP\EX18B\EX18B.** Choose AppWizard from Visual Workbench's Project menu. The options and the default class names are shown here:

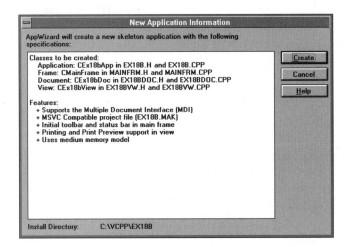

2. **Edit the EX18BDOC.H header file.** In the EX18A example, the document data consisted of strings stored in a *CStringArray* collection. Here we need an array of bounding rectangles for the circles. Because the *CRect* class is not derived from *CObject*, we can't use the *CObArray* class. We could use the TEMPLDEF program to generate a special array class for rectangles, but it's easier to use a normal fixed-size array, *m_ellipseArray*. That means, of course, that the document must contain a member variable, *m_nEllipseQty*, that tracks the array size. We'll also need a static member variable that specifies the number of printed lines (or records) per page. Here's the code that you'll need to add to the *CEx18bDoc* header file:

```
public:
    CRect  m_ellipseArray[50];
    int    m_nEllipseQty;
    static const int NEAR nLinesPerPage;
```

3. Edit the EX18BDOC.CPP implementation file. The document constructor initializes the ellipse array with some random values. This saves the trouble of writing serialization code. The static member variable, *nLinesPerPage*, needs to be initialized in the class implementation file.

```
CEx18bDoc::CEx18bDoc()
{
    int n1, n2, n3;
    // make 50 random circles
    srand((unsigned) time(NULL));
    m_nEllipseQty = 50;

    for (int i = 0; i < m_nEllipseQty; i++) {
        n1 = (long) rand() * 600L / RAND_MAX;
        n2 = (long) rand() * 600L / RAND_MAX;
        n3 = (long) rand() * 50L  / RAND_MAX;
        m_ellipseArray[i] = CRect(n1, -n2, n1 + n3, -(n2 + n3));
    }
}
```

```
const int NEAR CEx18bDoc::nLinesPerPage = 12;
```

4. Edit the EX18BVW.H header file. The *m_nPage* data member holds the document's current page number for printing. The public function prototypes are for overrides of application framework functions, and the private function prototypes are for the header and footer subroutines.

```
public:
    UINT m_nPage;
    virtual void OnPrint(CDC* pDC, CPrintInfo* pInfo);
protected:
    virtual void OnPrepareDC(CDC* pDC, CPrintInfo* pInfo = NULL);
private:
    void PrintPageHeader(CDC* pDC);
    void PrintPageFooter(CDC* pDC);
```

5. Edit the *OnDraw* function in EX18BVW.CPP. The overridden *OnDraw* function simply draws the bubbles in the view window:

```
void CEx18bView::OnDraw(CDC* pDC)
{
    int i, j;

    CEx18bDoc* pDoc = GetDocument();
    j = pDoc->m_nEllipseQty;
    for (i = 0; i < j; i++) {
        pDC->Ellipse(pDoc->m_ellipseArray[i]);
    }
}
```

6. **Insert the *OnPrepareDC* function in EX18BVW.CPP.** The view class is not a scrolling view, so the mapping mode must be set in this function.

```
void CEx18bView::OnPrepareDC(CDC* pDC, CPrintInfo* pInfo)
{
    pDC->SetMapMode(MM_LOENGLISH);
}
```

7. **Insert the *OnPrint* function in EX18BVW.CPP.** The *CView* default *OnPrint* function calls *OnDraw*. In this example, we want the printed output to be entirely different from the displayed output, so the *OnPrint* function must take care of the print output without calling *OnDraw*. *OnPrint* first sets the mapping mode to *MM_TWIPS* and then creates a fixed-pitch font. After printing the numeric contents of 12 *m_ellipseArray* elements, it deselects the font. You could have created the font once in *OnBeginPrinting*, but you wouldn't have noticed the increase in efficiency.

```
void CEx18bView::OnPrint(CDC* pDC, CPrintInfo* pInfo)
{
    int i,      nStart, nEnd, nHeight;
    char        temp[133];
    CPoint      point(720, -1440);
    CFont       font;
    TEXTMETRIC  tm;

    pDC->SetMapMode(MM_TWIPS);
    CEx18bDoc* pDoc = GetDocument();
    m_nPage = pInfo->m_nCurPage; // for PrintPageFooter's benefit
    nStart = (m_nPage - 1) * CEx18bDoc::nLinesPerPage;
    nEnd = nStart + CEx18bDoc::nLinesPerPage;
    // 14-point fixed-pitch font
    font.CreateFont(-280, 0, 0, 0, 400, FALSE, FALSE,
                    0, ANSI_CHARSET, OUT_DEFAULT_PRECIS,
                    CLIP_DEFAULT_PRECIS, DEFAULT_QUALITY,
```

```
                    DEFAULT_PITCH | FF_MODERN, "Courier New");
                    // Courier New is a TrueType font
  CFont* pOldFont = (CFont*) (pDC->SelectObject(&font));
  PrintPageHeader(pDC);
  pDC->GetTextMetrics(&tm);
  nHeight = tm.tmHeight + tm.tmExternalLeading;
  for (i = nStart; i < nEnd; i++) {
    if (i >= pDoc->m_nEllipseQty)
      break;
    wsprintf(temp, "%6d %6d %6d %6d %6d", i + 1,
             pDoc->m_ellipseArray[i].left,
             pDoc->m_ellipseArray[i].top,
             pDoc->m_ellipseArray[i].right,
             pDoc->m_ellipseArray[i].bottom);
    point.y -= nHeight;
    pDC->TextOut(point.x, point.y, temp);
  }
  PrintPageFooter(pDC);
  pDC->SelectObject(pOldFont);
}
```

8. **Edit the *OnPreparePrinting* function in EX18BVW.CPP.** The *OnPreparePrinting* function computes the number of pages in the document and then communicates that value to the application framework through the *SetMaxPage* function.

```
BOOL CEx18bView::OnPreparePrinting(CPrintInfo* pInfo)
{
    CEx18bDoc* pDoc = GetDocument();
    pInfo->SetMaxPage(pDoc->m_nEllipseQty /
                      CEx18bDoc::nLinesPerPage + 1);
    return DoPreparePrinting(pInfo);
}
```

9. **Insert the page header and footer functions in EX18BVW.CPP.** These private functions, called from *OnPrint*, print the page headers and the page footers. The page footer includes the page number, stored by *OnPrint* in the view class data member *m_nPage*. The *CDC GetTextExtent* function right-justifies the page number.

```
void CEx18bView::PrintPageHeader(CDC* pDC)
{
    char temp[133];

    CPoint point(0, 0);
```

(continued)

387

```
    pDC->TextOut(point.x, point.y, "Bubble Report");
    point += CSize(720, -720);
    wsprintf(temp, "%6.6s %6.6s %6.6s %6.6s %6.6s",
             (LPCSTR) "Index", (LPCSTR) "Left", (LPCSTR) "Top",
             (LPCSTR) "Right", (LPCSTR) "Bottom");
    pDC->TextOut(point.x, point.y, temp);
}

void CEx18bView::PrintPageFooter(CDC* pDC)
{
    char temp[133];

    CPoint point(0, -14400); // 10" down
    CEx18bDoc* pDoc = GetDocument();
    wsprintf(temp, "Document %s",(LPCSTR) pDoc->GetTitle());
    pDC->TextOut(point.x, point.y, temp);
    wsprintf(temp, "Page %d", m_nPage);
    CSize size = pDC->GetTextExtent(temp, strlen(temp));
    point.x += 11520 - size.cx;
    pDC->TextOut(point.x, point.y, temp); // right-justified
}
```

10. **Build and test the application.** For one set of random numbers, the bubble child window looks like this:

In Print Preview, the first page of the output should look like this:

Exercises for the Reader

Pretend that the function *OnPreparePrinting* can't compute the number of pages to be printed. Instead, modify *OnPrepareDC* to reset the *m_bContinuePrinting* flag (in the *CPrintInfo* structure) when there are no more elements to print.

The printing examples in this chapter have assumed a standard 8-inchby-10.5-inch printable area. The actual printable area depends on the installed printer driver, however. Some printers, such as the Hewlett-Packard LaserJet, can be switched between portrait and landscape mode. Try modifying the print examples to use the actual printable area dimensions stored in the *m_rectDraw* data member of the *CPrintInfo* structure. The rectangle is in logical coordinates as specified by *OnPrepareDC*, so you might have to do some mapping mode conversion.

CHAPTER NINETEEN

SPLITTER WINDOWS AND MULTIPLE VIEWS

Up to now, you've seen only one view attached to a document. If you've used a Windows-based word processor, you know that it's convenient to have two windows open simultaneously on various parts of a document. Both windows might contain a normal view, or one window might contain a page layout view and another might contain an outline view.

The application framework has several ways to present multiple views—the splitter window and multiple MDI child windows. You'll learn about both presentation options here, and you'll see that in each it's easy to make multiple view <u>objects</u> of the same view class (the normal view). It's slightly more difficult, though, to use two or more view <u>classes</u> in the same application (say, the outline view and the page layout view).

This chapter emphasizes the selection and presentation of multiple views. The examples depend on a document with data initialized in the *OnNewDocument* function. Look back to Chapter 15 for a review of document–view communication, and look ahead to Chapter 21 for a multiview example that exercises the full suite of application framework features.

The Splitter Window

A splitter window appears as a special type of frame window that holds several views in panes. The application can split the window on creation, or the user can split the window by choosing a menu command or by dragging a splitter box in the splitter window's scroll bar. After the window is split, the user can move the splitter bars with the mouse to adjust the relative sizes of the panes. Splitter windows can be used in both SDI and MDI applications.

You can see illustrations of splitter windows in the sections ahead, on pages 395 and 397.

The splitter window is represented by the class *CSplitterWnd*. As far as Windows is concerned, a *CSplitterWnd* object is an actual window that fully occupies the frame window (*CFrameWnd* or *CMDIChildWnd*) client area. The view windows occupy the splitter window pane areas. The splitter window does not take part in the command dispatch mechanism. The active view window (in the splitter pane) is logically connected directly to its frame window.

Multiple View Options

When you combine multiview presentation methods with application models, you get a number of permutations. Here are some of them:

- **SDI application with splitter window, single view class**—This chapter's first example, EX19A, covers this case. Each splitter window pane can be scrolled to a different part of the document. The programmer determines the maximum number of horizontal and vertical panes; the user makes the split at run time.

- **SDI application with splitter window, multiple view classes**—The EX19B example illustrates this case. The programmer determines the number of panes and the sequence of views; the user can change the pane size at run time.

- **MDI application with no splitter windows, single view class**—This is the standard MDI application you've seen already. The New Window menu item lets the user open a new child window for a document that's open already.

- **MDI application with no splitter windows, multiple view classes**— A small change to the standard MDI application allows the use of multiple views. As example EX19C shows, all that's necessary is replacing the New Window menu item with menu items and functions for each of the available view classes.

- **MDI application with splitter child windows**—This case is covered thoroughly in the *Class Library User's Guide*. The SCRIBBLE example illustrates the splitting of an MDI child window.

Dynamic and Static Splitter Windows

A dynamic splitter window allows the user to split the window at any time by choosing a menu item or by dragging a splitter box located on the scroll bar. The panes in a dynamic splitter window generally use the same view class. The top left pane is initialized to a particular view when the splitter window is created. In a dynamic splitter window, scroll bars are shared among the views. In a window with a single horizontal split, for example, the bottom scroll bar controls both views.

The panes of a static splitter window are defined when the window is first created, and they cannot be changed. The user can move the bars but cannot unsplit or resplit the window. Static splitter windows can accommodate multiple view classes, with the configuration set at creation time. In a static splitter window, each pane has separate scroll bars.

NOTE: You might have noticed a "splitter" class type option in the ClassWizard Add Class dialog. If you choose this option, you get a child window class, derived from *CMDIChildWnd*, that implements a dynamic splitter. This class is useful only in MDI applications such as SCRIBBLE. If you need an SDI splitter, you must follow the steps in this chapter's examples.

EX19A—A Single View Class
SDI Dynamic Splitter Example

In this example, the user can dynamically split the view into four panes. A four-way split produces four separate view objects, all managed by a single view class. We'll use the document and the view code from EX18A. The application class is standard AppWizard issue, but the main frame window class code has been modified.

CMainFrame

The application's main frame window class needs a splitter window data member and a prototype for an overridden *OnCreateClient* function. The following code has been added to the AppWizard-generated *CMainFrame* class declaration in MAINFRM.H:

```
protected:
    CSplitterWnd m_wndSplitter;
    virtual BOOL OnCreateClient(LPCREATESTRUCT lpcs,
                                CCreateContext* pContext);
```

The application framework calls the *CFrameWnd::OnCreateClient* virtual member function when the frame object is created. The base class version creates a single view window as specified by the document template. The overridden *OnCreateClient* version here (in MAINFRM.CPP) creates a splitter window instead, and the splitter window creates the first view.

```
BOOL CMainFrame::OnCreateClient(LPCREATESTRUCT lpcs,
                               CCreateContext* pContext)
{
    return m_wndSplitter.Create(this, 2, 2, CSize(1, 1), pContext);
}
```

The *CSplitterWnd Create* member function makes a dynamic splitter window. The *CSplitterWnd* object knows the view class because its name is embedded in the *CCreateContext* structure that's passed as a parameter to *Create*.

The second and third *Create* parameters (*2, 2*) specify that the window can be split into a maximum of two rows and two columns. The *CSize* parameter specifies the minimum pane size.

Resource Requirements

EX19A has an added Window main menu item and a pop-up menu with a Split item, as shown in Figure 19-1. The menu command ID is *ID_WINDOW_SPLIT*. The application framework recognizes this constant; its handler initiates the window-splitting action.

Figure 19-1.
The EX19A Window menu.

394

Testing the EX19A Application

When the application starts, you can split the window by choosing Split from the Window menu or by dragging the splitter boxes at the left and top of the scroll bars. Figure 19-2 shows a typical single view window with a four-way split. Multiple views share the scroll bars.

Figure 19-2.
A single view window with a four-way split.

EX19B—A Double View Class SDI Static Splitter Example

In EX19B, we'll extend EX19A by defining a second view class and allowing a static splitter window to show the two views. (The H and CPP files are cloned from the original view class.) This time the splitter window works a little differently. Instead of starting off as a single pane, the splitter is initialized with two panes. The user can move the bar between the panes by using the splitter box on the right scroll bar or by using the Window Split menu item.

CHexView

The *CHexView* class was written to allow programmers to appreciate poetry. As shown on the following page, it is essentially the same as *CStringView* except for the *OnDraw* member function:

```
void CHexView::OnDraw(CDC* pDC)
{
    // hex dump of document strings
    int       i, j, k, l, nHeight;
    long      n;
    char      temp[10];
    CString   outputLine;
    TEXTMETRIC tm;
    CFont·    font;

    CPoemDoc* pDoc = GetDocument();
    font.CreateFont(-160, 80, 0, 0, 400, FALSE, FALSE, 0, ANSI_CHARSET,
                    OUT_DEFAULT_PRECIS, CLIP_DEFAULT_PRECIS, DEFAULT_QUALITY,
                    DEFAULT_PITCH ! FF_SWISS, "Arial");
    CFont* pOldFont = (CFont*) pDC->SelectObject(&font);
    pDC->GetTextMetrics(&tm);
    nHeight = tm.tmHeight + tm.tmExternalLeading;

    j = pDoc->m_stringArray.GetSize();
    for (i = 0; i < j; i++) {
      wsprintf(temp, "%02x    ", i);
      outputLine = temp;
      l = pDoc->m_stringArray[i].GetLength();
      for (k = 0; k < l; k++) {
        n = pDoc->m_stringArray[i][k] & 0x00ff;
        wsprintf(temp, "%021x ", n);
        outputLine += temp;
      }
      pDC->TextOut(720, -i * nHeight - 720, outputLine);
    }
    pDC->SelectObject(pOldFont);
}
```

This function displays a hexadecimal dump of all strings in the document's *m_stringArray* collection. Notice the use of the subscript operator to access individual characters in a *CString* object.

CMainFrame

As in the previous example, the application's main frame window class needs a splitter window data member and a prototype for an overridden *OnCreateClient* function. The following code has been added to the AppWizard-generated *CMainFrame* class declaration file MAINFRM.H:

```
protected:
    CSplitterWnd m_wndSplitter;
    virtual BOOL OnCreateClient(LPCREATESTRUCT lpcs,
                                CCreateContext* pContext);
```

The implementation file, MAINFRM.CPP, needs both view class headers (and the prerequisite document header):

```
#include "poemdoc.h"
#include "stringvw.h"
#include "hexvw.h"
```

The overridden *OnCreateClient* function creates the splitter window as it did in EX19A, but this time it calls the *CSplitterWnd::CreateStatic* function, which is tailored for multiple view classes. The following calls to *CSplitterWnd::CreateView* attach the two view classes. As the second two *CreateStatic* parameters (*2, 1*) dictate, this splitter window contains only two panes, with an initial horizontal split 100 device units from the top of the window. The top pane is the string view; the bottom pane is the hex dump view. The user can change the splitter bar position but cannot change the view configuration.

```
BOOL CMainFrame::OnCreateClient(LPCREATESTRUCT lpcs,
                               CCreateContext* pContext)
{
    BOOL rtn = m_wndSplitter.CreateStatic(this, 2, 1);
    rtn |= m_wndSplitter.CreateView(0, 0, RUNTIME_CLASS(CStringView),
                                    CSize(100, 100), pContext);
    rtn |= m_wndSplitter.CreateView(1, 0, RUNTIME_CLASS(CHexView),
                                    CSize(100, 100), pContext);
    return rtn;
}
```

Testing the EX19B Application

When you start the EX19B application, the window should look like the one shown below. Notice the separate horizontal scroll bars for the two views.

EX19C—A Multiple View Class MDI Example

The final example, EX19C, uses the previous document and view classes to create a multiple view class MDI application without a splitter window. The logic is different from the logic in the other multiple view class application, EX19B. This time the action takes place in the application class rather than in the main frame class. As you study EX19C, you'll gain some more insight into the use of *CDocTemplate* objects.

This example was generated with the AppWizard Context Sensitive Help option. In Chapter 20, you'll be activating the context-sensitive help capability.

CEx19cApp

In the application class header file, EX19C.H, the following data members and function prototype have been added:

```
public:
    CMultiDocTemplate* m_pTemplate1;
    CMultiDocTemplate* m_pTemplate2;
    int ExitInstance();
```

The implementation file, EX19C.CPP, contains the following *#include* statements:

```
#include "poemdoc.h"
#include "stringvw.h"
#include "hexvw.h"
```

The *CEx19cApp InitInstance* member function has the following code inserted immediately after the *AddDocTemplate* function call:

```
m_pTemplate1 = new CMultiDocTemplate(IDR_POEMTYPE,
        RUNTIME_CLASS(CPoemDoc),
        RUNTIME_CLASS(CMDIChildWnd),
        RUNTIME_CLASS(CStringView));

m_pTemplate2 = new CMultiDocTemplate(IDR_POEMTYPE,
        RUNTIME_CLASS(CPoemDoc),
        RUNTIME_CLASS(CMDIChildWnd),
        RUNTIME_CLASS(CHexView));
```

The *AddDocTemplate* call generated by AppWizard established the primary document/frame/view combination for the application that is effective when the program starts. The two template objects above are secondary templates that can be activated in response to menu items.

Now all you need is an *ExitInstance* member function that cleans up the secondary templates:

```
int CEx19cApp::ExitInstance()
{
    delete m_pTemplate1;
    delete m_pTemplate2;
    return CWinApp::ExitInstance(); // saves profile settings
}
```

CMainFrame

The main frame class implementation file, MAINFRM.CPP, has both view class headers (and the prerequisite document header) included:

```
#include "poemdoc.h"
#include "stringvw.h"
#include "hexvw.h"
```

The base frame window class, *CMDIChildWnd*, has an *OnWindowNew* function that is normally connected to the standard Window New menu item. The following two command-handling functions are clones of *OnWindowNew*, adapted for the two view-specific templates that are defined in *InitInstance*. They create new child windows based on the specified view class.

```
void CMainFrame::OnWindowNew1() // ordinary text view
{
    CMDIChildWnd* pActiveChild = MDIGetActive();
    CDocument* pDocument;
    if (pActiveChild == NULL ||
        (pDocument = pActiveChild->GetActiveDocument()) == NULL)
    {
        TRACE0("Warning: No active document for WindowNew command\n");
        AfxMessageBox(AFX_IDP_COMMAND_FAILURE);
        return;         // command failed
    }

    // otherwise we have a new frame!
    CDocTemplate* pTemplate = ((CEx19cApp*) AfxGetApp())->m_pTemplate1;
    ASSERT_VALID(pTemplate);
    CFrameWnd* pFrame = pTemplate->CreateNewFrame(pDocument,
                                                  pActiveChild);
```

(continued)

```
    if (pFrame == NULL)
    {
        TRACE0("Warning: failed to create new frame\n");
        AfxMessageBox(AFX_IDP_COMMAND_FAILURE);
        return;          // command failed
    }

    pTemplate->InitialUpdateFrame(pFrame, pDocument);
}

void CMainFrame::OnWindowNew2() // hex dump view
{
    CMDIChildWnd* pActiveChild = MDIGetActive();
    CDocument* pDocument;
    if (pActiveChild == NULL ||
        (pDocument = pActiveChild->GetActiveDocument()) == NULL)
    {
        TRACE0("Warning: No active document for WindowNew command\n");
        AfxMessageBox(AFX_IDP_COMMAND_FAILURE);
        return;          // command failed
    }

    // otherwise we have a new frame!
    CDocTemplate* pTemplate = ((CEx19cApp*) AfxGetApp())->m_pTemplate2;
    ASSERT_VALID(pTemplate);
    CFrameWnd* pFrame = pTemplate->CreateNewFrame(pDocument,
                                                  pActiveChild);
    if (pFrame == NULL)
    {
        TRACE0("Warning: failed to create new frame\n");
        AfxMessageBox(AFX_IDP_COMMAND_FAILURE);
        return;          // command failed
    }

    pTemplate->InitialUpdateFrame(pFrame, pDocument);
}
```

NOTE: The function cloning above is a useful MFC library programming technique. You must first find a base class function that does almost what you want, and then you copy it from the \MSVC\MFC\SRC subdirectory into your derived class, changing it as required. The only danger is that subsequent versions of the MFC library will implement the original function differently.

Resource Requirements

The following two items have been added to the Window menu identified by *IDR_POEMTYPE*:

Menu Item	Command ID	Function
New &String Window	*ID_WINDOW_NEW1*	*OnWindowNew1* (replaces New Window item)
New &Hex Window	*ID_WINDOW_NEW2*	*OnWindowNew2*

ClassWizard was used to add the command-handling functions to the *CMainFrame* class.

Testing the EX19C Application

When you start the EX19C application, a text view child window appears. Choose New Hex Window from the Window menu. The application should look like this:

CONTEXT-SENSITIVE HELP

Most commercial Windows-based programs, including Visual Workbench, take advantage of the powerful WINHELP help engine that's included with Windows. The Microsoft Foundation Class (MFC) Library version 2.5 application framework allows you to use this same help engine for context-sensitive help in your own applications. This chapter first shows you how to construct and process a simple stand-alone help file that has a table of contents and allows the user to jump between topics. Next, you'll see how your MFC library program activates WINHELP with help context IDs that are derived from window and command IDs that are keyed to an AppWizard-generated help file. Finally, you'll learn how to modify the MFC library help message-handling system to customize the help capability.

The Windows WINHELP Program

If you've used commercial Windows-based applications, you've probably marveled at their sophisticated help screens with graphics, hyperlinks, and popups. At some software firms, including Microsoft, help authoring has been elevated to a profession in its own right. This section can't turn you into a help expert, but it can get you started by showing you how to prepare a simple no-frills help file.

Rich Text Format (RTF)

The Windows SDK documentation shows you how to format help files with an ASCII file format called Rich Text Format (RTF). We'll be using Rich Text Format too, but we'll be working in wysiwyg mode, thereby avoiding the direct use of awkward ASCII codes. You write with the same fonts, sizes, and styles that your user sees on the help screens. You'll definitely need a word processor that handles RTF. I've used Microsoft Word for Windows for this book, but many other word processors accommodate the RTF format.

NOTE: Several commercial Windows help tools are available, including RoboHELP from Blue Sky Software and The Windows Help Magician from Software Interphase. These products are easier to use than an ordinary word processor and can thus reduce the effort needed to produce help files. Some of these products are templates for Word for Windows; others are stand-alone programs.)

Writing a Simple Help File

We're going to write a simple help file with a table of contents and three topics. This help file is designed to be run directly from WINHELP, started from the Windows Program Manager. No C++ programming is involved. Here are the steps:

1. Create a \VCPP\EX20A subdirectory.

2. Write the main help text file. Use Microsoft Word for Windows (or another RTF-compatible word processor) to type text as shown here:

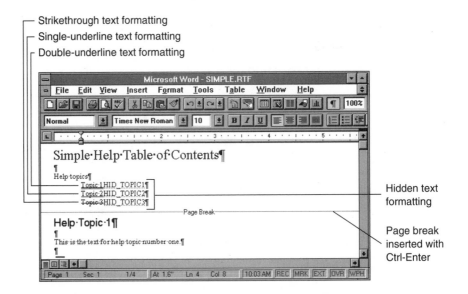

Be sure to apply the double-underline and hidden formats correctly and to insert the page break at the correct place.

3. Insert footnotes for the Table of Contents screen. The Table of Contents screen is the first topic screen in this help system. Turn on the word processor's footnote view, and then insert the following footnotes at the beginning of the topic title, using the specified custom footnote marks:

Footnote Mark	Text	Description
#	HID_CONTENTS	Help context ID
$	SIMPLE Help Contents	Topic title

When you're finished with this step, the document should look like this:

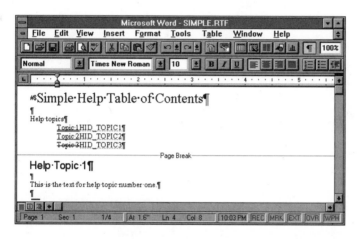

4. Insert footnotes for the Topic 1 screen. The Topic 1 screen is the second topic screen in the help system. Insert the following footnotes, using the specified custom footnote marks:

Footnote Mark	Text	Description
#	HID_TOPIC1	Help context ID
$	SIMPLE Help Topic 1	Topic title
K	SIMPLE Topics	Keyword text

5. Clone the Topic 1 screen. Copy the entire Topic 1 section of the document, including the page break, to the clipboard, and then paste two copies of the text into the document. The footnotes are copied along with the text. In the first copy, change all occurrences of *1* to *2*. In the second copy, change all occurrences of *1* to *3*. Don't forget to change the footnotes. With Word for Windows, it's a little difficult to see which footnote goes with which topic, so be careful. When you're finished with this step, the document text should look like that shown at the top of the following page:

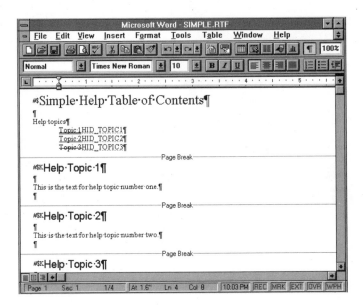

The footnotes should look like this:

6. Save the document. Save the document as \VCPP\EX20A\SIM-PLE.RTF. Specify Rich Text Format as the file type.

7. Write a help project file. Using your word processor, create a file named \VCPP\EX20A\SIMPLE.HPJ, as follows:

```
[OPTIONS]
CONTENTS=HID_CONTENTS
TITLE=SIMPLE Application Help
COMPRESS=true
WARNING=2

[FILES]
simple.rtf
```

This file specifies the context ID of the Table of Contents screen and the name of the RTF file that contains the help text. Be sure to save the file in text (ASCII) format.

8. Build the help file. At the MS-DOS command prompt, type the following MS-DOS commands:

```
cd \vcpp\ex20a
hc31 simple.hpj
```

This step runs the Windows Help Compiler with the project file SIMPLE.HPJ. The output is the help file SIMPLE.HLP. This example assumes that the \MSVC\BIN subdirectory is in your computer's search path. Use the MSVCVARS.BAT batch file in \MSV\BIN to set your computer's search path.

9. Run WINHELP with the new help file. From the Windows Program Manager, run WINHELP and then open the file \VCPP\EX20A\SIM-PLE.HLP. The Table of Contents screen should look like this:

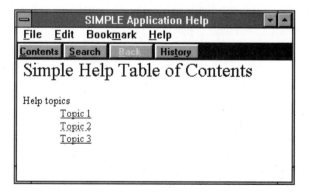

Now move the mouse cursor to Topic 1, and notice that the mouse cursor changes from an arrow to a pointing hand. When you press the left mouse button, the Topic 1 screen should appear as shown here:

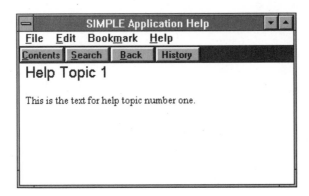

The *HID_TOPIC1* text in the Table of Contents screen links to the corresponding context ID (the # footnote) in the topic page. This link is known as a "jump."

The link to Topic 2 is coded as a pop-up jump. When you click on Topic 2, here's what you see:

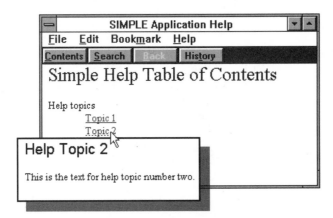

10. **Try the WINHELP Contents pushbutton.** Clicking this button should take you to the Table of Contents screen, as shown in step 9. WINHELP knows the ID of the Table of Contents screen because you specified it in the HPJ file.

11. Try the WINHELP Search pushbutton. When you click the Search button, WINHELP opens Help's Search dialog, which displays the Help file's list of keywords. In SIMPLE.HLP, all topics (excluding the table of contents) have the same keyword (the K footnotes), SIMPLE Topics. When you double-click on this keyword, you see all associated topic titles (the $ footnotes), as shown here:

What you have here is a two-level search hierarchy. The user can type the first few letters of the keyword and then select a topic from a list box. The more carefully you select your keywords and topic titles, the more effective your help system will be.

The Application Framework and WINHELP

You've seen WINHELP running as a stand-alone program. The application framework and WINHELP cooperate to give you context-sensitive help. Here's a summary of how this works:

1. You select the Context Sensitive Help option when you run AppWizard.

2. AppWizard generates Contents and Search items on your application's Help menu, and it creates one or more generic RTF files together with an HPJ file and a batch file that runs the Help Compiler.

3. AppWizard inserts a keyboard accelerator for the F1 key, and it maps the F1 key and the Help menu items to *CWinApp* member functions.

4. When your program runs, it calls WINHELP when the user presses F1 or chooses an item from the Help menu, passing a context ID that determines which help topic is displayed.

You now need to understand how WINHELP is called from another application and how your application generates context IDs for WINHELP.

Calling WINHELP

The *CWinApp* member function *WinHelp* activates WINHELP from within your application. If you look up *WinHelp* in the *Class Library Reference,* you'll see a long list of actions that the optional second parameter controls. Ignore the second parameter and pretend that *WinHelp* has only one unsigned long integer parameter, *dwData.* This parameter corresponds to a help topic. Suppose that the SIMPLE help file is available and that your program contains the statement

```
AfxGetApp()->WinHelp(HID_TOPIC1);
```

When the statement is executed, in response to the F1 key or some other event, the Topic 1 Help screen comes up, as it would if the user had clicked on Topic 1 in the Help Table of Contents screen.

"Wait a minute," you say. "How does WINHELP know what help file to use?" The name of the help file matches the application name. If the executable program name is SIMPLE.EXE, the help file is named SIMPLE.HLP.

NOTE: You can force WinHelp to use a different Help file by setting the *CWinApp* data member *m_pszHelpFilePath.*

"And how does WINHELP match the program constant *HID_TOPIC1* to the help file's context ID?" you ask. The Help project file must contain a MAP section that maps context IDs to numbers. If your application's RESOURCE.H file defines *HID_TOPIC1* as 101, the SIMPLE.HPJ MAP section looks like this:

```
[MAP]
HID_TOPIC1        101
```

The program's *#define* constant name doesn't have to match the help context ID; only the numbers must match. Making the names correspond, however, is good practice.

Using Search Strings

For a text-based application, you might need help based on a keyword rather than a numeric context ID. In that case, use the WinHelp *HELP_KEY* or *HELP_PARTIALKEY* option as follows:

```
CString string("find this string");
AfxGetApp()->WinHelp((DWORD) (LPCSTR) string, HELP_KEY);
```

The double cast for *string* is necessary because the first *WinHelp* parameter is multipurpose; its meaning depends on the value of the second parameter.

Help Context Aliases

The ALIAS section of the HPJ file allows you to equate one context ID to another. Suppose your HPJ file contained the following statements:

```
[ALIAS]
HID_TOPIC1 = HID_GETTING_STARTED

[MAP]
HID_TOPIC1        101
```

Your *RTF* files could use *HID_TOPIC1* and *HID_GETTING_STARTED* interchangeably. Both would be mapped to the help context 101 as generated by your application.

Determining the Help Context

You now have enough information to add a simple context-sensitive help system to the MFC library program. You define F1 (the standard MFC library Help key) as a keyboard accelerator, and then you write a command handler that maps the program's help context to a *WinHelp* parameter. You could invent your own method for mapping the program state to a context ID, but why not take advantage of the system that's already built into the application framework?

The application framework determines the help context based on the ID of the active program element. These identified program elements include menu commands, frame windows, dialog windows, message boxes, and control bars. A menu item might be identified as *ID_EDIT_CLEAR_ALL*, for example, and the main frame window usually has the identifier *IDR_MAINFRAME*. You might expect these identifiers to map directly to help contexts. *IDR_MAINFRAME*, for example, would map to a help context of the same name. But what if a frame ID and a command ID had the same numeric value? Obviously, you need a way to prevent these overlaps.

The application framework solves the overlap problem by defining a new set of help *#define* constants that are derived from program element IDs. These help constants are the sum of the element ID and a base value as follows:

Program Element	Element ID Prefix	Help Context ID Prefix	Base (Hexadecimal)
Menu item	*ID_*	*HID_*	10000
Frame or dialog	*IDR_, IDD_*	*HIDR_, HIDD_*	20000
Error message box	*IDP_*	*HIDP_*	30000
Nonclient areas	Other	*H....*	40000
Control bar	*IDW_*	*HIDW_*	50000

HID_EDIT_CLEAR_ALL (0x1E121) corresponds to *ID_EDIT_CLEAR_ALL* (0xE121), and *HIDR_MAINFRAME* (0x20002) corresponds to *IDR_MAIN-FRAME* (2).

Menu Access to Help

If you've checked the AppWizard Context Sensitive Help option, your application will have an Index item on its Help menu. This item brings up the Help Table of Contents screen, and the user can navigate the help file through jumps and searches.

F1 Help

Two separate context-sensitive help access methods are built into an MFC library application and are available if you've checked the AppWizard Context Sensitive Help option. The first is standard F1 help. The user presses F1; the program makes its best guess about the help context and then calls WINHELP. In this mode, it is possible to determine the menu item currently selected with the keyboard or the currently selected window (frame, view, dialog, or message box).

Shift-F1 Help

This second context-sensitive help mode is more powerful than the F1 mode. With Shift-F1 help, the program can identify the following help contexts:

- A menu item selected with the mouse cursor

- A toolbar button

- A frame window

- A view window

- A specific graphics element within a view window

- The status bar

- Various nonclient elements such as the system menu control

The user activates Shift-F1 help by pressing Shift-F1 or by clicking the Context Help toolbar button shown here:

In either case, the mouse cursor changes to

On the next mouse click, the help topic appears, with the position of the mouse cursor determining the context.

Shift-F1 help doesn't work with modal dialogs or message boxes.

Message Box Help—The *AfxMessageBox* Function

The global function *AfxMessageBox* displays application framework error messages. This function is similar to the *CWnd::MessageBox* member function except that it has a prompt ID as a parameter. The application framework maps this prompt ID to a help context ID and then calls WINHELP when the user presses F1. You can use *AfxMessageBox* for your own messages if you use prompt IDs that begin with *IDP_*. In your RTF file, use help contexts that begin with *HIDP_*.

There are two versions of *AfxMessageBox*. In the first version, the prompt string is specified by a pointer to a character-array parameter. In the second version, the prompt ID parameter specifies a string resource. If you use the second version, your executable program will be more efficient. Both *AfxMessageBox* versions take a style parameter that makes the message box display an exclamation point, a question mark, or another graphics symbol.

413

Generic Help

When context-sensitive help is enabled, AppWizard assembles a series of default help topics that are associated with standard MFC library program elements. Following are some of the standard topics:

- Menu and toolbar commands (File, Edit, and so forth)
- Nonclient window elements (maximize box, caption bar, and so forth)
- Status bar
- Error message boxes

These topics are contained in the files AFXCORE.RTF and AFXPRINT.RTF, which are contained, along with associated bitmap files, in the application's HLP subdirectory. Your job is to customize the generic help files.

NOTE: AppWizard generates AFXPRINT.RTF only if you specify the Printing And Print Preview option.

A Help Example—No Programming Required

If you followed the instructions for EX19C in Chapter 19, you selected the AppWizard Context Sensitive Help option. We'll now return to that example and explore the application framework's built-in help capability. You'll see how easy it is to link help topics to menu command IDs and frame window resource IDs. You edit RTF files, not CPP files.

Here are the steps for customizing the help for EX19C:

1. **From the EX19C project directory, run MAKEHELP.** At the MS-DOS prompt, type the following commands:

```
CD \VCPP\EX19C
MAKEHELP
```

The MAKEHELP batch file builds the application's ready-to-use HLP file from components located mostly in the project's HLP subdirectory. Be sure the \MSVC\BIN subdirectory is in your computer's search path. The project should also be on the same hard drive as Visual C++. (Some of the commands in the MAKEHELP batch file assume this.)

2. **Test the generic help file.** Run the EX19C application. Try the following experiments:

❑ Move the mouse cursor into the application's main frame window, and then press F1. You should see the generic Application Help screen, as shown here:

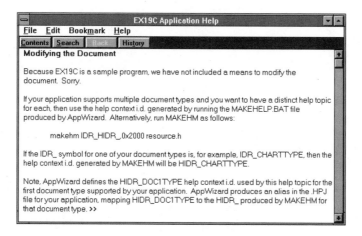

❑ Close the Help dialog and then press Alt-F, F1. This should open the Help topic for the File New command.

❑ Close the Help dialog, click the Context Help toolbar button (shown on page 413), and then choose Save from the File menu. Do you get the appropriate Help topic?

❑ Click the Context Help toolbar button again, and then select the frame window's title bar. You should get an explanation of a Windows title bar.

❑ Choose New from the EX19C File menu. Select the Poem document frame, and then press F1. You should see a generic Application Help screen with the title Modifying The Document.

3. Change the application title. The file AFXCORE.RTF, in the \VCPP-\EX19C\HLP directory, contains the string *<<YourApp>>* throughout. Replace it globally with *EX19C*.

4. Change the Modifying The Document help screen. The AFXCORE-.RTF file in the \VCPP\EX19C\HLP subdirectory contains text for the generic Application Help screen. Search for Modifying The Document, and then change the text to something appropriate for the application. This topic has the help context ID *HIDR_DOC1TYPE*. The EX19C.HPJ file provides the alias *HIDR_POEMTYPE*.

5. Add a topic for the Window New String Window menu item. The New String Window menu item was added to EX19C and thus didn't have associated help text. Add a topic to AFXCORE.RTF, as shown here:

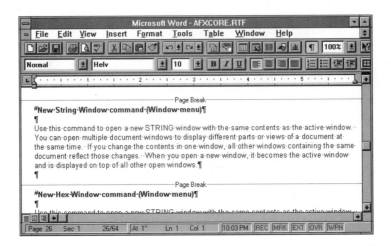

Notice the # footnote that links the topic to the context ID *HID_WIN-DOW_NEW1* as defined in HLP\EX19C.HM. The program's command ID for the New String Window menu item is, of course, *ID_WINDOW_NEW1*.

6. Rebuild the help file, and test the application. Run the MAKEHELP batch file again, and then rerun the EX19C program. Try the two new help links.

The MAKEHELP Process

The process of building the application's HLP file is complex. Part of the complexity results from the Help Compiler's nonacceptance of statements such as

```
HID_MAINFRAME = ID_MAINFRAME + 0x20000
```

Because of this nonacceptance, a special preprocessing program, MAKEHM.EXE, must read the RESOURCE.H file to produce a help map file that defines the help context values. At the top of the facing page is a diagram of the entire MAKEHELP process:

ON_COMMAND (ID_HELP, OnHelp)

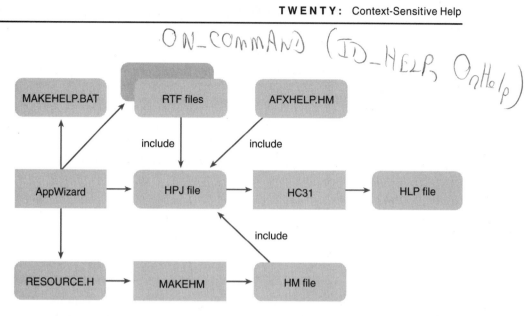

AppWizard generates the application's Help project file (HPJ). Its FILES section brings in the RTF files, and its MAP section contains *#include* statements for both the generic and the application-specific help map (HM) files. The Help Compiler, HC31, processes the project file to produce the help file that WINHELP reads.

Help Command Processing

You've seen the components of a help file, and you've seen the effects of F1 and Shift-F1. You know how the application element IDs are linked to help context IDs. What you haven't seen is the application framework's internal processing of the help requests. Why should you be concerned? Suppose you want to provide help on a specific view window instead of a frame window. What if you need help topics linked to specific graphics items in a view window? These and other needs can be met only by overriding the Help command processing functions.

Help command processing is different because it depends on whether the help request was an F1 request or a Shift-F1 request. The processing of each help request will be described separately.

F1 Processing

The F1 key is normally handled by a keyboard accelerator entry that AppWizard inserts in the RC file. The accelerator associates the F1 key with an *ID_HELP* command that is mapped to the *CWinApp* member function *OnHelp*.

ID_ON_HELP

417

NOTE: In an active modal dialog or menu selection in progress, the F1 key is processed by a Windows hook that causes the same *OnHelp* function to be called.

The *CWinApp::OnHelp* function sends a WM_COMMANDHELP message to the outermost frame window. In an SDI application, that message is handled by the main frame base class function, *CFrameWnd::OnCommandHelp*, which calls WINHELP with help context *HIDR_MAINFRAME*. The main frame window is the top-level window, and that is the starting point for daisy-chained WM_COMMANDHELP message processing. If you need to show help for a view window or another child window, you must map WM_COMMANDHELP in your derived frame class. Your *OnCommandHelp* function should then send the WM_COMMANDHELP message down the line to the active view window. When the view window gets the message, it calls WINHELP with an appropriate help context ID.

In an MDI application, the WM_COMMANDHELP message is mapped in both the *CMDIFrameWnd* class and the *CMDIChildWnd* class. If there are no MDI children, the frame window sets the context to *HIDR_MAINFRAME*; if there are one or more children, the frame window sends the message to the active child window, which sets the help context for the document. If you need Help for views, you must derive a class from *CMDIChildWnd* and then map the *OnCommandHelp* function in that derived class. This function then sends the WM_COMMANDHELP message down to the view.

Remember that F1 WM_COMMANDHELP processing is always in top-down order. The application first sends the message to the top-level window, which has the option of delegating the message to a child window. This routing is different from the normal command routing.

Shift-F1 Processing

When the user presses Shift-F1 or clicks the Context Help toolbar button, a mapped menu command message is sent to the *CWinApp* function *OnContextHelp*. When the user clicks the mouse again after positioning the mouse cursor, a WM_HELPHITTEST message is sent to the innermost window, where the mouse click is detected. If the message is not mapped in that window's class, the next outer window gets a chance at it.

In an SDI application, WM_HELPHITTEST is mapped to the *CFrameWnd* class member function *OnHelpHitTest*, which sets the help context to *HIDR_MAINFRAME*. In an MDI application, the message is mapped to both the *CMDIChildWnd* and the *CMDIFrameWnd* classes. If the mouse cursor is in the child window, the document help context is set; otherwise, the context is set to *HIDR_MAINFRAME*.

If you want a view-specific help context, simply map WM_HELPHIT-TEST in your view class and don't pass the message on to the frame. The *lParam* parameter of *OnHelpHitTest* contains the mouse coordinates in device units, relative to the upper left corner of the window's client area. The y value is in the high-order half; the x value is in the low-order half. You can use these coordinates to set the help context specifically for an item in the view.

Remember that Shift-F1 processing is always in bottom-up order. The message is first sent to the lowest-level window. If that window doesn't map the message, it's sent to the parent window.

A Help Command Processing Example—EX20B

This example, EX20B, is based on example EX19C from Chapter 19. It's a two-view MDI application with view-specific help added. The purpose of the added code is as follows:

- A new derived MDI child frame window class delegates the F1 help response to the active view object, and each of the two view classes has the necessary *OnCommandHelp* message handler.

- Each view class has an *OnHelpHitTest* message handler to process Shift-F1 help requests.

Header Requirements

The compiler recognizes help-specific identifiers only if the following *#include* statement is present:

```
#include <afxpriv.h>
```

In EX20B, the statement is in the STDAFX.H file.

CEx20bApp

You need a special MDI child frame window class, *CMDIHelpWnd*, to accommodate the new Help processing. This class is specified in the application class *AddDocTemplate* calls. Replace the EX19C.CPP line

```
RUNTIME_CLASS(CMDIChildWnd)
```

with

```
RUNTIME_CLASS(CMDIHelpWnd)
```

CMDIHelpWnd

The new class declaration is added to the MAINFRM.H header file as follows:

```
class CMDIHelpWnd : public CMDIChildWnd
{
    DECLARE_DYNCREATE(CMDIHelpWnd)
protected:
    //{{AFX_MSG(CMainFrame)
    afx_msg LRESULT OnCommandHelp(WPARAM wParam, LPARAM lParam);
    //}}AFX_MSG
    DECLARE_MESSAGE_MAP()
};
```

Here's the *CMDIHelpWnd* implementation code, inserted in MAINFRM.CPP.

```
IMPLEMENT_DYNCREATE(CMDIHelpWnd, CMDIChildWnd)

BEGIN_MESSAGE_MAP(CMDIHelpWnd, CMDIChildWnd)
    //{{AFX_MSG_MAP(CMDIHelpWnd)
    ON_MESSAGE(WM_COMMANDHELP, OnCommandHelp)
    //}}AFX_MSG_MAP
END_MESSAGE_MAP()

LRESULT CMDIHelpWnd::OnCommandHelp(WPARAM wParam, LPARAM lParam)
{
    if (lParam == 0) {
        if (m_nIDTracking > 0xe001) {
            // frame's own menu (system menu)
            lParam = HID_BASE_COMMAND + m_nIDTracking;
        }
        else {
            CView* pView = GetActiveView();
            if (pView) {
                // delegate the Help command to the view
                return pView->SendMessage(WM_COMMANDHELP, wParam, 0L);
            }
            else {
                lParam = HID_BASE_RESOURCE + IDR_MAINFRAME;
            }
        }
    }
    if (lParam != 0) {
        AfxGetApp()->WinHelp(lParam);
        return TRUE;
    }
    return FALSE;
}
```

The *OnCommandHelp* function first tests the *m_nIDTracking* data member to see whether the user was asking for help on a menu item. If no menu was open, the function tries to pass the WM_COMMANDHELP command message on to the active view. If no view is available, the function brings up the Help topic for the MDI client window. The document-specific topic isn't needed here because a document MDI child window can't exist without a view.

CStringView

The modified string view in STRINGVW.H needs message map function prototypes for both F1 help and Shift-F1 help:

```
afx_msg LRESULT OnCommandHelp(WPARAM wParam, LPARAM lParam);
afx_msg LRESULT OnHelpHitTest(WPARAM wParam, LPARAM lParam);
```

Here are the message map entries in STRINGVW.CPP:

```
ON_MESSAGE(WM_COMMANDHELP, OnCommandHelp)
ON_MESSAGE(WM_HELPHITTEST, OnHelpHitTest)
```

The *OnCommandHelp* message-handling member function in STRING-VW.CPP processes F1 help requests. It responds to the message sent from the MDI child frame and displays the help topic for the string view window.

```
LRESULT CStringView::OnCommandHelp(WPARAM wParam, LPARAM lParam)
{
    if (lParam == 0) {
        lParam = HID_BASE_RESOURCE + IDR_STRINGVIEW;
    }
    // context already determined above--we don't modify it
    AfxGetApp()->WinHelp(lParam);
    return TRUE;
}
```

Finally, the *OnHelpHitTest* member function handles Shift-F1 help.

```
LRESULT CStringView::OnHelpHitTest(WPARAM wParam, LPARAM lParam)
{
    return HID_BASE_RESOURCE + IDR_STRINGVIEW;
}
```

In a more complex application, you might want *OnHelpHitTest* to set the help context based on the mouse cursor position.

CHexView

The *CHexView* class processes help requests the same way the *CStringView* class does. Following is the necessary header code in HEXVW.H:

```
afx_msg LRESULT OnCommandHelp(WPARAM wParam, LPARAM lParam);
afx_msg LRESULT OnHelpHitTest(WPARAM wParam, LPARAM lParam);
```

Here are the message map entries in HEXVW.CPP:

```
ON_MESSAGE(WM_COMMANDHELP, OnCommandHelp)
ON_MESSAGE(WM_HELPHITTEST, OnHelpHitTest)
```

And here is the implementation code in HEXVW.CPP:

```
LRESULT CHexView::OnCommandHelp(WPARAM wParam, LPARAM lParam)
{
    if(lParam == 0) {
        lParam = HID_BASE_RESOURCE + IDR_HEXVIEW;
    }
    // context already determined above--we don't modify it
    AfxGetApp()->WinHelp(lParam);
    return TRUE;
}

LRESULT CHexView::OnHelpHitTest(WPARAM wParam, LPARAM lParam)
{
    return HID_BASE_RESOURCE + IDR_HEXVIEW;
}
```

Resource Requirements

Two new symbols were added to the resource file. Here are their values and corresponding help context IDs:

Symbol	Value	Help Context	Value
IDR_STRINGVIEW	101	*HIDR_STRINGVIEW*	0x20065
IDR_HEXVIEW	102	*HIDR_HEXVIEW*	0x20066

Help File Requirements

Two topics were added to the AFXCORE.RTF file with the help context IDs *HIDR_STRINGVIEW* and *HIDR_HEXVIEW* as shown in the screen on the facing page:

The generated EX20B.HM file, in the project's HLP subdirectory, should look like this:

```
// MAKEHELP.BAT generated Help Map file.  Used by EX20B.HPJ.

// Commands (ID_* and IDM_*)
HID_WINDOW_NEW1                     0x18000
HID_WINDOW_NEW2                     0x18001

// Prompts (IDP_*)

// Resources (IDR_*)
HIDR_MAINFRAME                      0x20002
HIDR_POEMTYPE                       0x20003
HIDR_STRINGVIEW                     0x20065
HIDR_HEXVIEW                        0x20066

// Dialogs (IDD_*)
HIDD_ABOUTBOX                       0x20064

// Frame Controls (IDW_*)
```

Build and Test the Application

Open a string child window and a hexadecimal child window. Test the action of F1 help and Shift-F1 help.

A PRACTICAL WINDOWS-BASED APPLICATION

The examples in the preceding chapters have illustrated specific Microsoft Foundation Class Library version 2.5 features. This chapter is different. It shows a complete two-view-class MDI application that combines most of the elements you've seen already, including

- Mouse capture and tracking
- Bit-block transfers
- A scrolling view
- Document–view interaction
- Dynamic array usage
- Serialization
- Wysiwyg printing
- Non-wysiwyg printing with pagination
- Menu command processing
- Dialog data exchange
- Context-sensitive help linked to the view

The application also illustrates the use of the list box as a central view element, and it shows the use of a document item class that streamlines the interface between view and document.

This chapter's presentation is a little different too. You won't see step-by-step instructions but rather selected code plus a summary of the resource requirements. The entire source is, of course, included on the companion disc. The class and file names are application-oriented and thus are not based on the chapter number.

The example is a materials planning application, named MATPLAN, that takes advantage of Windows' graphical user interface—the user can directly manipulate data with the mouse. I hope that the MATPLAN application will give you ideas for your own applications.

The MATPLAN Application

Have you ever planned a home project, a doghouse for example, that required plywood pieces cut from 4-foot-by-8-foot sheets? Or has your boss ever asked you to design a jet fighter that needed skin sections cut from sheets of titanium? The MATPLAN application addresses both these common, everyday problems.

Typically, the project design dictates the dimensions of the pieces of material. The challenge is to cut the pieces with a minimum amount of waste. MATPLAN uses a document that consists of an array of "piece" objects. The lengths, widths, and descriptions of the pieces are maintained through the list view; the user types the data for each piece in a dialog. The pieces are arranged through the graphical plan view; the user moves the pieces with the mouse on a grid that shows the material sheet boundaries.

Look at Figure 21-1 to get an idea of how MATPLAN works. Both the list view (in the top child window) and the plan view (in the bottom child window) are updated as the document's data changes.

When the user double-clicks on a line in the list view, a dialog appears, as shown in Figure 21-2.

The dialog's edit controls correspond to the columns in the list view. The x and y values represent the plan grid coordinates of the piece's top left corner. As the user moves the pieces in the plan view, the list view is updated to reflect the new coordinates. As the user changes the dimensions and descriptions in the list view, the plan view is updated accordingly. Of course, the computer could figure out how to lay out the pieces by itself, but that wouldn't be any fun. MATPLAN does offer some help to the user during the layout process. Overlapping pieces are displayed in black, and if the user double-clicks on a piece, it drops into place (like a piece in the TETRIS game).

MATPLAN fully supports the printer and Print Preview from both views. In the plan view, the entire grid of eight sheets is printed on one page. In the list view, list entries are printed report-style, three lines per page. (The lines-per-page is small to more easily illustrate paginated printing.)

426

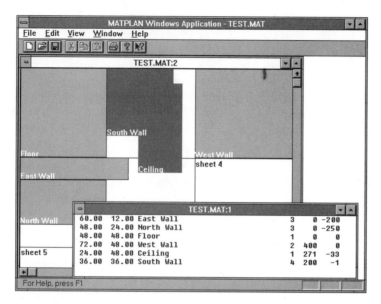

Figure 21-1.

The MATPLAN application in action, with two views active.

Figure 21-2.

The MATPLAN dialog.

The Anatomy of the MATPLAN Application

The MATPLAN application structure should start making sense quickly because of your work with this book's earlier examples. That's the idea behind programming with a standard application framework. First you identify the document and view and document classes, and then you analyze the other classes and find out how they interrelate.

Let's start with a list of the files and classes at the top of the next page:

Header File	Source Code File	Classes	Description
MATPLAN.H	MATPLAN.CPP	*CMatplanApp* *CAboutDlg*	Application class About dialog
MAINFRM.H	MAINFRM.CPP	*CMainFrame* *CMDISpecialChildWnd*	MDI main frame MDI child frame
MATDOC.H	MATDOC.CPP	*CMatplanDoc*	MATPLAN document
LISTVIEW.H	LISTVIEW.CPP	*CListView*	List view
PLANVIEW.H	PLANVIEW.CPP	*CPlanView*	Plan view
MATDLG.H	MATDLG.CPP	*CMatplanDialog*	Data entry dialog
MATPIECE.H	MATPIECE.CPP	*CPiece*	Document item
STDAFX.H	STDAFX.CPP		Standard class library include files
RESOURCE.H			Constants from App Studio

Now we'll discuss each class separately, and we'll look at some of the important member functions.

CMatplanApp

This class is the standard AppWizard-generated application class derived from *CWinApp*. Only its *InitInstance* and *ExitInstance* functions are unique.

InitInstance

As in the EX19C example, the *InitInstance* member function constructs two secondary document template objects, one for the list view and the other for the plan view, as shown below:

```
m_pTemplate1 = new CMultiDocTemplate(IDR_MATTYPE,
    RUNTIME_CLASS(CMatplanDoc),
    RUNTIME_CLASS(CMDISpecialChildWnd),
    RUNTIME_CLASS(CListView));

m_pTemplate2 = new CMultiDocTemplate(IDR_MATTYPE,
    RUNTIME_CLASS(CMatplanDoc),
    RUNTIME_CLASS(CMDISpecialChildWnd),
    RUNTIME_CLASS(CPlanView));
```

ExitInstance

This function destroys the templates constructed in *InitInstance*.

CMatplanDoc

This is the materials planning document class. It contains a dynamic array of *CPiece* object pointers, *m_pieceArray*, and is a friend to both view classes. This friendship allows the view class member functions to access the private piece array.

The piece array contains the primary copy of the application's data. The plan view accesses the *CPiece* objects directly, and the list view copies all the information contained in the array to and from its list box.

Constructor

The *CMatplanDoc* constructor illustrates the initialization of a dynamic array. The *CObArray SetSize* member function sets the initial array size to 0, but it sets the grow factor to 20. That means that the *new* operator is called only after the addition of every twentieth element to improve performance. The array elements are added in the *CListView* class with the *CObArray::SetAtGrow* member function.

```
CMatplanDoc::CMatplanDoc()
{
    m_pieceArray.SetSize(0, 20); // allocate mem 20 elements at a time
}
```

Serialize

The document class's *Serialize* function simply serializes *m_pieceArray*, which, in turn, serializes each *CPiece* object.

DeleteContents

A *CObArray* collection contains pointers to objects, not the objects themselves. This overridden virtual function not only removes the object pointers from the collection but also deletes the objects.

```
void CMatplanDoc::DeleteContents()
{
    for (int i = m_pieceArray.GetUpperBound(); i >= 0; i--) {
        delete m_pieceArray.GetAt(i);
    }
    m_pieceArray::RemoveAll();
}
```

OnEditClearAll

In addition to emptying the array, the *OnEditClearAll* function marks the document as modified and updates all views.

```
void CMatplanDoc::OnEditClearAll()
{    // gets rid of the old piece array in the document
    DeleteContents();
    SetModifiedFlag();
    UpdateAllViews(NULL);
}
```

OnUpdateEditClearAll

The Edit Clear All menu item should be grayed when the document's array is empty.

```
void CMatplanDoc::OnUpdateEditClearAll(CCmdUI* pCmdUI)
{
    pCmdUI->Enable(m_pieceArray.GetUpperBound() != -1);
}
```

OnUpdateFileSave

This update command UI function tests the modified flag and enables the toolbar disk (File Save) button accordingly.

CMainFrame

As in EX19C, this class, derived from *CMDIFrameWnd*, has command message handlers for the New List Window and New Plan Window menu items.

OnWindowNew1

This function opens a new MDI child frame window and associated list view, based on the document that is currently active. It is associated with the New List Window item on the Window menu and with the *ID_WINDOW_NEW1* constant.

OnWindowNew2

This function opens a new MDI child frame window and associated plan view, based on the document that is currently active. It is associated with the New Plan Window item on the Window menu and with the *ID_WINDOW-_NEW2* constant.

CMDISpecialChildWnd

This class, derived from *CMDIChildWnd*, exists only to support view-related, context-sensitive F1 help.

OnCommandHelp

This function handles the WM_COMMANDHELP message that the MDI main frame sends. It delegates the F1 help request to the active view.

CPiece

A MATPLAN document is composed of an array of *CPiece* objects. These pieces, known as document items, can draw and print themselves. This capability seems to violate the separation of view from document, but it's an accepted programming technique.

The *CPiece* class has data members for length, width, description, and position on the material grid. The length and width are maintained in physical coordinates—double-precision floating-point variables representing inches—and that's what the user edits in the dialog. Those physical coordinate values are converted to logical coordinates (1 logical unit = 0.01 inch) within the *CPiece* member functions, and subsequently they're converted to device coordinates.

Draw

The *CPiece Draw* function is called from the plan view *OnDraw* function for each piece in the array. The object's data members convey sufficient information to draw a rectangle representing the piece. If the *m_bOverlap* flag indicates that the piece overlaps another piece, the rectangle's fill color is black. *Draw* is designed to work with both the display and the printer.

```
void CPiece::Draw(CDC* pDC, int yChar)
{
    CRect rect;
    GetRect(rect);

    pDC->SelectStockObject(BLACK_PEN);
    if (m_bOverlap) {
        pDC->SelectStockObject(BLACK_BRUSH);
    }
```

(continued)

```
    else {
        pDC->SelectStockObject(GRAY_BRUSH);
    }
    pDC->Rectangle(rect);
    int hdcSave = pDC->SaveDC();
    pDC->SetTextColor((COLORREF) 0x00FFFFFF); // white
    pDC->SetBkMode(TRANSPARENT);
    pDC->IntersectClipRect(rect);  // restricts text to piece rectangle
    pDC->TextOut(rect.left, rect.bottom + yChar + 2, m_desc);
    pDC->RestoreDC(hdcSave);
}
```

The piece description is printed in white, and that works fine on the display and with many printers. Older HP LaserJet printers can't print fonts white-on-black, however.

PrintLine

The list view *OnDraw* function calls the *CPiece::PrintLine* function for each piece in the array. *PrintLine* is designed for printing only.

```
void CPiece::PrintLine(CDC* pDC, CPoint point)
{
    char temp[100];

    pDC->SetTextColor((COLORREF) 0x00000000); // black
    sprintf(temp, "%6.2f %6.2f %-30.30s%5ld%5ld%5ld",
            m_length, m_width, (const char*) m_desc, m_sheet, m_x, m_y);
    pDC->TextOut(point.x, point.y, temp);
}
```

MATPLAN uses a fixed-pitch font, and that allows use of the *sprintf* function. If you wanted a proportional font, you would have to compute the starting positions for each field.

Serialize

The *Serialize* function does disk I/O for all the *CPiece* data members except the flags *m_bNewList* and *m_bOverlap*.

```
void CPiece::Serialize(CArchive& ar)
{
    if (ar.IsStoring()) {
        ar << m_length << m_width << m_desc << m_sheet << m_x << m_y;
    }
    else {
        ar >> m_length >> m_width >> m_desc >> m_sheet >> m_x >> m_y;
    }
}
```

InsertInList, ExtractFromList

A *CPiece* object is represented by an entry in the *CListView* list box. These two functions transfer the piece object's data members to and from a specified (by index) list box entry, which consists of a single formatted string.

```
void CPiece::InsertInList(CListBox* pListBox, int index)
{    // copies data from this CPiece object into a list box entry
    char temp[100];

    sprintf(temp, "%6.2f %6.2f %-30.30s%5ld%5ld%5ld",
            m_length, m_width, (const char*) m_desc, m_sheet, m_x, m_y);
    pListBox->InsertString(index, temp);
}

void CPiece::ExtractFromList(CListBox* pListBox, int index)
{    // copies data from a list box entry into a CPiece object
    char temp1[100], temp2[100];

    // sscanf won't work here because the description
    //   can contain embedded spaces
    pListBox->GetText(index, temp1);
    strncpy(temp2, temp1, 6); temp2[6] = '\0';
    m_length = atof(temp2);
    strncpy(temp2, temp1+7, 6); temp2[6] = '\0';
    m_width= atof(temp2);
    strncpy(temp2, temp1+14, 30); temp2[30] = '\0';
    m_desc = temp2;
    strncpy(temp2, temp1+44, 5); temp2[5] = '\0';
    m_sheet = atol(temp2);
    strncpy(temp2, temp1+49, 5); temp2[5] = '\0';
    m_x = atol(temp2);
    strncpy(temp2, temp1+54, 5); temp2[5] = '\0';
    m_y = atol(temp2);
}
```

NOTE: In MATPLAN, <u>all</u> the document's data must be copied to or from the list box every time the document is updated. For large documents, performance suffers, and the document–view architecture is compromised. In Chapters 24 and 26, you'll see the *CRowView* class, which displays rows consisting of separate fields. This class eliminates the need for *strncpy* gymnastics, and it better supports the document–view architecture. With *CRowView*, the only rows copied are the rows actually being displayed.

CMatplanDialog

This modal dialog class, based on the dialog resource *IDD_FORM*, is the data entry form for material pieces. It works differently from the standard ClassWizard-generated dialog because it doesn't have individual data members for its edit controls. Instead, it has a single *CPiece* object pointer as a data member. The list view object owns the actual *CPiece* object.

Constructor

The *CMatplanDialog* constructor initializes the *m_pPiece* data member.

```
CMatplanDialog::CMatplanDialog(CWnd* pParentWnd, CPiece* pPiece)
        : CModalDialog(CMatplanDialog::IDD, pParentWnd)
{
    m_pPiece = pPiece; // this replaces ClassWizard's initialization
}
```

DoDataExchange

ClassWizard did not generate this *DoDataExchange* virtual function. It was hand-coded with references to *CPiece* data members. The Description field, for example, is referenced by the expression *m_pPiece->m_desc*. The first part is the *CMatplanDialog* data member that points to the view's *CPiece* object; the second part is the *CPiece* data member that holds the description string.

The *DoDataExchange* function also adjusts the default pushbutton. If the user is modifying an existing piece, the default button is the Update button; otherwise, it is the Insert button. Because we're taking control of the default pushbutton, overriding the virtual *OnOK* function is unnecessary. The function simply doesn't get called.

```
void CMatplanDialog::DoDataExchange(CDataExchange* pDX)
{
    // no data map here because we're using a CPiece object
    CDialog::DoDataExchange(pDX);
    DDX_Text(pDX, IDC_LENGTH, m_pPiece->m_length);
    DDV_MinMaxDouble(pDX, m_pPiece->m_length, 0.0, 96.0);
    DDX_Text(pDX, IDC_WIDTH, m_pPiece->m_width);
    DDV_MinMaxDouble(pDX, m_pPiece->m_width, 0.0, 96.0);
    DDX_Text(pDX, IDC_DESC, m_pPiece->m_desc);
    DDX_Text(pDX, IDC_SHEET, m_pPiece->m_sheet);
    DDV_MinMaxLong(pDX, m_pPiece->m_sheet, 0, 8);
```

```
    DDX_Text(pDX, IDC_X, m_pPiece->m_x);
    DDV_MinMaxLong(pDX, m_pPiece->m_x, 0, 800);
    DDX_Text(pDX, IDC_Y, m_pPiece->m_y);
    DDV_MinMaxLong(pDX, m_pPiece->m_y, -800, 0);

    if (m_pPiece->m_bNewList) {
        SetDefID(IDC_INSERT);
    }
    else {
        SetDefID(IDC_UPDATE);
    }
}
```

NOTE: The Visual C++ documentation might lead you to believe that ClassWizard's "foreign object" support can generate the
DDX code shown here. Unfortunately, this is not the case. The foreign object feature applies only to database "recordset" classes.

OnClickedCancel

This message map function is called in response to the dialog's Cancel button. *DoModal* then returns the *IDCancel* code.

```
void CMatplanDialog::OnClickedCancel()
{
    CDialog::OnCancel();
}
```

OnClear, OnDelete, OnInsert, OnUpdate

These command message handler functions are called in response to associ-
ated pushbuttons. Their main function is to pass the button's ID code to the
CDialog::EndDialog function, which establishes the return value from *Do-
Modal*. Here's the *OnInsert* function, which triggers a call to *DoDataExchange*:

```
void CMatplanDialog::OnInsert()
{
    if (!UpdateData(TRUE))
        return; // returns on error
    EndDialog(IDC_INSERT);
}
```

The *OnClear* function clears *CPiece* data members and sets the Insert button
as the default.

435

```
void CMatplanDialog::OnClear()
{
    m_pPiece->m_length = m_pPiece->m_width = 0.0;
    m_pPiece->m_desc = "";
    m_pPiece->m_sheet = m_pPiece->m_x = m_pPiece->m_y = 0;
    UpdateData(FALSE);
    SetDefID(IDC_INSERT); // insert is the next logical operation
    GotoDlgCtrl(GetDlgItem(IDC_LENGTH));
}
```

OnCascade

This virtual override is necessary to prevent the default *OnCancel* function being called when the user closes the dialog from the system menu or with the Esc key. This *OnCancel* function displays a message box through which the user confirms that he or she wants to exit the dialog. If the user chooses OK, *DoModal* returns the *IDCancel* code.

```
void CMatplanDialog::OnCancel()
{
    if (AfxMessageBox("Exit Dialog? (F1 for help)", MB_OKCANCEL,
                      IDP_EXIT_DLG) == IDOK)
    {
        CDialog::OnCancel();
    }
}
```

The *IDP_EXIT_DLG* symbol maps to a help context.

CListView

This is the MATPLAN <u>list</u> view class. A *CListView* object contains a pointer to a single *CListBox* object that occupies the entire view client area. It also contains pointers to a dialog object and to a *CPiece* object. Both the list box and the dialog pointer data members specify heap-allocated objects that belong to the view object. The *CPiece* pointer, however, specifies the current piece, which is associated with the selected item in the view's list box.

OnPrepareDC

The *OnPrepareDC* function sets the view's map mode and selects the font for printing.

```
void CListView::OnPrepareDC(CDC* pDC, CPrintInfo* pInfo)
{
    pDC->SetMapMode(MM_LOENGLISH);
```

```
    pDC->SelectObject(m_pPrintFont); // need to do it every page
}
```

OnDraw

This view's *OnDraw* function is not called for the display; it's called only for printing. It gets the document's piece array, and then it calls the *CPiece::PrintLine* member function for each piece that appears on the current page.

```
void CListView::OnDraw(CDC* pDC)
{   // called for Print/Print Preview ONLY, not for display
    CPoint  point(0, 0);
    CPiece* pPiece;
    int     nLineMin, nLineMax; // zero-based line numbers

    CMatplanDoc* pDoc = GetDocument();
    nLineMin = (m_nPage - 1) * CMatplanDoc::m_nLinesPerPage;
    nLineMax = nLineMin + CMatplanDoc::m_nLinesPerPage - 1;
    if (nLineMax > pDoc->m_pieceArray.GetUpperBound()) {
        nLineMax = pDoc->m_pieceArray.GetUpperBound();
    }
    point += m_drawOffset;
    point.y -= m_yChar * 2;  // space for col head & blank line
    for (int i = nLineMin; i <= nLineMax; i++) {
        pPiece = (CPiece*) (pDoc->m_pieceArray.GetAt(i));
        point.y -= m_yChar;
        pPiece->PrintLine(pDC, point);
    }
}
```

OnPrint

The application framework calls *OnPrint* for each printed page. The function prints the page header and then calls the *OnDraw* function. It also sets the value of the *m_nPage* data member so that the page footer function can access the current page.

```
void CListView::OnPrint(CDC* pDC, CPrintInfo* pInfo)
{
    // application framework calls OnPrepareDC prior to OnPrint
    PrintPageHeader(pDC);
    m_nPage = pInfo->m_nCurPage; // for OnDraw's and
                                 //  PrintPageFooter's benefit
    OnDraw(pDC);
    PrintPageFooter(pDC);
}
```

OnUpdate

This important virtual member function copies all the information in the document's *CPiece* array to the view's list box. It is called on File New, on File Open after the document has been read from disk, and when the document's *UpdateAllViews* function is called from some other view. *OnUpdate* is called by the application framework on File New, on File Open after the document has been read from disk, and when the document's *UpdateAllViews* function is called from some other view. If the piece array is empty, the *StartNewList* member function is called.

```
void CListView::OnUpdate(CView* pSender, LPARAM lHint, CObject* pHint)
{   // refreshes list box from array in document
    // when application starts, this function is called
    //  before the window is shown
    CPiece* pPiece;

    m_pListBox->ResetContent(); // empty the list box
    CMatplanDoc* pDoc = GetDocument();
    int nCount = pDoc->m_pieceArray.GetUpperBound();
    if (nCount == -1) {
        StartNewList();
    }
    else {
        // copy all data from the document's piece array
        //  to the view's list box
        for (int i = 0; i <= nCount; i++) {
            pPiece = (CPiece*) pDoc->m_pieceArray.GetAt(i);
            pPiece->InsertInList(m_pListBox, -1); // AddString
        }
    }
}
```

OnPreparePrinting

The *OnPreparePrinting* function is called immediately before the application framework's print dialog appears, and it sets the maximum page number based on the *CPiece* array size and the number of entries per page.

OnBeginPrinting, OnEndPrinting

A special fixed-pitch font is created in *OnBeginPrinting* and deleted in *OnEndPrinting*. This font exists for the duration of the print process.

OnCreate

The view's list box is created in this message handler. The list box uses a fixed-pitch font because that's an easy way to line up the columns.

```
int CListView::OnCreate(LPCREATESTRUCT lpcs)
{
    CRect rect;
    CFont font;

    // makes a list box the exact size of the window
    GetClientRect(&rect);
    rect.InflateRect(GetSystemMetrics(SM_CXBORDER),
                     GetSystemMetrics(SM_CYBORDER));
    m_pListBox->Create(WS_CHILD | WS_HSCROLL | WS_VSCROLL | WS_VISIBLE |
                       LBS_NOTIFY | LBS_NOINTEGRALHEIGHT,
                       rect, this, IDR_LISTBOX);
    // creates and attaches a fixed font to the list box

    font.CreateStockObject(SYSTEM_FIXED_FONT);
    m_pListBox->SetFont(&font);
    return CView::OnCreate(lpcs);
}
```

OnPaint

The base class *OnPaint* message handler calls *OnDraw*. We don't want to call *OnDraw* here, so we override *OnPaint*. The function must construct a *CPaintDC* object to validate the rectangle that contains the list box, thus assuring proper repainting of the list box.

```
void CListView::OnPaint()
{
    CPaintDC dc(this); // this statement is necessary to generate
                       //   the BeginPaint and EndPaint calls to
                       //   validate the rectangle
}
```

OnSize

This message handler ensures that the list box is resized every time the view window is resized.

```
void CListView::OnSize(UINT nType, int cx, int cy)
{
    CRect rect;
```

(continued)

439

```
if (m_pListBox) {
    GetClientRect(&rect);
    rect.InflateRect(GetSystemMetrics(SM_CXBORDER),
                     GetSystemMetrics(SM_CYBORDER));
    m_pListBox->MoveWindow(rect);
}
}
```

OnListBoxDblClk

When the user double-clicks on a list box entry, a dialog pops up, allowing the user to edit the length, width, and description for the selected piece. The user can also delete the piece or insert a new piece. If the list box is empty, the user obviously can't select an entry; so the user must close the view and use File New to create a new view.

```
void CListView::OnListBoxDblClk()
{   // called only if the list box is not empty
    int i = m_pListBox->GetCurSel();
    m_pPiece->ExtractFromList(m_pListBox, i);
    m_pPiece->m_bNewList = FALSE;
    m_pDialog = new CMatplanDialog(this, m_pPiece);
    int rtn = m_pDialog->DoModal();
    switch(rtn) {
    case IDC_UPDATE:
        m_pListBox->DeleteString(i);
        m_pPiece->InsertInList(m_pListBox, i);
        m_pListBox->SetCurSel(i);
        UpdatePlanDocument();
        break;
    case IDC_DELETE:
        m_pListBox->DeleteString(i);
        m_pListBox->SetCurSel(i);
        UpdatePlanDocument();
        break;
    case IDC_INSERT:
        m_pPiece->InsertInList(m_pListBox, i);
        m_pListBox->SetCurSel(i);
        UpdatePlanDocument();
        break;
    case IDCANCEL:
        break;
    case IDOK:
        default:
    default:
        ASSERT(0);
        break;
```

```
    }
    delete m_pDialog;
}
```

OnCommandHelp, OnHelpHitTest

These two functions process the WM_COMMANDHELP and WM_HELPHIT-
TEST messages, thus implementing context-sensitive help for the list view.

StartNewList

This private member function really doesn't create a new list—that's done
in *OnCreate*. *StartNewList*, called when the document *CPiece* array is empty,
brings up an empty dialog and invites the user to insert a new entry in the list
box, which, up to this point, is empty.

UpdatePlanDocument

This private member function copies the entire contents of the list box to
the document's *CPiece* array. It is called when the user changes an entry
through the dialog.

```
void CListView::UpdatePlanDocument()
{   // transfers all data from view (list box) to document
    CPiece* pPiece;
    int     i;

    CMatplanDoc* pDoc = GetDocument();

    // gets rid of the old piece list in the document
    for (i = pDoc->m_pieceArray.GetUpperBound(); i >= 0; i--) {
        pPiece = (CPiece*) pDoc->m_pieceArray.GetAt(i);
        delete pDoc->m_pieceArray.GetAt(i);
        pDoc->m_pieceArray.RemoveAt(i);
    }
    // copies all strings from view's list box to document's piece list
    int listLen = m_pListBox->GetCount();
    for (i = 0; i < listLen; i++) {
        pPiece = new CPiece;
        pPiece->ExtractFromList(m_pListBox, i);
        pDoc->m_pieceArray.SetAtGrow(i, pPiece);
    }
    pDoc->SetModifiedFlag();
    pDoc->UpdateAllViews(this); // except ourselves
}
```

CPlanView

This is the MATPLAN plan view class. It shows a visual representation of each piece as a rectangle. The user can position the pieces with the mouse, but the size of the pieces is controlled from the list view. As does the list view, the plan view has a pointer to the current piece. The plan view's list pointer refers to an element in the document's *CPiece* array.

OnDraw

The application framework calls this function both from *OnPaint* (for the display) and from *OnPrint* (for the printer). The mapping mode is the same for both destinations. For the display, *OnDraw* is passed a memory display context, but for the printer, *OnDraw* is passed a printer device context.

OnDraw calls the *Draw* member function for each piece in the document's array. The array order determines the drawing sequence so that the last piece in the list is always on top.

```
void CPlanView::OnDraw(CDC* pDC)
{
    CPiece* pPiece;
    DrawBackground(pDC);

    CMatplanDoc* pDoc = GetDocument();
    // draw all the pieces that are in the update region
    int nCount = pDoc-> m_pieceArray.GetUpperBound();
    for (int i = 0; i <= nCount; i++) {
        pPiece = (CPiece*) pDoc->m_pieceArray.GetAt(i);
        pPiece->Draw(pDC, m_yChar);
    }
}
```

OnPreparePrinting

The material grid fits on one printed page, so *OnPreparePrinting* sets the maximum page number to 1.

OnUpdate

The virtual *OnUpdate* function calls *ShowOverlap* to recalculate overlapping rectangles, and then it invalidates the client rectangle. This forces *OnDraw* to refresh the screen from the current document. *OnUpdate* is called by the application framework on File New, on File Open after the document has been read from disk, and when the document's *UpdateAllViews* function is called from some other view. The repaint process has not been optimized because the draw time of rectangles is not a concern. The draw time is more critical for complex shapes such as ellipses.

```
void CPlanView::OnUpdate(CView* pSender, LPARAM lHint, CObject* pHint)
{
    ShowOverlap();
    Invalidate(TRUE); // forces total redraw
}
```

OnInitialUpdate

The overridden *OnInitialUpdate* virtual function initializes the scroll view and creates a memory device context and bitmap to support the *BitBlt* calls when a rectangular piece is moved with the mouse. Note that the memory device context applies only to the display. For printing, the *OnDraw* function writes to the printer DC directly, so the gray rectangles are printed properly. The bitmap and device context are deleted in the view's destructor.

```
void CPlanView::OnInitialUpdate ()
{
    TEXTMETRIC tm;

    CSize totalSize = CSize(800, 800);
    CSize lineSize = CSize(totalSize.cx / 100, totalSize.cy / 100);
    SetScrollSizes(MM_LOENGLISH, totalSize, totalSize, lineSize);
    if (m_pMemDC->GetSafeHdc() == NULL)  {
        CClientDC cd(this);
        dc.GetTextMetrics(&tm);
        m_xChar = tm.tmAveCharWidth;
        m_yChar = tm.tmHeight + tm.tmExternalLeading;

        OnPrepareDC(&dc) ;
        CRect rectMax(CPoint(0, 0), totalSize);
        dc.LPtoDP(rectMax);

        m_pMemDC->CreateCompatibleDC(&dc);
        CBitmap* pBitmap = new CBitmap;
        pBitmap->CreateCompatibleBitmap(&dc, rectMax.right,
                                        -rectMax.bottom);
        CBitmap* pOldBitmap = (CBitmap*) (m_pMemDC->SelectObject (pBitmap));
    // This temp returned pointer doesn't remain valid past IDLE processing,
    //  therefore, we must save the handle instead.
        m_hOldBitmap = (HBITMAP) pOldBitmap->m_hObject;
        m_pMemDC->SetMapMode(MM_LOENGLISH);
```

(continued)

443

```
        }
        CScrollView::OnInitialUpdate();
}
```

OnPaint

The *OnPaint* message handler is overridden in this view to permit use of the memory device context and bitmap. *OnPaint* clears the bitmap, calls *OnDraw*, and then uses the *BitBlt* function to copy the piece rectangle from the memory device context to the display. This process ensures smooth movement of the rectangle.

```
void CPlanView::OnPaint()
{
    CRect updateRect;

    CPaintDC dc(this);
    OnPrepareDC(&dc);
    dc.GetClipBox(updateRect); // updateRect is already
                               //  in logical coordinates
    m_pMemDC->SelectClipRgn(NULL);
    m_pMemDC->IntersectClipRect(updateRect);
    m_pMemDC->PatBlt(updateRect.left, updateRect.top,
                updateRect.Width(), updateRect.Height(),
                WHITENESS);
    OnDraw(m_pMemDC);
    dc.BitBlt(updateRect.left, updateRect.top,
            updateRect.Width(), updateRect.Height(), m_pMemDC,
            updateRect.left, updateRect.top, SRCCOPY);
}
```

OnLButtonDown

When the user clicks on a piece rectangle, the mouse is captured, and piece movement can begin. The *OnLButtonDown* function sets the view's *m_pPiece* data member to point to the selected piece object.

```
void CPlanView::OnLButtonDown(UINT nFlags, CPoint point)
{
    CRect   rect;
    CPiece* pPiece;

    m_pPiece = NULL; // no piece selected
    CClientDC dc(this);
    OnPrepareDC(&dc);
    CMatplanDoc* pDoc = GetDocument();
```

```
        for (int i = pDoc->m_pieceArray.GetUpperBound(); i >= 0; i--) {
            pPiece = (CPiece*) pDoc->m_pieceArray.GetAt(i);
            pPiece->GetRect(rect);
            dc.LPtoDP(&rect);
            // PtInRect works only for device coordinates
            if (rect.PtInRect(point)) {
                SetCapture();
                m_bCaptured = TRUE;
                m_pPiece = pPiece;
                dc.DPtoLP(&point);
                m_mousePoint = point;
                ::SetCursor(::LoadCursor(NULL, IDC_CROSS));
                break;
            }
        }
    }
}
```

OnMouseMove

As the mouse moves, this function updates the *xy*-coordinates for the current
piece, which is stored in the document's *CPiece* array. If the user moves the
piece outside the view, the view is scrolled accordingly. This scrolling continues as long as the mouse is in motion. The *OnMouseMove* function invalidates
the union of the previous rectangle and the new rectangle.

```
void CPlanView::OnMouseMove(UINT nFlags, CPoint point)
{
    CSize offset;
    CRect clientRect, priorRect, newRect, invalidRect;

    if (m_bCaptured) {
        // let's work in device coords for scrolling
        CPoint scrollPos = GetDeviceScrollPosition();
        // scrolls in response to mouse movement outside client area
        GetClientRect(&clientRect);
        if (point.y > clientRect.bottom) {
            scrollPos.y += point.y - clientRect.bottom;
            SafeScrollTo(scrollPos);
        }
        if (point.y < 0) {
            scrollPos.y += point.y;
            SafeScrollTo(scrollPos);
        }
        if (point.x > clientRect.right) {
            scrollPos.x += point.x - clientRect.right;
```

(continued)

445

```
                SafeScrollTo(scrollPos);
        }
        if (point.x < 0) {
            scrollPos.x += point.x;
            SafeScrollTo(scrollPos);
        }

        CClientDC dc(this);
        OnPrepareDC(&dc);
        dc.DPtoLP(&point);
        offset = point - m_mousePoint;
        m_mousePoint = point;
        m_pPiece->GetRect(priorRect);
        dc.LPtoDP(&priorRect);
        m_pPiece->m_x += offset.cx;
        m_pPiece->m_y += offset.cy;
        m_pPiece->GetRect(newRect);
        dc.LPtoDP(&newRect);
        invalidRect.UnionRect(priorRect, newRect);
#ifdef _WIN32
        invalidRect.InflateRect(1, 1);
#endif
        InvalidateRect(&invalidRect, FALSE);
    }
}
```

OnLButtonUp

When the mouse button is released, mouse capture is turned off, and the
OnLButtonUp message handler calls *UpdateAllViews* to update the list view
with the new piece position. If the user has moved any part of the piece rectangle outside the grid boundaries, the piece is brought back into the grid.

```
void CPlanView::OnLButtonUp(UINT nFlags, CPoint point)
{
    CMatplanDoc* pDoc = GetDocument();
    if (m_bCaptured) {
        // if piece is outside view, move it back in now
        long length = (LONG) (m_pPiece->m_length / .24);
        long width = (LONG) (m_pPiece->m_width / .24);
        if ((m_pPiece->m_x <= 0)) {
            m_pPiece->m_x = 0;
        }
        if (m_pPiece->m_x + length > m_totalLog.cx) {
            m_pPiece->m_x = m_totalLog.cx - length;
        }
```

```
        if ((m_pPiece->m_y >= 0)) {
            m_pPiece->m_y = 0;
        }
        if (m_pPiece->m_y - width < -m_totalLog.cx) {
            m_pPiece->m_y = -m_totalLog.cy + width;
        }
        ReleaseCapture();
        m_bCaptured = FALSE;
        ShowOverlap();
        pDoc->SetModifiedFlag();
        pDoc->UpdateAllViews(this); // except this
    }
}
```

OnLButtonDblClk

This is the so-called TETRIS function. When the user double-clicks on a piece, the piece drops into place in the upper left corner of the sheet. If the upper left corner is occupied, the selected piece drops into the closest available position.

OnKeyDown

This message handler implements view scrolling from the keyboard.

OnCommandHelp, OnHelpHitTest

These two functions process the WM_COMMANDHELP and WM_HELP-HITTEST messages, thus implementing context-sensitive help for the plan view. The *OnHelpHitTest lParam* parameter contains the cursor position in device coordinates.

```
LRESULT CPlanView::OnHelpHitTest(WPARAM wParam, LPARAM lParam)
{
    TRACE("Mouse position = (%d, %d)\n",
        (int) HIWORD(lParam), (int) LOWORD(lParam));
    return HID_BASE_RESOURCE + IDR_PLANVIEW;
}
```

ShowOverlap

The *ShowOverlap* private member function computes which piece rectangles overlap other piece rectangles. The function sets the *m_bOverlap* flag for overlapping pieces.

447

SafeScrollTo

The *CScrollView* class establishes a logical size for the view window. The scroll bar control handlers are programmed to restrict scrolling to this area. No such restriction exists for the *CScrollView::ScrollToDevicePosition* function, however. The *SafeScrollTo* private member function wraps the *ScrollToDevicePosition* function in such a way that scrolling is limited to the logical window area.

```
void CPlanView::SafeScrollTo(CPoint posDev)
{   // executes scroll only if viewport is within window bounds
    CRect clientRect;

    GetClientRect(&clientRect);
    clientRect += posDev;
    if (clientRect.top < 0) {
        posDev.y = 0;
    }
    if (clientRect.bottom > m_totalDev.cy) {
        posDev.y = m_totalDev.cy;
    }
    if (clientRect.left < 0) {
        posDev.x = 0;
    }
    if (clientRect.right > m_totalDev.cx) {
        posDev.x = m_totalDev.cx;
    }
    ScrollToDevicePosition(posDev);
}
```

The MATPLAN Resource File

App Studio was used to enhance the application's resource file, which was originally generated by AppWizard.

The *IDD_FORM* Dialog

The most important element in MATPLAN.RC is the form dialog resource *IDD_FORM*. You've seen the form image in Figure 21-2 on page 427. Here are the dialog controls as input to App Studio:

Text	Text Control ID	Data Member
Width	*IDC_WIDTH*	*m_pPiece->m_width*
Length	*IDC_LENGTH*	*m_pPiece->m_length*
Description	*IDC_DESC*	*m_pPiece->m_desc*
Sheet #	*IDC_SHEET*	*m_pPiece->m_sheet*
x-coordinate	*IDC_X*	*m_pPiece->m_x*
y-coordinate	*IDC_Y*	*m_pPiece->m_y*

Button Caption	Button ID	*CMatplanDialog* Member Function
&CANCEL	*IDC_CANCEL*	*OnClickedCancel*
CLEA&R	*IDC_CLEAR*	*OnClear*
&DELETE	*IDC_DELETE*	*OnDelete*
&INSERT	*IDC_INSERT*	*OnInsert*
&UPDATE	*IDC_UPDATE*	*OnUpdate*

The *IDR_MATTYPE* Menu

The following table shows the new MATPLAN menu items:

Menu	Menu Item	Command ID
Edit	Clear All	*ID_EDIT_CLEAR_ALL*
Window	New List Window	*ID_WINDOW_NEW1*
	New Plan Window	*ID_WINDOW_NEW2*

Symbols

Here are the new symbols for MATPLAN:

Symbol	Description
IDP_EXIT_DLG	Dialog exit error prompt ID for help
IDR_LISTBOX	Identifier for list box child window
IDR_LISTVIEW	List view window ID for help
IDR_PLANVIEW	Plan view window ID for help

Header Files

The file STDAFX.H contains the following *#include* statements:

```
#include <afxwin.h>        // MFC core and standard components
#include <afxext.h>        // CPrintInfo
#include <afxpriv.h>       // help
```

Building and Testing the MATPLAN Application

After you build MATPLAN from the Visual Workbench, be sure to run MAKEHELP to create the Help file.

When you run MATPLAN, you must choose New from the File menu to start a new plan document. The Materials Data Entry Form dialog pops up to let you insert the first piece. After that, double-click on the list box to insert more pieces, and then, from the Window menu, choose New Plan Window. Move the pieces with the mouse, and double-click on a rectangle to test the autopositioning feature. Next, try Print Preview and Print for both views. Also check Help for the views, the dialog, and the dialog exit message box.

PART IV

ADVANCED TOPICS

MFC LIBRARY VERSION 2.5 PROGRAMS WITHOUT DOCUMENTS OR VIEWS

The document–view architecture is useful for many applications, but sometimes a simpler program structure is sufficient. This chapter illustrates three applications—a Single Document Interface (SDI) program, a dialog-based program, and a Multiple Document Interface (MDI) program. None of these programs use document, view, or document–template classes, but they use command routing and some other Microsoft Foundation Class Library features. When you build the examples, you don't use AppWizard, but you do use App Studio and ClassWizard. The source code for these applications is also on the companion disc.

The greatest benefit from avoiding documents and view is reduced code size. A normal do-nothing SDI application is about 66 KB (without debugging information), but a stripped-down version is only about 36 KB. If you don't need the document–view features such as serialization, print support, and control bars, why include them in your program? If you don't care about saving 30 KB, you can still learn more about Windows and the application framework by studying this chapter's examples.

The following three examples don't have a lot in common, but they all do use an application object of a class derived from *CWinApp*. The examples start to diverge in the application class's *InitInstance* function.

The EX22A Example—An SDI Application

This SDI "Hello, world!" example builds on the code you saw way back in Chapter 2. The application has only one window, an object of a class derived from *CFrameWnd*. All drawing occurs inside the frame window, and all messages are handled there. Besides the frame and application classes, here are the application's necessary elements:

- **A main menu.** You can have a Windows-based application without a menu; you don't even need a resource script. But EX22A has both. The application framework routes menu commands to message handlers in the frame class.

- **An icon.** An icon is necessary if the program is to be activated from Windows Program Manager. It's also useful when the application's main frame window is minimized. The icon is stored in the resource, along with the menu.

- **Window Close message command handler.** Many applications need to do special processing when their main window is closed. If you were using documents, you could override the *CDocument::SaveModified* function, as illustrated in Chapter 24. Here, to take control of the Close process, you must write message handlers to process "close" messages sent as a result of user actions and by Windows itself when it shuts down.

- **Precompiled headers.** Precompiled headers offer such a compile speed advantage that you can't afford not to use them. This demands two extra files in the project, but they are short and simple.

Except for the precompiled header files, STDAFX.H and STDAFX.CPP, all this example's code is combined into two files, EX22A.H and EX22A.CPP. The only other file is the resource script, EX22A.RC. The *AFX_MSG* brackets allow you to use ClassWizard to add message handlers. The listings for the EX22A header and implementation files are shown in Figure 22-1.

EX22A.H

```
// application class
#include "resource.h"
class CEx22aApp : public CWinApp
```

Figure 22-1. *(continued)*
The EX22A header and implementation file listings.

Figure 22-1. *continued*

```
{
public:
    virtual BOOL InitInstance();
};

// frame window class
class CMainFrame : public CFrameWnd
{
public:
    CMainFrame();
protected:
    //{{AFX_MSG(CMainFrame)
    afx_msg void OnPaint();
    afx_msg void OnClose();
    afx_msg BOOL OnQueryEndSession();
    afx_msg void OnFile();
    afx_msg void OnHlp();
    //}}AFX_MSG
    DECLARE_MESSAGE_MAP()
};
```

EX22A.CPP

```
#include "stdafx.h"
#include "ex22a.h"

CEx22aApp NEAR theApp; // the one and only CEx22aApp object

BOOL CEx22aApp::InitInstance()
{
    m_pMainWnd = new CMainFrame();
    ASSERT(m_pMainWnd != NULL); // error checking only
    m_pMainWnd->ShowWindow(m_nCmdShow);
    m_pMainWnd->UpdateWindow();
    return TRUE;
}

//////////////////////////////////////////////////////////////////////
BEGIN_MESSAGE_MAP(CMainFrame, CFrameWnd)
    //{{AFX_MSG_MAP(CMainFrame)
    ON_WM_PAINT()
    ON_WM_CLOSE()
    ON_WM_QUERYENDSESSION()
    ON_COMMAND(ID_FILE, OnFile)
    ON_COMMAND(ID_HLP, OnHlp)
```

(continued)

Figure 22-1. *continued*

```
    //}}AFX_MSG_MAP
END_MESSAGE_MAP()

/////////////////////////////////////////////////////////////////////
CMainFrame::CMainFrame()
{
    Create(NULL, "EX22A Application",
            WS_OVERLAPPEDWINDOW, rectDefault, NULL,
            MAKEINTRESOURCE(IDR_MAINFRAME));
}

/////////////////////////////////////////////////////////////////////
void CMainFrame::OnPaint()
{
    CPaintDC dc(this);
    dc.TextOut(0, 0, "Hello, world!");
}

/////////////////////////////////////////////////////////////////////
void CMainFrame::OnClose()
{
    if (AfxMessageBox("OK to close window?", MB_YESNO) == IDYES) {
        CFrameWnd::OnClose();
    }
}

/////////////////////////////////////////////////////////////////////
BOOL CMainFrame::OnQueryEndSession()
{
    // received when user quits Windows
    SendMessage(WM_CLOSE);
    return TRUE;
}

// menu command handlers
/////////////////////////////////////////////////////////////////////
void CMainFrame::OnFile()
{
    TRACE("Entering CMainFrame::OnFile\n");
}

/////////////////////////////////////////////////////////////////////
void CMainFrame::OnHlp()
```

(continued)

Figure 22-1. *continued*

```
{
    TRACE("Entering CMainFrame::OnHlp\n");
}
```

STDAFX.H

```
#include <afxwin.h>
```

STDAFX.CPP

```
#include "stdafx.h"
```

CEx22aApp

This is the standard Microsoft Foundation Class Library application class. All class library applications depend on the existence of a global object of a class derived from *CWinApp*.

InitInstance

This function is modeled on the *InitInstance* function you see in a typical full-scale MDI application. It simply creates a main frame window and shows it.

CMainFrame

This is the main frame window class, derived from *CFrameWnd*. It is the only window class in the application, and there is only one *CMainFrame* object.

Constructor

The *CMainFrame* constructor calls the *CFrameWnd::Create* function to create the window. The first parameter specifies the default application framework–defined window registration class (not to be confused with a C++ class) that attaches an icon resource with ID = 2. The last parameter specifies the menu resource.

> NOTE: Placing the window *Create* call in a window class constructor is a shortcut. Everything works fine unless you derive another class from *CMainFrame*. In that case, the base class *OnCreate* function gets called instead of the derived class *OnCreate* function. You would be more nearly correct to use two-phase construction here. The *Create* call would reside in its own base class or derived class member function, separate from the constructor.

OnPaint

If you've been using view classes, you're accustomed to using the virtual *OnDraw* function for painting in the window. Without the view class in the picture, you must use *OnPaint*.

OnClose

The *OnClose* function is called when the user closes the window. It's mapped here to allow the application to perform shutdown processing. In this application, a message box appears to confirm that you want to close the window.

OnQueryEndSession

When Windows itself shuts down, it sends the WM_QUERYENDSESSION message to all applications. If you had thought that the WM_CLOSE message is automatically sent in this case, you'd be wrong. Here the *OnQueryEndSession* function sends the WM_CLOSE message, which is handled by the *CMainFrame::OnClose* member function.

OnFile, OnHlp

These two dummy functions are linked to the application's menu, which lets you observe that command routing is operational.

Resource Requirements

The application framework expects the application's icon resource to have an ID of 2. Use the *IDR_MAINFRAME* identifier to be consistent with other programs, but be sure to check that it's set to 2 in RESOURCE.H. You can use *IDR_MAINFRAME* for the menu also.

It doesn't matter what's on the menu, but the message handlers expect the identifiers *ID_FILE* and *ID_HLP*.

The EX22B Example—A Dialog-Based Application

When a resizable main frame window is unnecessary, a dialog can be sufficient for an application's user interface. The dialog window appears straightaway when the user starts the application. Obviously, there's no way to iconize the program, but as long as the dialog is not system modal, the user can freely switch to other applications.

In this example, the dialog functions as a simple calculator, as shown in Figure 22-2. ClassWizard takes charge of defining the class data members and generating the dialog data exchange (DDX) function calls. The application's resource script, EX22B.RC, defines an icon as well as the dialog.

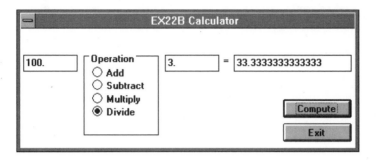

Figure 22-2.
The EX22B Calculator dialog.

The listings for the EX22B header and implementation files are shown in Figure 22-3. The precompiled header files, STDAFX.H and STDAFX.CPP, are the same as in the previous example.

EX22B.H

```
#include "resource.h"
class CEx22bDialog : public CDialog
{
public:
    CEx22bDialog();

// Dialog Data
    //{{AFX_DATA(CEx22bDialog)
    enum { IDD = IDD_EX22BDLG };
    double      m_d1;
    double      m_d2;
    double      m_d3;
    int         m_nOpr;
    //}}AFX_DATA

// Implementation
protected:
    virtual void DoDataExchange(CDataExchange* pDX); // DDX/DDV support
    //{{AFX_MSG(CEx22bDialog)
    afx_msg void OnCompute();
    //}}AFX_MSG
```

Figure 22-3.   *(continued)*
The EX22B header and implementation file listings.

459

Figure 22-3. *continued*

```
     DECLARE_MESSAGE_MAP()
};

class CEx22bApp : public CWinApp
{
private:
    CEx22bDialog m_dialog;
public:
    BOOL InitInstance();
};
```

EX22B.CPP

```
#include "stdafx.h"
#include "ex22b.h"

CEx22bApp NEAR theApp;

BOOL CEx22bApp::InitInstance()
{
    m_dialog.DoModal(); // returns when Exit button clicked
    return FALSE;
}


//////////////////////////////////////////////////////////////////////
BEGIN_MESSAGE_MAP(CEx22bDialog, CDialog)
    //{{AFX_MSG_MAP(CEx22bDialog)
    ON_BN_CLICKED(ID_COMPUTE, OnCompute)
    //}}AFX_MSG_MAP
END_MESSAGE_MAP()


//////////////////////////////////////////////////////////////////////
CEx22bDialog::CEx22bDialog() : CDialog(CEx22bDialog::IDD)
{
    //{{AFX_DATA_INIT(CEx22bDialog)
    m_d1 = 0;
    m_d2 = 0;
    m_d3 = 0;
    m_nOpr = 0; // changed from default -1
    //}}AFX_DATA_INIT
}


//////////////////////////////////////////////////////////////////////
void CEx22bDialog::DoDataExchange(CDataExchange* pDX)
```

(continued)

Figure 22-3. *continued*

```
{
    CDialog::DoDataExchange(pDX);
    //{{AFX_DATA_MAP(CEx22bDialog)
    DDX_Text(pDX, IDC_EDIT1, m_d1);
    DDX_Text(pDX, IDC_EDIT2, m_d2);
    DDX_Text(pDX, IDC_EDIT3, m_d3);
    DDX_Radio(pDX, IDC_RADIO1, m_nOpr);
    //}}AFX_DATA_MAP
}

///////////////////////////////////////////////////////////////////
void CEx22bDialog::OnCompute()
{
    UpdateData(TRUE);
    switch (m_nOpr) {
    case 0:  // add
        m_d3 = m_d1 + m_d2;
        break;
    case 1:  // subtract
        m_d3 = m_d1 - m_d2;
        break;
    case 2:  // multiply
        m_d3 = m_d1 * m_d2;
        break;
    case 3:  // divide
        if (m_d2 != 0.0) {
            m_d3 = m_d1 / m_d2;
        }
        else {
            AfxMessageBox("Divide by zero");
            m_d3 = 0.0;
        }
        break;
    default:
        TRACE("default m_nOpr = %d\n", m_nOpr);
    }
    UpdateData(FALSE);
}
```

TIP: If you need to open another modal dialog, pass *this* as the optional *pParentWind* parameter for the inner dialog constructor.

CEx22bApp

The EX22B application class is unique. Because there is no main window, there is no need for the *Run* function to translate and dispatch messages. All commands are handled within the application framework and the dialog.

Data Members

The variable *m_dialog* holds a dialog object of class *CEx22bDialog*. Because the object is embedded, the dialog is constructed and destroyed along with the application object.

InitInstance

The *CEx22bApp::InitInstance* function calls *DoModal* for *m_dialog*. After the user exits the dialog (through the *CDialog::OnCancel* function), *InitInstance* returns 0, thereby signaling the application framework to terminate the application immediately. The *CWinApp::Run* and *CWinApp::ExitInstance* functions are never called.

CEx22bDialog

This a standard dialog class derived from *CDialog*. The *AFX_MSG* brackets permit ClassWizard to operate on the code.

Data Members

ClassWizard helps you define data members for each dialog control. The edit controls have *double* values attached (*m_d1, m_d2, m_d3*), and the radio button group has an integer (*m_nOpr*) that takes on the value 0, 1, or 2.

Constructor

The constructor is tied to the dialog resource ID, *IDD_EX22BDLG*.

DoDataExchange

This function calls the DDX functions that ClassWizard assigned.

OnCompute

This notification message handler is activated by the dialog's Compute button and by the Enter key (because Compute is the default button).

Resource Requirements

The application's resource script, EX22B.RC, contains the dialog resource, identified as *IDD_EX22BDLG*, and a reference to the icon, *IDR_MAIN-FRAME* (set to 2). The dialog controls are listed in the following table, in their tabbing order:

Description	Type	ID	Tab Stop	Group
First Input	Edit control	*IDC_EDIT1*	X	
Add	Radio button	*IDC_RADIO1*	X	X
Subtract	Radio button	*IDC_RADIO2*	X	
Multiply	Radio button	*IDC_RADIO3*	X	
Divide	Radio button	*IDC_RADIO4*	X	
Second Input	Edit control	*IDC_EDIT2*	X	X
Result	Edit control (no input)	*IDC_EDIT3*		
Compute	Default pushbutton	*IDC_COMPUTE*		
Exit	Pushbutton	*IDOK*		

The Second Input edit control needs the Group property set to terminate the preceding radio button group.

The EX22C Example—An MDI Application

This bare-bones MDI example isn't as simple as the SDI example, EX22A. Remember, from Chapter 17, that an MDI application consists of a main frame window and one or more child windows. Also, a single MDI client window is attached to the main frame window, but the application framework keeps that window hidden. If you use EX22C as a prototype, you'll be doing most of your programming in classes derived from *CMDIChildWnd*. Child window objects can receive and process messages as did the frame window object in example EX22A.

The EX22C MDI program doesn't have all the features of a full-blown document–view MDI application, but it does have these basic elements:

■ **A main menu.** A full-blown MDI application has two (or more) menus. EX22C has only one menu, and that menu is attached to the main frame window. The MDI Window submenu (with the Cascade, Tile, and child selection items) is part of this main menu structure, but the items (along with the File Close item) are disabled when no child windows are present.

■ **An icon.** Every Windows-based program needs an icon. The EX22C resource script defines one for this application.

■ **Initial child window.** Many MDI applications open an empty child window on startup. EX22C is no exception. If you use EX22C as a prototype for your own MDI application, you can easily disable this feature.

■ **Window Close message command handler.** MDI window close logic is more complex than SDI window close logic because of the many windows involved. Child windows can be closed individually or as a result of the main frame window's closure. In the EX22C program, the main frame window sends WM_CLOSE messages to all child windows, and the child window message handlers can process these messages. The Window menu even has a Close All item, a feature not present in a standard document–view MDI application.

■ **Precompiled headers.** As in the previous examples, EX22C uses precompiled headers to speed compilation.

The listings for the EX22C header and implementation files are shown in Figure 22-4.

EX22C.H

```
#include "resource.h"

class CEx22cApp : public CWinApp
{
public:
    virtual BOOL InitInstance();
};

// MDI frame window class
class CMainFrame : public CMDIFrameWnd
{
public:
    CMainFrame();
protected:
    //{{AFX_MSG(CMainFrame)
    afx_msg void OnFileNew();
    afx_msg void OnWindowCloseAll();
    afx_msg void OnUpdateWindowCloseAll(CCmdUI* pCmdUI);
    afx_msg void OnClose();
```

Figure 22-4. *(continued)*

The EX22C header and implementation file listings.

Figure 22-4. *continued*

```
    afx_msg BOOL OnQueryEndSession();
    //}}AFX_MSG
    DECLARE_MESSAGE_MAP()
protected:
    BOOL CloseAllChildWindows();
};

// MDI child frame window class
class CChildFrame : public CMDIChildWnd
{
public:
    static int NEAR nChild;
    CChildFrame(BOOL bMaximized = FALSE);
protected:
    //{{AFX_MSG(CChildFrame)
    afx_msg void OnPaint();
    afx_msg void OnFileClose();
    afx_msg void OnClose();
    //}}AFX_MSG
    DECLARE_MESSAGE_MAP()
};
```

EX22C.CPP

```
#include "stdafx.h"
#include "ex22c.h"

CEx22cApp NEAR theApp; // the one and only CEx22cApp object

BOOL CEx22cApp::InitInstance()
{
    m_pMainWnd = new CMainFrame();
    m_pMainWnd->ShowWindow(m_nCmdShow);
    m_pMainWnd->UpdateWindow();
    new CChildFrame();
    return TRUE;
}


////////////////////////////////////////////////////////////////////////
BEGIN_MESSAGE_MAP(CMainFrame, CMDIFrameWnd)
    //{{AFX_MSG_MAP(CMainFrame)
    ON_WM_CLOSE()
    ON_WM_QUERYENDSESSION()
    ON_COMMAND(ID_FILE_NEW, OnFileNew)
    ON_COMMAND(ID_WINDOW_CLOSE_ALL, OnWindowCloseAll)
```

(continued)

Figure 22-4. *continued*

```
        ON_UPDATE_COMMAND_UI(ID_WINDOW_CLOSE_ALL, OnUpdateWindowCloseAll)
    //}}AFX_MSG_MAP
END_MESSAGE_MAP()

///////////////////////////////////////////////////////////////////////
CMainFrame::CMainFrame()
{
    Create(NULL, "EX22C Application",
            WS_OVERLAPPEDWINDOW,
            rectDefault, NULL,
            MAKEINTRESOURCE(IDR_MAINFRAME));
}

///////////////////////////////////////////////////////////////////////
void CMainFrame::OnClose()
{
    if (CloseAllChildWindows()) {
        CMDIFrameWnd::OnClose();
    }
}

///////////////////////////////////////////////////////////////////////
BOOL CMainFrame::OnQueryEndSession()
{
    return CloseAllChildWindows();
}

///////////////////////////////////////////////////////////////////////
void CMainFrame::OnFileNew()
{
    BOOL bMaximized = FALSE;
    // creates a new child window, maximized if active child is maximized
    CChildFrame* pActiveChild = (CChildFrame*) MDIGetActive(&bMaximized);
    new CChildFrame(bMaximized);
}

///////////////////////////////////////////////////////////////////////
void CMainFrame::OnWindowCloseAll()
{
    CloseAllChildWindows();
}

///////////////////////////////////////////////////////////////////////
void CMainFrame::OnUpdateWindowCloseAll(CCmdUI* pCmdUI)
```

(continued)

Figure 22-4. *continued*

```
{
    pCmdUI->Enable(MDIGetActive() != NULL);
}


//////////////////////////////////////////////////////////////////////////
BOOL CMainFrame::CloseAllChildWindows()
{
    // returns TRUE if all child windows permit closure
    CChildFrame* pChild;
    CChildFrame* pPrevChild = NULL;
    while ((pChild = (CChildFrame*) MDIGetActive()) != NULL) {
        if (pChild == pPrevChild)
            return FALSE; // closure not permitted
        pPrevChild = pChild;
        pChild->SendMessage(WM_CLOSE);
    }
    return TRUE;
}


//////////////////////////////////////////////////////////////////////////
BEGIN_MESSAGE_MAP(CChildFrame, CMDIChildWnd)
    //{{AFX_MSG_MAP(CChildFrame)
    ON_WM_PAINT()
    ON_WM_CLOSE()
    ON_COMMAND(ID_FILE_CLOSE, OnFileClose)
    //}}AFX_MSG_MAP
END_MESSAGE_MAP()

int NEAR CChildFrame::nChild = 1; // static

//////////////////////////////////////////////////////////////////////////
CChildFrame::CChildFrame(BOOL bMaximized /*= FALSE*/)
{
    char szTitle[30];
    wsprintf(szTitle, "EX22C Child Window %d", nChild++);
    CMainFrame* pFrameWnd = (CMainFrame*) AfxGetApp()->m_pMainWnd;
    Create(NULL, szTitle,
            WS_CHILD | WS_VISIBLE | WS_OVERLAPPEDWINDOW |
            (bMaximized ? WS_MAXIMIZE : 0),
            rectDefault, pFrameWnd);
}


//////////////////////////////////////////////////////////////////////////
void CChildFrame::OnPaint()
```

(continued)

467

Figure 22-4. *continued*

```
{
    CPaintDC dc(this);
    dc.TextOut(0, 0, "Hello, world!");
}


//////////////////////////////////////////////////////////////////////////
void CChildFrame::OnClose()

{
    if (AfxMessageBox("OK to close window?", MB_YESNO) == IDYES) {
        CMDIChildWnd::OnClose();
    }
}


//////////////////////////////////////////////////////////////////////////
void CChildFrame::OnFileClose()
{
    SendMessage(WM_CLOSE);
}
```

CEx22cApp

This is the standard application class again, derived from *CWinApp*.

InitInstance

In this MDI example, *InitInstance* performs one of the same functions that it performs in a document–view MDI application. It constructs an object of class *CMainFrame* and then shows the window. It also constructs the initial child window.

CMainFrame

You can use this class directly in your own minimalist MDI applications, or you can rename it and use it as a base class.

Constructor

The *CMainFrame* constructor creates the main frame window object. The note on page 457 about the EX22A two-phase constructor applies here also.

OnClose

The *CMainFrame::OnClose* function is called only when the user closes the main frame window from the system menu or with Alt-F4. Its purpose is to send WM_CLOSE messages to all the child windows. If this function weren't mapped, the child windows would be summarily destroyed without the opportunity to process the close message.

OnQueryEndSession

When Windows itself is shutting down, it sends the WM_QUERYEND-SESSION message to the main windows of all applications. If any application returns 0, Windows does not shut down. The message handler here does the same thing as *OnClose*.

OnFileNew

The File New menu item, through the *OnFileNew* message handler, causes construction of a new child window. If the current active child is maximized, the new child is maximized.

OnWindowCloseAll

The application's Window menu has a Close All item that is mapped to this function. The *OnWindowCloseAll* function sends a WM_CLOSE message to all child windows.

OnUpdateWindowCloseAll

The Window menu Close All item is enabled only when there is at least one child window.

CloseAllChildWindows

This is a protected member function that sends the WM_CLOSE message to the child windows. In a loop, the function sends the close message to the current active child window. If the active child refuses to be closed (the window stays active), the looping terminates, and the function returns failure status (*FALSE*).

CChildFrame

This class is derived from *CMDIChildWnd*. Add your own message handlers and *OnPaint* code to customize this class.

Data Members

The *CChildFrame* class has a static data member *nChild* that is incremented each time a new child window is created. This number is used in the child window titles.

Constructor

The *CChildFrame* constructor creates the child window object. If the optional *bMaximized* parameter is *TRUE*, the child window occupies the entire main frame client area. The window title includes a sequential window number from the static *nChild* data member. The note on page 457 about the EX22A two-phase constructor applies here also.

For Windows SDK Programmers

If you look at the *Create* function call in the constructor, you might think that the child frame is being created directly. Actually, the *CMDIChildWnd::Create* function loads a structure and then sends a WM_MDICREATE message to the MDI client window (owned by the main frame window). The client window then creates the child window.

OnPaint

As in EX22A, you must use *OnPaint* for painting in the window.

OnClose

This message handler is called in response to the WM_CLOSE message, sent by the main frame window or by the user's closing of a child window. This *OnClose* function displays a message box that asks the user for permission to close the window.

OnFileClose

This function is called when the user chooses Close from the File menu. It sends the WM_CLOSE message so that the *OnClose* member function can veto the window closing. The File Close menu item is disabled if there are no child windows.

Destroying *CMDIChildWnd* Objects

You might have noticed that child frame window objects are constructed with the *new* operator and not explicitly destroyed. These window objects are destroyed by the application framework in the *CWnd* virtual function *PostNCDestroy* (which is overridden in *CFrameWnd*) when the window itself is destroyed as a result of user action. Technical Note #17 in the MFC-NOTES.HLP file tells you which window objects are destroyed.

Resource Requirements

The EX22C program needs an icon resource with ID *IDR_MAINFRAME* set to 2. The EX22C Window menu, shown in Figure 22-5, uses the same ID.

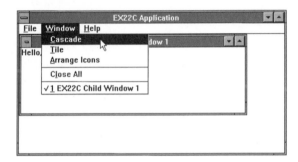

Figure 22-5.
The EX22C Window menu.

For Windows to insert the child window list at the bottom of the Window menu, the Window menu <u>must</u> be second from the right on the main menu.

Here are the command IDs for the menu items:

Menu Item	Command ID
File New	*ID_FILE_NEW*
File Close	*ID_FILE_CLOSE*
File Exit	*ID_APP_EXIT*
Window Cascade	*ID_WINDOW_CASCADE*
Window Tile	*ID_WINDOW_TILE_HORZ*
Window Arrange Icons	*ID_WINDOW_ARRANGE*
Window Close All	*ID_WINDOW_CLOSE_ALL*
Help	*ID_HELP*

CHAPTER TWENTY THREE

STORING BITMAPS IN A DOCUMENT—DIBS AND THE CLIPBOARD

In Chapter 10, you studied GDI bitmaps, and you saw how easy it was to load a device-independent bitmap (DIB) from a resource. Direct disk accessing of DIBs is more difficult, but this chapter presents a class, called *CDib*, that simplifies DIB processing. The EX23A example program, built around the *CDib* class, illustrates serialization of DIBs, direct file I/O, and transferring of GDI bitmaps through the Windows clipboard.

The Windows DIB Format

If you want to save bitmaps in a document file (or database) that other computers can read, you must use a device-independent format. The Windows DIB format is a good candidate because the Windows API directly supports it. Many applications, including Windows Paintbrush, process disk files in DIB format (BMP files). The standard DIB format supports monochrome, 16-color, and 256-color bitmaps, and it also supports 24-bit color bitmaps.

The DIB format has compression options for 16-color and 256-color bitmaps, and this compression can save substantial amounts of disk space and RAM. An uncompressed 16-color VGA screen dump bitmap, for example, requires 154 KB, but a compressed version might be as small as 30 KB.

A DIB is different from a GDI bitmap in that you have direct access to the DIB's data. As a matter of fact, you must allocate memory for the DIBs you create. In a DIB data structure, each pixel is represented by 1, 4, 8, or 24 adjacent bits. The bits are packed into bytes, which are organized by row and then by column, as shown in Figure 23-1, on the next page. Rows are padded to 4-byte boundaries, and a header provides the necessary access information. For the DIB header layout, look up the *BITMAPINFOHEADER* structure in the *Microsoft Windows 3.1 Programmer's Reference*. Figure 23-1 shows the layout of a 16-color DIB that is 10 pixels wide by 7 pixels high. Notice that the DIB requires 56 bytes of storage, plus the header.

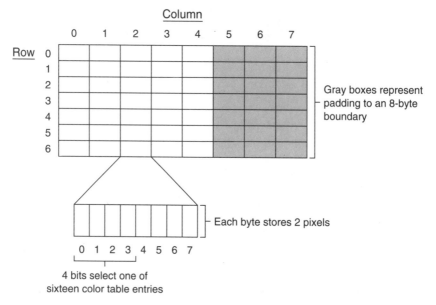

Figure 23-1.
The organization of a 16-color DIB.

DIBs, Colors, and Palettes

Refer to Chapter 5 for a description of the default color mapping for the common types of display boards in Windows systems. Be sure you're familiar with the standard pure colors that the VGA and 256-color display drivers support.

Because we are talking about a device-independent format, the DIB color information must be device-independent. A DIB contains its own color table. A 16-color DIB, for example, contains sixteen 24-bit absolute red-green-blue color values. Windows doesn't use dithered colors in bitmaps; it uses the closest matching pure color. Monochrome DIBs (with 1 bit per pixel) contain values for both the foreground and background colors.

When Windows displays a monochrome or a 16-color DIB (or converts it to a GDI bitmap) with a standard VGA display board, it chooses standard pure colors that most closely match the specified colors. You have no control over this process. Color palettes have no effect with a standard VGA display board.

With a 256-color display board, however, you have more flexibility. If you don't use color palettes (the default), Windows maps a DIB's colors to the driver's 20 standard colors. If you do use color palettes, Windows maps the DIB's colors as best it can to the colors that the display board supports; 20 palette colors are always reserved for the standard colors, but 236 palette colors can be changed to accommodate the bitmap.

Color palette programming is quite complex because you have to consider the interactions both among applications and among sibling MDI child windows. The 256-color display board can display only 256 colors at any time, as specified by the system palette. Suppose, for example, that a window gets the input focus and replaces the system palette's dark green entry with neon pink. Suppose a second window is showing a forest scene bitmap. Because you don't want neon pink trees, even in an inactive window, you must remap the inactive window's colors to enable Windows to choose another shade of green for the trees.

Inactive window programs can respond to the Windows message WM_PALETTE CHANGED, which is sent to <u>all</u> windows when the system palette is changed. When a program gets the input focus, it receives a WM_QUERYNEWPALETTE message if the system palette has been changed. In both cases, the program realizes its own color palette into the system palette. See the DIBLOOK program in the \MSVC\MFC\SAMPLES subdirectory for an example of the use of DIBs with color palettes. Remember that color palette programming applies only to color-intensive programs running on 256-color display boards.

A 24-bit DIB doesn't need a color table because the pixel groups specify colors directly. If you display a 24-bit DIB with a 24-bit display board, you don't need a color palette. If you display a 24-bit DIB with a 256-color display board, you can define your own 256-color palette that contains appropriate color values. Windows then matches the DIB's colors with the closest matching palette colors. If you don't define a palette, the DIB will be displayed with the 20 standard colors.

Passing Images via the Clipboard

As a Windows user, you're probably aware that the clipboard is a useful tool for transferring information among Windows-based programs. The clipboard can accommodate both text and image data, but the clipboard writer program and the clipboard reader program must agree on a format. The clipboard writer often provides data in several formats, and the reader chooses one that it understands. It's possible to transfer DIBs via the clipboard, but few programs use the DIB format. Many Windows programs use the GDI bitmap format, however, so that's the format we'll use in the EX23A example.

Bitmap Clipboard Rules

When you use the clipboard, first be aware that all applications must share one clipboard. Then be prepared to follow some strict rules when transferring GDI bitmaps via the clipboard.

- The clipboard must be open before you can transfer information. Call the *CWnd::OpenClipboard* member function. If it returns *TRUE*, you have exclusive access to the clipboard; otherwise, you know that another program is using it.

- If you are going to place information on the clipboard, you must first empty the clipboard with the Windows API function *EmptyClipboard*.

- The Windows API function *SetClipboardData* accepts a GDI bitmap handle (*HBITMAP*). The designated bitmap <u>cannot</u> be currently selected into a device context when you call *SetClipboardData*. You cannot use the bitmap again after you send it to the clipboard. This means that you'll have to copy the bitmap if your *OnDraw* function needs to display it.

- The clipboard deletes *HBITMAP* entities that have been sent to it. If you've used a *CBitmap* object, you can't delete that object until you've called the *CGdiObject* member function *Detach*. The *Detach* function separates the GDI bitmap handle from the C++ object so that the destructor doesn't delete the bitmap. *Detach* returns the bitmap handle.

- The Windows API function *GetClipboardData* returns a GDI bitmap handle (*HBITMAP*). The *CGdiObject::FromHandle* static function converts the handle to a temporary *CBitmap* object pointer. You don't have to worry about deleting this object or detaching the handle from it. You cannot, however, leave the bitmap selected into a device context. If you want to display the bitmap, you must copy it.

- When you're finished with the clipboard, you must use the Windows *CloseClipboard* function.

NOTE: Be careful with dialogs and message boxes that you create while the clipboard is open. If you don't make these dialogs system modal, the user could try to access the busy clipboard from another program.

DIBs in MFC Library Documents

Microsoft Foundation Class (MFC) Library version 2.5 application data is stored in *CDocument* objects and transferred to and from document files. If your application needs to save and retrieve images, those images must be stored in the document in device-independent format. In this chapter's example, EX23A, the document maintains an image in Windows DIB format.

Printing with DIBs

DIBs (device-independent bitmaps) are extremely useful for printing. Suppose you're trying to print a GDI bitmap that is selected into a memory device context that is compatible with the display. Most printer drivers won't show colors as gray shades if you call *BitBlt* or *StretchBlt*; they produce black-and-white output instead. If you send a DIB to the printer, however, you get the proper gray shades. The *CDib* class described below makes bitmap printing easy.

The *CDib* Class

The MFC Library has no *CDib* class, so we'll write our own. This class works fairly well, but it's designed as a teaching tool rather than as a piece of commercial software. You might want to add more error checking plus other features such as palette support and functions that access DIBs in resources. The *CDib* class is designed to be used directly. There are no virtual functions to implement in derived classes.

A *CDib* object represents a single device-independent bitmap. The image bits, together with all necessary decoding information, are contained within the object. There is no copy constructor or assignment operator because DIBs are often big, and it doesn't make much sense to copy them within a program. Also, there are no public data members.

A document can contain a single *CDib* object, or multiple *CDib* objects can exist in a document structure, such as a list or an array. Thus, DIBs can be serialized along with the rest of the document data.

Figure 23-2 on the following page shows the *CDib* class declaration:

CDIB.H

```
class CDib : public CObject
{
    DECLARE_SERIAL(CDib)
private:
    char huge* m_lpBuf;     // DIB data buffer
    DWORD     m_dwLength;   // total buffer length, including file header
    int       m_nBits;      // number of color bits per pixel
    // pointers for internal use
    LPBITMAPFILEHEADER m_lpBMFH;
    LPBITMAPINFOHEADER m_lpBMIH;
    LPBITMAPINFO       m_lpBMI;
    LPSTR              m_lpData;
public:
    CDib();
    CDib(CDC* pDC, int nBt = 0, BOOL bCompr = FALSE);
    // nBt = 0 means use default bits/pixel
    ~CDib();
    virtual void Serialize(CArchive &ar);
    BOOL Read(CFile* pFile);
    BOOL Write(CFile* pFile);
    CBitmap* MakeBitmap(CDC* pDC, CSize& bmSize);
    BOOL Display(CDC*, CPoint origin);
    BOOL Stretch(CDC*, CPoint origin, CSize size);
    int GetColorBits();
    DWORD GetLength();
    CSize GetSize();
    void SetMonoColors(DWORD dwForeground, DWORD dwBackground);
    BOOL GetMonoColors(DWORD& dwForeground, DWORD& dwBackground);
private:
    BOOL AllocateMemory(BOOL bRealloc = FALSE);
};
```

Figure 23-2.
The CDib *class declaration.*

Here's a rundown of the *CDib* member functions. (The implementation code is shown in Figure 23-3 beginning on page 485.)

■ **Default constructor**—You'll use the default constructor when you're loading a DIB from an archive or from a file. It creates an empty DIB object.

■ **Bitmap constructor**—Despite the absence of a *CBitmap* parameter, this second constructor makes a DIB from a GDI bitmap. The bitmap must have been previously selected into a memory device context.

Parameter	Description
pDC	A pointer to the memory device context into which the GDI bitmap is selected.
nBt	The number of color bits for the DIB; *0* means use the value from the GDI bitmap.
bCompr	*TRUE* for a compressed DIB (the default); *FALSE* for an uncompressed DIB.

■ **Destructor**—The *CDib* destructor frees all allocated DIB memory.

■ **Serialize**—See the *Class Library Reference* for a description of the *CObject* virtual *Serialize* function.

■ **Read**—This function reads a BMP file into the *CDib* object. The file must have been successfully opened.

Parameter	Description
pFile	A pointer to a *CFile* object. The corresponding disk file contains the DIB.
Return value	*TRUE* if successful.

■ **Write**—This function writes a BMP file from the *CDib* object. The file must have been successfully opened or created.

Parameter	Description
pFile	A pointer to a *CFile* object. The DIB will be written to the corresponding disk file.
Return value	*TRUE* if successful.

■ **MakeBitmap**—This function creates a GDI bitmap from the contents of the *CDib* object. The bitmap is then selected into the memory device context that is passed as a parameter. The bitmap size and number of color bits are set according to the DIB characteristics.

Parameter	Description
pDC	A pointer to the memory device context into which the GDI bitmap will be selected.
bmSize	A reference to a *CSize* object that holds the GDI bitmap size. The *MakeBitmap* function sets the value of this parameter.
Return value	A pointer to the previously selected GDI bitmap.

■ *Display*—This function sends this *CDib* object to the display (or printer) without creating an intermediate GDI bitmap. The function does no scaling under any circumstances.

Parameter	Description
pDC	A pointer to the display or printer device context that will receive the DIB image.
origin	A *CPoint* object that holds the logical coordinates at which the DIB will be displayed.
Return value	*TRUE* if successful.

■ *Stretch*—This function outputs this *CDib* object to the display (or printer) without creating an intermediate GDI bitmap. The bitmap will be stretched as necessary to fit the specified rectangle.

Parameter	Description
pDC	A pointer to the display or printer device context that will receive the DIB image.
origin	A *CPoint* object that holds the logical coordinates at which the DIB will be displayed.
size	A *CSize* object that represents the display rectangle's width and height in logical units.
Return value	*TRUE* if successful.

■ *GetColorBits*—This function returns the number of color bits per pixel for this *CDib* object. If the DIB is empty, *0* is returned.

■ *GetLength*—This function returns the total number of bytes in the *CDib* data buffer. This is the length of a corresponding BMP file. If the DIB is empty, *0* is returned.

■ *GetSize*—This function returns a *CSize* object that represents the width and height of the bitmap in pixels.

■ *SetMonoColors, GetMonoColors*—Monochrome DIBs contain the values for the bitmap's foreground and background colors. Because this information is not part of the GDI bitmap structure, we need functions to set and retrieve the two color values. *GetMonoColors* returns *TRUE* if the DIB is a monochrome bitmap.

DIB Access Functions

The *CDib* class uses four important Windows DIB access functions. None of these functions is a class library function, so you'll need to refer to the Windows SDK documentation (or the online help) for details. Here's a summary:

■ *SetDIBitsToDevice*—The *CDib Display* member function uses this function. It displays a DIB directly on the display or printer. No scaling occurs; one bitmap bit corresponds to one display pixel or one printer dot. This scaling restriction limits the function's usefulness. The function doesn't work like *BitBlt* because *BitBlt* uses logical coordinates.

■ *StretchDIBits*—The *CDib Stretch* member function uses this function. It displays a DIB directly on the display or printer in a manner similar to that of *StretchBlt.*

NOTE: If you call *SetDIBitsToDevice* or *StretchDIBits* for a compressed DIB, some printer drivers won't show gray shades correctly.

■ *GetDIBits*—The *CDib* bitmap constructor uses this function. It constructs a DIB from a GDI bitmap, using memory that you allocate. You have some control over the format of the DIB because you can specify the number of color bits per pixel and the compression. If you are using compression, you have to call *GetDIBits* twice, once to calculate the memory needed and again to generate the DIB data.

■ *CreateDIBitmap*—Contrary to its name, this function creates a GDI bitmap from a DIB. The *CDib::MakeBitmap* member function uses it. Before you call *CreateDIBitmap,* you must have a memory device context with a selected prototype bitmap that has the same characteristics as the bitmap you want *CreateDIBitmap* to create. If you want a 16-color bitmap, for example, you must first construct a 16-color prototype bitmap. If you don't first select the prototype bitmap into the memory device context, *CreateDIBitmap* provides a monochrome bitmap.

A strange thing happens when *CreateDIBitmap* processes a mono-chrome DIB. The function switches the image bits depending on the DIB's two color values. In the *CDib* class, we circumvent this behavior and preserve the original DIB bit values.

The EX23A Example

The EX23A example program uses a serializable document to hold a single *CDib* object. The one and only view class allows the display of the DIB in a scrolling view with a shrink-to-fit option. The view also supports the Printing and Print Preview features. The Edit menu has items for cutting, copying, and pasting bitmaps (in GDI format) to and from the clipboard. It also has Copy To and Paste From items for writing and reading BMP files. EX23A fully exploits the new *CDib* class.

As was the MATPLAN example in Chapter 21, this example is presented with code highlights and resource requirements. Here is a table of the files and classes:

Header File	Source Code File	Class	Description
EX23A.H	EX23A.CPP	*CEx23aApp*	Main application—from AppWizard
MAINFRM.H	MAINFRM.CPP	*CMainFrame*	SDI main frame—from AppWizard
EX23ADOC.H	EX23ADOC.CPP	*CEx23aDoc*	EX23A document
EX23AVW.H	EX23AVW.CPP	*CEx23aView*	Scrolling view class
BITSDLG.H	BITSDLG.CPP	*CBitsDialog*	Dialog for color bits and compression
CDIB.H	CDIB.CPP	*CDib*	DIB class
STDAFX.H	STDAFX.CPP		Precompiled headers

The application and main frame class consist of standard code generated by AppWizard, so they are not listed or described. The other classes are described together with their member functions.

CEx23aDoc

This document class contains a single <u>pointer</u> to a *CDib* object. Why not use an embedded object? Consider the problem of replacing the document's DIB with a new DIB just read from the clipboard or disk. With an embedded

CDib object, the class would need an assignment operator, or the serialization code would have to delete old data. With the *CDib* pointer, we simply delete the old object and construct a new one.

Constructor, Destructor

The *CEx23aDoc* constructor constructs the initial *CDib* object on the heap, and the destructor destroys it.

DeleteContents

This overridden application framework virtual function deletes the document's current *CDib* object and constructs a new, empty one. This function is crucial in SDI applications because it's called every time the user opens a new document or loads a document from disk.

```
void CEx23aDoc::DeleteContents()
{
    delete m_pDib;
    m_pDib = new CDib;
}
```

Serialize

This overridden application framework virtual function calls the *Serialize* function for the document's *CDib* object. Because the document class has no other data members to serialize, the resulting archive is equivalent to a BMP file.

OnEditClearAll

This message handler responds to the Edit Clear All menu item.

```
void CEx23aDoc::OnEditClearAll()
{
    DeleteContents();
    UpdateAllViews(NULL);
    SetModifiedFlag();
}
```

CBitsDialog

The *CBitsDialog* class is generated entirely by ClassWizard. It's based on the dialog resource discussed in the EX23A resource file section.

CDib

You've already seen the *CDib* class declaration and member function descriptions. Figure 23-3 lists the *CDib* implementation code. Below are a couple of important observations about the class.

Memory Allocation

Memory is allocated and freed with the WINDOWSX.H macros *GlobalAllocPtr*, *GlobalReAllocPtr*, and *GlobalFreePtr*. These functions are suitable for the large memory blocks that bitmaps often require. Memory is allocated in the private member function *AllocateMemory*.

Serialization of Large Bitmaps

Because so many bitmaps are larger than 64 KB, the *CDib* class must use <u>huge</u> pointers to manage data. The *CFile* class has the *ReadHuge* and *WriteHuge* member functions for reading and writing large data blocks, but there are no equivalent *CArchive* member functions. It's easy enough to get the archive's associated file object so that you can use the *CFile* functions for huge pointers. You must call the *CArchive Flush* function before reading or writing, however, to synchronize the archive's buffer. The *CDib::Serialize* function calls the *Read* and *Write* member functions, which are shared by the Edit menu's Paste From and Copy To handlers.

The *CDib::Write* function, shown below, is the first place where we've had to use the MFC library exception-handling mechanism. The *TRY* and *CATCH* macros work together to process errors where there is no error return value. These macros will be replaced when the C++ compiler officially supports exception handling.

```
BOOL CDib::Write(CFile* pFile)
{
    TRY {
        pFile->WriteHuge(m_lpBuf, m_dwLength);
    }
    CATCH (CException, e) {
        AfxMessageBox("Write error--possible disk full condition");
        return FALSE;
    }
    END_CATCH
    return TRUE;
}
```

CDIB.CPP

```cpp
#include "stdafx.h"
#include "resource.h"
#include "cdib.h"
#include <windowsx.h>  // for GlobalAllocPtr

IMPLEMENT_SERIAL(CDib, CObject, 0)

/////////////////////////////////////////////////////////////////
CDib::CDib()
{
    m_dwLength = 0L;
    m_nBits    = 0;
    m_lpBuf    = NULL;
}


/////////////////////////////////////////////////////////////////
CDib::CDib(CDC* pDC, int nBt, BOOL bCompr)
// pDC is memory DC ptr
// nBt is color bits per pixel (default = 0)
// bCompr is compression (default = TRUE)
{
// constructs a DIB from the contents of a bitmap
    BITMAP bm;
    int    nPaletteSize;

    CBitmap* pEmptyBitmap = new CBitmap;
    pEmptyBitmap->CreateCompatibleBitmap(pDC, 0, 0);
    CBitmap* pBitmap = (CBitmap*) (pDC->SelectObject(pEmptyBitmap));
    pBitmap->GetObject(sizeof(bm), &bm);
    if ((nBt == 1) || (nBt == 4) || (nBt == 8) || (nBt == 24)) {
        m_nBits = nBt;
    }
    else {   // nBt = 0
        m_nBits = bm.bmPlanes * bm.bmBitsPixel; // color bits per pixel
    }
    if (m_nBits == 1) {
        nPaletteSize = 2;
    }
    else {
        if (m_nBits == 4) {
            nPaletteSize = 16;
        }
```

Figure 23-3.

(continued)

The CDib *implementation code listing.*

Figure 23-3. *continued*

```
        else {
            if (m_nBits == 8) {
                nPaletteSize = 256;
            }
            else {
                nPaletteSize = 0; // no palette for 24-bit display
            }
        }
    }
    // fills out row to 4-byte boundary
    DWORD dwBytes = ((DWORD) bm.bmWidth * m_nBits) / 32;
    if (((DWORD) bm.bmWidth * m_nBits) % 32) {
        dwBytes ++;
    }
    dwBytes *= 4;

    m_dwLength = sizeof(BITMAPFILEHEADER) + sizeof(BITMAPINFOHEADER) +
                 sizeof(RGBQUAD) * nPaletteSize;
    if (!AllocateMemory()) return;

    m_lpBMIH->biSize = sizeof(BITMAPINFOHEADER);
    m_lpBMIH->biWidth = bm.bmWidth;
    m_lpBMIH->biHeight = bm.bmHeight;
    m_lpBMIH->biPlanes = 1;
    m_lpBMIH->biBitCount = m_nBits; // 1, 4, 8, or 24
    if (bCompr && (m_nBits == 4)) {
        m_lpBMIH->biCompression = BI_RLE4;
    }
    else {
        if (bCompr && (m_nBits == 8)) {
            m_lpBMIH->biCompression = BI_RLE8;
        }
        else {
            m_lpBMIH->biCompression = BI_RGB;
        }
    }
    m_lpBMIH->biSizeImage = 0;
    m_lpBMIH->biXPelsPerMeter = 0;
    m_lpBMIH->biYPelsPerMeter = 0;
    m_lpBMIH->biClrUsed = 0;
    m_lpBMIH->biClrImportant = 0;

    // calls GetDIBits with null data pointer to get size of DIB
    ::GetDIBits(pDC->GetSafeHdc(), (HBITMAP) pBitmap->GetSafeHandle(),
                0, (WORD) bm.bmHeight, NULL, m_lpBMI, DIB_RGB_COLORS);
```

(continued)

Figure 23-3. *continued*

```
    if (m_lpBMIH->biSizeImage == 0) {
        m_dwLength += dwBytes * bm.bmHeight;
        m_lpBMIH->biCompression = BI_RGB;
        // escape route for device drivers that don't do compression
        TRACE("Can't do compression\n");
    }
    else {
        m_dwLength += m_lpBMIH->biSizeImage;
    }
    if (!AllocateMemory(TRUE)) {
        return;
    }
    m_lpData = (LPSTR) m_lpBMIH + sizeof(BITMAPINFOHEADER) +
                sizeof(RGBQUAD) * nPaletteSize;
    m_lpBMFH->bfType = 0x4d42; // 'BM'
    m_lpBMFH->bfSize = m_dwLength;
    m_lpBMFH->bfReserved1 = 0;
    m_lpBMFH->bfReserved2 = 0;
    m_lpBMFH->bfOffBits = (char huge*) m_lpData - m_lpBuf;

    // second GetDIBits call to make DIB
    if (!::GetDIBits(pDC->GetSafeHdc(), (HBITMAP)
        pBitmap->GetSafeHandle(), 0, (WORD) bm.bmHeight, m_lpData,
        m_lpBMI, DIB_RGB_COLORS)) {
        m_dwLength = 0L;
    }
    delete pDC->SelectObject(pBitmap); // delete pEmptyBitmap
}


/////////////////////////////////////////////////////////////////////
CDib::~CDib()
{
    if (m_lpBuf) {
        GlobalFreePtr(m_lpBuf);  // free the DIB memory
    }
}


/////////////////////////////////////////////////////////////////////
void CDib::Serialize(CArchive& ar)
{
    ar.Flush();
    if (ar.IsStoring()) {
    {
        Write(ar.GetFile());
    }
```

(continued)

Figure 23-3. *continued*

```
    else
    {
    Read(ar.GetFile());
    }
}


/////////////////////////////////////////////////////////////////////
BOOL CDib::Read(CFile* pFile)
{
    // file assumed to be open
    ASSERT(m_dwLength == 0L); // DIB must be empty
    m_dwLength = pFile->GetLength();
    if (!AllocateMemory()) {
        return FALSE;
    }
    DWORD dwCount = pFile->ReadHuge(m_lpBuf, m_dwLength);
    if (dwCount != m_dwLength) {
        AfxMessageBox("Read error");
        return FALSE;
    }
    if (m_lpBMFH->bfType != 0x4d42) {
        AfxMessageBox("Invalid bitmap file");
        return FALSE;
    }
    ASSERT((m_lpBMIH->biBitCount == 1) || (m_lpBMIH->biBitCount == 4) ||
           (m_lpBMIH->biBitCount == 8) || (m_lpBMIH->biBitCount == 24));
    m_lpData = (LPSTR) m_lpBMFH + m_lpBMFH->bfOffBits;
    m_nBits = m_lpBMIH->biBitCount;
    return TRUE;
}


/////////////////////////////////////////////////////////////////////
BOOL CDib::Write(CFile* pFile)
{
    TRY {
        pFile->WriteHuge(m_lpBuf, m_dwLength);
    }
    CATCH (CException, e) {
        AfxMessageBox("Write error--possible disk full condition");
        return FALSE;
    }
    END_CATCH
    return TRUE;
}


/////////////////////////////////////////////////////////////////////
CBitmap* CDib::MakeBitmap(CDC* pDC, CSize& bmSize)
```

(continued)

Figure 23-3. *continued*

```
{
    // replaces the DC's existing bitmap with a new one from the DIB
    // returns the old one
    BITMAP bm;
    DWORD  dwFore, dwBack;
    // checks to see whether DIB buffer is properly loaded
    if (m_dwLength == 0L) {
        bmSize.cx = bmSize.cy = 0;
        return NULL;
    }

    // this code conditions the DC for mono or color
    int nPlanes = pDC->GetDeviceCaps(PLANES);
    int nBitsPixel = pDC->GetDeviceCaps(BITSPIXEL);
    CBitmap* pConfigBitmap = new CBitmap;
    char bits[100];
    if (m_lpBMIH->biBitCount == 1) {
        pConfigBitmap->CreateBitmap(1, 1, 1, 1, bits);
    }
    else {
        pConfigBitmap->CreateBitmap(1, 1, nPlanes, nBitsPixel, bits);
    }
    CBitmap* pOriginalBitmap =
        (CBitmap*) pDC->SelectObject(pConfigBitmap);

// CreateDIBitmap "switches bits" for mono bitmaps, depending on colors,
//   so we'll fool it
    if (GetMonoColors(dwFore, dwBack)) {
        SetMonoColors(0L, 0xFFFFFFFL);
    }

#ifdef _WIN32
    HBITMAP hBitmap = ::CreateDIBitmap(pDC->GetSafeHdc(), m_lpBMIH,
            CBM_INIT, (CONST BYTE*) (m_lpBuf + m_lpBMFH->bfOffBits),
            m_lpBMI, DIB_RGB_COLORS);
#else
    HBITMAP hBitmap = ::CreateDIBitmap(pDC->GetSafeHdc(), m_lpBMIH,
            CBM_INIT, (LPSTR) (m_lpBuf + m_lpBMFH->bfOffBits),
            m_lpBMI, DIB_RGB_COLORS);
#endif
    if (hBitmap == NULL) {
        TRACE("null bitmap\n");
        delete pDC->SelectObject(pOriginalBitmap); // del. config bitmap
        return NULL; // untested error logic
    }
```

(continued)

Figure 23-3. *continued*

```
    SetMonoColors(dwFore, dwBack);

    // Can't use CBitmap::FromHandle here because we need to
    //   delete the object later
    CBitmap* pBitmap = new CBitmap;
    pBitmap->Attach(hBitmap);
    pBitmap->GetObject(sizeof(bm), &bm);
    bmSize.cx = bm.bmWidth;
    bmSize.cy = bm.bmHeight;
    delete pDC->SelectObject(pBitmap); // delete configuration bitmap
    return pOriginalBitmap;
}


///////////////////////////////////////////////////////////////////
BOOL CDib::Display(CDC* pDC, CPoint origin)
{
    // direct to device--bypass the GDI bitmap
    if (!m_lpBuf) {
        return FALSE; // nothing to display
    }
    if (!::SetDIBitsToDevice(pDC->GetSafeHdc(), origin.x, origin.y,
        (WORD) m_lpBMIH->biWidth, (WORD) m_lpBMIH->biHeight, 0, 0, 0,
        (WORD) m_lpBMIH->biHeight, m_lpData, m_lpBMI,
        DIB_RGB_COLORS)) {
        return FALSE;
    }
    return TRUE;
}


///////////////////////////////////////////////////////////////////
BOOL CDib::Stretch(CDC* pDC, CPoint origin, CSize size)
{
    // direct to device--bypass the GDI bitmap
    if (!m_lpBuf) {
        return FALSE; // nothing to display
    }
    if (!::StretchDIBits(pDC->GetSafeHdc(), origin.x, origin.y,
        size.cx, size.cy, 0, 0, (WORD) m_lpBMIH->biWidth,
        (WORD) m_lpBMIH->biHeight, m_lpData, m_lpBMI,
        DIB_RGB_COLORS, SRCCOPY)) {
        return FALSE;
    }
    return TRUE;
}
```

(continued)

Figure 23-3. *continued*

```
/////////////////////////////////////////////////////////////////
int CDib::GetColorBits()
{
    return m_nBits;
}


/////////////////////////////////////////////////////////////////
DWORD CDib::GetLength()
{
    return m_dwLength;
}


CSize CDib::GetSize()
{
    return CSize((int) m_lpBMIH->biWidth, (int) m_lpBMIH->biHeight);
}


/////////////////////////////////////////////////////////////////
void CDib::SetMonoColors(DWORD dwForeground, DWORD dwBackground)
{
    if (m_nBits != 1) {
        return;
    }
    unsigned long far* pPalette = (unsigned long far*)
                    ((LPSTR) m_lpBMIH + sizeof(BITMAPINFOHEADER));
    *pPalette = dwForeground;
    *(++pPalette) = dwBackground;
    return;
}


/////////////////////////////////////////////////////////////////
BOOL CDib::GetMonoColors(DWORD& dwForeground, DWORD& dwBackground)
{
    if (m_nBits != 1) {
        return FALSE;
    }
    unsigned long far* pPalette = (unsigned long far*)
                    ((LPSTR) m_lpBMIH + sizeof(BITMAPINFOHEADER));
    dwForeground = *pPalette;
    dwBackground = *(++pPalette);
    return TRUE;
}


/////////////////////////////////////////////////////////////////
BOOL CDib::AllocateMemory(BOOL bRealloc) // bRealloc default = FALSE
```

(continued)

491

Figure 23-3. *continued*

```
{
    if (bRealloc) {
        m_lpBuf = (char huge*) GlobalReAllocPtr(m_lpBuf,
                                              m_dwLength, GHND);
    }
    else {
        m_lpBuf = (char huge*) GlobalAllocPtr(GHND, m_dwLength);
    }
    if (!m_lpBuf) {
        AfxMessageBox("Unable to allocate DIB memory");
        m_dwLength = 0L;
        m_nBits = 0;
        return FALSE;
    }
    m_lpBMFH = (LPBITMAPFILEHEADER) m_lpBuf;
    m_lpBMIH = (LPBITMAPINFOHEADER) (m_lpBuf + sizeof(BITMAPFILEHEADER));
    m_lpBMI = (LPBITMAPINFO) m_lpBMIH;
    return TRUE;
}
```

CEx23aView

This class, derived from *CScrollView*, does most of the application's work. All the Edit menu items are routed to *CEx23aView* except for Edit Clear All. The view's most important data member, *m_pDisplayMemDC*, is a pointer to the memory device context that's used throughout the application. Other data members hold the size of the view and the view's GDI bitmap. The *m_bShrink-ToFit* member, controlled from the View menu, indicates whether the bitmap occupies the whole view.

The *CEx23aView* class uses the MM_TEXT mapping mode so that it can take advantage of the *CScrollView* shrink-to-fit feature. When the shrink-to-fit mode is active, the entire view is visible in the window; otherwise, the view scrolls normally.

Constructor, Destructor

The *CEx23aView* constructor and destructor take care of routine housekeeping. The destructor ensures that the view's memory display context and last bitmap are deleted.

```
CEx23aView::CEx23aView() : m_totalSize(800, 1050) // 8" x 10.5" when
                                                  //  printed
```

```
{
    m_pDisplayMemDC = new CDC;  // DC lasts for the life of the view
    m_bShrinkToFit = FALSE;
}

CEx23aView::~CEx23aView()
{
    delete m_pDisplayMemDC->SelectObject
        (CBitmap::FromHandle(m_hOldDisplayBitmap));
    delete m_pDisplayMemDC;
}
```

OnCreate

As in any view class derived from *CScrollView*, the *OnCreate* message handler must set the scroll sizes. The *OnCreate* function also sets the shrink-to-fit mode flag, and it sets up the memory device context for later use. The display mapping mode is MM_TEXT, but the print mapping mode is a modified MM_LOENGLISH.

```
int CEx23aView::OnCreate(LPCREATESTRUCT lpCreateStruct)
{
    if (CScrollView::OnCreate(lpCreateStruct)) {
        return -1;
    }

    // 'prime the pump' with an empty bitmap
    CClientDC dc(this);
    m_pDisplayMemDC->CreateCompatibleDC(&dc);
    CBitmap* pEmptyBitmap = new CBitmap;
    pEmptyBitmap->CreateCompatibleBitmap(&dc, 0, 0);
    CBitmap* pOldBitmap =
        (CBitmap*) m_pDisplayMemDC->SelectObject(pEmptyBitmap);
    // so we'll have an old bitmap to switch to at the end
    m_hOldDisplayBitmap = (HBITMAP) pOldBitmap->GetSafeHandle();
    return 0;
}
```

OnInitialUpdate

As is true in any view class derived from *CScrollView*, the overridden *OnInitial-Update* function must set the scroll sizes. The display mapping mode is MM_TEXT, but the *OnPrint* function sets the printer mapping mode to modified MM_LOENGLISH. Thus, one pixel on the screen maps to 0.01 inch on the printer.

```
void CEx23aView::OnInitialUpdate()
{
    CScrollView::OnInitialUpdate();
    if (m_bShrinkToFit) {
        SetScaleToFitSize(m_totalSize);
    }
    else {
        SetScrollSizes(MM_TEXT, m_totalSize);
    }
}
```

OnDraw

This function is actually four functions in one. The *DRAW_ALT* preprocessor constant determines which alternative drawing code is compiled. Here's a list of the alternatives with their key bitmap display function calls:

■ **Alternative 1—*StretchBlt*:** Even though the application's bitmap is stored in the document as a DIB, the view keeps a GDI bitmap in memory, selected into the *m_pDisplayMemDC* memory display context. Every time a DIB is read from disk, this bitmap is refreshed. It's more efficient to draw from a GDI bitmap than directly from a DIB because the color conversion is done once when the DIB is read. In the *StretchBlt* display alternative, the bitmap occupies the entire view—800 by 1050 logical units.

```
pDC->StretchBlt(0, 0, m_totalSize.cx, m_totalSize.cy,
        m_pDisplayMemDC, 0, 0, m_bmSize.cx,
        m_bmSize.cy, SRCCOPY);
```

The *StretchBlt* call above works in both scroll mode and shrink-to-fit mode. In shrink-to-fit mode, the bitmap size exactly matches the window size. Scroll mode can slow *StretchBlt* because we're mapping bits to a much larger area than the window. A second version of the code chops down the bitmap size to match the window rectangle.

```
pDC->StretchBlt(clientRect.left, clientRect.top,
        clientRect.Width(), clientRect.Height(),
        m_pDisplayMemDC,
        (int) ((long) m_bmSize.cx * (long) clientRect.left /
                (long) m_totalSize.cx),
        (int) ((long) m_bmSize.cy * (long) clientRect.top /
                (long) m_totalSize.cy),
        (int) ((long) m_bmSize.cx * (long) clientRect.Width() /
                (long) m_totalSize.cx),
        (int) ((long) m_bmSize.cy * (long) clientRect.Height() /
                (long) m_totalSize.cy), SRCCOPY);
```

■ **Alternative 2—*BitBlt*:** With this alternative, the bitmap bits are mapped directly to pixels, but only in scroll mode. If the bitmap size is 400 by 525 pixels, for example, the bitmap occupies the top left quadrant of the view. In the view's shrink-to-fit mode, the bitmap pixels are mapped to logical units in such a way that the 800-by-1050-unit document occupies the entire window. Display update is faster in scroll mode than it is in shrink-to-fit mode.

```
pDC->BitBlt(0, 0, m_bmSize.cx, m_bmSize.cy,
            m_pDisplayMemDC, 0, 0, SRCCOPY);
```

■ **Alternative 3—*CDib::Stretch*:** This alternative produces the same result as Alternative 2. This time the bitmap is rendered directly from the DIB.

```
GetDocument()->m_pDib->Stretch(pDC, CPoint(0, 0), m_bmSize);
```

■ **Alternative 4—*CDib::Display*:** This alternative does not produce the same result as Alternative 2. The bitmap pixels are always mapped one-to-one to the display (or printer).

```
GetDocument()->m_pDib->Display(pDC, CPoint(0, 0));
```

OnEditCopy

This command message handler is called in response to the Edit Copy menu item. Its job is to send a GDI bitmap to the clipboard, but remember that a bitmap can't be sent if it's selected into a device context. We need a bitmap selected, though, to create it and to display it. The *OnEditPaste* function solves the problem with two GDI bitmaps. First the function calls the *CDib MakeBitmap* function to create a new bitmap from the document's DIB. *MakeBitmap* then selects the new bitmap into the memory device context and returns the previously selected bitmap, which contains the same bit pattern. The deselected bitmap is passed to the clipboard.

```
void CEx23aView::OnEditCopy()
{
    CBitmap* pBitmap =
        GetDocument()->m_pDib->MakeBitmap(m_pDisplayMemDC, m_bmSize);
    if (pBitmap) {
        VERIFY(OpenClipboard());
        VERIFY(::EmptyClipboard());
        VERIFY(::SetClipboardData(CF_BITMAP, pBitmap->Detach()));
        VERIFY(::CloseClipboard());
        delete pBitmap;
    }
}
```

OnEditCopyTo

This function copies the document's *CDib* object to a device-independent bitmap disk file, usually with a BMP extension. It's called in response to the Edit Copy To menu item. This function does not involve GDI bitmaps or the memory display contents. It merely writes out the data in the document's *CDib* object.

OnEditCut

The *OnEditCut* message handler, called in response to the Edit Cut menu item, first calls *OnEditCopy* and then clears the document. When the document is cleared, its *CDib* object is reset and the view's *OnUpdate* function is called. The *OnUpdate* function loads the view's GDI bitmap from an empty DIB and thus clears the view window.

OnEditPaste

This command message handler is called in response to the Edit Paste menu item. It gets a GDI bitmap from the clipboard and then converts it to a DIB for storage in the document. It also updates the view's memory device context so that *OnDraw* displays the new bitmap. The *OnEditPaste* function uses a dialog of class *CBitsDialog* to query the user for some DIB specifications. The user can decide whether the DIB will use 1, 4, 8, or 24 bits per pixel and whether the DIB will be stored in compressed format.

First the clipboard GDI bitmap is selected into the view's memory device context, and then a *CDib* object is constructed from the GDI bitmap, replacing the existing *CDib* object. The new DIB is used to construct a second, identical, GDI bitmap, which is selected into the device context, thereby deselecting the clipboard's bitmap. The corresponding C++ bitmap object doesn't have to be deleted because it's a temporary object.

The *OnEditPaste* function displays, through the Windows debug window, the available clipboard formats. If a particular application does not copy GDI bitmaps to the clipboard, at least you'll know which formats it does copy.

OnEditPasteFrom

This command message handler is called in response to the Edit Paste From menu item. It reads a device-independent bitmap file, usually a file with a BMP extension, into the document's *CDib* object. In the process, the file is converted to a GDI bitmap for the *OnDraw* function.

A new, empty *CDib* object is constructed to replace the existing object, and then the *CDib::Read* function reads data from an open file. The *MakeBitmap* function creates the GDI bitmap that is selected into the memory device context. The previously selected bitmap is deleted.

OnPrint

The *OnPrint* function prepares the printer device context for the *OnDraw* function. What we have here is a custom mapping mode that's really "upside-down MM_LOENGLISH." There are 100 logical units per inch, but, unlike in the real MM_LOENGLISH mode, *y* values increase from top to bottom. We can't simply use MM_LOENGLISH because that mapping mode is incompatible with the view's shrink-to-fit capability.

```
void CEx23aView::OnPrint(CDC* pDC, CPrintInfo* pInfo)
{
    int nHsize = (int) (pDC->GetDeviceCaps(HORZSIZE) * 1000L / 254L);
    int nVsize = (int) (pDC->GetDeviceCaps(VERTSIZE) * 1000L / 254L);
    pDC->SetMapMode(MM_ANISOTROPIC);
    pDC->SetWindowExt(nHsize, nVsize);
    pDC->SetViewportExt(pDC->GetDeviceCaps(HORZRES),
                        pDC->GetDeviceCaps(VERTRES));
    OnDraw(pDC);
}
```

OnUpdate

The application framework calls the view's *OnUpdate* function when the document changes. This overridden function makes a new GDI bitmap from the document's *CDib* object.

```
void CEx23aView::OnUpdate(CView* pSender, LPARAM lHint, CObject* pHint)
{
    delete GetDocument()->m_pDib->MakeBitmap(m_pDisplayMemDC, m_bmSize);
    if (!m_bShrinkToFit) {
        ScrollToPosition(CPoint(0, 0));
    }
    Invalidate();
}
```

The Update Command UI Functions

The *OnUpdateEditPaste* and *OnUpdateEditCopy* functions enable the Edit menu items and corresponding toolbar buttons according to the status of the clipboard and the document.

The EX23A Resource File

The EX23A.RC resource script was generated by AppWizard and enhanced with App Studio. There are a new dialog and some extra menu items:

The *IDD_BITS* Dialog Resource

The *IDD_BITS* dialog is arranged as shown in Figure 23-4.

Figure 23-4.
The EX23A Color Bits dialog layout from App Studio.

This dialog appears when you paste a bitmap from the clipboard into the application. Notice the default OK and Cancel buttons. Add the radio buttons and the check box with data members as shown in the table below:

Button Caption	Type	Group	Symbol	Data Member
1 (mono)	Radio	Yes	*IDC_BITS1*	*m_nBits*
4 (16 colors)	Radio	No	*IDC_BITS4*	
8 (256 colors)	Radio	No	*IDD_BITS*	
24	Radio	No	*IDC_BITS24*	
Compression	Check box	Yes	*IDC_COMPRESSION*	*m_bCompression*

The *IDR_MAINFRAME* Menu Resource

You must add the items in the following table to the standard menu. Use ClassWizard to define the functions.

Menu	Menu Item	Command ID	Function	Update UI Function
Edit	Clear All	*ID_EDIT_CLEAR_ALL*	*OnEditClearAll*	
	Cut	*ID_EDIT_CUT*	*OnEditCut*	*OnUpdate-EditCut*
	Copy	*ID_EDIT_COPY*	*OnEditCopy*	*OnUpdate-EditCopy*
	Copy To	*ID_EDIT_COPY_TO*	*OnEditCopyTo*	*OnUpdate-EditCopyTo*
	Paste	*ID_EDIT_PASTE*	*OnEditPaste*	*OnUpdate-EditPaste*
	Paste From	*ID_EDIT_PASTE_FROM*	*OnEditPasteFrom*	
View	Shrink To Fit	*ID_VIEW_SHRINK*	*OnViewShrink*	*OnUpdate-ViewShrink*

Testing the EX23A Application

Try building EX23A with all four drawing alternatives (as determined by the value of *DRAW_ALT* in EX23AVW.CPP). Try scroll mode and shrink-to-fit mode with all alternatives. Remember that File Save is different from Edit Copy To. The former creates a class library archive file with the DIB extension, and the latter creates a standard BMP file. The two formats are not compatible. Figure 23-5 shows the EX23A display with drawing Alternative 2 in scroll mode.

Figure 23-5.
The EX23A display.

Bitmap Manipulation

Every bitmap you've seen so far has originated in another program. You can build and modify bitmaps in your own programs if you want to. You've already seen how the *CBitmap* member function *CreateCompatibleBitmap* can create a blank bitmap of a specified size. The *CBitmap* member functions *GetBitmapBits* and *SetBitmapBits* allow you to copy bytes from and to a GDI bitmap. If you use these functions, you must carefully account for the bitmap's number of planes, bits per pixel, and byte alignment. These parameters are hardware-dependent, but they are readily available from the *BITMAP* structure returned by the *CGdiObject::GetObject* member function.

Bitmap access might be easier if you use the hardware-independent DIB format. You have direct access to the bits, and the format is fixed. Be careful, though, that the DIBs you work with are not compressed.

CHAPTER TWENTY-FOUR

DATABASE MANAGEMENT WITH MICROSOFT ODBC

Microcomputers became popular, in part, because businesspeople saw them as a low-cost means of tracking inventory, processing orders, printing payroll checks, and so forth. These applications required fast access to individual records in a large database. One of the first microcomputer database tools was dBASE II, a single-user product with its own programming language and file format. Today, Microsoft Windows programmers have a wide choice of programmable database management systems (DBMS's), including Powersoft PowerBuilder, Borland Paradox, Microsoft Access, and Microsoft FoxPro. Most of these products can access both local data and remote data on a central computer. The latter case requires the addition of "database server" software such as ORACLE or Microsoft SQL Server.

How do you, as an MFC programmer, fit into the picture? Beginning with version 1.5, Visual C++ contains all the components you'll need to write C++ database applications for Windows. The key element is the ODBC (Microsoft's Open Database Connectivity) standard, which consists of an extensible set of dynamic link libraries (DLLs) that provide a standard database application programming interface. ODBC is based on a standardized version of Structured Query Language (SQL). With ODBC and SQL, you can write database access code that is independent of any database product.

Visual C++ includes tools and MFC classes for ODBC, and that's the subject of this chapter. You'll learn the basics of ODBC, and you'll see two sample programs—one that is hard-coded for a particular database table and another, more dynamic, application that lets you view any table in any database. Along the way, you'll see the MFC dialog bar in action, you'll use a class that provides a scrolling row view of a database table, and you'll learn how to control the MFC application shutdown sequence.

Database Management vs. Serialization

The serialization process, introduced in Chapters 16 and 17, ties a document object to a disk file. All the document's data must be read into memory when the document is opened, and all the data must be written back to disk when an updated document is closed. Obviously, you can't serialize a document that's bigger than the available virtual memory. Even if the document is small enough to fit in memory, you might not need to read and write all the data every time the program runs.

You could, of course, program your own random-access disk file, thus inventing your own database management system (DBMS), but you probably have enough other work to do. Besides, using a real DBMS gives you many advantages, including these:

- **Use of standard file formats**—Many people think of dBASE/Xbase DBF files when they think of database formats. This is only one database file format, but it's a popular one. A lot of data is distributed in DBF files, and many programs can read and write in this format. Recently, the Microsoft Access MDB format has become popular too. With the MDB format, all of a database's tables and indexes can be contained in a single disk file.

- **Indexed file access**—If you need quick access to records by key (a customer name, for example), you need indexed file access. You could always write your own B-tree file access routines, but that's a tedious job that's been done already. All DBMS's contain efficient indexed access routines.

- **Data integrity safeguards**—Many professional DBMS products have procedures for protecting their data. One example is transaction processing. A transaction encompasses a series of related changes. If the entire transaction can't be processed, it is rolled back so that the database reverts to its original state before the transaction.

- **Multiuser access control**—If your application doesn't need multiuser access now, it might in the future. Most DBMS's provide record locking to prevent interference among simultaneous users. Some multiuser DBMS's use the client-server model, which means that most processing is handled on a single database server computer; the workstations handle the user interface. Other multiuser DBMSs handle database processing on the workstations, and they control each workstation's access to shared files.

SQL

You could not have worked in the software field without at least hearing about SQL, a standard database access language with its own grammar. In the SQL world, a database is a collection of tables that consist of rows and columns. Many DBMS products support SQL, and many programmers know SQL. The SQL standard is continually evolving, and SQL grammar varies between products. SQL extensions, such as binary large object ("blob") capability, allow storage of pictures, sound, and complex data structures.

The ODBC Standard

The Microsoft Open Database Connectivity (ODBC) standard defines not only the rules of SQL grammar but also the C-language programming interface to an SQL database. It's now possible for a single compiled C or C++ program to access any DBMS that has an ODBC driver. The ODBC Software Development Kit (SDK), which is included with Visual C++, contains drivers for DBF files, Access MDB databases, Microsoft Excel XLS files, Microsoft FoxPro files, ASCII text files, and SQL Server databases. Other database companies, including Oracle, Informix, Progress, Ingres, and Gupta, provide ODBC drivers for their own DBMS's.

If you develop an MFC program with the dBASE/Xbase driver, for example, you can run the same program with an Access database driver. No recompilation is necessary—the program simply loads a different DLL.

Not only can C++ programs use ODBC, but other DBMS programming environments can take advantage of this new standard. You could write a C++ program to update an SQL Server database, and then you could use an off-the-shelf ODBC-compatible report writer to format and print the data. ODBC thus separates the user interface from the actual database management process. You no longer have to buy your interface tools from the same company that supplies the database engine.

Some people have publicly criticized ODBC because it doesn't let programmers take advantage of the special features of some particular DBMS. Well, that's the whole point! Programmers need only learn one application programming interface (API), and they can choose their software components based on price, performance, and support. No longer will developers be locked into buying all their tools from their database supplier.

What's the future of ODBC? That's a difficult question. Microsoft is driving the standard, but it isn't actually "selling" ODBC; it's giving ODBC away for the purpose of promoting other products. Another company, Q+E

Software, is supporting ODBC along with its own proprietary multi-DBMS access library. Q+E sells ODBC drivers, which it claims have a performance advantage over Microsoft's "free" drivers. Meanwhile, there are noises about Microsoft publishing a new OLE interface for database access. (See Chapter 25 for an explanation of OLE and interfaces.) Will OLE supersede ODBC? Perhaps later, but for the time being ODBC is an efficient standard that works.

The ODBC Architecture

ODBC has a unique DLL-based architecture that makes the system fully modular. A small top-level DLL, ODBC.DLL, defines the API. ODBC.DLL calls database-specific DLLs, known as drivers, during program execution. With the help of the ODBC.INI file (maintained by the ODBC Administrator module in the Windows Control Panel), ODBC.DLL tracks which database-specific DLLs are available and thus allows a single program to access data in several DBMS's simultaneously. A program could, for example, keep some local tables in DBF format and use other tables controlled by a database server. Figure 24-1 shows the ODBC DLL hierarchy.

ODBC SDK Programming

If you program directly at the ODBC C-language API level, you must know about three important ODBC elements: the environment, the connection, and the statement. All three are accessed through handles. First you need an environment, which establishes the link between your program and the ODBC system. An application usually has only one environment handle.

Next you need one or more connections. The connection references a specific driver and data source combination. You might have several connections to subdirectories that contain DBF files, and you might have connections to several SQL servers on the same network. A specific ODBC connection can be hard-wired into a program, or the user can be allowed to choose from a list of available drivers and data sources.

ODBC.DLL has a built-in Windows dialog that lists the connections that are defined in the INI file. Once you have a connection, you need an SQL statement to execute. The statement might be a query, such as

```
SELECT FNAME, LNAME, CITY FROM AUTHORS
WHERE STATE = 'UT'
```

Figure 24-1.
Typical ODBC architecture.

Or the statement could be an update statement, such as

UPDATE AUTHORS SET PHONE = '801 232-5780'
WHERE ID = '357-86-4343'

Because query statements need a program loop to process the returned rows, your program might need several statements active at the same time. Many ODBC drivers allow multiple active statement handles per connection.

Look again at the SQL statement on page 504. Suppose there were 10 authors in Utah. ODBC lets you define the query result as a block of data called a "rowset," which is associated with an SQL statement. Through the ODBC SDK function *SQLExtendedFetch,* your program can move through the 10 selected records, forward and backward, by means of an ODBC cursor. This cursor is a programmable pointer into the rowset.

What if, in a multiuser situation, another program modified (or deleted or added) a Utah author record while your program was stepping through the rowset? With an ODBC Level 2 driver, the rowset would probably be dynamic, and ODBC could update the rowset whenever the database changed. A dynamic rowset is called a "dynaset." Most of today's ODBC drivers are Level 1, however, and they don't support dynasets. Visual C++ includes the ODBC cursor library module ODBCCURS.DLL, which supports static rowsets called "snapshots." When the *SELECT* statement is executed, ODBC makes what amounts to a local copy of the 10 author records and builds an in-memory list of pointers to those records. These records are guaranteed not to change once you've scrolled into them, so in a multiuser situation, you might need to requery the database periodically to rebuild the snapshot.

The MFC ODBC Classes

With the MFC classes for Windows, you use C++ objects instead of window handles and device context handles; with the MFC ODBC classes, you use objects instead of connection handles and statement handles. The environment handle is stored in a global variable and is not represented by a C++ object. The two principal ODBC classes are *CDatabase* and *CRecordset*. Objects of class *CDatabase* represent ODBC connections to data sources, and objects of class *CRecordset* represent scrollable rowsets (usually snapshots). The Visual C++ documentation uses the term "recordset" instead of "rowset" to be consistent with Microsoft Visual Basic and Access. You seldom derive classes from *CDatabase*, but you always derive classes from *CRecordset* to match the columns in your database tables.

> NOTE: *CRecordView* is another important MFC ODBC class, but this user interface class is "one step removed" from the database and is not covered in this chapter. A very good example of a *CRecordView* application can be found by choosing Books Online, Database Classes, and Part 1: Database Tutorial.

For the author query on page 504, you would derive (with the help of ClassWizard) a *CAuthorSet* class from *CRecordset* that had data members for first name, last name, city, and zip code. Your program would construct a *CAuthorSet* object (typically embedded in the document) and call its inherited *Open* member function. Using the values of parameters and data members, *CRecordset::Open* constructs and opens a *CDatabase* object; it issues an

SQL *SELECT* statement and then moves to the first record. Your program would then call other *CRecordset* member functions to position the ODBC cursor and exchange data between the database fields and the *CAuthorSet* data members. When the *CAuthorSet* object is deleted, the recordset is closed, and under certain conditions, the database is closed and deleted. Figure 24-2 shows the relationships between the C++ objects and ODBC components.

Figure 24-2.
MFC ODBC class database relationships.

It's important to recognize that the *CAuthorSet* object contains data members that represent only one row in a table, the so-called "current record." The *CRecordset* class, together with the underlying ODBC rowset code, manages the database snapshot.

NOTE: It's possible to have several active snapshots per data source, and you can use multiple data sources within the same program.

The EX24A Example

You can use AppWizard to generate a complete forms-oriented database application, and that's what the Database Tutorial is all about. If customers or users wanted a straightforward business database application like that, however, they probably wouldn't call in a Visual C++ programmer; instead, they might use a less technical tool, such as Microsoft Access. Visual C++ and the MFC ODBC classes are more appropriate for a complex application that might have an incidental need for database access. As you'll see in EX24B, you can also use the classes to make your own general-purpose database query tool.

The EX24A program isolates the database access code from user interface code so that you can see how to add ODBC database capability to any MFC application. You'll be using ClassWizard to generate a *CRecordset* class, but you won't be using the *CRecordView* class that AppWizard always generates when you ask for a database application.

The application is fairly simple. It displays the rows from the student database table in a scrolling view, as shown in the screen on page 512. The student table is part of the Student Registration (Microsoft Access version 1.1) sample database that's included with Visual C++.

Here are the steps for building the EX24A example:

1. **Run ODBC Administrator to verify ODBC data source installation.** Start the ODBC Administrator module from the Windows Control Panel. If the ODBC icon isn't there, or if Student Registration doesn't appear among the data sources, rerun the Visual C++ Setup program. The required database is contained in the file \MSVC\MFC\SAMPLES-\ENROLL\STDREG.MDB.

   > NOTE: If you're using Visual C++ 1.5 under Windows NT, look for the ODBC Administrator icon in the Microsoft ODBC group, not in the Control Panel.

2. **Run AppWizard to produce \VCPP\EX24A\EX24A.** Choose App-Wizard from Visual Workbench's Project menu. Specify an SDI application with *CScrollView* as the view's class type. Select the Include Header Files option from the Database Options dialog. The options and the default class names are shown in the screen at the top of the facing page:

3. Choose ClassWizard from Visual Workbench's Browse menu.

Click the Add Class button, and then fill in the Add Class dialog as shown here:

4. Select the Student Registration STUDENT table for the *CEx24aSet*

class. When you click the Create Class button in the Add Class dialog, ClassWizard displays the SQL Data Sources dialog. Select the Student Registration data source, as shown here:

509

NOTE: If more data sources are installed on your computer, the SQL Data Sources list box will show their names along with Student Registration.

After you select the data source, ClassWizard prompts you to select a table. Pick STUDENT, as shown here:

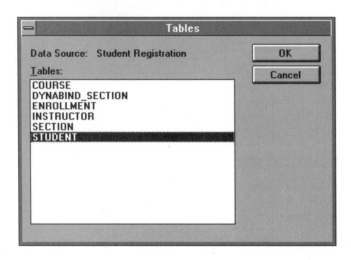

5. Examine the data members that ClassWizard generates. Click the Member Variables tab for the newly generated *CEx24aSet* class. ClassWizard should have generated data members based on student column names, as shown here:

6. Declare an embedded recordset object in EX24ADOC.H. Add the following lines in the *CEx24aDoc* class declaration:

```
public:
    CEx24aSet m_ex24aSet;
```

7. Edit the EX24ADOC.CPP file. Add the line

```
#include "ex24aset.h"
```

just before the line

```
#include "ex24adoc.h"
```

8. Declare a recordset pointer in EX24AVW.H. Add the following lines in the *CEx24aView* class declaration:

```
public:
    CEx24aSet* m_pSet;
```

9. Edit the *OnDraw* and *OnInitialUpdate* functions in EX24AVW.CPP:

```
void CEx24aView::OnDraw(CDC* pDC)
{
    int  y = 0;
    char temp[21];

    if (m_pSet->IsBOF()) {
      return;
    }
    m_pSet->MoveFirst();   // fails if recordset is empty
    while (!m_pSet->IsEOF()) {
      wsprintf(temp, "%ld", m_pSet->m_StudentID);
      pDC->TextOut(0, y, temp);
      pDC->TextOut(500, y, m_pSet->m_Name);
      wsprintf(temp, "%d", m_pSet->m_GradYear);
      pDC->TextOut(2500, y, temp);
      m_pSet->MoveNext();
      y -= 200;  // 0.2 inch down
    }
}
void CEx24aView::OnInitialUpdate()
{
    CScrollView::OnInitialUpdate();
    CSize sizeTotal;

    sizeTotal.cx = 8000;
    sizeTotal.cy = 10500;
```

(continued)

```
SetScrollSizes(MM_HIENGLISH, sizeTotal);

m_pSet = &GetDocument()->m_ex24aSet;
// remember that docs/views are reused in SDI apps!
if (m_pSet->IsOpen()) {
  m_pSet->Close();
}
m_pSet->Open();
}
```

Also in EX24AVW.CPP, add the line

```
#include "ex24aset.h"
```

just before the line

```
#include "ex24adoc.h"
```

10. Edit the EX24A.CPP file. Add the line

```
#include "ex24aset.h"
```

just before the line

```
#include "ex24adoc.h"
```

11. Build and test the application. Does the resulting screen look like the one shown here?

Adding ODBC Capability to an MFC Application

If you need to add ODBC capability to an existing MFC application, make the following changes to the project:

1. Add the following line at the end of STDAFX.H:

   ```
   #include "afxdb.h"
   ```

2. In the Linker Input dialog, under Project Options, add ODBC to the list of libraries.

3. Edit the RC file in text mode. After the line

   ```
   "#include ""afxprint.rc"
   "     // printing/print preview resources\r\n"
   ```

   add the line

   ```
   "#include ""afxdb.rc""          // Database resources\r\n"
   ```

   And after the line

   ```
   #include "afxprint.rc"          // printing/print preview resources
   ```

   add the line

   ```
   #include "afxdb.rc"          // Database resources
   ```

The EX24A Program Elements

The following is a discussion of the major elements in the EX24A program.

Connection of the Recordset Class to the Application

When ClassWizard generates the *CEx24aSet* class, it adds the CPP file to the project—and that's all. It's up to you to link the recordset to your view and to your document. By embedding a *CEx24aSet* object inside the *CEx24a-Document* class, you ensure that the recordset object will be constructed when the application starts.

The view could always get the recordset via the document, but it's more efficient if the view keeps its own recordset pointer. Notice how the view's *OnInitialUpdate* function sets the *m_pSet* data member.

NOTE: If you run AppWizard with the Database Support option, AppWizard generates a class derived from *CRecordset*, a class derived from *CDatabaseView*, and all the necessary linkage as just described. We're not using AppWizard in this mode because we don't want a form-based application.

The *CEx24aView* Class's *OnInitialUpdate* Member Function

The job of the *OnInitialUpdate* function is to open the recordset that's associated with the view. The recordset constructor was called with a NULL database pointer parameter, so the *CRecordset::Open* function knows it must construct a *CDatabase* object and link that database one-to-one with the recordset. But how does *Open* know what data source and table to use? It calls two *CRecordset* virtual functions, *GetDefaultConnect* and *GetDefaultSQL*. ClassWizard generates implementations of these functions in your derived recordset class, as shown here:

```
CString CEx24aSet::GetDefaultConnect()
{
    return "ODBC;DSN=Student Registration;";
}
CString CEx24aSet::GetDefaultSQL()
{
    return "STUDENT";
}
```

GetDefaultSQL is a pure virtual function, so the derived class must implement it. *GetDefaultConnect*, on the other hand, has a base class implementation that brings up an ODBC dialog that prompts the user for the data source name.

Because documents are reused in SDI applications, the *OnInitialUpdate* function must close any open recordset before it opens a new recordset. The *IsOpen* member function makes the test.

The *CEx24aView* Class's *OnDraw* Member Function

As in any document-view application, the *OnDraw* function is called every time the view is invalidated and once for every printed page. Here *OnDraw* inefficiently slogs through every row in the recordset and paints its column values with the *CDC::TextOut* function. The principal *CRecordset* member functions it calls are *MoveFirst* and *MoveNext*. *MoveFirst* will fail if the recordset is empty, so a prior call to *IsBOF* is necessary to detect the beginning-of-file condition. The *IsEOF* member function detects the end-of-file for the recordset and terminates the row loop.

Remember that ClassWizard generated *CEx24aSet* class data members for the recordset's columns. This means that the recordset class, and now the view class, are both hard-coded for the student record. The *CRecordset* member functions call a pure virtual function *DoFieldExchange* that ClassWizard generates based on the data members *m_StudentID*, *m_Name*, and *m_Grad-Year*. Here is the code for this example's derived recordset class:

```
void CEx24aSet::DoFieldExchange(CFieldExchange* pFX)
{
    //{{AFX_FIELD_MAP(CEx24aSet)
    pFX->SetFieldType(CFieldExchange::outputColumn);
    RFX_Long(pFX, "StudentID", m_StudentID);
    RFX_Text(pFX, "Name", m_Name);
    RFX_Int(pFX, "GradYear", m_GradYear);
    //}}AFX_FIELD_MAP
}
```

Each SQL data type has a field exchange (*RFX_*) function. These functions are quite complex and are called many times during database processing. You might first think, as I did, that the *RFX_* functions are like the *CDialog DDX_* functions and thus actually transfer data between the database and the data members. This is not the case. The primary purpose of the *RFX_* functions is to "bind" the database columns to the data members so that the underlying ODBC functions, such as *SQLExtendedFetch*, can transfer the column data. To this end, the *DoFieldExchange* function is called from *CRecordSet::Open*. *DoFieldExchange* is also called by the *Move* functions for the purpose of reallocating strings and clearing status bits.

Because the *DoFieldExchange* function is so tightly integrated with MFC database processing, you are advised not to call this function directly in your programs. In the next example, EX24B, you'll learn how to write a *DoFieldExchange* function that is not hard-coded for specific columns.

The MFC Dialog Bar

You haven't seen the *CDialogBar* class yet because it didn't make sense to use it in the earlier example. (A dialog bar is a child of the frame window that is arranged according to a dialog template resource and that routes commands in a manner similar to that of a toolbar.) It fits well in the ODBC example, however. Look at Figure 24-4 on page 532, which shows the EX24B example in operation. The dialog bar contains edit controls for the SQL sort and filter strings, and it has a pushbutton to re-execute the query. The button sends a command message that can be handled in the view, and it can be disabled by an update command UI handler. Most dialog bars reside at the top of the frame window, immediately under the toolbar.

It's surprisingly easy to add a dialog bar to an application. You don't even need a new derived class. Here are the steps:

1. Use App Studio to lay out the dialog. Apply the following styles:

    Style = Child
    Border = None
    Visible = unchecked

    You can choose a horizontally oriented bar for the top or bottom of the frame, or you can choose a vertically oriented bar for the left or right of the frame. Add any controls you need, including buttons and edit controls.

2. Declare an embedded *CDialogBar* object in your derived main frame class declaration, like this:

```
CDialogBar m_wndMyBar;
```

3. Add dialog bar object creation code in your main frame class *OnCreate* member function, like this:

```
if (!m_wndMyBar.Create(this, IDD_MY_BAR, CBRS_TOP, ID_MY_BAR)) {
  TRACE("Failed to create dialog bar\n");
  return -1;
}
```

    IDD_MY_BAR is the dialog resource ID assigned in App Studio. The *CBRS_TOP* style tells the application framework to place the dialog bar at the top of the frame window. *ID_MY_BAR* is the dialog bar's control window ID, which should be within the range 0xE800–0xE820 to ensure that the print preview window preempts the dialog bar.

Application Shutdown

Up to now, you haven't been too concerned about the process of shutting down an application. With ordinary document-oriented MFC library applications, your calling the *CDocument::SetModifiedFlag* function ensured that the application framework would prompt the user to save documents. With the EX24A ODBC application, you were OK because the database was closed automatically when the document was destroyed. But what if you want to force the user to disconnect from the data source before he or she closes the document?

The application framework provides the means for trapping the user's attempt to exit the application. It's all done at the document level through the virtual *CDocument::SaveModified* member function. The application framework calls this function whenever a document is to be closed, even if the closing was triggered by the user's attempt to close the application's main frame window or to shut down Windows. If *SaveModified* returns 0, the application framework doesn't close the document. In the EX24B example, the derived document class overrides *SaveModified* to check whether the database is still connected.

A Row–View Class

Database applications are often built around scrolling lists of database records. The EX24A example was a feeble attempt in this direction. The EX24B example goes further. If you've read other books about programming for Windows, you know that authors spend lots of time on the problem of scrolling lists. This is a tricky programming exercise that must be repeated over and over again. Why not encapsulate a scrolling list in a base class? All the ugly details would be hidden, and you could get on with the business of writing your application.

The *CRowView* class, adapted from the class of the identical name in the \MSVC\MFC\SAMPLES\CHKBOOK directory, does the job. Through its use of virtual callback functions, it serves as a model for other derivable base classes. *CRowView* has some limitations, and it's not built to industrial-strength specifications, but it works well in the ODBC example. Figure 24-3 contains the complete listing.

ROWVIEW.H

```
// rowview.h : interface of the CRowView class
//
// This class implements the behavior of a scrolling view that
//   presents multiple rows of fixed-height data.  A row view is
//   similar to an owner-draw list box in its visual behavior; but
//   unlike a list box, a row view has all the benefits of a
//   view (as well as a scroll view), including--perhaps most
//   important--printing and print preview.
/////////////////////////////////////////////////////////////////
```

Figure 24-3. *(continued)*
The CRowView *listing.*

Figure 24-3. *continued*

```
class CRowView : public CScrollView  // abstract base class
{
DECLARE_DYNAMIC(CRowView)

// Construction/destruction
protected:
    CRowView();
    virtual ~CRowView();

// Attributes
protected:
    int m_nRowWidth;            // width of row in
                               //  logical units
    int m_nRowHeight;           // height of row in
                               //  logical units
    int m_nCharWidth;           // avg character width in
                               //  logical units
    int m_nPrevSelectedRow;     // index of most recently
                               //  selected row
    int m_nPrevRowCount;        // most recent row count,
                               //  before update
    int m_nRowsPerPrintedPage;  // how many rows fit on a
                               //  printed page
// Operations-Attributes
protected:
    virtual void UpdateRow(int nInvalidRow); // called by derived
                                             //  class OnUpdate
    virtual void CalculateRowMetrics(CDC* pDC)
            { GetRowWidthHeight(pDC, m_nRowWidth, m_nRowHeight,
                               m_nCharWidth); }
    virtual void UpdateScrollSizes();
    virtual CRect RowToWndRect(CDC* pDC, int nRow);
    virtual int RowToYPos(int nRow);
    virtual void RectLPtoRowRange(const CRect& rectLP,
                                 int& nFirstRow, int& nLastRow,
                                 BOOL bIncludePartiallyShownRows);
    virtual int LastViewableRow();

// Overridables
protected:
    virtual void GetRowWidthHeight(CDC* pDC, int& nRowWidth,
                                   int& nRowHeight,
                                   int& nCharWidth) = 0;
    virtual int GetActiveRow() = 0;
    virtual int GetRowCount() = 0;
```

(continued)

Figure 24-3. *continued*

```
    virtual void OnDrawRow(CDC* pDC, int nRow, int y,
                            BOOL bSelected) = 0;
    virtual void ChangeSelectionNextRow(BOOL bNext) = 0;
    virtual void ChangeSelectionToRow(int nRow) = 0;


// Implementation
protected:
    // standard overrides of MFC classes
    virtual void OnInitialUpdate();
    virtual void OnDraw(CDC* pDC);  // overridden to draw
                                    //  this view
    virtual void OnPrepareDC(CDC* pDC,
                            CPrintInfo* pInfo = NULL);
    virtual BOOL OnPreparePrinting(CPrintInfo* pInfo);
    virtual void OnBeginPrinting(CDC* pDC, CPrintInfo* pInfo);
    virtual void OnPrint(CDC* pDC, CPrintInfo* pInfo);

// Generated message map functions
protected:
    //{{AFX_MSG(CRowView)
    afx_msg void OnKeyDown(UINT nChar, UINT nRepCnt,
                            UINT nFlags);
    afx_msg void OnSize(UINT nType, int cx, int cy);
    afx_msg void OnLButtonDown(UINT nFlags, CPoint point);
    //}}AFX_MSG
    DECLARE_MESSAGE_MAP()
};
```

ROWVIEW.CPP

```
// rowview.cpp : implementation of the CRowView class (MM_TEXT)
//
#include "stdafx.h"
#include "resource.h" // for IDS_TOO_MANY_ROWS
#include "rowview.h"
#include <limits.h> // for INT_MAX

#ifdef _DEBUG
#undef THIS_FILE
static char BASED_CODE THIS_FILE[] = __FILE__;
#endif

IMPLEMENT_DYNAMIC(CRowView, CScrollView)
```

(continued)

Figure 24-3. *continued*

```
/////////////////////////////////////////////////////////////////
// CRowView

BEGIN_MESSAGE_MAP(CRowView, CScrollView)
    //{{AFX_MSG_MAP(CRowView)
    ON_WM_KEYDOWN()
    ON_WM_SIZE()
    ON_WM_LBUTTONDOWN()
    //}}AFX_MSG_MAP
    // Standard printing commands
    ON_COMMAND(ID_FILE_PRINT, CView::OnFilePrint)
    ON_COMMAND(ID_FILE_PRINT_PREVIEW, CView::OnFilePrintPreview)
END_MESSAGE_MAP()


/////////////////////////////////////////////////////////////////
// CRowView construction, initialization, and destruction

CRowView::CRowView()
{
    m_nPrevSelectedRow = 0;
}


CRowView::~CRowView()
{
}


/////////////////////////////////////////////////////////////////
// CRowView updating and drawing

void CRowView::OnInitialUpdate()
{
    m_nPrevRowCount = GetRowCount();
    m_nPrevSelectedRow = GetActiveRow();
    OnUpdate(this, 0, NULL);
}


/////////////////////////////////////////////////////////////////
void CRowView::UpdateRow(int nInvalidRow)
{
    int nRowCount = GetRowCount();
    // If the number of rows has changed, adjust
    //   the scrolling range.
    if (nRowCount != m_nPrevRowCount) {
      UpdateScrollSizes();
      m_nPrevRowCount = nRowCount;
    }
```

(continued)

Figure 24-3. *continued*

```
// When the currently selected row changes, scroll the view
//  so that the newly selected row is visible, and ask the
//  derived class to repaint the selected and previously
//  selected rows.

CClientDC dc(this);
OnPrepareDC(&dc);

// Determine the range of the rows that are currently fully
//  visible in the window.  We want to do discrete
//  scrolling so that the next or previous row is always
//  fully visible.

int   nFirstRow, nLastRow;
CRect rectClient;

GetClientRect(&rectClient);
dc.DPtoLP(&rectClient);
RectLPtoRowRange(rectClient, nFirstRow, nLastRow, FALSE);

// If necessary, scroll the window so that the newly
//  selected row is visible.

CPoint pt = GetDeviceScrollPosition();
BOOL   bNeedToScroll = TRUE;

if (nInvalidRow < nFirstRow) {
  // The newly selected row is above those currently
  //  visible in the window. Scroll so that the newly
  //  selected row is at the very top of the window.
  //  The last row in the window might be only
  //  partially visible.
  pt.y = RowToYPos(nInvalidRow);
}
else if (nInvalidRow > nLastRow){
  // The newly selected row is below those currently
  //  visible in the window.  Scroll so that the newly
  //  selected row is at the very bottom of the window.
  //  The first row in the window might be only
  //  partially visible.
  pt.y = max(0, RowToYPos(nInvalidRow+1) -
          rectClient.Height());
}
```

(continued)

Figure 24-3. *continued*

```
      else {
        bNeedToScroll = FALSE;
      }
      if (bNeedToScroll) {
        ScrollToDevicePosition(pt);
        // Scrolling will cause the newly selected row to be
        //  redrawn in the invalidated area of the window.

        OnPrepareDC(&dc);  // Need to prepare the DC again
                           //  because ScrollToDevicePosition()
                           //  will have changed the viewport
                           //  origin. The DC is used some
                           //  more below.
      }

      CRect rectInvalid = RowToWndRect(&dc, nInvalidRow);
      InvalidateRect(&rectInvalid);

      // Give the derived class an opportunity to repaint the
      //  previously selected row, perhaps to un-highlight it.

      int nSelectedRow = GetActiveRow();
      if (m_nPrevSelectedRow != nSelectedRow) {
        CRect rectOldSelection =
                    RowToWndRect(&dc, m_nPrevSelectedRow);
        InvalidateRect(&rectOldSelection);
        m_nPrevSelectedRow = nSelectedRow;
      }
    }
    //////////////////////////////////////////////////////////////
    void CRowView::UpdateScrollSizes()
    {
      // UpdateScrollSizes() is called when it is necessary to
      //  adjust the scrolling range or page/line sizes. There
      //  are two occasions when this is necessary:
      //
      // 1. when a new row is added--see UpdateRow()
      // 2. when the window size changes--see OnSize()

      CRect rectClient;
      GetClientRect(&rectClient);

      CClientDC dc(this);
      CalculateRowMetrics(&dc);
```

(continued)

Figure 24-3. *continued*

```
    // The vertical scrolling range is the total display
    //  height of all the rows..
    CSize sizeTotal(m_nRowWidth, m_nRowHeight *
                (min(GetRowCount(), LastViewableRow())));

    // The vertical per-page scrolling distance is equal to the
    //  number of rows that can be displayed in the current
    //  window, less one row for paging overlap.
    CSize sizePage(m_nRowWidth / 5, max(m_nRowHeight,
                ((rectClient.bottom / m_nRowHeight) - 1) *
                m_nRowHeight));

    // The vertical per-line scrolling distance is equal to the
    //  height of the row.
    CSize sizeLine(m_nRowWidth / 20, m_nRowHeight);

    SetScrollSizes(MM_TEXT, sizeTotal, sizePage, sizeLine);
}


/////////////////////////////////////////////////////////////////
void CRowView::OnDraw(CDC* pDC)
{
    if (GetRowCount() == 0) {
      return;
    }
    // The window has been invalidated and needs to be
    //  repainted, or a page needs to be printed (or previewed).
    // First, determine the range of rows that need to be
    //  displayed or printed.

    int    nFirstRow, nLastRow;
    CRect rectClip;
    pDC->GetClipBox(&rectClip); // Get the invalidated region.
    RectLPtoRowRange(rectClip, nFirstRow, nLastRow, TRUE);

    // Draw each row in the invalidated region of the window,
    //  or on the printed (previewed) page.

    int nActiveRow = GetActiveRow();
    int nRow, y;
    int nLastViewableRow = LastViewableRow();

    for (nRow = nFirstRow, y = m_nRowHeight * nFirstRow;
        nRow <= nLastRow; nRow++, y += m_nRowHeight) {
      if (nRow >= (nLastViewableRow - 1)) {
```

(continued)

523

Figure 24-3. *continued*

```
        CString strWarning;
        strWarning.LoadString(IDS_TOO_MANY_ROWS);
        pDC->TextOut(0, y, strWarning);
        break;
    }
    // Prepare for highlighting or un-highlighting the row,
    //   depending on whether it is the currently
    //   selected row. And paint the background (behind the
    //   text) accordingly.
    CBrush brushBackground;
    COLORREF crOldText, crOldBackground;
    if (!pDC->IsPrinting()) {
      if (nRow == nActiveRow) {
        brushBackground.CreateSolidBrush(
                      ::GetSysColor(COLOR_HIGHLIGHT));
        crOldBackground = pDC->SetBkColor(
                      ::GetSysColor(COLOR_HIGHLIGHT));
        crOldText = pDC->SetTextColor(
                      ::GetSysColor(COLOR_HIGHLIGHTTEXT));
      }
      else {
        brushBackground.CreateSolidBrush(
                      ::GetSysColor(COLOR_WINDOW));
      }
      CRect rectSelection;
      pDC->GetClipBox(&rectSelection);
      rectSelection.top = y;
      rectSelection.bottom = y + m_nRowHeight;
      pDC->FillRect(&rectSelection, &brushBackground);
    }
    OnDrawRow(pDC, nRow, y, nRow == nActiveRow);
    // Restore the DC. (MOVED FROM DERIVED CLASS)
    if (!pDC->IsPrinting() && (nRow == nActiveRow)) {
      pDC->SetBkColor(crOldBackground);
      pDC->SetTextColor(crOldText);
    }
  }
}


/////////////////////////////////////////////////////////////
// Implementation
int CRowView::RowToYPos(int nRow)
{
    return (nRow * m_nRowHeight);
}
```

(continued)

Figure 24-3. *continued*

```
//////////////////////////////////////////////////////////////////
CRect CRowView::RowToWndRect(CDC* pDC, int nRow)
{
    CRect clientRect;

    GetClientRect(clientRect);
    pDC->DPtoLP(clientRect);
    CRect rect(clientRect.left, nRow * m_nRowHeight,
            clientRect.right, (nRow + 1) * m_nRowHeight);
    pDC->LPtoDP(&rect);
    return rect;
}


//////////////////////////////////////////////////////////////////
int CRowView::LastViewableRow()
{
    return (INT_MAX / m_nRowHeight - 1);
}


//////////////////////////////////////////////////////////////////
void CRowView::RectLPtoRowRange(const CRect& rect,
                               int& nFirstRow,
                               int& nLastRow,
                               BOOL bIncludePartiallyShownRows)
{
    int nRounding = bIncludePartiallyShownRows ?
                    0 : (m_nRowHeight - 1);
    nFirstRow = (rect.top + nRounding) / m_nRowHeight;
    nLastRow = min((rect.bottom - nRounding) / m_nRowHeight,
                GetRowCount() - 1);
}


//////////////////////////////////////////////////////////////////
void CRowView::OnPrepareDC(CDC* pDC, CPrintInfo* pInfo)
{
    // The size of text that is displayed, printed, or
    //   previewed changes depending on the DC.  We explicitly
    //   call OnPrepareDC() to prepare CClientDC objects used
    //   for calculating text positions and to prepare the text
    //   metric member variables of the CRowView object. The
    //   application framework also calls OnPrepareDC() before
    //   passing the DC to OnDraw().
```

(continued)

525

Figure 24-3. *continued*

```
    CScrollView::OnPrepareDC(pDC, pInfo);
    CalculateRowMetrics(pDC);
}


/////////////////////////////////////////////////////////////////////
// Overrides of CView for implementing printing

BOOL CRowView::OnPreparePrinting(CPrintInfo* pInfo)
{
    return DoPreparePrinting(pInfo);
}


/////////////////////////////////////////////////////////////////////
void CRowView::OnBeginPrinting(CDC* pDC, CPrintInfo* pInfo)
{
    // OnBeginPrinting() is called after the user has committed
    //  to printing by OKing the Print dialog and after the
    //  application framework has created a CDC object for the
    //  printer or print preview.
    // This is the best opportunity to set up the page range.
    // Given the CDC object, we can determine how many rows
    //  will fit on a page, so we can in turn determine how
    //  many printed pages represent the entire document.

    int nPageHeight = pDC->GetDeviceCaps(VERTRES);
    CalculateRowMetrics(pDC);
    m_nRowsPerPrintedPage = nPageHeight / m_nRowHeight;
    int nPrintableRowCount = LastViewableRow() + 1;
    if (GetRowCount() < nPrintableRowCount) {
      nPrintableRowCount = GetRowCount();
    }
    pInfo->SetMaxPage((nPrintableRowCount +
                    m_nRowsPerPrintedPage - 1) /
                    m_nRowsPerPrintedPage);
    pInfo->m_nCurPage = 1;  // Start previewing at page 1.
}


/////////////////////////////////////////////////////////////////////
void CRowView::OnPrint(CDC* pDC, CPrintInfo* pInfo)
{
    // Print the rows for the current page.

    int yTopOfPage = (pInfo->m_nCurPage -1) *
                    m_nRowsPerPrintedPage * m_nRowHeight;
```

(continued)

Figure 24-3. *continued*

```
    // Orient the viewport so that the first row to be printed
    //  has a viewport coordinate of (0, 0).
    pDC->SetViewportOrg(0, -yTopOfPage);

    // Draw as many rows as will fit on the printed page.
    // Clip the printed page so that there is no partially
    //  shown row at the bottom of the page (the same row that
    //  will be fully shown at the top of the next page).

    int nPageWidth = pDC->GetDeviceCaps(HORZRES);

    CRect rectClip = CRect(0, yTopOfPage, nPageWidth, yTopOfPage +
                           m_nRowsPerPrintedPage * m_nRowHeight);
    pDC->IntersectClipRect(&rectClip);
    OnDraw(pDC);
}


/////////////////////////////////////////////////////////////////
// CRowView commands

void CRowView::OnSize(UINT nType, int cx, int cy)
{
    UpdateScrollSizes();
    CScrollView::OnSize(nType, cx, cy);
}


/////////////////////////////////////////////////////////////////
void CRowView::OnKeyDown(UINT nChar, UINT nRepCnt, UINT nFlags)
{
    CRect clientRect;

    GetClientRect(clientRect);
    CClientDC dc(this);
    dc.DPtoLP(clientRect);

    switch (nChar)
    {
      case VK_HOME:
          ChangeSelectionToRow(0);
          break;
      case VK_END:
          ChangeSelectionToRow(min(GetRowCount() - 1,
                               LastViewableRow() - 2));
          break;
```

(continued)

527

Figure 24-3. *continued*

```
        case VK_UP:
            ChangeSelectionNextRow(FALSE);
            break;
        case VK_DOWN:
            ChangeSelectionNextRow(TRUE);
            break;
        case VK_LEFT:
            if (clientRect.Width() < GetTotalSize().cx) {
                OnHScroll(SB_LINELEFT, 0, NULL);
            }
            break;
        case VK_RIGHT:
            if (clientRect.Width() < GetTotalSize().cx) {
                OnHScroll(SB_LINERIGHT, 0, NULL);
            }
            break;
        case VK_PRIOR:
            if (clientRect.Height() < GetTotalSize().cy) {
                OnVScroll(SB_PAGEUP, 0, NULL);
            }
            break;
        case VK_NEXT:
            if (clientRect.Height() < GetTotalSize().cy) {
                OnVScroll(SB_PAGEDOWN, 0, NULL);
            }
            break;
        default:
            CScrollView::OnKeyDown(nChar, nRepCnt, nFlags);
    }
}


/////////////////////////////////////////////////////////////////
void CRowView::OnLButtonDown(UINT, CPoint point)
{
    CClientDC dc(this);
    OnPrepareDC(&dc);
    dc.DPtoLP(&point);

    CRect rect(point, CSize(1,1));
    int   nFirstRow, nLastRow;
    RectLPtoRowRange(rect, nFirstRow, nLastRow, TRUE);

    if (nFirstRow <= (GetRowCount() - 1)) {
      ChangeSelectionToRow(nFirstRow);
    }
}
```

The Scrolling Problem

You've seen the *CScrollView* base class used in EX24A. The scroll view's window consists of an area as large as 32,767 units high by 32,767 units wide, only a small part of which is visible on the screen. Suppose you had a list of 2000 database query result rows, each 14 units high. Your view class *OnDraw* function could use the *CDC::TextOut* function to paint all 2000 records each time the list was updated. This would work, but it would be terribly slow. As you've probably guessed, the trick is to paint only those rows that fall within the invalid rectangle that corresponds to the display screen—and this is what *CRowView* does.

Dividing the Work Between Base and Derived Classes

Because the *CRowView* class (itself derived from *CScrollView*) is designed to be a base class, it is as general as possible. *CRowView* relies on its derived class to access and paint the row's data. The EX24B example's document class obtains its row data from a scrollable database, but the CHKBOOK example uses a random-access disk file. The *CRowView* class serves both examples effectively. It supports the concept of a selected row that is highlighted in the view. Through the *CRowView* virtual member functions, the derived class is alerted when the user changes the selected row.

The *CRowView* Pure Virtual Member Functions

Classes derived from *CRowView* must implement the following pure virtual member functions:

- **GetRowWidthHeight**—This function returns the character width and height of the currently selected font, and the width of the row, based on average character widths. As the device context switches between printer and display, the returned font metric values change accordingly.

- **GetActiveRow**—The base class calls this function frequently, so if another view changes the selected row, this view can track it.

- **ChangeSelectionNextRow, ChangeSelectionToRow**—These two functions serve to alert the derived class that the user has changed the selected row. The derived class can then update the document (and other views) if necessary.

- **OnDrawRow**—The *OnDrawRow* function is called by the *CRowView::OnDraw* function to draw a specific row.

529

Other *CRowView* Functions

Three other *CRowView* functions are available to be called by derived classes and the application framework. These are *UpdateRow*, *UpdateScrollSizes*, and *OnPrint*.

- ■ *UpdateRow*—This public function triggers a view update when the row selection changes. Normally, only the newly selected row and the deselected row are invalidated, and this means that the final invalid rectangle spans both rows. If the total number of rows has changed, *UpdateRow* calls *UpdateScrollSizes*.

- ■ *UpdateScrollSizes*—This is a virtual function, so you can override it if necessary. The *CRowView* implementation updates the size of the view, which invalidates the visible portion. *UpdateScrollSizes* is called by *OnSize* and by *OnUpdate* (after the user executes a new query).

- ■ *OnPrint*—The *CRowView* class overrides this function to cleverly adjust the viewport origin and clipping rectangle so that *OnDraw* can paint on the printed page as it does in the visible portion of a window.

Programming a Dynamic Recordset

The recordset you saw in EX24A had a *DoFieldExchange* function that was hard-coded for the columns in a specific database table. For a dynamic recordset class, we need to determine the column names and data types at run time. That information is always available from an ODBC data source, and the sample program \MSVC\MFC\SAMPLES\CATALOG has recordset classes *CTables* and *CColumns* that retrieve the necessary data.

We have a sequencing problem here: If we construct and open the main recordset, as we did in EX24A, we'll get an error because *DoField-Exchange* gets called before we've defined the columns. We must construct a *CDatabase* object first, make a *CTables* recordset to select a table, make a *CColumns* recordset, and, finally, make the main recordset. All recordsets are attached to the same *CDatabase* object.

Here are the steps to follow for creating the main recordset:

1. Use the default constructor to make a *CDatabase* object. It's a good idea to embed this object in the document.

2. Call the *Open* member function for the *CDatabase* object. Depending on the parameters you supply, the function can prompt the user to select the data source.

3. Construct a *CTables* object, using the *CDatabase* pointer as a constructor parameter. Open this recordset to obtain a list of table names. Let the user choose a table.

4. Construct the main recordset object, passing a pointer to the *CDatabase* object as a parameter to the constructor. You can store a pointer to this recordset in a document data member. Because you passed in a database pointer, the virtual *CRecordset* functions *GetDefaultConnect* and *GetDefaultSQL* won't be called.

5. Construct a *CColumns* object, again using the *CDatabase* pointer as a constructor parameter. Set the *CColumns* data member *m_strTableNameParam* to the table name. Open this recordset to get each column's name. Also, obtain each column's data type and allocate storage for the data transfer that will occur later under the control of *DoFieldExchange*.

6. Finally, open the main recordset, passing the table name (from step 3) as a parameter. This works if you have written a *DoFieldExchange* function that references the names and storage locations that were set up in step 5.

To clean up, you must first delete the main recordset (which closes it) and then close or delete the database. The table and column recordsets take care of themselves if you declare them on the stack.

Counting the Rows in a Recordset

The ODBC library doesn't provide an accurate count of the rows in a recordset until you've read past the end. Until that time, the count returned from the *CRecordset::GetRecordCount* member function is a "high-water mark" only. It returns only the last row read. The *GetStatus* member function returns a *CRecordsetStatus* object, which has a data member *m_bRecordCountFinal* indicating whether the count is final.

The EX24B Example

Now we'll put everything together and build another working program—an MDI application that connects to any ODBC data source. The application dynamically displays tables in scrolling view windows, and it allows the user to enter filter and sort strings, which are stored in the document along with data source and table information. AppWizard generates the usual MDI main frame, document, application, and view classes, and we change the view class base to *CRowView* and add the ODBC-specific code. Figure 24-4 shows the EX24B program in operation.

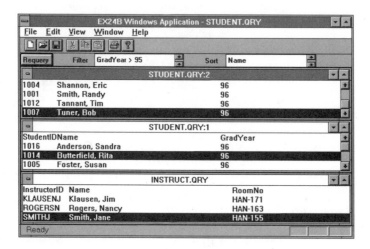

Figure 24-4.
The EX24B program in operation.

The document's File menu has the commands ODBC Connect and ODBC Disconnect. The user must choose ODBC Connect to attach a recordset to an empty document and then choose ODBC Disconnect prior to closing the document or attaching another recordset.

You can learn a lot about this application by looking at the three view windows. The two views on the top are tied to the same document, STUDENT.QRY, and the bottom view is tied to another document, INSTRUCT.QRY. The dialog bar shows the SQL statement that's associated with the active view window.

The EX24B example is presented with source code listings and resource requirements. Here's a table of the files and classes:

Header File	Source Code File	Class	Description
EX24B.H	EX24B.CPP	*CEx24bApp*	Main application
MAINFRM.H	MAINFRM.CPP	*CMainFrame*	MDI main frame
EX24BDOC.H	EX24BDOC.CPP	*CEx24bDoc*	EX24B document
EX24BVW.H	EX24BVW.CPP	*CEx24bView*	Scrolling database view class
EX24BSET.H	EX24BSET.CPP	*CEx24bSet*	Recordset class
ROWVIEW.H	ROWVIEW.CPP	*CRowView*	Row view base class
COLUMNST.H	COLUMNST.CPP	*CColumns*	Column rowset class from CATALOG
TABLESET.H	TABLESET.CPP	*CTables*	Table rowset class from CATALOG
TABLESEL.H	TABLESEL.CPP	*CTableSelect*	Table selection dialog class
STDAFX.H	STDAFX.CPP		Precompiled headers

Now we'll go through the application's classes one at a time, excluding *CRowView* and the classes borrowed from CATALOG. You'll see the important data members and the principal member functions.

CEx24bApp

The application class is the unmodified output from AppWizard.

CMainFrame

This class is the standard output from AppWizard except for the addition of the dialog bar, which is created in the *OnCreate* member function.

CEx24bDoc

The document class manages the database connections and recordsets. Each document object can support one main recordset attached to one data source. A document object can have several views attached. Data sources (represented by *CDatabase* objects) are not shared among document objects; each document has its own.

Data Members

The important *CEx24bDoc* data members are as follows:

m_pEx24bSet	A pointer to the document's recordset object
m_database	The document's embedded *CDatabase* object
m_strTableName	The name of the selected table
m_strConnect	The connection string that identifies the ODBC data source
m_strFilter	The filter string (example: GradYear > 95) that becomes part of an SQL statement
m_strSort	The sort string (example: GradYear, StudentID)
m_bConnected	A flag that is *TRUE* when the document is connected to a recordset

The sort and filter strings are also data members of the recordset class, but they're duplicated in the document class so that we can serialize them.

OnNewDocument

This overridden *CDocument* function sets the default database connection string.

OnFileConnect

This function is called in response to the ODBC Connect command on the File menu. It creates the recordset and allocates storage for the recordset's *DoFieldExchange* function according to the steps listed above. Notice the use of the TRY/CATCH block to detect SQL processing errors. Notice also that *OnFileConnect*, together with *OnFileDisconnect* and *OnQueryRequery*, calls *UpdateAllViews*.

```
void CEx24bDoc::OnFileConnect()
{
    char errorMsg[201];

    BeginWaitCursor();
    if (m_database.Open(NULL, FALSE, TRUE, m_strConnect) == 0) {
        EndWaitCursor();
        return;
    }
    m_strConnect = m_database.GetConnect();
```

```
CTableSelect tableDlg(&m_database);
tableDlg.m_strSelection = m_strTableName;
if (tableDlg.DoModal() != IDOK) {
  m_database.Close();  // escape route
  EndWaitCursor();
  return;
}
m_strTableName = tableDlg.m_strSelection;

m_pEx24bSet = new CEx24bSet(&m_database);
m_pEx24bSet->Initialize(m_strTableName);  // get column info
m_pEx24bSet->m_strFilter = m_strFilter;
m_pEx24bSet->m_strSort = m_strSort;
PutFilterSort();

TRY {
  m_pEx24bSet->Open(CRecordset::snapshot, m_strTableName,
                    CRecordset::readOnly);
}
CATCH(CDBException, e) {
  sprintf(errorMsg, "ODBC %s", (const char*) e->m_strError);
  AfxMessageBox(errorMsg);
  UpdateAllViews(NULL);
  m_bConnected = FALSE;
  EndWaitCursor();
  return;
}
END_CATCH
UpdateAllViews(NULL);
m_bConnected = TRUE;
EndWaitCursor();
}
```

OnFileDisconnect

This function is called in response to the ODBC Disconnect command on the File menu.

```
void CEx24bDoc::OnFileDisconnect()
{
    GetFilterSort();
    delete m_pEx24bSet; // destructor calls Close
    m_database.Close();
    m_pEx24bSet = NULL;
    m_bConnected = FALSE;
    UpdateAllViews(NULL);
}
```

OnQueryRequery

This message handler is called in response to the Requery button on the dialog bar. It reads the sort and filter string values and regenerates the recordset. Note that the *CRecordset::Requery* function doesn't process the sort and filter strings, so we close and reopen the recordset instead.

```
void CEx24bDoc::OnQueryRequery()
{
    char errorMsg[201];
    BeginWaitCursor();
    GetFilterSort();
    m_pEx24bSet->m_strFilter = m_strFilter;
    m_pEx24bSet->m_strSort = m_strSort;
    m_pEx24bSet->Close();  // do this instead for
                           //  now--less efficient
    TRY {
      m_pEx24bSet->Open(CRecordset::snapshot,
                        m_strTableName, CRecordset::readOnly);
    }
    CATCH(CDBException, e) {
      sprintf(errorMsg, "ODBC %s", (const char*) e->m_strError);
      AfxMessageBox(errorMsg);
    }
    END_CATCH

    UpdateAllViews(NULL);
    EndWaitCursor();
}
```

PutFilterSort, GetFilterSort

These utility functions move the document's sort and filter strings to and from the edit controls on the dialog bar.

SaveModified

This virtual function, called by the application framework when the user tries to close a document, checks to see whether the document's database connection is open. If it is, the document is not closed, and the program warns the user with a message box.

Serialize

The *Serialize* function reads and writes the data members *m_strConnect*, *m_strTableName*, *m_strFilter*, and *m_strSort*.

CEx24bView

This class is derived from *CRowView* and thus implements the necessary virtual functions.

Data Members

The view class uses the integer variable *m_nSelectedRow* to track the currently selected row. The recordset pointer is held in *m_pSet*.

OnUpdate

This virtual *CView* function is called through the application framework when the document's contents change in response to a new connection, a requery, or a disconnect. If several views are active for a given document, all views reflect the current query, but each can maintain its own current row and scroll position. *OnUpdate* also sets the value of the *m_pSet* data member. This can't be done in *OnInitialUpdate* because the recordset is not open at that point.

GetRowWidthHeight, GetActiveRow, ChangeSelectionNextRow, ChangeSelectionToRow

These functions are implementations of the *CRowView* class pure virtual functions. They take care of drawing a specified query result row, and they track the current selection.

GetRowCount

Remember that the recordset doesn't know the record count until you've read past the end of the data. This overridden virtual function sets the view's count value to a large number (*MAX_ROWS*) until it can determine the true recordset row count.

```
int CEx24bView::GetRowCount()
{
    CRecordsetStatus rStatus;
    int nRows = 0;
    if (m_pSet != NULL && m_pSet->IsOpen()) {
        m_pSet->GetStatus(rStatus);
        if (rStatus.m_bRecordCountFinal) {
            nRows = (int) m_pSet->GetRecordCount() + 1;
        }
```

(continued)

```
     else {
       nRows = MAXROWS;
       }
    }
    return nRows;
}
```

OnDrawRow, DrawDataRow

The *OnDrawRow* virtual function is called from *CRowView* member functions
to do the actual work of drawing a designated row. *OnDrawRow* reads the
recordset's current row and then calls the *CRecordset::Move* function to position the cursor and read the data. The TRY/CATCH block detects cata-
strophic errors resulting from unreadable data. The *DrawDataRow* helper
function steps through the columns and prints the values from the memory
that was allocated when the recordset was initialized.

```
void CEx24bView::OnDrawRow(CDC* pDC, int nRow, int y, BOOL bSelected)
{
    int x = 0;
    int i;
    int nFields = (int) m_pSet->m_nFields;
    CRecordsetStatus rStatus;
    char errorMsg[201];

    if (nRow == 0) {     // title row
      for (i = 0; i < nFields; i++) {
        pDC->TextOut(x, y, m_pSet->m_arrayName[i]);
        x += m_pSet->m_nColWidth[i] * m_nCharWidth;
      }
    }
    else {
      m_pSet->GetStatus(rStatus);
      TRY {
        m_pSet->Move(nRow - (int) rStatus.m_lCurrentRecord - 1);
        if (m_pSet->IsEOF()) {
          m_pSet->MoveLast();
        }
        else {
          DrawDataRow(pDC, y);
        }
      }
      CATCH(CDBException, e) {
        sprintf(errorMsg, "ODBC %s SHUT DOWN THE APP NOW!!!",
              (const char*) e->m_strError);
        AfxMessageBox(errorMsg);
```

```
        // Figure out some way to escape from here.
    }
    END_CATCH
}
}

void CEx24bView::DrawDataRow(CDC* pDC, int y)
{
    int     x = 0;
    char    temp[101];
    CString strTime;
    int     nFields = (int) m_pSet->m_nFields;

    for (int i = 0; i < nFields; i++) {
        switch (m_pSet->m_nDatType[i]) {
        case SQL_BIT:
            *((BOOL*) m_pSet->m_arrayValue[i]) ?
                pDC->TextOut(x, y, "T") : pDC->TextOut(x, y, "F");
            break;
        case SQL_TINYINT:
            sprintf(temp, "%d",
                    (int) *((BYTE*) m_pSet->m_arrayValue[i]));
            pDC->TextOut(x, y, temp);
            break;
        case SQL_SMALLINT:
            sprintf(temp, "%d",
                    *((int*) m_pSet->m_arrayValue[i]));
            pDC->TextOut(x, y, temp);
            break;
        case SQL_INTEGER:
            sprintf(temp, "%ld",
                    *((long*) m_pSet->m_arrayValue[i]));
            pDC->TextOut(x, y, temp);
            break;
        case SQL_REAL:
            sprintf(temp, "%10.2f",
                    (double) *((float*) m_pSet->m_arrayValue[i]));
            pDC->TextOut(x, y, temp);
            break;
        case SQL_FLOAT:
        case SQL_DOUBLE:
            sprintf(temp, "%10.2f",
                    *((double*) m_pSet->m_arrayValue[i]));
            pDC->TextOut(x, y, temp);
            break;
        case SQL_DATE:
```

(continued)

```
      case SQL_TIME:
      case SQL_TIMESTAMP:
          strTime = ((CTime*)
            m_pSet->m_arrayValue[i])->Format("%A, %B %d, %Y");
          pDC->TextOut(x, y, temp);
          break;
      case SQL_BINARY:
      case SQL_VARBINARY:
          pDC->TextOut(x, y, "binary");
          break;
      case SQL_DECIMAL:
      case SQL_NUMERIC:
      case SQL_CHAR:
      case SQL_VARCHAR:
          pDC->TextOut(x, y,
                      *((CString*) m_pSet->m_arrayValue[i]));
          break;
      case SQL_LONGVARCHAR:
      case SQL_LONGVARBINARY:
          pDC->TextOut(x, y, "long binary");
          break;
      default:
          ASSERT(FALSE);
      }
      x += m_pSet->m_nColWidth[i] * m_nCharWidth;
  }
}
```

CEx24bSet

This recordset class does most of the work for dynamic database access and thus could serve as a building block in your own applications.

Data Members

The important *CEx24bSet* data members are as follows:

m_arrayName	A dynamic string array that holds the column names
m_arrayValue	A dynamic void pointer array that holds the current row's values
m_nColWidth	An integer array of column widths (depends on column name lengths)
m_nDatType	An integer array of ODBC data types (SQL_CHAR, SQL_INTEGER, and so on)

Initialize

The code in this member function could have been put in the constructor, but it's better to put it in a separate function because the database access might fail. The *Initialize* function allocates memory for each column according to the data type. The *DoFieldExchange* function uses this memory when it binds the columns.

```
void CEx24bSet::Initialize(const char* pchTableName)
{
// second construction phase

    void* pVar = NULL;

    m_nFields = 0;
    CColumns columns(m_pDatabase);  // closed on destruction
    columns.m_strTableNameParam = pchTableName;
    columns.Open();
    while (!columns.IsEOF()) {
      m_arrayName.Add(columns.m_strColumnName);
      m_nColWidth[m_nFields] = max(((int) columns.m_lLength + 2),
                        columns.m_strColumnName.GetLength());
      // data types defined in sql.h and sqlext.h
      m_nDatType[m_nFields] = columns.m_nDataType;
      switch (columns.m_nDataType) {
      case SQL_BIT:
          pVar = new BOOL;
          break;
      case SQL_TINYINT:
          pVar = new BYTE;
          break;
      case SQL_SMALLINT:
          pVar = new int;
          break;
      case SQL_INTEGER:
          pVar = new long;
          break;
      case SQL_REAL:
          pVar = new float;
          break;
      case SQL_FLOAT:
      case SQL_DOUBLE:
          pVar = new double;
          break;
      case SQL_DATE:
      case SQL_TIME:
```

(continued)

```
        case SQL_TIMESTAMP:
            pVar = new CTime;
            break;
        case SQL_BINARY:
        case SQL_VARBINARY:
            pVar = new CByteArray;
            break;
        case SQL_DECIMAL:
        case SQL_NUMERIC:
        case SQL_CHAR:
        case SQL_VARCHAR:
            pVar = new CString;
            break;
        case SQL_LONGVARCHAR:
        case SQL_LONGVARBINARY:
            pVar = new CLongBinary;
            break;
        default:
            ASSERT(FALSE);
        }
        m_arrayValue.Add(pVar);
        columns.MoveNext();
        m_nFields++;
    }
}
```

DoFieldExchange

This function binds the allocated memory to the columns. Remember that the *Open* member function calls *DoFieldExchange*, so the memory must have been allocated before the recordset's *Open* function is called.

```
void CEx24bSet::DoFieldExchange(CFieldExchange* pFX)
{
    pFX->SetFieldType(CFieldExchange::outputColumn);
    for (int i = 0; i < (int) m_nFields; i++) {
      switch (m_nDatType[i]) {
      case SQL_BIT:
          RFX_Bool(pFX, m_arrayName[i],
                  *((BOOL*) m_arrayValue[i]));
          break;
      case SQL_TINYINT:
          RFX_Byte(pFX, m_arrayName[i],
                  *((BYTE*) m_arrayValue[i]));
          break;
      case SQL_SMALLINT:
          RFX_Int(pFX,  m_arrayName[i],
```

```
                *((int*) m_arrayValue[i]));
            break;
        case SQL_INTEGER:
            RFX_Long(pFX, m_arrayName[i],
                    *((long*) m_arrayValue[i]));
            break;
        case SQL_REAL:
            RFX_Single(pFX, m_arrayName[i],
                    *((float*) m_arrayValue[i]));
            break;
        case SQL_FLOAT:
        case SQL_DOUBLE:
            RFX_Double(pFX, m_arrayName[i],
                    *((double*) m_arrayValue[i]));
            break;
        case SQL_DATE:
        case SQL_TIME:
        case SQL_TIMESTAMP:
            RFX_Date(pFX, m_arrayName[i],
                    *((CTime*) m_arrayValue[i]));
            break;
        case SQL_BINARY:
        case SQL_VARBINARY:
            RFX_Binary(pFX, m_arrayName[i],
                    *((CByteArray*) m_arrayValue[i]));
            break;
        case SQL_DECIMAL:
        case SQL_NUMERIC:
        case SQL_CHAR:
        case SQL_VARCHAR:
            RFX_Text(pFX, m_arrayName[i],
                    *((CString*) m_arrayValue[i]));
            break;
        case SQL_LONGVARCHAR:
        case SQL_LONGVARBINARY:
            RFX_LongBinary(pFX, m_arrayName[i],
                        *((CLongBinary*) m_arrayValue[i]));
            break;
        default:
            ASSERT(FALSE);
        }
    }
}
```

Destructor

The *CEx24bSet* destructor frees the memory allocated by the *Initialize* member function, as shown on the following page.

```
CEx24bSet::~CEx24bSet()
{
    for (int i = 0; i < (int) m_nFields; i++) {
        switch (m_nDatType[i]) {
        case SQL_DECIMAL:
        case SQL_NUMERIC:
        case SQL_CHAR:
        case SQL_VARCHAR:
            delete (CString*) m_arrayValue[i];
            break;
        case SQL_BINARY:
        case SQL_VARBINARY:
            delete (CByteArray*) m_arrayValue[i];
            break;
        case SQL_LONGVARCHAR:
        case SQL_LONGVARBINARY:
            delete (CLongBinary*) m_arrayValue[i];
        default:
            delete m_arrayValue[i];
        }
    }
}
```

CTableSelect

This is a ClassWizard-generated dialog class that contains a list box used for selecting the table.

Data Members

The important *CTableSelect* data members are as follows:

m_pDatabase	A pointer to the recordset's *CDatabase* object
m_strSelection	The ClassWizard-generated variable that corresponds to the list-box selection

Constructor

The constructor takes a database pointer parameter, which it uses to set the *m_pDatabase* data member.

```
CTableSelect::CTableSelect(CDatabase* pDatabase,
                           CWnd* pParent /*=NULL*/)
                : CDialog(CTableSelect::IDD, pParent)
{
    //{{AFX_DATA_INIT(CTableSelect)
    m_strSelection = "";
```

```
    //}}AFX_DATA_INIT
    m_pDatabase = pDatabase;
}
```

OnInitDialog

This self-contained function creates, opens, and reads the data source's list of tables, and it puts the table name strings in the dialog's list box.

```
BOOL CTableSelect::OnInitDialog()
{
    CListBox* pLB = (CListBox*) GetDlgItem(IDC_LIST1);
    CTables tables(m_pDatabase);   // db passed via constructor
    tables.Open();                 // closed on table's
                                   //   destruction
    while (!tables.IsEOF()) {
      TRACE("table name = %s\n", tables.m_strName);
      if (tables.m_strName.Left(4) != "MSYS") {
       . pLB->AddString(tables.m_strName);
      }
      tables.MoveNext();
    }
    return CDialog::OnInitDialog();
}
```

OnDblclkList1

It's handy for the user to choose a list-box entry with a double-click. This function is mapped to the appropriate list-box notification message.

```
void CTableSelect::OnDblclkList1()
{
    OnOK();  // double-click on list-box item exits dialog
}
```

The EX24B Resource File

This application uses a dialog bar, so you'll need a dialog resource for it. Figure 24-4 on page 532 shows the dialog bar. The dialog resource ID is *IDD_QUERY_BAR*. The controls are listed here:

Control	ID
Button	*IDC_REQUERY*
Edit	*IDC_FILTER*
Edit	*IDC_SORT*

The dialog resource ID is *IDD_QUERY_BAR*, and the following styles are set:

Style = Child
Border = None
Visible = unchecked

There's also a table selection dialog resource, *IDD_TABLE_SELECT*, which has a list-box control with ID *IDC_LIST1*. That dialog is shown here:

The File menu has two added items:

Menu Item	Command ID
ODBC Connect	*ID_FILE_CONNECT*
ODBC Disconnect	*ID_FILE_DISCONNECT*

Running the EX24B Program

You can run the EX24B program with any ODBC data source, including SQL Server databases. Be careful, though, with Microsoft Access version 2.0. The Access 2.0 Setup program installs something that looks like an ODBC driver—its name shows up in the ODBC data source list. This driver is intended only for use within the Microsoft Office suite of programs. It will <u>not</u> work with the MFC 1.5 ODBC classes. If you need to read and write Access 2.0 files, you'll have to get a real ODBC driver from Microsoft or from a third-party supplier.

Going Further with ODBC

You'll find the *CRecordset* and *CDatabase* classes adequate for most ODBC work. There are member functions for adding and deleting records and for setting up database transactions. The *CRecordset::Open* function is flexible enough to accommodate general SQL *SELECT* statements and calls to stored procedures. The *CDatabase::ExecuteSQL* function allows you to bypass the recordset entirely when you execute an SQL statement. This works only if the SQL statement is <u>not</u> a query, because you need access to the ODBC statement handle for query processing. If you want to do your own queries without recordsets, you'll have to work directly at the ODBC SDK level.

OLE AND OLE AUTOMATION

OLE is a much bigger subject than one chapter in a Visual C++ book can cover. The Microsoft Foundation Class (MFC) libraries do make OLE programming easier, but you need to understand the underlying OLE architecture—particularly the Common Object Model (COM)—before you can use the MFC library effectively. This chapter focuses on two things:

- COM theory in the context of the MFC application framework.

- OLE Automation (an OLE feature). This OLE feature is important because it's the bridge between C++, Visual Basic for Applications (VBA), and other languages.

Learning COM theory and OLE Automation will give you a head start in understanding the inner workings of other OLE features, such as Visual Editing, drag-and-drop, structured storage, and OLE Controls.

Learning OLE

OLE stands for Object Linking and Embedding, but that now-insufficient title is left over from a previous incarnation, OLE version 1.0. OLE version 2.0 is a whole lot more. It's the beginning of Microsoft's new object-oriented operating system—a brand-new application programming interface (API) for Windows applications. Sounds pretty grandiose, doesn't it? If you found this book in a bookstore, you might have noticed other OLE books on the shelf, particularly Kraig Brockschmidt's 1000-page *Inside OLE 2* and the two volumes of the *OLE 2 Programmer's Reference*. (Both titles were published by Microsoft Press. The two reference volumes are supplied as WINHELP files in Visual C++.) Did you get the feeling that maybe you didn't know as much as you thought you did? You should have!

Let me tell you my experience. I was feeling pretty good about myself because I had mastered the C++ language, Windows programming, and MFC. I thought I really was ahead of the game—but then there was this obscure API for linking and embedding that had undergone a version change. No problem, I thought, because the MFC developers had promised that their OLE classes wouldn't change much. Then I started digging in. Pretty soon I began to see references to "interfaces," and I had no clue what an interface was. Shortly thereafter, I attended some OLE seminars at a conference, and I saw dozens of incomprehensible APIs on Microsoft PowerPoint slides. Suddenly it dawned on me that I was at the very bottom of yet another learning curve!

Kraig Brockschmidt, a true Microsoft insider who's a very bright guy, refers to "six months of mental fog." He's not kidding. Perhaps it won't be as bad for you. You've got Brockschmidt's book, this chapter, and the MFC OLE classes to help you. But if your boss or client has asked for an OLE application by the middle of next week, you could be in trouble. Don't make the same mistake I did. Don't depend on the MFC OLE classes to shield you from the underlying OLE architecture. That would be like using MFC to program Windows applications with no understanding of Windows messages and device contexts.

A few other words of advice:

- Know the C++ language cold.

- Read Brockschmidt's book.

In this chapter, I'll try to rephrase (in abbreviated form) Brockschmidt's "Component Object Model" tutorial in terms of the application framework. Brockschmidt's book addresses all the important OLE features that I ignore, but it doesn't cover OLE Automation. As I was writing this chapter, I was not aware of any books specifically about OLE Automation.

The Common Object Model (COM)

As far as I'm concerned, the Common Object Model (COM) is what OLE is really about. OLE is a superset of COM that has some nice features, such as Visual Editing, drag-and-drop, and automation, but COM encompasses a new modular software architecture. You really need to learn COM before you can master the OLE features that build on it.

COM used to stand for "Component Object Model," but as this book was in the final editing stages, Microsoft Corporation and Digital Equipment

Corporation announced a deal allowing the COM standard to be supported by both companies. Watch for COM, which now includes structured storage, to appear on the Windows, Macintosh, and UNIX platforms.

The Problem That COM Solves

The "problem" is that there isn't a standard way for Windows program modules to communicate with one another. "But," you say, "there's the DLL interface, the VBX standard, Dynamic Data Exchange (DDE), the clipboard, the old OLE 1, and the Windows API itself. Aren't they good enough?" Well, no. You can't build an object-oriented operating system for the future out of these ad hoc, unrelated standards. With the OLE Common Object Model, however, you can, and that's precisely what Microsoft is doing.

The Essence of COM

What's wrong with the old standards? Lots. The Windows API has too large a programming "surface area"—350 separate functions. VBXs don't work in the 32-bit world. With DDE, there's a complicated system of applications, topics, and items. How you call a DLL is totally application-specific, and your approach depends on whether client and DLL are both 32-bit, both 16-bit, or one of each. COM provides a unified, expandable, object-oriented Windows communications protocol that already supports

- A standard way for a client EXE to call a DLL

- A general-purpose way for one EXE to control another EXE on the same computer (the DDE replacement)

- A replacement for the VBX control, called an OLE Control

- A language-independent binary standard for linking 16-bit and 32-bit applications

In the immediate future, Microsoft Corporation will expand COM to handle communications between programs running on separate processors and even different processor types.

So what is COM? That's an easier question to ask than to answer. COM is a protocol that connects one software module with another, and then drops out of the picture. After the connection is made, the two modules can communicate through a mechanism called an "interface." Interfaces require no statically or dynamically linked entry points or hard-coded addresses other than the few general-purpose COM functions that get the communication process started. An interface (more precisely, a COM interface) is an

OLE term that you'll be seeing a lot of. Follow along, and you'll begin to understand what an interface really is.

What Is a COM Interface?

Appendix A of this book uses a planetary-motion simulation (suitable for NASA or Nintendo) to illustrate C++ inheritance and polymorphism. I'll stick with that same example here, because it's useful to show what COM adds to the plain-vanilla C++ approach used in the appendix. The example here, however, is independent of Appendix A.

Imagine a spaceship that travels through our solar system under the influence of the sun's gravity. In ordinary C++, you could declare a *CSpaceship* class and write a constructor that sets the spaceship's initial position and acceleration. Then you could write a member function named *Fly* that obeyed Kepler's laws in order to move the spaceship from one position to the next— say, over a period of 0.1 second. *Fly* would be an ordinary nonvirtual member function. You could also write a *Display* function that painted an image of the spaceship in a window.

Now, if we move to COM, the spaceship code lives in a separate EXE or DLL (the "server"), which is a COM module. A "client" program can't call *Fly* or any *CSpaceship* constructor because COM provides a standard global function call to gain access to the spaceship. Before we tackle real COM, let's do a "COM simulation" in which both the server and the client code are statically linked in the same EXE file. For our standard global function, we'll invent a function named *GetClassObject*, with three parameters:

```
BOOL GetClassObject(const long& lClsid, const long& lRid,
                    void** ppvObj);
```

> NOTE: Real COM functions return a special error code structure of type *HRESULT*. For tutorial purposes, I'll show an ordinary Boolean return instead. Assume the return value is *TRUE* if a function was successful.

The first *GetClassObject* parameter, *lClsid*, is a 32-bit number (real COM uses 128 bits) that uniquely identifies the *CSpaceship* class. The second parameter, *lRid*, is the unique identifier of the interface that we want. Now let's back up to the design of *CSpaceship*. We haven't talked about spaceship interfaces yet. A COM interface is a C++ base class (actually, a C++ *struct*) that declares a group of pure virtual functions. These functions completely control some aspect of derived class behavior. For *CSpaceship*, let's choose an interface named *IMotion*, which controls the spaceship object's position. For simplicity's sake, we'll declare just two functions, *Fly* and *GetPosition*, and we'll make the position value an integer. The *Fly* function moves the spaceship, and the *GetPosition* function returns a reference to the current position. Here are the declarations:

```
struct IMotion
{
    virtual void Fly() = 0;
    virtual int& GetPosition() = 0;
};

class CSpaceship : public IMotion
{
protected:
    int m_nPosition;
public:
    CSpaceship() { m_nPosition = 0; }
    void Fly();
    int& GetPosition();
};
```

The actual code for the spaceship-related functions, including *GetClassObject,* is in the server part of the program. The client part calls the *GetClassObject* function to construct the spaceship and to obtain an *IMotion* pointer. Both parts have access to the class declarations at compile time. Here's how the client calls *GetClassObject*:

```
IMotion* pMot;
GetClassObject(CLSID_CSpaceship, IID_IMotion, (void**) &pMot);
```

Assume for now that COM can use the unique identifiers *CLSID_C-Spaceship* and *IID_IMotion* to find the specific *GetClassObject* function for spaceships. If the call is successful, *pMot* points to a *CSpaceship* object that *Get-ClassObject* somehow constructs. As you can see, the *CSpaceship* class implements the *Fly* and *GetPosition* functions, and our main program can call them for the one particular spaceship object:

```
int nPos = 50;
pMot->GetPosition() = nPos;
pMot->Fly();
nPos = pMot->GetPosition();
TRACE("new position = %d\n", nPos);
```

Now the spaceship is off and flying, and we're controlling it entirely through the *pMot* pointer. Notice that *pMot* is not technically a pointer to a *CSpaceship* object, but in this case, a *CSpaceship* pointer and an *IMotion* pointer are the same because *CSpaceship* is derived from *IMotion*. You can see how the virtual functions work here: it's classic C++ polymorphism.

Let's make things a little more complex by adding a second interface, *IVisual*, that handles the spaceship's visual representation. One function is enough—*Display*. Here's the whole base class:

```
struct IVisual
{
    virtual void Display() = 0;
};
```

Are you getting the idea that COM wants you to associate functions in groups? (You're not imagining it.) But why? Well, in your space simulation, you probably want other kinds of objects in addition to spaceships. Imagine that the *IMotion* and *IVisual* interfaces are being used for other classes. Perhaps the *CSun* class has an implementation of *IVisual* but does not have an implementation of *IMotion*, and perhaps the *CSpaceStation* class has other interfaces as well. If you "published" your *IMotion* and *IVisual* interfaces, perhaps other space simulation software companies would adopt them. Or perhaps they wouldn't.

Think of an interface as a contract between two software modules. The idea is that interface declarations never change. If you want to upgrade your spaceship code, you don't change the *IMotion* or *the IVisual* interface; rather, you add a new interface, such as *ICrew*. The existing spaceship clients can continue to run with the old interfaces, and new client programs can use the new *ICrew* interface as well. These client programs can find out, at run time, which interfaces a particular spaceship software version supports.

Consider the *GetClassObject* function as a more powerful alternative to the C++ constructor. With the ordinary constructor, you obtain one object with one batch of member functions. With the *GetClassObject* function, you obtain the object plus your choice of interfaces. As you'll see later, you start with one interface, and then you use that interface to get other interfaces to the same object.

So how do you program <u>two</u> interfaces for *CSpaceship*? You could use C++ multiple inheritance, but that isn't the preferred way. With MFC, you would use "nested classes" instead. Not all C++ programmers are familiar with nested classes, so I'll offer a little help. Here's a first cut at nesting interfaces within the *CSpaceship* class:

```
class CSpaceship
{
protected:
    int m_nPosition;
public:
    CSpaceship() { m_nPosition = 0; }
```

```
class XMotion : public IMotion
{
private:
    int m_nAcceleration;
public:
    XMotion() { m_nAcceleration = 101; }
    virtual void Fly();
    virtual int& GetPosition();
} m_xMotion;

class XVisual : public IVisual
{
private:
    int m_nColor;
public:
    XVisual() { m_nColor = 102; }
    virtual void Display();
} m_xVisual;

friend class XVisual;
friend class XMotion;
};
```

NOTE: The MFC library provides a series of macros that make it easy to declare and implement nested classes that support interfaces. These macros, described in Technical Note #38 in the MFCNOTES.HLP file, generate code that is similar to the code above. In the MFC universe, the *CSpaceship* class declaration might look something like this:

```
BEGIN_INTERFACE_PART(CMotion, IMotion)
    STDMETHOD_(void, Fly) ();
    STDMETHOD_(int&, GetPosition) ();
END_INTERFACE_PART(CMotion)
BEGIN_INTERFACE_PART(CVisual, IVisual)
    STDMETHOD_(void, Display) ();
END_INTERFACE_PART(CVisual)

DECLARE_INTERFACE_MAP()
```

The *BEGIN_INTERFACE_PART* macro also generates prototypes for certain other functions, namely *QueryInterface, AddRef*, and *Release*, which are described later in this chapter. In the *CSpaceship* implementation file, you would use other macros in the manner shown at the top of the following page:

555

```
BEGIN_INTERFACE_MAP(CSpaceship, CCmdTarget)
    INTERFACE_PART(CSpaceship, IID_IMotion, Motion)
    INTERFACE_PART(CSpaceship, IID_IVisual, Visual)
END_INTERFACE_MAP()
```

Notice that the implementations of *IMotion* and *IVisual* are contained within the "parent" *CSpaceship* class. Be aware that *m_xMotion* and *m_xVisual* are really embedded data members of *CSpaceship*. Indeed, you could have implemented *CSpaceship* strictly with embedding. Nesting, however, brings two things to the party: First, nested class member functions can access parent class data members without the need for separate *CSpaceship** data members; second, the nested classes are neatly packaged along with the parent and are invisible outside the parent. Look at the code for the *GetPosition* member function:

```
int& CSpaceship::XMotion::GetPosition()
{
    METHOD_PROLOGUE(CSpaceship, Motion) // makes pThis
    return pThis->m_nPosition;
}
```

Notice also the double scope resolution operators that are necessary for nested class member functions. *METHOD_PROLOGUE* is an MFC macro that uses the C *offsetof* operator to generate a *this* pointer to the parent class, *pThis*. The compiler always knows the offset from the beginning of parent class data to the beginning of nested class data. *GetPosition* can thus access the *CSpaceship* data member *m_nPosition*.

Now, suppose you <u>have</u> two interface pointers, *pMot* and *pVis,* for a particular *CSpaceship* object. (Don't worry yet about how you got the pointers.) You can call interface member functions in the following manner:

```
pMot->Fly();
pVis->Display();
```

What's happening under the hood? In C++, each <u>class</u> (at least a class that has virtual functions and is not an abstract base class) has a virtual function table, aka vtbl. In this example, that means there are vtbls for *CSpaceship::XMotion* and *CSpaceship::XVisual*. For each <u>object</u>, there's a pointer to the object's data, the first element of which is a pointer to the class's vtbl. The pointer relationships are shown in the illustration at the top of the facing page:

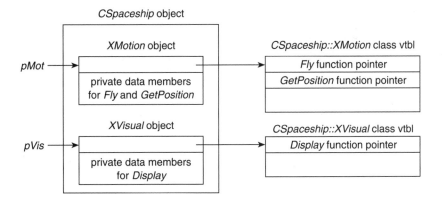

NOTE: Theoretically, it's possible to program OLE in C. If you look at the OLE header files, you'll see code such as this:

```
#ifdef __cplusplus
// C++-specific headers
#else
/* C-specific headers */
#endif
```

In C++, interfaces are declared as C++ *structs*, often with inheritance; in C, they're declared as C *typedef structs* with no inheritance. In C++, coding vtbls in your derived classes is easy; in C, you must "roll your own" vtbls, and that gets tedious. It's important to realize, however, that in neither language do the interface declarations have data members, constructors, or destructors. Therefore, you can't rely on the interface having a virtual destructor, but that's not a problem because you never invoke a destructor for an interface.

The *IUnknown* Interface and the *QueryInterface* Member Function

Let's get back to the problem of obtaining your interface pointers in the first place. OLE declares a very special interface named *IUnknown* for this purpose. As a matter of fact, all interfaces are derived from *IUnknown*, which has a member function, *QueryInterface*, that returns an interface pointer based on the interface ID you feed it. All this assumes that you have one interface pointer to start with, either an *IUnknown* pointer or a pointer to a derived interface such as *IMotion*. Let's enhance *CSpaceship* to add a public data

557

member of type *IUnknown**, which provides a back door for obtaining the first interface pointer. Here's the next iteration of our spaceship classes:

```
struct IUnknown
{
    virtual BOOL QueryInterface(const long& lRid, void** ppvObj) = 0;
};

struct IMotion : public IUnknown
{
    virtual void Fly() = 0;
    virtual int& GetPosition() = 0;
};

struct IVisual : public IUnknown
{
    virtual void Display() = 0;
};

class CSpaceship
{
public:
    IUnknown* m_pUnknown;
protected:
    int m_nPosition;
public:
    CSpaceship() {
        m_nPosition = 0;
        m_pUnknown = &m_xMotion;
    }

    class XMotion : public IMotion
    {
    private:
        int m_nAcceleration;
    public:
        XMotion() { m_nAcceleration = 101; }
        virtual void Fly();
        virtual int& GetPosition();
        virtual BOOL QueryInterface(const long& lRid, void** ppvObj);
    } m_xMotion;

    class XVisual : public IVisual
    {
    private:
        int m_nColor;
```

```
public:
    XVisual() { m_nColor = 102; }
    virtual void Display();
    virtual BOOL QueryInterface(const long& lRid,
                                    void** ppvObj);
} m_xVisual;

    friend class XVisual;
    friend class XMotion;
};
```

What do the vtbls look like now? For each derived class, the compiler builds a vtbl with the base class function pointers on top, as shown here:

CSpaceship::XMotion vtbl

QueryInterface function pointer
Fly function pointer
GetPosition function pointer

CSpaceship::XVisual vtbl

QueryInterface function pointer
Display function pointer

Notice that the *CSpaceship* constructor sets *m_pUnknown*. Now there's a way for *GetClassObject* to get the *IUnknown* pointer for a given *CSpaceship* object. Here's the code for the *XMotion QueryInterface* function:

```
BOOL CSpaceship::XMotion::QueryInterface(const long& lRid,
                                            void** ppvObj)
{
    switch (lRid) {
    case IID_IUnknown:
    case IID_IMotion:
        *ppvObj = &m_xMotion;
        break;
    case IID_IVisual:
        *ppvObj = &m_xVisual;
        break;
    default:
        *ppvObj = NULL;
        return FALSE;
    }
    return TRUE;
}
```

Because *IMotion* is derived from *IUnknown*, an *IMotion* pointer will be OK if the caller asks for an *IUnknown* pointer. At the top of the following page is a *GetClassObject* function that uses *m_pUnknown* to obtain the first interface pointer for the newly constructed *CSpaceship* object:

```
BOOL GetClassObject(const long& lClsid, const long& lRid,
                    void** ppvObj)
{
    ASSERT(lClsid == CLSID_CSpaceship);
    CSpaceship* pObj = new CSpaceship();
    IUnknown* pUnk = pObj->m_pUnknown;
    return pUnk->QueryInterface(lRid, ppvObj);
}
```

Now your client program can call *QueryInterface* to obtain an *IVisual* pointer:

```
IMotion* pMot;
IVisual* pVis;
GetClassObject(CLSID_CSpaceship, IID_IMotion, (void**) &pMot);
pMot->Fly();
pMot->QueryInterface(IID_IVisual, (void**) &pVis);
pVis->Display();
```

Notice that the client uses a *CSpaceship* object, but it <u>never</u> has an actual *CSpaceship* pointer. Thus the client cannot directly access *CSpaceship* data members, even if they're public.

> **NOTE:** In the MFC library, the INTERFACE macros shown in the note beginning on page 555 work together to build a table that *QueryInterface* uses to obtain the interface pointers. If a client requests an *IUnknown* pointer, MFC retrieves the first interface pointer in the table. Thus, MFC doesn't need an *m_pUnknown* pointer like the one we've put in the *CSpaceship* class.

OLE has its own graphic representation for interfaces and COM classes. Interfaces are shown as small circles (or jacks) with lines attached to their class. The *IUnknown* interface, which every COM class supports, is at the top, and the others are on the left. The *CSpaceship* class can be represented like this:

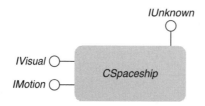

Reference Counting: The *AddRef* and *Release* Functions

COM interfaces don't have virtual destructors, so it isn't cool to write a statement such as this:

```
delete pMot;  // Don't do this.
```

OLE has a strict protocol for deleting objects, and the *IUnknown* virtual functions *AddRef* and *Release* are the key. Each COM class has a data member—*m_dwRef*, for example—that keeps count of how many "users" an object has. Each time the server program returns a new interface pointer (as in *QueryInterface*), the program calls *AddRef*, which increments *m_dwRef*. When the client program is finished with the pointer, it calls *Release*. When *m_dwRef* goes to 0, the object destroys itself. Here's an example of a *Release* function for the *CSpaceship::XMotion* class:

```
DWORD CSpaceship::XMotion::Release()
{
    METHOD_PROLOGUE(CSpaceship, Motion) // makes pThis
    if (pThis->m_dwRef == 0)
      return 0;
    if (--pThis->m_dwRef == 0L) {
      delete pThis; // the spaceship object
      return 0;
    }
    return pThis->m_dwRef;
}
```

In MFC OLE programs, the object's constructor sets *m_dwRef* to 1. This means it isn't necessary to call *AddRef* after the object is first constructed.

Class Factories

Object-oriented terminology gets a little fuzzy sometimes. Smalltalk programmers, for example, talk about "objects" the way that C++ programmers talk about "classes." The OLE reference documentation often uses the term "component object" when it really should use "component class." What OLE calls a "class factory" is really an "object factory." A class factory is a class that supports a special OLE interface named *IClassFactory*. This interface, like all interfaces, is derived from *IUnknown*. *IClassFactory*'s principal member function is *CreateInstance*, which is declared like this:

```
virtual BOOL CreateInstance(const long& lRid, void** ppvObj) = 0;
```

What does all this mean? It means that we screwed up when we let *GetClassObject* construct the *CSpaceship* object directly. We were supposed to construct a class factory object and then call *CreateInstance* to cause the class factory (object factory) to construct the actual spaceship object.

Why use a class factory? We've already seen that we can't call the target class constructor directly; we have to let the server decide how to construct objects. The server provides the class factory for this purpose and thus encapsulates the creation step, as it should. Locating and launching server modules, and thus establishing the class factory, is expensive, but constructing objects with *CreateInstance* is cheap. We can, therefore, allow a single class factory to create multiple objects.

Now let's do things the right way. First, we declare a new class, *CSpaceshipFactory*. To keep things simple, we'll derive the class from *IClassFactory* so that we don't have to deal with nested classes, and in addition, we'll add the code that tracks references:

```
struct IClassFactory : public IUnknown
{
    virtual BOOL CreateInstance(const long& lRid, void** ppvObj) = 0;
};

class CSpaceshipFactory : public IClassFactory
{
private:
    DWORD m_dwRef;
public:
    CSpaceshipFactory() {
      m_dwRef = 1;
      m_pObj = NULL;
    }
    // IUnknown functions
    virtual BOOL QueryInterface(const long& lRid,
                                void** ppvObj);
    virtual DWORD AddRef();
    virtual DWORD Release();
    // IClassFactory function
    virtual BOOL CreateInstance(const long& lRid,
                                void** ppvObj);
};
```

Next, we write the *CreateInstance* member function:

```
BOOL CSpaceshipFactory::CreateInstance(const long& lRid, void** ppvObj)
{
    CSpaceship* pObj = new CSpaceship();
    IUnknown* pUnk = pObj->m_pUnknown;
    return pUnk->QueryInterface(lRid, ppvObj);
}
```

Finally, here's the new *GetClassObject* function, which constructs a class factory object and returns an *IClassFactory* interface pointer:

```
BOOL GetClassObject(const long& lClsid, const long& lRid,
                    void** ppvObj)
{
    ASSERT(lClsid == CLSID_CSpaceship && lRid == IID_IClassFactory);
    CSpaceshipFactory* pObj = new CSpaceshipFactory();
    *ppObj = pObj;
}
```

The *CSpaceship* and *CSpaceshipFactory* classes work together and share the same class ID. Now the client code looks like this (without error checking logic):

```
IMotion* pMot;
IVisual* pVis;
IClassFactory* pFac;
GetClassObject(CLSID_CSpaceship, IID_IClassFactory, (void**) &pFac);
pFac->CreateInstance(IID_IMotion, &pMot);
pMot->QueryInterface(IID_IVisual, (void**) &pVis);
pMot->Fly();
pVis->Display();
```

Notice that the *CSpaceshipFactory* class implements the *AddRef* and *Release* functions. It must do this because *AddRef* and *Release* are pure virtual functions in the *IClassFactory* base class. We'll start using these functions in the next iteration of the program.

NOTE: The MFC library uses one class, aptly named *COleObject-Factory*, for all class factory objects. Each factory object contains a *CRuntimeClass* pointer for the target class so that *CreateInstance* can dynamically construct an object of that class.

COM and MFC—The *CCmdTarget* Class

The last batch of code was getting pretty close to the real thing, but we've got one more step to take. As you can guess, there's some code and data that can be "factored out" of our spaceship COM classes into a base class. That's exactly what MFC does, and the base class is *CCmdTarget*, the standard base class for document and window classes. *CCmdTarget*, in turn, is derived from *CObject*. We won't put too much in *CCmdTarget*—only the reference counting logic and the pointer to *IUnknown*. The *CCmdTarget* functions *InternalAddRef* and *InternalRelease* can be called in derived COM classes. Because we're using *CCmdTarget*, we'll bring *CSpaceshipFactory* in line with *CSpaceship*, and we'll use a nested class for the *IClassFactory* interface.

We can also do some factoring inside our *CSpaceship* class. The *QueryInterface* function can be "delegated" from the nested classes to the parent class helper function *InternalQueryInterface*, which calls *InternalAddRef*. Each *QueryInterface* function calls *AddRef*, but *CreateInstance* calls *InternalQueryInterface*, followed by a call to *InternalRelease*. Now, when the first interface pointer is returned by *CreateInstance*, the spaceship object has a reference count of 1. A subsequent *QueryInterface* call increments the count to 2, and in this case, the client must call *Release* twice to destroy the spaceship object.

One last thing—we'll make the class factory object a global object. That way we won't have to call its constructor. When the client calls *Release*, there is no problem because the class factory's reference count is 2 by the time the client receives it. (The *CSpaceshipFactory* constructor set the reference count to 1, and *QueryInterface*, called by *GetClassObject*, set the count to 2.)

> **NOTE:** The MFC macro *IMPLEMENT_OLECREATE* takes care of defining a global class factory object of the class *COleObject-Factory*.

A Working COM Example

Figures 25-1, 25-2, and 25-3 show code for a working "simulated OLE" program, EX25A. This is a QuickWin program that uses a class factory to construct an object of class *CSpaceship*, calls its interface functions, and then releases the spaceship. The SHIP.H header file, shown in Figure 25-1, contains all the class declarations that are used in the "client" and "server" programs. SHIP.CPP, shown in Figure 25-2 (beginning on page 569), is the client, which calls *GetClassObject*; and CLIENT.CPP, shown in Figure 25-3 (beginning on page 573), is the server, which implements *GetClassObject*. What's phony here is that both client and server code are linked within the same EX25A.EXE program. Thus OLE is not required to make the connection at run time. (You'll see how that's done later in this chapter.)

SHIP.H

```
# ship.h
#include <stddef.h> // for offsetof in METHOD_PROLOGUE

//----------Definitions and Macros------------------------------------
#define IID_IUnknown          0
#define IID_IClassFactory     1
#define IID_IMotion           2
#define IID_IVisual           3
#define CLSID_CSpaceship      10

// this macro for 16-bit Windows only
#define METHOD_PROLOGUE(theClass, localClass) \
 theClass* pThis = ((theClass*)((char*)(this) - \
 offsetof(theClass, m_x##localClass))); \

//----------Interface Declarations------------------------------------
struct IUnknown
{
    IUnknown() {
        printf("Entering IUnknown constructor %p\n", this);
    }
    virtual BOOL QueryInterface(const long& lRid,
                                void** ppvObj) = 0;
    virtual DWORD Release() = 0;
    virtual DWORD AddRef() = 0;
};

struct IClassFactory : public IUnknown
{
    IClassFactory() {
        printf("Entering IClassFactory constructor %p\n", this);
    }
    virtual BOOL CreateInstance(const long& lRid,
                                void** ppvObj) = 0;
};

struct IMotion : public IUnknown
{
    IMotion() {
        printf("Entering IMotion constructor %p\n", this);
    }
    virtual void Fly() = 0;  // pure
    virtual int& GetPosition() = 0;
};
```

Figure 25-1.   *(continued)*

The SHIP.H file.

Figure 25-1. *continued*

```
struct IVisual : public IUnknown
{
    IVisual() {
        printf("Entering IVisual constructor %p\n", this);
    }
    virtual void Display() = 0;
};

//----------Class Declarations----------------------------------------
class CSimulatedCmdTarget      // 'simulated' CSimulatedCmdTarget
{
public:
    IUnknown* m_pUnknown;       // not needed in real MFC
    DWORD     m_dwRef;

protected:
    CSimulatedCmdTarget() {
        printf("Entering CSimulatedCmdTarget constructor %p\n",
               this);
        m_dwRef = 1;            // implied first AddRef
    }
    virtual ~CSimulatedCmdTarget() {
        printf("Entering CSimulatedCmdTarget destructor %p\n",
               this);
    }
    DWORD InternalRelease() {
        printf("Entering CSimulatedCmdTarget::InternalRelease --\
 RefCount = %ld\n", m_dwRef);
        if (m_dwRef == 0)
          return 0;
        if (--m_dwRef == 0L) {
          printf("deleting\n");
          delete this;
          return 0;
        }
        return m_dwRef;
    }
    DWORD InternalAddRef() {
        return ++m_dwRef;
    }
};

class CSpaceship;
```

(continued)

Figure 25-1. *continued*

```
class CSpaceshipFactory : public CSimulatedCmdTarget
{
public:
    CSpaceshipFactory() {
        printf("Entering CSpaceshipFactory constructor %p\n",
                this);
        m_pUnknown = &m_xClassFactory;
     }
    ~CSpaceshipFactory() {
        printf("Entering CSpaceshipFactory destructor %p\n",
                this);
    }
    class XClassFactory : public IClassFactory
    {
    public:
        XClassFactory() {
            printf("Entering XClassFactory constructor %p\n",
                    this);
        }
        virtual BOOL QueryInterface(const long& lRid,
                                      void** ppvObj);
        virtual DWORD Release();
        virtual DWORD AddRef();
        virtual BOOL  CreateInstance(const long& lRid,
                                      void** ppvObj);
    } m_xClassFactory;
    friend class XClassFactory;
};


class CSpaceship : public CSimulatedCmdTarget
{
private:
    int m_nPosition; // We can access this from all the interfaces.
public:
    BOOL InternalQueryInterface(const long& lRid,
                                  void** ppvObj);
    CSpaceship() {
        printf("Entering CSpaceship constructor %p\n", this);
        m_nPosition = 100;
        m_pUnknown = &m_xMotion;
    }
    ~CSpaceship() {
        printf("Entering CSpaceship destructor %p\n", this);
    }
```

(continued)

Figure 25-1. *continued*

```
class XMotion : public IMotion
{
private:
    int m_nAcceleration;
public:
    XMotion() {
        printf("Entering XMotion constructor %p\n", this);
        m_nAcceleration = 101;
    }
    virtual BOOL QueryInterface(const long& lRid,
                               void** ppvObj);
    virtual DWORD Release();
    virtual DWORD AddRef();
    virtual void  Fly();
    virtual int&  GetPosition();
} m_xMotion;

class XVisual : public IVisual
{
private:
    int m_nColor;
public:
    XVisual() {
        printf("Entering XVisual constructor\n");
        m_nColor = 102;
    }
    virtual BOOL QueryInterface(const long& lRid,
                               void** ppvObj);
    virtual DWORD Release();
    virtual DWORD AddRef();
    virtual void Display();
} m_xVisual;

    friend class XVisual;  // These must be at the bottom!
    friend class XMotion;
    friend class CSpaceshipFactory::XClassFactory;
};

BOOL GetClassObject(const long& lClsid, const long& lRid,
                    void** ppvObj);
```

SHIP.CPP

```
// ship.cpp  pseudo-OLE QuickWin application
#include <afx.h>
#include "ship.h"

CSpaceshipFactory NEAR factory;

//---------Member Functions---------------------------------------
BOOL CSpaceshipFactory::XClassFactory::QueryInterface(
                    const long& lRid, void** ppvObj)
{
    printf("Entering CSpaceshipFactory::XClassFactory::\
 QueryInterface -- lRid = %d\n", lRid);
    METHOD_PROLOGUE(CSpaceshipFactory,
                    ClassFactory) // makes pThis
    if (lRid == IID_IUnknown || lRid == IID_IClassFactory) {
      *ppvObj = this;
      pThis->InternalAddRef ();    // Client can't release
                                   //  the factory object.
      return TRUE;
    }
    return FALSE;
}


BOOL CSpaceshipFactory::XClassFactory::CreateInstance(
                    const long& lRid, void** ppvObj)
{
    printf("Entering CSpaceshipFactory::XClassFactory::\
 CreateInstance\n");
    METHOD_PROLOGUE(CSpaceshipFactory,
                    ClassFactory) // makes pThis
    ASSERT(lRid == IID_IUnknown);
    CSpaceship* pObj = new CSpaceship();
    if pObj->InternalQueryInterface(lRid, ppvObj)) {
      pObj->InternalRelease(); // balance reference count
      return TRUE;
    }
    return FALSE;
}

DWORD CSpaceshipFactory::XClassFactory::Release()
{
    printf("Entering CSpaceshipFactory::XClassFactory::Release\n");
```

Figure 25-2.
The SHIP.CPP file.

(continued)

569

Figure 25-2. *continued*

```
    METHOD_PROLOGUE(CSpaceshipFactory,
                    ClassFactory) // makes pThis
    return pThis->InternalRelease();
    // delegate to CSimulatedCmdTarget
}

DWORD CSpaceshipFactory::XClassFactory::AddRef ()
{
    printf("Entering CSpaceshipFactory::XClassFactory::AddRef\n");
    METHOD_PROLOGUE(CSpaceshipFactory,
                    ClassFactory) // makes pThis
    return pThis->InternalAddRef ();
    // delegate to CSimulatedCmdTarget
}

BOOL CSpaceship::InternalQueryInterface(const long& lRid,
                                        void** ppvObj)
{
    printf("Entering CSpaceship::InternalQueryInterface --\
lRid = %d\n", lRid);
    switch (lRid) {
    case IID_IUnknown:
    case IID_IMotion:
        *ppvObj = &m_xMotion;       // Both IMotion and IVisual are
                                    // derived from IUnknown, so
                                    // either pointer will do.

        break;
    case IID_IVisual:
        *ppvObj = &m_xVisual;
        break;
    default:
        *ppvObj = NULL;
        return FALSE;
    }
    InternalAddRef ();
    return TRUE;
}

BOOL CSpaceship::XMotion::QueryInterface(const long& lRid,
                                         void** ppvObj)
{
    printf("Entering CSpaceship::XMotion::QueryInterface --\
lRid = %d\n", lRid);
    METHOD_PROLOGUE(CSpaceship,
                    Motion)         // makes pThis
```

(continued)

Figure 25-2. *continued*

```
    return pThis->InternalQueryInterface(lRid, ppvObj);
    // delegate to CSpaceship
}

DWORD CSpaceship::XMotion::Release()
{
    printf("Entering CSpaceship::XMotion::Release\n");
    METHOD_PROLOGUE(CSpaceship,
                    Motion)          // makes pThis
    return pThis->InternalRelease();
    // delegate to CSimulatedCmdTarget
}

DWORD CSpaceship::XMotion::AddRef ()
{
    printf("Entering CSpaceship::XMotion::AddRef\n");
    METHOD_PROLOGUE(CSpaceship,
                    Motion)          // makes pThis
    return pThis->InternalAddRef ();
    // delegate to CSimulatedCmdTarget
}

void CSpaceship::XMotion::Fly()
{
    printf("Entering CSpaceship::XMotion::Fly\n");
    METHOD_PROLOGUE(CSpaceship,
                    Motion)          // makes pThis
    printf("this = %p, pThis = %p\n", this, pThis);
    printf("m_nPosition = %d\n", pThis->m_nPosition);
    printf("m_nAcceleration = %d\n", m_nAcceleration);
}

int& CSpaceship::XMotion::GetPosition()
{
    printf("Entering CSpaceship::XMotion::GetPosition\n");
    METHOD_PROLOGUE(CSpaceship,
                    Motion)          // makes pThis
    printf("this = %p, pThis = %p\n", this, pThis);
    printf("m_nPosition = %d\n", pThis->m_nPosition);
    printf("m_nAcceleration = %d\n", m_nAcceleration);
    return pThis->m_nPosition;
}

BOOL CSpaceship::XVisual::QueryInterface(const long& lRid,
                                         void** ppvObj)
```

(continued)

Figure 25-2. *continued*

```
{
    printf("Entering CSpaceship::XVisual::QueryInterface --\
lRid = %d\n", lRid);
    METHOD_PROLOGUE(CSpaceship,
                    Visual)        // makes pThis
    return pThis->InternalQueryInterface(lRid, ppvObj);
    // delegate to CSpaceship
}

DWORD CSpaceship::XVisual::Release()
{
    printf("Entering CSpaceship::XVisual::Release\n");
    METHOD_PROLOGUE(CSpaceship,
                    Visual)        // makes pThis
    return pThis->InternalRelease();
    // delegate to CSimulatedCmdTarget
}

DWORD CSpaceship::XVisual::AddRef ()
{
    printf("Entering CSpaceship::XVisual::AddRef\n");
    METHOD_PROLOGUE(CSpaceship,
                    Visual)        // makes pThis
    return pThis->InternalAddRef ();
    // delegate to CSimulatedCmdTarget
}

void CSpaceship::XVisual::Display()
{
    printf("Entering CSpaceship::XVisual::Display\n");
    METHOD_PROLOGUE(CSpaceship,
                    Visual)        // makes pThis
    printf("this = %p, pThis = %p\n", this, pThis);
    printf("m_nPosition = %d\n", pThis->m_nPosition);
    printf("m_nColor = %d\n", m_nColor);
}

//----------simulates OLE server ----------------------------
// In real OLE, this would be DllGetClassObject, which would
// be called whenever a client called CoGetClassObject.

BOOL GetClassObject(const long& lClsid, const long& lRid,
                    void** ppvObj)
{
    ASSERT(lClsid == CLSID_CSpaceship &&
```

(continued)

Figure 25-2. *continued*

```
            lRid == IID_IClassFactory);
    return factory.m_pUnknown->QueryInterface(IID_IClassFactory,
                                              ppvObj);
}
```

CLIENT.CPP

```
// client.cpp  pseudo-OLE QuickWin application
#include <afx.h>
#include "ship.h"

//----------Main Program----------------------------------------------
int main() // simulates OLE client program
{
    printf("Entering client main\n");
    IUnknown*       pUnk;  // If you declare these void*,
                           //  you lose type-safety.
    IMotion*        pMot;
    IVisual*        pVis;
    IClassFactory*  pClf;

    GetClassObject(CLSID_CSpaceship, IID_IClassFactory,
                   (void**) &pClf);

    pClf->CreateInstance(IID_IUnknown, (void**) &pUnk);
    pUnk->QueryInterface(IID_IMotion,  (void**) &pMot);
    pMot->QueryInterface(IID_IVisual,  (void**) &pVis);
    // All three pointers should work.
    printf("main: pUnk = %p, pMot = %p, pDis = %p\n",
           pUnk, pMot, pVis);

    // Test all the interface virtual functions.
    pMot->Fly();
    int nPos = pMot->GetPosition();
    pVis->Display();

    pClf->Release();

    pUnk->Release();
    pMot->Release();
    pVis->Release();
    return 0;
}
```

Figure 25-3.
The CLIENT.CPP file.

573

NOTE: You can ignore the warning Visual C++ gives when you build EX25A.

OLE and the Windows Registration Database

In the EX25A example, the server was statically linked to the client, a clearly bogus circumstance. In real OLE, the server is either a DLL or a separate EXE. When the client calls the real OLE equivalent of *GetClassObject*, OLE steps in and finds the correct server, which might already be in memory or might be on disk. How does OLE make the connection? It looks up the class's unique 128-bit class ID number in the Windows registration database, the file REG.DAT in the \WINDOWS directory. Thus, the <u>class</u> must be registered permanently on your computer.

If you run the Windows REGEDIT program with the */v* parameter, you will see a screen similar to the one shown in Figure 25-4. This figure shows three class IDs, two that are associated with EXEs and one that is associated with a DLL. Now we'll switch over to the "real" OLE function, *CoGetClassObject*. (*Co* stands for "common object.") It has the same parameters as the tutorial *GetClassObject*, but instead of calling the server directly, it looks up the class ID in the registration database and then figures out what to do.

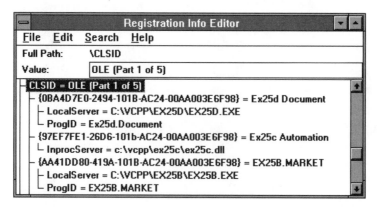

Figure 25-4.
Three class IDs in the registration database.

What if you don't want to track those ugly class ID numbers in your client program? No problem. OLE supports another type of registration database entry, which translates a human-readable class <u>name</u> into the corresponding class ID. Figure 25-5 shows the REG.DAT entries. The OLE function *CLSIDFromProgID* reads the database and performs the translation.

```
┌─────────────────────────────────────────────────────┐
│ ─          Registration Info Editor          ▼ ▲    │
├─────────────────────────────────────────────────────┤
│ File  Edit  Search  Help                            │
├─────────────────────────────────────────────────────┤
│ Full Path:    \Ex25d.Document                       │
├─────────────────────────────────────────────────────┤
│ Value:        Ex25d Document                        │
├─────────────────────────────────────────────────────┤
│ \                                              ▲    │
│  ┌───────────────────────────────────────────┐      │
│  │ Ex25d.Document = Ex25d Document           │      │
│  └ CLSID = {0BA4D7E0-2494-101B-AC24-00AA003E6F98}   │
│  ─ Ex25c.auto = Ex25c Automation                    │
│    └ CLSID = {97EF7FE1-26D6-101b-AC24-00AA003E6F98} │
│  ─ EX25B.MARKET = EX25B.MARKET                      │
│    └ CLSID = {AA41DD80-419A-101B-AC24-00AA003E6F98} ▼│
└─────────────────────────────────────────────────────┘
```

Figure 25-5.
Three "human-readable" class names in the registration database.

As you'll see later in this chapter, when you get to OLE Automation, MFC provides some easy-to-call functions that do the work of the OLE functions *CLSIDFromProgID* and *CoGetClassObject*.

How does the registration information get into REG.DAT? In two ways. First, REGEDIT has an ASCII file import facility that accepts data in a REG file such as this one:

```
REGEDIT
HKEY_CLASSES_ROOT\Ex25b.Document = Ex25b Document
HKEY_CLASSES_ROOT\Ex25b.Document\CLSID =
 {0BA4D7E0-2494-101B-AC24-00AA003E6F98}
HKEY_CLASSES_ROOT\CLSID\{0BA4D7E0-2494-101B-AC24-00AA003E6F98} =
 Ex25b Document
HKEY_CLASSES_ROOT\CLSID\{0BA4D7E0-2494-101B-AC24-00AA003E6F98}\LocalServer
 = C:\OLE2\EX25B\EX25B.EXE
HKEY_CLASSES_ROOT\CLSID\{0BA4D7E0-2494-101B-AC24-00AA003E6F98}\ProgID =
 Ex25b.Document
```

Notice that REG.DAT is organized as a hierarchical database with a root node and branches. REGEDIT can load a REG file in batch mode, or you can load such a file through the REGEDIT File menu.

Second, instead of using REGEDIT, you can program your client application to call OLE functions that update REG.DAT directly. MFC conveniently wraps these functions with the function *COleObjectFactory::UpdateRegistryAll*, which finds all your program's global class factory objects and registers their names and class IDs.

Run-Time Object Registration

You've just seen how the REG.DAT file registers OLE classes. Class factory <u>objects</u> also must be registered, and it's a shame that the same word, "register," is used in both contexts. Objects are registered at run time, and the registration information is maintained in memory by the OLE DLLs. MFC provides the *COleObjectFactory* member functions *Register* and *RegisterAll* for this purpose. (You'll see how these are used later.)

How a COM Client Calls a DLL Server

We're beginning with a DLL server instead of an EXE server because the program interactions are simpler. I'll show pseudo-code here because you're going to be using the MFC library classes, which hide much of the detail. If you want to see actual COM code, refer to Chapter 4 of *Inside OLE 2* by Kraig Brockschmidt (Microsoft Press).

Different levels of indentation show code for the client, COM, and the DLL server.

```
Client          COM            DLL Server

CLSID lClsid;
IClassFactory* pClf;
IUnknown* pUnk;
CoInitialize(NULL); // initialize COM
CLSIDFromProgID("servername", &lClsid);
                COM uses REG.DAT to look up the class ID from "servername"
CoGetClassObject(lClsid, IID_IClassFactory, (void**) &pClf );
                COM uses the class ID to look for a server in memory
                if (server DLL is not loaded already) {
                   COM gets DLL filename from REG.DAT
                   Loads the server DLL into memory
                }
                                if (server just loaded) {
                                   Global factory objects are constructed
                                   InitInstance called (MFC only)
                                }
                COM calls DLL's global exported DllGetClassObject
                                DllGetClassObject returns IClassFactory*
                COM returns IClassFactory* to client
pClf->CreateInstance(IID_IUnknown, (void**) &pUnk);
                                class factory's CreateInstance function called
                                (called directly—through the server's vtbl)
                                constructs object of "servername" class
                                returns requested interface pointer
pClf->Release();
pUnk->Release();

                                "servername" Release is called through vtbl
                                if (refcount == 0) {
                                   object destroys itself
                                }
```

CoFreeUnusedLibraries();
        COM calls DLL's global exported DllCanUnloadNow
            DllCanUnloadNow called
              if (all DLL's objects destroyed) {
                Exit DLL
              }
COMUninitialize(); // just prior to exit
        COM releases resources
client exits
              Windows unloads the DLL if it is still loaded and
              no other programs are using it

Some important points are worth noting. First, the DLL's exported *DllGetClassObject* function is called in response to the client's *CoGetClassObject* call. Second, the class factory interface address returned is the actual physical address of the class factory vtbl pointer in the DLL. And third, when the client calls *CreateInstance*, or <u>any</u> <u>other</u> <u>interface</u> <u>function</u>, the call is direct (through the server's vtbl).

The COM linkage between a client EXE and a server DLL is quite efficient. It's just as efficient as the linkage to any C++ virtual function in a large-model application, plus there's full C++ parameter and return type checking at compile time. The only penalty for using ordinary DLL linkage is the extra step of looking up the class ID in REG.DAT when the DLL is first loaded.

> **NOTE:** The MFC library version 2.5 contains the exported functions *DllGetClassObject* and *DllCanUnloadNow*. If you're using MFC, you don't have to write these functions in your COM server DLL. All you do is include the function names in your server project's DEF file.

How a COM Client Calls an EXE Server

The COM linkage to a separate EXE file is more complicated than the linkage to a DLL server. The EXE server is in a different operating system process, and a 16-bit/32-bit mismatch is possible. In the future, the server might be on a different computer, in which case the client wouldn't be able to directly access any interfaces in the server. Don't worry, though. Write your programs as though a direct connection exists. COM takes care of the details through a process called "marshaling."

With marshaling, Windows messages are invisibly exchanged, and data is transferred through shared memory blocks. Someone, however, has to write the marshaling code for each interface. If you use standard interfaces such as *IUnknown* and *IClassFactory*, the marshaling code is provided by COM. If you invent your own interfaces, such as *IMotion* and *IVisual*, you're stuck with the tedious job of writing the marshaling code. That's why few software firms develop their own interfaces but rather rely on existing COM interfaces, such as *IDispatch* (which you'll see later).

Here's the pseudo-code interaction between an EXE client and an EXE server. Compare it to the DLL version on pages 576 and 577. Notice that the client side calls are exactly the same.

```
Client              COM              EXE Server
CLSID lClsid;
IClassFactory* pClf;
IUnknown* pUnk;
CoInitialize(NULL); // initialize COM
CLSIDFromProgID("servername", &lClsid);
          COM uses REG.DAT to look up the class ID from "servername"
CoGetClassObject(lClsid, IID_IClassFactory, (void**) &pClf );
          COM uses the class ID to look for a server in memory
          if (server EXE is not loaded already, or if we need another instance) {
            COM gets EXE filename from REG.DAT
            Loads the server EXE into memory
          }
                        if (just loaded) {
                          Global factory objects are constructed
                          InitInstance called (MFC only)
                           CoInitialize(NULL);
                           for each factory object {
                             CoRegisterClassObject(...);
                              returns IClassFactory* to COM
                           }
                        }
          COM returns the requested interface pointer to the client
             (client's pointer is a "proxy" for server's interface pointer)
pClf->CreateInstance(IID_IUnknown, (void**) &pUnk);
                        class factory's CreateInstance function called
                        (called indirectly through marshaling)
                        constructs object of "servername" class
                        returns requested interface pointer indirectly
pClf->Release();
pUnk->Release();

                        "servername" Release is called indirectly
                        if (refcount == 0) {
                         object destroys itself
                        }
                        if (all objects released) {
                         server exits gracefully
                        }
```

CoUninitialize(); // just prior to exit
             COM calls Release for any objects this client has failed to release
                          server exits if this causes all objects to be released
             COM releases resources
client exits

As you can see, COM plays an important role in the communication between the client and the server. COM keeps a global list of class factory objects that contains the name of the EXE or DLL in which they're located. COM does not, however, keep track of individual COM objects such as the *CSpaceship* object. Those objects are responsible for destroying themselves through the *AddRef/Release* mechanism. COM does step in when a client exits. If that client is using an EXE server, COM "listens in" on the communication and keeps track of the reference count on each object. COM disconnects from server objects when the client exits, and, under certain circumstances, this causes those objects to be released. Don't depend on this behavior, however. Make sure that your client program releases all its interface pointers prior to exit.

MFC and OLE

We've been talking about the lowest level of OLE up to this point—COM. MFC provides some COM support, including

- Macros for nesting interface implementations

- *IUnknown* support in *CCmdTarget*

- The *COleObjectFactory* class

- Special versions of OLE initialization and uninitialization functions

- Library-based DLL export functions

If you wrote general-purpose COM client and server programs, however, you'd write them pretty much as you see them written in the pseudo-code shown in the previous two sections.

When you start using the other OLE features, such as compound documents, in-place editing, and drag-and-drop, MFC will do a lot more for you. Beginning on page 580, the rest of the chapter shows how MFC helps you write OLE Automation clients and servers.

579

Containment vs. Inheritance

In normal C++ programming, you frequently use inheritance to factor common behavior into a reusable base class. The *CPersistentFrame* class (discussed in Chapter 14) and the *Orbiter* base class (discussed in Appendix A) are examples of reusability through inheritance.

COM uses "containment" instead of inheritance. If the planetary-motion simulation example from Appendix A were to be translated to OLE, there would be "outer" *Spaceship* and *Planet* classes plus an "inner" *Orbiter* class. The outer classes would implement the *IVisual* interface directly, but those outer classes would "delegate" their *IMotion* interfaces to the inner class. The result would look something like this:

An alternative to containment is "aggregation," in which, in this example, the orbiter's *IMotion* interface pointer would be exposed directly to the client. Aggregation is more complex because the outer class's *IUnknown* interface needs to be connected with the inner class's. See Brockschmidt's *Inside OLE 2* for a detailed discussion of aggregation, and see Technical Note #38 in the MFCNOTES.HLP file for a description of MFC aggregation support.

OLE Automation

After reading the first part of this chapter, you know what an interface is, and you've already seen two standard OLE interfaces, *IUnknown* and *IClassFactory*. Now you're ready for "applied" OLE, or at least one aspect of it, OLE Automation. Later in this chapter, you'll learn how to use the *IDispatch* interface for communication between C++ programs and Visual Basic for Applications programs.

Connecting C++ with Visual Basic for Applications (VBA)

Not all programmers for Windows are going to be C++ programmers, especially if they have to learn the intricacies of OLE. There's talk of a programming "division of labor," in which C++ programmers will produce reusable modules and VBA programmers will consume those modules by integrating them into applications. You can prepare for this eventuality now by learning how to make your software "VBA-friendly." OLE Automation is one tool that's available now and supported by MFC. Another tool, the OLE Control, is on the way. OLE Controls use the *IDispatch* interface, so you can apply what you learn here to this upcoming technology.

Two factors are working on behalf of OLE Automation's success. First, Visual Basic for Applications (VBA) is now the programming standard in most Microsoft applications, including Word, Excel, and Access, not to mention Visual Basic itself. All these applications support OLE Automation, which means they can be linked to other OLE Automation–compatible components, including those written in C++ and VBA. For example, you can write a C++ program that uses the text processing capability of Word, or you can write a C++ matrix inversion program that can be called from a VBA macro in an Excel worksheet.

Second, dozens of software companies are providing OLE Automation interfaces for their applications, mostly for the benefit of VBA programmers. With a little extra effort you can use these interfaces from C++. You can, for example, write an MFC program that controls Shapeware's Visio drawing program.

OLE Automation isn't just for C++ and VBA. Software-tools companies are already announcing OLE-compatible Basic-like languages that you can license for your own programmable applications. There's even a version of Smalltalk that supports OLE Automation!

Automation Controllers and Automation Servers

A clearly defined master–slave relationship is always present in an OLE Automation communication dialog. The master is the automation controller (or client), and the slave is the automation server. The controller initiates the interaction by constructing a server object (it might have to load the server program) or by attaching to an existing object in a server program that is already running. The controller then calls interface functions in the server and releases those interfaces when it's finished. Here are some interaction scenarios:

- A C++ automation controller uses a Microsoft or third-party application as a server. The interaction could trigger the execution of VBA code in the server.

581

- A C++ automation server is used from inside a Microsoft application (or a Visual Basic application), which acts as the automation controller. Thus, VBA code can construct and use C++ objects.

- A C++ automation server is used by a C++ automation controller.

- A Visual Basic program can use an Automation-aware application such as Excel. In this case, VB is the controller, and Excel is the server.

Microsoft Excel—A Better Visual Basic Than Visual Basic

Some of the examples in this chapter depend on VBA. Microsoft Visual Basic serves well as an automation controller, but you can't use VB as an automation server. Microsoft Excel, on the other hand, works as either a controller or a server. You can, therefore, adapt the Excel controller examples to work with VB, but you need Excel if you want to see how OLE Automation applications can be controlled from a C++ program.

I strongly recommend, however, that you get a copy of Excel 5.0 (or later), but not just because it runs as both an automation controller and a server. This product contains a version of VBA that's more up-to-date than the version in Visual Basic 3.0. What's really interesting is that the old Lotus-style macro system has been superseded by VBA. (Old macros are still supported, of course.) You don't have to wedge code inside worksheet cells anymore. Instead, you write VBA code that accesses worksheet cells in an object-oriented manner. It's easy to add visual programming elements such as pushbuttons.

This chapter isn't meant to be an Excel tutorial, but I have included a simple Excel workbook. (A workbook is a file that can contain multiple worksheets plus separate VBA code.) This workbook demonstrates a VBA macro that executes from a pushbutton. You can use Excel to load EX25A.XLS from the \VCPP\EX25A subdirectory, or you can key in the example from scratch. Figure 25-6 shows the actual spreadsheet with the button and sample data. You highlight cell A4 and click the Process Col button. A VBA program iterates down the column and draws a hatched pattern on cells that have numeric values greater than 10. Figure 25-7 shows the macro code itself, which is stored in a separate section of the workbook, which I've named Macros.

Figure 25-6.
An Excel spreadsheet that uses VBA code.

Figure 25-7.
The VBA code for the Excel spreadsheet.

If you want to create the example yourself, follow these steps:

1. Start Excel with a new workbook, choose Macro from the Insert menu, and choose Module.

2. Type in the macro code shown in Figure 25-7.

3. Double-click the word Module1 at the bottom of the screen, and change the name to *Macros*.

4. Click the Sheet1 tab, and choose Toolbars from the View menu. Check the Forms check box to display the Forms toolbar. Click OK.

5. Click the Create Button control, and drag in the upper left corner of the worksheet to create a pushbutton. Assign the button to the *ProcessColumn* macro.

6. Size the pushbutton, and type the caption shown in Figure 25-6.

7. Type some numbers in the column starting at cell A4; then select A4, and click the button to test the program.

Pretty easy, isn't it?

Let's look at one Excel VBA statement from the macro above and analyze it:

```
Selection.Offset(1, 0).Range("A1").Select
```

The first element, Selection, is a "property" of an implied "object," the Excel Application. The Selection property in this case is assumed to be a *Range* object that represents a rectangular array of cells. The second element, *Offset*, is a "method" of the *Range* object that returns another *Range* object based on the two parameters. In this case, the returned *Range* object is the one-cell range that begins one row down from the original range. The third element, *Range*, is a method of the *Range* object that returns yet another range. This time it's the upper left cell in the second range. Finally, the *Select* method causes Excel to highlight the selected cell and makes it the new Selection property of the Application.

As the program iterates through the loop, the statement above moves the selected cell down the worksheet one row at a time. This style of programming takes some getting used to, but you can't afford to ignore it. The real value here is that you now have all the capabilities of the Excel spreadsheet and graphics engine available to you in a seamless programming environment.

Properties, Methods, and Collections

The distinction between a property and a method is somewhat artificial. Basically, a property is a value that can be both set and retrieved. You can, for example, set and get the Selection property for an Excel Application. Another example is Excel's Width property, which applies to many object types. Some Excel properties are read-only; most are read-write. Properties don't officially have parameters, but some properties are "indexed." The property index acts a lot like a parameter. It doesn't have to be an integer, and there can be more than one element in the index (row and column, for example). You won't find indexed properties in Excel, but Excel VBA can handle indexed properties in OLE Automation servers.

Methods are more flexible than properties. They can have zero or many parameters, they can either set or retrieve object data, or they can perform some action, such as showing a window. Excel's *Select* method is an example of an action method. The *Offset* method returns an object based on two parameters.

Excel supports collection objects. An example is the Worksheets object, which is returned by the *Worksheets* method of the Workbook object. The *Worksheets* method has an *index* parameter that specifies the individual Worksheets object you want. What's the difference between a collection and an indexed property? With an indexed property, the controller can't delete or insert elements; with a collection, it can.

The Problem That OLE Automation Solves

You've already learned that an OLE interface is the ideal way for Windows programs to communicate with one another, but you've learned that it's mostly impractical to design your own OLE interfaces. OLE Automation provides a general-purpose interface, *IDispatch*, that serves the needs of both C++ and VBA programmers. As you might guess from your glimpse of Excel VBA, this interface involves objects, methods, and properties.

You can write OLE interfaces that have functions with any parameter types and return values you specify. *IMotion* and *IVisual* are examples. If you're going to let VBA programmers in, however, you can't be fast and loose anymore. You can solve the communication problem with one interface that has only a single member function that's smart enough to accommodate methods and properties as defined by VBA. Needless to say, *IDispatch* has such a function, and it's named *Invoke*. You use *IDispatch::Invoke* for COM objects that can be constructed and used in either C++ or VBA programs.

Now you're beginning to see what OLE Automation does. It funnels all intermodule communication through the *IDispatch::Invoke* function. How does a controller first connect to its server? Because *IDispatch* is merely another OLE interface, all the registration logic supported by COM comes into play. Automation servers can be DLLs or EXEs, and they can be accessed over a network as soon as OLE supports that feature.

The *IDispatch* Interface

IDispatch is the heart of OLE Automation. It's fully supported by OLE marshaling, as are *IUnknown* and *IClassFactory*, and it's very well supported by the MFC library. At the server end, you need a COM class with an *IDispatch* interface (plus the prerequisite class factory, of course). At the controller end, you use standard OLE techniques to obtain an *IDispatch* pointer. (As you'll see, MFC and the Wizards take care of a lot of these details for you.)

Remember that *Invoke* is the principal member function of *IDispatch*. If you looked up *IDispatch::Invoke* in OLESDKV2.HLP, you'd see a really ugly set of parameters. Don't worry about those now. MFC steps in on both sides of the *Invoke* call, using a data-driven scheme to call server functions based on dispatch map parameters you define with macros.

Invoke isn't the only *IDispatch* member function. Another function your controller might call is *GetIDsOfNames*. From the VBA programmer's point of view, properties and methods have ASCII names, but C++ programmers prefer more efficient integer indexes. *Invoke* uses integers to specify properties and methods, so *GetIDsOfNames* is useful at the start of a program to convert each name to a number if you don't know the index numbers at compile time. You've already seen that *IDispatch* supports ASCII names for methods. In addition, the interface supports ASCII names for a method's parameters. The *GetIDsOfNames* function returns those parameter names along with the method name. Unfortunately, the MFC *IDispatch* implementation doesn't support named parameters.

OLE Automation Programming

Suppose you're writing an automation server in C++. You've got some choices to make. Do you want a DLL server or an EXE server? What kind of user interface do you want? Does the server need a user interface at all? Can users run your server EXE as a stand-alone application? If the server is an EXE, will it be SDI or MDI? Can the user shut down the server directly?

If your server is a DLL, OLE linkage will be more efficient than with an EXE server because no marshaling is required. With a DLL, however, your user interface options are limited. A modal dialog is about your only option—no frame window. Be aware that DLL automation servers can connect quite happily to VBA controllers. As with any DLL, only one copy of the DLL is in memory, and that DLL can support multiple OLE Automation server objects controlled by one or many automation controller programs.

With an EXE server, you must be careful to distinguish between a server program and a server object. When a controller calls *IClassFactory::Create-Instance* to construct a server object, the server's class factory constructs the object, but OLE might or might not need to start the server program. Here are some scenarios:

- The server class is programmed to require a new instance of the program for each object constructed. Assuming the server program is able to run in multi-instance mode, OLE will start a new instance in response to the second and following *CreateInstance* calls, each of which returns an *IDispatch* pointer.

- A special case of the scenario above, specific to MFC applications: The server class is an MFC document class in an SDI application. Each time a controller calls *CreateInstance*, a new instance of the server application starts, complete with a document object, a view object, and an SDI main frame window.

- The server class is programmed to allow multiple objects in a single program instance. Each time a controller calls *CreateInstance*, a new server object is constructed. There is only one instance of the server program, however.

- A special case of the scenario above, specific to MFC applications: The server class is an MFC document class in an MDI application. There is a single instance of the server application with one MDI main frame window. Each time a controller calls *CreateInstance*, a new document object is constructed, along with a view object and an MDI child frame window.

There's one more interesting case. Suppose a server EXE is running before the controller needs it. Then the controller decides to access a server object that already exists. You'll see this case with Excel. The user might have Excel already on the desktop, and the controller needs access to Excel's one and only Application object. Here the controller calls the OLE function *GetActiveObject*, which provides an interface pointer for an existing server object. If the call fails, the controller can create the object with *CoCreateInstance*.

For server object deletion, the normal COM rules apply. Automation objects have reference counts, and they delete themselves when the controller calls *Release* and the reference count goes to 0. In an MDI server, if the automation object is an MFC document, its destruction causes the corresponding MDI child window to close. In an SDI server, the destruction of the document object causes the server to exit. The controller is responsible for calling *Release* for each *IDispatch* interface before exit. For EXE servers, OLE will intervene if the controller exits without releasing an interface, thus allowing the server to exit. You can't always depend on this intervention, however, so make sure your controller cleans up its interfaces!

With generic OLE, a client application often obtains multiple interface pointers for a single server object. Look back at the spaceship example, in which the simulated OLE server class had both an *IMotion* pointer and an *IVisual* pointer. With OLE Automation, however, there's usually only a single (*IDispatch*) pointer per object. As in all OLE programming, you must be careful to release all your interface pointers. In Excel, for example, many methods return an *IDispatch* pointer to new or existing objects. If you fail to release a pointer, the Debug version of MFC alerts you with a memory leak dump when the controller program exits.

The MFC *IDispatch* Implementation

If you read the *OLE 2 Programmer's Reference, Volume 2,* you'll notice that OLE provides an implementation for the *IDispatch* interface, which you can activate by calling the function *CreateStandardDispatch*. This built-in implementation uses an OLE Automation feature called a "type library." A type library is a table, optionally bound into the server's resources, that allows a controller to query the server for the ASCII names of objects, methods, and properties. A controller could, for example, contain a browser that allows the user to explore the server's capabilities.

The OLE type library is not directly supported by MFC. MFC implements its own version of *IDispatch* that is driven by a dispatch map rather than by a type library. MFC programs don't call *CreateStandardDispatch* at all. Consequently, it isn't possible to write browsers for automation servers that were written with MFC (unless you make the extra effort to create your own type library and use the *ITypeLib* interface).

An MFC OLE Automation Server

Let's look at what happens in an MFC automation server, in this case a simplified version of the EX25D alarm clock program that is discussed later in this chapter. In MFC, the *IDispatch* implementation is part of the *CCmdTarget* class. You write an automation server class, *CClockServ*, for example, that is derived from *CCmdTarget*, and this class's CPP file contains a dispatch map:

```
BEGIN_DISPATCH_MAP(CClockServ, CCmdTarget)
    //{{AFX_DISPATCH_MAP(CClockServ)
    DISP_PROPERTY(CClockServ, "Time", m_time, VT_VARIANT)
    DISP_PROPERTY_PARAM(CClockServ, "Figure", GetFigure,
                        SetFigure, VT_VARIANT, VTS_I2)
    DISP_FUNCTION(CClockServ, "RefreshWin", Refresh,
                  VT_EMPTY, VTS_NONE)
    DISP_FUNCTION(CClockServ, "ShowWin", ShowWin, VT_BOOL,
                  VTS_I2)
    //}}AFX_DISPATCH_MAP
END_DISPATCH_MAP()
```

Looks a little like an MFC message map, doesn't it? The *CClockServ* class header file contains related code:

```
public:
    //{{AFX_DISPATCH(CClockServ)
    VARIANT m_time;
    afx_msg VARIANT GetFigure(short n);
    afx_msg void SetFigure(short n,
                           const VARIANT FAR& vNew);
    afx_msg void Refresh();
    afx_msg BOOL ShowWin(short n);
    //}}AFX_DISPATCH
    DECLARE_DISPATCH_MAP()
```

What's all this stuff mean? It means that the *CClockServ* class has the following properties and methods:

Name	Type	Description
Time	Property	Linked directly to class data member *m_time*.
Figure	Property	Indexed property, accessed through member functions *GetFigure* and *SetFigure;* first parameter is the index, second (for *SetFigure*) is the string value. (The figures are the "12," "3," "6," and "9" that appear on the clock face.)
RefreshWin	Method	Linked to class member function *Refresh*—no parameters or return value.
ShowWin	Method	Linked to class member function *ShowWin*— short integer parameter, Boolean return value.

How does the MFC dispatch map relate to *IDispatch* and the *Invoke* member function? The dispatch map macros generate internal data tables that MFC's *Invoke* implementation can read. A controller gets an *IDispatch* pointer for *CClockServ* (connected through the *CCmdTarget* base class), and it calls *Invoke* with some obscure sequence of parameters. MFC's implementation of *Invoke*, buried somewhere inside *CCmdTarget*, uses the dispatch map to decode the supplied parameters and either calls one of your member functions or accesses *m_time* directly.

As you'll see when you get to the examples, ClassWizard can generate the automation server class for you, and it can help you code the dispatch map.

An MFC OLE Automation Controller

Let's move on to the controller's end of the automation dialog. How does an MFC automation controller program call *Invoke*? MFC provides a base class *COleDispatchDriver* for this purpose. To shield you from the complexities of the OLE *Invoke* parameter sequence, *COleDispatchDriver* has three member functions—*InvokeHelper*, *GetProperty*, and *SetProperty*. Each of these functions calls *Invoke* for an *IDispatch* pointer that links to the server. The *COleDispatchDriver* object incorporates the *IDispatch* pointer.

Let's suppose our controller program has a class *CClockControl*, derived from *COleDispatchDriver*, that controls *CClockServ* objects in an automation server. Here are the functions that get and set the Time property:

```
VARIANT CClockControl::GetTime()
{
    VARIANT result;
    GetProperty(1, VT_VARIANT, (void*)&result);
    return result;
}

void CClockControl::SetTime(const VARIANT& propVal)
{
    SetProperty(1, VT_VARIANT, &propVal);
}
```

Here are the functions for the indexed Figure property:

```
VARIANT CClockControl::GetFigure(short i)
{
    VARIANT result;
    static BYTE BASED_CODE parms[] = VTS_I2;
    InvokeHelper(2, DISPATCH_PROPERTYGET, VT_VARIANT,
                (void*)&result, parms, i);
    return result;
}

void CClockControl::SetFigure(short i, const VARIANT& propVal)
{
    static BYTE BASED_CODE parms[] = VTS_I2 VTS_VARIANT;
    InvokeHelper(2, DISPATCH_PROPERTYPUT, VT_EMPTY, NULL,
                parms, i, &propVal);
}
```

And finally, here are the functions that access the server's methods:

```
void CClockControl::RefreshWin()
{
    InvokeHelper(3, DISPATCH_METHOD, VT_EMPTY, NULL, NULL);
}

BOOL CClockControl::ShowWin(short i)
{
    BOOL result;
    static BYTE BASED_CODE parms[] = VTS_I2;
    InvokeHelper(4, DISPATCH_METHOD, VT_BOOL,
                (void*)&result, parms, i);
    return result;
}
```

The function parameters identify the property or method, its return value, and its parameters. You'll learn more about dispatch function parameters later, but for now take special note of the first parameter for the *InvokeHelper*, *GetProperty*, and *SetProperty* functions. This is the unique integer index, or dispatch ID, for the property or method. Because you're using compiled C++, you can establish these IDs at compile time. If you're using an MFC automation server with a dispatch map, the indexes are determined by the map sequence, beginning with 1. If you don't know a server's dispatch indexes, you can call the *IDispatch* member function *GetIDsOfNames* to convert the ASCII property or method names to integers.

The illustration at the top of the following page shows the interactions between the controller and the server:

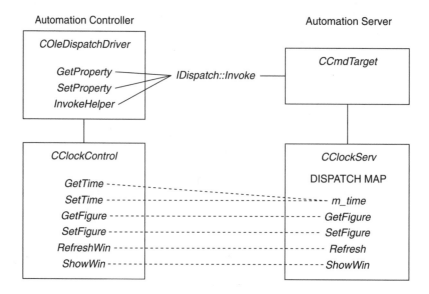

The solid lines show the actual connections through the MFC base classes and the *Invoke* function. The dotted lines represent the resulting logical connections between controller class members and server class members.

Some automation servers, including Excel, use a type library. This type library is bound into the EXE file, but the information is also included in a separate type library file with a TLB or an ODL extension. ClassWizard can access this type library file to generate a class derived from *COleDispatch-Driver*. This generated class contains member functions for all the server's methods and properties with hard-coded dispatch IDs. Sometimes you need to do some surgery on this generated code, but that's better than writing the functions from scratch.

The *VARIANT* Type

No doubt you've noticed the *VARIANT* type used in both automation controller and server functions in the previous example. *VARIANT* is an all-purpose data type that *IDispatch::Invoke* uses to transmit parameters and return values. The *VARIANT* type is the natural type to use when exchanging data with VBA. Let's look at a <u>simplified</u> version of the *VARIANT* definition in the VARIANT.H header file:

```
struct tagVARIANT {
    VARTYPE vt; // unsigned short integer type code
    unsigned short wReserved1;
    unsigned short wReserved2;
    unsigned short wReserved3;
    union {
        short       iVal;              // VT_I2   short integer
        long        lVal;              // VT_I4   long integer
        float       fltVal;            // VT_R4   4-byte float
        double      dblVal;            // VT_R8   8-byte IEEE float
        DATE        date;              // VT_DATE stored as dbl
                                       //   date.time
        BSTR        bstrVal;           // VT_BSTR
        IUnknown    FAR* punkVal;      // VT_UNKNOWN
        IDispatch   FAR* pdispVal;     // VT_DISPATCH
        short       FAR* piVal;        // VT_BYREF!VT_I2
        long        FAR* plVal;        // VT_BYREF!VT_I4
        float       FAR* pfltVal;      // VT_BYREF!VT_R4
        double      FAR* pdblVal;      // VT_BYREF!VT_R8
        DATE        FAR* pdate;        // VT_BYREF!VT_DATE
        BSTR        FAR* pbstrVal;     // VT_BYREF!VT_BSTR
        IUnknown    FAR* FAR* ppunkVal; // VT_BYREF!VT_UNKNOWN
        IDispatch   FAR* FAR* ppdispVal // VT_BYREF!VT_DISPATCH
    }
};

typedef struct tagVARIANT VARIANT;
```

As you can see, the *VARIANT* type is a C structure that contains a type code *vt*, some filler bytes, and a big *union* of types that you already know about. If *vt* is VT_I2, for example, we can read the *VARIANT*'s value from *iVal*. If *vt* is VT_R8, we want *dblVal*.

A *VARIANT* object can contain actual data or a pointer to data. If *vt* has the VT_BYREF bit set, you must access a pointer in *piVal, plVal,* and so on. Note that a *VARIANT* object can contain an *IUnknown* or *IDispatch* pointer. This means that you can pass a complete *COM* object via an OLE Automation call, but if you want VBA to process that object, its class should have an *IDispatch* interface.

Strings are special. The *BSTR* type is yet another way to represent character strings. A *BSTR* variable is a far pointer to a 0-terminated character array with a character count in front. A *BSTR* variable could, therefore, contain binary characters, including 0s. If you had a *VARIANT* object with *vt* = VT_BSTR, memory would look like this:

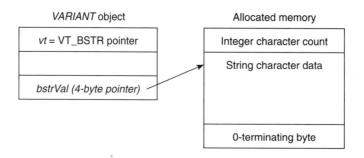

Because the string has a terminating 0, you can use *bstrVal* as though it were an ordinary *char* pointer, but you have to be very, very careful about memory cleanup. You can't simply delete the string pointer because the allocated memory begins with the character count. OLE provides the *SysAllocString* and *SysFreeString* functions for allocating and deleting *BSTR* objects.

OLE supplies some useful functions for *VARIANT*s, including *Variant-Init*, *VariantClear*, *VariantCopy*, *VariantCopyInd*, and *VariantChangeType*. If a *VARIANT* object contains a *BSTR*, these functions ensure that memory is allocated and cleared properly. The *VariantInit* and *VariantClear* functions set *vt* to VT_EMPTY. All the variant functions are global functions and take a *VARIANT** parameter.

The *CVariant* Class

It makes a lot of sense to write a C++ class to wrap the *VARIANT* structure. Constructors call *VariantInit*, and the destructor calls *VariantClear*. The class can have a constructor for each standard type, and it can have a copy constructor and assignment operator that call *VariantCopy*. When a *VARIANT* object goes out of scope, its destructor is called, and memory is cleaned up automatically.

Let's go ahead and write a variant class named, naturally, *CVariant*. Here's the declaration:

```
class CVariant : public tagVARIANT
{
public:
    CVariant();
    CVariant(const CVariant FAR& rv);
    CVariant(const tagVARIANT FAR& rv);
    CVariant(const char*);
    CVariant(int nYr, int nMo, int nDa, int nHr,
            int nMn, int nSc);
    CVariant(double);
    CVariant(short);
```

```
    CVariant(long);
    ~CVariant();
    void GetYMD(int& nYr, int& nMo, int& nDa) const;
    void GetHMS(int& nHr, int& nMn, int& nSc) const;
    BOOL ChangeType(VARTYPE vtDest, tagVARIANT FAR& vDest);
    const CVariant& operator=(const CVariant FAR& rv);
    const CVariant& operator=(const tagVARIANT FAR& rv);
};
```

And here are some selected member function implementations:

```
CVariant::CVariant()
{
    ::VariantInit(this);
}


CVariant::CVariant(const CVariant FAR& rv) // copy constructor
{
    ::VariantInit(this);
    ::VariantCopyInd(this, (CVariant FAR*) &rv);
    // ensures that destination is not a pointer
}


CVariant::CVariant(const char* pchArg)
{
    ::VariantInit(this);
    vt = VT_BSTR;
    bstrVal = ::SysAllocString(pchArg); // allocates BSTR
}
CVariant::CVariant(long lArg)
{
    ::VariantInit(this);
    vt = VT_I4;
    lVal = lArg;
}


CVariant::~CVariant()
{
    ::VariantClear(this);
}


const CVariant& CVariant::operator=(const CVariant FAR& rv) // assignment
                                                            //  operator
{
    ::VariantCopyInd(this, (CVariant FAR*) &rv);    // releases destination
                                                    //  first
    return *this;
}
```

595

The complete source for the *CVariant* class is in CVARIANT.H and CVARIANT.CPP in the EX25C subdirectory.

Now let's see how the *CVariant* class helps us write the server's *GetFigure* function that you saw referenced previously in the sample dispatch map. Assume that the server stores strings for four figures in a class data member like this:

```
private:
    CString m_figure[4];
```

Here's what we'd have to do if we used the *VARIANT* structure directly:

```
VARIANT CClockServ::GetFigure(short n)
{
    VARIANT vResult;
    ::VariantInit(&vResult);
    vResult.vt = VT_BSTR;
    vResult.bstrVal = ::SysAllocString(m_figure[n]);
    return vResult; // copies vResult without copying BSTR
                    // BSTR still must be freed later
}
```

Here's the equivalent, with a *CVariant* return value:

```
CVariant CClockServ::GetFigure(short n)
{
    return CVariant(m_figure[n]);
}
```

Here the function is constructing a temporary *CVariant* object with an explicit constructor. The compiler invokes the copy constructor to construct a second object that is passed back to the calling program—all in one statement. Isn't C++ wonderful? The only problem is that the *CVariant* class trips up ClassWizard. If you change *VARIANT* return types to *CVariant* types in the AFX_DISPATCH section of the server's dispatch class header, ClassWizard can no longer maintain the dispatch map. You can solve the problem by moving the *CVariant*-related functions outside the //}} brackets. It's OK to leave the server dispatch function <u>parameters</u> as *const VARIANT FAR&*, however, because you can always cast a *VARIANT* pointer to a *CVariant* pointer inside the function. Here's the *SetFigure* function:

```
void CClockServ::SetFigure(short n, const VARIANT FAR& vNew)
{
    CVariant vTemp;
    if ((((CVariant*) &vNew)->ChangeType(VT_BSTR, vTemp)) {
      m_figure[n] = vTemp.bstrVal;
    }
}
```

Leave your <u>controller</u> dispatch function variant parameters typed as *const VARIANT&*, because that allows you to call those functions either a *VARIANT* object or a *CVariant* object. Here's an example of a call to the *CClockControl::SetFigure* function shown on the previous page:

```
pClockControl->SetFigure(0, CVariant("XII"));
```

Parameter and Return Type Conversions for *Invoke*

All *IDispatch::Invoke* parameters and return values are processed internally as *VARIANT* objects. Remember that. The MFC implementation of *Invoke* is smart enough to convert between a *VARIANT* and whatever type you supply (where possible), so you have some flexibility in declaring parameter and return types. Suppose, for example, that your controller's *GetFigure* function specifies a return type of *BSTR*. If a server returns an *int* or a *long*, all is OK: OLE and MFC convert the number to a string. Suppose your server declares a *long* parameter and the controller supplies an *int*. Again, no problem. Even though, theoretically, OLE and MFC can handle *BSTR* parameters and return values, your life will be easier if you use *VARIANT* parameters and return values instead.

> **NOTE:** An MFC automation controller specifies the expected return type as a VT_ parameter to the *COleDispatchDriver* functions *GetProperty*, *SetProperty*, and *InvokeHelper*. An MFC automation server specifies the expected parameter types as VTS_ parameters in the *DISP_PROPERTY* and *DISP_FUNCTION* macros.

Unlike C++, VBA is not a strongly typed language. VBA variables are often stored internally as *VARIANT*s. Take an Excel spreadsheet cell value, for example. A spreadsheet user can type a text string, an integer, a floating-point number, or a date/time into the cell. VBA treats the cell value as a *VARIANT* and returns a *VARIANT* object to an automation controller. If your controller function declares a *VARIANT* return value, it can test *vt* and process the data accordingly.

VBA uses yet another date/time format. Variables of type *DATE* hold both the date and the time in one *double* value. The fractional part represents time (.25 is 6:00 AM), and the whole part represents the date (number of days since December 30, 1899). I recommend using *VARIANT*s instead of *DATE*s for dispatch function return values and parameters. The *CVariant* class has a constructor that takes integer time and date values as parameters, its *GetTime* and *GetDate* member functions extract numerical values, and the

ChangeType member function can convert a date to an ASCII string. Be aware that Excel sometimes returns a date in a *VARIANT* with *vt* set to VT_R8 instead of VT_DATE.

What if you specified *VARIANT* for all your controller's return values and all your server's parameters? That would work, but then you'd be doing unnecessary conversions. If you know a function returns a short integer, you should declare a short integer return value.

Here's a useful table of dispatch function return types:

Server Returns	Controller Declares	Controller Function Return Type
void	VT_EMPTY	N/A
indeterminate (VBA)	VT_VARIANT	*CVariant*
short integer	VT_I2	short
long integer	VT_I4	long
BSTR	VT_VARIANT	*CVariant*
float	VT_R4	float
double	VT_R8	double
date/time	VT_VARIANT	*CVariant*
IDispatch*	VT_DISPATCH	*LPDISPATCH*

And here's a table of dispatch function parameter types:

Controller Passes	Controller Parameter Type	Server Dispatch Map	Server Function Parameter Type
indeterminate (VBA)	N/A	VTS_VARIANT	const *VARIANT FAR&*
short integer	short	VTS_I2	short
long integer	long	VTS_I4	long
BSTR	*VARIANT**	VTS_VARIANT	const *VARIANT FAR&*
float	float	VTS_R4	float
double	double	VTS_R8	double
date/time	*VARIANT**	VTS_VARIANT	const *VARIANT FAR&*
IDispatch*	*LPDISPATCH*	VTS_DISPATCH	*LPDISPATCH*

One last item concerning *Invoke* parameters: A dispatch function can have <u>optional</u> <u>parameters</u>. If the server declares trailing parameters as *VARIANT*s, the controller doesn't have to supply them. If the controller calls the function without supplying an optional parameter, the *VARIANT* object's *vt* value on the server end is VT_ERROR.

NOTE: Some dispatch functions pass a legitimate OLE error code in a *VARIANT* parameter. If you don't know whether a parameter is omitted or represents a real error, test the value of *vt.scode* for *DISP_E_PARAMNOTFOUND*.

OLE Automation Examples

The remainder of this chapter presents four sample programs. The first three programs are OLE Automation servers—an EXE server with no user interface, a DLL server, and a multi-instance SDI EXE server. Each of these programs comes with a Microsoft Excel driver workbook. The last sample program is an MFC OLE Automation controller program that drives the three servers and also runs Excel.

The EX25B Automation Server EXE—No User Interface

The AUTOCLIK example is a good demonstration of an MDI framework application with the document object as the automation server. (To find the AUTOCLIK example, click on Books Online, OLE Classes, Tutorial, and Chapters 6-9.) The EX25B example is different because it has no user interface. There is one automation-aware class, and in the first version of the program a single instance of the server supports the construction of multiple automation objects. In the second version, a new instance starts up each time an automation controller creates an object.

The EX25B application is an answer to a real need in the financial marketplace. There are already countless programs that analyze the past behavior of the stock market, but what an investor really wants is the <u>future</u> prices of stocks. My original version of the program downloaded all the world's political and economic data from the information superhighway to produce very accurate predictions, but Microsoft Press said there wasn't room on the companion disc for all the source code. So I was forced to abbreviate the program and reduce its accuracy. Sorry.

The example is tied to an automation server named EX25B.MARKET. This server has a single method, *GetIndustrialsAverage* (the same name as the

C++ *CMarket* member function), that takes a date parameter and returns an integer value. You supply the date, and the program tells you the closing Dow Jones industrials average for that day. You can use Excel to control the server, as shown in Figure 25-8. A macro reads the dates from column C and then calls *GetIndustrialsAverage* to put values in column D.

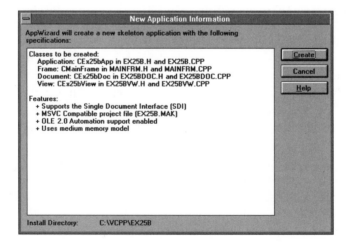

Figure 25-8.
This Excel workbook is controlling the EX25B server.

Here are the steps for creating the program from scratch:

1. **Run AppWizard to create the EX25B project in the \VCPP\EX25B directory.** Turn off all general options, and check the Automation Support check box in the OLE Options dialog. The options and the default class names are shown here:

NOTE: AppWizard generates an SDI application with an automation-aware document class. All the necessary OLE initialization calls, *#includes*, and resources are present. You'll be chopping out the document, view, and frame classes, and then you'll be using ClassWizard to add a new automation-aware class named *CMarket*. The final result, less the *CMarket* files, could serve as a prototype for your own automation servers that don't have a user interface. You could further reduce the EXE file size by eliminating unused resources.

2. **From MS-DOS or from Windows' File Manager, delete the following files from the EX25B project:**

EX25B.CLW
EX25BDOC.CPP
EX25BDOC.H
EX25BVW.CPP
EX25BVW.H
MAINFRM.CPP
MAINFRM.H

and then choose Edit from the Visual Workbench's Project menu to remove the three CPP files from the project.

3. **Edit the EX25B.CPP file, as follows.** Remove the following *#include* lines:

```
#include "mainfrm.h"
#include "ex25bdoc.h"
#include "ex25bvw.h"
```

Take out all references to the About dialog, and then remove the following statement:

```
static const CLSID BASED_CODE clsid =
{ 0xba4d7e0, 0x2494, 0x101b, { 0xac, 0x24, 0x0, 0xaa,
                               0x0, 0x3e, 0x6f, 0x98 } };
```

Replace the *InitInstance* member function with the following code:

```
BOOL CEx25bApp::InitInstance()
{
    TRACE("Entering CEx25bApp::InitInstance\n");
    if (!AfxOleInit()) {
```

(continued)

```
      AfxMessageBox(IDP_OLE_INIT_FAILED);
      return FALSE;
    }
    if (RunEmbedded() || RunAutomated()) {
      COleTemplateServer::RegisterAll();
      return TRUE;
    }
    AfxMessageBox("EX25B cannot be run stand-alone\n");
    COleObjectFactory::UpdateRegistryAll();
    return FALSE;
}
```

Add the following *ExitInstance* function for diagnostic purposes:

```
int CEx25bApp::ExitInstance()
{
    TRACE("Entering CEx25bApp::ExitInstance\n");
    return CWinApp::ExitInstance();
}
```

4. Edit the EX25B.H file, as follows. Add the *ExitInstance* prototype:

```
virtual int  ExitInstance();
```

Remove the following lines:

```
COleTemplateServer m_server;
afx_msg void OnAppAbout();
```

5. Run ClassWizard from App Studio, and then let ClassWizard rebuild its database.

6. Click the OLE Automation tab, and use the Add Class dialog to add the *CMarket* class, as shown here:

Be sure to check the OLE Automation and OLE Createable check boxes.

7. Use the Add Method dialog to add the *GetIndustrialsAverage* method, as shown here:

Close the MFC Class Wizard dialog and exit App Studio.

8. **Add *TRACE* statements to the *CMarket* constructor and destructor.**

9. **Edit the *GetIndustrialsAverage* member function in MARKET.CPP as follows:**

```
short CMarket::GetIndustrialsAverage(const VARIANT FAR& Date)
{
    TRACE("CMarket::GetIndustrialsAverage - %p, Date = % of \n",
        this, Date.dblVal);
    long lRand = rand();
    return (short) (Date.dblVal - 30600.0) +
        (short) (lRand * 40 / RAND_MAX) - 20;
}
```

10. **Build the EX25B program, and run it once to register the server in REG.DAT.**

11. **Set up three Excel macros in a new workbook file, EX25B.XLS, as follows:**

```
Dim Market As Object
```

(continued)

```
Sub LoadMarket()
    Set Market = CreateObject("ex25b.market")
End Sub

Sub UnloadMarket()
    Set Market = Nothing
End Sub

Sub GetIndustrialsAverage()
    Do Until ActiveCell.Value = ""
        Ave = Market.GetIndustrialsAverage(ActiveCell.Value)
        Selection.Offset(0, 1).Value = Ave
        Selection.Offset(1, 0).Range("A1").Select
    Loop
End Sub
```

12. **Arrange an Excel worksheet as shown here:**

Attach the macros to the pushbuttons (use the right mouse button).
Enter your list of dates, starting at cell A4.

13. **Click the Load Market Program button, select cell A4, and then click the Get Industrials Averages button.** Click the Unload Market Program button. Watch the debug window while the EX25B program executes. Observe, from the *TRACE* statements, the sequence of the *InitInstance, ExitInstance*, constructor, and destructor calls.

> NOTE: Sometimes you need to click the buttons twice. The first click switches the focus to the worksheet, and the second click runs the macro. The hourglass cursor tells you the macro is working.

14. **Phone your stockbroker, and then send me 10 percent of your profits.**

What's happening in this program? Look closely at the *CEx25bApp-::InitInstance* function. When you run the program directly from Windows' Program Manager or File Manager, it displays a message box and then quits, but not before it updates the REG.DAT file. The *COleObjectFactory::Update-RegistryAll* function hunts for global class factory objects, and the *CMarket* class's *IMPLEMENT_OLECREATE* macro invocation defines such an object. (The *IMPLEMENT_OLECREATE* line was generated because you checked ClassWizard's Ole Createable box for *CMarket.*) The unique class ID and the server name, EX25B.MARKET, are added to the registration database.

When Excel now calls *CreateObject*, OLE loads the EX25B program, which contains the global factory for *CMarket* objects; OLE then calls the factory object's *CreateInstance* function to construct the *CMarket* object and return an *IDispatch* pointer. Here's the *CMarket* class that ClassWizard generated, with unnecessary detail (and the *GetIndustrialsAverage* function) omitted:

```
class CMarket : public CCmdTarget
{
    DECLARE_DYNCREATE(CMarket)
protected:
    CMarket();          // protected constructor used by
                        //  dynamic creation
public:
    virtual ~CMarket();
    virtual void OnFinalRelease();
protected:
    DECLARE_OLECREATE(CMarket)
    // Generated OLE dispatch map functions
    //{{AFX_DISPATCH(CMarket)
    afx_msg short GetIndustrialsAverage(const VARIANT FAR& Date);
    //}}AFX_DISPATCH
    DECLARE_DISPATCH_MAP()
};


IMPLEMENT_DYNCREATE(CMarket, CCmdTarget)


CMarket::CMarket()
{
    EnableAutomation();

    // To keep the application running as long as an OLE Automation
    //  object is active, the constructor calls AfxOleLockApp.

    AfxOleLockApp();
}
```

(continued)

```
CMarket::~CMarket()
{
    // To terminate the application when all objects are created
    //  with OLE Automation, the destructor calls AfxOleUnlockApp.

    AfxOleUnlockApp();
}

void CMarket::OnFinalRelease()
{
    // When the last reference for an automation object is released,
    //  OnFinalRelease is called.  This implementation deletes the
    //  object.  Add additional cleanup required for your object before
    //  deleting it from memory.

    delete this;
}

BEGIN_DISPATCH_MAP(CMarket, CCmdTarget)
    //{{AFX_DISPATCH_MAP(CMarket)
    DISP_FUNCTION(CMarket, "GetIndustrialsAverage",
                 GetIndustrialsAverage, VT_I2, VTS_VARIANT)
    //}}AFX_DISPATCH_MAP
END_DISPATCH_MAP()

IMPLEMENT_OLECREATE(CMarket, "EX25B.MARKET", 0xaa41dd80, 0x419a,
                    0x101b, 0xac, 0x24, 0x0, 0xaa, 0x0, 0x3e,
                    0x6f, 0x98)
```

This first version of the program runs in single-instance mode, as does the AUTOCLIK program. If a second automation controller asks for a new *CMarket* object, OLE calls the class factory *CreateInstance* function again, and the existing instance constructs another *CMarket* object on the heap. You can verify this by making a copy of the EX25B.XLS workbook (under a different name) and loading both the original and the copy. Click the Load Market Program button in each workbook and watch the debug window. *InitInstance* should be called only once.

A small change in the EX25B program makes it behave differently. To have a new instance of EX25B start up each time a new server object is requested, follow these steps:

1. Add the following macro in MARKET.H:

```
#define IMPLEMENT_OLECREATE2(class_name, external_name, \
    l, w1, w2, b1, b2, b3, b4, b5, b6, b7, b8) \
```

```
static const char BASED_CODE _szProgID_##class_name[] = external_name; \
COleObjectFactory NEAR class_name::factory(class_name::guid, \
    RUNTIME_CLASS(class_name), TRUE, _szProgID_##class_name); \
const GUID CDECL BASED_CODE class_name::guid = \
    { l, w1, w2, { b1, b2, b3, b4, b5, b6, b7, b8 } };
```

This macro is the same as the standard MFC *IMPLEMENT_OLECREATE* macro, except the original *FALSE* parameter (after the *RUNTIME_CLASS* parameter) has been changed to *TRUE*.

2. In MARKET.CPP, change the *IMPLEMENT_OLECREATE* macro invocation to *IMPLEMENT_OLECREATE2*.

3. Restart Windows. This step is necessary because OLE "remembers" that EX25B is a single-instance program even after the program exits.

4. Build and test the program from Excel. Use the same two workbooks and note that *InitInstance* gets called each time you click the Load Market Program button.

> NOTE: The EX25B program on the companion disc uses the *IMPLEMENT_OLECREATE2* macro.

The EX25C Automation Server DLL

You could easily convert EX25B from an EXE to a DLL. The *CMarket* class would be exactly the same, and the Excel driver would be similar. It's more interesting, though, to write a new application, this time with a minimal user interface (UI). We'll use a modal dialog because it's about the most complex UI we can use in an automation server DLL.

AppWizard isn't much help here. We need a program that's specifically designed to be an automation-server DLL. The EX25C program on the companion disc (bound into this book) is a starting point for your own DLL programs; simply copy it and modify it for your own needs.

The EX25C program is fairly simple. An automation server class, identified by the registered name EX25C.AUTO, has the following properties and method:

LongData	Long integer property
TextData	String property
DisplayDialog	Method—no parameters, Boolean return

DisplayDialog displays the EX25C OLE Data Gathering dialog shown in Figure 25-9 on the following page. An Excel macro passes two cell values to the DLL and then updates the same cells with the updated values.

Figure 25-9.
The EX25C OLE Data Gathering dialog in action.

Here are the steps for building and testing the EX25C server DLL:

1. **From the Visual Workbench, open the project in the \VCPP\EX25C directory.** Build the project to produce the EX25C.DLL file in the project directory.

2. **Use REGEDIT to load the data in EX25C.REG.** (Because EX25C is a DLL, you can't run it directly to update the registration database.) If you haven't already done so, add a Program Manager icon that runs \WINDOWS\REGEDIT.EXE with the */v* parameter. Start REGEDIT, choose Merge Registration File from the File menu, and specify \VCPP\EX25C\EX25C.REG.

3. **Load the Excel workbook file \VCPP\EX25C\EX25C.XLS.** Type an integer in cell C3, and type some text in cell D3, as shown here:

Click the Load DLL button, and then click the Gather Data button. Edit the data, click OK, and watch the new values appear in the spreadsheet.

4. **Click the Unload DLL button and watch the debug window to be sure the DLL's *ExitInstance* function is called.**

Now let's look at the EX25C code. Like an MFC EXE, an MFC DLL has an application class (derived from *CWinApp*) and a global application object. The overridden *InitInstance* member function in EX25C.CPP looks like this:

```
BOOL CEx25cDLL::InitInstance()
{
    // any DLL initialization goes here
    TRACE("EX25C.DLL CEx25cDLL::InitInstance\n");
    SetDialogBkColor(); // gray dialogs in the DLL as well
    // do not call AfxOleInit or ::OleInitialize
    // OLE is already initialized by the client app
    COleTemplateServer::RegisterAll();
    return TRUE;
}
```

There's also an *ExitInstance* function for diagnostic purposes only. The EX25C.CPP file also contains code for the *CPromptDlg* class, but that class is a standard class derived from *CDialog*. The file PROMPT.H contains the *CPromptDlg* class header.

The *CEx25cAuto* class, the automation server class initially generated by ClassWizard (with the OLE Createable option), is more interesting. This class is exposed to OLE under the name EX25C.AUTO. Figure 25-10 shows the header file EX25CAUT.H.

EX25CAUT.H

```
// ex25caut.h : header file
//
#include "cvariant.h"


///////////////////////////////////////////////////////////////////////
// CEx25cAuto command target

class CEx25cAuto : public CCmdTarget
{
    DECLARE_DYNCREATE(CEx25cAuto)
protected:
    CEx25cAuto(); // protected constructor used by dynamic creation

// Implementation
public:
    virtual ~CEx25cAuto();
    virtual void OnFinalRelease();

protected:
    // Generated message map functions
    //{{AFX_MSG(CEx25cAuto)
        // NOTE - the ClassWizard will add and remove member
        //    functions here.
```

Figure 25-10. *(continued)*

The EX25CAUT.H file.

Figure 25-10. *continued*

```
    //}}AFX_MSG
    DECLARE_MESSAGE_MAP()

    DECLARE_OLECREATE(CEx25cAuto)

    CVariant m_textData; // moved here to keep
                         //   ClassWizard happy
    // Generated OLE dispatch map functions
    //{{AFX_DISPATCH(CEx25cAuto)
    long m_longData;
    afx_msg BOOL DisplayDialog();
    //}}AFX_DISPATCH
    DECLARE_DISPATCH_MAP()
};
```

Figure 25-11 shows the implementation file EX25CAUT.CPP.

EX25CAUT.CPP

```
// ex25caut.cpp : implementation file
//

#include "stdafx.h"
#include "ex25cres.h"        // ex25c resources
#include "ex25caut.h"
#include "prompt.h"

#ifdef _DEBUG
#undef THIS_FILE
static char BASED_CODE THIS_FILE[] = __FILE__;
#endif

/////////////////////////////////////////////////////////////////////
// CEx25cAuto

IMPLEMENT_DYNCREATE(CEx25cAuto, CCmdTarget)

BEGIN_MESSAGE_MAP(CEx25cAuto, CCmdTarget)
    //{{AFX_MSG_MAP(CEx25cAuto)
        // NOTE - the ClassWizard will add and remove mapping
        //   macros here.
    //}}AFX_MSG_MAP
END_MESSAGE_MAP()
```

Figure 25-11.   *(continued)*
The EX25CAUT.CPP file.

Figure 25-11. *continued*

```
BEGIN_DISPATCH_MAP(CEx25cAuto, CCmdTarget)
    //{{AFX_DISPATCH_MAP(CEx25cAuto)
    DISP_PROPERTY(CEx25cAuto, "LongData", m_longData, VT_I4)
    DISP_PROPERTY(CEx25cAuto, "TextData", m_textData,
                    VT_VARIANT)
    DISP_FUNCTION(CEx25cAuto, "DisplayDialog", DisplayDialog,
                    VT_BOOL, VTS_NONE)
    //}}AFX_DISPATCH_MAP
END_DISPATCH_MAP()

IMPLEMENT_OLECREATE(CEx25cAuto, "Ex25c.auto", 0x97ef7fe1,
                    0x26d6, 0x101b, 0xac, 0x24, 0x0, 0xaa,
                    0x0, 0x3e, 0x6f, 0x98)

CEx25cAuto::CEx25cAuto() : m_textData("default")
{
    TRACE("Entering CEx25cAuto constructor %p\n", this);
    m_longData = 0L;
    EnableAutomation();

    // To keep the application running as long as an OLE
    //  Automation object is active, the constructor calls
    //  AfxOleLockApp.
    AfxOleLockApp();
}

CEx25cAuto::~CEx25cAuto()
{
    // To terminate the application when all objects are
    //  created with OLE Automation, the destructor
    //  calls AfxOleUnlockApp.

    TRACE("Entering CEx25cAuto destructor %p\n", this);
    AfxOleUnlockApp();
}

void CEx25cAuto::OnFinalRelease()
{
    // When the last reference for an automation object is
    //  released, OnFinalRelease is called. This implementation
    //  deletes the object. Add additional cleanup required for
    //  your object before deleting it from memory.
```

(continued)

Figure 25-11. *continued*

```
      TRACE("Entering CEx25cAuto::OnFinalRelease %p\n", this);
      delete this;
}


/////////////////////////////////////////////////////////////////////
// CEx25cAuto message handlers

BOOL CEx25cAuto::DisplayDialog()
{
    TRACE("Entering CEx25cAuto::DisplayDialog %p\n", this);
    BOOL bRet = TRUE;
    AfxLockTempMaps();  // see MFC Tech Note #3
    TRY {
        CPromptDlg dlg(CWnd::GetActiveWindow());
        ASSERT(m_textData.vt = VT_BSTR);
        dlg.m_strTextData = m_textData.bstrVal;
        dlg.m_longData = m_longData;
        if (dlg.DoModal() == IDOK) {
            m_textData = CVariant(dlg.m_strTextData);
            m_longData = dlg.m_longData;
            bRet = TRUE;
        }
        else {
            bRet = FALSE;
        }
    }
    CATCH_ALL(e) {
        TRACE("Exception: failure to display dialog\n");
        bRet = FALSE;
    }
    END_CATCH_ALL
    AfxUnlockTempMaps();
    return bRet;
}
```

The two properties, LongData and TextData, are represented by class data members *m_longData* and *m_textData*. Because we've changed *m_textData* from a *VARIANT* to a *CVariant* object, we must move its declaration out of ClassWizard's sight. The *DisplayDialog* member function, which is the *DisplayDialog* method, is ordinary except for two things. First, the dialog's parent window must be set to the client application's main window. The static *CWnd::GetActiveWindow* function provides this window to the dialog's constructor. Second, the *AfxLockTempMaps* and *AfxUnlockTempMaps* functions are necessary for cleaning up temporary object pointers that would normally be deleted in an EXE program's idle loop.

The registration file EX25C.REG, in case you were wondering, was written manually using the class ID that ClassWizard generated in the *IMPLEMENT_OLECREATE* macro invocation. Here's the file:

```
REGEDIT
HKEY_CLASSES_ROOT\Ex25c.auto = Ex25c Automation
HKEY_CLASSES_ROOT\Ex25c.auto\CLSID =
 {97EF7FE1-26D6-101b-AC24-00AA003E6F98}
HKEY_CLASSES_ROOT\CLSID\{97EF7FE1-26D6-101b-AC24-00AA003E6F98} =
 Ex25c Automation
HKEY_CLASSES_ROOT\CLSID\{97EF7FE1-26D6-101b-AC24-
 00AA003E6F98}\InprocServer = c:\vcpp\ex25c\ex25c.dll
```

What about the Excel code? Here are the three macros and the global declarations:

```
Dim Dllserv As Object
Declare Sub CoFreeUnusedLibraries Lib "COMPOBJ" ()

Sub LoadDllServ()
    Set Dllserv = CreateObject("ex25c.auto")
    Range("C3").Select
    Dllserv.LongData = Selection.Value
    Range("D3").Select
    Dllserv.TextData = Selection.Value
End Sub

Sub RefreshDllServ() 'Gather Data button
    Range("C3").Select
    Dllserv.LongData = Selection.Value
    Range("D3").Select
    Dllserv.TextData = Selection.Value
    Dllserv.DisplayDialog
    Range("C3").Select
    Selection.Value = Dllserv.LongData
    Range("D3").Select
    Selection.Value = Dllserv.TextData
End Sub

Sub UnloadDllServ()
    Set Dllserv = Nothing
'Excel should do this, but it doesn't
    Call CoFreeUnusedLibraries
End Sub
```

The first line in *LoadDLLServ* creates a server object as identified by the registered name *ex25c.auto*. The *RefreshDllServ* macro accesses the server object's LongData and TextData properties. The first time you run *Load-DLLServ*, it loads the DLL and constructs an *ex25c.auto* object. The second time you run *LoadDLLServ*, something curious happens: A second object is constructed, and the original one is destroyed. (You'll learn why later.) If you run *LoadDLLServ* from another copy of the workbook, you get two separate *ex25c.auto* objects. Of course, there's only one copy of the EX25C DLL in memory at any time.

Notice the call to the OLE function *CoFreeUnusedLibraries*. This is necessary because Excel doesn't try to unload the DLLs that it isn't using. You'll see later that MFC controller programs have better manners; they call *CoFreeUnusedLibraries* in their idle loops, so you don't have to.

The EX25D SDI Automation Server EXE

This last OLE server example illustrates the use of a document server class in a multi-instance SDI application. This server demonstrates an indexed property plus a method that constructs a new OLE object.

The first automation server you saw, EX25B, didn't have a user interface. The global class factory constructed a *CMarket* object that did the server's work. What if you want your EXE server to have a window? If you've bought into the MFC document–view architecture, you'll want the document, view, and frame with all the benefits they provide.

Suppose you made a regular MFC application and then added an OLE createable class such as *CMarket*. How do you attach the *CMarket* object to the document and view? From a *CMarket* class member function, you could navigate through the application object and main frame to the current document or view, but you'd have a tough time in an MDI application if you encountered several server objects and several documents. There is a better way. You make the document class itself the OLE createable class, and you have the full support of AppWizard for this task, and that's true both in MDI and in SDI applications.

The MDI AUTOCLIK example demonstrates how OLE triggers the construction of new document, view, and child frame objects each time an automation controller creates a new server object. Because the EX25D example is an SDI program, OLE starts a new instance each time the controller creates an object. Immediately after it starts the program, OLE constructs not only the automation-aware document, but also the view and the main frame window.

Now's a good time to experiment with the EX25D application, which was first generated by AppWizard with the OLE Automation Support option checked. It's a Windows alarm-clock program that's designed to be manipulated from an automation controller such as Excel. It has properties and methods as shown in this table:

Time	Date Property
RefreshWin	Method that invalidates the view window and brings the main frame window to the top
ShowWin	Method that shows the application's main window
CreateAlarm	Method that creates a *CAlarm* object and returns its *IDispatch* pointer
Figure	Indexed property for the four figures on the clock face

Here are the steps for building and running EX25D:

1. From the Visual Workbench, open the project in the \VCPP\EX25D directory. Build the project to produce the EX25D.EXE file in the project directory.

2. Run the program once to register it in REG.DAT. The program is designed to be executed only as an OLE Automation server. When you run it from Program Manager or the Visual Workbench, it updates the registration database and exits.

3. Load the Excel workbook file \VCPP\EX25D\EX25D.XLS. The worksheet should look like the one shown here:

Click the Load Clock button, and then click the Set Alarm button. (There is a long delay after you click each button.) The clock should appear as shown on the following page, with the "A" indicating the alarm setting:

Watch the debug window to see when *InitInstance* is called and when the document object is constructed.

4. Click the Unload Clock button, and watch the debug window to be sure the *ExitInstance* function is called.

AppWizard did most of the work of setting up the document as an automation server. In the derived application class *CEx25dApp*, it generated a data member for the server:

```
public:
    COleTemplateServer m_server;
```

and in the *InitInstance* function (in EX25D.CPP), it generated the following code that connects the server object (the document) to the application's document template:

```
CSingleDocTemplate* pDocTemplate;
pDocTemplate = new CSingleDocTemplate(
    IDR_MAINFRAME,
    RUNTIME_CLASS(CEx25dDoc),
    RUNTIME_CLASS(CMainFrame),      // main SDI frame window
    RUNTIME_CLASS(CEx25dView));
AddDocTemplate(pDocTemplate);
m_server.ConnectTemplate(clsid, pDocTemplate, TRUE);
```

Now all the plumbing is in place for OLE to construct the document, together with the view and frame. When the objects are constructed, however, the main window is not made visible. That's your job. You must write a method that shows the window.

The following *UpdateRegistry* call updates REG.DAT with contents of the *IDR_MAINFRAME* string resource:

```
m_server.UpdateRegistry(OAT_DISPATCH_OBJECT);
```

The following dispatch map shows the properties and methods for the *CEx25dDoc* class. Notice that the *m_time* data member (for the Time property) is out of ClassWizard's view because its type was changed from *VARIANT* to *CVariant*. Also, the Figure property is an indexed property and thus inaccessible to ClassWizard.

```
BEGIN_DISPATCH_MAP(CEx25dDoc, CDocument)
    DISP_PROPERTY(CEx25dDoc, "Time", m_time, VT_VARIANT)
    //{{AFX_DISPATCH_MAP(CEx25dDoc)
    DISP_FUNCTION(CEx25dDoc, "RefreshWin", Refresh,
                    VT_EMPTY, VTS_NONE)
    DISP_FUNCTION(CEx25dDoc, "ShowWin", ShowWin,
                    VT_EMPTY, VTS_NONE)
    DISP_FUNCTION(CEx25dDoc, "CreateAlarm", CreateAlarm,
                    VT_DISPATCH, VTS_VARIANT)
    //}}AFX_DISPATCH_MAP
    DISP_PROPERTY_PARAM(CEx25dDoc, "Figure", GetFigure,
                    SetFigure, VT_VARIANT, VTS_I2)
END_DISPATCH_MAP()
```

The *RefreshWin* and *ShowWin* methods aren't very interesting, but the *CreateAlarm* method is worth a close look. Here's the corresponding *Create-Alarm* member function:

```
LPDISPATCH CEx25dDoc::CreateAlarm(const VARIANT FAR& time)
{
    m_pAlarm = new CAlarm(time); // m_pAlarm is a CAlarm*
                                 //   data member
    return m_pAlarm->GetIDispatch(FALSE);
}
```

We've chosen to have the server create an alarm object when a controller calls *CreateAlarm*. *CAlarm* is an automation server class that we've generated with ClassWizard. It is <u>not</u> OLE createable, and that means there's no *IMPLEMENT_OLECREATE* macro and no class factory. The *CreateAlarm* function constructs a *CAlarm* object and returns an *IDispatch* pointer. (The *FALSE* parameter for *CCmdTarget::GetIDispatch* means that the reference count is not incremented; the *CAlarm* object already has a reference count of 1 when it is constructed.)

The *CAlarm* class is declared in ALARM.H as follows:

```
#include "cvariant.h"

class CAlarm : public CCmdTarget
{
public:
    CAlarm(const VARIANT FAR& time);
public:
    virtual ~CAlarm();
    virtual void OnFinalRelease();

protected:
    // Generated message map functions
    //{{AFX_MSG(CAlarm)
    // NOTE - the ClassWizard will add and remove
    //  member functions here.
    //}}AFX_MSG
    DECLARE_MESSAGE_MAP()
public:
    CVariant m_time;  // ClassWizard wants a VARIANT
    // Generated OLE dispatch map functions
    //{{AFX_DISPATCH(CAlarm)
    //}}AFX_DISPATCH
    DECLARE_DISPATCH_MAP()
};
```

Notice the absence of the *DECLARE_DYNCREATE* macro.

ALARM.CPP contains a dispatch map, as follows:

```
BEGIN_DISPATCH_MAP(CAlarm, CCmdTarget)
    //{{AFX_DISPATCH_MAP(CAlarm)
    DISP_PROPERTY(CAlarm, "Time", m_time, VT_VARIANT)
    //}}AFX_DISPATCH_MAP
END_DISPATCH_MAP()
```

Why do we have a *CAlarm* class? We could have added an "Alarm Time" property in the *CEx25dDoc* class instead, but then we would have needed another property or method to turn the alarm on and off. By using the *CAlarm* class, what we're really doing is setting ourselves up to support multiple alarms—a "collection" of alarms.

To implement an OLE Automation collection, we would write another class, *CAlarms*, which would contain the methods *Add*, *Remove*, and *Item*. *Add* and *Remove* are self-explanatory; *Item* returns an *IDispatch* pointer for a collection element identified by an index, numeric or otherwise. We would also implement a read-only Count property that returned the number of elements. The document class (which owns the collection) would have an *Alarms* method with an optional *VARIANT* parameter. If the parameter were omitted, the method would return the *IDispatch* pointer for the collection. If the parameter specified an index, the method would return an *IDispatch* pointer for the selected alarm.

If we wanted our collection to support the VBA "For Each" syntax, we'd have some more work to do. We'd add an *IEnumVARIANT* interface to the *CAlarms* class and implement the *Next* member function to step through the collection. Finally, we'd add a *CAlarms* method called *_NewEnum* that returned an *IEnumVARIANT* interface pointer. If we wanted the collection to be really general, we'd allow separate enumerator objects (with an *IEnumVARIANT* interface) and we'd implement the other *IEnumVARIANT* functions—*Skip, Reset,* and *Clone.*

The Figures property is an indexed property, and that makes it interesting. The Figures property represents the four figures on the clock face—twelve, three, six, and nine. It's a *CString* array, so we can use Roman numerals. Here's the declaration in the EX25DDOC.H:

```
public:
    CString m_figure[4];
```

and here are the *GetFigure* and *SetFigure* functions in EX25DDOC.CPP:

```
CVariant CEx25dDoc::GetFigure(short n)
{
    return CVariant(m_figure[n]);
}


void CEx25dDoc::SetFigure(short n, const VARIANT FAR& vNew)
{
    CVariant vTemp;
    if (((CVariant*) &vNew)->ChangeType(VT_BSTR, vTemp)) {
       m_figure[n] = vTemp.bstrVal;
    }
}
```

These functions tie back to the *DISP_PROPERTY_PARAM* macro in the *CEx25dDoc* dispatch map. The first parameter is the index number, specified as a short integer by the last macro parameter. Property indexes don't have to be integers, and the index can have several components (row and column number, for example). The *ChangeType* call in *SetFigure* is necessary because the controller might otherwise pass numbers instead of strings.

You've just seen collection properties and indexed properties. What's the difference? A controller can't add or delete elements of an indexed property, but it can add elements to a collection, and it can delete elements.

What draws the clock face? As you might expect, it's the *OnDraw* member function of view class. This function uses *GetDocument* to get a pointer to the document object, and then it accesses the document's property data members and method member functions.

Finally, here's the Excel macro code:

```
Dim Clock As Object
Dim Alarm As Object

Sub LoadClock()
    Set Clock = CreateObject("ex25d.document")
    Range("A3").Select
    n = 0
    Do Until n = 4
        Clock.figure(n) = Selection.Value
        Selection.Offset(0, 1).Range("A1").Select
        n = n + 1
    Loop
    RefreshClock
    Clock.ShowWin
End Sub

Sub RefreshClock()
    Clock.Time = Now()
    Clock.RefreshWin
End Sub

Sub CreateAlarm()
    Range("E3").Select
    Set Alarm = Clock.CreateAlarm(Selection.Value)
    RefreshClock
End Sub

Sub UnloadClock()
    Set Clock = Nothing
End Sub
```

Notice the Set Alarm statement in the *CreateAlarm* macro. It calls the *CreateAlarm* method to return an *IDispatch* pointer, which is stored in an object variable. If the macro is run a second time, a new alarm is created, but the original one is destroyed because its reference count goes to 0.

WARNING: You've seen a modal dialog in a DLL (EX25C), and you've seen a main frame window in an EXE (EX25D). Be careful with modal dialogs in EXEs. It's OK to have an About dialog that is invoked directly by the server program, but it isn't a good idea to invoke a modal dialog in a server method function.

The problem is that, once the modal dialog is on the screen, the user can switch back to the controller program. MFC controllers handle this situation with a special "Server Busy" message box, which appears right away. Excel does something similar, but it waits 30 seconds, and this could confuse the user. If you want to see this effect, uncomment the *OnAppAbout* line in *CEx25dDoc-::CreateAlarm*.

The EX25E Automation Controller Program

So far, you've seen C++ OLE Automation server programs. Now you'll see a C++ Automation controller program that runs all the previous servers and also controls Microsoft Excel. The EX25E program was originally generated by AppWizard, but without any OLE options. It was marginally easier to add the OLE code than it would have been to rip out the server-specific code. If you do use AppWizard to build such an automation controller, follow these steps to make it OLE-aware:

1. Choose Project from Visual Workbench's Options menu, and then add the following library names to the Input section of the Linker dialog: *compobj, storage, ole2, ole2disp, ole2nls,* and *mfcoleui.*

2. Add the following line at the end of STDAFX.H:

   ```
   #include <afxdisp.h>
   ```

3. In the project's resource file, add the following string, with ID equal to *IDP_OLE_INIT_FAILED*:

   ```
   OLE initialization failed. Make sure that the OLE
    libraries are the correct version.
   ```

4. Add the following code at the beginning of the application class's *InitInstance* function:

   ```
   if (!AfxOleInit())    {
       AfxMessageBox(IDP_OLE_INIT_FAILED);
       return FALSE;
   }
   ```

To prepare EX25E, open the project in \VCPP\EX25E and do the build. When you run the application, you'll see a standard SDI application with a menu structure such as the one shown in Figure 25-12 on the following page:

File	Edit	Market OLE	DDL OLE	Clock OLE	Excel OLE	View	Help
		Load	Load	Load	Load		
		Get Average	Get Data	Create Alarm	Execute		
		Unload	Unload	Refresh Time			
				Unload			

Figure 25-12.
A sample menu structure for a standard SDI application.

If you have built and registered all the servers, you can test them from EX25E. Notice that the DLL doesn't have to be in the \WINDOWS\SYSTEM directory because OLE finds it through the registration database. For some servers, you'll have to watch the debug window to verify that the test results are correct. The program is reasonably modular. Menu commands and update command UI events are mapped to the view class. Each server object has its own C++ controller class and an embedded data member in EX25E-VW.H. We'll look at each part separately.

The Market Controller Class for EX25B.EXE

The *CMarketControl* class is designed to interact with the EX25B automation server. That server, as you'll remember, has one method, *GetIndustrials-Average,* and no properties. We'll use the method name for our controller class's member function, although this isn't necessary. Like the server's method, this function takes a date in a *VARIANT* parameter and returns a short integer.

There's one trick we'll use here and in all the automation controllers that aren't generated by ClassWizard. We'll use a class *enum* to make dispatch IDs that match the server's. In the EX25B server, the one and only dispatch map entry has an ID of 1 because 1 is the starting number. *DID_GET-AVERAGE,* then, is equal to 1, and thus the server's *GetIndustrialsAverage* method is linked to the controller's *GetIndustrialsAverage* member function through the *IDispatch::Invoke* function. Here's the *CMarketControl* header, which is contained in MARKETC.H:

```
class CMarketControl : public COleDispatchDriver
{
// Attributes
public:
    enum { DID_ZERO, DID_GETAVERAGE };
    short GetIndustrialsAverage(const VARIANT& propVal);
};
```

The class implementation file, MARKETC.CPP, is shown next. The *parms* variable contains a list of codes, each of which corresponds to a parameter; in this case, it contains a list of only one item—a *VARIANT*. The parameters themselves are supplied as trailing arguments to *InvokeHelper*, which can process a variable number of arguments as *printf* does.

```
#include "stdafx.h"
#include "marketc.h"

short CMarketControl::GetIndustrialsAverage(const VARIANT& vTime)
{
    short  result;
    static BYTE BASED_CODE parms[] = VTS_VARIANT;
    InvokeHelper(DID_GETAVERAGE, DISPATCH_METHOD, VT_I2,
                 (void*)&result, parms, &vTime);
    return result;
}
```

The *CEx25eView* class has a data member *m_marketc* of class *CMarketControl*. The *CEx25eView* member functions for the Market server are listed here:

```
void CEx25eView::OnMarketGetAverage()
{
    BeginWaitCursor();
    int nAvg = m_marketc.GetIndustrialsAverage(
               CVariant(1994, 8, 1, 0, 0, 0));
    TRACE("CEx25eView::OnMarketGetAverage -- nAvg = %d\n",
          nAvg);
    EndWaitCursor();
}


void CEx25eView::OnUpdateMarketGetAverage(CCmdUI* pCmdUI)
{
    pCmdUI->Enable(m_marketc.m_lpDispatch != NULL);
}


void CEx25eView::OnMarketLoad()
{
    BeginWaitCursor();
    VERIFY(m_marketc.CreateDispatch("ex25b.market") == TRUE);
    EndWaitCursor();
}


void CEx25eView::OnUpdateMarketLoad(CCmdUI* pCmdUI)
{
    pCmdUI->Enable(m_marketc.m_lpDispatch == NULL);
}
```

(continued)

```
void CEx25eView::OnMarketUnload()
{
    BeginWaitCursor();
    m_marketc.ReleaseDispatch();
    EndWaitCursor();
}

void CEx25eView::OnUpdateMarketUnload(CCmdUI* pCmdUI)
{
    pCmdUI->Enable(m_marketc.m_lpDispatch != NULL);
}
```

Notice the use of the base class *CreateDispatch* and *ReleaseDispatch* functions for loading and unloading the server program. In the second version of EX25B, *ReleaseDispatch* always causes the instance to exit. The *COleDispatch-Driver::m_lpDispatch* data member is useful for enabling and disabling menu choices. (See the note on page 633.)

The Controller Class for EX25C.DLL

We'll use the *CDLLControl* class to represent the EX25C.AUTO server. This class was not generated by AppWizard or ClassWizard; you must write your own controller classes for MFC automation servers. Here's the class header file (DLLCONT.H):

```
#include "cvariant.h"

class CDLLControl : public COleDispatchDriver
{
// Attributes
public:
    enum { DID_ZERO, DID_LONGDATA, DID_TEXTDATA, DID_DISPDIALOG };
    CVariant GetTextData();
    void SetTextData(const VARIANT& propVal);
    long GetLongData();
    void SetLongData(long propVal);
    BOOL DisplayDialog();

// Operations
public:
    void ShowWin();
    void RefreshWin();
};
```

And here are the member functions from DLLCONT.CPP:

```
CVariant CDLLControl::GetTextData()
{
    CVariant result;
    GetProperty(DID_TEXTDATA, VT_VARIANT, (void*)&result);
```

```
        return result;
    }

    void CDLLControl::SetTextData(const VARIANT& propVal)
    {
        SetProperty(DID_TEXTDATA, VT_VARIANT, &propVal);
    }

    long CDLLControl::GetLongData()
    {
        long result;
        GetProperty(DID_LONGDATA, VT_I4, (void*)&result);
        return result;
    }

    void CDLLControl::SetLongData(long propVal)
    {
        SetProperty(DID_LONGDATA, VT_I4, propVal);
    }

    BOOL CDLLControl::DisplayDialog()
    {
        BOOL result;
        InvokeHelper(DID_DISPDIALOG, DISPATCH_METHOD, VT_BOOL,
                     NULL, NULL);
        return result;
    }
```

Notice that each property requires separate *Get* and *Set* functions, even though the property is represented by a data member in the server. Also notice that *CDLLControl* uses an *enum* for dispatch IDs. Be careful here when you modify the server: ClassWizard sometimes changes the server's dispatch map sequence, thus requiring you to update the *enum* in the controller.

The view class header has a data member *m_dllControl* of class *CDLLControl*. Here are two DLL-related command handler member functions from EX25EVW.CPP:

```
void CEx25eView::OnDllLoad()
{
    BeginWaitCursor();
    VERIFY(m_dllControl.CreateDispatch("ex25c.auto") == TRUE);
    m_dllControl.SetTextData(CVariant("test"));  // testing
    m_dllControl.SetLongData(79L);     // testing
    EndWaitCursor();
}

void CEx25eView::OnDllGetData()
```

(continued)

```
{
    m_dllControl.DisplayDialog();
    CVariant vData = m_dllControl.GetTextData();
    ASSERT(vData.vt == VT_BSTR);
    long lData = m_dllControl.GetLongData();
    TRACE("CEx25eView::OnDllGetData -- long = %ld, text = %s\n",
        lData, (const char FAR*) vData.bstrVal);
}
```

The Controller Class for EX25D.EXE

The file CLOCKC.H contains the header for the *CClockControl* class, which controls the EX25D automation server.

```
#include "cvariant.h"

class CClockControl : public COleDispatchDriver
{
// Attributes
public:
    // These need to be in the same sequence as the server's
    //  dispatch map. If the server changes, update these.
    enum { DID_ZERO, DID_TIME, DID_REFRESH,
           DID_SHOW, DID_CREATEALARM, DID_FIGURE };
    CVariant GetFigure(short i);
    void SetFigure(short i, const VARIANT&);
    CVariant GetTime();
    void SetTime(const VARIANT&);

// Operations
public:
    void ShowWin();
    void RefreshWin();
    LPDISPATCH CreateAlarm(const VARIANT& time);
};
```

The code for the *GetFigure* and *SetFigure* functions is shown on page 619. Here's the *CClockControl::CreateAlarm* member function:

```
LPDISPATCH CClockControl::CreateAlarm(const VARIANT& vTime)
{
    LPDISPATCH result;
    static    BYTE BASED_CODE parms[] = VTS_VARIANT;
    InvokeHelper(DID_CREATEALARM, DISPATCH_METHOD, VT_DISPATCH,
                (void*)&result, parms, &vTime);
    return result;
}
```

There's a class for the alarm controller as well, and it's declared in ALARMC.H:

```
#include "cvariant.h"

class CAlarmControl : public COleDispatchDriver
{
// Attributes
public:
    // These need to be in the same sequence as the server's
    // dispatch map. If the server changes, update these.
    enum { DID_ZERO, DID_TIME };
    CVariant GetTime();
    void SetTime(const VARIANT&);
};
```

The view class has data members *m_alarmc* and *m_clockc*. Here's the view command handler that calls *CClock::CreateAlarm*:

```
void CEx25eView::OnClockCreateAlarm()
{
    TRACE("Entering CEx25eView::OnClockCreateAlarm\n");

    // the following code demonstrates use of
    // GetIDsOfNames -- not required
    char    FAR* szMember = "CreateAlarm";
    DISPID dispid;
    VERIFY(m_clockc.m_lpDispatch->GetIDsOfNames(IID_NULL,
           &szMember, 1, 0, &dispid) == S_OK);
    TRACE("GetIDsOfNames: dispid = %d\n", dispid);

    CAlarmDialog dlg;
    if (dlg.DoModal() == IDOK) {
      LPDISPATCH pAlarm = m_clockc.CreateAlarm(CVariant(0, 0,
             0, dlg.m_hours, dlg.m_minutes, dlg.m_seconds));
      m_alarmc.AttachDispatch(pAlarm);       // releases prior
                                             //   object!
      m_clockc.RefreshWin();

      CVariant vTime = m_alarmc.GetTime(); // test property
                                           //   access
      CVariant vStringTime;
      vTime.ChangeType(VT_BSTR, vStringTime);
    }
}
```

The *CClockControl::CreateAlarm* function causes the server to construct a clock object and return an *IDispatch* pointer with a reference count of 1. The *COleDispatchDriver::AttachDispatch* function connects that pointer to the *m_alarmc* object, but if that object already has a dispatch pointer, the old pointer is released. That's why, if you watch the debug window, you'll see that the old EX25D instance exits immediately after you ask for a new instance.

You'll have to test this behavior with the Excel driver because EX25E disables the Load menu choice when the clock is running.

Controlling Microsoft Excel

The EX25E program contains code that loads Excel, creates a workbook, and reads and writes cells from the active worksheet. Controlling Excel is exactly like controlling an MFC automation server, but you need to know about a few Excel peculiarities.

If you study Excel VBA, you'll notice that there are over 100 "objects" you can use in your programs. All of these objects are accessible through OLE Automation, but if you write an MFC automation controller program, you'll need to know about the objects' properties and methods. Ideally, you'd like a C++ class for each object, complete with member functions coded to the proper dispatch IDs.

Because Excel uses a type library, there's a binary file named XLEN50.OLB in the EXCEL directory that contains all the information you need for writing your classes. ClassWizard can read this file to automatically create C++ classes for individual Excel objects. If you click the Read Type Library button in the ClassWizard OLE Automation page and you select XLEN50.OLB, you'll see the objects listed, as shown in Figure 25-13. You select an object and specify a class name and filenames.

Figure 25-13.
ClassWizard can create C++ classes for the Excel objects listed in XLEN50.OLB.

CAUTION: Visual C++ version 1.5 requires you to use the object name as the class name. If you type *CRange* in place of *Range*, ClassWizard generates code for <u>all</u> the Excel objects. Perhaps this problem will be fixed in a later version.

You might need to edit the generated code to suit your needs. Let's look at an example. If you use ClassWizard to generate a controller class for the Worksheet object, you get a *Range* member function:

```
VARIANT Worksheet::Range(const VARIANT& Cell1,
                         const VARIANT& Cell2)
{
    VARIANT result;
    static BYTE BASED_CODE parms[] = VTS_VARIANT VTS_VARIANT;
    InvokeHelper(0xc5, DISPATCH_METHOD, VT_VARIANT,
             (void*)&result, parms, &Cell1, &Cell2);
    return result;
}
```

The trouble is that you know (from the documentation) that the *Range* method returns a dispatch pointer, not a *VARIANT*, and that you can call the method with either a single cell (1 parameter) or a rectangular area specified by two cells (2 parameters). Remember: You can omit optional parameters in a call to *InvokeHelper*. Now it makes sense to replace the generated *Range* function with two overloaded functions:

```
LPDISPATCH Worksheet::Range(const VARIANT& Cell1,
                            const VARIANT& Cell2)
{
    TRACE("Entering Worksheet::Range(Cell1, Cell2)\n");
    LPDISPATCH result;
    static BYTE BASED_CODE parms[] = VTS_VARIANT VTS_VARIANT;
    InvokeHelper(0xc5, DISPATCH_METHOD, VT_DISPATCH,
             (void*)&result, parms, &Cell1, &Cell2);
    return result;
}

LPDISPATCH Worksheet::Range(const VARIANT& Cell1)
{
    TRACE("Entering Worksheet::Range(Cell1)\n");
    LPDISPATCH result;
    static BYTE BASED_CODE parms[] = VTS_VARIANT;
    InvokeHelper(0xc5, DISPATCH_METHOD, VT_DISPATCH,
             (void*)&result, parms, &Cell1);
    return result;
}
```

How do you know which functions to fix up? They're the functions you decide to use in your program. You'll have to read the Excel VBA reference manual to figure out the required parameters and return values. Perhaps someday soon someone will write a set of Excel controller classes.

The EX25E program uses the following Excel objects and thus contains corresponding classes, as shown in this table:

Object/Class	View Class Data Member	Header File	Implementation File
Application	*m_excel*	app.h	app.cpp
Range	*m_range[5]*	range.h	range.cpp
Worksheet	*m_worksheet*	wksheet.h	wksheet.cpp
Workbooks	*m_workbooks*	wkbooks.h	wkbooks.cpp

The following view member function, *OnExcelLoad,* handles the Excel OLE Load menu command. This function must work if the user already has Excel running on the desktop. The OLE *GetActiveObject* function tries to return an *IUnknown* pointer for Excel. *GetActiveObject* requires a class ID, so we must first call *CLSIDFromProgID.* If *GetActiveObject* is successful, we call *QueryInterface* to get an *IDispatch* pointer, and we attach it to the view's *m_excel* controller object of class *Application.* If *GetActiveObject* is unsuccessful, we call *COleDispatchDriver::CreateDispatch,* as we did for the other servers.

```
void CEx25eView::OnExcelLoad()
{   // if Excel is already running, attach to it,
    //   otherwise start it
    LPDISPATCH pDisp;
    LPUNKNOWN pUnk;
    CLSID clsid;
    TRACE("Entering CEx25eView::OnExcelLoad\n");
    BeginWaitCursor();
    ::CLSIDFromProgID("excel.application.5", &clsid);
    // from REG.DAT
    if (::GetActiveObject(clsid, NULL, &pUnk) == S_OK) {
      TRACE("attaching\n");
      VERIFY(pUnk->QueryInterface(IID_IDispatch,
          (void FAR* FAR*) &pDisp) == S_OK);
      m_excel.AttachDispatch(pDisp);
      pUnk->Release();
    }
    else {
      TRACE("creating\n");
```

```
            VERIFY(m_excel.CreateDispatch("excel.application.5")
                == TRUE);
        }
        EndWaitCursor();
    }
```

OnExcelExecute is the command handler for Excel OLE Execute. Its first task is to find the Excel main window and bring it to the top. We must write some Windows code here because the Excel developers weren't kind enough to supply a method for this purpose. We must also create a workbook if no workbook is currently open.

We have to watch our method return values closely. The *Workbooks Add* method, for example, returns an *IDispatch* pointer for a Workbook object and, of course, increments the reference count. If we generated a class for Workbook, we could call *AttachDispatch* so that *Release* would be called when the Workbook object was destroyed. Because we don't need a Workbook class, we'll simply release the pointer ourselves at the end of the function. If we don't clean up our pointers properly, we'll get memory leak messages from the Debug version of MFC.

The rest of the *OnExcelExecute* function accesses the cells in the worksheet. You can see how easy it is to get and set numbers, dates, strings, and formulas. The C++ code is similar to the VBA code you would write to do the same job.

```
void CEx25eView::OnExcelExecute()
{
    TRACE("Entering CEx25eView::OnExcelExecute\n");
    LPDISPATCH pRange, pWorkbooks;

    CWnd* pWnd = CWnd::FindWindow("XLMAIN", NULL);
    if (pWnd != NULL) {
        TRACE("Excel window found\n");
        pWnd->ShowWindow(SW_SHOWNORMAL);
        pWnd->UpdateWindow();
        pWnd->BringWindowToTop();
    }

    m_excel.SetSheetsInNewWorkbook(1);

    VERIFY(pWorkbooks = m_excel.Workbooks());
    m_workbooks.AttachDispatch(pWorkbooks);

    LPDISPATCH pWorkbook = NULL;
    if (m_workbooks.GetCount() == 0) {
```

(continued)

```
    // Add returns a Workbook pointer, but we don't
    //  have a Workbook class
    pWorkbook = m_workbooks.Add(); // save pointer for later release
}
LPDISPATCH pWorksheet = m_excel.Worksheets(CVariant("sheet1"));
VERIFY(pWorksheet != NULL);

m_worksheet.AttachDispatch(pWorksheet);
m_worksheet.Select();

VERIFY(pRange = m_worksheet.Range(CVariant("A1")));
m_range[0].AttachDispatch(pRange);

VERIFY(pRange = m_worksheet.Range(CVariant("A2")));
m_range[1].AttachDispatch(pRange);

VERIFY(pRange = m_worksheet.Range(CVariant("A3")));
m_range[2].AttachDispatch(pRange);

VERIFY(pRange = m_worksheet.Range(CVariant("A3"),
        CVariant("C5")));
m_range[3].AttachDispatch(pRange);

VERIFY(pRange = m_worksheet.Range(CVariant("A6")));
m_range[4].AttachDispatch(pRange);

m_range[4].SetValue(CVariant(1994, 4, 24, 15, 47, 8));
CVariant timeDate = m_range[4].GetValue();
CVariant varDate, stringDate;
if (timeDate.ChangeType(VT_DATE, varDate)) {
  // allows for returned R8 date
  if (varDate.ChangeType(VT_BSTR, stringDate)) {
    TRACE("string date = %s\n", stringDate.bstrVal);
  }
}
m_range[0].SetValue(CVariant("test string"));

CVariant vResult0 = m_range[0].GetValue();
if (vResult0.vt == VT_BSTR) {
  TRACE("vResult0 = %s\n", vResult0.bstrVal);
}

m_range[1].SetValue(CVariant(3.14159));

CVariant vResult1 = m_range[1].GetValue();
if (vResult1.vt == VT_R8) {
  TRACE("vResult1 = %f\n", vResult1.dblVal);
}
```

```
    m_range[2].SetFormula(CVariant("=$A2*2.0"));

    CVariant vResult2 = m_range[2].GetValue();
    if (vResult2.vt == VT_R8) {
      TRACE("vResult2 = %f\n", vResult2.dblVal);
    }

    CVariant vResult2a = m_range[2].GetFormula();
    if (vResult2a.vt == VT_BSTR) {
      TRACE("vResult2a = %s\n", vResult2a.bstrVal);
    }

    m_range[3].FillRight();
    m_range[3].FillDown();

// cleanup
    if (pWorkbook != NULL) {
        pWorkbook->Release();
    }
}
```

WARNING: If you compile EX25E with the Debug build option, you'll get an ASSERT dialog box at OLEDISP2.CPP line 352. This is an MFC 2.5 bug. This statement should be commented out and the library should be rebuilt.

NOTE: EX25E is a C++ automation controller program that runs EX25B, a C++ automation server, via the Get Averages command on the Market OLE menu. A TRACE statement in EX25E prints in the Debug Messages window the value that EX25B calculates. Earlier we used Microsoft Excel as the controller, which put the calculated value in a cell.

OLE and the Future

At the time this book went to press, OLE was still very new, yet a number of "early adopter" companies had jumped into it. I interviewed only two developers, but, interestingly, both of them were building complex modular systems and were using the Common Object Model as the underlying architecture. To this end, they had developed their own interfaces. Neither was very interested in connecting to outside applications, but both were considering OLE Automation for a VBA interface. One developer was looking closely at OLE Structured Storage. What are you going to do with OLE? Please tell me. I'd like to know.

You've probably heard of Microsoft's Cairo. I was a little fuzzy about what Cairo was, thinking first that it was a new operating system. After talking to the experts, I discovered that it's a "shell" that will run inside new versions of Windows. Think of the Cairo shell as a Visual Basic form. Instead of being populated by VBXs, it contains "Cairo-aware apps" that might end up being similar to OLE Controls. These applications must implement specified OLE interfaces, and they can use other interfaces supported by Cairo. The short story is this: If you want to write applications for Cairo, you'd better learn OLE now. Good luck!

DYNAMIC LINK LIBRARIES (DLLs)

The dynamic link library (DLL) has always been an important part of Windows-based programming. Now Microsoft Foundation Class (MFC) Library version 2.5 programmers can take advantage of this powerful programming technique. You'll find that a class library DLL is somewhat different from the normal C-language API DLLs you might have worked with before. This chapter points out the differences and shows you how to build and use a class library DLL. You'll start by using MFC250.DLL, which packages the entire MFC library. Then you'll extend this ready-made DLL by writing your own custom DLL.

Why Use a DLL?

DLLs are Windows-based program modules that can be loaded and linked at run time. Many applications can benefit by being split into a series of main programs and DLLs. Suppose you are developing a large integrated accounting system. This job is too big for a single executable program. You might have separate programs, or modules, for Payroll, Accounts Receivable, and so forth, but these programs have a lot of functionality in common. All modules might share the same list management and database access classes, for example. If you put the shared code in one or more DLLs, the individual modules will be smaller on disk and therefore quicker to load. If the user has both the Payroll and the Accounts Receivable program loaded at the same time, only one copy of the DLL code will be in memory, shared by the two client applications.

Another use for DLLs is national language support. If you isolate language-dependent functions and resources into DLLs for, say, the English,

French, or Spanish language, the user can choose the proper DLL during the installation process or at run time. You'll probably think of other uses for DLLs in your own applications.

Conventional DLLs

Even if you haven't written your own Windows DLLs, you've probably used the DLLs that come with Windows or those that other software vendors produce. File dialog and drag-and-drop support, for instance, are in the Windows DLLs COMMDLG.DLL and SHELL.DLG. The EX24A example used ODBC.DLL, which, in turn, loaded another DLL for the selected DBMS. Using a C-language API DLL is no big deal. You simply ensure that your make file includes a reference to the DLL's import library, and you ensure that the DLL file is available on disk at run time. You call a DLL C function the same way you call a function that's in your own project.

Conventional C-language API DLLs have one important characteristic: They can be used with any C compiler and with other languages and programming environments. A database DLL written in Borland C, for example, can be called from a Microsoft C program, from a Microsoft Visual Basic program, or from a Toolbook script.

You can think of a conventional DLL as an independent program with its own instance handle, its own global memory, its own heap, and its own resources. The DLL shares the client's stack, however. DLLs do not have their own Windows message loops. The DLL is loaded at startup or when needed, and it is unloaded after the last client application terminates. If the conventional DLL allocates memory, that memory is released when the DLL terminates, not when a client terminates. Often a DLL's API will require the client to allocate memory. The client passes a buffer address to the DLL, the DLL operates on the buffer, and then the client frees the memory. With ODBC, for example, the client allocates a buffer for column data, and the DLL writes in the buffer.

There are several DLL linkage options. The import library is the most common option for compiled C programs. The client uses a symbolic name to call a DLL function, and Windows matches calls to DLL function addresses when the DLL is loaded. The functions can be matched symbolically or through ordinal numbers. The ordinal method, in which each DLL function is assigned a unique integer, is more efficient. Interpreted-language Windows environments often use DLLs in a more dynamic manner. They can select and load DLLs at run time, and they can call DLL functions without prior address resolution.

A DLL can be updated without client recompilation if the existing function prototypes remain exactly the same. If you change a function name, return data type, or parameter data type, you should count on recompiling the client applications.

Visual C++ supports the creation of conventional DLLs written with the MFC library classes but with a C-language external interface. Technical Note #11 in the MFCNOTES.HLP file describes the process of writing what is known as a user DLL (_USRDLL). The sample program in the \MSVC-\MFC\SAMPLES\DLLTRACE subdirectory illustrates such a DLL. This chapter focuses on a different kind of DLL—the MFC library DLL that's compatible with the C++ language.

The MFC Library DLL

An MFC library DLL can accommodate entire C++ classes. You can use these DLL-resident classes the same way you use statically linked classes. You can construct objects of DLL-resident classes, and you can use them as base classes. There are some major differences between conventional DLLs and class library DLLs, however.

MFC Library DLL Usage Restricted to Microsoft C++ Compilers

Unlike conventional DLLs, MFC library DLLs can be used only in Microsoft MFC library applications. Why the restriction? The Microsoft C++ compiler uses special internal function names that combine the class name, function name, return data type, parameter data types, and public/protected/private access. With the Microsoft C++ compiler, for example, the function

```
CWnd* GetDescendantWindow(int nID) const
```

is assigned the mangled (or decorated) name

```
?GetDescendantWindow@CWnd@@RFCPEV1@H@Z
```

Other compilers use different name-mangling algorithms, so if a Borland C++ client program contained a *GetDescendantWindow* call, the Borland mangled name wouldn't match the Microsoft mangled name.

The MFC Library Classes as a DLL

The easiest way to use the MFC library DLL technology in your application is to use the MFC250 and MFC250D DLLs included with Visual C++. These DLLs contain all the MFC library functionality, with some minor exceptions such as time formatting. MFC200.DLL is the release version, and MFC250D.DLL is the debugging equivalent. Converting a statically linked class library application to a DLL-based application is easy. You simply change some Visual Workbench options (or change some switches in your make file for NMAKE), as shown later in this chapter.

For Windows SDK Programmers

If you've written a Windows DLL client application in the SDK environment, you're probably used to exporting client callback functions (functions in the client program that are called by Windows and by the DLL). You have undoubtedly used the Windows *MakeProcInstance* function for these exported functions. Forget this stuff. With Microsoft C/C++ versions 7.0 and later (with the /GA switch), these exports are unnecessary.

Do you want your MFC library applications to be DLL-based? Your answer depends on your needs. You should develop your applications first with static linking for easier debugging. If you're distributing a large suite of programs that each use many MFC library features, using MFC250.DLL will conserve your users' disk space and memory. If, on the other hand, you have a few small programs, using MFC250.DLL might lead to a larger net program size because the MFC library DLL approach forces you to use the large memory model and because MFC250.DLL contains <u>all</u> the MFC library classes and functions.

Here are some actual numbers for you. The size of the MFC250.DLL file is 298 KB. The medium-model statically linked MATPLAN.EXE example program from Chapter 21 is about 124 KB, and the large-model equivalent is about 148 KB. With the DLL, the MATPLAN.EXE file's size is 43 KB. It's obviously not worth using the DLL if you're distributing only a single MATPLAN-type application.

Using MFC250D.DLL in an Application

Now it's time to turn on the computer. It's so easy to switch an application from using the static MFC library to using the dynamic library that we don't need a separate project for it. Simply choose any project from an earlier chapter. The MATPLAN example from Chapter 21 is fine. If you want to double-check on the option settings, look at the EX26B project, which uses MFC250D.DLL plus an extension DLL.

Here are the steps for converting a statically linked project to a dynamically linked one:

1. In Visual Workbench's Project Options dialog, <u>uncheck</u> the Use Microsoft Foundation Classes check box.

2. In the C/C++ Compiler Options dialog, change the following Common To Both build options:

   ❏ Memory Model: Set "Model" to "Large."

   ❏ Preprocessor: Add "_AFXDLL" to "Symbols and Macros to Define."

   ❏ Windows Prolog/Epilog: Check the "Generate for __far Functions" check box.

3. In the Project's Linker Options dialog, add *MFC250* at the <u>head</u> of the Input Library list for the Release Specific build option.

4. In the Project's Linker Options dialog, add *MFC250D* at the <u>head</u> of the Input Library list for the Debug Specific build option.

If you want to reduce the size of your client EXE file, eliminate redundant resources from your resource script. To do so, start App Studio and choose Set Includes from App Studio's File menu. Delete the references to the standard AFX resources from the Compile-Time Directives list box in the Set Includes dialog box that appears, and then click OK. Remember that the application framework searches the client resources before it searches the MFC250.DLL resources, so you can override standard AFX resources if necessary.

You must select Rebuild All from the Visual Workbench Project menu after you make the changes listed above.

MFC Library Extension DLLs

If you want to add new classes to the MFC library DLL, you should not rebuild MFC250.DLL but rather write your own MFC library extension DLL that client programs can load along with MFC250.DLL. When you write your extension DLL, you must follow some clearly defined conventions, which are highlighted in this chapter's first example.

WARNING: If you modify MFC250.DLL, you could create problems for other applications that depend on Microsoft's version of the DLL.

MFC Library DLL Memory Usage

In an MFC library extension DLL, memory is managed by the client application—which means that if you use the *new* operator in the MFC library DLL (*new* and *delete* are specially overloaded for DLLs), client application memory will be allocated. When the client application terminates, all its allocated memory is released, including memory allocated in DLL functions. Now the DLL is starting to look less like an independent program and more like part of the client application! As in conventional DLLs, the DLL and the client application share the stack. The DLL owns the global variables.

> NOTE: A statically linked MFC library application references global variables, defined inside the class library, that identify per-application elements such as the current application object, the current instance handle, and the current resource handle. A class library DLL moves these global variables to a fixed location in the client application's stack segment.

Required Code for Extension DLLs

Each class library extension DLL you write must contain boilerplate code similar to the following code. The *LibMain* function is the DLL equivalent of *WinMain*, and Windows calls it when the DLL is loaded. The DLL initialization function, named *InitMyDLL* here, is optionally called from your client application. You'll see why later.

```
#include <afxdllx.h>          // prior #include <afxwin.h> assumed

extern AFX_EXTENSION_MODULE NEAR extensionDLL = {NULL, NULL};

extern "C" int CALLBACK LibMain(HINSTANCE hInstance, WORD, WORD, LPSTR)
{
    // do not allocate memory or use TRACE, ASSERT, or MessageBox here
    AfxInitExtensionModule(extensionDLL, hInstance);
    return 1; // OK
}

// following DLL initialization function is called from the client app
extern "C" extern void WINAPI InitMyDLL()
{
    new CDynLinkLibrary(extensionDLL);
}
```

Searching for Resources

Both a DLL and a client application can have their own resources. Suppose a program contains the following code:

```
CString strError;
strError.LoadString(IDS_ERROR1);
```

Where does the application framework search for the string identified by *IDS_ERROR1*—in the class library client application's resources or in the DLL's? The default behavior (assuming that you've written the DLL initialization function discussed in the previous section) is to search for resources in this sequence:

1. Client application resources

2. Your extension DLL resources

3. MFC250 standard AFX resources

NOTE: Because MFC250.DLL contains the standard AFX resources, your project's AppWizard-generated RC file need not duplicate them. You can choose Set Includes from App Studio's File menu and then remove the following lines from your resource script file:

```
#include "afxres.rc"
#include "afxprint.rc"
```

and you can use the Visual Workbench editor to remove many of the string resource definitions (such as the file and edit menu prompts). Because the application framework searches the client resources before it searches the MFC250.DLL resources, you can override standard AFX resources if you need to.

You can change the default search behavior by forcing a DLL to search its own resources first. The following code switches the application framework's instance handle from the client application to a DLL, accessing the resource, and then it switches the instance handle back to the client application:

```
HINSTANCE hInstResourceClient = AfxGetResourceHandle();
AfxSetResourceHandle(extensionDLL.hModule);    // uses DLL's instance
                                               // handle
strError.LoadString(IDS_ERROR1);
AfxSetResourceHandle(hInstResourceClient);     // restores client's
                                               // instance handle
```

Inline Constructors

Do <u>not</u> use inline constructors for DLL-resident classes. Inline constructors complicate the process of exporting class member functions.

Extension DLL Exports

You must specifically "export" selected extension DLL functions and variables. Which ones do you export? That depends on whether you are constructing objects from a DLL-resident class or deriving classes from a DLL-resident class. Here are some rules:

A DLL-Resident Class Used Directly

- Export all nonvirtual member functions that your client program calls directly.

- You don't need to export virtual functions that are declared in a base class. (Note: This rule applies to classes that do not have inline constructors. You should not use inline constructors for classes you intend to use in a DLL.)

- If the class has a message map, export the static *messageMap* entry, as shown on the facing page.

  NOTE: The use of the *RUNTIME_CLASS* macro is restricted. In a client application, you cannot dynamically create objects of DLL-resident classes. This means, for example, that you can't place a view class in a DLL and then use it in your client application's *AddDocTemplate* call. You can place the *AddDocTemplate* call in the DLL's initialization function, however, as the example program in the \MSVC\MFC\SAMPLES\DLLHUSK subdirectory illustrates.

A DLL-Resident Class Used for Derivation

- Export all public nonvirtual member functions that your client program calls directly.

- Export all nonvirtual member functions that a derived class might want to call.

- Export all virtual member functions (except pure virtual functions).

■ Export the *CRuntimeClass* entry, as shown below.

■ If the class has a message map, export the static *messageMap* entry, as shown below.

You export a DLL function by listing its mangled name, together with an ordinal number, in the EXPORTS section of the DLL's DEF file. If your DLL contained a view class *CMyBaseView* with an overridden *OnDraw* function, for example, you would export the *OnDraw* function with a line such as this:

```
?OnDraw@CMyBaseView1@@VECXPEVCDC@@@Z                    @101 NONAME
```

The function's arbitrary (but unique) ordinal number is 101.

The *CRuntimeClass* entry is exported like this:

```
?classCMyBaseView@CMyBaseView@@2UCRuntimeClass@@A      @114 NONAME
```

and the *messageMap* entry is exported as follows:

```
?messageMap@CMyBaseView@@1UAFX_MSGMAP@@A              @115 NONAME
```

The project's MAP file is the source for these exported mangled names. In Visual Workbench, click on the Miscellaneous category in the Linker Options dialog, and then set Other Options to /MAP:FULL. For each exported function, search the MAP file for the function name, and then extract the mangled name on the previous line. For the run time class and message map entries, use the lines shown above, with your own class name substituted for *CMyBaseView*.

> **NOTE:** The DLL project switch settings ensure that all far functions have the proper prolog and epilog code for export. Do <u>not</u> use the *_export* keyword in your DLL source. This option has undesirable side effects in the class library environment. In particular, it precludes the use of space-saving ordinals in the executable program.

Static Class Data Members

You can define static data members for your DLL classes, but be careful that the definitions don't allocate memory. You can, for example, define a static *CRect* object like this:

```
const CRect NEAR CMyView::rect(10, 10, 500, 400);
```

but you <u>cannot</u> define a *CString* object like this:

```
const CString NEAR CMyView::string("test"); // don't do this in a DLL
```

The latter definition causes major problems because the *new* operator is called before the application framework has had a chance to install the correct *new* implementation.

Extension DLL Run-Time Class Identification

As mentioned in the note on page 642, the *RUNTIME_CLASS* macro, when used in a client program, doesn't work for a class that is resident in a class library extension DLL. The *GetRuntimeClass* function does work, however, if you have declared the class to be dynamic.

Creating the DLL

Visual Workbench has a specific project type for Windows-based DLLs. When you select this option, the linker produces a DLL file, and the compiler and linker switches are set accordingly. Be sure the DLL file is available to its client applications at run time. Windows version 3.1 first searches for DLLs in the subdirectories specified in the PATH environment variable, and then it searches the \WINDOWS and \WINDOWS\SYSTEM subdirectories. If you install the necessary extension DLLs in the client project's own subdirectory, you will eliminate the chance of conflict with other DLLs with the same names. If you install the DLLs in the \WINDOWS\SYSTEM subdirectory, all applications can share them.

Creating the Import Library

You must create an import library for your class library extension DLL. Even though Visual Workbench generates an import library, that library does not correspond to your DEF file and is therefore useless. Use the Visual C++ IMPLIB utility from the command line as follows (substituting your application's name for *myapp*):

```
implib myapp.lib myapp.def
```

Once the import library is created, be sure that the linker can find it when you are building a client project. Copy the import library to the \MSVC\MFC\LIB subdirectory or choose Options Directory from the Visual Workbench menu to modify the library search path.

Debug and Release DLL Versions

After you have switched from static linking to dynamic linking, you might still need to debug your extension DLLs and client applications. It's good practice to maintain both a debug and a release version of your extension

DLLs. By convention, the debug version name ends with a D. You'll need separate DEF files too because the DEF file contains the name of the DLL. Also, you'll want separate import libraries that follow the DLL naming convention.

EX26A—Writing Your Own Class Library Extension DLL

The EX26A example project combines the *CStudent* class (from Chapter 15), the *CPersistentFrame* class (from Chapter 14), and the *CRowView* class (from Chapter 24) into a single dynamic link library, EX26AD.DLL. (EX26A.DLL is the companion release version.) The *CRowView* and *CPersistentFrame* classes are included because they are typical class library base classes. The *CStudent* class is included to demonstrate that the objects of a DLL-resident class can be serialized in a client application.

The EX26A classes have mostly the same source code as their statically linked counterparts, except for some added code that demonstrates resource searching and runtime class access. This chapter's second example, EX26B, is a client application that uses the EX26A DLL.

The EX26A subdirectory actually contains two projects—EX26A.MAK for the release DLL and EX26AD.MAK for the debugging DLL. It also contains two separate DEF files—EX26A.DEF and EX26AD.DEF. The source code is split into the following source code files, which the two projects share:

Header File	Source Code File	Class	Description
STDAFX.H	EX26A.CPP		*LibMain* function and DLL initializer
PERSIST.H	PERSIST.CPP	*CPersistentFrame*	SDI persistent frame base class
ROWVIEW.H	ROWVIEW.CPP	*CRowView*	Row view base class
STUDENT.H	STUDENT.CPP	*CStudent*	Student record class

A resource file, EX26A.RC, contains the *CRowView IDS_TOO_MANY_ROWS* error message string.

You've seen the *CStudent*, *CPersistentFrame*, and *CRowView* code before. The *CStudent* class was modified to eliminate the inline constructor and to add the constructor, as shown at the top of the following page:

```
CStudent::CStudent(const char* szName, long lGrade): m_name(szName)
{
    m_lGrade = lGrade;
}
```

The code in EX26A.CPP is almost identical to the DLL boilerplate code listed previously. For this application, the DLL initializer function is named *InitEx26aDLL*.

The EX26AD.DEF File

Figure 26-1 shows the complete DEF file for the project (debugging version). Only those functions used in the EX26B example are exported. The EX26A.DEF file is identical except for the library name. You can use this file as a prototype for your own extension DLL DEF files.

```
LIBRARY     EX26AD
DESCRIPTION  'ROWVIEW/PERSISTENTVIEW DLL'
EXETYPE WINDOWS
CODE    LOADONCALL MOVEABLE DISCARDABLE
DATA    PRELOAD MOVEABLE SINGLE

SEGMENTS
    _TEXT    PRELOAD MOVEABLE DISCARDABLE
    WEP_TEXT PRELOAD MOVEABLE DISCARDABLE

HEAPSIZE  1024

EXPORTS
    WEP @1 RESIDENTNAME PRIVATE ;; required WEP entry point (uses library WEP)

    ; Explicitly exported initialization routine
    INITEX26ADLL                                              @2 NONAME;

; CRowView
    ; Constructor and Destructor
    ??0CRowView@@JEC@XZ                                       @100 NONAME
    ??1CRowView@@NEC@XZ                                       @101 NONAME
    ; operations/attributes
    ?RowToWndRect@CRowView@@NEC?EVCRect@@PEVCDC@@H@Z           @102 NONAME
    ?LastViewableRow@CRowView@@NECHXZ                         @103 NONAME
    ?RowToYPos@CRowView@@NECHH@Z                              @104 NONAME
    ?RectLPtoRowRange@CRowView@@NECXAFVCRect@@AEH1H@Z         @105 NONAME
    ?UpdateRow@CRowView@@NECXH@Z                              @106 NONAME
```

Figure 26-1. *(continued)*
The EX26AD.DEF file listing.

Figure 26-1. *continued*

```
    ; Virtual overrides (called by framework)
    ?OnPreparePrinting@CRowView@@NECHPEUCPrintInfo@@@Z            @107 NONAME
    ?OnBeginPrinting@CRowView@@NECXPEVCDC@@PEUCPrintInfo@@@Z       @108 NONAME
    ?OnDraw@CRowView@@NECXPEVCDC@@@Z                              @109 NONAME
    ?OnInitialUpdate@CRowView@@NECXXZ                            @110 NONAME
    ?OnPrepareDC@CRowView@@NECXPEVCDC@@PEUCPrintInfo@@@Z          @111 NONAME
    ?OnPrint@CRowView@@NECXPEVCDC@@PEUCPrintInfo@@@Z              @112 NONAME
    ?UpdateScrollSizes@CRowView@@NECXXZ                          @113 NONAME
    ; runtime class & message map
    ?classCRowView@CRowView@@2UCRuntimeClass@@A                  @114 NONAME
    ?messageMap@CRowView@@1UAFX_MSGMAP@@A                        @115 NONAME

; CPersistentFrame
    ; Constructor and Destructor
    ??0CPersistentFrame@@JEC@XZ                                  @200 NONAME
    ??1CPersistentFrame@@NEC@XZ                                  @201 NONAME
    ;
    ?ActivateFrame@CPersistentFrame@@NECXH@Z                     @202 NONAME
    ; runtime class & message map
    ?classCPersistentFrame@CPersistentFrame@@2UCRuntimeClass@@A  @203 NONAME
    ?messageMap@CPersistentFrame@@1UAFX_MSGMAP@@A                @204 NONAME

; CStudent
    ; Constructors
    ??0CStudent@@REC@XZ                                          @300 NONAME
    ??0CStudent@@REC@PFDJ@Z                                      @301 NONAME
```

(Note: The *CRowView* member functions *GetRowWidthHeight, GetActiveRow, GetRowCount, OnDrawRow, ChangeSelectionNextRow,* and *ChangeSelectionToRow* don't need to be exported because they are pure virtual functions and therefore must be overridden in derived classes.)

Visual Workbench Options for the EX26AD Project

Following are the Visual Workbench options for the EX26AD class library extension DLL. The instructions assume you are starting a new project. (AppWizard doesn't generate MAK files for DLL projects.)

1. In Visual Workbench's Project Options dialog, set Project Type to "Windows dynamic link library (DLL)."

2. While still in the Project Options dialog, <u>uncheck</u> the "Use Microsoft Foundation Classes" check box.

3. In the C/C++ Compiler Options dialog, change the following Debug Specific build options for the categories shown:

❏ Memory Model: Set "Model" to "Large."

❏ Preprocessor: Add "_AFXDLL" to "Symbols and Macros to Define."

❏ Windows Prolog/Epilog: Check the "Generate for __far Functions" check box.

❏ Precompiled Headers: Precompile through Header—"STDAFX.H"
Precompile with Source—"EX26A.CPP"

4. In the Linker Options dialog, add *MFC250D* at the head of the Input Libraries list for the Debug Specific build option.

Creating the Import Library and Copying the DLL

After you have successfully built the EX26AD project, use the command line

```
implib \msvc\mfc\lib\ex26ad.lib ex26ad.def
```

to create a debug import library that is accessible to the client project link step. You might want to make a batch file for this job. Next, copy the new extension DLL to the \WINDOWS\SYSTEM directory.

EX26B—Using an MFC Library Extension DLL

The EX26B project consists of an SDI MFC library application that uses the EX26AD DLL that you built in the previous section. The EX26B program also relies on MFC250D.DLL, as do all MFC library DLL client applications. You can use the new DLL with the EX14A, EX15B, and EX24A examples, but it's more fun to build a new program that uses all three EX26A classes. The new program is yet another student list variation.

Here are the source code files involved in the EX26B project:

Header File	Source Code File	Class	Description
EX26B.H	EX26B.CPP	*CEx26bApp*	Main application class
PERSIST.H		*CPersistentFrame*	SDI persistent frame base class
MAINFRM.H	MAINFRM.CPP	*CMainFrame*	Main frame class (derived from *CPersistentFrame*)

(continued)

Header File	Source Code File	Class	Description
EX26BDOC.H	EX26BDOC.CPP	*CEx26bDoc*	Document class
ROWVIEW.H	ROWVIEW.CPP	*CRowView*	Row view base class
EX26BVW.H	EX26BVW.CPP	*CEx26bView*	View class (derived from *CRowView*)
STUDENT.H		*CStudent*	Student record class
STUDLG.H	STUDLG.CPP	*CStudentDialog*	Student modal dialog class
STDAFX.H	STDAFX.CPP		Precompiled headers

Following are descriptions of the new classes for EX26B.

CEx26bApp

This class is the standard AppWizard-generated SDI application class, except for the call to the DLL initialization routine at the beginning of *InitInstance*.

EX26B.H

```
extern "C" extern void WINAPI InitEx26aDLL();
```

EX26B.CPP

```
#ifdef_AFXDLL
    InitEx26aDLL(); // necessary for DLL resource access and IsKindOf
#endif
```

CEx26bDoc

The document class contains an embedded object pointer array that is called *m_studentArray*. This array is emptied in the *DeleteContents* member function.

CEx26bView

The *CEx26bView* class is derived from *CRowView* and is similar to the *CEx24bView* class from the ODBC example. The *OnDrawRow* function is perhaps the most interesting overridden pure virtual function.

```
void CEx26bView::OnDrawRow(CDC* pDC, int nRow, int y, BOOL bSelected)
{
    // Gets the data for the specific student
```

(continued)

```
CStudent* pStudent = (CStudent*)
                    (GetDocument()->m_studentArray[nRow]);

TEXTMETRIC tm;
pDC->GetTextMetrics(&tm);
char grade[10];

// Displays the student record in one line of text
pDC->TextOut(STUDENT_NAME_COL*tm.tmAveCharWidth, y, pStudent->m_name);
_itoa((int) (pStudent->m_lGrade), grade, 10);
pDC->TextOut(STUDENT_GRADE_COL*tm.tmAveCharWidth, y, grade, strlen(grade));
}
```

The *OnLButtonDblClk* message handler brings up the student dialog for the row that has been selected.

```
void CEx26bView::OnLButtonDblClk(UINT, CPoint point)
{
    LONG lHint = 1L;

// Brings up a dialog for the selected student record
// First click selected the row, so we don't have to here
    CStudent* pStudent1;
    CStudent* pStudent2;
    int ret;

    CEx26bDoc* pDoc = GetDocument();
    if (GetRowCount()) { // there's at least one student record
        CStudentDialog dlg(IDB_UPDATE);
        pStudent1 = (CStudent*)
                    (pDoc->m_studentArray[m_nSelectedStudent]);
        dlg.m_name = pStudent1->m_name;
        dlg.m_lGrade = pStudent1->m_lGrade;
        ret = dlg.DoModal();
        switch(ret) {
        case IDB_UPDATE:
            pStudent1->m_name = dlg.m_name;
            pStudent1->m_lGrade = dlg.m_lGrade;
            break;
        case IDB_INSERT:
            pStudent2 = new CStudent(dlg.m_name, dlg.m_lGrade);
            pDoc->m_studentArray.InsertAt(m_nSelectedStudent, pStudent2);
            break;
        case IDB_DELETE:
            lHint = 0L;
            pDoc->m_studentArray.RemoveAt(m_nSelectedStudent);
            break;
```

```
            case IDB_CANCEL:
                break;
            default:
                ASSERT(0);
                break;
        }
    }
    else {
        CStudentDialog dlg(IDB_INSERT);
        pStudent2 = new CStudent("", 0); // array was empty
        dlg.m_name = pStudent2->m_name;
        dlg.m_lGrade = pStudent2->m_lGrade;
        ret = dlg.DoModal();
        if (ret == IDB_INSERT) {
            pStudent2->m_name = dlg.m_name;
            pStudent2->m_lGrade = dlg.m_lGrade;
            pDoc->m_studentArray.InsertAt(0, pStudent2);
        }
    }
    pDoc->SetModifiedFlag();
    pDoc->UpdateAllViews(NULL, lHint);
}
```

NOTE: This is an example of the use of "hints" to optimize the repainting of the view data. When *OnUpdate* is called from *On-InitialUpdate*, the *lHint* parameter is *0*, which causes existing lines to be erased. If the user modifies or inserts a line, *lHint* is set to *1* and the old data is not erased, thereby reducing screen flicker. If the user deletes a line, *lHint* is set to *0*.

CStudentDialog

The code for this class is compatible with ClassWizard. The behavior is similar to that of the *CMatplanDialog* class from Chapter 21. The *DoModal* return value indicates which button the user clicked.

Building and Testing the EX26B Program

Building the EX26B class library DLL extension client application is similar to building an MFC250D.DLL client application: You compile with the large memory model, and you specify MFC250D.DLL and EX26AD.DLL to the linker. Don't forget to uncheck the Use Microsoft Foundation Classes option in the Project Options dialog and to define _AFXDLL. The Input category of the Linker Options dialog is shown in Figure 26-2 on the following page.

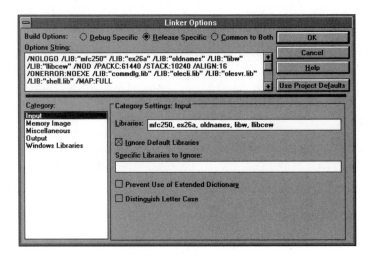

Figure 26-2.
The Linker Options dialog showing libraries.

If you did everything right when you built the EX26A example, the EX26AD import library and DLL will be available. You should be able to build and run the EX26B client application. The output should look something like that shown in Figure 26-3.

If you double-click in an empty frame or on a student record in the row view, an editing dialog pops up as shown. Document file I/O and printing are implemented.

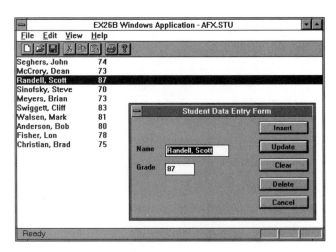

Figure 26-3.
The EX26B screen with student list.

> NOTE: If you look in the debug window after EX26B exits, you'll notice some messages regarding undeleted GDI objects. These messages result from a DLL-related bug in the Windows Debug Kernel. Ignore them.

Accessing Resources

The EX26A DLL and the EX26B client each contain diagnostic code that allows you to see how the application framework finds resources. A string resource, *IDS_TOO_MANY_ROWS* (with value *3*), is defined in <u>both</u> the DLL resource script and the client resource script. The string values are a little different, however, as shown here:

Resource Script	Value of *IDS_TOO_MANY_ROWS*
EX26A.RC	EX26A: You have exceeded the storage capacity of the scrolling view
EX26B.RC	EX26B: You have exceeded the storage capacity of the scrolling view

This difference allows you to see which resources were accessed.

The *CRowView* constructor (located in \VCPP\EX26A\ROWVIEW.CPP) contains the following code:

```
    CString strRes;
    strRes.LoadString(IDS_TOO_MANY_ROWS);
    TRACE("resource string = %s\n", (const char*) strRes);

#ifdef _AFXDLL
    HINSTANCE hInstResourceClient = AfxGetResourceHandle();
    AfxSetResourceHandle(extensionDLL.hModule);     // uses client's
                                                    //  instance handle
    strRes.LoadString(IDS_TOO_MANY_ROWS);
    TRACE("resource string = %s\n", (const char*) strRes);
    AfxSetResourceHandle(hInstResourceClient);      // restores client's
                                                    //  instance handle
#endif
```

The first *LoadString* call exercises the class library resource search capability. Because the *InitInstance* function, in the client file EX26B.CPP, contains the following code:

```
#ifdef _AFXDLL
    InitEx26aDLL();
#endif
```

the first *LoadString* call uses the <u>client's</u> resource. If you remove the *Init-Ex26aDLL* call, *LoadString* fails, returning a null string.

The second *LoadString* call above uses the DLL's resource.

The *CEx26bView* constructor (located in \VCPP\EX26B\EX26BVW.CPP) contains the following code:

```
CString strRes;
strRes.LoadString(IDS_TOO_MANY_ROWS);
TRACE("resource string = %s\n", (const char*) strRes);
```

The *LoadString* call here always uses the client's resource, whether or not the *InitEx26aDLL* call is present.

PART V

APPENDIXES

A P P E N D I X   A

A CRASH COURSE IN THE C++ LANGUAGE

Have you ever started reading a C++ textbook and given up because there was too much detail and you weren't motivated? If so, this appendix is for you. It's based on an example that I used when I taught myself C++, but it's flavored by my experience learning the classes of Microsoft Foundation Class (MFC) Library version 2.5. It's not meant to be comprehensive, and each C++ expert will find something to complain about, but I think it serves well as a C++ crash course.

As you read this appendix, you'll be hit straightaway by the essence of C++—classes and objects—and then you'll learn how to "wire" objects together to build an application. Important details are introduced as you need them, but I recommend that you keep a C++ textbook close at hand. The more you already know about C programming, the better.

An Introduction to Classes and Objects

The class is the language element that C++ programmers use to write modular, maintainable programs. This section teaches you how the class encapsulates code and data. Later sections introduce two other C++ features you might have heard about: inheritance and polymorphism.

Because classes and objects are such important C++ concepts, you must understand them thoroughly before proceeding. Understanding C's *struct* and *typedef* syntax will help you get started.

User-Defined Types in C

A C++ class declaration is an outgrowth of the C structure declaration. In C, the following code declares a structure with the name *xy*, but the compiler allocates no storage:

657

```
struct xy {
    double x;
    double y;
};
```

After you declare the structure, you can use *xy* instances in your C code this way:

```
struct xy topLeft = { 0.0, 0.0 };
struct xy bottomRight = { 1.0, 1.0 };
printf("topLeft = (%f, %f)\n", topLeft.x, topLeft.y);
printf("bottomRight = (%f, %f)\n", bottomRight.x, bottomRight.y);
```

If you use the C *typedef* syntax, the code becomes a little cleaner:

```
typedef struct xy {
    double x;
    double y;
} XY;
```

The type definition *XY* now substitutes for the more awkward *struct xy*:

```
XY topLeft = { 0.0, 0.0 };
XY bottomRight = { 1.0, 1.0 };
printf("topLeft = (%f, %f)\n", topLeft.x, topLeft.y);
printf("bottomRight = (%f, %f)\n", bottomRight.x, bottomRight.y);
```

Instances of *XY*, such as *topLeft* and *bottomRight*, correspond to C++ objects. Each occupies storage on the stack, and you can get away with writing simple assignment statements such as

```
bottomRight = topLeft;
```

However, the C compiler doesn't understand statements such as

```
bottomRight = topLeft + 1;
```

Moving to C++

Now let's recode the previous example in C++, using real classes and objects. Here's the simplest form of the class declaration:

```
class XY {
public:
    double x;
    double y;
};
```

The *public* keyword allows direct access to *x* and *y*, as though *x* and *y* were structure members.

Here's the code to make an *XY* object:

```
XY bottomRight; // an uninitialized object
bottomRight.x = 1.0;
bottomRight.y = 1.0;
printf("bottomRight = (%f, %f)\n", bottomRight.x, bottomRight.y);
```

The class elements *x* and *y*, called data members, were individually assigned values because, for most classes, the C++ compiler won't accept a statement such as

```
XY bottomRight = { 1.0, 1.0 };
```

> **NOTE:** The compiler does indeed accept the statement above for the simple *XY* class, but it won't accept it after you add the class's constructor, described in the following section.

C++ has structures too, but I was well into my C++ career before I realized that C++ structures were different from C structures. Instead of declaring an *XY* class, you could declare a C++ *XY* structure like this:

```
struct XY {
    double x;
    double y;
};
```

In C++ the only difference between a class and a structure is that structure members are, by default, publically accessible. C++ structures can have member functions (which you'll see later), and they can participate in C++ inheritance (which you'll also see later).

Constructors

You've seen how awkward it is to initialize the data members of an *XY* object with assignment statements. As you'll see later, C++ classes, unlike C structures, can contain "member functions" as well as data members. Member functions have full access to all data members of the class. All C++ classes have one or more special member functions, called "constructors," that are called to initialize objects. If you don't specify a constructor function in your class definition, the compiler generates a "default" constructor with no arguments. This default constructor calls the constructors for any C++ objects that are data members of the class. When the compiler generates a call to the default constructor, the compiler assigns storage for an object of the class but does not initialize values of built-in types. Indeed, in the previous example, the *XY* default constructor is called in the function shown at the top of the following page:

```
void func()
{
    XY bottomRight;  // XY object bottomRight constructed on the stack
                     // x and y values are uninitialized
}
```

NOTE: Many beginning C++ programmers try to call default constructors by writing code in this way:

```
XY bottomRight();  // don't do this!
```

The compiler interprets the statement as a forward declaration of a function named *bottomRight* that returns an object of type *XY*—clearly not the intended result.

A reasonable "explicit" constructor for the *XY* class would take two double-precision arguments. Here is a new *XY* class declaration with this constructor added:

```
class XY {
public:
    double x, y;
    XY(double xarg, double yarg)  { x = xarg; y = yarg; }
};
```

The constructor function name is always the same as the class name, and the constructor always returns nothing. In this example, the constructor is defined "inline," which means that the compiler directly substitutes the two assignment statements wherever the constructor is called. Now the previous example code becomes

```
XY bottomRight(1.0, 1.0);  // object named bottomRight of class XY
printf("bottomRight = (%f, %f)\n", bottomRight.x, bottomRight.y);
```

Yes, it's a little weird to write a function named *XY* and then to call it by the name *bottomRight*, but that's just the way C++ works. It makes sense if you consider that, for the default constructor, the statement

```
XY topLeft;
```

is analogous to

```
double x;
```

Both result in the creation of an entity on the stack—a C++ object of class *XY* or standard type *double*. Now, with the two-argument constructor, the statement

```
XY bottomRight(1.0, 1.0);
```

is a logical extension of

```
XY bottomRight;
```

Because you have written your own constructor, the compiler does not generate a default constructor. The compiler now rejects the statement

```
XY bottomRight;
```

If you write your own default (empty argument list) constructor that sets the data members to *0*, the class declaration, with two constructors, looks like this:

```
class XY {
public:
    double x, y;
    XY() { x = 0.0; y = 0.0; }
    XY(double xarg, double yarg)    {x = xarg; y = yarg;}
};
```

Now two functions are called *XY*, a situation clearly not generally allowed in C. The C++ compiler does permit multiple declarations and, furthermore, can tell from the function call statement which version of *XY()* you want. Therefore, both of the following statements are legal in the same program:

```
XY topLeft;
XY bottomRight(1.0, 1.0);
```

Destructors

No discussion of constructors would be complete without a companion discussion of "destructors." A destructor is another special C++ member function; its name is the class name preceded by a tilde (~). Each class has one and only one destructor function, and that function takes no arguments and returns nothing. The destructor is automatically called for any stack or global object when that object goes out of scope.

Even though we have no need for an explicit *XY* destructor, we'll write one anyway. This time, neither the constructors nor the destructor will be inline, so we can show off some new C++ notation.

```
class XY {
public:
    double x, y;
    XY();   // default constructor
    XY(double xarg, double yarg);
    ~XY();  // destructor
};
```

(continued)

661

```
XY::XY()
{
    printf("XY default constructor called\n");
    x = y = 0.0;
}

XY::XY(double xarg, double yarg)
{
    printf("XY explicit constructor called\n");
    x = xarg;
    y = yarg;
}

XY::~XY()
{
    printf("XY destructor called\n");
}
```

Now for an explanation of the new notation: The tilde character preceding the class name identifies the destructor and is part of the function name. The *XY::* prefix, used for both the constructor and the destructor definitions, tells the compiler that a function is a member function of the *XY* class.

If you made the following function call

```
void func() {
    XY bottomRight(1.0, 1.0);
    printf("the x coordinate is: %5.1f\n", bottomRight.x);

}
```

the output would be

```
XY explicit constructor called
the x coordinate is: 1.0
XY destructor called
```

Notice that the destructor is called automatically when the *bottomRight* object goes out of scope at the end of *func*'s execution.

If you don't write a destructor, the compiler generates a default destructor for you. For data members that are C++ objects, the default constructor calls those objects' destructors. When the compiler generates a call to a destructor for an object, the compiler generates code that releases storage occupied by that object.

Other Member Functions

You've seen the constructor and destructor member functions, and you know that they're always present, even if the compiler has to generate them for you. You can also write your own special-purpose class member functions.

Suppose you need member functions that retrieve the *x* and *y* values of an *XY* object. Here is the class declaration that includes the inline member functions *Getx* and *Gety*:

```
class XY {
public:
    double x, y;
    XY();
    XY(double xarg, double yarg);
    double Getx() const { return x; }
    double Gety() const { return y; }
};
```

Getx and *Gety* can directly access all data members of their class functions, as can other member functions (including constructors and destructors).

> **NOTE:** The *const* modifier used with *Getx* and *Gety* indicates that these functions do not modify class data members. This means that the compiler rejects any statements inside these functions that write to data members.

In the application code, *assert* is a C/C++ diagnostic macro that tests the given condition:

```
XY bottomRight(1.0, 1.0);
assert(bottomRight.Getx() == 1.0);
```

The notation *bottomRight.Getx()* means "Call the *Getx* member function for the object *bottomRight*." That's all there is to it.

> **NOTE:** In Microsoft Foundation Class (MFC) Library version 2.5 code, you'll see the MFC library *ASSERT* macro used instead of the C/C++ *assert* macro.

Private vs. Public Class Members

Up to now, the *x* and *y* data members in our *XY* class have been "public" and thus accessible throughout the program, as they are in a C structure. C++ allows a class's data to be hidden. If you designate a data member as "private," it is inaccessible outside the class; only class member functions can get at it.

Now that the *XY* class has member functions that return the coordinate values, we can write a useful program that doesn't require direct access to any data members. Here is the new class declaration:

```
class XY {
private:
    double x, y;
```

(continued)

```
public:
    XY();
    XY(double xarg, double yarg);
    double Getx() const;
    double Gety() const;
};
```

Class members are private by default, so technically we could eliminate the *private* keyword. The program is easier to read, however, if we leave it in.

Now the same application code still works:

```
XY bottomRight(1.0, 1.0);
assert(bottomRight.Getx() == 1.0);
```

But, outside the class, the compiler no longer accepts statements such as

```
bottomRight.x = 1.0;
```

The *x* data member is now private and accessible only through the *Getx* member function. This clearly illustrates C++'s encapsulation feature. Encapsulation is particularly useful in more complex classes, where a need exists for tight control over internal data access.

Member functions can also be private. A private member function, sometimes called a "helper" function, isn't callable outside the class, but it is accessible to other member functions of the same class. As with any member function, a private member function can be named anything you want, even something like *sqrt*, because you know it won't conflict with other like-named functions, even global ones.

Global Functions

Sometimes you need to write new class-related functions without changing the class declaration or writing a derived class. If, for example, you need a function *Show* that displays the values of the *XY* data members, you could write a global function such as this:

```
void Show(XY xy)
{
    printf("x = %f, y = %f\n", xy.Getx(), xy.Gety());
}
```

This technique works only when the existing class member functions provide all the necessary access to the data members (or if the data members are public). An alternative method is the friend function, described later, which does require a change to the *XY* class declaration.

Even though *Show* is global, it won't conflict with other *Show* functions because the compiler matches the calls according to parameter types.

C++ Encapsulation—A Recap

You've just learned about one of the big three C++ features: encapsulation. The data elements in the *XY* class example, *x* and *y*, are encapsulated with a set of useful functions that operate on them. The resulting *XY* class is a modular programming unit that, as you will see, you can use as a building block in an application.

Inheritance and Polymorphism—An Example

You're probably bored with the *XY* class by now, so let's move on to something out of this world. We'll create a two-dimensional simulation of the solar system, adaptable to both video games and StarWars defense projects. This exercise in object-oriented design lets you relate C++ objects to physical entities.

We want a computer program containing objects that represent heavenly bodies (such as planets and moons) and spaceships, that move in the sun's gravitational field. Ultimately we'd like to display the moving planets and spaceships on the screen, but we'll leave that as an exercise for the reader.

The *Orbiter* Base Class and Virtual Functions

An important step in object-oriented design, after initially identifying classes, is arranging the classes into a hierarchy with common functionality factored out to a "base class." In the solar system example, we define a base class *Orbiter* that has functionality common to both planets and spaceships. An orbiter is aware of Kepler's laws and thus knows how to move in the sun's gravitational field.

Here's the first try at an *Orbiter* class declaration:

```
class Orbiter {
private:             // data members
    double m_mass; // 'm_' is the prefix convention for data members
    XY      m_current, m_prior, m_thrust;
public:              // member functions
    Orbiter(XY current, XY prior, double mass); // constructor
    XY GetPosition() const;
    void Fly();
};
```

Notice your old friend the *XY* class. Objects of class *XY* represent sun-based position coordinates that are "embedded" within an *Orbiter* object, as is the standard type *m_mass*.

The *GetPosition* member function returns an object of class *XY* that corresponds to the orbiter's current position. (Later you'll learn how references make this process more efficient.) The *Fly* member function (not shown) applies a formula to the current and prior coordinate values, thus moving the orbiter through space. On the next iteration, the new prior coordinates are set to this iteration's current coordinates.

The *m_thrust* data member is included in the *Orbiter* class, even though planets don't have thrust, because the *Fly* member function needs thrust for its calculations, and we want a single general *Fly* function. For planets, *m_thrust* is always (0, 0).

Before we can "derive" the planet and spaceship classes from *Orbiter*, we must fix a few things. First, if the *Orbiter* data members are all private, they will be totally inaccessible to the derived classes. The C++ *protected* keyword allows a derived class to access base-class data members.

Next we need a member function that displays an orbiter. This *Display* function must be implemented differently for each derived *Orbiter* class because, for example, spaceships look different from planets. The C++ keyword *virtual* in the base-class declaration identifies *Display* as a function of this special category. Here is the new class declaration:

```
class Orbiter {
protected:
    double m_mass;
    XY      m_current, m_prior, m_thrust;
public:
    Orbiter(XY current, XY prior, double mass) {
        m_current = current;
        m_prior = prior;
        m_mass = mass;
    }
    XY GetPosition() const;
    void Fly();
    virtual void Display() const;
};
```

Now, if you have an array of orbiters, including planets, spaceships, and other space junk, you call the *Fly* function to update positions, and you call *Display* to show the objects on the screen. You call the same *Fly* function for each object, but which *Display* function you call depends on the object's class. The use of the virtual *Display* function illustrates the C++ polymorphism feature.

The following example assumes that *orbiterArray* contains pointers to a mixture of objects of classes derived from *Orbiter*:

```
extern Orbiter* orbiterArray[];
for(int i = 0; i < MAX; i++) {
    orbiterArray[i]->Fly();
    orbiterArray[i]->Display();
}
```

This example uses pointers to *Orbiter* objects rather than the objects themselves. You'll see more object pointer usage later.

Pure Virtual Functions

In the example above, a program could construct objects of class *Orbiter*, but that doesn't make sense because an orbiter is an abstract concept. You can prevent construction of *Orbiter* base-class objects by declaring one or more functions as "pure virtual" with this syntax:

```
virtual void Display() const = 0; // '= 0' means pure virtual
```

Now *Orbiter* is officially an "abstract base class," and the compiler forces all derived classes (which are used for constructing objects) to provide implementations of the *Display* member function.

Derived Classes

We'll be writing two classes derived from *Orbiter*: *Planet* and *Spaceship*. The *Planet* derived class isn't very interesting. Perhaps all it needs is its own *Display* function and, of course, a constructor. Here's the declaration:

```
class Planet : public Orbiter {
public:
    Planet(XY current, XY prior, double mass) :
        Orbiter(current, prior, mass) {}
    void Display() const;
};
```

The first line says that the *Planet* class is publicly derived from the *Orbiter* class. Any derived class inherits all the data members and member functions (except constructors and destructors) of its base class. For a publicly derived class, inherited public base-class members are public, and inherited protected base-class members are protected. All the derived classes in this book are publicly derived.

The colon (:) notation in the *Planet* class constructor declaration means that the base-class (*Orbiter*) constructor is called first to make the *Orbiter* component of the *Planet* object. Any *Planet*-specific code (nothing, in this case) is then executed. Actually, all the memory for both the base-class and the derived-class data members is allocated prior to execution of any constructor code.

667

NOTE: If you had not included the *Orbiter* constructor as part of the *Planet* constructor, the compiler would have rejected the statement. Why? The compiler would have tried to use a default *Orbiter* constructor, but, because you had declared only an explicit three-argument *Orbiter* constructor, the compiler would have given up.

The *Spaceship* class is more complex than the *Planet* class because it has its own data members and a new member function:

```
class Spaceship : public Orbiter {
private:
    double m_fuel;
    XY      m_orientation;
public:
    Spaceship(XY current, XY prior, XY thrust, double mass,
            double fuel, XY orientation) :
        Orbiter(current, prior, mass) {
            m_fuel = fuel;
            m_orientation = orientation;
            m_thrust = thrust; // m_thrust is an Orbiter data member
        }
    void Display() const;
    void FireThrusters();
};
```

Now you must provide constructor code to initialize the spaceship-specific data members.

Virtual Functions Called in Base Classes

You've seen the virtual *Display* function called for elements of an *Orbiter* object array. Virtual functions can be called in a base class as well as from outside the class. Suppose that the *Orbiter::Fly* function needs to compute angular momentum and that this computation is specific to the derived class. If the *Orbiter* class contains the following declaration

```
protected:
    virtual XY GetAngularMomentum() const = 0;
```

then derived classes are obliged to provide override functions.

Embedded Objects

What about the *XY* objects embedded in the *Planet* and *Spaceship* objects? When are they constructed? Here things get complicated, but you must understand the process to prepare yourself for the more complex C++ class

668

interrelationships you'll see in MFC library programming. Before you go any further, however, you need to know about copy constructors and assignment operators.

Copy Constructors

Like the default constructor, the copy constructor is a class member function that the compiler often generates. Indeed, the compiler frequently generates invisible calls to the copy constructor, sometimes where you least expect them.

The purpose of the copy constructor is to make a new object of the same class from an existing object that is passed as an argument. An inline copy constructor for the *XY* class looks like this:

```
XY(const XY& xy) {
    x = xy.x;
    y = xy.y;
}
```

> **NOTE:** The *const* modifier indicates that the function does not modify the values referenced by the *xy* parameter. The absence of *const* would alert you to the possibility that the function might indeed modify the values.

If you don't define a copy constructor for a class, the compiler generates one for you that simply does a memberwise copy of all the object's data. (The compiler can safely optimize this to a bitwise copy when appropriate.) Because the *XY* class is so simple, the default copy constructor is sufficient. For more complex classes, such as those that require memory allocation or other special processing, the default copy constructor isn't sufficient. It's good practice to write copy constructors for all but the most trivial classes.

The notation *const XY&* that you saw earlier in the *Orbiter* class declaration is a C++ *reference,* and its use is required in copy constructors. The compiler passes the address of the *XY* object as an argument to the *XY* copy constructor rather than passing a copy of the object itself. It's like passing a pointer, but the notation is cleaner. You'll see references again, and you'll learn why they're more than a pointer substitute.

An obvious use for a compiler-generated copy constructor call is in code such as the following example:

```
XY alpha(1.0, 2.0);
XY beta = alpha;
XY gamma(alpha); // same result as preceding statement
```

Here two new *XY* objects, *beta* and *gamma*, are constructed from the existing object *alpha*.

Less obvious is the copy constructor call in the following sequence:

```
void func(XY xy);
XY alpha(2.0, 3.0);
func(alpha);
```

Here the *alpha* object is constructed on the calling program's stack using the explicit constructor, and then the copy constructor is called to copy the *alpha* object to the argument list for *func.*

Assignment Operators

The assignment operator is a lot like a copy constructor except that it operates on an existing object rather than creating a new object. The compiler generates default assignment operators, and it generates calls to them. The assignment operator is an example of a C++ overloaded operator, which you'll learn more about later in this appendix. You need to understand the use of assignment operators now, however.

If you were to write your own inline assignment operator for the *XY* class, it would look like this:

```
const XY& operator=(const XY& xy) { // uses references
    x = xy.x;                       // copies the values
    y = xy.y;
    return *this;
}
```

> **NOTE:** The returned *XY* reference permits assignment operators to be "chained," as in the statement
>
> ```
> xy1 = xy2 = XY(0.0, 0.0);
> ```

The first *const* modifier indicates that the result of the assignment can be used only where a *const* parameter is specified. If *ClearContents* is declared as a non-*const XY* member function, the compiler rejects this statement:

```
(xy1 = xy2).ClearContents();
```

but the compiler accepts the statement

```
(xy1 = xy2).Getx();
```

because *Getx* is declared a *const* function. (See also the section titled "Use of the *this* Pointer," later in this appendix.)

This code illustrates an obvious use of the assignment operator:

```
XY alpha(1.0, 2.0);
XY beta(3.0, 4.0);
beta = alpha;
```

Here the contents of *alpha* are copied to *beta*, overwriting the latter's previous contents.

Here's another example:

```
class Container {
private:
    XY m_point;
public:
    Container(XY point) { m_point = point; }
};
```

When an object of class *Container* is constructed, the *XY* default constructor is called to make an *m_point* object before the body of the *Container* constructor is executed. The assignment statement

```
m_point = point;
```

triggers a call to the *XY* assignment operator.

The compiler-generated default assignment operator does a memberwise copy of all the object's data, and that's sufficient for the *XY* class. Plan to write your own assignment operators for more complex classes.

Reference Parameters: *const* vs. non-*const*

Remember that reference parameters are just disguised pointer parameters. If you see a reference parameter in a function declaration, you can assume the programmer used it for one of two reasons. Perhaps the function uses the parameter to change a variable in the calling program, or possibly the programmer wanted to avoid copying a large object onto the function's call stack. Fortunately, there's an easy way to determine the real reason. In the first case, the reference will be non-*const*, and in the second case, the reference will be *const*.

Consider the following global function:

```
void TimesTwo(XY& xy) { xy.x *= 2.0; xy.y *= 2.0; }
```

and its usage:

```
XY pos(1.0, 2.0);
TimesTwo(pos);
assert(pos.x == 2.0 && pos.y == 4.0);
```

Here the function *TimesTwo* definitely changes the value of its non-*const* parameter. Some would argue that this parameter usage violates C++ encapsulation—a member function would be more correct. Naturally, the *x* and *y* data members must be public, or *TimesTwo* must be a friend of the class.

Now let's see the usage of a *const* reference parameter. We'll revisit the global *Show* function and make it more efficient:

```
void Show(const XY& xy)  {
    printf("x = %f, y = %f\n", xy.Getx(), xy.Gety());
}
```

Show now cannot change the value of the *XY* object in the calling program. Not only does a statement (inside *Show*) such as

```
xy.x = 5.0;
```

generate a compile error, the statement also causes any calls to non-*const XY* member functions to generate errors. Calling *Getx* and *Gety* would be illegal unless we had the foresight to declare *Getx* and *Gety* as *const* functions (which we did). *Getx* and *Gety* promise not to change the object, so it's OK to call them for a *const XY* reference.

C++ References At Work

The following application code constructs our home planet:

```
XY current(100.0, 200.0); // constructs current XY coordinate pair
XY prior(100.1, 200.1);   // constructs prior XY coordinate pair
Planet earth(current, prior, 1.0E+10); // constructs Earth object
```

If you use the following versions of the class declarations that you've already seen:

```
class XY {
public:
    double x, y;
    XY() { x = 0.0; y = 0.0; }          // default constructor
    XY(double xarg, double yarg)        // explicit constructor
        { x = xarg; y = yarg; }
    XY(const XY& xy) {                  // copy constructor
        x = xy.x;
        y = xy.y;
    }
    const XY& operator=(const XY& xy) { // assignment operator
        x = xy.x;
        y = xy.y;
```

```
            return *this;
    }
};

class Orbiter {
protected:
    double m_mass;
    XY      m_current, m_prior, m_thrust;
public:
    Orbiter(XY current, XY prior, double mass) {
        m_current = current;
        m_prior = prior;
        m_mass = mass;
    }
    XY GetPosition() const;
    void Fly();
    virtual void Display() = 0;
};

class Planet : public Orbiter {
public:
    Planet(XY current, XY prior, double mass)
        : Orbiter(current, prior, mass) { }
    void Display();
};
```

the following sequence of *XY* constructor calls is necessary to make an object
named *earth*:

1. The explicit *XY* constructor creates *current* and *prior* objects on the
   stack.

2. The *XY* copy constructor copies the *current* and *prior* objects to the
   Planet constructor's argument list.

3. The *XY* copy constructor copies the *current* and *prior* objects from
   the *Planet* constructor's argument list to the *Orbiter* constructor's
   argument list.

4. The *XY* default constructor (required) creates *m_current* and
   m_prior members and initializes them to (0, 0).

5. The *XY* assignment operator copies the *current* and *prior* objects
   from the *Orbiter* constructor's argument list to the corresponding
   data members.

Wow! That's a lot of construction! For efficiency's sake, we'll rearrange the *Orbiter* and *Planet* code, particularly that of the constructors:

```
class Orbiter {
protected:
    double m_mass;
    XY      m_current, m_prior, m_thrust;
public:
    Orbiter(XY& current, XY& prior, double mass)
        : m_current(current), m_prior(prior), m_mass(mass) { }
    const XY& GetPosition() const;
    void Fly();
    virtual void Display() = 0;
};

class Planet : public Orbiter {
public:
    // copy constructor and assignment operator not shown
    Planet(XY& current, XY& prior, double mass)
        : Orbiter(current, prior, mass) { }
    void Display();
};
```

You'll notice that the *Orbiter* and *Planet* constructors use *XY* references now. Also, the *Orbiter* constructor is quite different. We've dropped the statements

```
m_current = current;
m_prior = prior;
m_mass = mass;
```

and substituted the clause

```
: m_current(current), m_prior(prior), m_mass(mass) { }
```

> **NOTE:** C++ allows the function syntax *m_mass(mass)* even though *m_mass* is a data member of a built-in data type (double).

Now, instead of generating two calls to the *XY* default constructor and two calls to the assignment operator, the compiler simply generates two calls to the *XY* copy constructor ahead of the mass assignment (in the *Orbiter* constructor body). This should give you some insight into the real meaning of the constructor colon syntax: The statements after the colon, including (but not limited to) calls to the base class and contained object constructors, are executed before the constructor body.

For variety's sake, we'll rewrite the "create Earth" code as follows:

```
Planet earth(XY(100.00, 200.00), XY(100.01, 200.01), 1.0E+10);
```

Here you see another variation of constructor call syntax for the two *XY* objects. Now the *XY* constructor calls for planet Earth are as follows:

1. Temporary current and prior objects are constructed in the constructor's argument list with the explicit *XY* constructor.

2. The *m_current* and *m_prior* objects are constructed, with the *XY* copy constructor, from the objects from step 1. Those objects were passed all the way down to the *Orbiter* constructor as references, thereby avoiding extra copy operations.

Returning References

A function can return a reference, which is equivalent to returning a pointer, and these references can be *const* or non-*const*. Here's a new version of *Getx* that returns a *const* reference to an *XY* object:

```
const double& XY::GetConstRefx() const { return x; }
```

The *GetConstRefx* function can be used on the right side of an assignment statement but, because the reference is *const*, not on the left side. Thus the statement

```
topLeft.GetConstRefx() = 3.0;  // topLeft is an object of class XY
```

causes a compiler error. If you removed the *const* keyword from the reference, the statement would be allowed, and you could use the function to modify the state of the *topLeft* object.

In both cases, the *m_thrust* embedded object is constructed with the default *XY* constructor, which sets both the *x* and *y* components to 0.

> **NOTE:** If you write a C++ function that returns a reference, you could end up making the same mistake that beginning C programmers often make. Here's the classic C example:
>
> ```
> double *GetNumber()
> {
>     double result = (double) rand() / (double) RAND_MAX;
>     return &result; /* don't do this */
> }
> ```
>
> The function returns a pointer to stack memory that will be used for something else after the function returns.

Here's the C++ equivalent with a reference:

```
double& GetNumber()
{
    double result = (double) rand() / (double) RAND_MAX;
    return result; // don't do this either
}
```

It's just as wrong as the C example because the compiler is still returning a pointer to a temporary variable.

Construction of Embedded Objects—A Summary

You've seen the construction sequence for a *Planet* object. The *Spaceship* class is more interesting because both the *Orbiter* and *Spaceship* classes have their own embedded objects. Here's the construction sequence for a *Spaceship* object:

1. The compiler already knows how much total memory a *Spaceship* object (including all embedded objects) requires, so that amount of memory is allocated.

2. The *m_current, m_prior,* and *m_thrust* embedded objects are constructed.

3. The *Orbiter* constructor function is called.

4. The *m_orientation* embedded object is constructed.

5. The *Spaceship* constructor function is called.

The class design and initial *Spaceship* constructor call determine exactly which constructors (default, explicit, or copy) are called, but the list above is an accurate summary.

Destruction of Embedded Objects

Consider what happens when an object of class *Spaceship* is destroyed. The *Spaceship* class is interesting because it's a derived class with embedded objects defined both in the base class and in the derived class. Here's the sequence of events:

1. The compiler-generated *Spaceship* destructor is called.

2. The *m_orientation* embedded object is destroyed.

3. The compiler-generated *Orbiter* destructor is called.

4. The *m_current*, *m_prior*, and *m_thrust* embedded objects are destroyed.

5. The memory allocated for the *Spaceship* object is freed.

Notice that this destruction sequence is the exact opposite of the construction sequence.

Allocation of Objects on the Heap

So far, all objects have been allocated on the stack, and, except for the virtual *Display* function, the objects have been referenced directly. You'll recall that stack objects are destroyed when they go out of scope. As you do in C with the help of the run-time library, when you program in C++ you allocate objects on the heap so that their memory remains in use until you specifically free it. You keep track of heap objects with pointers.

The C++ *new* and *delete* Operators

The operators *new* and *delete* are roughly equivalent to the C *malloc* and *free* functions. You can use *new* to allocate raw storage this way:

```
char* pCommBuffer = new char[4096];
```

More often, however, you'll use *new* to construct objects on the heap this way:

```
Planet* pEarth = new Planet(XY(100.0, 200.0), XY(100.1, 200.1),
1.0E+10);
```

The variable *pEarth* contains the address of an object of class *Planet* and is thus a pointer. Note that the constructor syntax for heap allocation is different from the syntax for stack allocation.

To get rid of *pEarth*, simply call the *Planet* destructor this way:

```
delete pEarth;
```

All the contained objects are destroyed, as they are when a stack-allocated *Planet* object goes out of scope.

Referring to Objects Through Pointers

You can see that pointers go hand in hand with heap-allocated objects. You could use pointers to stack objects, but then you'd be vulnerable to a common programming error—the use of a pointer to an object that has gone out of scope.

Pointer Declarations—A C++ Coding Convention

The following pointer examples illustrate a C++ coding convention that is used both in this book and in the Microsoft Foundation Class Library documentation. In pointer declarations, the asterisk always appears next to the type name rather than next to the variable name; this is different from the usual C convention. For example:

```
char *szLastName; /* C-style pointer declaration */
char* szLastname; // C++/class library-style pointer declaration
```

This convention has two advantages:

- It differentiates between pointer declarations and dereference operators.

    The following statement, at first glance, appears to assign the first characters of the *szLastName* string the value of the *szDefault* pointer:

    ```
    char *szLastName = szDefault;
    ```

    With the C++ notation, however, the statement clearly declares a new pointer and assigns it the value of *szDefault*:

    ```
    char* szLastName = szDefault;
    ```

- It's compatible with the C++ reference notation.

    References are always indicated by an ampersand (&) following the type name to distinguish them from the "address of" operator. References to pointers, then, are shown this way:

    ```
    XY*& pxy;
    ```

The disadvantage of the convention shows up in multiple declarations in a single statement. With the familiar C notation, the following statement declares three character pointers:

```
char *a, *b, *c;
```

With the new convention, the following statement declares one pointer and two individual character variables:

```
char* a, b, c;  // perhaps not what you wanted
```

If you consistently use the new convention, you must use separate statements for each declaration, like this:

```
char* a; char* b; char* c;
```

Once you have a pointer to an object, you can call its class member functions using this convenient notation:

```
pEarth->Fly();
```

Pointers are necessary if you want to reference objects polymorphically. For example, you could construct an object of class *Planet*, but you would store its pointer as an *Orbiter* pointer this way:

```
Orbiter* pAny = new Planet(XY(100.0, 200.0), XY(100.1, 200.1), 1.0E+10);
```

C++ allows this conversion because the *Planet* class is derived from *Orbiter*. You could not convert an *Orbiter* pointer to a *Planet* pointer without a specific (and dangerous) cast operator.

Now you can call *Orbiter* virtual functions this way:

```
pAny->Display();
```

At run time, the *Display* function of the *Planet* class is called because a compiler-generated structure (called a "vtbl") maps *pAny* to the correct function in the *Planet* class.

Virtual Destructors

Be aware that destructors are not inherited, that the compiler generates a default destructor for each class if you do not explicitly write one, and that a derived-class destructor <u>always</u> calls its base-class destructor. What if you had a pointer to an object of an unknown class derived from *Orbiter* and you wanted to destroy that object? If you called the *Orbiter* default destructor, it would destroy only those object elements specified by the *Orbiter* class itself. Suppose you constructed a *Spaceship* object on the heap, assigned its address to an *Orbiter* pointer, and then deleted the pointer like this:

```
Orbiter* pAny = new Spaceship(current, prior, thrust, mass,
                             fuel, orientation);
delete pAny;
```

The *Spaceship* object's deletion would be incomplete. In particular, the destructor for the *XY* object *m_orientation* would not be called.

How do you solve this problem? You declare a "virtual destructor" for the *Orbiter* class:

```
virtual ~Orbiter() { }
```

You don't need any code or declarations for derived-class destructors unless you're not satisfied with the compiler-generated defaults.

If you repeat the previous example now, the statement

```
delete pAny;
```

calls the proper derived-class destructor, in this case the destructor for class *Spaceship*, which first destroys all elements particular to spaceships, including *m_orientation*, and then calls the *Orbiter* destructor.

Allocation of Global Objects

You've seen stack objects, heap objects, and objects contained in other objects. Global objects are constructed before your main program is called, and they are destroyed after the main program exits. Like global variables, global objects are accessible to all functions in your program.

Suppose you have encapsulated all the Microsoft non-Windows graphics functions (declared in GRAPH.H) in a C++ class called *GraphScreen*. The program skeleton would look like this:

```
class GraphScreen {
private:
    // misc. data members
public:
    GraphScreen();  // constructor that initializes the display for
                    //   graphics
    ~GraphScreen(); // destructor that resets the screen back to
                    //   text mode
    void MoveTo(int x, int y);
    void LineTo(int x, int y);
    // more member functions
};

GraphScreen screen; // a single global screen object

void main() {
    screen.MoveTo(100, 200);
    screen.LineTo(200, 200);  // draws a line from (100, 200) to
                              //   (200, 200)
}
```

Because the *GraphScreen* constructor is called before *main*, it can do any necessary video mode initialization. Because the destructor is called automatically after *main* exits, it can reset the video.

Object Interrelationships—Pointer Data Members

You'll recall that the *Planet* class provided for several embedded *XY* objects. Because an *XY* object is only 16 bytes long, and because these objects are not shared among *Planet* objects, it's reasonable to make them embedded objects. A benefit of this arrangement is the automatic destruction of all *XY* objects when the *Planet* object is destroyed. A restriction is that the compiler must see the *XY* class declaration before the *Planet* class declaration.

What if you want to establish a relationship between two existing objects? Suppose your universe contains moons, in addition to planets and spaceships, and you want to associate each moon to its planet. Our moon has little effect on the motion of the Earth around the sun, but the Earth profoundly affects the moon's motion. The Earth has only one moon, but other planets have several moons. It makes sense, then, for the *Moon* class to have a *Planet* pointer data member, as shown below:

```
class Planet;

class Moon : public Orbiter {
private:
    Planet* m_pPlanet; // pointer to associated Planet object
public:
    Moon(XY& current, XY& prior, double mass, Planet* pPlanet)
        : Orbiter(current, prior, mass), m_pPlanet(pPlanet) { }
    void Display() const { } // necessary because Display is pure
virtual
    Planet* GetPlanet() const { return m_pPlanet; }
    void SetPlanet(const Planet* pPlanet) { m_pPlanet = pPlanet; }
};
```

The *Moon* constructor takes a *Planet* pointer as an argument. The *GetPlanet* and *SetPlanet* member functions allow access to the pointer. Notice that the compiler doesn't have to see the complete *Planet* class declaration prior to the *Moon* declaration. The forward declaration

```
class Planet;
```

is sufficient because the compiler merely has to reserve space for a pointer, and all object pointers are the same size. The size of the *Moon* object itself is of no consequence.

Now, when you construct a *Moon* object, you must include a *Planet* object pointer in the constructor call:

```
Planet* pEarth = new Planet(XY(100.00, 200.00),
                            XY(100.01, 200.01), 1.0E+10);
Moon* pMoon = new Moon(XY(100.10, 200.10),
                       XY(100.11, 200.11), 1.0E+10, pEarth);
```

Please be careful when deleting interrelated objects. If, in this example, you deleted the *earth* object, your program would crash if it continued to use the dependent *Moon* object.

.

> NOTE: The addition of moons to the solar system seriously complicates the *Orbiter::Fly* function. Now an *Orbiter* object's state is no longer solely dependent on current and prior sun-based co-ordinates. We must make *Fly* a virtual function with a special version for moons, or we must rewrite *Fly* to process gravitational interactions among all heavenly bodies.

Use of the *this* Pointer

The C++ language provides a self-reference syntax that allows a program to obtain a pointer to the current object. This pointer, denoted by the keyword *this*, can be used as a function call parameter, and it can be returned by a member function or an overloaded operator. In the following example, a *Planet* class member function connects to a specified *Moon* object:

```
void Planet::ConnectToMoon(Moon* pMoon) {
    pMoon->SetPlanet(this); // this planet object
}
```

References to Pointers

Most C++ textbooks explain references and illustrate pointer usage. Few, however, give good examples of references to pointers, a feature used in some MFC library classes. You've already seen the separate *Moon* class member functions *SetPlanet* and *GetPlanet*. You can combine these two functions into one easy-to-use function like this:

```
Planet*& Moon::GetPlanet() { return m_pPlanet; }
```

The returned reference to a pointer is, in effect, a double pointer; therefore, you can place *GetPlanet* on either the right or the left of an assignment statement:

```
XY      xy11, xy12, xy21, xy22, xy31, xy32;
double mass1, mass2, mass3;

Planet* pEarth = new Planet(xy11, xy12, mass1);
Planet* pMars = new Planet(xy21, xy22, mass2);
Moon*   pMoon = new Moon(xy31, xy32, mass3, pEarth);
assert(pMoon->GetPlanet() == pEarth); // rvalue
pMoon->GetPlanet() = pMars;           // lvalue
assert(pMoon->GetPlanet() == pMars);  // rvalue
```

If you're confused, consider the more C-like equivalent notation:

```
Planet** Moon::GetPlanet() { return &m_pPlanet; }

*(pMoon->GetPlanet()) = pMars;
```

Does that make it any better?

In the MFC library classes, the declaration

```
Planet*& Moon::GetPlanet();
```

is often paired with the declaration

```
Planet* Moon::GetPlanet() const;
```

This second overloaded variation allows *GetPlanet* to be used (on the right side of an assignment statement) with *const* pointers to *Planet* objects. The following example shows use of the *const* variation of *GetPlanet*:

```
const Moon* cpMoon = new Moon(xy1, xy2, mass, pEarth);
Planet* pPlanet = cpMoon->GetPlanet();
```

The compiler will not accept the second statement unless the second *GetPlanet* declaration is present. For more information on *const* pointers, refer to a C++ textbook.

Friend Classes and Friend Functions

Sometimes two classes are closely related, and the C++ "friendship" feature can formalize this relationship. Class friendship is similar to human friendship. For example, you are free to declare yourself a friend to the president of the United States, but that doesn't give you the right to show up at the White House for dinner. If, on the other hand, the president declares you a friend, chances are you can drop by any time, as long as you bring a campaign contribution.

Friend Classes

Moving from Washington, D.C., out to space for a minute, it would be handy if *Moon* objects could directly access *Planet* data members, particularly the planet's mass and current position. This is possible only if the *Planet* class is declared a friend to class *Moon* like this:

```
class Planet : public Orbiter {
    friend class Moon;  // no prior declaration required
public:
    // constructors and other member functions
};
```

Now the following code is allowed in <u>all</u> *Moon* class member functions:

```
double Moon::MassProduct() {
    return GetPlanet()->m_mass * m_mass; // planet's mass * moon's mass
}
```

You could restrict friendship to the *MassProduct* member function like this:

```
class Planet : public Orbiter {
    friend double Moon::MassProduct();
public:
    // constructors and other member functions
};
```

Global Friend Functions

Suppose, in a particular application, that the *XY* class represents a vector and that you need the tangent of the vector's angle. You could write an ordinary *tan* member function as follows:

```
double XY::tan() {
    if (y != 0.0) {
        return x / y;
    }
    else {
        return 0.0;
    }
}
```

You could then call *tan* as you would any class member function:

```
XY      vector(1.0, 1.0);
double result = vector.tan();
```

If you want a more familiar calling syntax, however, you can declare *tan* as a global friend function to class *XY* as follows:

```
class XY {
    friend double tan(const XY& xy);
private:
    double x, y;
public:
    // constructors, etc.
};

double tan(const XY& xy) {
    if (xy.y != 0.0) {
        return xy.x / xy.y;
    }
```

```
    else {
        return 0.0;
    }
}
```

You now call the new *tan* function like this:

```
XY      vector(1.0, 1.0);
double result = tan(vector);
```

There won't be a conflict with the standard library *tan* functions because the compiler selects the proper function by looking at the parameter types.

Static Class Members

What if you needed a count of all currently active space orbiters? You could define a global variable, but that would compromise encapsulation. C++ provides static data members and static member functions that are associated with a class rather than with any specific object.

Static Data Members

Here's the *Orbiter* class declaration with a static integer data member, *nCount*:

```
class Orbiter {
protected:
    double m_mass;
    XY      m_current, m_prior, m_thrust;
public:
    static int nCount;
    Orbiter(XY& current, XY& prior, double mass);
    const XY& GetPosition() const;
    void Fly();
    virtual void Display() const = 0;
};
```

There will be only one copy of *nCount*, no matter how many orbiter objects there are. The class declaration above declares the class, but it doesn't reserve memory for *nCount*. You must write your own global definition code, to appear only once in the link, similar to the following:

```
int Orbiter::nCount = 0; // initialization is optional
```

Because the variable is declared public, you can use it in your program like this:

```
Orbiter::nCount++;
```

Of course, if you access *nCount* inside an *Orbiter* member function, such as a constructor, you can omit *Orbiter::.*

If you declare a constant static data member like this:

```
static const int nMaxCount;
```

you can still initialize it globally like this:

```
const int Orbiter::nMaxCount = 256;
```

Enumerated Types—A Static Data Member Shortcut

If your class needs a constant static integer, you can use a shortcut that avoids a separate initialization statement. You simply place an *enum* statement in your class declaration like this:

```
enum { nMaxCount = 256 };
```

Static Member Functions

If the static *Orbiter* data member *nCount* were private, you would need a static member function to access it. If you define a public function *Count* that returns a reference to an integer, you can use it on either side of an assignment statement:

```
public:
    static int& Count() { return nCount; }
```

Here's some code that uses the new *Count* function:

```
int nOldCount = Orbiter::Count()++;
int nNewCount = Orbiter::Count();
assert(nNewCount == nOldCount + 1);
```

A more interesting use of static class member functions is the construction of objects. Suppose you need to construct a new orbiting object but you don't know until run time which derived *Orbiter* class you want. Here's a static construction function that uses a *switch* statement to choose the object class:

```
static Orbiter* Orbiter::MakeNew(int selection, XY& current, XY& prior,
                                 double mass, XY& thrust, double fuel,
                                 XY& orientation, Planet* pPlanet)
{
    switch (selection) {
    case 0:
        return new Planet(current, prior, mass);
    case 1:
        return new Spaceship(current, prior, thrust, mass, fuel,
                             orientation);
```

```
    case 2:
        return new Moon(current, prior, mass, pPlanet);
    default:
        return NULL;
    }
}
```

Now you can fill up an array of *Orbiter* pointers:

```
Orbiter* pOrbiterArray[MAX]
XY       current, prior, thrust, orientation;
double   mass, fuel;
Planet*  pPlanet;

for (int i = 0; i < MAX; i++) {
    pOrbiterArray[i] = Orbiter::MakeNew(i % 3, current, prior, mass,
                                        thrust, fuel, orientation,
                                        pPlanet);
}
```

Once you stuff the *Planet, Spaceship,* and *Moon* pointers into the *Orbiter* pointer array, how do you ever sort out which is which? Of course, you don't need to know the class if you simply call *Fly* and *Display* and then destroy the objects. If you do need to know the class, C++ doesn't help much. You could, of course, add an *Orbiter* data member and associated access functions that indicate the class. As you'll see in MFC code, the MFC library's run-time class mechanism lets you determine an object's class at run time.

Overloaded Operators

You might not write many overloaded operators in the early stages of class library programming, but you will certainly use the ones that class libraries provide. The more you know about writing overloaded operators, though, the easier it will be to use them.

Overloaded operators are useful because they can make C++ application code easier to write and read, but some programmers get carried away. Use overloaded operators only when their meanings are intuitive and natural. After all, they are nothing but substitutes for member function calls, and sometimes member function calls make more sense.

Member Function Operators

Many overloaded operators are implemented as class member functions. In this appendix's examples, *XY* objects are mostly *xy*-coordinate pairs, and the obvious thing to do with coordinate pairs is to add and subtract them. At the top of the following page is the code for the add and subtract operators:

```
XY XY::operator +(const XY& xy) const { // add
    return XY(x + xy.x, y + xy.y);
}

XY XY::operator -(const XY& xy) const { // subtract
    return XY(x - xy.x, y - xy.y);
}
```

(The declarations are shown in the section titled "Separating Class Declarations from Code," later in this chapter.)

Notice the use of references. For the *XY* class, with its small-size objects, you could get away without the references, but you've already seen how references make the code more efficient, and you've seen that they're required for assignment operators.

Now you use the + operator like this:

```
XY xy1(1.0, 2.0), xy2(3.0, 4.0);
XY xy3 = xy1 + xy2; // should be (4.0, 6.0)
```

That was easy. What about some more operators? The unary minus is another useful one. Notice that it doesn't have an argument.

```
XY XY::operator -() const { // unary minus
    return XY(-x, -y);
}
```

What about the multiply operator? It doesn't make sense to multiply one coordinate pair by another, but you can multiply a coordinate pair by a scalar. Here's the code for the * and *= operators:

```
XY operator *(double mult) { // scalar multiply
    return XY(x * mult, y * mult);
}

const XY& operator *=(const double mult) {
    x *= mult;
    y *= mult;
    return *this;
}
```

And here's the application code:

```
XY xy1(1.0, 2.0);
XY xy2 = xy1 * 3.0; // should be (3.0, 6.0)
xy2 *= 2.0;         // should be (6.0, 12.0)
```

And now for something a little more difficult. In the *Spaceship* class, you might have noticed an *XY* data member called *m_orientation*. This isn't really a coordinate pair but a representation of an angle. (There's a possible case for a derived *XY* class here.) You could, of course, represent an angle by a scalar radian or a degree value, but subsequent math is easier if you store the angle as a cosine/sine pair. We'll now expropriate the C++ right-shift and left-shift operators and make them rotation operators for *XY* objects:

```
XY operator >>(const XY& xy) const { // rotate cos/sin pair plus
    return XY(x * xy.x - y * xy.y, y * xy.x + x * xy.y);
}

XY operator <<(const XY& xy) const { // rotate cos/sin pair minus
    return XY(x * xy.x + y * xy.y, y * xy.x - x * xy.y);
}
```

The formulas are standard trigonometric identities that require no use of the *sin* or *cos* function.

Here are the new rotation operators in use:

```
XY angle1(0.707, 0.707);      // 45 degrees
XY rotation(0.0, 1.0);        // 90 degrees
XY angle2 = angle1 >> rotation; // should be (-.707, .070), 135 degrees
```

In a video game application I designed, the player controlled the spaceship's master rotation angle from the keyboard. The spaceship outline points were stored in an array of polar coordinates consisting of an *XY* angle and a scalar distance from the center of the ship. For each point, the *XY* value was rotated by the current angle and then multiplied by the scalar value, yielding a new *xy*-coordinate pair for the display.

Conversion Operators

Both C and C++ allow extensive automatic conversion among built-in types. Consider these statements:

```
int    radians = 2;
double result = atan(radians);
```

The function *atan* expects a *double* argument, so the compiler converts the integer *radians* to a *double* before passing it to the function.

What about conversions for your own classes? You must write them yourself, of course. Suppose you have a *String* class that contains a character array *m_pch*. The following operator function returns a constant pointer to an object's internal array:

```
String::operator const char*() const
{
    return (const char*) m_pch;
}
```

689

You can now use a *String* argument anywhere the compiler expects a *const char** argument—for example:

```
String s1("test");      // construct S1 from character array
String s2;
char   c1[20];
int    n = strlen(s1);  // OK
strcpy(s2, s1);         // won't compile because first parameter is not
                        //  const
strcpy(c1, s1);         // OK
```

We purposely didn't declare a (non-*const*) *char** operator because getting data into a *String* object isn't as easy as extracting it.

The class library provides a useful string class called *CString* that has this same overloaded *const char** conversion operator. You'll use this operator quite frequently when you write class library programs.

Global Operators

The operators you've seen so far are class member functions. Suppose you need a new operator but you don't want to derive a new class. If your class has public data members and member functions sufficient to access the required data, you can write stand-alone global operators for your class.

Because we "forgot" to write a divide member function operator for the *XY* class, we'll write one now, but the code is a little different from the overloaded multiply operator you've seen already:

```
XY operator / (const XY& xy, const double div) // scalar divide helper
{
    return XY(xy.x / div, yx.y / div);
}
```

Notice that the data members *x* and *y* must be public, or if they are not, you must write *XY* member functions that access them.

Global operators can enhance the arithmetic capabilities of a class. The *XY* multiply member function operator that you've already seen is called by this expression:

```
XY xy2 = xy1 * 3.0;
```

But it won't work for this expression:

```
XY xy2 = 3.0 * xy1;
```

For the second case, you need a multiply helper operator such as this one:

```
XY operator *(const double mult, const XY& xy)  // scalar multiply
{
    return XY(xy.x * mult, xy.y * mult);
}
```

Separating Class Declarations from Code

In the previous examples, class declarations have been mixed with code. The modularity of C++ depends, however, on the separation of the class implementation code from the class declaration. Class "users" need only the declarations; class "authors" write the code and might choose to deliver it in compiled, linkable form only.

Often, as in the case of the class library, all the class declarations are combined into one or several H files, and the code, broken into small, independently linkable modules, is stored in a LIB file. Application programmers include the H file in their C++ source code, and then they link with the corresponding library.

Below is a view of what the solar system header might look like (minus the moon):

```
// SOLAR.H class declaration file

class XY { // all member functions are inline
private:
    double x, y;
public:
    XY();
    XY(double xarg, double yarg);
    XY(const XY& xy);
    const XY& operator =(const XY& xy);
    XY operator +(const XY& xy) const;
    XY operator -(const XY& xy) const;
    XY operator *(const XY& xy) const;
    XY operator /(const XY& xy) const;
    XY operator -() const;
};


class Orbiter {

protected:
    double m_mass;
    XY      m_current, m_prior, m_thrust;
public:
    static int nCount;
    Orbiter(XY& current, XY& prior, double mass); // inline
    const XY& GetPosition() const;
    void Fly();
    virtual void Display() const = 0;
};
```

(continued)

```
class Planet : public Orbiter {
public:
    // copy constructor and assignment operator not shown
    Planet(XY& current, XY& prior, double mass) :
        Orbiter(current, prior, mass) { }
    void Display();
};

class Spaceship : public Orbiter {
private:
    double m_fuel;
    XY      m_orientation;
public:
    // copy constructor and assignment operator not shown
    Spaceship(XY& current, XY& prior, XY& thrust,
            double mass, double fuel, XY& orientation); // inline
    void Display();
    void FireThrusters();
};
// **** all XY class inline functions here ****
```

Some programmers choose to nest *#include* files, but this requires that code not be inadvertently included more than once, and it complicates make file dependencies. Class library programs, by convention, don't generally nest their *#include* files. Your class library CPP files will always show you exactly which header files are included.

Notice that all the inline functions are grouped at the bottom of the header. This isn't necessary for the solar system example, but it makes the declaration more readable, and it allows the inline functions to be moved to a separate *#include* file. Some applications require the separation because inline code might depend on prior declarations.

The non-inline functions—*Orbiter::Fly, Orbiter::GetPosition, Planet::Display, Spaceship::Display,* and *Spaceship::FireThrusters*—are kept in CPP files. You choose how to split them up. If you put them all in one file, they are all linked even if only one is used (unless you set the compiler's function-level linking option). Often you'll separate member functions by class. A class code file is a good place for static data member definitions.

("del_info");
lock(info_cnt, &info_pkt, CURR_DB) ==
wait until locks are available */
ect and delete abstract */

A P P E N D I X   B

MESSAGE MAP FUNCTIONS IN THE MICROSOFT FOUNDATION CLASS LIBRARY

HANDLERS FOR WM_COMMAND MESSAGES

Map Entry	Function Prototype
ON_COMMAND(<id>, <memberFxn>)	afx_msg void memberFxn( );
ON_COMMAND_EX(<id>, <memberFxn>)	afx_msg BOOL memberFxn(UINT);

HANDLERS FOR CHILD WINDOW NOTIFICATION MESSAGES

Map Entry	Function Prototype
Generic Control Notification Codes	
ON_CONTROL(<wNotifyCode>, <id>, <memberFxn>)	afx_msg void memberFxn( );
User Button Notification Codes	
ON_BN_CLICKED(<id>, <memberFxn>)	afx_msg void memberFxn( );
ON_BN_DISABLE(<id>, <memberFxn>)	afx_msg void memberFxn( );
ON_BN_DOUBLECLICKED(<id>, <memberFxn>)	afx_msg void memberFxn( );
ON_BN_HILITE(<id>, <memberFxn>)	afx_msg void memberFxn( );

(continued)

HANDLERS FOR CHILD WINDOW NOTIFICATION MESSAGES *continued*

Map Entry	Function Prototype
User Button Notification Codes, continued	
ON_BN_PAINT(<id>, <memberFxn>)	afx_msg void memberFxn( );
ON_BN_UNHILITE(<id>, <memberFxn>)	afx_msg void memberFxn( );
Combo Box Notification Codes	
ON_CBN_CLOSEUP(<id>, <memberFxn>)	afx_msg void memberFxn( ); [†]
ON_CBN_DBLCLK(<id>, <memberFxn>)	afx_msg void memberFxn( );
ON_CBN_DROPDOWN(<id>, <memberFxn>)	afx_msg void memberFxn( );
ON_CBN_EDITCHANGE(<id>, <memberFxn>)	afx_msg void memberFxn( );
ON_CBN_EDITUPDATE(<id>, <memberFxn>)	afx_msg void memberFxn( );
ON_CBN_ERRSPACE(<id>, <memberFxn>)	afx_msg void memberFxn( );
ON_CBN_KILLFOCUS(<id>, <memberFxn>)	afx_msg void memberFxn( );
ON_CBN_SELCHANGE(<id>, <memberFxn>)	afx_msg void memberFxn( );
ON_CBN_SELENDCANCEL(<id>, <memberFxn>)	afx_msg void memberFxn( ); [†]
ON_CBN_SELENDOK(<id>, <memberFxn>)	afx_msg void memberFxn( ); [†]
ON_CBN_SETFOCUS(<id>, <memberFxn>)	afx_msg void memberFxn( );
Edit Control Notification Codes	
ON_EN_CHANGE(<id>, <memberFxn>)	afx_msg void memberFxn( );
ON_EN_ERRSPACE(<id>, <memberFxn>)	afx_msg void memberFxn( );
ON_EN_HSCROLL(<id>, <memberFxn>)	afx_msg void memberFxn( );
ON_EN_KILLFOCUS(<id>, <memberFxn>)	afx_msg void memberFxn( );
ON_EN_MAXTEXT(<id>, <memberFxn>)	afx_msg void memberFxn( );
ON_EN_SETFOCUS(<id>, <memberFxn>)	afx_msg void memberFxn( );
ON_EN_UPDATE(<id>, <memberFxn>)	afx_msg void memberFxn( );
ON_EN_VSCROLL(<id>, <memberFxn>)	afx_msg void memberFxn( );
List Box Notification Codes	
ON_LBN_DBLCLK(<id>, <memberFxn>)	afx_msg void memberFxn( );
ON_LBN_ERRSPACE(<id>, <memberFxn>)	afx_msg void memberFxn( );
ON_LBN_KILLFOCUS(<id>, <memberFxn>)	afx_msg void memberFxn( );
ON_LBN_SELCHANGE(<id>, <memberFxn>)	afx_msg void memberFxn( );
ON_LBN_SETFOCUS(<id>, <memberFxn>)	afx_msg void memberFxn( );

[†]For Windows 3.1 only.

HANDLERS FOR WINDOWS NOTIFICATION MESSAGES

Map Entry	Function Prototype
ON_WM_ACTIVATE( )	afx_msg void OnActivate(UINT, CWnd*, BOOL);
ON_WM_ACTIVATEAPP( )	afx_msg void OnActivateApp(BOOL, HANDLE);
ON_WM_ASKCBFORMATNAME( )	afx_msg void OnAskCbFormatName(UINT, LPSTR);
ON_WM_CANCELMODE( )	afx_msg void OnCancelMode( );
ON_WM_CHANGECBCHAIN( )	afx_msg void OnChangeCbChain(HWND, HWND);
ON_WM_CHAR( )	afx_msg void OnChar(UINT, UINT, UINT);
ON_WM_CHARTOITEM( )	afx_msg int OnCharToItem(UINT, CWnd*, UINT);
ON_WM_CHILDACTIVATE( )	afx_msg void OnChildActivate( );
ON_WM_CLOSE( )	afx_msg void OnClose( );
ON_WM_COMPACTING( )	afx_msg void OnCompacting(UINT);
ON_WM_COMPAREITEM( )	afx_msg int OnCompareItem(LPCOMPAREITEMSTRUCT);
ON_WM_CREATE( )	afx_msg int OnCreate(LPCREATESTRUCT);
ON_WM_CTLCOLOR( )	afx_msg HBRUSH OnCtlColor(CDC*, CWnd*, UINT);
ON_WM_DEADCHAR( )	afx_msg void OnDeadChar(UINT, UINT, UINT);
ON_WM_DELETEITEM( )	afx_msg void OnDeleteItem(LPDELETEITEMSTRUCT);
ON_WM_DESTROY( )	afx_msg void OnDestroy( );
ON_WM_DESTROYCLIPBOARD( )	afx_msg void OnDestroyClipboard( );
ON_WM_DEVMODECHANGE( )	afx_msg void OnDevModeChange(LPSTR);
ON_WM_DRAWCLIPBOARD( )	afx_msg void OnDrawClipboard( );
ON_WM_DRAWITEM( )	afx_msg void OnDrawItem(LPDRAWITEMSTRUCT);
ON_WM_DROPFILES()	afx_msg void OnDropFiles(HANDLE); †
ON_WM_ENABLE( )	afx_msg void OnEnable(BOOL);
ON_WM_ENDSESSION( )	afx_msg void OnEndSession(BOOL);
ON_WM_ENTERIDLE( )	afx_msg void OnEnterIdle(UINT, CWnd*);
ON_WM_ERASEBKGND( )	afx_msg BOOL OnEraseBkgnd(CDC*);
ON_WM_FONTCHANGE( )	afx_msg void OnFontChange( );
ON_WM_GETDLGCODE( )	afx_msg UINT OnGetDlgCode( );
ON_WM_GETMINMAXINFO( )	afx_msg void OnGetMinMaxInfo(LPPOINT);
ON_WM_HSCROLL( )	afx_msg void OnHScroll(UINT, UINT, CWnd*);
ON_WM_HSCROLLCLIPBOARD( )	afx_msg void OnHScrollClipboard(CWnd*, UINT, UINT);
ON_WM_ICONERASEBKGND( )	afx_msg void OnIconEraseBkgnd(CDC*);
ON_WM_INITMENU( )	afx_msg void OnInitMenu(CMenu*);
ON_WM_INITMENUPOPUP( )	afx_msg void OnInitMenuPopup(CMenu*, UINT, BOOL);

† For Windows 3.1 only.

(continued)

HANDLERS FOR WINDOWS NOTIFICATION MESSAGES *continued*

Map Entry	Function Prototype
ON_WM_KEYDOWN( )	afx_msg void OnKeyDown(UINT, UINT, UINT);
ON_WM_KEYUP( )	afx_msg void OnKeyUp(UINT, UINT, UINT);
ON_WM_KILLFOCUS( )	afx_msg void OnKillFocus(CWnd*);
ON_WM_LBUTTONDBLCLK( )	afx_msg void OnLButtonDblClk(UINT, CPoint);
ON_WM_LBUTTONDOWN( )	afx_msg void OnLButtonDown(UINT, CPoint);
ON_WM_LBUTTONUP( )	afx_msg void OnLButtonUp(UINT, CPoint);
ON_WM_MBUTTONDBLCLK( )	afx_msg void OnMButtonDblClk(UINT, CPoint);
ON_WM_MBUTTONDOWN( )	afx_msg void OnMButtonDown(UINT, CPoint);
ON_WM_MBUTTONUP( )	afx_msg void OnMButtonUp(UINT, CPoint);
ON_WM_MDIACTIVATE( )	afx_msg void OnMDIActivate(BOOL, CWnd*, CWnd*);
ON_WM_MEASUREITEM( )	afx_msg void OnMeasureItem(LPMEASUREITEMSTRUCT);
ON_WM_MENUCHAR( )	afx_msg LONG OnMenuChar(UINT, UINT,CMenu*);
ON_WM_MENUSELECT( )	afx_msg void OnMenuSelect(UINT, UINT, HMENU);
ON_WM_MOUSEACTIVATE( )	afx_msg int OnMouseActivate(CWnd*, UINT, UINT);
ON_WM_MOUSEMOVE( )	afx_msg void OnMouseMove(UINT, CPoint);
ON_WM_MOVE( )	afx_msg void OnMove(int, int);
ON_WM_NCACTIVATE( )	afx_msg BOOL OnNcActivate(BOOL);
ON_WM_NCCALCSIZE( )	afx_msg void OnNcCalcSize(LPRECT);
ON_WM_NCCREATE( )	afx_msg BOOL OnNcCreate(LPCREATESTRUCT);
ON_WM_NCDESTROY( )	afx_msg void OnNcDestroy( );
ON_WM_NCHITTEST( )	afx_msg UINT OnNcHitTest(CPoint);
ON_WM_NCLBUTTONDBLCLK( )	afx_msg void OnNcLButtonDblClk(UINT, CPoint);
ON_WM_NCLBUTTONDOWN( )	afx_msg void OnNcLButtonDown(UINT, CPoint);
ON_WM_NCLBUTTONUP( )	afx_msg void OnNcLButtonUp(UINT, CPoint);
ON_WM_NCMBUTTONDBLCLK( )	afx_msg void OnNcMButtonDblClk(UINT, CPoint);
ON_WM_NCMBUTTONDOWN( )	afx_msg void OnNcMButtonDown(UINT, CPoint);
ON_WM_NCMBUTTONUP( )	afx_msg void OnNcMButtonUp(UINT, CPoint);
ON_WM_NCMOUSEMOVE( )	afx_msg void OnNcMouseMove(UINT, CPoint);
ON_WM_NCPAINT( )	afx_msg void OnNcPaint();
ON_WM_NCRBUTTONDBLCLK( )	afx_msg void OnNcRButtonDblClk(UINT, CPoint);
ON_WM_NCRBUTTONDOWN( )	afx_msg void OnNcRButtonDown(UINT, CPoint);
ON_WM_NCRBUTTONUP( )	afx_msg void OnNcRButtonUp(UINT, CPoint);
ON_WM_PAINT( )	afx_msg void OnPaint( );

(continued)

HANDLERS FOR WINDOWS NOTIFICATION MESSAGES *continued*

Map Entry	Function Prototype
ON_WM_PAINTCLIPBOARD( )	afx_msg void OnPaintClipboard(CWnd*, HANDLE);
ON_WM_PALETTECHANGED( )	afx_msg void OnPaletteChanged(CWnd*);
ON_WM_PALETTEISCHANGING( )	afx_msg void OnPaletteIsChanging(CWnd*);
ON_WM_PARENTNOTIFY( )	afx_msg void OnParentNotify(UINT, LONG);
ON_WM_QUERYDRAGICON( )	afx_msg HCURSOR OnQueryDragIcon( );
ON_WM_QUERYENDSESSION( )	afx_msg BOOL OnQueryEndSession( );
ON_WM_QUERYNEWPALETTE( )	afx_msg BOOL OnQueryNewPalette( );
ON_WM_QUERYOPEN( )	afx_msg BOOL OnQueryOpen( );
ON_WM_RBUTTONDBLCLK( )	afx_msg void OnRButtonDblClk(UINT, CPoint);
ON_WM_RBUTTONDOWN( )	afx_msg void OnRButtonDown(UINT, CPoint);
ON_WM_RBUTTONUP( )	afx_msg void OnRButtonUp(UINT, CPoint);
ON_WM_RENDERALLFORMATS( )	afx_msg void OnRenderAllFormats( );
ON_WM_RENDERFORMAT( )	afx_msg void OnRenderFormat(UINT);
ON_WM_SETCURSOR( )	afx_msg BOOL OnSetCursor(CWnd*, UINT, UINT);
ON_WM_SETFOCUS( )	afx_msg void OnSetFocus(CWnd*);
ON_WM_SHOWWINDOW( )	afx_msg void OnShowWindow(BOOL, UINT);
ON_WM_SIZE( )	afx_msg void OnSize(UINT, int, int);
ON_WM_SIZECLIPBOARD( )	afx_msg void OnSizeClipboard(CWnd*, HANDLE);
ON_WM_SPOOLERSTATUS( )	afx_msg void OnSpoolerStatus(UINT, UINT);
ON_WM_SYSCHAR( )	afx_msg void OnSysChar(UINT, UINT, UINT);
ON_WM_SYSCOLORCHANGE( )	afx_msg void OnSysColorChange( );
ON_WM_SYSCOMMAND( )	afx_msg void OnSysCommand(UINT, LONG);
ON_WM_SYSDEADCHAR( )	afx_msg void OnSysDeadChar(UINT, UINT, UINT);
ON_WM_SYSKEYDOWN( )	afx_msg void OnSysKeyDown(UINT, UINT, UINT);
ON_WM_SYSKEYUP( )	afx_msg void OnSysKeyUp(UINT, UINT, UINT);
ON_WM_TIMECHANGE( )	afx_msg void OnTimeChange( );
ON_WM_TIMER( )	afx_msg void OnTimer(UINT);
ON_WM_VKEYTOITEM( )	afx_msg int OnVKeyToItem(UINT, CWnd*, UINT);
ON_WM_VSCROLL( )	afx_msg void OnVScroll(UINT, UINT, CWnd*);
ON_WM_VSCROLLCLIPBOARD( )	afx_msg void OnVScrollClipboard(CWnd*, UINT, UINT);
ON_WM_WINDOWPOSCHANGED( )	afx_msg void OnWindowPosChanged(WINDOWPOS FAR*);[†]
ON_WM_WINDOWPOSCHANGING( )	afx_msg void OnWindowPosChanging(WINDOWPOS FAR*);[†]
ON_WM_WININICHANGE( )	afx_msg void OnWinIniChange(LPSTR);

[†]For Windows 3.1 only.

USER-DEFINED MESSAGE CODES

Map Entry	Function Prototype
ON_MESSAGE(<message>, <memberFxn>)	afx_msg LONGmemberFxn(UINT, LONG);
ON_REGISTERED_MESSAGE(<nMessageVariable>, <memberFxn>)	afx_msg LONG memberFxn(UINT, LONG);

A P P E N D I X   C

MICROSOFT WINDOWS FUNCTIONS USED IN THIS BOOK

The Visual C++ printed documentation (and online help) covers all the Microsoft Foundation Class (MFC) Library classes and functions. The MFC library wraps a significant number of Windows Software Development Kit (SDK) functions, but at times you must call Windows SDK functions directly. The Windows SDK functions are documented in the Visual C++ online help and in printed manuals that are available separately. This appendix summarizes those Windows SDK functions that are used in this book's examples. This is by no means a complete list of unwrapped Windows functions. Refer to the Windows 3.1 SDK online help for details.

Windows SDK Function	Purpose
CloseClipboard	Closes the Windows clipboard. The *CWnd::OpenClipboard* member function opens the clipboard.
CreateDIBitmap	Creates a GDI bitmap from a device-independent bitmap and optionally sets bits in the bitmap.
CreateSolidBrush	Creates a brush that has a specified solid color. Returns an HBRUSH handle.
DeleteObject	Deletes a GDI object from Windows memory. The *CGdiObject::DeleteObject* function requires an object pointer, but you'll need this *DeleteObject* function if you have an HGDIOBJ handle instead.
DispatchMessage	Dispatches a Windows message that was retrieved by the *GetMessage* and *PeekMessage* functions.
EmptyClipboard	Empties the Windows clipboard.

(continued)

699

continued

Windows SDK Function	Purpose
EnumClipboardFormats	Retrieves the currently available clipboard formats. Should be called in a loop.
GetClipboardData	Retrieves a handle to the clipboard data as specified by the format parameter.
GetDIBits	Converts a device-independent bitmap to a GDI bitmap.
GetKeyState	Gets the state of a specified virtual key.
GetSysColor	Gets the color of a specified display element such as the window background or the title bar.
GetSystemMetrics	Retrieves the widths and heights of various Windows display elements such as windows, borders, and fonts. Also indicates whether the current version of Windows is a debugging version and whether a mouse is present.
IsClipboardFormatAvailable	Tests whether the clipboard contains a specified format.
LoadCursor	Loads a specified mouse cursor from a resource or loads a standard Windows mouse cursor. Used with *SetCursor*.
PeekMessage	Retrieves a message from the application's message queue and, except for WM_PAINT messages, removes it from the queue. The function does not wait for a message to become available but returns 0 if the queue is empty. *PeekMessage* is often used with *DispatchMessage* and *TranslateMessage* to yield control during a long compute process.
RegCloseKey	Releases a key in the Windows registration database. When all keys are released, the database is updated.
RegCreateKey	Creates or opens a Windows registration database key.
RegSetValue	Sets the value of an open key to a text string.
SetClipboardData	Transfers data to the clipboard. The clipboard must have been previously opened.
SetCursor	Changes the Windows mouse cursor as specified by the cursor resource created by *LoadCursor*.
SetDIBitsToDevice	Displays a device-independent bitmap without scaling.
StretchDIBits	Displays a device-independent bitmap with scaling.
TranslateMessage	Translates a virtual key code to a character. Used with *PeekMessage* and *DispatchMessage*.

A P P E N D I X   D

VISUAL C++, VERSION 2.0 FOR WINDOWS NT

As this book was going to press, Microsoft was introducing Visual C++ 2.0, which includes the Microsoft Foundation Class (MFC) Library version 3.0. This new product runs only under Windows NT and under the beta version of Chicago (the new 32-bit successor to Windows 3.1). Visual C++ 2.0 generates 32-bit applications only; the CD-ROM, however, contains a maintenance upgrade of the 16-bit Visual C++ 1.5, which includes MFC version 2.51.

Visual C++ 2.0 contains many new features not found in version 1.5, including:

- Seamless integration between the Visual Workbench and App Studio

- Compiler support for templates and exceptions

- MFC support for NT features, such as threads and Bézier curves

- MFC and DLL support for new user interface features, such as tabbed dialogs

- Tools for creating OLE Controls (but without App Studio support)

It should be obvious by now that you'll need to switch to 32-bit Windows if you want to keep up with Microsoft's new developments. The plan is for users to convert to Chicago as soon as possible after it is released, thus relegating 16-bit Windows to pen computers and dishwasher controllers. It will be a fine day for developers when 16-bit programming finally fades away.

Speaking of Chicago, there'll be another version of Visual C++ when Chicago is released. This new version will support all the Chicago user interface features and fully integrate OLE Controls. Watch for a new edition of this book after that version is released.

32-Bit Programming

Programs written for Windows NT use a flat 32-bit memory model. All pointers and integers are 32 bits wide. The modifiers *near* and *far* have no meaning, and there are no segments. This makes 32-bit programming easier than 16-bit programming. Here's a list of common type sizes (in bits):

Type	Size in Windows 3.1	Size in 32-Bit Windows
BYTE	8	8
double	64	64
DWORD	32	32
float	32	32
int	16	32
long	32	32
long double	80	64
LONG (lParam)	32	32
short	16	16
SHORT	16	16
UINT (wParam)	16	32
WORD	16	16

The application programming interface used in Windows NT is commonly referred to as the Win32 API. With Win32, all handles (including *HWND*s and *HDC*s) for Windows NT are 32 bits wide, and GDI functions take 32-bit parameters. Some device coordinates are still returned as 16-bit values, however. For example, the WM_LBUTTONDOWN message returns the *x* and *y* cursor coordinates packed in the *lParam* parameter, which is still 32 bits wide.

Many Win32 functions look the same as their Windows 3.1 counterparts. Take the *SetPixel* function, for example:

```
DWORD SetPixel(HDC hDC, int X, int Y, COLORREF crColor);
```

The declaration is the same for both Win32 and Windows 3.1. The widths of the *hDC*, *X*, and *Y* parameters are different, however.

In the area of file input/output, the Win32 API is very different. For example, the old *_lread* and *_lwrite* functions have been replaced by the new functions *ReadFile* and *WriteFile*. There are hundreds of brand-new functions too, supporting features such as threads, multibyte characters, and Bézier curves.

Porting 16-Bit MFC Library Applications to Windows NT

Because the MFC library was designed for portability, it's easy to port most applications from Windows 3.1 to Windows NT. Simply recompile and relink. If your application uses the *CFile* class, for example, the MFC library connects to the new Win32 file functions. The compiler will catch most incompatibilities, which usually involve direct calls to Windows-based functions rather than calls to MFC library functions. Here's an example of one change that was made in the *CDib* class from the Chapter 23 example EX23A:

```
#ifdef _WIN32
    HBITMAP hBitmap = ::CreateDIBitmap(pDC->GetSafeHdc(), m_lpBMIH,
            CBM_INIT, (CONST BYTE*) (m_lpBuf + m_lpBMFH->bfOffBits),
            m_lpBMI, DIB_RGB_COLORS);
#else
    HBITMAP hBitmap = ::CreateDIBitmap(pDC->GetSafeHdc(), m_lpBMIH,
            CBM_INIT, (LPSTR) (m_lpBuf + m_lpBMFH->bfOffBits),
            m_lpBMI, DIB_RGB_COLORS);
#endif
```

Notice that the fourth *CreateDIBitmap* parameter has changed between Windows NT and Windows 3.1. The preprocessor statements ensure that the code compiles in both environments.

The above change was about the only change I made when I ported the examples in this book. Recompilation under Windows NT did expose a few bugs, however, but those were easy to fix. I couldn't port the examples that use Visual Basic controls or extension DLLs (EX08A, EX11C, EX26A, and EX26B). Why? Because with the Win32 API, the *wParam* message parameter is 32 bits wide, and this means that some messages pack the *lParam* and *wParam* parameters differently. Because the MFC library decodes message parameters for you, you're mostly insulated from these changes. If your program handles the WM_COMMAND message directly, for example, you must allow for the packing differences. The files WINDOWSX.H and WINDOWSX.H16 contain "message-cracker macros" that help you write portable code.

> HINT: Applications generated by AppWizard under Windows 3.1 often include the file VER.H. The equivalent Windows NT file is WINVER.H. If you copy WINVER.H to VER.H in the \MSVCNT\INCLUDE subdirectory, your ported applications will compile.

Archive Portability Between Windows 3.1 and Win32

As summarized in Chapter 16, the MFC library *CArchive* class supports built-in types that are the same size in both Windows environments. Thus *int* is not supported, but *LONG* is. Most archive files written under Windows 3.1 can be read under Windows NT. Notice that the sizes for *CRect*, *CPoint*, and *CSize* objects are different, so archive files that contain these items are not portable.

Some MFC Library Features for Windows 3.1 Not Supported Under Win32

A few MFC library and tool features for Windows 3.1 are not supported under Win32. These include:

- Visual Basic controls—The Visual Basic control API is inherently a 16-bit API that uses pointers and data structures that are not compatible with Win32. The controls themselves are 16-bit DLLs and thus won't run with 32-bit applications. For the time being, Visual Basic controls are not supported by the MFC library, AppWizard, or App Studio.

- Microsoft Windows for Pen Computing classes—You wouldn't expect to use Windows NT for pen computing applications, so the pen classes *CHEdit* and *CBEdit* aren't supported.

- App Studio EXE, RES, and DLL editing capability—In the Windows NT environment, App Studio can edit only RC files.

Enhanced MFC 3.0 Library Features

In addition to the new features listed earlier, MFC 3.0 includes the following improvements:

- *CTime* class enhancements—The *CTime* class has been extended to support the system and file times offered by Windows NT.

- Collection memory restrictions removed—Under Windows 3.1, array collection (*CObArray*, *CStringArray*, and so on) size was limited to 64 KB for small and medium memory models, and the number of array elements was limited to 32-KB elements for all models; under Win32, array size is limited only by available memory.

Windows NT Debugging Considerations

Visual C++ 2.0 contains a Windows-hosted debugger similar to the one included in Visual C++ 1.5, as well as a symbolic debugger, NTSD. Both these debuggers can display the output of *TRACE* and *afxDump* statements if you've built your application with the Debug build option. You don't have to set the compiler and linker debugging information options to get trace output from the debugger.

Windows NT has no equivalent of DBWIN, so you must use one of the debuggers to get trace output. Also, the Windows 3.1 Debug kernel has no equivalent, which means you can't determine which GDI objects are not deleted. Windows NT does release all GDI memory when an application terminates, however. Once you've written a 32-bit class library application, it might be a good idea to port it back to Windows 3.1 to test it with the Debug kernel.

The Win32s Subsystem

When you buy Visual C++ 2.0, you get the Win32s Software Development Kit (SDK), which enables 32-bit applications to run under Windows 3.1. The Win32s SDK is a collection of DLLs plus a device driver that you can ship with your application. You can view Win32s as a mapping layer between the Win32 API and the underlying Windows 3.1 system. Many Windows NT functions are not supported under Win32s—in particular, multiple threads and the advanced Windows NT file system calls. These functions are "stubbed out" to return error codes.

Be aware that Windows NT can run many existing Windows 3.1 binary programs (including Visual C++ 1.5) using its Windows on Win32 (WOW) component. So why bother with Win32s, which requires use of a mapping layer and the distribution of extra DLLs? The answer is that 32-bit programs run faster than 16-bit programs, particularly if they are compute-intensive. Some CAD programs run twice as fast in 32-bit mode, despite the inefficiencies of the mapping layer.

Multiplatform Development Strategy

Multiplatform development is easy if you're programming to the lowest common denominator of 32-bit and 16-bit platforms. Unfortunately, 16-bit Windows is not a true subset of 32-bit Windows, and that complicates matters. You can't use VBXs, for example, in a 32-bit application. If you wrote a 16-bit

Windows application with MFC 2.5, and you didn't use VBXs or direct SDK calls, you could easily recompile and relink that application for Windows NT, using the same source code.

What if you wanted to take advantage of new Windows NT features, such as threads and Bézier curves? What if your application uses Windows features not supported by MFC? Take serial communication, for instance. Suppose you want your application to download information from an online service. Windows 3.1 provides a set of communications functions (supported by the standard communications driver) that depend on the WM_COMM-NOTIFY message. Windows NT doesn't use WM_COMMNOTIFY but rather provides a new set of functions, including one called *WaitCommEvent*, that beg for multithread programming. Win32s supports neither communications interface but requires you to implement something called "universal thunks."

How do you deal with platform incompatibilities? First you analyze the market to determine which platforms you need to support. If you determine that you must support several platforms, you begin the design process by isolating the functionality that is common to all platforms. Most of this common functionality can be handled by the class library.

Next you design the platform-dependent components to be as modular as possible. C++ classes can help you with this process. In the hypothetical serial communications example discussed above, Windows 3.1 might dictate that you write a *CComm* class that is derived from *CWnd* (to map the WM_-COMMNOTIFY message). For Windows NT, your *CComm* class wouldn't use any MFC library elements; rather, it would encapsulate a separate communication thread that would handle the download task. The *CComm* class member functions would be identical in both cases, however.

INDEX

Special Characters

Numbers

A

C

X

Y